Readings for Writers

ninth edition

Readings for Writers

ninth edition

Jo Ray McCuen
Glendale College

Anthony Winkler

Harcourt Brace College Publishers

Fort Worth Philadelphia San Diego New York Orlando Austin San Antonio
Toronto Montreal London Sydney Tokyo

Publisher	Christopher P. Klein
Executive Editor	Michael Rosenberg
Acquisitions Editor	John Meyers
Product Manager	Ilse Wolfe West
Developmental Editor	Terri House/Van Strength
Project Editor	Betsy Cummings
Art Director	Candice Johnson Clifford
Production Manager	Kathleen Ferguson

Cover Image and Details: © 1998 by Celia Johnson/SIS

ISBN: 0-03-064422-4

Library of Congress Catalog Card Number: 97-71822

Copyright © 1998, 1995, 1992, 1989, 1986, 1983, 1980, 1977, 1974 by Harcourt Brace & Company

Address for Editorial Correspondence: Harcourt Brace College Publishers, 301 Commerce Street, Suite 3700, Fort Worth, TX 76102.

Copyrights and acknowledgments appear on pages 831–836 which constitutes a continuation of the copyright page.

Address for Orders: Harcourt Brace College Publishers, 6277 Sea Harbor Drive, Orlando, FL 32887-6777. 1-800-782-4479.

Web site address: http://www.hbcollege.com

Harcourt Brace & Company will provide supplements or supplement packages to those adopters qualified under our adoption policy. Please contact your sales representative to learn how you qualify. If as an adopter or potential user you receive supplements you do not need, please return them to your sales representative or send them to: Attn: Returns Department, Troy Warehouse, 465 South Lincoln Drive, Troy, MO 63379.

Printed in the United States of America

1 2 3 4 5 6 7 8 9 0   039   11 10 9 8 7 6 5 4 3 2

In fond memory of
Matthew Milan, Jr.,
our first editor.

Preface

▼▼▼

When the first edition of *Readings for Writers* was published in 1974, our rationale behind it was simple: to assemble a book with a wide variety of readings grouped under the unique labeling sequence of *Advice, Discussion,* or *Examples.* Twenty-four years later, the ninth edition of *Readings for Writers* remains true to its original design. Its selections are still grouped under its unique labeling sequence that shows how each reading is meant to be used. No piece is included as mere window dressing. Every selection has a specific role to play in helping teach students how to write.

Containing one hundred-twenty selections from a rich variety of writers and sources, the ninth edition of *Readings for Writers* continues to be a diverse collection. Its selections consist of seventy-four essays (ten of them by students), fourteen poems, twelve excerpts (from books and other sources), five short stories, five paragraphs, three speeches, three long student papers, one letter, one editorial, one article, and one diary entry. In addition, the book contains the reproductions of ten paintings and photographs, one for each *Issue For Critical Thinking and Debate* topic.

This ninth edition, however, is no mere clone of its predecessors but has its own special features. First among them is the greater voice we have given to student writers. All ten student essays in this edition are new, especially commissioned for this book, and reproduced in two drafts. The first is a rough draft with the student's own handwritten changes, the second a final draft ready to be submitted. The student writer then weighs in with a personal opinion on the writing process under the headings of *How I Write, How I Wrote This Essay,* and *My Writing Tip.* The result is not only a faithful reflection of how all writers actually write—with the inevitably messy first drafts—but also provides some nuggets of practical advice fellow students should find both useful and engaging.

In a new edition of any reader the most obvious change is the selections. Twenty-six selections are new to this edition including the following: "A Diarist on Diarists" by Gail Godwin; "Books" by Allan Bloom; "Drug Use: The Continuing Epidemic" by Linda Kunce; "A Good War Will Set Gen X Straight" by Brian Gabriel; and "Putting in a Good Word for Guilt" by Ellen Goodman. Back are the favorites "A, B, and C: The Human Elements in Mathematics" by Stephen Lealock; "Three Bears in Search of an Author," by Dan Greenberg; and "The Odour of Cheese," by Jerome K. Jerome. All three are hilarious and perennial favorites of long-time users.

We feature ten running *Issues for Critical Thinking and Debate.* We have replaced the issues of *Crime and Punishment, Immigrant Culture versus American Culture,* and *Poverty* with *Racism, The Values of a New Generation,* and *Homelessness.* As before, each issue consists of two pieces by professionals followed by a student opinion and is designed to stimulate class discussion that will, in turn, give students a hot topic to write about.

We continue many of the extras that users have grown to expect from *Readings for Writers.* Every selection is still followed by an accurate word count in parentheses, making *Readings for Writers* a practical and usable book for reading courses or for readers who wish to check their reading speed. We still end every chapter with three kinds of writing assignments: general assignments; Writing Assignments For A Specific Audience, which asks students to write for a specific, imagined audience; and Collaborative Writing Project, meant to involve several students in a joint writing assignment.

The main appeal of *Readings for Writers* has always been its diversity of selections that offer something for readers of every conceivable type and taste. To this end, we continue to roam the literary globe in search of writers and topics that are compelling. Contributors to this edition range from a former big-game hunter in India writing about why tigers become man eaters, to a New York lawyer tackling the incendiary topic of sex predators, to a diarist sharing with us what she has learned over the years about other diarists. In one selection readers sit in on a discussion of Shakespeare's *Hamlet* with elders of a West African tribe; in another they witness a young Massachusetts mother's slow and painful descent into homelessness. As ever, all the wide variety of selections have one common and overriding aim: to stimulate students to do their best writing.

We appreciate the dedication of the editorial, marketing, and production staff at Harcourt Brace. We thank John Meyers for his editorial direction. We are grateful for the contributions of our developmental editors, Terri House and Van Strength, who, with John, guided the book through the revision process. We appreciate the hard work of Ilse Wolfe West for her continued efforts in marketing this text. Finally, we thank Candice Clifford, Kathleen Ferguson, and Nancy Marcus Land for their contributions throughout the production of the text.

We gratefully acknowledge the help and advice of many colleagues. Numbered among them, for this edition, are Darnell Eckersley, Southwest College; Shelly Jaffray, Rancho Santiago Community College; Ruby Lewis, Grambling State University; Lori Pangborne, Cyprus College; and Richard Tracz, Oakton Community College.

JO RAY MCCUEN
ANTHONY C. WINKLER

Contents

▼▼▼

Chapter Four
Planning and Organizing   199

Chapter Five
Developing Paragraphs   255

Chapter Eight
Analyzing: Comparison/Contrast,
Division/Classification, and Causal Analysis   519

Chapter Nine
Argumentation 621

Thematic Table of Contents

▼▼

(Alphabetically listed within sections.)

THINKING

Guidelines for Critical Reading

▼▼▼

Critical reading means reading with a conscious effort to see both sides of an issue, draw valid conclusions, and detect bias. It means burrowing below your immediate reaction and trying to fathom the underlying meaning of a piece of writing. This is not the sort of reading you do when you read a detective novel or a pulp magazine. But it is the best way to read, although perhaps the most strenuous, because it helps you to learn. Here are ten guidelines to help you read critically.

Understand What You Read

Reread difficult passages, looking up in a dictionary all the unfamiliar words. You cannot form an opinion of what you have read unless you understand what the author is saying.

Imagine an Opposing Point of View for All Opinions

If a writer says that the Arab punishment of cutting off the hands of a thief is more humane than the American equivalent of imprisonment, reverse the argument and see what happens. In other words, look for reasons that support the other side.

Search for Biases and Hidden Assumptions

Be alert to the biases of the writer. For example, an atheist arguing for abortion will not attribute a soul to the unborn fetus; a devout

Catholic will. To ferret out possible biases and hidden assumptions, check the author's age, sex, education, and ethnic background. These and other personal biographical facts might have influenced the opinions expressed in the work, but you cannot know to what extent unless you know something about the author. (That is the rationale behind the use of biographical headnotes, which accompany the articles in this book.)

Separate Emotion from Fact

Talented writers frequently color an issue with emotionally charged language, thus casting their opinions in the best possible light. For example, a condemned murderer may be described in sympathetic language that draws attention away from a horrifying crime. Be alert to sloganeering, to bumper-sticker philosophizing about complex issues. Emotion is no solution to complicated problems.

If the Issue Is New to You, Look Up the Facts

If you are reading about an unfamiliar issue, be willing to fill in the gaps in your knowledge with research. For example, if you are reading an editorial that proposes raising home insurance rates for families taking care of foster children, you will want to know why. Is it because foster children do more damage than natural children? Is it because natural parents are apt to file lawsuits against foster parents? You can find answers to these questions by asking representatives of the affected parties: the State Department of Social Services, typical insurance agencies, foster parents associations, the County Welfare Directors Association, any children's lobby, and others. To make a critical judgment you must know, and carefully weigh, the facts.

Use Insights from One Subject to Illuminate or Correct Another

Be prepared to apply what you already know to whatever you read. History can inform psychology; literature can give you insights into geography. For example, if a writer in psychology argues that most oppressed people develop a psychology of defeat that gives them a subconscious desire to be subjugated and makes them prey to tyrants, your knowledge of American history should tell you otherwise. As proof that oppressed people often fight oppression unto death, you can point to the Battle of Fallen Timbers in 1794, the Battle of Tippecanoe in 1811, and the Black Hawk War of 1832—conflicts in which the Indians fought desperately to retain their territories rather than go meekly to the reservations. In other words, you can use what you have learned from history to refute a falsehood from psychology.

Evaluate the Evidence

Critical readers do not accept evidence at face value. They question its source, its verifiability, its appropriateness. Here are some practical tips for evaluating evidence:

- Verify a questionable opinion by cross-checking with other sources. For example, if a medical writer argues that heavy smoking tends to cause serious bladder diseases in males, check the medical journals for conformation of this view. Diligent research often turns up a consensus of opinion among the experts in any field.

- Check the date of the evidence. In science, especially, evidence varies from year to year. Before 1987, no one really knew exactly how the immune system worked. Then Susumu Tonegawa, a geneticist at the Massachusetts Institute of Technology, discovered how the immune system protects the body from foreign substances by the manufacture of antibodies. In 1980, the evidence would say that the workings of the immune system were a mystery; that evidence would be inaccurate in 1987.

- Use common sense in evaluating evidence. For example, if a writer argues that a child's handwriting can accurately predict his or her life as an adult, your own experience with human nature should lead you to reject this conclusion as speculative. No convincing evidence exists to corroborate it.

Ponder the Values That Give an Argument Its Impetus

In writing the Declaration of Independence, Thomas Jefferson based his arguments on the value that "all men are created equal." On the other hand, Karl Marx based the arguments of his *Communist Manifesto* on the value that the laborer is society's greatest good. Critical reading means thinking about the values implicit in an argument. For instance, to argue that murderers should be hanged in public to satisfy society's need for revenge is to value revenge over human dignity. On the other hand, to argue that democracy can exist only with free speech is to highly value freedom of speech.

Look for Logical Fallacies

These typical logical flaws occur in a wide range of arguments: the *ad hominem* attack (attacking the person instead of the issue or argument); the *ad populum* appeal (the use of simplistic popular slogans to convince); the *false analogy* (comparing situations that have no bearing on each other); *begging the question* (arguing in circles); and *ignoring the question* (focusing on matters that are beside the point). For a better understanding of logical fallacies, review Chapter Nine, "Argumentation."

Don't Be Seduced by Bogus Claims

Arguments are often based on unsubstantiated claims. For example, a writer may warn that "recent studies show women becoming increasingly hostile to men." Or, another writer might announce, "Statistics have shown beyond doubt that most well-educated males oppose gun control." You should always remain skeptical of these and similar claims when they are unaccompanied by hard-headed evidence. A proper claim will always be documented with verifiable evidence.

Readings for Writers

▼▼

ninth edition

▼▼▼

Chapter One

DEFINING RHETORIC

INTRODUCTION: WHAT IS RHETORIC?

Rhetoric is the art of writing and speaking persuasively. It is made up of all those strategies and techniques a writer will use to make a case or drive home a point. All of us are occasionally speakers and writers who try to make a point or sway an audience and can therefore benefit from mastering the art of forceful expression.

Many theories exist about the teaching of writing, and many schools of thought contend for the beginner's discipleship. We have our own theory: You learn to write well by first writing less well. If you write long and often enough, eventually you will write better. Then, after an apprenticeship whose length will vary with your particular gifts, you will begin to write well. That is the way one learns to write— by the painful process of effort and error. One learns what works and what does not; one accumulates a certain habit of phrasing and expression. But mainly, one absorbs the underlying technique that is most likely to yield the best writing—namely, constant revision.

The indispensable lessons that rhetoric and its study can teach are many and varied, but the most important of all is the lesson of keeping an eye on the audience. Writers do not write for themselves. Even the solitary diarist conceptualizes a part of the writing self as listener, reader, audience, and it is to this attentive part that the words and phrases of a diary are aimed. Some students assume everything about an instructor except this single obvious fact—that he or she is a paid audience for the student's work. It is to the instructor that you must direct your essay, taking into account personal quirks of taste and inclinations that any audience can be expected to have. If you can produce writing that will please the instructor, it is highly likely that you can do the same later for the boss or for the salespeople whom you might one day try to spur on with the written word.

Collected in this chapter are essays, speeches, a short story, and a love letter, that exemplify the collected wisdom as well as contemporary practice of rhetoric. We begin with Donald Murray's "What—and How—to Write When You Have No Time to Write." Tilly Warnock, a seasoned writing instructor, shares her own formulas for warding off writing fears. Martin Luther King, Jr.'s speech shows us a practiced rhetorician hard at work persuading a nation to acknowledge and remedy the injustice of racism; following this is a gifted English poet who died tragically young and who croons to his beloved in a romantic letter. The section ends with an editor's written response to a little girl's question, "Is there a Santa Claus?"

In the arena of debate, we get our first whiff of rhetorical gunpowder. The issue is the so-called political correctness movement on college campuses that allegedly aims to stifle free speech with political orthodoxy. A magazine writer details case after case of this movement, ascribing outrageous utterances to various partisans, while a former Harvard student argues that political correctness on campus is a myth perpetuated by conservatives.

We learn to write well by constantly revising. But we also absorb standards and strategies of rhetoric by peering over the shoulders of skilled writers at work. That is what these selections will allow you to do.

A D V I C E

▼▼

Donald Murray

WHAT—AND HOW—TO WRITE WHEN YOU HAVE NO TIME TO WRITE

DONALD MURRAY (b. 1924) is a Pulitzer Prize-winning journalist who has made it part of his life's work to teach others how to write. He writes a much-read weekly column for *The Boston Globe* as well as feature articles for a variety of magazines. Many teachers of composition rely on Murray's books for teaching strategies. Among his most influential books are: *Shoptalk, Expecting the Unexpected, Learning by Teaching, The Craft of Revision,* and *Crafting a Life* (1995). Murray is Professor Emeritus of English at the University of New Hampshire.

We begin this book with practical advice from this prolific writer who is also a popular and successful college teacher. To make the reader's job easy, the author summarizes his ideas into "ten little habits of mind and craft."

1   The less time I have for writing, the more important it is that I write. Writing gives me a necessary calm, what Robert Frost called "a momentary stay against confusion." Writing slows down the rush of life, forcing awareness and reflection. As writing increases my awareness, language clarifies that vision. What is vague and general becomes concrete and specific as I find the words. These words connect with other words in phrase and sentence, placing the immediate experience in the context of my life. I read the story of my life by writing it. I also receive the gift of concentration and escape the swirling problems of my life as I follow paragraph and page toward meaning.

2   I write fragments in slivers of time, always with interruptions, and yet, when I look back, I am surprised that the writing caught on the fly has produced a lifetime of productivity. I have come to realize that very little published writing is produced during sustained periods of composition without interruption. You have to arrange a life in which part of your mind is writing all the time; that's when the seeds of writing are sown and then cultivated. The writing is harvested in short periods of time between the busy chores that crowd the day.

3   Graham Greene said, "If one wants to write, one simply has to organize one's life in a mass of little habits." Here are ten little habits of mind and craft that I realize, looking back, made me a productive writer—without long writing days free of interruption.

4   1. Don't wait for an idea.

5   If you know what you want to say, you've probably said it before, or it's not worth saying. Writing is thinking, and thought begins not with a conclusion but with an itch, a hint, a clue, a question, a doubt, a wonder, a problem, an answer without a question, an image that refuses to be forgotten. Such fragments are caught on the wing, when I think my mind is somewhere else.

6   My four-year-old grandson told his mother, "I know Grandpa is a writer because he's always writing in his wallet." It is not a wallet, but a container for the 3×5 cards that are always in my shirt pocket with three pens. In a shoulder case that is not far from me night and day is the spiral daybook in which I talk to myself, capturing and playing with fragments of language that may become a draft.

7   2. Listen to your own difference.

8   People who want to write look at what is being published, but the writers who are published have looked within themselves, found their own vision of the world, heard their own voices. Sandra Cisneros said, "Write about what makes you different."

9   As I look back, I realize that what made me strange to my family, classmates and teachers, friends and neighbors, colleagues and editors, is what has produced the writing that has been read. In the wonderful way of art, what is most personal, eccentric, individual, becomes most universal. When I have tried to become someone else I have failed; when I have been myself I have succeeded.

10   3. Avoid long writing sessions.

11   Most people believe, as I once did, that it is necessary to have long, uninterrupted days in which to write. But there are no such days. Life intrudes. I try to follow the counsel of Horace, Pliny, and so many others through the centuries: *nulla dies sine linea*—never a day without a line.

12   How long does it take me to write? My weekly columns take 71 years of living and about forty-five minutes of writing. I write in bursts of twenty minutes, five, fifteen, thirty, sixty; ninety minutes is the maximum amount of writing time that is effective for me.

13   And how much writing do I produce? I've finished a book averaging 300 words a day. These days I try to average 500 words a day. The important thing is not the time or the words, but the habit, that dailyness of the writing.

14   4. Break long writing projects into brief daily tasks.

15   Books are written a page at a time, and I find it helpful—essential—to break a book into units that can be finished in a short morning's writing: lead for Ch. 3, scene in court, description of experiment, interview with source, column on writing time.

16   5. Write in the morning.

17   Most writers write in the early morning before the world intrudes. They harvest the product of their subconscious. Each hour of the day

becomes less efficient as the writer is not only interrupted, but increasingly aware of all the professional and family concerns that crowd the mind. An 800-word column I can write in 45 minutes in the morning takes me three hours in the afternoon.

18   6. Know tomorrow's task today.

19   I set myself a single writing task and know what it is the night before. I don't know what I am going to write, but I assign the writing problem to my subconscious at the end of the morning writing session or before I go to bed, and part of my mind works on it as I go about my living.

20   7. Seek instructive failure.

21   Effective writing is the product of instructive failure. You try to say what you cannot yet say, but in the attempt you discover—draft by draft—*what* you have to say and *how* you can say it. Failure is essential. Failure occurs when the words race ahead of thought, producing insights that may be developed through revision. The writer should seek to fail, not to say what has been said before, but what has not yet been said and is worth saying.

22   8. Focus on what works.

23   Once failure has revealed what you want to say, you should develop the topic by concentrating on what works, rather than focusing on correcting errors. Most errors will not occur if you develop what works and, at the end of the drafting process, you can solve any problems that remain. I revise mostly by layering, writing over—and over—what has been written.

24   9. Keep score.

25   As you write, it is important to suspend critical judgment until after a draft is finished. It's helpful to count words—or pages or hours—so that you can tell yourself that you have written without assessing how well you have written until the piece is finished.

26   10. Let it go.

27   Hardest of all is to let it go. The draft never equals the dream. The draft will expose your private thoughts and feelings to the world, but when you are published, what you most feared would appear foolish, your readers often find most profound. You have given words to their private thoughts and feelings.

28   Writing produces writing. When writing you are more aware of the world and your own reaction to it. As a writer, you relive your life hundreds of times, and when you are in your seventies, as I am, you'll come to your writing desk and discover you have even more to say than you imagined when you were 17 years old and dreaming of a writing life.

(1,289 words)

VOCABULARY

sustained (2)	eccentric (9)	assessing (25)
daybook (6)	suspend (25)	

D I S C U S S I O N

▼▼

Tilly Warnock
_____

HOW I WRITE

TILLY WARNOCK (b. 1942) is an Associate Professor at the University of Wyoming. She received her PhD from the University of Southern California and is the author of *Writing Is Critical Action* (1989).

> *Do writing teachers practice what they preach? That intriguing question formed the basis of the book* Writers on Writing *(1985) from which this article comes. The author, who was once the director of the Writing Center at the University of Wyoming, candidly admits that much of what she preaches about writing she does not practice. She also shares with us many of the techniques she has taught to, and learned from, her students to encourage their growth as writers.*

1   One cold July night several years ago at Vedauwoo, during the Wyoming Conference on Freshman and Sophomore English, several people were talking beside the fire when one man began explaining how exhausted he was from revising his textbook. We asked how he writes. He described his writing process in detail but seemed particularly pleased with the stage when he passes his draft to his wife, who is not in English, so that she can detect the b.s. in his work. Because I was delighted by his account, I asked if he included such collaboration as a common stage for writers in his textbook. He drew himself to full height, a large shadow against the flames and silhouettes of the mysteriously shaped mountains, and replied indignantly, "Every word I write is my own." The conversation ended.

2   I want to admit right away that no words I write are my own and that I never write alone. I also want to confess that I spent many years of my life with the golden dream of having a book dedicated to me, not of writing one but of inspiring one. I wanted to be the power behind

the throne, or, in the words of Ernest Hemingway, to be that "most essential gift for a good writer, a built-in shock-proof shit-detector." I did not want to take risks myself: I wanted to be "the one without whom not."

3   At a certain point, I began to want not the upper hand but the writing hand to be my own. Instead of motivating someone else to write, I wanted to relax—in an important sense of that word which I will try to develop later—and write for myself.

4   With this change in attitude toward myself and toward writing, I began scrounging around to find words to help me write and to see myself as a writer. I had been teaching writing for many years and had published several articles on composition and literature, but I could not call myself a writer. I still cannot, but I can now say confidently that I am writing.

5   I feel presumptuous, though, describing how I write. The rat in the basement—as a colleague, Fred Homer, refers to writing fears—creeps up to remind me that I cannot write, not real writing. Of course I write articles for publication and talks for conferences. I have become a whiz at writing abstracts for conference papers, before-the-fact-writing; and through two humanities proposals I have learned to bureaucratize my imagination, as Kenneth Burke says. I also write letters, grocery lists, and class notes, and I am presently revising a manuscript on Burke's rhetoric of the symbol. I do not like to write reviews of books I do not like, although I enjoy writing reviews of books I learn from. I began writing poems only last summer during a Wyoming Writing Project institute in Gillette, Wyoming, and I have never finished a work of fiction. But I will. (Having written this, several days later I finally finished a short story, which certainly needs revision but which I pushed through to the end.)

6   In one sense, then, I have learned to write, but my attitude is that I am still learning. Past tense is inappropriate. The biggest rat in my basement remains the definition I still have of writers as people who have published several novels, several very good novels. I strongly encourage students to name and erase such destructive rats, but my excuse for believing the rat who says I cannot write is that I grew up in the land of Carson McCullers, Flannery O'Connor, Alice Walker, and Eudora Welty. I am like Mary Anne Bocquin, English Department chair at Green River High School, who says she never wrote a poem because she felt she was not worthy even to kiss the hem of a poet's garment. We talked about how most poets don't even wear robes anymore; she has begun writing poems. The early drafts, early works, and comments about writing by Welty, Walker, and others have helped me understand writers primarily as people who write and work hard at it.

7   How did I take the plunge? How am I still learning to write? How do I help students begin writing and join the community of writers? How am I learning to overcome the excuses of time, busywork, head-tripping, and hems of garments to avoid writing? Most important, I believe, I am learning to write, not alone, but with others.

Take a Deep Breath, Reach Out, and Write

8   William Stafford gives me a gentle push in *Writing the Australian Crawl* when he explains how swimmers must have faith that the water will keep them afloat and how writers must have faith that the writing will keep them afloat. The only way to write is to write, not to spend hours, days, and years talking about writing.

9   Stafford also suggests how to take the plunge when he describes how he sits daily beside an open window, with pen and paper in hand, waiting for the nibble. He says that on any given day nothing may happen, but he knows for sure that if he is not ready and waiting, he will not get the catch. I try to write daily, but I do not have a certain window, scheduled time, or enough confidence yet to claim such time and space for myself. Those are some of my excuses, but I now recognize them as excuses, and I now realize that I need to write daily, so that I won't feel frazzled. I constantly struggle with the feeling that I am not worth the writing.

10   Of course, I do write daily in another sense. I write lists that I then rewrite throughout the day. The only time earlier when I was a list-maker was when I was pregnant. Then I made lists of things to do, so that when I awoke, I could cross "nap" off of my list and feel a sense of accomplishment. I put away lists when my children were young because then there was no question about what I had to do. As they grew older, I realized that I was making lists again. Although I feared the meaning in my messages, I knew I was not pregnant with a child: I was pregnant with ideas and images. Now I keep lists of titles, ideas, images, and people to guide my writing.

11   While the lists are bait for the hook, I also like to wait with pen and paper—at present a fine-point black Bic and narrow-ruled paper—not having any notion of where the writing will take me. Don Murray writes so compellingly about writing for surprise and discovery that for several years I have tried to give myself the pleasure of beginning with blank mind and paper at least for a few minutes a day.

12   Murray's own writing, as well as his ideas about writing, also help me to become more patient with myself and with writing. I have often wrestled with my writing as it would turn into something alive that I could not control, like the slime children play with that oozes out of cupped palms. As I begin to have faith that the writing will keep me afloat, not that I have to make it happen and control it, my interaction

with language is changing. Kenneth Burke discusses how we do to language but also how language does unto us, and for Burke, symbolic action is the dancing of attitudes. I am beginning to relax, in that important sense of the term which I alluded to earlier. I knew from sports and from dancing that fighting the water or the music only prevents motion. Ideally, we cannot know the dancer from the dance as we are performing.

13   In addition to keeping in shape through some form of daily writing, with faith that the writing will keep me afloat if I let it, I also let my head fill with writing. In graduate school, my head was always working on a current project as I drove the Los Angeles freeways to and from classes. Because of time constraints, I had to write in my head as I drove, and I would arrive home and race inside to get down on paper what was spilling out of my head. This writing in the head was not figuring out what I wanted to write before clothing thoughts in words; it was letting ideas happen, letting them spark each other, and letting voices speak in dialogue.

14   On about the second day during writing project institutes, teachers often comment of their embarrassment at writing in strange places, during dinner, during the middle of conversations, even at traffic lights. We assure ourselves that as long as two writing project teachers aren't at the same light, others are safe. Teachers confess that they are no longer listening to family and friends in the same way; even though part of their minds seem to be writing all of the time, their attentiveness seems to be heightened. As the writing continues, teachers discuss how writing begins to enter their dreams.

15   Writing in the head is not scary, at least not yet. There is no loss of identity or concern for others, and voices in the head do not distract from voices outside. In fact, inner writing seems to make life richer. I have also realized that I was exerting enormous energy keeping the writing out. Again, I am learning to relax and letting the writing happen and the ideas nibble. In a recent writing project institute, when Bob Burk, a biology teacher at Green River High School, created a new term—relaxive writing—a variant of reflexive and expressive, he gave the name for something I have been feeling for some time.

16   As I listen more attentively to myself and to others, I realize that in my teaching I am guilty of the do-what-I-say-not-what-I-do approach. Although I profess that writing teachers must be *writing* teachers and that people who write can call themselves writers, I teach what I want students to believe and act upon, but what I do not fully enact myself. I repeatedly say that people don't have to play in the NBA in order to call themselves basketball players and that people don't have to publish novels to call themselves writers. That applies to students but not to me. What helps is for me to write regularly and to read widely. I also remember Stafford's gentle nudge to reach out and write. What else helps?

Lower Your Standards

17   When Stafford was asked if he ever gets writer's block, he replied that he doesn't: he just lowers his standards. This may sound like blasphemy to teachers but not to writers. Lowering standards is a way in to writing, a way in to raising standards ultimately. Stafford's phrase has generated numerous other rag-tag theories and mixed metaphors that have helped me and my students learn to write.

18   In addition to the paltry draft fear, the I-have-nothing-to-say syndrome, which can be alleviated by lowering one's standards, the dry well theory has also arisen in my classes. Many writers are afraid that if we write what's in our heads, we will run out of words and ideas; therefore, we tend to write without disclosing much until the conclusion, where we place gently the golden egg. Of course, few readers want to wait until the end to find substance.

19   I encourage writers, myself included, to replace the dry well image with the belief that writing can prime the pump, instead of draining it. The more the well is pumped, the greater the yield. If that variation doesn't work, we use another, the squeeze play image, which encourages writers to write what they have in mind right away, instead of waffling around, with the belief that the more they say specifically the more they will have to say. By boldly casting the line, to use another image, the writer elicits numerous nibbles. Students comment on how a writer is like a magician who draws a long string of colorful scarves from a seemingly empty hand, or who releases numerous clowns from a miniature car. All of these scraps of images and mixed metaphors are reflections of my own fears as well as of students' fears; we are all writers together.

20   The drafts produced by the dry well fear may look like discovery drafts, in which writers write to discover ideas that emerge at the ends of sentences, paragraphs, and papers. Writers learn to read both kinds of drafts critically in order to locate the watershed moments. One revision strategy for such drafts is to flip-flop the sentence, paragraph, or paper, so that the main point is put up-front. We have named another strategy for such drafts, the pluck it method, by which the writer extracts the gem or kernel and begins again.

21   Donald Graves has suggested, although in other words, that the dry well fear is taught by teachers. In his article, "Break the Welfare Cycle: Let Writers Choose Their Topics," he explains that when we give students topics we teach them that they don't have anything to write. He advocates also that we *let*, not make, students write, with the confidence based on research that children do have subjects to write on and that they want to write—when the writing means making meaning.

22   Another variation on the dry well fear also has developed in classes, which helps us lower our standards. Perhaps because of living

in mineral-rich, yet dry, Wyoming, we developed the oil well theory. In classes I noticed that some students write freely, without stopping to look up or read, filling a page quickly, whereas others write hesitantly, stopping frequently to think and reread, getting very few words down on paper. Gushers became our name for those who can't seem to stop writing, and eekers became our name for those who can't seem to start. Gushers write without shifting to the role of critical reader of their own text, while eekers shift immediately to the role of critical reader, sometimes even before they have written a word.

23   These two terms describe extremes in writers; neither is good nor bad, and neither fully describes a particular writer. But with these terms, people begin to see themselves as writers and to recognize tendencies in their writing processes, as specific actions, attitudes, and textual features begin to cluster around the terms. For example, gushers tend to work whole to part, while eekers work part to whole. Gushers focus on the overall feel or gist and tend to omit letters, endings, words, sentences, and transitions. For them, everything seems to flow together, and so there is no gap between themselves and their readers. Gushers tend to write run-on sentences, omit specific details for development, and omit markings of tense, possession, and punctuation. In contrast, eekers focus on specifics, such as words, a sentence, an image. They seem acutely aware of the distance between them and their readers, and so they seldom omit a word, ending, letter.

24   The oil well theory has become common in my writing classes, and students who begin to see themselves in terms of certain tendencies seek strategies that will compensate. For example, gushers often seek a strategy that gives order and control, such as a cluster or outline, whereas eekers benefit from free writing, and brainstorming. Writers who tend in one direction, but not too far, often seek strategies that give a balance of freedom and restraint, such as list-order-label and questions.

25   As I watched my students use these terms to help them lower their standards and write, I began to recognize my own tendencies. I am a gusher in that I like the initial bursts of writing, but I have difficulty pushing through to the end. Assembling footnotes and polishing irritate me. But I am a gusher only when I am writing freely, on my own to get started. Less and less, I like to write an assignment. I remember vividly the tall pile of yellow legal paper beside my desk after a psycholinguistics exam, when I could not for forty-five minutes get started because I wanted the first paragraph to be just right. Certainly tendencies in writing are affected by rhetorical contexts, purposes, and audiences.

26   As a gusher, I have learned to recognize and name the various ways I revise. My most common strategy is the rolling dough method. Ideas pour out very quickly and fully, often the initial burst being a

condensed form of the final paper. What I then do is roll out the mass of dough many times—rolling out, reforming, rolling out again to gain the right texture. The physical act of rolling out the ideas seems to help me fill in gaps. The method is time-consuming in that I start from the top many times, but the revisionary actions are very satisfying, unlike the actions that produce the layered look. I recognized in D. H. Lawrence's drafts that he rewrites by the rolling dough method—for example, beginning *Lady Chatterley's Lover* in full several times. In contrast, James Joyce's manuscripts reveal him to be a writer of the layered look school of revision. A single page of the drafts of *Ulysses* is a palimpsest. Several other revision strategies that have also emerged in classes are the collage method, in which small chunks of writing are assembled; the poker hand method, in which written pieces are arrayed like cards to determine which will work best for the particular game and players; and the cut and tape method.

27   All of these strategies are ways for me and students to lower our standards so that we can begin to write and rewrite. Naming our strategies helps us to integrate them, as it creates a code language for our particular community of writers. Most of these strategies, however, are text-centered; they are essential but not sufficient. What else helps?

Let the Lawn Die

28   Annie Dillard has said that in order to write, people have to let the lawn die. This dictum reflects the importance of the writer's relationship to the surrounding situation. Virginia Woolf has made us aware of the importance of a room of one's own, but we also know how difficult it is to claim time for writing—since life must go on and we feel it cannot without us. She has also helped us kill the Angel in the House. Although Agatha Christie has said that "the best time for planning a book is while you're doing the dishes," if one does dishes more than one writes, the book never is written.

29   Unless we are in a place where writing counts most, letting go of other activities is difficult. Teachers, for example, are often afraid that if they write with their students someone might think they are not on the job. Many writers share the experience of having been asked what they are doing. When they reply that they are writing, someone responds, "Well, since you aren't doing anything, would you mind doing this chore for me?"

30   But letting the lawn die means more than claiming time and space for writing, letting go of other duties. It also means taking more risks and responsibilities in writing. One way of letting the lawn die is to identify theories and rules that inhibit writing. I remember a student who came into the Writing Center several years ago with a draft of her

review of *The Ugly American*. As usual, she first talked about her review, which sounded exceptionally clear and convincing. At that time, instead of asking her to read it aloud as I do now, I looked at the draft and was horrified by the contorted syntax and indirection. I asked her a question and once again she talked clearly, but she wrote again with the same contorted writing. After several talk-write sequences, I finally realized that in writing she did not use "I." When I asked why, she said that she was not supposed to, at least that's what she had been taught. The unreadable text was a result of her ingenuity in expressing her views on the book without using the first person pronoun. Once free of the forbidden "I" rule, she wrote clearly and intelligently.

31   Often I discover that I am holding on to a rule as if for life. I might have acquired it as a warning but have since concretized it. I have found myself trying to avoid "and" at the price of clarity, and for a time I wrote as if every other paragraph had to include someone else's authoritative voice. Certainly I, and students, are operating with numerous tacit rules that inhibit writing, but the more we talk about the ones we can identify, the more we reveal.

32   Two useful variations on the let-the-lawn-die theory are the chuck it and tuck it methods. Learning to throw away writing is often painful, and it has to be taught or encouraged. Bob Boba, a junior high teacher in Big Piney, gets his students on the first day to ball up a piece of paper and throw it in the trash can. Then everyone retrieves a piece of crumpled paper and begins writing. For many years I would worry a piece of writing to death, but I could not throw it away. I learned, though, that nothing I write has such importance. Whenever I have a clipping that won't sprout but which I think might, I tuck it away for a while, like bulbs in the winter. Don Murray says that whenever he likes a sentence particularly well, he knows it will probably have to go. In classes, we learn to distinguish ideas, metaphors, and private terms that help the writer get started but that have no meaning for the reader.

33   Ironically, letting the lawn die usually does not mean that the lawn will die. Having been raised in Georgia, I know that lawns grow on their own and that kudzu thrives on isolated back roads. Although the Laramie perspective has made me doubtful, as I cultivate with care the blue flax and yellow daisies that grow as weeds elsewhere, I try to let the lawn die. What else helps?

Listen to the Voices

34   One night after dinner, as we were all talking about how we write, my son, Walter, tried to exit unnoticed as he juggled the three oranges and two ice cream sandwiches for his after-dinner snack. We asked how he writes. He paused, put down his nourishment, and replied, "Oh, I just listen to the voices," indicating the general area behind him between

his left shoulder and ear. He continued to explain that he sometimes writes from his forehead, especially when a teacher tells him what to write, but he knows that the writing is good when he writes the voices.

35   From Walter and others, I am learning to listen to the voices, the disembodied voices in my own head, who speak not always one at a time but often as in a chorus or shouting match. Instead of trying to control the voices in my head, I try to listen to them as to a dialogue I am overhearing. I also have begun to listen to the voices around me: family, friends, students, radio announcers, and television characters.

36   For several years, Kenneth Burke's image in *The Philosophy of Literary Form* of how people learn language has been very important to me, but I have lately begun to see it as an image of myself participating in the conversations in my head:

> Imagine that you enter a parlor. You come late. When you arrive, others have long preceded you, and they are engaged in a heated discussion, too heated for them to pause and tell you exactly what it is about. In fact, the discussion had already begun long before any of them got there, so that no one present is qualified to retrace for you all the steps that had gone before. You listen for a while, until you decide that you have caught the tenor of the argument; then you put in your oar. Someone answers; you answer him; another comes to your defense; another aligns himself against you, to either the embarrassment or gratification of your opponent, depending upon the quality of your ally's assistance. However, the discussion is interminable. The hour grows late, you must depart. And you do depart, with the discussion still vigorously in progress.
>
> (*The Philosophy of Literary Form*, pp. 110–111)

I also find it helpful not to enter the inner conversation sometimes but just to listen.

37   Listening to voices does not mean only listening to internal voices. I hear my students in writing give voice to themselves and others, and I learn. Mike, who is now a graduate student in biology with several publications, wrote the following in a freshman English class several years ago:

> I don't know why in the hell I am here. I hate to write. I have flunked English four times in three different states. I don't want to be here. My palms are sweaty and I am mad.

I heard Mike that day, and I am still listening to him as he writes in various voices.

38   Throughout last semester, I heard Rhonda voice her perspectives on returning to school and my own writing grew:

As I loaded my two-year old daughter, Elaine, into the old Ford truck and drove up the country lane, I tore our family apart, leaving my five-year-old son, David, behind with his father and grandmother on the small ranch that had been my home for nine years of a troubled marriage.

39   Judy also gave voice to herself in writing and helped me to hear myself and others:

I was a junior in high school when my mother sank down on the freshly vacuumed suburban home. Her size five shoulders shook as she passed a hand over her carefully mascaraed eyes. An absurd, tight smile stretched to grimace proportions. With dread resolution my mother announced, "I just can't do it anymore."

But my mother did go on. She rose the next morning as if last night's scene was someone else's property. By eight in the morning she had already made breakfast, put the house in order, showered, dressed and was ready for an eight-hour day. At lunch she would do the grocery shopping, at five she would attend exercise class, by seven supper would be on the table and then the remaining evening would be devoted to laundry. That was seven years ago and I have yet to see my mother erupt in anger and bitterness. But it is still there, smouldering in coals until fanned by a wisp of discontent when it will flame hot and consume itself again.

I am becoming a woman now. And I am angry.

40   Gary is an older student who, after being an accountant for many years, has returned to school. Through a series of drafts he experimented with various voices. The first appeared in an in-class, short writing about a job:

I wonder what they do with wool these days—bet it isn't handled like it was in 1946—one of the jobs I had during part of a summer when I was in high school.

He wrote on this job again for an in-class free writing four days later:

I worked as a laborer in an old warehouse for a part of one summer between my freshman and sophomore years in high school. The job was working with wool.

A month later he returned to the piece:

The wool sacks stood on end, slightly sloped, each leaning against its neighbor, holding one another from falling. They appeared as a ghostlike army, row on row, separated by narrow aisles, in the shadowy darkness of the long warehouse.

At this point, Gary decided to let the writing become fiction, and he allowed the voices of the other boys with whom he had worked to speak in his writing.

41   Our voices seem to come when we stop and write—lower our standards, let the lawn die, and listen. I am glad that my son, Walter, trusts the voices that he hears. I am also glad that Alice Walker wrote *The Color Purple* with its chorus of voices, and I am glad she described in her collected essays, *In Search of Our Mothers' Gardens*, how she moved around the country, so that her characters could feel at home and speak clearly.

42   I am glad also in this writing to give voice to the many professional and student writers whose words encourage me to learn to write. While this clutter of rag-tag theories, images, and metaphors has helped me in the past, by writing them in this form they allow me now to move beyond them to a new language. I am not sure what the new language will be, but I am fairly certain that it will be a language already well used by others. I am also fairly certain that I will never learn to write but that I will continue learning, with the help of others.

(4,911 words)

VOCABULARY

alluded (12)	elicits (19)	inhibit (30)
constraints (13)	psycholinguistics (25)	contorted (30)
reflexive (15)	palimpsest (26)	concretized (31)
syndrome (18)	collage (26)	tacit (31)
waffling (19)	dictum (28)	disembodied (35)

THE FACTS

1. What "golden dream" does the author confess to having had many years of her life?

2. What does the author mean by "the rat in the basement"? What kind of rats live in your personal basement?

3. What reply did author William Stafford make when asked how he avoids writer's block?

4. What terms does the author use, based on her residence in Wyoming, to distinguish two extreme kinds of writers? Into which category do you fall?

5. According to the author Agatha Christie, when is the best time to plan a book?

THE STRATEGIES

1. The author is an English teacher writing an essay for a monograph or specialized textbook. Given these background facts, what is most notable about her style?

2. How does the author use her opening paragraph to engage our interest? How is her opening tied in with her closing?

3. What is the point of all the questions in paragraph 7?

4. What transition sentence does the writer employ in both paragraphs 27 and 33? Do you think this repetition deliberate or an oversight?

5. What is the author's principal source of supporting details behind her explanations of how she writes? How effective do you find these details?

THE ISSUES

1. The author expends a great deal of ink expressing what she fears about writing and cataloguing antidotes to these fears she and her students have devised. What is your opinion of such microscopic self-scrutiny about one's writing fears? Do you think it healthy or unhelpful?

2. What rats in the basement do you suffer from as you grope to develop as a writer? How do you cope with them?

3. To what kind of writing does the author's advice seem particularly to apply? How useful do you find her varied strategies for dealing with your own struggles to write?

4. What is your opinion of collegiate or secondary school writing courses? How have they helped or hindered your own growth as a writer?

5. The author tells the story of a student who went to contorted lengths to avoid using "I" in her prose, and admits to having had a similar fixation about not using "and." What similar fixation of grammar or style have you personally suffered from in your own writing?

SUGGESTIONS FOR WRITING

1. As a college student, you have probably already taken one or two courses on how to write. Based on your experiences of success and failure in these courses, write an essay suggesting how you would teach writing if you were an instructor.

2. How do you write? Write an essay giving details to answer that question.

E X A M P L E S

▼▼

Martin Luther King, Jr.

I HAVE A DREAM

MARTIN LUTHER KING, JR. (1929–1968), American clergyman and black civil rights leader, was born in Atlanta and educated at Morehouse College, Crozer Theological Seminary, and Boston University (Ph.D., 1955). A lifelong advocate of nonviolent resistance to segregation, he led a boycott of blacks in Montgomery, Alabama (1955–1956) against the city's segregated bus system and organized a massive march on Washington in 1963, during which he delivered his famous "I Have a Dream" speech. In 1964 he was awarded the Nobel Peace Prize. Dr. King was assassinated April 4, 1968, on the balcony of a motel in Memphis, Tennessee, where he had journeyed in support of the city's striking sanitation workers.

In August 1963, more than two hundred thousand blacks and whites gathered peacefully in Washington, D.C., to focus attention on black demands for civil rights. The marchers gathered at the Lincoln Memorial, where Dr. King delivered this impassioned speech.

1   Five score years ago, a great American, in whose symbolic shadow we stand today, signed the Emancipation Proclamation. This momentous decree came as a great beacon of light of hope to millions of Negro slaves who had been seared in the flames of withering injustice. It came as a joyous daybreak to end the long night of their captivity.

2   But one hundred years later, the Negro still is not free. One hundred years later, the life of the Negro is still sadly crippled by the manacles of segregation and the chains of discrimination.

3   One hundred years later, the Negro lives on a lonely island of poverty in the midst of a vast ocean of material prosperity. One hundred years later, the Negro is still languished in the corners of American society and finds himself an exile in his own land. So we have come here today to dramatize a shameful condition.

4   In a sense we have come to our nation's capital to cash a check. When the architects of our republic wrote the magnificent words of the Constitution and the Declaration of Independence, they were

signing a promissory note to which every American was to fall heir. This note was a promise that all men, yes, black men as well as white men, would be granted the unalienable rights of life, liberty, and the pursuit of happiness.

5   It is obvious today that America has defaulted on this promissory note insofar as her citizens of color are concerned. Instead of honoring this sacred obligation, America has given the Negro people a bad check, which has come back marked "insufficient funds."

6   But we refuse to believe that the bank of justice is bankrupt. We refuse to believe that there are insufficient funds in the great vaults of opportunity of this nation. So we have come to cash this check—a check that will give us upon demand the riches of freedom and the security of justice.

7   We have also come to this hallowed spot to remind America of the fierce urgency of now. This is no time to engage in the luxury of cooling off or to take the tranquilizing drug of gradualism. Now is the time to make real the promises of democracy. Now is the time to rise from the dark and desolate valley of segregation to the sunlit path of racial justice. Now is the time to lift our nation from the quick sands of racial injustice to the solid rock of brotherhood. Now is the time to make justice a reality for all of God's children.

8   It would be fatal for the nation to overlook the urgency of the movement and to underestimate the determination of the Negro. This sweltering summer of the Negro's legitimate discontent will not pass until there is an invigorating autumn of freedom and equality. 1963 is not an end but a beginning. Those who hope that the Negro needed to blow off steam and will now be content will have a rude awakening if the nation returns to business as usual.

9   There will be neither rest nor tranquility in America until the Negro is granted his citizenship rights. The whirlwinds of revolt will continue to shake the foundations of our nation until the bright day of justice emerges.

10   But there is something that I must say to my people who stand on the warm threshold which leads into the palace of justice. In the process of gaining our rightful place we must not be guilty of wrongful deeds.

11   Let us not seek to satisfy our thirst for freedom by drinking from the cup of bitterness and hatred. We must forever conduct our struggle on the high plane of dignity and discipline. We must not allow our creative protest to degenerate into physical violence. Again and again we must rise to the majestic heights of meeting physical force with soul force.

12   The marvelous new militancy which has engulfed the Negro community must not lead us to a distrust of all white people, for many of our white brothers, as evidenced by their presence here today, have

come to realize that their destiny is tied up with our destiny and they have come to realize that their freedom is inextricably bound to our freedom. This offense we share mounted to storm the battlements of injustice must be carried forth by a biracial army. We cannot walk alone.

13   And as we walk, we must make the pledge that we shall always march ahead. We cannot turn back. There are those who are asking the devotees of civil rights, "When will you be satisfied?" We can never be satisfied as long as the Negro is the victim of the unspeakable horrors of police brutality.

14   We can never be satisfied as long as our bodies, heavy with the fatigue of travel, cannot gain lodging in the motels of the highways and the hotels of the cities. We cannot be satisfied as long as the Negro's basic mobility is from a smaller ghetto to a larger one.

15   We can never be satisfied as long as our children are stripped of their selfhood and robbed of their dignity by signs stating "for whites only." We cannot be satisfied as long as a Negro in Mississippi cannot vote and a Negro in New York believes he has nothing for which to vote. No, we are not satisfied, and we will not be satisfied until justice rolls down like waters and righteousness like a mighty stream.

16   I am not unmindful that some of you have come here out of excessive trials and tribulation. Some of you have come fresh from narrow jail cells. Some of you have come from areas where your quest for freedom left you battered by the storms of persecution and staggered by the winds of police brutality. You have been the veterans of creative suffering. Continue to work with the faith that unearned suffering is redemptive.

17   Go back to Mississippi; go back to Alabama; go back to South Carolina; go back to Georgia; go back to Louisiana; go back to the slums and ghettos of the Northern cities, knowing that somehow this situation can, and will be changed. Let us not wallow in the valley of despair.

18   So I say to you, my friends, that even though we must face the difficulties of today and tomorrow, I still have a dream. It is a dream deeply rooted in the American dream that one day this nation will rise up and live out the true meaning of its creed—we hold these truths to be self evident, that all men are created equal.

19   I have a dream that one day on the red hills of Georgia, sons of former slaves and sons of former slave-owners will be able to sit down together at the table of brotherhood.

20   I have a dream that one day, even the state of Mississippi, a state sweltering with the heat of injustice, sweltering with the heat of oppression, will be transformed into an oasis of freedom and justice.

21   I have a dream my four little children will one day live in a nation where they will not be judged by the color of their skin but by the content of their character. I have a dream today!

22   I have a dream that one day, down in Alabama, with its vicious racists, with its governor having his lips dripping with the words of interposition and nullification, that one day, right there in Alabama, little black boys and black girls will be able to join hands with little white boys and white girls as sisters and brothers. I have a dream today!

23   I have a dream that one day every valley shall be exalted, every hill and mountain shall be made low, the rough places shall be made plain, and the crooked places shall be made straight and the glory of the Lord will be revealed and all flesh shall see it together.

24   This is our hope. This is the faith that I go back to the South with.

25   With this faith we will be able to hew out of the mountain of despair a stone of hope. With this faith we will be able to transform the jangling discords of our nation into a beautiful symphony of brotherhood.

26   With this faith we will be able to work together, to pray together, to struggle together, to go to jail together, to stand up for freedom together, knowing that we will be free one day. This will be the day when all of God's children will be able to sing with new meaning—"my country 'tis of thee; sweet land of liberty; of thee I sing; land where my fathers died, land of the pilgrim's pride; from every mountain side, let freedom ring"—and if America is to be a great nation, this must become true.

27   So let freedom ring from the prodigious hilltops of New Hampshire.

28   Let freedom ring from the mighty mountains of New York.

29   Let freedom ring from the heightening Alleghenies of Pennsylvania.

30   Let freedom ring from the snow-capped Rockies of Colorado.

31   Let freedom ring from the curvaceous slopes of California.

32   But not only that.

33   Let freedom ring from Stone Mountain of Georgia.

34   Let freedom ring from Lookout Mountain of Tennessee.

35   Let freedom ring from every hill and molehill of Mississippi, from every mountainside, let freedom ring.

36   And when we allow freedom to ring, when we let it ring from every village and hamlet, from every state and city, we will be able to speed up that day when all of God's children—black men and white men, Jews and Gentiles, Catholics and Protestants—will be able to join hands and to sing in the words of the old Negro spiritual, "Free at last, free at last; thank God Almighty, we are free at last."

(1,643 words)

VOCABULARY

momentous (1)	invigorating (8)	sweltering (20)
manacles (2)	degenerate (11)	interposition (22)
languished (3)	militancy (12)	nullification (22)
unalienable (4)	inextricably (12)	exalted (23)
hallowed (7)	tribulation (16)	prodigious (27)
gradualism (7)	redemptive (16)	curvaceous (31)

THE FACTS

1. The speech begins "Five score years ago, . . ." Why was this beginning especially appropriate?

2. What grievances of black Americans does Dr. King summarize in paragraphs 2 and 3 of this speech?

3. What does Dr. King caution his listeners against in paragraph 11?

4. What attitude toward white people does the speaker urge upon his audience?

5. Although Dr. King speaks out mainly against injustices committed against blacks in the South, he is also critical of the North. What can be inferred from this speech about the living conditions of blacks in the North during the early 1960s?

THE STRATEGIES

1. One critic has written of this speech that its purpose was to intensify the values of the black movement. What characteristic of its style can you point to that might be said to have served this purpose?

2. Paragraphs 4 through 6 of the speech are linked through the use of an extended analogy. What is this analogy?

3. What common rhetorical device does the speech frequently use to emphasize its points?

4. It is often said that speakers and writers use paragraphs differently. How are the paragraphs of this speech especially adapted for oral delivery? What is the most obvious difference between these paragraphs and the ones a writer might use?

5. What is the function of the brief paragraph 32?

THE ISSUES

1. Since *black* is a term widely used in the United States to designate people whose skin color may range from dark brown to sepia, what definition of blackness does our society seem implicitly to use?

2. What, in your opinion, is the basis of racial prejudice?

3. Will the United States ever have a black president? Defend your answer.

4. Does prejudice in the United States against black men exceed or equal the prejudice against black women? Explain the difference, if there is one, and justify your answer.

5. What stereotypes do you hold about black people? Write them down along with an explanation of how you arrived at them. Share them with your classmates.

SUGGESTIONS FOR WRITING

1. Write an essay analyzing the extensive use of metaphors in this speech. Comment on their effectiveness, bearing in mind the audience for whom the speech was intended.

2. Write an essay analyzing the oral style of this speech. Point out specific techniques of phrasing, sentence construction, paragraphing, and so on, that identify this composition as a speech. Suggest how a writer might have alternately phrased some passages if this work had been written to be read rather than delivered.

▼▼▼

John Keats

LETTER TO FANNY BRAWNE

JOHN KEATS (1795–1821), among the greatest of English poets, was born the son of a livery stable keeper and apprenticed to a surgeon in 1811. Through his friendship with the poet and critic Leigh Hunt (1784–1859), who presided over a literary circle, Keats soon gave up surgery and began to write poetry. His first book of poetry appeared in 1817 and was savagely attacked by critics as belonging to the "Cockney school" of poetry. A subsequent volume, *Lamia, Isabella, The Eve of St. Agnes, and Other Poems* (1820), is regarded as the greatest collection of poetry published in the century. Keats contracted tuberculosis and died at the age of 25 in Rome, nursed by a faithful friend, the artist Joseph Severn.

*Keats wrote this letter to his beloved Fanny Brawne (1800–1865) from
Shanklin, Isle of Wight, where he had gone on holiday. Like Keats
himself, Fanny also had her share of critics, many of whom initially
described her as a "cold, hard, haughty young woman." But with the
discovery of letters Fanny herself had written about her poet lover, the
opinion of scholars has substantially changed, with many now regarding her as "a young woman of remarkable perception and imagination" who would have been "intellectually fitted to become the wife
of Keats." Twelve years after the death of Keats, Fanny married Louis
Lindo, who was twelve years her junior. She bore him three children
and shares his grave in Brompton Cemetery, Kensington.*

TO FANNY BRAWNE
25 July 1819

Sunday Night.

My sweet Girl,

   I hope you did not blame me much for not obeying your request of
a Letter on Saturday: we have had four in our small room playing at
cards night and morning leaving me no undisturb'd opportunity to
write. Now Rice[1] and Martin[2] are gone I am at liberty. Brown to my
sorrow confirms the account you give of your ill health. You cannot
conceive how I ache to be with you: how I would die for one hour—for
what is in the world? I say you cannot conceive; it is impossible you
should look with such eyes upon me as I have upon you: it cannot be.
Forgive me if I wander a little this evening, for I have been all day employ'd in a very abstr[a]ct Poem[3] and I am in deep love with you—two
things which must excuse me. I have, believe me, not been an age in letting you take possession of me; the very first week I knew you I wrote
myself your vassal; but burnt the Letter as the very next time I saw you
I thought you manifested some dislike to me. If you should ever feel for
Man at the first sight what I did for you, I am lost. Yet I should not
quarrel with you, but hate myself if such a thing were to happen—only
I should burst if the thing were not as fine as a Man as you are as a
Woman. Perhaps I am too vehement, then fancy me on my knees, especially when I mention a part of your Letter which hurt me; you say
speaking of Mr. Severn[4] "but you must be satisfied in knowing that I
admired you much more than your friend." My dear love, I cannot believe there ever was or ever could be any thing to admire in me especially as far as sight goes—I cannot be admired, I am not a thing to be

---

[1] James Rice, Jr., attorney (1792–1832) and friend of Keats.
[2] John Martin (1791–1855), publisher and bookseller.
[3] Probably *Hyperion*.
[4] Joseph Severn (1793–1879) painter and deathbed companion of Keats.

admired. You are, I love you; all I can bring you is a swooning admiration of your Beauty. I hold that place among Men which snubnos'd brunettes with meeting eyebrows do among women—they are trash to me—unless I should find one among them with a fire in her heart like the one that burns in mine. You absorb me in spite of myself—you alone: for I look not forward with any pleasure to what is call'd being settled in the world; I tremble at domestic cares—yet for you I would meet them, though if it would leave you the happier I would rather die than do so. I have two luxuries to brood over in my walks, your Loveliness and the hour of my death. O that I could have possession of them both in the same minute. I hate the world: it batters too much the wings of my self-will, and would I could take a sweet poison from your lips to send me out of it. From no others would I take it. I am indeed astonish'd to find myself so careless of all cha[r]ms but yours—remembring as I do the time when even a bit of ribband was a matter of interest with me. What softer words can I find for you after this—what it is I will not read. Nor will I say more here, but in a Postscript[5] answer any thing else you may have mentioned in your Letter in so many words—for I am distracted with a thousand thoughts. I will imagine you Venus tonight and pray, pray, pray to your star like a Heathen.

Your's ever, fair Star,
John Keats.

(628 words)

VOCABULARY

vassal (1)   manifested (1)   vehement (1)

THE FACTS

1. What excuse does Keats give for not writing sooner?

2. According to Keats, how long was it before he knew himself to be in love with Fanny?

3. What does Fanny say in her letter that Keats refuses to believe about himself?

4. What two luxuries does Keats say he has to brood over in his walks?

5. What feelings does Keats have about the world that he expresses in this letter?

---

[5] Omitted here.

THE STRATEGIES

1. What are the rhetorical pressures faced by a writer who sits down to compose a love letter? What consolations does the occasion offer a writer?

2. How does this particular love letter differ from one that might be written today? What specific features earmark it as not modern?

3. What rhetorical role does a man traditionally assume when he writes a love letter to a woman, and how does Keats conform to this expected convention?

4. How do you think this letter might have differed if it been written by a woman passionately in love with a man?

5. What is the implication of the image in the last line of this letter? In what conventional terms does this implication cast Keats, the lover, and Fanny, the beloved?

THE ISSUES

1. What might a modern psychologically minded reader conclude about Keats from what he says in this letter?

2. A contemporary of Keats wrote about the poet, "a genius more purely poetical never existed." What about this letter might strike a modern reader as "purely poetical"?

3. What are some of the common stereotypes prevalent in popular thinking about the poetic temperament? Which, if any, of these stereotypes are evident in this letter?

4. What about this love letter might some modern women find offensive?

5. Keats relegates to a postscript (not included in this version) answers to some practical everyday questions Fanny apparently asked him in her letter. Why do you think he chose to do this? What does this gesture imply about him?

SUGGESTIONS FOR WRITING

1. Write an essay discussing the kinds of rhetorical problems and pressures involved in composing a love letter.

2. If you are a woman, write an essay discussing what you think men would like to read in a love letter sent to them. If you are a man, write an essay discussing what you think women want to read in a love letter sent to them. Get together with your male or female

counterpart and compare the observations in your respective essays.

▼▼

Francis P. Church

EDITORIAL: IS THERE A SANTA CLAUS?

FRANCIS P. CHURCH (1839–1906), editorial writer and journalist, was born in Rochester, New York, and educated at Columbia College. A former editor of Galaxy magazine, he became the editorial writer for the *New York Sun* in 1874.

VIRGINIA O'HANLON (1890–1971) grew up to become a teacher and school principal in the New York City public school system. Frequently called upon at Christmas to read the editorial she had prompted with her innocent letter, she once wryly remarked, "I am anonymous from January to November."

> *Editorial writers usually work in anonymity, crafting essays that reflect the collective wisdom of the newspapers that employ them. This editorial had become so seasonally famous that following the death of Church in 1906,* The Sun *broke its policy of anonymity to credit him with writing it. Church wrote the editorial on September 21, 1897, in response to a letter from eight-year-old Virginia O'Hanlon.*

Dear Editor: I am 8 years old.
Some of my little friends say there is no Santa Claus.
Papa says "If you see it in *The Sun* it's so."
Please tell me the truth; is there a Santa Claus?

Virginia O'Hanlon.
115 West Ninety-fifth Street.

1   Virginia, your little friends are wrong. They have been affected by the skepticism of a skeptical age. They do not believe except they see. They think that nothing can be which is not comprehensible by their little minds. All minds, Virginia, whether they be men's or children's are little. In this great universe of ours man is a mere insect, an ant, in his intellect, as compared with the boundless world about him, as measured by the intelligence capable of grasping the whole of truth and knowledge.

2   Yes, Virginia, there is a Santa Claus. He exists as certainly as love and generosity and devotion exist, and you know that they abound and give to your life its highest beauty and joy. Alas! how dreary would be the world if there were no Santa Claus. It would be as dreary as if there

were no Virginias. There would be no childlike faith then, no poetry, no romance to make tolerable this existence. We should have no enjoyment, except in sense and sight. The eternal light with which childhood fills the world would be extinguished.

3   Not believe in Santa Claus! You might as well not believe in fairies! You might get your papa to hire men to watch in all the chimneys on Christmas Eve to catch Santa Claus but even if they did not see Santa Claus coming down, what would that prove? Nobody sees Santa Claus, but that is no sign that there is no Santa Claus. The most real things in the world are those that neither children nor men can see. Did you ever see fairies dancing on the lawn? Of course not, but that's no proof that they are not there. Nobody can conceive or imagine all the wonders there are unseen and unseeable in the world.

4   You may tear apart the baby's rattle and see what makes the noise inside, but there is a veil covering the unseen world which not the strongest man, nor even the united strength of all the strongest men that ever lived, could tear apart. Only faith, fancy, poetry, love, romance, can push aside that curtain and view and picture the supernal beauty and glory beyond. Is it all real? Ah, Virginia, in all this world there is nothing else real and abiding.

5   No Santa Claus! Thank God! he lives, and he lives forever. A thousand years from now, Virginia, nay, ten times ten thousand years from now, he will continue to make glad the heart of childhood.

(463 words)

VOCABULARY

supernal (4)

THE FACTS

1. What does Church say has affected the belief of Virginia's doubting friends?

2. With what qualities does Church equate Santa Claus?

3. Why, according to Church, would the world be dreary without Santa Claus?

4. What, according to Church, are the most real things in the world?

THE STRATEGIES

1. Who is the audience of this editorial? What obvious adaptations did Church make to accommodate its audience?

2. What two meanings does the author seem to assign to Santa Claus? Why do you think this was necessary, and how does he make this dual meaning clear?

3. How would you characterize the tone of these two sentences, "Not believe in Santa Claus! You might as well not believe in fairies!"

4. In paragraph 4, the author writes that only "faith, fancy, poetry, love, romance, can push aside that curtain." What meaning do you think he intends for the word "fancy"?

THE ISSUES

1. Some religious groups oppose the concept of Santa Claus. What rationale do you think exists for this opposition?

2. What effect do you think Santa Claus has had on the celebration of Christmas?

3. What do you think would have been the response of subscribers if *The Sun* had published an editorial admitting that Santa Claus is a myth?

4. What harm, if any, do you think a belief in Santa Claus can cause a child? What good can you foresee, which Church touches on in his editorial?

SUGGESTIONS FOR WRITING

1. Write an essay telling how belief in Santa Claus affected you as a child.

2. In an essay, say how you discovered that Santa Claus was a myth and how the discovery made you feel.

ISSUE FOR CRITICAL THINKING AND DEBATE

▾▾

POLITICAL CORRECTNESS

"Political correctness" is a phrase that has been much used lately. But exactly what it means depends on whom you ask. *Toward the Tower*, a painting by Remedios Varo that leads off this section, hints of the meaning commonly ascribed to this term. It graphically suggests political

Remedios Varo (1908–1963), Toward the Tower, *1961. Oil on masonite, 48³/₈ × 39³/₈ inches. By permission of Walter Gruen, Mexico City. Copyright © 1997 Artists Rights Society (ARS)/VEGAP, Madrid.*

correctness in a group of identically clad girls on bicycles being led by a grotesque man and a uniformed nun out of what looks like a castle. The absurd procession of blank-faced girls daintily lined up on silly bicycles behind a ridiculous looking man and an impassive nun suggests the authoritarian conformity that is allegedly practiced by the politically correct.

To conservatives, "political correctness" conjures up the existence of so-called "thought police" on campus who are bent on rigidly enforcing political orthodoxy among students. To liberals, it is a bogeyman phrase invented by conservatives to smear any who disagree with their particular brand of political straitlacedness. That the debate over this elusive term comes down to competing interpretations only makes the issue murkier.

Nor does clarity come from reading the furious charges being hurled by either side. Conservatives, for example, claim that followers of political correctness are humorless leftwingers bent on replacing the heritage of western civilization with a wishy-washy multiculturalism that welcomes every creed and doctrine, no matter how eccentric or alien. Under the umbrella of political correctness, charge the conservatives, is the belief that all lifestyles are acceptable and deserving of respect, even those that depart from traditional heterosexual monogamy. And to the politically correct, no dissent from this accommodating orthodoxy is allowed.

For their part, the liberals charge conservatives not only with making up the term "political correctness" but also with inventing fictitious events to prove its existence. What is involved, say the liberals, is the unwillingness of stuffed-shirt conservatives to tolerate any but the narrowest and most traditional lifestyles or creeds. To ban the harassment of feminists and gays on campus by enforcing a strict speech code, the liberals argue, is to demand civility in public debate, not orthodoxy. To teach the cultural contributions of blacks and other minorities in the curriculum is merely to be realistic and truthful, not politically correct.

Both sides—liberal as well as conservative—are represented in the essays of this section. John Taylor, a political writer for *New York* magazine, cites examples of what he terms a "new sort of fundamentalism" on campus. He shows us professors allegedly harassed by jeering students over innocent statements; he quotes the so-called new radicals spouting a mishmash of outrageous opinions.

Rosa Ehrenreich, a former student at Harvard, answers by debunking Taylor's thesis about the existence of campus radicals who function as thought police. She argues that political correctness was invented by conservatives such as former President George Bush because the bogus issue played well in public debate. She tackles one or two instances cited by Taylor and shows them in an entirely different light. The student essayist weighs in with a humorous piece about using euphemisms to skirt sensitive issues in these politically tense times.

Political correctness—whether a fact or figment of campus life—clearly demarks the seismic fault-line that splits liberals and conservatives, the left from the right. And as a symbol of this political division, if nothing else, it undeniably exists.

▼▼

John Taylor

ARE YOU POLITICALLY CORRECT?

JOHN TAYLOR (b. 1955), political columnist for *New York* magazine, was born in Yokosuka, Japan, to diplomat parents. Educated at the University of Chicago, he is the author of two books, *Storming the Magic Kingdom: Wall Street, the Raiders, and the Battle for Disney* (1987), and *Circuits of Ambition: The Culture of Wealth and Power in the 80's* (1989).

1   "Racist."
"Racist!"
"The man is a racist!"
"A *racist!*"

2   Such denunciations, hissed in tones of self-righteousness and contempt, vicious and vengeful, furious, smoking with hatred—such denunciations haunted Stephan Thernstrom for weeks. Whenever he walked through the campus that spring, down Harvard's brick paths, under the arched gates, past the fluttering elms, he found it hard not to imagine the pointing fingers, the whispers. Racist. There goes *the racist*. It was hellish, this persecution. Thernstrom couldn't sleep. His nerves were frayed, his temper raw. He was making his family miserable. And the worst thing was that he didn't know who was calling him a racist, or why.

3   Thernstrom, 56, a professor at Harvard University for 25 years, is considered one of the preeminent scholars of the history of race relations in America. He has tenure. He has won prizes and published numerous articles and four books and edited the *Harvard Encyclopedia of American Ethnic Groups.* For several years, Thernstrom and another professor, Bernard Bailyn, taught an undergraduate lecture course on the history of race relations in the United States called "Peopling of America." Bailyn covered the Colonial era. Thernstrom took the class up to the present.

4   Both professors are regarded as very much in the academic mainstream, their views grounded in extensive research on their subject, and both have solid liberal democratic credentials. But all of a sudden, in the fall of 1987, articles began to appear in the *Harvard Crimson* accusing Thernstrom and Bailyn of "racial insensitivity" in "Peopling of America." The sources for the articles were anonymous, the charges vague, but they continued to be repeated, these ringing indictments.

5   Finally, through the intervention of another professor, two students from the lecture course came forward and identified themselves

as the sources for the articles. When asked to explain their grievances, they presented the professors with a six-page letter. Bailyn's crime had been to read from the diary of a southern planter without giving equal time to the recollections of a slave. This, to the students, amounted to a covert defense of slavery. Bailyn, who has won two Pulitzer Prizes, had pointed out during the lecture that no journals, diaries, or letters written by slaves had ever been found. He had explained to the class that all they could do was read the planter's diary and use it to speculate about the experience of slaves. But that failed to satisfy the complaining students. Since it was impossible to give equal representation to the slaves, Bailyn ought to have dispensed with the planter's diary altogether.

6   Thernstrom's failures, according to the students, were almost systematic. He had, to begin with, used the word *Indians* instead of *Native Americans*. Thernstrom tried to point out that he had said very clearly in class that *Indian* was the word most Indians themselves use, but that was irrelevant to the students. They considered the word racist. Thernstrom was also accused of referring to an "Oriental religion." The word *Oriental*, with its imperialist overtones, was unacceptable. Thernstrom explained that he had used the word as an adjective, not as a noun, but the students weren't buying any wriggling, sophistic evasions like that.

7   Even worse, they continued, Thernstrom had assigned a book to the class that mentioned that some people regarded affirmative action as preferential treatment. That was a racist opinion. But most egregiously, Thernstrom had endorsed, in class, Patrick Moynihan's emphasis on the breakup of the black family as a cause of persistent black poverty. That was a racist idea.

8   All of these words and opinions and ideas and historical approaches were racist. *Racist!* They would not be tolerated.

9   The semester was pretty much over by then. But during the spring, when Thernstrom sat down to plan the course for the following year, he had to think about how he would combat charges of racism should they crop up again. And they assuredly would. All it took was one militant student, one word like *Oriental* taken out of context, one objection that a professor's account of slavery was insufficiently critical or that, in discussing black poverty, he had raised the "racist" issue of welfare dependency. And a charge of racism, however unsubstantiated, leaves a lasting impression. "It's like being called a Commie in the fifties," Thernstrom says. "Whatever explanation you offer, once accused, you're always suspect."

10   He decided that to protect himself in case he was misquoted or had comments taken out of context, he would need to tape all his lectures. Then he decided he would have to tape his talks with students in his office. He would, in fact, have to tape everything he said on the subject of

race. It would require a tape-recording system worthy of the Nixon White House. Microphones everywhere, the reels turning constantly. That was plainly ridiculous. Thernstrom instead decided it would be easier just to drop the course altogether. "Peopling of America" is no longer offered at Harvard.

11   When The CHRISTIAN-Fundamentalist uprising began in the late seventies, Americans on the left sneered at the Bible thumpers who tried to ban the teaching of evolution in public schools, at the troglodytes who wanted to remove *The Catcher in the Rye* from public libraries. They heaped scorn on the evangelists who railed against secular humanism and the pious hypocrites who tried to legislate patriotism and Christianity through school prayer and the Pledge of Allegiance. This last effort was considered particularly heinous. Those right-wing demagogues were interfering with individual liberties! They were trying to indoctrinate the children! It was scandalous and outrageous, and unconstitutional too.

12   But curiously enough, in the past few years, a new sort of fundamentalism has arisen precisely among those people who were the most appalled by Christian fundamentalism. And it is just as demagogic and fanatical. The new fundamentalists are an eclectic group; they include multiculturalists, feminists, radical homosexuals, Marxists, New Historicists. What unites them—as firmly as the Christian fundamentalists are united in the belief that the Bible is the revealed word of God—is their conviction that Western culture and American society are thoroughly and hopelessly racist, sexist, oppressive. "Racism and sexism are pervasive in America and fundamentally present in all American institutions," declares a draft report on "race and gender enrichment" at Tulane University. A 1989 report by a New York State Board of Education task force was even more sweeping: "Intellectual and educational oppression . . . has characterized the culture and institutions of the United States and the European American world for centuries."

13   The heart of the new fundamentalists' argument is not just that, as most everyone would agree, racism and sexism historically have existed within political systems designed to promote individual liberties. They believe that the doctrine of individual liberties *itself* is inherently oppressive. At the University of Pennsylvania, an undergraduate on the "diversity education committee" wrote a memo to committee members describing her "deep regard for the individual and my desire to protect the freedoms of all members of society." The tone was earnest and sincere. The young woman clearly considered herself an idealist of the Jeffersonian persuasion. Individual freedom, she seemed to indicate, was a concept to be cherished above all else.

14   But in the prevailing climate, Thomas Jefferson and all the Founding Fathers are in disrepute. (The Constitution, according to the 1989

SPECIFIC MANIFESTATIONS OF OPPRESSION:

As you can see from the above definition of oppression, people can be oppressed in many ways and for many reasons because they are perceived to be different. As groups of people begin the process of realizing that they are oppressed, and why, new words tend to be created to express the concepts that the existing language cannot. Thus, some of the words below may be familiar to you while others may be new.

ABLEISM: oppression of the differently abled, by the temporarily able.

AGEISM: oppression of the young and the old, by young adults and the middle-aged in the belief that others are "incapable" or unable to take care of themselves.

ANTI-SEMITISM: oppression of Jewish peoples in the belief that they are members of an inferior group because of ethnic identity and religion.

CLASSISM: oppression of the working-class and non-propertied, by the upper- and middle-class.

ETHNOCENTRISM: oppression of cultures other than the dominant one in the belief that the dominant way of doing things is the superior way.

HETEROSEXISM: oppression of those of sexual orientations other than heterosexual, such as gays, lesbians, and bisexuals; this can take place by not acknowledging their existence. Homophobia is the fear of lesbians, gays, or bisexuals.

LOOKISM: the belief that appearance is an indicator of a person's value; the construction of a standard for beauty/attractiveness; and oppression through stereotypes and generalizations of both those who do not fit that standard and those who do.

RACISM: the belief that one group of people are superior to another and therefore have the right to dominate, and the power to institute and enforce their prejudices and discriminations.

RELIGIOUS DISCRIMINATION: oppression of religions other than the dominant one in the belief that the dominant way of worship is the only correct way.

SEXISM: stereotyping of males and females on the basis of their gender; the oppression of women by society in the belief that gender is an indication of ability.

Handout at Smith College.

New York State report, is "the embodiment of the White Male with Property Model.") One college administrator had no patience with the young woman's naïve and bourgeois sentiments. He returned her memo with the word *individual* underlined. "This is a 'RED FLAG' phrase today, which many consider RACIST," the administrator wrote. "Arguments that champion the individual over the group ultimately privilege the 'INDIVIDUALS' belonging to the largest or dominant group."

15   Defenders of Western culture try to point out that other civilizations—from the Islamic and the Hindu to the Confucian and the Buddhist—are rife with racism and sexism. They find it odd that while Eastern Europeans are rushing to embrace Western democracy, while the pro-democracy movement in China actually erected a replica of the Statue of Liberty in Tiananmen Square, this peculiar intellectual cult back in the States continues to insist that Western values are the source of much of the world's evil.

16   But one of the marvels of the new fundamentalism is the rationale it has concocted for dismissing all dissent. Just as Christian fundamentalists attack nonbelievers as agents of Satan, so the politically correct dismiss their critics as victims of, to use the famous Marxist phrase, "false consciousness." Anyone who disagrees is simply too soaked in the oppressors' propaganda to see the truth. "Racism and sexism are subtle and, for the most part, subconscious or at least subsurface," the Tulane report continues. "It is difficult for us to see and overcome racism and sexism because we are all a product of the problem, i.e., we are all the progeny of a racist and sexist society."

17   This circular reasoning enables the new fundamentalists to attack not just the opinions of their critics but the right of their critics to disagree. Alternate viewpoints are simply not allowed. Though there was little visible protest when Louis Farrakhan was invited to speak at the University of Wisconsin, students at the University of Northern Colorado practically rioted when Linda Chavez, a Hispanic member of the Reagan administration who opposes affirmative action and believes immigrants should be encouraged to learn English, was asked to talk. The invitation was withdrawn. Last February, Patrick Moynihan declared during a lecture at Vassar that America was "a model of a reasonably successful multiethnic society." Afterward, he got into an argument with a black woman who disagreed with him, and when she claimed the senator had insulted her, militant students occupied a school building until Moynihan returned his lecture fee. "The disturbing factor in the success of totalitarianism is . . . the true selflessness of its adherents," Hannah Arendt wrote in *The Origins of Totalitarianism*. "The fanaticized members can be reached by neither experience nor argument."

18   It is this sort of demand for intellectual conformity, enforced with harassment and intimidation, that has led some people to compare the

atmosphere in universities today to that of Germany in the thirties. "It's fascism of the left," says Camille Paglia, a professor at the University of the Arts in Philadelphia and the author of *Sexual Personae*. "These people behave like the Hitler Youth."

19   It reminds others of America in the fifties. "This sort of atmosphere, where a few highly mobilized radical students can intimidate everyone else, is quite new," Thernstrom says. "This is a new McCarthyism. It's more frightening than the old McCarthyism, which had no support in the academy. Now the enemy is within. There are students and faculty who have no belief in freedom of speech."

20   And it reminds still others of China during the Cultural Revolution of the sixties, when thought criminals were paraded through towns in dunce caps. "In certain respects, the University of Pennsylvania has become like the University of Peking," says Alan Kors, a professor of history.

21   Indeed, schools like Berkeley and Carleton require courses in race relations, sometimes called "oppression studies." A proposed course book for a required writing seminar at the University of Texas contains, instead of models of clarity like E. B. White, essays such as "is not so gd [sic] to be born a girl," by Ntozake Shange. Many schools— including Stanford, Pennsylvania, and the University of Wisconsin— have adopted codes of conduct that require students who deviate from politically correct thinking to undergo thought reform. When a student at the University of Michigan read a limerick that speculated jokingly about the homosexuality of a famous athlete, he was required to attend gay-sensitivity sessions and publish a piece of self-criticism in the student newspaper called "Learned My Lesson."

22   But is any of this so awful? In the minds of its advocates, thought reform is merely a well-intentioned effort to help stop the spread of the racial tensions that have proliferated in universities in recent years. "I don't know of any institution that is saying you have to adore everyone else," says Catharine Stimpson, dean of the graduate school at Rutgers. "They are saying you have to learn to live with everyone. They are taking insulting language seriously. That's a good thing. They're not laughing off anti-Semitic and homophobic graffiti."

23   After all, it is said, political indoctrination of one sort or another has always taken place at universities. Now that process is simply being made overt. And anyway, all these people complaining about the loss of academic freedom and the decline in standards are only trying to disguise their own efforts to retain power. "The attack on diversity is a rhetorical strategy by neoconservatives who have their own political agenda," says Stimpson. "Under the guise of defending objectivity and intellectual rigor, which is a lot of mishmash, they are trying to preserve the cultural and political supremacy of white heterosexual males."

24   If the debate over what students should be taught has become an openly political power struggle, that is only because, to the politically correct, *everything* is political. And nothing is more political, in their view, than the humanities, where much of the recent controversy has been centered.

25   For most of the twentieth century, professors in the humanities modeled themselves on their counterparts in the natural sciences. They thought of themselves as specialists in the disinterested pursuit of the truth. Their job, in the words of T. S. Eliot, was "the elucidation of art and the correction of taste," and to do so they concentrated on what Matthew Arnold called "the best that has been thought and written."

26   That common sense of purpose began to fracture in the sixties. The generation of professors now acquiring prominence and power at universities—Elaine Showalter, the head of the English department at Princeton; Donna Shalala, chancellor of the University of Wisconsin; James Freedman, the president of Dartmouth—came of age during that period. They witnessed its upheavals and absorbed its political commitments.

27   And by and large, they have retained them.

28   Which means that, though much of the country subsequently rejected the political vision of the sixties, it has triumphed at the universities. "If the undergraduate population has moved quietly to the right in recent years, the men and women who are paid to introduce students to the great works and ideas of our civilization have by and large remained true to the emancipationist ideology of the sixties," writes Roger Kimball in his book, *Tenured Radicals.* The professors themselves eagerly admit this. "I see my scholarship as an extension of my political activism," said Annette Kolodny, a former Berkeley radical and now the dean of the humanities faculty at the University of Arizona.

29   In the view of such activists, the universities were hardly the havens of academic independence they pretended to be. They had hopelessly compromised their integrity by accepting contracts from the Pentagon, but those alliances with the reviled "military-industrial Establishment" were seen as merely one symptom of a larger conspiracy by white males. Less obviously, but more insidiously, they had appointed themselves guardians of the culture and compiled the list of so-called Great Books as a propaganda exercise to reinforce the notion of white-male superiority. "The canon of great literature was created by high-Anglican ass——s to underwrite their social class," Stanley Hauerwas, a professor at Duke's Divinity School, put it recently.

30   Several schools of French critical theory that became fashionable during the seventies provided the jargon for this critique: Semiotics and Lacanian psychoanalysis argued that language and art conveyed subliminal cultural prejudices, power configurations, metaphoric

representations of gender. Deconstruction declared that texts, to use the preferred word, had no meaning outside themselves. "There is no such thing as literal meaning . . . there is no such thing as intrinsic merit," wrote Stanley Fish, the head of Duke's English department.

31   That being the case, any attempt to assign meaning to art, literature, or thought, to interpret it and evaluate it, was nothing more than an exercise in political power by the individual with the authority to impose his or her view. It then followed that the only reason to require students to read certain books is not to "correct taste" or because the books were "the best that has been thought or written" but because they promoted politically correct viewpoints. That ideological emphasis also applied to scholarship generally. "If the work doesn't have a strong political thrust, I don't see how it matters," said Eve Sedgwick, a professor of English at Duke and the author of such papers as "Jane Austen and the Masturbating Girl."

32   This agenda can produce a rather remarkable, not to say outré, reading list. Catharine Stimpson has declared that her ideal curriculum would contain the little-known book *Stars in My Pocket Like Grains of Sand*. "Like many contemporary speculative fictions," Stimpson wrote, "*Stars in My Pocket* finds conventional heterosexuality absurd. The central characters are two men, Rat Korga and Marq Dyeth, who have a complex but ecstatic affair. Marq is also the product of a rich 'nurture stream.' His ancestry includes both humans and aliens. His genetic heritage blends differences. In a sweet scene, he sees three of his mothers."

Ethnic and Ideological Purity

33   The multicultural and ethnic-studies programs now in place at most universities tend to divide humanity into five groups—whites, blacks, Native Americans, Hispanics, and Asians. (Homosexuals and feminists are usually included on the grounds that, though they are not a distinct ethnic group, they, too, have been oppressed by the "whitemale," to use the neologism of black literature professor Houston Baker, and prevented from expressing their "otherness.") These are somewhat arbitrary categories, and, in fact, the new fundamentalists have two contradictory views about just what constitutes an ethnic group and who can belong.

34   On the one hand, there is a reluctance to confer ethnic status on certain groups. At the University of Washington, a student-faculty Task Force on Ethnicity denied Jews, Italians, and Irish-Americans certification as ethnic groups. Status as an oppressed ethnic group is guarded even more jealously. The Washington task force also decided that a required ethnic-studies program exploring the pervasiveness of racism in America would not take up the subject of anti-Semitism. The

reason, *Commentary* quoted professor Johnnella Butler as having said, was that "anti-Semitism is not institutionalized in this country."

35   At the same time, the racial credentials of people aspiring to membership in the officially sanctioned ethnic categories are examined with an attention to detail associated with apartheid. Recently, a Hispanic who had been turned down for an affirmative-action promotion in the San Francisco fire department filed a complaint because the person who got the job instead was from Spain rather than Latin America. Colleges are becoming equally obsessed with such distinctions. Three years ago, the faculty at Hampshire College in Amherst began interviewing candidates for a professorship in Latin American literature. The professor, of course, needed to be Latin. *Pure* Latin. One woman who applied for the job was turned down because, though she was Argentine, she had, like many Argentines, Jewish and Italian blood, and thus her Third World ethnicity was considered insufficiently pure. Her heritage made her, in the words of one faculty member, "Eurocentric."

36   But even as these standards become increasingly exacting, more and more groups are clamoring for oppressed status. While supporters of American involvement in the Vietnam War were denounced as "war criminals" at the University of Michigan in the sixties, the school now counts Vietnam veterans as an oppressed group. In fact, the politically correct have concluded that virtually *any*one with *any* sort of trait, anxiety, flaw, impediment, or unusual sexual preference qualifies for membership in an oppressed group. This past fall, a handout from the Office of Student Affairs at Smith College explained that many people are *unaware* they are oppressed, though with help they are finding out: "As groups of people begin the process of realizing that they are oppressed, and why, new words tend to be created to express the concepts that the existing language cannot."

37   This obsessive tendency to see oppression everywhere is creating a sort of New Age caste system. The Smith handout listed various categories of oppression that ranged from "classism" and "ageism" to "ableism" (identified as "oppression of the differently abled by the temporarily able") and "lookism," which was revealed to be "the construction of a standard for beauty/attractiveness; and oppression through stereotypes and generalizations of both those who do not fit that standard and those who do." Heightism may be next. In a joke now making the rounds, short people are demanding to be known as "the vertically challenged."

38   But joking isn't allowed! Even the most harmless, lighthearted remarks can lead to virulent denunciations. In October, Roderick Nash, a professor at the University of California at Santa Barbara, pointed out during a lecture on environmental ethics that there is a movement to start referring to pets as animal companions. (Apparently, domesti-

cated animals are offended by the word *pet.*) Nash then made some sort of off-the-cuff observation about how women who pose for *Penthouse* are still called Pets (and not *Penthouse* Animal Companions). Inevitably, several female students filed a formal sexual-harassment complaint against him. Susan Rode, one of the signers, said, "Maybe this will make more people aware in other classes and make other faculty watch what they say."

39   Indeed, making people *watch what they say* is the central preoccupation of politically correct students. Stephan Thernstrom is not the only professor who has been forced to give up a course on race relations. Reynolds Farley, one of the leading scholars on race relations, dropped a course he had taught for nearly ten years at the University of Michigan after he was accused of racial insensitivity for reading Malcolm X's description of himself as a pimp and a thief and for discussing the southern defense of slavery. "Given the climate at Michigan," Farley said, "I could be hassled for anything I do or don't say in that class."

40   *Watch what you say:* And it's not enough just to avoid racism. One must display absolute ideological purity. The search committee at Hampshire College also considered a highly qualified Chicano candidate for the Latin American-literature post. Unfortunately for him, in his dissertation on Chicano literature he drew parallels between Shakespeare and Mexican writers. This demonstrated dangerous "Eurocentric" tendencies. Certain faculty members, doubting the candidate's ethnic purity as well, wondered whether someone of Mexican heritage was *really* Latin American. They thought a Puerto Rican might be better. He didn't get the job.

41   It was finally offered to Norman Holland, who seemed both ethnically and ideologically pure. But this past summer, Holland's contract was not renewed, and Holland claims it is because he also was branded "Eurocentric." Though the school's official position is that Holland was an ineffective teacher, two of the professors who reviewed his work insinuated that he had a European bias. Holland, one professor declared, had "focused mainly on Western Europe to the exclusion of cultural issues Third World students perceive as uniquely relevant." "I suppose I committed certain kinds of sins," says Holland. "When I was teaching *One Hundred Years of Solitude,* I would talk about colonial rape, but I would also talk about how the novel originated in Europe and how García Márquez was working in that tradition and addressing ideas in Proust and Joyce. I didn't limit myself to considering it as a sociological document."

42   "Misogynistic!"
       "Patriarchal!"
       "Gynophobic!"

"Phallocentric!"

43   Last fall, Camille Paglia attended a lecture by a "feminist theorist" from a large Ivy League university who had set out to "decode" the subliminal sexual oppressiveness in fashion photography. The feminist theorist stood at the front of the room showing slides of fashion photography and cosmetics ads and exposing, in the style of Lacanian psychoanalysis, their violent sexism. She had selected a Revlon ad of a woman with a heavily made-up face who was standing up to her chin in a pool of water. When it came up on the screen, she exclaimed, "Decapitation!"

44   She showed a picture of a black woman who was wearing aviator goggles and had the collar of her turtleneck sweater pulled up. "Strangulation!" she shouted. "Bondage!"

45   It went on like this for the entire lecture. When it was over, Paglia, who considers herself a feminist, stood up and made an impassioned speech. She declared that the fashion photography of the past 40 years is great art, that instead of decapitation she saw the birth of Venus, instead of strangulation she saw references to King Tut. But political correctness has achieved a kind of exquisitely perfect rigidity among the group known as the gender feminists, and she was greeted, she says, "with gasps of horror and angry murmuring. It's a form of psychosis, this slogan-filled machinery. The radical feminists have contempt for values other than their own, and they're inspiring in students a resentful attitude toward the world."

46   Indeed, the central tenet of gender feminism is that Western society is organized around a "sex/gender system." What defines the system, according to Sandra Harding, a professor of philosophy at the University of Delaware and one of its exponents, is "male dominance made possible by men's control of women's productive and reproductive labor."

47   The primary arena for this dominance is, of course, the family, which Alison Jaggar, a professor at the University of Cincinnati and the head of the American Philosophical Association's Committee on the Status of Women in Philosophy, sees as "a cornerstone of women's oppression." The family, in Jaggar's view, "enforces heterosexuality" and "imposes the prevailing masculine and feminine character structures on the next generation."

48   This position makes gender feminists, as Christina Sommers has written in an article in *Public Affairs Quarterly*, from which some of these quotes were taken, "oddly unsympathetic to the women whom they claim to represent." But that poses no problem. Women who have decided to get married and raise families, women who want to become mothers, are, naturally, victims of false consciousness. The radical feminists are fond of quoting Simone de Beauvoir, who said, "No woman should be authorized to stay at home and raise children . . .

precisely because if there is such a choice, too many women will make that one."

49   Jaggar, for one, would like to abolish the family altogether and create a society where, with the aid of technology, "one woman could inseminate another . . . men . . . could lactate . . . and fertilized ova could be transferred into women's or even men's bodies." All that is preventing this, according to the gender feminists, is "phallocentricity" and "androcentricity," the view that society is organized around the male and his sexual organs. The feminists, ablaze with revolutionary rhetoric, have set out to overthrow this system. "What we feminists are doing," the philosopher Barbara Minnich has said, "is comparable to Copernicus shattering our geocentricity, Darwin shattering our species-centricity. We are shattering androcentricity, and the change is as fundamental, as dangerous, as exciting."

50   But unlike the pre-Copernican view that the Earth was at the center of the universe, androcentricity is not, in the view of the gender feminists, merely a flawed theory. It is a moral evil, dedicated to the enslavement of women. And since most of Western culture, according to this view, has been a testament to "male power and transcendence," it is similarly evil and must be discarded. This includes not only patriarchal books like the Bible and sexist subjects like traditional history, with its emphasis on great men and great deeds, but also the natural sciences and even the very process of analytical thinking itself. "To know is to f—" has become a radical-feminist rallying cry. Indeed, scientific inquiry itself is seen as "the rape of nature." A project sponsored by the state of New Jersey to integrate these views into college campuses has issued a set of "feminist scholarship guidelines" that declares "mind was male. Nature was female, and knowledge was created as an act of aggression—a passive nature had to be interrogated, unclothed, penetrated, and compelled by man to reveal her secrets."

51   To certain women, however, this is just a veiled restatement of the old idea that women don't make good scientists. "As a liberal feminist, I encourage women to study science," says Christina Sommers. "I'm not impugning science itself as hostile to the female sensibility."

52   But it is not just the coldly analytical and dualistic structures of male thinking that the gender feminists find so contemptible. It is males themselves, or at least heterosexual males. After all, heterosexuality is responsible for the subjugation of women, and so, in the oppressive culture of the West, any woman who goes on a date with a man is a prostitute. "Both man and woman might be outraged at the description of their candlelight dinner as prostitution," Jaggar has written. "But the radical feminist argues this outrage is simply due to the participants' failure or refusal to perceive the social context in which the dinner occurs." In other words, they are victims of—what else?—false consciousness.

53   This eagerness to see all women as victims, to describe all male behavior with images of rape and violation, may shed some light on the phenomenon of date rape, a legitimate issue that has been exaggerated and distorted by a small group with a specific political agenda. As with the hysteria a few years ago over the sexual abuse of children, endless talk shows, television news stories, and magazine articles have been devoted to date rape, often describing it as "an epidemic" that, as the Chicago *Tribune* put it, "makes women campus prisoners" and forces them, as at Brown, to list supposed rapists on bathroom walls.

54   Much of this discussion starts off with the claim that one in four female students is raped by a date. The figure seems staggeringly high, and debate tends to focus on whether actual rape or merely the reporting of rape is on the rise. But the journalist Stephanie Gutmann has pointed out in *Reason* magazine the gross statistical flaws in the survey of date rape that produced this figure. According to Gutmann, "the real story about campus date rape is not that there's been any significant increase of rape on college campuses, at least of the acquaintance type, but that the word *rape* is being stretched to encompass any type of sexual interaction."

55   In fact, rape under the new definition does not have to involve physical assault at all. Andrea Parrot, a professor at Cornell who has promoted the idea of the date-rape epidemic, has declared that "any sexual intercourse without mutual desire is a form of rape." In other words, a woman is being raped if she has sex when not in the mood, even if she fails to inform her partner of that fact. As a former director of Columbia's date-rape-education program told Gutmann, "Every time you have an act of intercourse, there must be explicit consent, and if there's no explicit consent, then it's rape. . . . Stone silence throughout an entire physical encounter with someone is not explicit consent." And rape is no longer limited to actual intercourse. A training manual at Swarthmore College states that "acquaintance rape . . . spans a spectrum of incidents and behaviors ranging from crimes legally defined as rape to verbal harassment and inappropriate innuendo."

56   It is no surprise then that Catherine Nye, a University of Chicago psychologist interviewed by Gutmann, found that 43 percent of the women in a widely cited rape study "had not realized they had been raped." In other words, they were victims of, yes, false consciousness. But by the definition of the radical feminists, all sexual encounters that involve any confusion or ambivalence constitute rape. "Ordinary bungled sex—the kind you regret in the morning or even during—is being classified as rape," Gutmann says. "Bad or confused feelings after sex becomes someone else's fault." Which is fine with the feminists. "In terms of making men nervous or worried about overstepping their bounds, I don't think that's a bad thing," Parrot said. Indeed, since it encourages a general suspicion of all men, it's a good thing. As

Parrot has put it, "Since you can't tell who has the potential for rape simply by looking, be on your guard with every man."

Afrocentrism

57   For all their fury, the gender feminists are surpassed in ideological rage by an even more extreme wing of the politically correct: the Afrocentrists. Afrocentrists argue that not only is Western culture oppressive, it isn't even really *Western.* Key accomplishments, from mathematics and biology to architecture and medicine, were in fact the work of Africans. "Very few doctors, African-American or otherwise in America, are aware of the fact that when they take their medical oath, the hypocratic [*sic*] oath, they actually swear to Imhotep, the African God of Medicine," Asa Hilliard, a professor of Afro-American history at Georgia State, has written.

58   The theory that Africa was the true source of Western civilization hinges on the claim that the ancient Egyptians were black. "The first 12 dynasties plus dynasties 18 and 25 were native-black-African dynasties," Hilliard has asserted. Traditional Egyptologists generally believe that while blacks, from Nubia to the south, were active in Egyptian society, ancient Egyptians, like their contemporary counterparts, tended to be of Semitic stock. But to the Afrocentrists, that explanation is merely part of the long-running conspiracy by Western whites to deny the African contribution to civilization.

59   The conspiracy began, in the Afrocentric view, when the ancient Greeks "stole" African philosophy and science from the Egyptians. To claim European credit for these discoveries, Romans and, later, Christians burned the library of Alexandria in Egypt. The conspiracy has continued ever since. Napoleon's soldiers shot off the nose and lips of the Sphinx to obliterate its Negroid features. Beethoven and Robert Browning were actually blacks whose ethnicity has been hidden. "African history has been lost, stolen, destroyed, and suppressed," Hilliard maintains.

60   Leonard Jeffries, chairman of the black-studies department at City College and one of the most extreme exponents of Afrocentrism, has worked up a sort of anthropological model to explain why Europeans have oppressed Africans. The human race, according to Jeffries, is divided into the "ice people" and the "sun people." The ethnic groups descended from the ice people are materialistic, selfish, and violent, while those descended from the sun people are nonviolent, cooperative, and spiritual. In addition, blacks are biologically superior to whites, Jeffries maintains, because they have more melanin, and melanin regulates intellect and health.

61   Despite the spiritual benevolence one might expect from a "sun person," Jeffries is known for making the sort of hostile denunciations

that, if he were at the other end of the political spectrum, would no doubt provoke howls of indignation. He called Diana Ross an "international whore" for her involvement with white men. And he applauded the destruction of the Challenger space shuttle because it would deter white people from "spreading their filth throughout the universe."

62   Jeffries's wild remarks are excused by the politically correct on the grounds that to be a racist, you have to have "institutional power," and since blacks do not have "institutional power," they cannot be considered racist. The somewhat flimsy propositions of Afrocentrism are excused with equal finesse. First of all, since everything is political, there has never been disinterested scholarship, only power plays by various groups to justify their own claims. And even if there are some holes in Afrocentrism, the approach is useful because it raises the "self-esteem" of black students.

63   Such was the reasoning of the New York State Board of Education's Task Force on Minorities, to which Leonard Jeffries was a consultant. Its report suggested that "all curricular materials [including math and science] be prepared on the basis of multicultural contributions." As a result, the report said, children from minority cultures "will have higher self-esteem and self-respect, while children from European cultures will have a less arrogant perspective." The notion has already been put into effect in public schools in Portland, Indianapolis, and Washington, D.C., where students are taught subjects like Yoruba mathematics and ancient-Egyptian astronomy.

64   The idea that the "self-esteem" of student—rather than historical relevance—should be the basis for including material in textbooks does have its critics. Among the most prominent is Diane Ravitch, who has said the idea "that children can learn only from the experiences of people from the same race" represents a sort of "racial fundamentalism." The success of Chinese students in math is due not to a "Sinocentric" approach to numbers but to hard work. If the "self-esteem" model had any validity, Italian American students—the descendants of Caesar and Michelangelo—would excel in school, but in fact they have the highest dropout rate of any white group in New York City schools. By promoting a brand of history "in which everyone is either a descendant of victims or oppressors," Ravitch has declared, "ancient hatreds are fanned and re-created in each new generation."

65   Ravitch naturally was branded a racist for this position. Participants at a recent Afrocentrism conference in Atlanta derided her as "Miss Daisy." She has been attacked in the *City Sun* and on black television and radio programs. As a result, she has received so many threats that when we first agreed to meet, she was afraid to tell me where she lived. "They've written saying things like 'We're going to get you, bitch. We're going to beat your white ass.'"

Moonies in the Classroom

66   The supreme irony of the new fundamentalism is that the generation that produced the free-speech movement in Berkeley and rebelled against the idea of *in loco parentis*—that university administrators should act as surrogate parents—is now trying to restrict speech and control the behavior of a new generation of students. The enterprise is undertaken to combat racism, of course, and it is an article of faith among the politically correct that the current climate of racial hostility can be traced to the Reagan and Bush presidencies, to conservative-Republican efforts to gut civil-rights legislation and affirmative-action programs. However true that may he, scholars like Shelby Steele, a black essayist and English professor, have also argued that the separatist movements at universities—black dorms, Native American student centers, gay-studies programs, the relentless harping on "otherness"—have heightened tensions and contributed to the culture of victimization. "If you sensitize people from day one to look at everything in terms of race and sex, eventually they will see racism and sexism at the root of everything," says Alan Kors. "But not all the problems and frustrations in life are due to race and gender."

67   Furthermore, they say, instead of increasing self-esteem, schools that offer an Afrocentric education will only turn out students who are more resentful, and incompetent, than ever. Indeed, while the more rabid Afrocentrics have claimed that crack and AIDS are conspiracies by whites to eliminate blacks, it could just as easily be argued that white indulgence of Afrocentric education represents a conspiracy to provide blacks with a useless education that will keep them out of the job market.

68   Of course, to make such a statement is invariably to provoke a charge of racism. But part of the problem with this reaction is that it trivializes the debate. In fact, it makes debate impossible. But that is just as well, according to the new fundamentalists. Debate, and the analytic thinking it requires, is oppressive. It's logocentric. It favors the articulate at the expense of the inarticulate. It forces people to make distinctions, and since racism is the result of distinctions, they should be discouraged. "I have students tell me they don't need to study philosophy because it's patriarchal and logocentric," says Christina Sommers. "They're unteachable and scary. It's like having a Moonie in the classroom."

69   Resistance to this sort of robotic sloganeering is beginning. "Today, routinized righteous indignation has been substituted for rigorous criticism," Henry Louis Gates, a black English professor at Duke, recently declared. Some professors are actually arguing that colleges should begin to emphasize what whites, homosexuals, minorities, and women

have in common rather than dwelling constantly on "difference." In November, writing in the *Stanford Daily* about a proposal to require Stanford students to take a course in diversity, David Kennedy, chairman of American studies at Stanford and previously a champion of multiculturalism, said, "I worry that the proposal will add to the already considerable weight that Stanford culture places on racial and ethnic divisiveness, rather than shared participation. I question whether this is socially wise and, further, whether it is intellectually true to the lived experience of members of this society."

70   A few emboldened administrators are actually suggesting that it is not unreasonable for Western culture to enjoy a certain prominence at American colleges. In an address to incoming Yale students in September, Donald Kagan, dean of the college, encouraged them to center their undergraduate studies around Western culture. He argued that the West "has asserted the claims of the individual against those of the state, limiting its power and creating a realm of privacy into which it cannot penetrate." The West's tradition of civil liberties has produced "a tolerance and respect for diversity unknown in most cultures."

71   But many of the Yale freshmen—or "freshpeople," as the *Yale Daily News* puts it—considered the dean's statements "quite disturbing." And the dean was denounced with the obligatory mind-numbing litany.

72   "Paternalistic!"
        "Racist!"
        "Fascist!"

(7,278 words)

VOCABULARY

denunciations (2)	progeny (16)	virulent (38)
indictments (4)	overt (23)	misogynistic (42)
covert (5)	disinterested (25)	gynophobic (42)
sophistic (6)	elucidation (25)	phallocentric (42)
egregiously (7)	insidiously (29)	lactate (49)
troglodytes (11)	Lacanian	androcentricity (49)
heinous (11)	psychoanalysis (30)	impugning (51)
demagogues (11)	subliminal (30)	subjugation (52)
eclectic (12)	intrinsic (30)	innuendo (55)
inherently (13)	outré (32)	finesse (62)
bourgeois (14)	neologism (33)	*in loco parentis* (62)
concocted (16)	Eurocentric (35)	logocentric (68)

THE FACTS

1. Of what "crime" was professor Baylin accused by students who thought him racist? What was professor Thernstrom's crime?

2. Who are the "new fundamentalists"?

3. What rationale does the new fundamentalism use in dismissing all dissent?

4. Which group does the author see as being the driving force behind the emergence of the new fundamentalism of political correctness?

5. Into which five primary groups does the author claim ethnic-studies programs tend to divide humanity?

THE STRATEGIES

1. What are the advantages of the opening used in this article? How does the author use his opening in his closing?

2. In paragraphs 11 and 12, what tactic does the author use to define the nature of the political correctness movement? What is your opinion of the legitimacy of this tactic?

3. In making his case against the "new fundamentalism," what are the author's primary sources of facts? What weakness can you discern in these sources?

4. Reread paragraphs 18 through 20. What objection to the argument here might a scrupulous logician make?

5. In paragraphs 22 and 23, the author outlines the justification for the political correctness movement. What is his purpose?

THE ISSUES

1. The author cites a report from the New York State Board of Education task force that declares, "Intellectual and educational oppression . . . has characterized the culture and institutions of the United States and the European American world for centuries." What is your opinion of the accuracy of this statement?

2. The author implies that the "political correctness" movement is sweeping college campuses throughout the nation. What instances of this can you find and cite on your own campus, or does your experience refute his contention?

3. The author says that the function of the humanities in the university was formerly thought to be, in T. S. Eliot's words, "the elucidation of art and the correction of taste." What is your opinion of this

alleged function? Can the "correction of taste" be simply scholarly and apolitical or does the attempt to "correct taste" necessarily imply a political subtext?

4. Why do you think so much of the politically correct movement has come to focus on the humanities?

5. What do you think is the greatest possible good that could come from the politically correct movement? What, the greatest possible harm?

SUGGESTIONS FOR WRITING

1. Write an essay on the political correctness movement as it applies, or does not apply, to your particular campus.

2. Analyze the logic of this article in an essay, commenting on whether or not you think the author has sensationalized the issue.

▼▼▼

Rosa Ehrenreich

WHAT CAMPUS RADICALS?
THE PC UNDERGRAD IS A USEFUL SPECTER

ROSA EHRENREICH (b. 1970) was born in New York City and educated at Harvard and Oxford. She presently attends law school at Yale. She has written a book about her experiences at Oxford, *A Garden of Paper Flowers*, whose publication is upcoming.

1 A national survey of college administrators released last summer found that "political correctness" is not the campus issue it has been portrayed to be by pundits and politicians of the political right. During the 1990–91 academic year, according to the survey's findings, faculty members complained of pressure from students and fellow professors to alter the political and cultural content of their courses at only *5 percent* of all colleges. So much for the influence of the radicals, tenured or otherwise.

2 The survey's findings came as no real surprise to me. The hegemony of the "politically correct" is not a problem at Harvard, where I've just completed my undergraduate education, or at any other campus I visited during my student years. But then none among those who have escalated the P.C. debate in the past year—Dinesh D'Souza[1] and

---

[1] Dinesh D'Souza (b. 1961) conservative writer.

Roger Kimball[2], George Will and George Bush, *Time* and *New York* magazines—is actually interested in what is happening on the campuses. In all the articles and op-ed pieces published on P.C., multiculturalism, etc., very few student voices have been heard. To be a liberal arts student with progressive politics today is at once to be at the center of a raging national debate and to be completely on the sidelines, watching others far from campus describe you and use you for their own ends.

3   For instance: During the spring semester of my freshman year at Harvard, Stephan Thernstrom, an American history professor, was criticized by several black students for making "racially insensitive" comments during lectures. The incident made the *Harvard Crimson* for a few days, then blew over after a week afterlife, however, in the P.C. debate. Here is how it was described last January in a *New York* magazine cover story by John Taylor on, in the author's words, the "moonies in the classroom" propagating the "new fundamentalism":

4   "Racist." "Racist!" "The man is a racist!" "A *racist!*"
Such denunciations, hissed in tones of self-righteousness and contempt, vicious and vengeful, furious, smoking with hatred—such denunciations haunted Stephan Thernstrom for weeks. Whenever he walked through the campus that spring, down Harvard's brick paths, under the arched gates, past the fluttering elms, he found it hard not to imagine the pointing fingers, the whispers.

5   The operative word here is "imagine." Taylor seriously distorted what actually happened. In February of 1988, several black female students told classmates that they had been disturbed by some "racially insensitive" comments made by Professor Thernstrom. Thernstrom, they said, had spoken approvingly of Jim Crow laws, and had said that black men, harboring feelings of inadequacy, beat their female partners. The *students,* fearing for their grades should they anger Professor Thernstrom by confronting him with their criticisms—this is not an unusual way for college students to think things through, as anyone who's been an undergraduate well knows—never discussed the matter with him. They told friends, who told friends, and the *Crimson* soon picked up word of the incident and ran an article.

6   Professor Thernstrom, understandably disturbed to learn of the matter in the *Crimson*, wrote a letter protesting that no students had ever approached him directly with such criticisms. He also complained that the students' vague criticisms about "racial insensitivity" had "launched a witchhunt" that would have "chilling effect upon freedom of expression." Suddenly, Professor Thernstrom was to be understood

---

[2] Roger Kimball (b. 1953) conservative Catholic writer of *Tenured Radicals: How Politics Has Corrupted Our Higher Education* (1990).

as a victim, falsely smeared with the charge of racism. But no one had ever accused him of any such thing. "I do not charge that [Thernstrom] is a racist," Wendi Grantham, one of the students who criticized Thernstrom, wrote in the *Crimson* in response to his letter. Grantham believed the professor gave "an incomplete and over-simplistic presentation of the information. . . . I am simply asking questions about his presentation of the material. . . . " As for the professor's comment that the criticisms were like a "witch-hunt," Grantham protested that Thernstrom had "turned the whole situation full circle, proclaimed himself victim, and resorted to childish name-calling and irrational comparisons . . . 'witch-hunt' [is] more than a little extreme. . . . " But vehement, even hysterical language is more and more used to demonize students who question and comment. Terms like "authoritarian" and "Hitler youth" have been hurled at students who, like Grantham, dare to express any sort of criticism of the classroom status quo.

7   In my four years as a student at Harvard, I found few signs of a new fascism of the left. For that matter, there are few signs of the left at all. The Harvard-Radcliffe Democratic Socialists Club collapsed due to lack of members, as did the left-wing newspaper, the *Subterranean Review*. As to the neoconservative charge that the traditional political left has been supplanted by a feminist-gay-multicultural left: In my senior year the African-American Studies department and the Women's Studies committee each had so few faculty that the same woman served as chair of both. I got through thirty-two courses at Harvard, majoring in the history and literature of England and America, without ever being required to read a work by a black woman writer, and of my thirty-two professors only two were women. I never even *saw* a black or Hispanic professor. (Fewer than 10 percent of tenured professors at Harvard are women, and fewer than 7 percent are members of minorities.)

8   Perhaps, as some conservatives have maintained, even a few radical professors can reach hundreds of students, bending their minds and sending them, angry and politicized, out into society upon graduation. To cure such fears, drop by Harvard's Office of Career Services. Most staffers there spend their days advising those who would be corporate execs, financial consultants, and investment bankers. Nearly 20 percent of the class of 1990 planned to go to law school. This compares with 10 percent who claimed that they would eventually go into government or one of what Career Services calls the "helping professions."

9   President Bush, speaking at the University of Michigan's commencement exercises last spring, went on about radical extremists on campus. It would be interesting to know how he calculated this rise in radicalism. Two thirds of Harvard students wholeheartedly supported the Gulf War, according to one *Crimson* poll. That's more support for the war than was found in the country at large. And during my years at Harvard I found that most women on campus, including those who

consider themselves politically liberal, would not willingly identify themselves as feminists.

10   The very notion of "politicization" makes most Harvard students nervous. I discovered this in the fall of 1989, when I was elected president of Harvard's community service organization, Phillips Brooks House Association. I had been reckless enough to suggest that volunteers would benefit from having some awareness of the social and political issues that affected the communities in which they did their volunteer work. I was promptly attacked in the *Crimson* for trying to inappropriately "politicize" public service. The paper also suggested that under my leadership volunteer training might mimic a "party line," with Brooks House as a "central planning office." This used to be called red-baiting. (So much for the liberal campus media.)

11   Meanwhile—and unremarked upon by D'Souza, et al.—the campus right thrives nationally. Two new right-wing vehicles have popped up on Harvard's campus in recent years. The Association Against Learning in the Absence of Religion and Morality (AALARM) initially made a splash with its uninhibited gay-bashing. The magazine *Peninsula*, closely tied to AALARM, bears an uncanny editorial resemblance to the notorious *Dartmouth Review*, claims to uphold Truth, and has a bizarre propensity for centerfold spreads of mangled fetuses. And older, more traditional conservative groups have grown stronger and more ideological. The Harvard Republican Club, once a stodgy and relatively inactive group, suffered a rash of purges and resignations as more moderate members were driven out by the far right. It is inactive no more.

12   There *are* those on the left who are intolerant and who could stand to lighten up a bit—these are the activists whom *progressive* and *liberal* students mockingly called "politically correct" years before the right appropriated the term, with a typical lack of irony. But on the whole, intolerance at Harvard—and, I suspect, elsewhere—is the province mostly of extreme conservatism. Posters put up at Harvard by the Bisexual, Gay and Lesbian Students Association are routinely torn down. I don't recall any Republican Club posters being ripped up or removed.

13   The day after the bombing started in Iraq, I went to an event advertised as "a nonpartisan rally to support our troops," sponsored by the Republican Club. After the scheduled speakers—and several other nonscheduled speakers—had finished, I tried to speak. The rally organizers promptly turned off the microphone. I kept speaking, saying that I supported the troops but not the war. I added that I had been disturbed to hear it said by rally organizers—and applauded by the audience—that the time for debate was over. In a democracy, I said, the time for debate is never over.

14   I would have gone on, but at this point a group of men in the audience felt the need to demonstrate their conviction that there should be no debate. They began to loudly chant "victory" over and over, quite effectively drowning me out. By way of contrast, supporters of the war

were listened to in polite silence by the crowd at an anti-war rally the next day.

15   In the classroom, too, right-wing political views are heard without disruption. One of Harvard's largest core courses, taken by nearly half of all undergraduates while I was there, is Social Analysis 10, Principles of Economics. It was taught during my undergrad years by two of President Reagan's top economic advisers, Martin Feldstein and Larry Lindsay. Students did not rise up *en masse* to protest the course's right-wing political bias; instead, they sat scribbling feverishly in their notebooks: Ec-10 had a notoriously steep grading curve. (No one seemed worried that each year some 750 innocent Harvard students were being lectured to by the engineers of what George Bush, in one of his more forthright moments, once referred to as "voodoo economics.")

16   There are many other politically conservative professors at Harvard whose courses are quite popular—Richard Pipes on Russian history and Samuel P. Huntington on modern democracy, to name two of the most prominent—and in their classrooms, as in all undergrad classrooms I was in, free and open discussion did quite well. I took many classes in which fearless conservatives rushed to take part in entirely civil discussions about the efficacy and justice of affirmative action, about whether books like *Uncle Tom's Cabin* and Frederick Douglass's autobiography are "really *literature*," as opposed to just interesting historical documents, and about whether it's at all fair or even interesting to condemn Jefferson for owning slaves even as he decried slavery. These are all valid questions, and all sides deserve a hearing—which, in my experience, is exactly what they always got.

17   And my experience was not unique. Most other Harvard students seemed to agree that there's no such thing as a cadre of P.C. thought police. Last winter the Republican Club laid huge sheets of poster board across several dining-hall tables and put up a sign asking students to scribble down their responses to the question "Is there free speech at Harvard?" The vast majority of students wrote things like "What's the big deal? Of course there's free speech here." And the lively, cheerful discussion going on among the students gathered around the tables attested to that fact.

18   Conservatives like D'Souza and Kimball charge that traditional Western culture courses barely exist anymore at schools like Harvard, because of some mysterious combination of student pressure and the multiculturalist, post-structuralist tendencies of radical professors. Writing in the *Atlantic Monthly* last year, Caleb Nelson, a former editor of the conservative *Harvard Salient*, complained that in the 1989–90 Harvard course catalogue:

19   No core Literature and Arts course lists any of the great nineteenth-century British novelists among the authors studied, nor does any

list such writers as Virgil, Milton, and Dostoevsky. In the core's history areas even students who . . . took every single course would not focus on any Western history before the Middle Ages, nor would they study the history of the Enlightenment, the Renaissance, the American Civil War, or a host of other topics that one might expect a core to cover.

20   Nelson's major complaint is that Harvard is not properly educating all of its students. I agree with him here; in Caleb Nelson, Harvard has let us all down by producing a student so poorly educated that he's unable even to read the course catalogue.

21   I have the 1989–90 catalogue in front of me as I write, and a quick sampling of some of the entries gives us, from the Literature and Arts and the Historical Study sections of the core curriculum, the following courses: Chaucer, Shakespeare, The Bible and Its Interpreters, Classical Greek Literature and 5th-Century Athens, The Rome of Augustus, The British Empire, The Crusades, The Protestant Reformation. Perhaps Chaucer and Shakespeare are somehow, to Caleb Nelson, not "such writers" as Milton and Dostoevsky and the Protestant Reformation is a historically trivial topic.

22   Nelson also worries that students will have "no broad look on . . . philosophy"—by which he really means Western philosophy. Yet in the Moral Reasoning section of the core, seven of the ten courses listed have at least four of the following authors on their primary reading lists: Plato, Aristotle, Thucydides, Machiavelli, Locke, Kant, Rousseau, Hume, Mill, Nietzsche, Marx, and Weber. There is one course devoted to a non-Western philosopher: Confucius. The remaining two Moral Reasoning courses focus, respectively, on the writings of "Aristotle . . . [and] Maimonides," and of "Jesus as presented in the Gospels."

23   These courses are far more representative of those taken by most Harvard undergraduates than the titillating and much denounced 1991 English course on Cross-Dressing and Cultural Anxiety—a graduate seminar listed in the course catalogue but ultimately never held. But then, if you are a right-winger looking for something to replace the commies on campus—remember them?—you aren't going to sell books or raise funds or win votes complaining about undergrads studying Confucian Humanism and Moral Community.

24   Many of the loudest complainers about P.C. thought police are those who are doing their best to curb free expression in other areas. It doesn't appear to bother Dinesh D'Souza that the word "abortion" cannot be uttered at a federally funded family clinic.[3] More broadly, the

---

[3] Under a rule promulgated by the Bush administration but promptly rescinded by Bill Clinton.

brouhaha about political conformity on campus serves as a perfect smoke screen, masking from Americans—from ourselves—the rigid political conformity *off* campus: the blandness of our political discourse, the chronic silence in Washington on domestic matters, the same faces returned to office each year, the bipartisanship that keeps problems from becoming issues. During the Gulf War, the number of huge yellow bouquets in public places rivaled the number of larger-than-life photos of Saddam Hussein displayed on Iraqi billboards. Patriotically correct.

25   The campuses are no more under siege by radicals than is the society at large. It has been clever of the Kimballs and D'Souzas to write as if it were so. It is always clever of those in ascendance to masquerade as victims. Rebecca Walkowitz, the newly elected president of the *Harvard Crimson*, understands perfectly how this dynamic works. Referring to the 1988 incident involving Professor Thernstrom and several of his black students, Walkowitz has said: "People call the *Crimson* and ask me what we 'did to that man.' It's important to remember who has the power here, because it's not students. Who would dare criticize a professor for political reasons now? In addition to fearing for your grade, you'd fear being pilloried in the national press."

(2,661 words)

VOCABULARY

specter (title)	appropriated (12)	brouhaha (24)
pundits (1)	cadre (17)	ascendance (25)
hegemony (2)	titillating (23)	pilloried (25)

THE FACTS

1. What did the survey of college administrators reveal about the presence and pressure of campus radicals?

2. On what does the writer blame the controversy about the existence of political correctness on campuses?

3. According to the author, how does "the very notion of 'politicization'" make Harvard students typically feel?

4. What was the attitude of Harvard students toward the Gulf War?

5. According to the quoted testimony of a president of the *Harvard Crimson*, why would students dare not criticize a professor?

THE STRATEGIES

1. What is the thesis of this article, and where is it stated?

2. In rebutting the charge that left-wing fascism is taking over the universities, the author mainly focuses her attention on Harvard. What is the logic behind this strategy?

3. What do you see as the most serious weakness of the author's argument?

4. In paragraph 12, the author admits that "there are those on the left who are intolerant and who could stand to lighten up a bit. . . ." Why does she make this admission? What does making it contribute to her argument?

5. How does the author use irony and sarcasm to support her argument that the so-called political correctness movement is a myth? Point to at least two instances.

THE ISSUES

1. Which of these two essays on political correctness do you regard as presenting the stronger argument? Why?

2. What inference can be made about Ehrenreich's politics? Where do you think she falls on the political spectrum, and what effect does this conclusion have on your judgment of her argument?

3. Without actually saying so, of what common journalistic fault does the author accuse John Taylor's report of political correctness on campus? What is your opinion of this implied charge?

4. What argument do you think conservatives have against multiculturalist? What is your opinion of this argument?

5. The author writes that during her tenure at Harvard she never even saw an African American or a Hispanic professor. What obligation does a university have to include representatives of ethnic minorities on its faculty? How would such inclusions benefit a university?

SUGGESTIONS FOR WRITING

1. In an essay, side with one of these two writers, explaining which you find more convincing and why.

2. The author quotes the president of the *Harvard Crimson* on the intimidation of students who fear that standing up to a professor will jeopardize their grades. Write an essay exploring the effect grading has on your relationship with your professors.

I

First Draft

Carlye Ketchum, University of Tennessee

Sheer Confusion

I am not sure when or how it all got started, but I know that
things have not been the same since. I'm speaking of Political
Correctness. I don't know about you, but I tend to feel a little
overwhelmed by it all. There seems to be so much that is correct
and incorrect that a regular person can easily get lost in it. I
know that I do not ever want to offend anyone, but where do we
draw the line? When does not trying to hurt someone's feelings
become so intense that it is just silly?

[better wording] I have no problem with someone demanding respect, ~~I understand not wanting to be called something that is offensive, but who decides what is or is not offensive and how does the general public get access to this information.~~ **[delete]** **[useless]** **[add new transition]** What is
the difference between being called a "waitress" or a "server"? No **[transition better here]**
[comma needed] matter what you call it, you are still taking orders and bringing
food to people. I know, "server" is one of those unisex words, so
we can use it to describe either a female or male, but I have
always thought that was the purpose of the word "waiter." And
"stewardesses," now that is a whole other can of worms. Should
[quotation marks needed] we say "excuse me, steward," or "excuse me, Ma'am," or "excuse

Ketchum 2

me, flight attendant? ~~I~~ [or] I am confused. And when I call my father's [his]

[comma needed] office, am I speaking with my father's "secretary" or "executive [quotation marks needed]

assistant?" Are people who are not ~~very~~ tall "short" or "vertically [wordy]

challenged?"

I am afraid to even bring up race —

~~And dare I even bring up race,~~ or do I mean cultural heritage?

[Race] [term]

~~That~~ is the worst, to contend with simply because it has the most [better]

potential to offend someone. Do we have to [c]ensor ~~what we~~ [our references (more exact)]

~~refer~~ to people ~~as~~ depending on who [m] we are around at that [Correct pronoun]

moment, should we just always go with "Native [quotation marks needed]

American" or do some people think it is all right to just say

"Indian?" But if we say "Indian," aren't we referring to people that

originate from India? I feel the most threatened with what to call

black people. Should I say "people of color," or "African American?" I [better phrasing]

am stuck. And, white people, "Caucasian" or can I stick with "white [should I call]

people?" My vote is that we just stick with the universal ~~theme~~ [all] [label] of [better word]

American for everybody. And how incorrect would it be of me [move to end of para. Too choppy.]

to leave out other ethnicities, you know the ones marked

"Other" on all of those tests we took in high school, how

politically incorrect was that? I mean, is it "Oriental," or "Asian," or

should we take the time to learn exactly, what part of the world

each person's family originated (from)? ~~What do we call~~ [better phrasing]

[not needed] ~~homosexuals without offending anyone? Are only men gay and~~

~~women are lesbian? Or are they both gay? Or is it better to just~~

~~say homosexual?~~ New paragraph added here

The confusion does not end with race; it has been taken to even further extremes.

[helps explain]) Why do we even have to put such emphasis on what we call

people? People are the same, no matter what you call them. I hope

True respect is not found in a term; it is found in a

person's attitude.   └ semicolon needed

[left margin, vertical:] I think that if you are born in America you are an American, period. In saying this I do not mean to nullify the importance of a person's heritage, but again, where do we draw the line?

Ketchum 3

political
correctness

that in writing this essay I have offend~ed~ as few people as humanly *clearer*

possible. I am sure that ~it~ matters to someone, but to me, all of *better phrasing*

dithering this is as insignificant as saying "soft drink" ~or~ "soda," although ~in~ *rather than*

being a southerner I usually just go with Coke.

New ¶ Add on page 2 of essay

I could be wrong, but I believe that political correctness started with good intentions and over time **has** been taken to extremes. In the beginning I think (emphasizing) political correctness was a way to remind people *that* prejudice and the names and connotations associated with prejudice were unacceptable in an educated society. For far too many years insulting names and attitudes were a part of our society, and sometimes for no other reason than families passing down prejudices that had been in their family for years. Kids take on their parents' values, good or bad, so now it has become the job of society, primarily schools and the entertainment industry, to be politically correct. They must display a standard for kids and adults alike to learn and follow. All of that is very important and has helped to change society and its future, but where do we draw the line? Political correctness has been taken to such an extreme, there is no longer a clear definition of what is (right and wrong.

that — *that*

1

Final Draft

Carlye Ketchum, University of Tennessee

Sheer Confusion

I am not sure when or how it all got started, but I know that things have not been the same since. I'm speaking of Political Correctness. I don't know about you, but I tend to feel a little overwhelmed by it all. There seems to be so much that is correct and incorrect that a regular person can easily get lost in it. I know that I do not ever want to offend anyone, but where do we draw the line? When does not trying to hurt someone's feelings become so intense that it is just silly?

What is the difference between being called a "waitress" or a "server"? No matter what you call it, you are still taking orders and bringing food to people. I know, "server" is one of those unisex words, so we can use it to describe either a female or male, but I have always thought that was the purpose of the word "waiter." And "stewardesses," now that is a whole other can of worms. Should we say "excuse me, steward," or "excuse me, Ma'am," or "excuse me, flight attendant"? I am confused. And when I call my father's office, am I speaking with my father's "secretary" or his "executive assistant"? Are people who are not tall "short" or "vertically challenged"?

I am afraid to even bring up race—or do I mean cultural heritage? Race is the worst term to contend with simply because it has the most potential to offend someone. Do we have to censor our references to people depending on whom we are around at that moment? For instance, should we just always go with "Native American" or do some people think it is all right to just say "Indian"? But if we say "Indian," aren't we referring to people that originate from India? I feel the most threatened with what to call black people. Should I say "people of color," or "African American"? I am stuck. And should I call white people, "Caucasian" or can I stick with "white people"? I think that if you are born in America you are an American, period. In saying this I do not mean to nullify the importance of a person's heritage, but again, where do we draw the line? And how incorrect would it be of me to leave out other ethnicities, you know the ones marked "Other" on all of those tests we took in high school? How politically incorrect was that? I mean, is it "Oriental," or "Asian," or should we take the time to learn exactly from what part of the world each person's family originated? My vote is that we just all stick with the universal label of American for everybody.

I could be wrong, but I believe that political correctness started with good intentions and over time has been taken to extremes. In the beginning I think emphasizing political correctness was a way to remind people that prejudice and the names and connotations associated with prejudice are unacceptable in an educated society. For far too many years insulting names and attitudes were a part of our society, and sometimes for no other reason than families passing down prejudices that had been in their family for years.

Kids take on their parents' values, good or bad, so now it has become the job of society, primarily schools and the entertainment industry, to be politically correct. They must display a standard for kids and adults alike to learn and follow. All of that is very important and has helped to change society and its future, but where do we draw the line? Political correctness has been taken to such an extreme that there is no longer a clear definition of what is right and wrong.

The confusion does not end with race; it has been taken to even further extremes. Why do we even have to put such emphasis on what we call people? People are the same, no matter what you call them. True respect is not found in a term; it is found in a person's attitude. I hope that in writing this essay I have offended as few people as humanly possible. I am sure that political correctness matters to someone, but to me, all of this dithering is as insignificant as saying "soft drink" rather than "soda," although being a southerner I usually just go with Coke.

How I Write

I can only write when the mood strikes me. Sitting down at the computer with the thought "write something now" just doesn't work for me. I find that I do my best writing when I am just sitting in my room or on my bed or anywhere I feel comfortable. I know this is outdated of me, but I also always prefer to write my first draft with pen and paper as opposed to using the keyboard. If a paper involves any research, I would always much rather check out the books I need rather than read them in the library. That way, I can take them someplace quiet where I can really focus on what I am trying to get out of them. I take notes as I go, making sure to jot down where I thought a specific note would help in the essay (i.e., what it would back up).

How I Wrote This Essay

I first wrote most of this essay with pen and paper in my room at my desk. I asked a few friends if they could think of any blurry examples of political correctness, but they were not much help. I then typed out a draft that I printed and made corrections on. The only part of this essay that really gave me trouble was the opening. I ended up calling a friend with whom I have great political arguments, and there was my inspiration.

My Writing Tip

Always give yourself plenty of time to write, or you will regret it. I also find it really helpful to type my first draft, then leave it a few hours. I just go away and do something else. When I come back to it, I always have a fresh outlook that helps me with the revision.

CHAPTER WRITING ASSIGNMENTS

1. Select any two paragraphs, one from an article in the *Reader's Digest* and another from an article in *The New Yorker*. Analyze the differences in the language (diction, phrasing, sentence style, and paragraph length) and speculate on the intended audience of each magazine.

2. Write an essay on the meaning and practice of rhetoric as exemplified in this chapter.

3. Rewrite the John Keats letter in the English and style that someone might use in a love letter today.

WRITING ASSIGNMENTS FOR A SPECIFIC AUDIENCE

1. To an imagined audience of African American readers, direct an essay arguing for or against the idea that race relations in America have gotten better since Dr. King's speech was delivered.

2. Write an essay aimed at an audience of eighth-graders explaining to them what they can expect to encounter later in high school and college writing courses.

COLLABORATIVE WRITING PROJECT

Dividing your group into two teams, investigate and research the debate raging among English instructors between the so-called "product" and "process" approach to teaching writing. If necessary, interview faculty members who are practitioners of your assigned approach. Each team will report on its findings and defend its position before the other. Finally, each team will write an essay explaining exactly what is entailed by the approach, outlining its drawbacks and merits.

▼▼▼

Chapter Two

THE WRITER'S VOICE

INTRODUCTION: WHAT IS A WRITER'S VOICE?

We all possess a range of speaking tones that we unconsciously inflect to signal moods from despair to cheerfulness. We alter these speaking tones without even thinking, making sophisticated adjustments to them on the spot. A similar technique is also within the power of writers. A letter to a banker will not sound like a *billet-doux* to a lover, and if it does, then either the banker or the lover is in for trouble. In sum, we do not always write in the same style. Yet mysteries persist: What is a writer's style? How does it differ from the writer's voice?

Most writers do not sit down to write consciously in a certain style. They do, however, try to project a certain voice onto the page. Sometimes this voice is deliberately assumed, but often it is chosen for the writer by the psychology of audience and material, by the need and occasion that make the writing necessary.

Here is an example. You, the boss, sit down to write a memo to your employees. Your position goes to your head, and you write:

Illumination of the overhead fixtures must be extinguished by the final person exiting the premises.

This notice tells the reader two things. First, it tells the reader to turn out the lights before leaving the room. Second, it tells the reader that you are the boss and you say so. That is not the only kind of notice you could have written. You might, for example, have written this equivalent:

The last person to leave this room must turn out the overhead lights.

This makes the point but you think it also makes you sound awfully humble.

The difference between these two is not one of content, but of tone or style. It is tone of voice when you are composing the memo, for what you tried to do was not write in a certain style but to sound like the boss; to the reader, however, it is your style. Voice goes in; style comes out: that is the formula to remember.

With some justification, many writing teachers approach voice and style as if they are always related to the writer's psychology. If you had confidence in your authority as the boss, if you really felt comfortable with your power, you wouldn't think it necessary to sound like God in every memo you wrote. So if you must sound like the Almighty in your memos, perhaps it is because you really don't feel at ease with the idea of being the boss. Many similar mishaps of voice or style in student papers can be traced to a psychological uncertainty about the material, to an unconfident attitude, or even to the writer's resistance to the assignment.

Behind this line of thinking lurks that age-old advice instructors often hand out to student writers: "Be yourself." Don't try to write in a voice that is not truly your own; don't try to put on airs in your writing. This is genuinely good advice, for the pompous voice affected by the writer always comes out for the reader as a pompous style. As computer programmers say: "Garbage in, garbage out." "Sincerity in, sincerity out" is also a happier truth.

The articles in this chapter grapple with the perennial problem of voice and style. Paul Roberts tells us how to make our writing more readable. F. L. Lucas discusses what makes a good style. Then we are treated to a range of highly individualistic styles, from the lyrical broken English of Bartolomeo Vanzetti to the voice of a child recollecting a memorable encounter with religion. Stephen Leacock makes us laugh as he pokes fun at typical mathematical problems handed to students in class. Dan Greenburg tells the famous Goldilock tale in two different styles. The chapter ends with a poem and a debate about AIDS, which has become a particularly virulent epidemic throughout the world.

A D V I C E

▼▼▼

Paul Roberts

HOW TO SAY NOTHING IN FIVE HUNDRED WORDS

PAUL MCHENRY ROBERTS (1917–1967) taught college English for over twenty years, first at San Jose State College and later at Cornell University. He wrote several books on linguistics, including *Understanding Grammar* (1954), *Patterns of English* (1956), and *Understanding English* (1958).

> *Freshman composition, like everything else, has its share of fashions. In the 1950s, when this article was written, the most popular argument raging among student essayists was the proposed abolition of college football. With the greater social consciousness of the early 1960s, the topic of the day became the morality of capital punishment. Topics may change, but the core principles of good writing remain constant, and this essay has become something of a minor classic in explaining them. Be concrete, says Roberts; get to the point; express your opinions colorfully. Refreshingly, he even practices what he preaches. His essay is humorous, direct, and almost salty in summarizing the working habits that all good prose writers must cultivate.*

1   It's Friday afternoon, and you have almost survived another week of classes. You are just looking forward dreamily to the weekend when the English instructor says: "For Monday you will turn in a five-hundred-word composition on college football."

2   Well, that puts a good hole in the weekend. You don't have any strong views on college football one way or the other. You get rather excited during the season and go to all the home games and find it rather more fun than not. On the other hand, the class has been reading Robert Hutchins in the anthology and perhaps Shaw's "Eighty-Yard Run," and from the class discussion you have got the idea that the instructor thinks college football is for the birds. You are no fool. You can figure out what side to take.

3   After dinner you get out the portable typewriter that you got for high school graduation. You might as well get it over with and enjoy Saturday and Sunday. Five hundred words is about two double-spaced pages with normal margins. You put in a sheet of paper, think up a title, and you're off:

Why College Football Should Be Abolished

College football should be abolished because it's bad for the school and also for the players. The players are so busy practicing that they don't have any time for their studies.

This, you feel, is a mighty good start. The only trouble is that it's only thirty-two words. You still have four hundred and sixty-eight to go, and you've pretty well exhausted the subject. It comes to you that you do your best thinking in the morning, so you put away the typewriter and go to the movies. But the next morning you have to do your washing and some math problems, and in the afternoon you go to the game. The English instructor turns up too, and you wonder if you've taken the right side after all. Saturday night you have a date, and Sunday morning you have to go to church. (You can't let English assignments interfere with your religion.) What with one thing and another, it's ten o'clock Sunday night before you get out the typewriter again. You make a pot of coffee and start to fill out your views on college football. Put a little meat on the bones.

Why College Football Should Be Abolished

In my opinion, it seems to me that college football should be abolished. The reason why I think this to be true is because I feel that football is bad for the colleges in nearly every respect. As Robert Hutchins says in his article in our anthology in which he discusses college football, it would be better if the colleges had race horses and had races with one another, because then the horses would not have to attend classes. I firmly agree with Mr. Hutchins on this point, and I am sure that many other students would agree too.

One reason why it seems to me that college football is bad is that it has become too commercial. In the olden times when people played football just for the fun of it, maybe college football was all right, but they do not play college football just for the fun of it now as they used to in the old days. Nowadays college football is what you might call a big business. Maybe this is not true at all schools, and I don't think it is especially true here at State, but certainly this is the case at most colleges and universities in America nowadays, as Mr. Hutchins points out in his very interesting article. Actually the coaches and alumni go around to the high schools and offer the high school stars large salaries to come to their colleges and play football for them. There was one case where a high school star was offered a convertible if he would play football for a certain college.

Another reason for abolishing college football is that it is bad for the players. They do not have time to get a college education, because they are so busy playing football. A football player has to practice every afternoon from three to six and then he is so tired that he can't concentrate on his studies. He just feels like dropping off to sleep after dinner, and then the next day he goes to his classes without having studied and maybe he fails the test.

(Good ripe stuff so far, but you're still a hundred and fifty-one words from home. One more push.)

Also I think college football is bad for the colleges and the universities because not very many students get to participate in it. Out of a college of ten thousand students only seventy-five or a hundred play football, if that many. Football is what you might call a spectator sport. That means that most people go to watch it but do not play it themselves.

(Four hundred and fifteen. Well, you still have the conclusion, and when you retype it, you can make the margins a little wider.)

These are the reasons why I agree with Mr. Hutchins that college football should be abolished in American colleges and universities.

4   On Monday you turn it in, moderately hopeful, and on Friday it comes back marked "weak in content" and sporting a big "D."

5   This essay is exaggerated a little, not much. The English instructor will recognize it as reasonably typical of what an assignment on college football will bring in. He knows that nearly half of the class will contrive in five hundred words to say that college football is too commercial and bad for the players. Most of the other half will inform him that college football builds character and prepares one for life and brings prestige to the school. As he reads paper after paper all saying the same thing in almost the same words, all bloodless, five hundred words dripping out of nothing, he wonders how he allowed himself to get trapped into teaching English when he might have had a happy and interesting life as an electrician or a confidence man.

6   Well, you may ask, what can you do about it? The subject is one on which you have few convictions and little information. Can you be expected to make a dull subject interesting? As a matter of fact, this is precisely what you are expected to do. This is the writer's essential task. All subjects, except sex, are dull until somebody makes them interesting. The writer's job is to find the argument, the approach, the angle, the wording that will take the reader with him. This is seldom easy, and it is particularly hard in subjects that have been much discussed: College Football, Fraternities, Popular Music, Is Chivalry Dead?, and the like. You will feel that there is nothing you can do with such subjects except repeat the old bromides. But there are some things you can do which will make your papers, if not throbbingly alive, at least less insufferably tedious than they might otherwise be.

Avoid the Obvious Content

7   Say the assignment is college football. Say that you've decided to be against it. Begin by putting down the arguments that come to your mind: it is too commercial, it takes the students' minds off their studies, it is hard on the players, it makes the university a kind of circus instead of an intellectual center, for most schools it is financially ruinous. Can you think of any more arguments, just offhand? All right. Now when you write your paper, *make sure that you don't use any of the material on this list.* If these are the points that leap to your mind, they will leap to everyone else's too, and whether you get a "C" or a "D" may depend on whether the instructor reads your paper early when he is fresh and tolerant or late, when the sentence "In my opinion, college football has become too commercial," inexorably repeated, has brought him to the brink of lunacy.

8   Be against college football for some reason or reasons of your own. If they are keen and perceptive ones, that's splendid. But even if they are trivial or foolish or indefensible, you are still ahead so long as they are not everybody else's reasons too. Be against it because the colleges don't spend enough money on it to make it worthwhile, because it is bad for the characters of the spectators, because the players are forced to attend classes, because the football stars hog all the beautiful women, because it competes with baseball and is therefore unAmerican and possibly Communist-inspired. There are lots of more or less unused reasons for being against college football.

9   Sometimes it is a good idea to sum up and dispose of the trite and conventional points before going on to your own. This has the advantage of indicating to the reader that you are going to be neither trite nor conventional. Something like this:

> We are often told that college football should be abolished because it has become too commercial or because it is bad for the players. These arguments are no doubt very cogent, but they don't really go to the heart of the matter.

Then you go to the heart of the matter.

Take the Less Usual Side

10   One rather simple way of getting into your paper is to take the side of the argument that most of the citizens will want to avoid. If the assignment is an essay on dogs, you can, if you choose, explain that dogs are faithful and lovable companions, intelligent, useful as guardians of the house and protectors of children, indispensable in police work—in short, when all is said and done, man's best friends. Or you can suggest that those big brown eyes conceal, more often than not, a vacuity of mind and an inconstancy of purpose; that the dogs you have known

most intimately have been mangy, ill-tempered brutes, incapable of instruction; and that only your nobility of mind and fear of arrest prevent you from kicking the flea-ridden animals when you pass them on the street.

11   Naturally personal convictions will sometimes dictate your approach. If the assigned subject is "Is Methodism Rewarding to the Individual?" and you are a pious Methodist, you have really no choice. But few assigned subjects, if any, will fall in this category. Most of them will lie in broad areas of discussion with much to be said on both sides. They are intellectual exercises, and it is legitimate to argue now one way and now another, as debaters do in similar circumstances. Always take the side that looks to you hardest, least defensible. It will almost always turn out to be easier to write interestingly on that side.

12   This general advice applies where you have a choice of subjects. If you are to choose among "The Value of Fraternities" and "My Favorite High School Teacher" and "What I Think About Beetles," by all means plump for the beetles. By the time the instructor gets to your paper, he will be up to his ears in tedious tales about a French teacher at Bloombury High and assertions about how fraternities build character and prepare one for life. Your views on beetles, whatever they are, are bound to be a refreshing change.

13   Don't worry too much about figuring out what the instructor thinks about the subject so that you can cuddle up with him. Chances are his views are no stronger than yours. If he does have convictions and you oppose him, his problem is to keep from grading you higher than you deserve in order to show he is not biased. This doesn't mean that you should always cantankerously dissent from what the instructor says; that gets tiresome too. And if the subject assigned is "My Pet Peeve," do not begin, "My pet peeve is the English instructor who assigns papers on 'my pet peeve.'" This was still funny during the War of 1812, but it has sort of lost its edge since then. It is in general good manners to avoid personalities.

Slip Out of Abstraction

14   If you will study the essay on college football [near the beginning of this essay], you will perceive that one reason for its appalling dullness is that it never gets down to particulars. It is just a series of not very glittering generalities: "football is bad for the colleges," "it has become too commercial," "football is big business," "it is bad for the players," and so on. Such round phrases thudding against the reader's brain are unlikely to convince him, though they may well render him unconscious.

15   If you want the reader to believe that college football is bad for the players, you have to do more than say so. You have to display the evil. Take your roommate, Alfred Simkins, the second-string center. Picture

poor old Alfy coming home from football practice every evening, bruised and aching, agonizingly tired, scarcely able to shovel the mashed potatoes into his mouth. Let us see him staggering up to the room, getting out his econ textbook, peering desperately at it with his good eye, falling asleep and failing the test in the morning. Let us share his unbearable tension as Saturday draws near. Will he fail, be demoted, lose his monthly allowance, be forced to return to the coal mines? And if he succeeds, what will be his reward? Perhaps a slight ripple of applause when the third-string center replaces him, a moment of elation in the locker room if the team wins, of despair if it loses. What will he look back on when he graduates from college? Toil and torn ligaments. And what will be his future? He is not good enough for pro football, and he is too obscure and weak in econ to succeed in stocks and bonds. College football is tearing the heart from Alfy Simkins and, when it finishes with him, will callously toss aside the shattered hulk.

16   This is no doubt a weak enough argument for the abolition of college football, but it is a sight better than saying, in three or four variations, that college football (in your opinion) is bad for the players.

17   Look at the work of any professional writer and notice how constantly he is moving from the generality, the abstract statement, to the concrete example, the facts and figures, the illustrations. If he is writing on juvenile delinquency, he does not just tell you that juveniles are (it seems to him) delinquent and that (in his opinion) something should be done about it. He shows you juveniles being delinquent, tearing up movie theatres in Buffalo, stabbing high school principals in Dallas, smoking marijuana in Palo Alto. And more than likely he is moving toward some specific remedy, not just a general wringing of the hands.

18   It is no doubt possible to be *too* concrete, too illustrative or anecdotal, but few inexperienced writers err this way. For most the soundest advice is to be seeking always for the picture, to be always turning general remarks into seeable examples. Don't say, "Sororities teach girls the social graces." Say, "Sorority life teaches a girl how to carry on a conversation while pouring tea, without sloshing the tea into the saucer." Don't say, "I like certain kinds of popular music very much." Say, "Whenever I hear Gerber Sprinklittle play 'Mississippi Man' on the trombone, my socks creep up my ankles."

Get Rid of Obvious Padding

19   The student toiling away at his weekly English theme is too often tormented by a figure: five hundred words. How, he asks himself, is he to achieve this staggering total? Obviously by never using one word when he can somehow work in ten.

20   He is therefore seldom content with a plain statement like "Fast driving is dangerous." This has only four words in it. He takes thought, and the sentence becomes:

> In my opinion, fast driving is dangerous.

Better, but he can do better still:

> In my opinion, fast driving would seem to be rather dangerous.

If he is really adept, it may come out:

> In my humble opinion, though I do not claim to be an expert on this complicated subject, fast driving, in most circumstances, would seem to be rather dangerous in many respects, or at least so it would seem to me.

Thus four words have been turned into forty, and not an iota of content has been added.

21   Now this is a way to go about reaching five hundred words, and if you are content with a "D" grade, it is as good a way as any. But if you aim higher, you must work differently. Instead of stuffing your sentences with straw, you must try steadily to get rid of the padding, to make your sentences lean and tough. If you are really working at it, your first draft will greatly exceed the required total, and then you will work it down, thus:

> It is thought in some quarters that fraternities do not contribute as much as might be expected to campus life.
> Some people think that fraternities contribute little to campus life.

> The average doctor who practices in small towns or in the country must toil night and day to heal the sick.
> Most country doctors work long hours.

> When I was a little girl, I suffered from shyness and embarrassment in the presence of others.
> I was a shy little girl.

> It is absolutely necessary for the person employed as a marine fireman to give the matter of steam pressure his undivided attention at all times.
> The fireman has to keep his eye on the steam gauge.

22   You may ask how you can arrive at five hundred words at this rate. Simple. You dig up more real content. Instead of taking a couple

of obvious points off the surface of the topic and then circling warily around them for six paragraphs, you work in and explore, figure out the details. You illustrate. You say that fast driving is dangerous, and then you prove it. How long does it take to stop a car at forty and at eighty? How far can you see at night? What happens when a tire blows? What happens in a head-on collision at fifty miles an hour? Pretty soon your paper will be full of broken glass and blood and headless torsos, and reaching five hundred words will not really be a problem.

Call a Fool a Fool

23   Some of the padding in freshman themes is to be blamed not on anxiety about the word minimum but on excessive timidity. The student writes, "In my opinion, the principal of my high school acted in ways that I believe every unbiased person would have to call foolish." This isn't exactly what he means. What he means is, "My high school principal was a fool." If he was a fool, call him a fool. Hedging the thing about with "in-my-opinion's" and "it-seems-to-me's" and "as-I-see-it's" and "at-least-from-my-point-of-view's" gains you nothing. Delete these phrases whenever they creep into your paper.

24   The student's tendency to hedge stems from a modesty that in other circumstances would be commendable. He is, he realizes, young and inexperienced, and he half suspects that he is dopey and fuzzy-minded beyond the average. Probably only too true. But it doesn't help to announce your incompetence six times in every paragraph. Decide what you want to say and say it as vigorously as possible, without apology and in plain words.

25   Linguistic diffidence can take various forms. One is what we call *euphemism.* This is the tendency to call a spade "a certain garden implement" or women's underwear "unmentionables." It is stronger in some eras than others and in some people than others but it always operates more or less in subjects that are touchy or taboo: death, sex, madness, and so on. Thus we shrink from saying "He died last night" but say instead "passed away," "left us," "joined his Maker," "went to his reward." Or we try to take off the tension with a lighter cliché: "kicked the bucket," "cashed in his chips," "handed in his dinner pail." We have found all sorts of ways to avoid saying *mad:* "mentally ill," "touched," "not quite right upstairs," "feebleminded," "innocent," "simple," "off his trolley," "not in his right mind." Even such a now plain word as *insane* began as a euphemism with the meaning "not healthy."

26   Modern science, particularly psychology, contributes many polysyllables in which we can wrap our thoughts and blunt their force. To many writers there is no such thing as a bad schoolboy. Schoolboys are maladjusted or unoriented or misunderstood or in the need of guidance or lacking in continued success toward satisfactory integration of

the personality as a social unit, but they are never bad. Psychology no doubt makes us better men and women, more sympathetic and tolerant, but it doesn't make writing any easier. Had Shakespeare been confronted with psychology, "To be or not to be" might have come out, "To continue as a social unit or not to do so. That is the personality problem. Whether 'tis a better sign of integration at the conscious level to display a psychic tolerance toward the maladjustments and repressions induced by one's lack of orientation in one's environment or—" But Hamlet would never have finished the soliloquy.

27   Writing in the modern world, you cannot altogether avoid modern jargon. Nor, in an effort to get away from euphemism, should you salt your paper with four-letter words. But you can do much if you will mount guard against those roundabout phrases, those echoing polysyllables that tend to slip into your writing to rob it of its crispness and force.

Beware of Pat Expressions

28   Other things being equal, avoid phrases like "other things being equal." Those sentences that come to you whole, or in two or three doughy lumps, are sure to be bad sentences. They are no creation of yours but pieces of common thought floating in the community soup.

29   Pat expressions are hard, often impossible, to avoid, because they come too easily to be noticed and seem too necessary to be dispensed with. No writer avoids them altogether, but good writers avoid them more often than poor writers.

30   By "pat expressions" we mean such tags as "to all practical intents and purposes," "the pure and simple truth," "from where I sit," "the time of his life," "to the ends of the earth," "in the twinkling of an eye," "as sure as you're born," "over my dead body," "under cover of darkness," "took the easy way out," "when all is said and done," "told him time and time again," "parted the best of friends," "stand up and be counted," "gave him the best years of her life," "worked her fingers to the bone." Like other clichés, these expressions were once forceful. Now we should use them only when we can't possibly think of anything else.

31   Some pat expressions stand like a wall between the writer and thought. Such a one is "the American way of life." Many student writers feel that when they have said that something accords with the American way of life or does not they have exhausted the subject. Actually, they have stopped at the highest level of abstraction. The American way of life is the complicated set of bonds between a hundred and eighty million ways. All of us know this when we think about it, but the tag phrase too often keeps us from thinking about it.

32   So with many another phrase dear to the politician: "this great land of ours," "the man in the street," "our national heritage." These

may prove our patriotism or give a clue to our political beliefs, but otherwise they add nothing to the paper except words.

Colorful Words

33   The writer builds with words, and no builder uses a raw material more slippery and elusive and treacherous. A writer's work is a constant struggle to get the right word in the right place, to find that particular word that will convey his meaning exactly, that will persuade the reader or soothe him or startle or amuse him. He never succeeds altogether—sometimes he feels that he scarcely succeeds at all—but such successes as he has are what make the thing worth doing.

34   There is no book of rules for this game. One progresses through everlasting experiment on the basis of ever-widening experience. There are few useful generalizations that one can make about words as words, but there are perhaps a few.

35   Some words are what we call "colorful." By this we mean that they are calculated to produce a picture or induce an emotion. They are dressy instead of plain, specific instead of general, loud instead of soft. Thus, in place of "Her heart beat," we may write, "her heart *pounded, throbbed, fluttered, danced.*" Instead of "He sat in his chair," we may say, "he *lounged, sprawled, coiled.*" Instead of "It was hot," we may say, "It was *blistering, sultry, muggy, suffocating, steamy, wilting.*"

36   However, it should not be supposed that the fancy word is always better. Often it is as well to write "Her heart beat" or "It was hot" if that is all it did or all it was. Ages differ in how they like their prose. The nineteenth century liked it rich and smoky. The twentieth has usually preferred it lean and cool. The twentieth century writer, like all writers, is forever seeking the exact word, but he is wary of sounding feverish. He tends to pitch it low, to understate it, to throw it away. He knows that if he gets too colorful, the audience is likely to giggle.

37   See how this strikes you: "As the rich, golden glow of the sunset died away along the eternal western hills, Angela's limpid blue eyes looked softly and trustingly into Montague's flashing brown ones, and her heart pounded like a drum in time with the joyous song surging in her soul." Some people like that sort of thing, but most modern readers would say, "Good grief," and turn on the television.

Colored Words

38   Some words we would call not so much colorful as colored—that is, loaded with associations, good or bad. All words—except perhaps structure words—have associations of some sort. We have said that the meaning of a word is the sum of the contexts in which it occurs. When we hear a word, we hear with it an echo of all the situations in which we have heard it before.

39   In some words, these echoes are obvious and discussible. The word *mother,* for example, has, for most people, agreeable associations. When you hear *mother* you probably think of home, safety, love, food, and various other pleasant things. If one writes, "She was like a mother to me," he gets an effect which he would not get in "She was like an aunt to me." The advertiser makes use of the associations of *mother* by working it in when he talks about his product. The politician works it in when he talks about himself.

40   So also with such words as *home, liberty, fireside, contentment, patriot, tenderness, sacrifice, childlike, manly, bluff, limpid.* All of these words are loaded with associations that would be rather hard to indicate in a straightforward definition. There is more than a literal difference between "They sat around the fireside" and "They sat around the stove." They might have been equally warm and happy around the stove, but *fireside* suggests leisure, grace, quiet tradition, congenial company, and *stove* does not.

41   Conversely, some words have bad associations. *Mother* suggests pleasant things, but *mother-in-law* does not. Many mothers-in-law are heroically lovable and some mothers drink gin all day and beat their children insensible, but these facts of life are beside the point. The point is that *mother* sounds good and *mother-in-law* does not.

42   Or consider the word *intellectual.* This would seem to be a complimentary term, but in point of fact it is not, for it has picked up associations of impracticality and ineffectuality and general dopiness. So also such words as *liberal, reactionary, Communist, socialist, capitalist, radical, schoolteacher, truck driver, undertaker, operator, salesman, huckster, speculator.* These convey meaning on the literal level, but beyond that—sometimes, in some places—they convey contempt on the part of the speaker.

43   The question of whether to use loaded words or not depends on what is being written. The scientist, the scholar, try to avoid them; for the poet, the advertising writer, the public speaker, they are standard equipment. But every writer should take care that they do not substitute for thought. If you write, "Anyone who thinks that is nothing but a Socialist (or Communist or capitalist)" you have said nothing except that you don't like people who think that, and such remarks are effective only with the most naive readers. It is always a bad mistake to think your readers more naive than they really are.

Colorless Words

44   But probably most student writers come to grief not with words that are colorful or those that are colored but with those that have no color at all. A pet example is *nice,* a word we would find it hard to dispense with in casual conversation but which is no longer capable of adding

much to a description. Colorless words are those of such general meaning that in a particular sentence they mean nothing. Slang adjectives like *cool* ("That's real cool") tend to explode all over the language. They are applied to everything, lose their original force, and quickly die.

45   Beware also of nouns of very general meaning, like *circumstances, cases, instances, aspects, factors, relationships, attitudes, eventualities,* etc. In most circumstances you will find that those cases of writing which contain too many instances of words like these will in this and other aspects have factors leading to unsatisfactory relationships with the reader resulting in unfavorable attitudes on his part and perhaps other eventualities, like a grade of "D." Notice also what *etc.* means. It means "I'd like to make this list longer, but I can't think of any more examples."

(5,080 words)

VOCABULARY

contrive (5)   vacuity (10)   jargon (27)
bromides (6)   warily (22)   polysyllables (27)
inexorably (7)   diffidence (25)   elusive (33)
cogent (9)   euphemism (25)   induce (35)

DISCUSSION

▼▼▼

F. L. Lucas

WHAT IS STYLE?

F. L. LUCAS (1894–1967) was for many years a distinguished scholar and lecturer at Cambridge. In his teaching, he placed particular emphasis on the classics and on good writing. Lucas tried his hand at virtually every literary form; yet his best work was in the field of literary criticism, where he was prolific. Among his principal works are *The Decline and Fall of the Romantic Ideal* (1934), *Greek Poetry for Everyman* (1951), *Greek Drama for Everyman* (1954), and *The Art of Living* (1959).

Style belongs to that category of things about which people commonly say: I don't know what it is but I know what I like. We all think that we can recognize and appreciate style when we see it, but few of us would undertake to define it. Literary style is possibly the most elu-sive kind of all. In this essay, originally published in March 1960, F. L. Lucas surveys what some famous people have written and said about style, and gives us some suggestions for improving our own.

1   When it was suggested to Walt Whitman that one of his works should be bound in vellum, he was outraged—"Pshaw!" he snorted, "—hang-ings, curtains, finger bowls, chinaware, Matthew Arnold!" And he might have been equally irritated by talk of style; for he boasted of "my barbaric yawp"—he would *not* be literary; his readers should touch not a book but a man. Yet Whitman took the pains to rewrite *Leaves of Grass* four times, and his style is unmistakable. Samuel But-ler maintained that writers who bothered about their style became unreadable but he bothered about his own. "Style" has got a bad name by growing associated with precious and superior persons who, like Oscar Wilde, spend a morning putting in a comma, and the after-noon (so he said) taking it out again. But such abuse of "style" is mis-use of English. For the word means merely "a way of expressing oneself, in language, manner, or appearance"; or, secondly, "a *good* way of so expressing oneself"—as when one says, "Her behavior never lacked style."

2   Now there is no crime in expressing oneself (though to try to im-press oneself on others easily grows revolting or ridiculous). Indeed one cannot help expressing oneself, unless one passes one's life in a cupboard. Even the most rigid Communist, or Organization-man, is compelled by Nature to have a unique voice, unique fingerprints, unique handwriting. Even the signatures of the letters on your break-fast table may reveal more than their writers guess. There are bluster-ing signatures that swish across the page like cornstalks bowed before a tempest. There are cryptic signatures, like a scrabble of lightning across a cloud, suggesting that behind is a lofty divinity whom all must know, or an aloof divinity whom none is worthy to know (though, as this might be highly inconvenient, a docile typist sometimes inter-prets the mystery in a bracket underneath). There are impetuous squiggles implying that the author is a sort of strenuous Sputnik streaking around the globe every eighty minutes. There are florid sig-natures, all curlicues and danglements and flamboyance, like the youthful Disraeli (though these seem rather out of fashion). There are humble, humdrum signatures. And there are also, sometimes, signa-tures that are courteously clear, yet mindful of a certain simple grace and artistic economy—in short, of style.

3   Since, then, not one of us can put pen to paper, or even open his mouth, without giving something of himself away to shrewd observers, it seems mere common sense to give the matter a little thought. Yet it

does not seem very common. Ladies may take infinite pains about having style in their clothes, but many of us remain curiously indifferent about having it in our words. How many women would dream of polishing not only their nails but also their tongues? They may play freely on that perilous little organ, but they cannot often be bothered to tune it. And how many men think of improving their talk as well as their golf handicap?

4   No doubt strong silent men, speaking only in gruff monosyllables, may despise "mere words." No doubt the world does suffer from an endemic plague of verbal dysentery. But that, precisely, is bad style. And consider the amazing power of mere words. Adolf Hitler was a bad artist, bad statesman, bad general, and bad man. But largely because he could tune his rant, with psychological nicety, to the exact wave length of his audiences and make millions quarrelsome-drunk all at the same time by his command of windy nonsense, skilled statesmen, soldiers, scientists were blown away like chaff, and he came near to rule the world. If Sir Winston Churchill had been a mere speechifier, we might well have lost the war; yet his speeches did quite a lot to win it.

5   No man was less of a literary aesthete than Benjamin Franklin; yet this tallow-chandler's son, who changed world history, regarded as "a principal means of my advancement" that pungent style which he acquired partly by working in youth over old *Spectators;* but mainly by being Benjamin Franklin. The squinting demagogue, John Wilkes, as ugly as his many sins, had yet a tongue so winning that he asked only half an hour's start (to counteract his face) against any rival for a woman's favor. "Vote for you!" growled a surly elector in his constituency. "I'd sooner vote for the devil!" "But in case your friend should not stand . . . ?" Cleopatra, the ensnarer of world conquerors, owed less to the shape of her nose than to the charm of her tongue. Shakespeare himself has often poor plots and thin ideas; even his mastery of character has been questioned; what does remain unchallenged is his verbal magic. Men are often taken, like rabbits, by the ears. And though the tongue has no bones, it can sometimes break millions of them.

6   "But," the reader may grumble, "I am neither Hitler, Cleopatra, nor Shakespeare. What is all this to me?" Yet we all talk—often too much; we all have to write letters—often too many. We live not by bread alone but also by words. And not always with remarkable efficiency. Strikes, lawsuits, divorces, all sorts of public nuisance and private misery, often come just from the gaggling incompetence with which we express ourselves. Americans and British get at cross-purposes because they use the same words with different meanings. Men have been hanged on a comma in a statute. And in the valley of Balaclava a mere verbal ambiguity, about *which* guns were to be captured, sent the whole Light Brigade to futile annihilation.

7   Words can be more powerful, and more treacherous, than we sometimes suspect; communication more difficult than we may think. We are all serving life sentences of solitary confinement within our own bodies; like prisoners, we have, as it were, to tap in awkward code to our fellow men in their neighboring cells. Further, when A and B converse, there take part in their dialogue not two characters, as they suppose, but six. For there is A's real self—call it A_1; there is also A's picture of himself—A_2; there is also B's picture of A—A_3. And there are three corresponding personalities of B. With six characters involved even in a simple tête-à-tête, no wonder we fall into muddles and misunderstandings.

8   Perhaps, then, there are five main reasons for trying to gain some mastery of language:

> We have no other way of understanding, informing, misinforming, or persuading one another.

> Even alone, we think mainly in words; if our language is muddy, so will our thinking be.

> By our handling of words we are often revealed and judged. "Has he written anything?" said Napoleon of a candidate for an appointment. "Let me see his *style.*"

> Without a feeling for language one remains half-blind and deaf to literature.

> Our mother tongue is bettered or worsened by the way each generation uses it. Languages evolve like species. They can degenerate; just as oysters and barnacles have lost their heads. Compare ancient Greek with modern. A heavy responsibility, though often forgotten.

9   Why and how did I become interested in style? The main answer, I suppose, is that I was born that way. Then I was, till ten, an only child running loose in a house packed with books, and in a world (thank goodness) still undistracted by radio and television. So at three I groaned to my mother, "Oh, I *wish* I could read," and at four I read. Now travel among books is the best travel of all, and the easiest, and the cheapest. (Not that I belittle ordinary travel—which I regard as one of the three main pleasures in life.) One learns to write by reading good books, as one learns to talk by hearing good talkers. And if I have learned anything in writing, it is largely from writers like Montaigne, Dorothy Osborne, Horace Walpole, Johnson, Goldsmith, Montesquieu, Voltaire, Flaubert and Anatole France. Again, I was reared on Greek and Latin, and one can learn much from translating Homer or the Greek Anthology, Horace or Tacitus, if one is thrilled by the originals and tries, however vainly, to recapture some of that thrill in English.

10   But at Rugby I could *not* write English essays. I believe it stupid to torment boys to write on topics that they know and care nothing about. I used to rush to the school library and cram the subject, like a python swallowing rabbits; then, still replete as a postprandial python, I would tie myself in clumsy knots to embrace those accursed themes. Bacon was wise in saying that reading makes a full man; talking, a ready one; writing, an exact one. But writing from an empty head is futile anguish.

11   At Cambridge, my head having grown a little fuller, I suddenly found I *could* write—not with enjoyment (it is always tearing oneself in pieces)—but fairly fluently. Then came the War of 1914–18; and though soldiers have other things than pens to handle, they learn painfully to be clear and brief. Then the late Sir Desmond MacCarthy invited me to review for the *New Statesman:* it was a useful apprentice-ship, and he was delightful to work for. But I think it was well after a few years to stop; reviewers remain essential, but there are too many books one *cannot* praise, and only the pugnacious enjoy amassing ene-mies. By then I was an ink-addict—not because writing is much plea-sure, but because not to write is pain; just as some smokers do not so much enjoy tobacco as suffer without it. The positive happiness of writing comes, I think, from work when done—decently, one hopes, and not without use—and from the letters of readers which help to re-assure, or delude, one that so it is.

12   But one of my most vivid lessons came, I think, from service in a war department during the Second World War. Then, if the matter one sent out was too wordy, the communication channels might choke; yet if it was not absolutely clear, the results might be serious. So I emerged, after six years of it, with more passion than ever for clarity and brevity, more loathing than ever for the obscure and the verbose.

13   For forty years at Cambridge I have tried to teach young men to write well, and have come to think it impossible. To write really well is a gift inborn; those who have it teach themselves; one can only try to help and hasten the process. After all, the uneducated sometimes express themselves far better than their "betters." In language, as in life, it is possible to be perfectly correct—and yet perfectly tedious, or odious. The literate last letter of the doomed Vanzetti[1] was more moving than most professional orators; 18th Century ladies, who should have been spanked for their spelling, could yet write far better letters than most professors of English; and the talk of Synge's Irish peasants seems to me vastly more vivid than the latter styles of Henry James. Yet Synge averred that his characters owed far less of their eloquence to what he invented for them than to what he had overheard in the cottages of Wicklow and Kerry.

---

[1] See p. 91.—Ed.

> CHRISTY. It's little you'll think if my love's a poacher's, or an earl's
> itself, when you'll feel my two hands stretched around you, and I
> squeezing kisses on your puckered lips, till I'd feel a kind of pity for
> the Lord God in all ages sitting lonesome in His golden chair.
>
> PEGEEN. That'll be right fun, Christy Mahon, and any girl would
> walk her heart out before she'd meet a young man was your like for
> eloquence, or talk at all.

14   Well she might! It's not like that they talk in universities—more's
the pity.

15   But though one cannot teach people to write well, one can sometimes teach them to write rather better. One can give a certain number
of hints, which often seem boringly obvious—only experience shows
they are not.

16   One can say: Beware of pronouns—they are devils. Look at even
Addison, describing the type of pedant who chatters of style without
having any:

> Upon enquiry I found my learned friend had dined that day with Mr.
> Swan, the famous punster; and desiring *him* to give me some account
> of Mr. Swan's conversation, *he* told me that *he* generally talked in the
> Paronomasia, that *he* sometimes gave it to the Ploce, but that in *his*
> humble opinion *he* shone most in the Antanaclasis.

17   What a sluttish muddle of *he* and *him* and *his!* It all needs reword-
ing. Far better repeat a noun, or a name, than puzzle the reader, even
for a moment, with ambiguous pronouns. Thou shalt not puzzle thy
reader.

18   Or one can say: Avoid jingles. The B.B.C. news bulletins seem compiled by earless persons, capable of crying around the globe: "The
enemy is *reported* to have seized this im*port*ant *port,* and reinforce-
ments are hurrying up in sup*port.*" Any fool, once told, can hear such
things to be insupportable.

19   Or one can say: Be sparing with relative clauses. Don't string them
together like sausages, or jam them inside one another like Chinese
boxes or the receptacles of Buddha's tooth. Or one can say: Don't flaunt
jargon, like Addison's Mr. Swan, or the type of modern critic who gur-
gles more technical terms in a page than Johnson used in all his *Lives*
or Sainte-Beuve in thirty volumes. But dozens of such snippety precepts, though they may sometimes save people from writing badly, will
help them little toward writing well. Are there no general rules of a
more positive kind, and of more positive use?

20   Perhaps. There *are* certain basic principles which seem to me observed by many authors I admire, which I think have served me and
which may serve others. I am not talking of geniuses, who are a law to
themselves (and do not always write a very good style, either); nor of

poetry, which has different laws from prose; nor of poetic prose, like Sir Thomas Browne's or De Quincey's which is often more akin to poetry; but of the plain prose of ordinary books and documents, letters and talk.

21   The writer should respect truth and himself; therefore honesty. He should respect his readers; therefore courtesy. These are two of the cornerstones of style. Confucius saw it, twenty-five centuries ago: "The Master said, The gentleman is courteous, but not pliable: common men are pliable, but not courteous."

22   First, honesty. In literature, as in life, one of the fundamentals is to find, and be, one's true self. One's true self may indeed be unpleasant (though one can try to better it); but a false self, sooner or later, becomes disgusting—just as a nice plain woman, painted to the eyebrows, can become horrid. In writing, in the long run, pretense does not work. As the police put it, anything you say may be used as evidence against you. If handwriting reveals character, writing reveals it still more. You cannot fool *all* your judges *all* the time.

23   Most style is not honest enough. Easy to say, but hard to practice. A writer may take to long words, as young men to beards—to impress. But long words, like beards, are often the badge of charlatans. Or a writer may cultivate the obscure, to seem profound. But even carefully muddied puddles are soon fathomed. Or he may cultivate eccentricity, to seem original. But really original people do not have to think about being original—they can no more help it than they can help breathing. They do not need to dye their hair green. The fame of Meredith, Wilde or Bernard Shaw might now shine brighter, had they struggled less to be brilliant; whereas Johnson remains great, not merely because his gifts were formidable but also because, with all his prejudice and passion, he fought no less passionately to "clear his mind of cant."

24   Secondly, courtesy—respect for the reader. From this follow several other basic principles of style. Clarity is one. For it is boorish to make your reader rack his brains to understand. One should aim at being impossible to misunderstand—though men's capacity for misunderstanding approaches infinity. Hence Molière and Po Chu-i tried their work on their cooks; and Swift his on his men-servants—"which, if they did not comprehend, he would alter and amend, until they understood it perfectly." Our bureaucrats and pundits, unfortunately, are less considerate.

25   Brevity is another basic principle. For it is boorish, to waste your reader's time. People who would not dream of stealing a penny of one's money turn not a hair at stealing hours of one's life. But that does not make them less exasperating. Therefore there is no excuse for the sort of writer who takes as long as a marching army corps to pass a given point. Besides, brevity is often more effective; the half can say more than the whole, and to imply things may strike far deeper than to state them at length. And because one is particularly apt to waste words on

preambles before coming to the substance, there was sense in the Scots professor who always asked his pupils—"Did ye remember to tear up that fir-r-st page?"

26   Here are some instances that would only lose by lengthening.

> *It is useless to go to bed to save the light, if the result is twins.* (Chinese proverb.)
>
> *My barn is burnt down—*
>
> > *Nothing hides the moon.* (Complete Japanese poem.)
>
> *Je me regrette.*[2] (Dying words of the gay Vicomtesse d'Houdetot.)
>
> *I have seen their backs before.* (Wellington, when French marshals turned their backs on him at a reception.)
>
> *Continue until the tanks stop, then get out and walk.* (Patton to the Twelfth Corps, halted for fuel supplies at St. Dizier, 8/30/44.)

27   Or there is the most laconic diplomatic note on record: when Philip of Macedon wrote to the Spartans that, if he came within their borders, he would leave not one stone of their city, they wrote back the one word—"If."

28   Clarity comes before even brevity. But it is a fallacy that wordiness is necessarily clearer. Metternich when he thought something he had written was obscure would simply go through it crossing out everything irrelevant. What remained, he found, often became clear. Wellington, asked to recommend three names for the post of Commander-in-Chief, India, took a piece of paper and wrote three times—"Napier." Pages could not have been clearer—or as forcible. On the other hand the lectures, and the sentences, of Coleridge became at times bewildering because his mind was often "wiggle-waggle"; just as he could not even walk straight on a path.

29   But clarity and brevity, though a good beginning, are only a beginning. By themselves, they may remain bare and bleak. When Calvin Coolidge, asked by his wife what the preacher had preached on, replied "Sin," and, asked what the preacher had said, replied, "He was against it," he was brief enough. But one hardly envies Mrs. Coolidge.

30   An attractive style requires, of course, all kinds of further gifts—such as variety, good humor, good sense, vitality, imagination. Variety means avoiding monotony of rhythm, of language, of mood. One needs to vary one's sentence length (this present article has too many short sentences; but so vast a subject grows here as cramped as a djin in a bottle); to amplify one's vocabulary; to diversify one's tone. There are books that petrify one throughout, with the rigidly pompous solemnity of an owl perched on a leafless tree. But ceaseless facetiousness

---

[2] "I shall miss myself."—Ed.

can be as bad; or perpetual irony. Even the smile of Voltaire can seem at times a fixed grin, a disagreeable wrinkle. Constant peevishness is far worse, as often in Swift; even on the stage too much irritable dialogue may irritate an audience, without its knowing why.

31   Still more are vitality, energy, imagination gifts that must be inborn before they can be cultivated. But under the head of imagination two common devices may be mentioned that have been the making of many a style—metaphor and simile. Why such magic power should reside in simply saying, or implying, that A is like B remains a little mysterious. But even our unconscious seems to love symbols; again, language often tends to lose itself in clouds of vaporous abstraction, and simile or metaphor can bring it back to concrete solidity; and, again, such imagery can gild the gray flats of prose with sudden sunglints of poetry.

32   If a foreigner may for a moment be impertinent, I admire the native gift of Americans for imagery as much as I wince at their fondness for slang. (Slang seems to me a kind of linguistic fungus; as poisonous, and as short-lived, as toadstools.) When Matthew Arnold lectured in the United States, he was likened by one newspaper to "an elderly macaw pecking at a trellis of grapes"; he observed, very justly, "How lively journalistic fancy is among the Americans!" General Grant, again, unable to hear him, remarked: "Well, wife, we've paid to see the British lion, but as we can't hear him roar, we'd better go home." By simile and metaphor, these two quotations bring before us the slightly pompous, fastidious, inaudible Arnold as no direct description could have done.

33   Or consider how language comes alive in the Chinese saying that lending to the feckless is "like pelting a stray dog with dumplings," or in the Arab proverb: "They came to shoe the pasha's horse, and the beetle stretched forth his leg"; in the Greek phrase for a perilous cape—"stepmother of ships"; or the Hebrew adage that "as the climbing up a sandy way is to the feet of the aged, so is a wife full of words to a quiet man"; in Shakespeare's phrase for a little England lost in the world's vastness—"in a great Poole, a Swan's nest"; or Fuller's libel on tall men—"Ofttimes such who are built four stories high are observed to have little in their cockloft"; in Chateaubriand's "I go yawning my life"; or in Jules Renard's portrait of a cat, "well buttoned in her fur." Or, to take a modern instance, there is Churchill on dealing with Russia:

> Trying to maintain good relations with a Communist is like wooing a crocodile. You do not know whether to tickle it under the chin or beat it over the head. When it opens its mouth, you cannot tell whether it is trying to smile or preparing to eat you up.

34   What a miracle human speech can be, and how dull is most that one hears! Would one hold one's hearers, it is far less help, I suspect, to

read manuals on style than to cultivate one's own imagination and imagery.

35   I will end with two remarks by two wise old women of the civilized 18th Century.

36   The first is from the blind Mme. du Deffand (the friend of Horace Walpole) to that Mlle. de Lespinasse with whom, alas, she was to quarrel so unwisely: "You must make up your mind, my queen, to live with me in the greatest truth and sincerity. You will be charming so long as you let yourself be natural, and remain without pretension and without artifice." The second is from Mme. de Charrière, the Zélide whom Boswell had once loved at Utrecht in vain, to a Swiss girl friend: "Lucinde, my clever Lucinde, while you wait for the Romeos to arrive, you have nothing better to do than become perfect. Have ideas that are clear, and expressions that are simple." *("Ayez des idées nettes et des expressions simples.")* More than half the bad writing in the world, I believe, comes from neglecting those two very simple pieces of advice.

37   In many ways, no doubt, our world grows more and more complex; sputniks cannot be simple; yet how many of our complexities remain futile, how many of our artificialities false. Simplicity too can be subtle—as the straight lines of a Greek temple, like the Parthenon at Athens, are delicately curved, in order to look straighter still.

(4,043 words)

VOCABULARY

curlicues (2)	annihilation (6)	verbose (12)
endemic (4)	tête-à-tête (7)	odious (13)
aesthete (5)	degenerate (8)	averred (13)
tallow-chandler (5)	replete (10)	pedant (16)
demagogue (5)	postprandial (10)	
gaggling (6)	pugnacious (11)	

THE FACTS

1. Why, according to the author, did "style" get a bad name?

2. What are the two basic principles of good writing style? What other principles follow from the second?

3. What are some other gifts of an attractive style listed in paragraph 30?

4. What are two common literary devices that have made many a style? According to paragraph 32, who has a particular gift for these devices?

5. Lucas ends his essay with some pertinent advice from two women. Who are they and what is their advice?

THE STRATEGIES

1. What is the difference between "expressing" and "impressing" as discussed in paragraph 2?

2. In paragraph 4 Lucas states that skilled statesmen, soldiers, and scientists were "blown away like chaff" by Adolf Hitler's "windy nonsense." What would happen to Lucas's style if you substituted "drowned" for "blown away"?

3. Paragraph 5 alludes to Benjamin Franklin, John Wilkes, Cleopatra, and Shakespeare as people who owed their charm or success to their verbal style. Whom else can you add to the list? Give reasons for your choices.

4. In paragraph 9 Lucas suggests that people learn to write by reading good books. What purpose is served by the list of nine authors that follows?

5. What is the rhetorical function of paragraph 34?

THE ISSUES

1. What is the difference, if any, between "class" and "style" when each word is used to designate an individual's personal conduct and mode of living?

2. The author says that we all express a self no matter how hard we may try to efface it. Does it not follow, then, that we all have "style"? Why or why not?

3. Lucas comes from a highly elitist background in which privilege and status dictated advancement and social preferment. How does his definition of style implicitly reflect this background? Or does it?

4. What is your opinion of the adage "Style is the man"? How does it apply or not apply to Lucas's idea of style?

5. Lucas implies that growing up in a world undistracted by radio and television helped him to develop early as a writer and reader. What effect, if any, have radio and television had on your own development as a reader and writer?

SUGGESTIONS FOR WRITING

1. Lucas's essay was first published as a magazine article in March 1960. Write an essay quoting and evaluating particular passages and opinions to which a modern reader, especially a feminist, might take offense.

2. Write an essay explaining the effect you think the media have had on your own development as a reader and writer. Say how this effect might have been overcome or lessened.

E X A M P L E S

▼▼

Bartolomeo Vanzetti

REMARKS ON THE LIFE OF SACCO AND ON HIS OWN LIFE AND EXECUTION

BARTOLOMEO VANZETTI (1888–1927) was born of peasant stock in northern Italy, where he worked as a baker's apprentice before migrating to the United States in 1908. In the U.S. he worked as a laborer and became an avowed anarchist. In 1920, along with Nicolo Sacco, another Italian immigrant, Vanzetti was arrested for the murder of a guard during a payroll robbery. While in prison awaiting execution, he wrote his autobiography. Maintaining their innocence to the end, and despite the worldwide public protest mounted in their behalf, Sacco and Vanzetti were executed on August 22, 1927.

These four paragraphs are assembled from the writings and sayings of Vanzetti. The first three paragraphs are notes from a speech. Vanzetti intended to deliver them in court before his sentencing but was barred from doing so by the judge. The final paragraph is a transcription from an interview given by Vanzetti in April 1927 to Philip D. Strong, a reporter for the North American Newspaper Alliance. The entire excerpt illustrates the lyricism and elegance of simple words cast in idiomatic sentences.

1 I have talk a great deal of myself but I even forgot to name Sacco. Sacco too is a worker from his boyhood, a skilled worker lover of work, with a good job and pay, a good and lovely wife, two beautiful children and a neat little home at the verge of a wood, near a brook. Sacco is a heart, a faith, a character, a man; a man lover of nature and of mankind. A man who gave all, who sacrifice all to the cause of Liberty

and to his love for mankind; money, rest, mundane ambitions, his own wife, his children, himself and his own life. Sacco has never dreamt to steal, never to assassinate. He and I have never brought a morsel of bread to our mouths, from our childhood to today—which has not been gained by the sweat of our brows. Never. His people also are in good position and of good reputation.

2   Oh, yes, I may be more witful, as some have put it, I am a better babbler than he is, but many, many times in hearing his heartful voice ringing a faith sublime, in considering his supreme sacrifice, remembering his heroism I felt small small at the presence of his greatness and found myself compelled to fight back from my throat to not weep before him—this man called thief and assassin and doomed. But Sacco's name will live in the hearts of the people and in their gratitude when Katzmann's* and your bones will be dispersed by time, when your name, his name, your laws, institutions, and your false god are but a *deem rememoring of a cursed past in which man was wolf to the man.* . . .

3   If it had not been for these thing . . . I might have live out my life talking at street corners to scorning men. I might have die, unmarked, unknown, a failure. Now we are not a failure. This is our career and our triumph. Never in our full life could we hope to do such work for tolerance, for joostice, for man's onderstanding of man as now we do by accident.

4   Our words—our lives—our pains—nothing! The taking of our lives—lives of a good shoemaker and a poor fish-peddler—all! That last moment belongs to us—that agony is our triumph.

(390 words)

VOCABULARY

mundane (1)
sublime (2)

THE FACTS

1. What kind of man does the excerpt make Sacco out to be?

2. What does Vanzetti claim to be better at than Sacco?

3. According to Vanzetti, how might his life have turned out were it not for his trial and conviction?

---

* Frederick G. Katzmann was the district attorney who prosecuted the case.—Ed.

THE STRATEGIES

1. The author was an Italian with a frail grasp of the American speech idiom. What effect does his grammatical errors have on the way he expresses himself?

2. How would you characterize the diction of this excerpt? Is it lofty? Plain?

3. Why do some editors include this excerpt in poetry anthologies? What is poetic about it?

THE ISSUES

1. Because of his beliefs, Vanzetti was labeled a philosophical anarchist. What is a philosophical anarchist?

2. In the final paragraph, Vanzetti calls his impending execution with Sacco "our triumph." What do you think he meant by that?

3. The Sacco and Vanzetti trial was made famous mainly because of the intense media attention it drew. What restrictions, if any, do you think should be imposed on media coverage of sensational criminals and trials? Why? Justify your answer.

SUGGESTIONS FOR WRITING

1. Copy this excerpt, correcting its grammatical and spelling errors as you go. Add any words that are necessary to make it grammatical. Write a paragraph on which version you think is more effective, the original or the corrected one, giving your reasons.

2. Without doing any further research into Vanzetti, and using this excerpt as your only evidence, write an impressionistic description of the kind of man you think he was. Be specific in your references to passages in the excerpt.

TERM PAPER SUGGESTION

Write a term paper on the Sacco-Vanzetti trial. Reach your own conclusion as to whether or not it was a fair trial, and support your belief.

▼▼

Langston Hughes

SALVATION

LANGSTON HUGHES (1902–1967) was born in Joplin, Missouri, and educated at Columbia University, New York, and Lincoln University, Pennsylvania. He worked at odd jobs in this country and in France before becoming established as a writer. His lifelong interest was the promotion of black art, history, and causes. In addition to many collections of poetry, Hughes wrote a novel, *Not Without Laughter* (1930), and an autobiography, *The Big Sea* (1940).

In this selection from The Big Sea, *Hughes recounts a dramatic incident from his childhood. The incident is narrated from the perspective of a twelve-year-old boy and demonstrates a skillful writer's use of language to re-create the innocent voice of childhood.*

1   I was saved from sin when I was going on thirteen. But not really saved. It happened like this. There was a big revival at my Auntie Reed's church. Every night for weeks there had been much preaching, singing, praying, and shouting, and some very hardened sinners had been brought to Christ, and the membership of the church had grown by leaps and bounds. Then just before the revival ended, they held a special meeting for children, "to bring the young lambs to the fold." My aunt spoke of it for days ahead. That night I was escorted to the front row and placed on the mourners' bench with all the other young sinners, who had not yet been brought to Jesus.

2   My aunt told me that when you were saved you saw a light, and something happened to you inside! And Jesus came into your life! And God was with you from then on! She said you could see and hear and feel Jesus in your soul. I believed her. I had heard a great many old people say the same thing and it seemed to me they ought to know. So I sat there calmly in the hot, crowded church, waiting for Jesus to come to me.

3   The preacher preached a wonderful rhythmical sermon, all moans and shouts and lonely cries and dire pictures of hell, and then he sang a song about the ninety and nine safe in the fold, but one little lamb was left out in the cold. Then he said: "Won't you come? Won't you come to Jesus? Young lambs, won't you come?" And he held out his arms to all us young sinners there on the mourners' bench. And the little girls cried. And some of them jumped up and went to Jesus right away. But most of us just sat there.

4   A great many old people came and knelt around us and prayed, old women with jet-black faces and braided hair, old men with work-gnarled hands. And the church sang a song about the lower lights are burning, some poor sinners to be saved. And the whole building rocked with prayer and song.

5   Still I keep waiting to *see* Jesus.

6   Finally all the young people had gone to the altar and were saved, but one boy and me. He was a rounder's son named Westley. Westley and I were surrounded by sisters and deacons praying. It was very hot in the church, and getting late now. Finally Westley said to me in a whisper: "God damn! I'm tired o' sitting here. Let's get up and be saved." So he got up and was saved.

7   Then I was left all alone on the mourners' bench. My aunt came and knelt at my knees and cried, while prayers and songs swirled all around me in the little church. The whole congregation prayed for me alone, in a mighty wail of moans and voices. And I kept waiting serenely for Jesus, waiting, waiting—but he didn't come. I wanted to see him, but nothing happened to me. Nothing! I wanted something to happen to me, but nothing happened.

8   I heard the songs and the minister saying: "Why don't you come? My dear child, why don't you come to Jesus? Jesus is waiting for you. He wants you. Why don't you come? Sister Reed, what is this child's name?"

9   "Langston," my aunt sobbed.

10   "Langston, why don't you come? Why don't you come and be saved? Oh, Lamb of God! Why don't you come?"

11   Now it was really getting late. I began to be ashamed of myself, holding everything up so long. I began to wonder what God thought about Westley, who certainly hadn't seen Jesus either, but who was now sitting proudly on the platform, swinging his knickerbockered legs and grinning down at me, surrounded by deacons and old women on their knees praying. God had not struck Westley dead for taking his name in vain or for lying in the temple. So I decided that maybe to save further trouble, I'd better lie, too, and say that Jesus had come, and get up and be saved.

12   So I got up.

13   Suddenly the whole room broke into a sea of shouting, as they saw me rise. Waves of rejoicing swept the place. Women leaped in the air. My aunt threw her arms around me. The minister took me by the hand and led me to the platform.

14   When things quieted down, in a hushed silence, punctuated by a few ecstatic "Amens," all the new young lambs were blessed in the name of God. Then joyous singing filled the room.

15   That night, for the last time in my life but one—for I was a big boy twelve years old—I cried. I cried, in bed alone, and couldn't stop. I

buried my head under the quilts, but my aunt heard me. She woke up and told my uncle I was crying because the Holy Ghost had come into my life, and because I had seen Jesus. But I was really crying because I couldn't bear to tell her that I had lied, that I had deceived everybody in the church, and I hadn't seen Jesus, and that now I didn't believe there was a Jesus any more, since he didn't come to help me.

(889 words)

VOCABULARY

gnarled (4)   punctuated (14)   ecstatic (14)

THE FACTS

1. How does Westley's attitude differ from the narrator's? Is Westley more realistic and less gullible, or is he simply more callous and less sensitive than the narrator? Comment.

2. The narrator holds out to the last minute and finally submits to being saved. What is his motive for finally giving in?

3. Who has been deceived in the story? The aunt by the narrator? The narrator by the aunt? Both the narrator and the aunt by the minister? Everybody by the demands of religion? Comment.

4. What insight does the narrator come to at the end of the story? What has he learned?

5. The story is told as a flashback to when Hughes was a boy. What is his attitude toward the experience as he retells it?

THE STRATEGIES

1. The story is narrated from the point of view of a twelve-year-old boy. What techniques of language are used in the story to create the perspective of a boy? How is the vocabulary appropriate to a boy?

2. In his article on "How to Say Nothing in Five Hundred Words," Paul Roberts urges the use of specific details in writing. How does Hughes make use of such details?

3. The description in paragraph 4 is vivid but compressed. How does Hughes achieve this effect?

THE ISSUES

1. Marx wrote that "religion . . . is the opium of the people." What is your view of this sentiment? How does it apply or not apply to this excerpt?

2. The little girls were the first to break down and offer themselves to be saved. The last two holdouts were boys. How do you explain this different reaction of the two sexes?

3. What do you think would have likely happened if the narrator had not gone up to be saved?

4. Religions often use ovine terms *(sheep, lamb, flock)* to refer to their congregations. What do you think is the origin of this usage? What does this usage imply about the members?

SUGGESTIONS FOR WRITING

1. Describe an experience of your own where group pressure forced you into doing something you did not believe in.

2. Write a brief biographical sketch of Westley, fantasizing on the kind of man you believe he grew into and the kind of life he eventually led.

▼▼▼

Stephen Leacock

A, B, AND C: THE HUMAN ELEMENT IN MATHEMATICS

STEPHEN LEACOCK (1869–1944), Canadian economist and humorist, was born in England and educated at the University of Toronto and the University of Chicago. He was the author of numerous genial satires and comical essays, published under such titles as *Literary Lapses* (1910) and *Winnowed Wisdom* (1926).

> *The word* tone *is often used in literary criticism to designate an author's implied attitude toward his or her subject. Considerable variations in tone may exist on the page, and endless techniques can be used to achieve it. The following burlesque, from* Literary Lapses, *is done in a comical and sardonic tone, achieved primarily through ridiculous exaggeration.*

1   The student of arithmetic who has mastered the first four rules of his art, and successfully striven with money sums and fractions, finds

himself confronted by an unbroken expanse of questions known as problems. These are short stories of adventure and industry with the end omitted, and though betraying a strong family resemblance, are not without a certain element of romance.

2   The characters in the plot of a problem are three people called A, B, and C. The form of the question is generally of this sort:

3   "A, B, and C do a certain piece of work. A can do as much work in one hour as B in two, or C in four. Find how long they work at it."

4   Or thus:

"A, B, and C are employed to dig a ditch. A can dig as much in one hour as B can dig in two, and B can dig twice as fast as C. Find how long, etc., etc."

5   Or after this wise:

"A lays a wager that he can walk faster than B or C. A can walk half as fast again as B, and C is only an indifferent walker. Find how far, and so forth."

6   The occupations of A, B, and C are many and varied. In the older arithmetics they contented themselves with doing "a certain piece of work." This statement of the case, however, was found too sly and mysterious, or possibly lacking in romantic charm. It became the fashion to define the job more clearly and to set them at walking matches, ditch-digging, regattas, and piling cord wood. At times, they became commercial and entered into partnership, having with their old mystery a "certain" capital. Above all they revel in motion. When they tire of walking-matches—A rides on horseback or borrows a bicycle and competes with his weaker-minded associates on foot. Now they race on locomotives; now they row; or again they become historical and engage stage-coaches; or at times they are aquatic and swim. If their occupation is actual work they prefer to pump water into cisterns, two of which leak through holes in the bottom and one of which is watertight. A, of course, has the good one; he also takes the bicycle, and the best locomotive, and the right of swimming with the current. Whatever they do they put money on it, being all three sports. A always wins.

7   In the early chapters of the arithmetic, their identity is concealed under the names John, William, and Henry, and they wrangle over the division of marbles. In algebra they are often called X, Y, Z. But these are only their Christian names, and they are really the same people.

8   Now to one who has followed the history of these men through countless pages of problems, watched them in their leisure hours dallying with cord wood, and seen their panting sides heave in the full frenzy of filling a cistern with a leak in it, they become something more than mere symbols. They appear as creatures of flesh and blood, living men with their own passions, ambitions, and aspirations like the rest of us. Let us view them in turn. A is a full-blooded blustering fellow, of energetic temperament, hot-headed and strong-willed. It is

he who proposes everything, challenges B to work, makes the bets, and bends the others to his will. He is a man of great physical strength and phenomenal endurance. He has been known to walk forty-eight hours at a stretch, and to pump ninety-six. His life is arduous and full of peril. A mistake in the working of a sum may keep him digging a fortnight without sleep. A repeating decimal in the answer might kill him.

9   B is a quiet, easy-going fellow, afraid of A and bullied by him, but very gentle and brotherly to little C, the weakling. He is quite in A's power, having lost all his money in bets.

10   Poor C is an undersized, frail man, with a plaintive face. Constant walking, digging, and pumping has broken his health and ruined his nervous system. His joyless life has driven him to drink and smoke more than is good for him, and his hand often shakes as he digs ditches. He has not the strength to work as the others can, in fact, as Hamlin Smith has said, "A can do more work in one hour than C in four."

11   The first time that ever I saw these men was one evening after a regatta. They had all been rowing in it, and it had transpired that A could row as much in one hour as B in two, or C in four. B and C had come in dead fagged and C was coughing badly. "Never mind, old fellow," I heard B say, "I'll fix you up on the sofa and get you some hot tea." Just then A came blustering in and shouted, "I say, you fellows, Hamlin Smith has shown me three cisterns in his garden and he says we can pump them until tomorrow night. I bet I can beat you both. Come on. You can pump in your rowing things, you know. Your cistern leaks a little, I think, C." I heard B growl that it was a dirty shame and that C was used up now, but they went, and presently I could tell from the sound of the water that A was pumping four times as fast as C.

12   For years after that I used to see them constantly about town and always busy. I never heard of any of them eating or sleeping. Then owing to a long absence from home, I lost sight of them. On my return I was surprised to no longer find A, B, and C at their accustomed tasks; on inquiry I heard that work in this line was now done by N, M, and O, and that some people were employing for algebraical jobs four foreigners called Alpha, Beta, Gamma, and Delta.

13   Now it chanced one day that I stumbled upon old D, in the little garden in front of his cottage, hoeing in the sun. D is an aged labouring man who used occasionally to be called in to help A, B, and C. "Did I know 'em, sir?" he answered, "why, I knowed 'em ever since they was little fellows in brackets. Master A, he were a fine lad, sir, though I always said, give me Master B for kind-heartedness-like. Many's the job as we've been on together, sir, though I never did no racing nor aught of that, but just the plain labour, as you might say. I'm getting a bit too old and stiff for it nowadays, sir—just scratch about in the garden here

and grow a bit of a logarithm, or raise a common denominator or two. But Mr. Euclid he use me still for them propositions, he do."

14   From the garrulous old man I learned the melancholy end of my former acquaintances. Soon after I left town, he told me, C had been taken ill. It seems that A and B had been rowing on the river for a wager, and C had been running on the bank and then sat in a draught. Of course the bank had refused the draught and C was taken ill. A and B came home and found C lying helpless in bed. A shook him roughly and said, "Get up, C, we're going to pile wood." C looked so worn and pitiful that B said, "Look here, A, I won't stand this, he isn't fit to pile wood tonight." C smiled feebly and said, "Perhaps I might pile a little if I sat up in bed." Then B, thoroughly alarmed, said, "See here, A, I'm going to fetch a doctor; he's dying." A flared up and answered, "You've no money to fetch a doctor." "I'll reduce him to his lowest terms," B said firmly, "that'll fetch him." C's life might even then have been saved but they made a mistake about the medicine. It stood at the head of the bed on a bracket, and the nurse accidentally removed it from the bracket without changing the sign. After the fatal blunder C seems to have sunk rapidly. On the evening of the next day, as the shadows deepened in the little room, it was clear to all that the end was near. I think that even A was affected at the last as he stood with bowed head, aimlessly offering to bet with the doctor on C's laboured breathing, "A," whispered C, "I think I'm going fast." "How fast do you think you'll go, old man?" murmured A. "I don't know," said C, "but I'm going at any rate."—The end came soon after that. C rallied for a moment and asked for a certain piece of work that he had left downstairs. A put it in his arms and he expired. As his soul sped heavenward A watched its flight with melancholy admiration. B burst into a passionate flood of tears and sobbed, "Put away his little cistern and the rowing clothes he used to wear, I feel as if I could hardly ever dig again."—The funeral was plain and unostentatious. It differed in nothing from the ordinary, except that out of deference to sporting men and mathematicians, A engaged two hearses. Both vehicles started at the same time, B driving the one which bore the sable parallelopiped containing the last remains of his ill-fated friend. A on the box of the empty hearse generously consented to a handicap of a hundred yards, but arrived first at the cemetery by driving four times as fast as B. (Find the distance to the cemetery.) As the sarcophagus was lowered, the grave was surrounded by the broken figures of the first book of Euclid.—It was noticed that after the death of C, A became a changed man. He lost interest in racing with B, and dug but languidly. He finally gave up his work and settled down to live on the interest of his bets.—B never recovered from the shock of C's death; his grief preyed upon his intellect and it became deranged. He grew moody and spoke only in

monosyllables. His disease became rapidly aggravated, and he presently spoke only in words whose spelling was regular and which presented no difficulty to the beginner. Realizing his precarious condition he voluntarily submitted to be incarcerated in an asylum, where he abjured mathematics and devoted himself to writing the History of the Swiss Family Robinson in words of one syllable.

(1,776 words)

VOCABULARY

arduous (8)

plaintive (10)

transpired (11)

garrulous (14)

draught (14)

unostentatious (14)

deference (14)

parallelopiped (14)

sarcophagus (14)

languidly (14)

deranged (14)

incarcerated (14)

abjured (14)

THE FACTS

1. What, according to the author, are "short stories of adventure and industry with the end omitted"?

2. What were the early names of the three principal arithmetic characters?

3. What sort of character is A?

4. What are the names of the replacements of A, B, and C?

5. What was the eventual fate of A, B, and C?

THE STRATEGIES

1. Where does the writer first establish that humor is his aim? How does he do this?

2. What technique does the author use in his descriptions of A, B, and C for humorous effect?

3. In paragraph 14, the author writes: "It seems that A and B had been rowing for a wager, and C had been running on the bank and then caught a draught. Of course the bank had refused the draught and C was taken ill." What humorous device is being used here?

4. When C dies, we are told that "his soul sped heavenward." Why do you think the author mentions that C went to heaven?

5. The writer mentions Hamlin Smith twice without identifying him. If you had to guess, who do you think Hamlin Smith is?

THE ISSUES

1. To whom is this humorous piece most likely to appeal? To whom is it least likely to appeal?

2. What do you think is the nationality of A, B, and C, if you had to guess from their dialogue?

3. What underlying charge does this piece seem to make about math problems?

4. Why do we think a piece like this funny?

5. What is your opinion of algebra and algebra problems?

SUGGESTIONS FOR WRITING

1. Write an essay about your own experiences with impossible arithmetic or algebra problems.

2. Using the technique of attributing human characteristics to inanimate or symbolic objects, write an essay in which you treat some common objects in your life as if they were human.

▼▼

Dan Greenburg

THREE BEARS IN SEARCH OF AN AUTHOR

DAN GREENBURG (1936–   ) was born in Chicago and educated at the University of California, Los Angeles. His published works include *How to Be a Jewish Mother* (1964), *Kiss My Firm but Pliant Lips* (1965), and *Scoring: A Sexual Memoir* (1972).

What is style? How do we recognize the differences between two styles? In "Three Bears in Search of an Author" Dan Greenburg presents two versions of the Goldilocks story, one written in the style of The Catcher in the Rye *by J. D. Salinger, and the other in the style of* A Farewell to Arms *by Ernest Hemingway.*

I. Catch Her in the Oatmeal

1   If you actually want to hear about it, what I'd better do is I'd better warn you right now that you aren't going to believe it. I mean it's a true *story* and all, but it still sounds sort of phony.

2   Anyway, my name is Goldie Lox. It's sort of a boring name, but my parents said that when I was born I had this very blonde hair and all. Actually I was born bald. I mean how many babies get born with blonde hair? None. I mean I've *seen* them and they're all wrinkled and red and slimy and everything. And bald. And then all the phonies have to come around and tell you he's as cute as a bug's ear. A bug's ear, boy, that really kills me. You ever *seen* a bug's ear? What's cute about a bug's *ear*, for Chrissake! Nothing, that's what.

3   So, like I was saying, I always seem to be getting into these very stupid situations. Like this time I was telling you about. Anyway, I was walking through the forest and all when I see this very interesting house. A *house*. You wouldn't think anybody would be living way the hell out in the goddam *forest*, but they were. No one was home or anything and the door was open, so I walked in. I figured what I'd do is I'd probably horse around until the guys that lived there came home and maybe asked me to stay for dinner or something. Some people think they *have* to ask you to stay for dinner even if they *hate* you. Also I didn't exactly feel like going home and getting asked a lot of lousy questions. I mean that's *all* I ever seem to do.

4   Anyway, while I was waiting I sort of sampled some of this stuff they had on the table that tasted like oatmeal. *Oatmeal.* It would have made you puke, I mean it. Then something very spooky started happening. I started getting dizzier than hell. I figured I'd feel better if I could just rest for a while. Sometimes if you eat something like lousy oatmeal you can feel better if you just rest for awhile, so I sat down. That's when the goddam *chair* breaks in half. No kidding, you start feeling lousy and some stupid *chair* is going to break on you every time. I'm not kidding. Anyway I finally found the crummy bedroom and I lay down on this very tiny bed. I was really depressed.

5   I don't know how long I was asleep or anything but all of a sudden I hear this very strange voice say, "Someone's been sleeping in *my* sack, for Chrissake, and there she is!" So I open my eyes and here at the foot of the bed are these three crummy *bears. Bears!* I swear to God. By that time I was *really* feeling depressed. There's nothing more depressing than waking up and finding three *bears* talking about you, I mean.

6   So I didn't stay around and shoot the breeze with them or anything. If you want to know the truth, I sort of ran out of there like a madman or something. I do that quite a little when I'm depressed like that.

7　　On the way home, though, I got to figuring. What probably happened is these bears wandered in when they smelled this oatmeal and all. Probably bears *like* oatmeal. I don't know. And the voice I heard when I woke up was probably something I dreamt.

8　　So that's the story.

9　　I wrote it all up once as a theme in school, but my crummy teacher said it was too *whimsical*. Whimsical. That killed me. You got to meet her sometime, boy. She's a real queen.

2. A Farewell to Porridge

10　In the late autumn of that year we lived in a house in the forest that looked across the river to the mountains, but we always thought we lived on the plain because we couldn't see the forest for the trees.

11　　Sometimes people would come to the door and ask if we would like to subscribe to *The Saturday Evening Post* or buy Fuller brushes, but when we would answer the bell they would see we were only bears and go away.

12　　Sometimes we would go for long walks along the river and you could almost forget for a little while that you were a bear and not people.

13　　Once when we were out strolling for a very long time we came home and you could see that someone had broken in and the door was open.

14　　*"La porte est ouverte!"* said Mama Bear. "The door should not be open." Mama Bear had French blood on her father's side.

15　　"It is all right," I said. "We will close it."

16　　"It should not have been left open," she said.

17　　"It is all right," I said. "We will close it. Then it will be good like in the old days."

18　　*"Bien,"* she said. "It is well."

19　　We walked in and closed the door. There were dishes and bowls and all manner of eating utensils on the table and you could tell that someone had been eating porridge. We did not say anything for a long while.

20　　"It is lovely here," I said finally. "But someone has been eating my porridge."

21　　"Mine as well," said Mama Bear.

22　　"It is all right," I said, "It is nothing."

23　　"Darling," said Mama Bear, "do you love me?"

24　　"Yes I love you."

25　　"You really love me?"

26　　"I really love you. I'm crazy in love with you."

27　　"And the porridge? How about the porridge?"

28　　"That too. I really love the porridge too."

29   "It was supposed to be a surprise. I made it as a surprise for you, but someone has eaten it all up."

30   "You sweet. You made it as a surprise. Oh, you're lovely," I said.

31   "But it is gone."

32   "It is all right," I said. "It will be all right."

33   Then I looked at my chair and you could see someone had been sitting in it and Mama Bear looked at her chair and someone had been sitting in that too and Baby Bear's chair is broken.

34   "We will go upstairs," I said and we went upstairs to the bedroom but you could see that someone had been sleeping in my bed and in Mama Bear's too although that was the same bed but you have to mention it that way because that is the story. Truly. And then we looked in Baby Bear's bed and there she was.

35   "I ate your porridge and sat in your chairs and I broke one of them," she said.

36   "It is all right," I said. "It will be all right."

37   "And now I am lying in Baby Bear's bed."

38   "Baby Bear can take care of himself."

39   "I mean that I am sorry. I have behaved badly and I am sorry for all of this."

40   "*Ça ne fait rien,*" said Mama Bear, "It is nothing." Outside it had started to rain again.

41   "I will go now," she said. "I am sorry." She walked slowly down the stairs.

42   I tried to think of something to tell her but it wasn't any good. "Good-by," she said.

43   Then she opened the door and went outside and walked all the way back to her hotel in the rain.

(1,366 words)

VOCABULARY

Porridge (no. 2 heading)
whimsical (9)

THE FACTS

1. In the first narration, what is the narrator's opinion of blonde babies?

2. In the second narration, what foreign language does Mama Bear occasionally use? Why?

3. In the first narration, what was the teacher's reaction to the narrator's composition about his experience?

4. At the end of the second narration, what is the weather?

5. What does the narrator of the first story do quite often when she is depressed?

THE STRATEGIES

1. How do the two stories differ in points of view? What difference does this make?

2. Compare the word choice in the two stories? What is the difference?

3. Which of the two stories is more dramatic? What technique adds drama?

4. What is the personality of the narrator revealed in each story?

5. Which narration do you prefer? Why?

THE ISSUES

1. What is the purpose of writing these two different accounts of the famous Goldilocks tale?

2. How does the title relate to the purpose of the stories?

3. What part of Hemingway and Salinger's styles did the author catch? Were you able to recognize the styles? Why?

4. What makes both Salinger and Hemingway authors of fine reputations—despite their styles as reflected in Greenburg's satire?

5. Should students try to develop a distinctive, recognizable style? Give reasons for your answer.

SUGGESTIONS FOR WRITING

1. Write a third "bear story" in the style of someone you know well who has a distinctive personality.

2. Write the story of "Little Red Riding Hood" in the style of either J. D. Salinger or Ernest Hemingway.

▼▼▼

Wislawa Szymborska

IN PRAISE OF DREAMS

WISLAWA SZYMBORSKA (b. 1923) is a Polish poet who won the 1996 Nobel Prize for Literature. Little known in the United States until she was warmly acclaimed by the Nobel Prize Committee, she has written volumes of poetry, sketching out the political and social turmoil suffered by her homeland during World War II and its aftermath. Her poetry is both delicate and incisive, sad as well as exuberant. The poem reprinted here comes from a book titled *View with a Grain of Sand* (1996), translated from Polish by Stanislaw Baranczak and Claire Cavanagh.

Voice is often a pronounced element in poetry because of the brevity of the form. Notice how the voice of this poem reveals a dreamlike, internal joy.

In my dreams
I paint like Vermeer van Delft.

I speak fluent Greek
and not only with the living.

5   I drive a car
that does what I say.

I am talented.
I write epic poems.

I hear voices
10   no less often than saints do.

You would be amazed
at my skill in piano playing.

I fly properly
all by myself.

15   Sliding off the roof
I fall onto soft grass.

I do not find it hard
to breathe underwater.

I cannot complain:
20   I discovered Atlantis.

It's a relief to wake up
just before dying.

I turn sideways comfortably
when wars break out.

25   I am, but am not forced to be,
a child of his age.

Some years ago
I saw two suns.

And the day before yesterday a penguin.
30   I saw it quite clearly.

(155 words)

VOCABULARY

Vermeer van Delft (2)   epic (8)   Atlantis (20)

THE FACTS

1. In what state of mind is the speaker throughout the poem?

2. What is the reference implied in lines 9 and 10?

3. In the context of the poem, what do two suns and a penguin have in common? (See lines 27–30.)

4. What specific dreams does the speaker have? List them.

5. What does it mean to be "a child of his age"? (see line 26)

THE STRATEGIES

1. Do you believe it was difficult or easy to translate this poem from the Polish? Give reasons for your answer.

2. The poem is written in couplets. What does this technique do for the poem?

3. In line 8, the speaker mentions "epic poems." Why? What does the term add to the meaning of the thought?

4. How would you classify the poet's style? Describe its characteristics.

5. What is the effect of the repetitious use of "I"?

THE ISSUES

1. How does the title of the poem enhance its meaning?

2. For most of the poem, the poet pretends to have talents recognized by most cultures (the ability to paint, speak a foreign language, drive a car, play the piano, and so forth). But occasionally she turns to different images. What are some of the unusual images? How do you explain the shift?

3. What does the speaker mean when she says, "I turn sideways comfortably when wars break out"? Explain her meaning in your own words.

4. What are the voices heard by the poet? Speculate on what they might be.

5. What are some of your dream accomplishments? What do you think dreaming about accomplishments does to reality?

SUGGESTIONS FOR WRITING

1. Using your own natural voice to the best of your ability, describe a dream that embodies an important desire you have for your life.

2. Write an essay in which you explore the importance of having fantasies in which you are successful or are able to overcome difficult obstacles.

ISSUE FOR CRITICAL THINKING AND DEBATE

▼▼

AIDS

The painting *San la Muerte* by Mirta Toledo suggests a chilling image of AIDS as a germ cell of death. And indeed, AIDS, an acronym for Acquired Immune Deficiency Syndrome, is death lurking inside the cells of body fluids—blood, semen, even saliva. Even though recent drug therapies offer hope, AIDS robs the body of its natural defenses, exposing the helpless victim to ravaging by nature's microbial vandals. AIDS sufferers die of rare cancers and pneumonias, plundered by germs a healthy person would dismiss with a sneeze, cannibalized by bacilluses running amok over defenseless organs.

Since its recognition in the early 1980s, AIDS has surged through the communal bloodstream in a loathsome tidal plague. According to the World Health Organization (WHO), in 1992, some 10 to 12 million adults and 1 million children were HIV positive—infected with the retrovirus that causes AIDS. By the year 2000 that number could exceed 40 million. Typically, the stricken AIDS victim will incur an average lifetime medical bill of $102,000 and still succumb to the disease within five years after it becomes active.

Of all the diseases that afflict modern humans, AIDS is undoubtedly the most politicized partly because of whom it affects and how it is transmitted. In the United States, the Centers for Disease Control estimate that some 65 percent of male victims acquired AIDS through unprotected homosexual intercourse while 50 percent of its female victims were infected through the sharing of contaminated needles. Heterosexual contact accounts for 3 percent of the cases while the transfusion of tainted blood was implicated in only 1 percent.

Because of the ambivalence of society toward homosexuals and drug abusers, some oddly judgmental attitudes toward AIDS victims have emerged in the public debate. Tennis champion Arthur Ashe, who caught the disease from a blood transfusion, is everybody's innocent victim; on the other hand, basketball star Magic Johnson, who revealed that he had tested HIV positive, was so hounded by questions about whether he had caught the disease through heterosexual promiscuity or covert homosexuality that he was driven to repeated denials of any alleged bisexuality. Overlooked during all this finger-pointing is one stark fact: AIDS is democratically deadly for everyone who gets it regardless of how it was caught.

The two essayists in this section reflect the widely differing opinions evoked by AIDS and its victims. Amanda Bennett and Anita

Mirta Toledo, San la Muerte. *India ink and acrylic on paper, 30 × 38 cm. Copyright © Mirta Toledo/Fort Worth 1993.*

Sharpe are probing and journalistic. Their research leads them to question the publicized notion that everyone is at risk for AIDS. Donna Ferentes, on the other hand, writing about her homosexual brother whose illness she sees as symbolic of his alienation from God and his family, gives us the Catholic perspective. She sees AIDS as God's attempt to teach a lesson to His erring children and is bitter about what she calls the "homosexual death dance" being performed over her dying brother.

With most other diseases, the public's attitude is usually one of sympathy and thankfulness for being spared the affliction. But with AIDS, the grim death that awaits victims is made even worse by sanctimonious speculation about how the disease was caught. As the English economist John Maynard Keynes said, "In the long run, we're all dead," and whether the end comes from senility, AIDS, or from slipping on a banana peel should make little difference to a compassionate and humane heart.

▼▼

Amanda Bennett
Anita Sharpe

WHO'S REALLY AT RISK FOR AIDS?

AMANDA BENNETT (b. 1952) is a staff reporter for the *Wall Street Journal*. After receiving her education at Harvard, she spent several years working as a journalist in China and writing articles about the various aspects of Chinese life. She is the author of a book on China, titled *The Man Who Stayed Behind* (1992) and the co-author of two other books: *The Death of the Organization Man* (1990) and *The Quiet Room* (1994).

ANITA SHARPE (b. 1955) is a staff reporter for the *Wall Street Journal*.

Nine years after the 1987 "America Responds to AIDS" campaign, many scientists and doctors are worrying that the warning "Everyone gets AIDS" may be less than honest. But, even more important, they suggest that such a message may have a potentially deadly effect on funding for AIDS prevention. A careful reading of the following essay will help you decide whether or not the worry is justified.

1   In the summer of 1987, federal health officials made the fateful decision to bombard the public with a terrifying message: Anyone could get AIDS.

2   While the message was technically true, it was also highly misleading. Everyone certainly faced some danger, but for most heterosexuals, the risk from a single act of sex was smaller than the risk of ever getting hit by lightning. In the U.S., the disease was, and remains, largely the scourge of gay men, intravenous drug users, their sex partners and their newborn children.

3   Nonetheless, a bold public-relations campaign promised to sound a general alarm about AIDS, lifting it from a homosexual concern to a

national obsession and accelerating efforts to eradicate the disease. For people devoted to public health, it seemed the best course to take.

4   But nine years after the America Responds to AIDS campaign first hit the airwaves, many scientists and doctors are raising new questions. Increasingly, they worry that the everyone-gets-AIDS message— still trumpeted not only by government agencies but by celebrities and the media—is more than just dishonest: It is also having a perverse, potentially deadly effect on funding for AIDS prevention.

5   The emphasis on the broad reach of the disease has virtually ensured that precious funds won't go where they are most needed. For instance, though homosexuals and intravenous drug users now account for 83% of all AIDS cases reported in the U.S., the federal AIDS-prevention budget includes no specific allocation for programs for homosexual and bisexual men. And needle-exchange programs, widely seen as among the most effective methods available in fighting infection among drug users, are denied any federal funding.

6   Much of the Centers for Disease Control's $584 million AIDS-prevention budget goes instead to programs to combat the disease among heterosexual women, college students and others who face a relatively low risk of becoming infected. Federally funded testing programs alone, which primarily serve low-risk groups, account for roughly 20% of the entire budget.

7   Some scientists charge that tens of thousands of infections a year could be averted if only practical assistance were directed to the right people. Instead of aiming general warnings at non-drug-using heterosexuals, these critics say, the government should use the bulk of its anti-AIDS money to teach homosexual men to avoid unprotected anal sex and to dissuade addicts from sharing infected needles.

8   "You can't stop this epidemic if you spend the money where the epidemic hasn't happened," says Ron Stall, associate professor of epidemiology at the University of California in San Francisco.

9   Helene Gayle, who is in charge of AIDS prevention at the CDC, agrees that "increasingly, it is important to shift strategies to meet the epidemic." She says that the CDC, by giving communities more freedom to decide how to spend federal AIDS money, is now seeking to direct more help to those who need it most.

10   But she defends the CDC's pivotal decision in 1987 to emphasize the universality of AIDS: "One should not underestimate the fear and confusion this disease caused early on," Dr. Gayle says. "We needed to build a base of understanding before we could go for the jugular."

11   Certainly, powerful political and social forces at work nine years ago made it nearly impossible for health officials to focus attention on those most at risk, a reconstruction of events of that year shows. And though, as Dr. Gayle says, the CDC is now trying to revamp its AIDS-prevention efforts, the same forces that shaped public policy in 1987

are making it difficult for the government to change directions, even now.

12   By 1987, CDC officials already had a fairly clear picture of where and how AIDS was spreading—and how much risk different groups faced. The disease was proving less likely to be transmitted through vaginal intercourse than many had feared. A major study that was just being completed put the average risk from a one-time heterosexual encounter with someone not in a high-risk group at one in five million without use of a condom, and one in 50 million for condom users.

13   Homosexuals, needle-sharing drug users and their sex partners, however, were in grave danger. A single act of anal sex with an infected partner, or a single injection with an AIDS-tainted needle, carried as much as a one in 50 chance of infection. For people facing these risks, it was fair to say AIDS was truly a modern-day plague.

14   A key player in the CDC's earliest AIDS-prevention efforts was Walter Dowdle, a virologist who was a veteran of the war on herpes and had helped create the CDC's anti-AIDS office in the early 1980s. Like most people in his operation, he understood that AIDS had to be fought hardest in the places it was most prevalent.

15   But by the spring of 1987, Dr. Dowdle had already been rebuffed repeatedly in efforts to prepare AIDS warnings aimed directly at high-risk groups. TV networks were refusing to air announcements advocating the use of condoms. And Dr. Dowdle had failed in his attempt to disseminate a brochure that mentioned condoms as effective in slowing the spread of AIDS. At the time, all AIDS material had to be cleared by the president's Domestic Policy Council, and the Reagan White House objected to pro-condom messages on moral grounds. The 1986 brochure went into the White House for review and never came out.

16   Searching for clues about how to proceed, CDC officials began a series of internal meetings at their red-brick headquarters on Clifton Road in Atlanta. They also reached outside for high-powered marketing help, retaining Steve Rabin, then a senior vice president of the advertising giant Ogilvy & Mather. In August, Mr. Rabin, openly gay and deeply committed to the effort, ran focus groups in a half-dozen cities to gauge attitudes toward the disease.

17   The results were discouraging: In city after city, the focus groups made clear that concern about AIDS hadn't taken hold in much of the country, despite the widely publicized announcement two years earlier that Rock Hudson had the disease. With some exceptions in big cities like New York and San Francisco, homosexuals continued to engage casually in unprotected sex, as did heterosexuals everywhere. The prevailing attitude: It was somebody else's problem.

18   For gays and drug users, this view was flatly wrong and potentially fatal. Moreover, the focus-group results highlighted a huge policy issue:

Would the public support funding for AIDS prevention and research if the majority of heterosexuals believed they and their families were only minimally at risk? Would they be compassionate toward the victims of the disease?

19   Poll data suggested otherwise. A 1987 Gallup Poll showed that 25% of Americans thought that employers should have the right to fire AIDS victims. In that same poll, 43% felt that AIDS was a punishment for moral decline. In meetings within the CDC, many people, including Messrs. Dowdle and Rabin, expressed particular concern about the growth of housing and job discrimination against people with AIDS.

20   It was in this environment that the idea of presenting AIDS as an equal-opportunity scourge began to form. Politicians, including Republican Sen. Jesse Helms of North Carolina, were blocking campaigns aimed at gays anyway. And homosexual and minority groups were concerned about being linked too closely with the disease. Some CDC scientists, watching the spread of the disease among heterosexuals in Africa, worried that AIDS might yet make inroads among non-drug-using heterosexuals in the U.S. In any event, CDC officials believed that fighting AIDS was everyone's responsibility, even if everyone wasn't equally at risk of getting it.

21   "We were drawing on gut instinct," recalls Paula Van Ness, who had come to the CDC after serving as chief executive of the AIDS Project, a community program in Los Angeles. "The aim was, we thought we should get people talking about AIDS and we wanted to reduce the stigma." Earlier, in Los Angeles, she had reached out directly to high-risk groups: "Don't go out without your rubbers!" warned a motherly woman in one announcement the AIDS Project had sponsored. But now, on the national scene, she too felt that such a direct approach was impossible.

22   Dr. Dowdle, burned by the response to his earlier, more targeted efforts, agreed with his colleagues that the CDC's best bet was to present AIDS as everyone's problem: "As long as this was seen as a gay disease or, even worse, a disease of drug abusers, that pushed the disease way down the ladder" of people's priorities, he says.

23   After considerable soul-searching and debate, officials fixed on a dramatic approach they believed would do the most good in the long run: a high-powered PR and advertising campaign to spread a sobering yet politically palatable message nationwide.

24   In subsequent meetings in the summer and fall of 1987, the CDC team developed the idea of filming people with AIDS and building a series of public-service announcements around what they had to say. Subjects wouldn't be identified as gay, and the dangers of intravenous drug use would get little attention.

25   Early on, the staffers stumbled on their defining slogan when they interviewed the son of a rural Baptist minister. As Ms. Van Ness recalls

it, the man said, "If I can get AIDS, anyone can." His remark "wasn't scripted. That's what he actually said." Other similar public-service announcements were prepared, all with the same personal approach. "If you want your audience to be more receptive about this, you had to touch their hearts," Ms. Van Ness says.

26   The CDC's award-winning campaign, deftly pitched to a general audience, was launched in October 1987 and featured 38 TV spots, eight radio announcements and six print ads. The initial ads steered clear of specific advice on how to avoid AIDS, instead focusing on the universality of the disease and counseling Americans to discuss it with their families.

27   It wasn't until the spring of 1988, when the government mailed its *Understanding AIDS* brochure to 117 million U.S. households, that the risks of anal sex and drug abuse were underlined. But even this brochure accentuated the broader risk; it featured a prominent photo of a female AIDS victim saying that "AIDS is not a we 'they' disease, it's an 'us' disease."

28   As public relations, the CDC campaign and parallel warnings from other groups proved to be remarkably effective, particularly because these messages were reinforced by various public agencies and the media. According to one poll, during the last three months of 1989, 80% of U.S. adults said they saw an AIDS-related public-service announcement on television.

29   Millions of people were thus sold and resold on the message: Though AIDS started in the homosexual population it was inexorably spreading, stalking high-school students, middle-class husbands, suburban housewives, doctors, dentists and even their unwitting patients.

30   In late 1991, Magic Johnson dramatically boosted the perception that everyone was at risk when he announced that his infection was due to promiscuous heterosexual behavior. Talk shows and magazines pursued the theme relentlessly. Even late last year, Redbook magazine—written for a largely middle-class female audience—carried a major story about married women called, "Could I have AIDS?" In it, the author wrote: "My mind automatically telescopes to AIDS every time I get sick."

31   Meanwhile, the CDC itself was producing research that made clear that heterosexual fears were exaggerated. And some CDC scientists, including then-epidemiology chief Harold W. Jaffe, publicly railed against the everyone-gets-AIDS message and urged that assistance be targeted to those who most needed it. But his opinion, along with the internal research on which it was based, was typically drowned out by the countervailing mass-media campaign.

32   Fear of AIDS spread—and remains. Gallup surveys show that by 1988, 69% of Americans thought AIDS "was likely" to become an

epidemic, compared with 51% a year earlier, before the PR campaign got in full swing. By 1991, most thought that married people who had an occasional affair would eventually face substantial risk.

33   Yet, as CDC officials well knew, many of the images presented by the anti-AIDS campaign created a misleading impression about who was likely to get the disease. The blonde, middle-aged woman in the CDC's brochure was an intravenous drug user who had shared AIDS-tainted needles, although she wasn't identified as such in the brochure. The Baptist minister's son who said, "If I can get AIDS, anyone can," was gay, although the public-service announcement featuring him didn't say so.

34   Ryan White, perhaps the epidemic's most compelling symbol, had been diagnosed in 1984, at the age of 13, after receiving a transfusion from an AIDS-tainted blood-clotting agent used in the treatment of hemophilia. Barred by his school, shunned by neighbors, he emerged with his family as a forceful opponent of discrimination against AIDS patients. But five years before he died in 1990, the availability of a blood test for the human immunodeficiency virus, which causes AIDS, had nearly eliminated the infection from America's blood-products supply. (Similarly, activist Elizabeth Glaser, who spoke at the 1992 Democratic Convention, was infected through a blood transfusion well before AIDS testing began.)

35   Meanwhile, Kimberly Bergalis became famous for a particularly rare case: She and five other Florida patients apparently acquired their infections from their dentist, who later died of AIDS. But although the CDC has tracked down and tested thousands of patients of hundreds of HIV-positive doctors and dentists, that single Florida dentist remains the only documented case in the U.S. of a health professional's passing the virus on to patients.

36   Research continued to show that AIDS among heterosexuals had largely settled into an inner-city nexus, a world bounded by poverty and poor health care and beset by rampant drug use. AIDS was also on the rise in some poor rural communities. Yet government ads typically didn't address the heterosexual group at greatest risk, a group that a CDC researcher would later define as "generally young, minority, indigent women who use 'crack' cocaine, have multiple sex partners, trade sex for 'crack' or other drugs or money, and have [other sexually transmitted diseases] such as syphilis and herpes."

37   Though scientists and anti-AIDS activists knew that the government-nurtured fear of AIDS among upscale, non-drug-using heterosexuals was exaggerated, not everyone thought this was a bad thing. Indeed, many credited rampant fear with achieving pro-family goals that no amount of moralizing alone could have accomplished. In a 1991 Gallup Poll, 57% of respondents said they believed that AIDS had

already made their married friends "less likely to fool around." Singles reported being less apt to have one-night stands and more reluctant to date more than one person.

38   Moreover, there was no question that even mainstream heterosexuals bore some risk of AIDS and that greater caution would reduce their already-low rate of infection. "I don't see that much downside in slightly exaggerating [AIDS risk]" says John Ward, chief of the CDC branch that keeps track of AIDS cases. "Maybe they'll wear a condom. Maybe they won't sleep with someone they don't know."

39   The marketing campaign also appeared to be having another key desired effect: to mobilize support for public funding of AIDS research and prevention. Federal funding for AIDS-related medical research soared from $341 million in 1987 to $655 million in 1988, the year after the CDC's campaign began. (This year, the figure stands at $1.65 billion.) Meanwhile, the CDC's prevention dollars leapt from $136 million in 1987 to $304 million in 1988; $584 million was allocated for 1996.

40   Even the gay community, though not specifically targeted for assistance, began to see the wisdom of the everyone-gets-AIDS campaign. "This was a time of decreases in government funding," according to Jeff Amory, who headed the San Francisco AIDS Office in the 1980s. "Meanwhile, AIDS money was increasing."

41   It took a while before people realized that much of the money pouring in wasn't reaching the groups most at risk. In 1990, Mr. Amory took part in a telephone survey of about 50 HIV/AIDS groups funded by the CDC. Fewer than 10% even mentioned gay men as among their constituencies. (Mr. Amory died in November, after his interview with this newspaper.)

42   Meanwhile, the rush to testing meant that people at low risk were using up more and more of the available AIDS-prevention money just to discover they weren't infected. In 1994, 2.4 million tests were administered at government-funded locations, more than 10 times the number in 1985. Only 13% of those tests were given to homosexual or bisexual men or intravenous drug users.

43   As the CDC's biggest single prevention program, AIDS testing in 1995 accounted for about $136 million of the agency's total $589 million AIDS-prevention budget for that year. "It was not efficient or effective in picking up HIV-positive people," says Eric Goosby, director of the HIV/AIDS Policy Office of the U.S. Public Health Service, which oversees the CDC and other health agencies.

44   Moreover, because treating drug-addiction wasn't directly part of the CDC's mandate, stopping the spread of AIDS among needle-sharing addicts fell "between the cracks," says Dr. James W. Curran, who was director of the anti-AIDS office at the CDC until late last year and is now dean of the School of Public Health at Emory University in Atlanta.

45   State funding for AIDS prevention—tracking public attitudes toward the disease—was also being directed largely toward low-risk groups, says Patricia E. Franks, a senior researcher at UCSF, who spearheaded a study of California AIDS spending between 1989 and 1992. The study found that while 85% of AIDS cases were concentrated among men who had sex with men, programs targeting this group received only 9% of all state AIDS prevention dollars.

46   Spending for women, in contrast, grew to 29% of the state money in 1992 from 13% in 1989, even though HIV rates among women of childbearing age held steady at less than one-tenth of 1% from 1988 through 1992.

47   California health officials say they believe spending on high-risk groups has improved in the past few years. But Wayne Sauseda, director of the California Office of AIDS, concedes that "it's hard to take money away from groups already receiving grants." In California's last three-year state funding cycle, "we were being deluged by proposals from low- and no-risk population groups," Mr. Sauseda says. "We got two proposals for every one from a high-risk group."

48   Typical of the requests from low-risk groups, he says, were proposals to offer education on college campuses. "No one would say coeds are not at any risk," says Mr. Sauseda. "But in California, that's not our first priority."

49   AIDS officials in other states report similar frustrations. In 1994, the CDC turned to a community-planning process for dispensing AIDS funds, a system that theoretically allows local people to allocate dollars to groups most in need. But various community planners say it has been tough to redirect the funds, in large part because public attitudes have become so entrenched.

50   In Oregon, for example, many community AIDS workers "are unwilling to acknowledge that youth who are truly at risk [are] young gay men," says Robert McAlister, the state's HIV program manager. Thus, most of Oregon's AIDS-prevention money is still spent on counseling and testing that primarily serves low-risk individuals. "When Magic Johnson made his statement, we got overwhelmed with clients demanding service," Dr. McAlister says. "You start to cut corners. If we try to serve everybody, we wind up serving everybody poorly."

51   Having helped shape current attitudes and set AIDS-prevention policies in motion, the Centers for Disease Control finds itself in a serious bind. So far, AIDS has killed 320,000 Americans, according to the CDC. Between 650,000 and 900,000 others are currently infected with the virus that causes the illness.

52   Overall, rates of new HIV infections appear to be declining from their peak in the mid-1980s. Nonetheless, as many as 40,000 people, mostly gay men, drug users and their sex partners, will contract the virus this year alone. Despite this, the CDC aims its current education

campaign, called "Respect Yourself, Protect Yourself," at a broad spectrum of young adults, rather than targeting the high-risk groups. A current focus of the campaign is to discourage premarital sex among heterosexuals.

53   The CDC also has been emphasizing that women constitute a growing proportion of AIDS cases. But close analyses of the data indicate that the vast majority of these victims are drug users or sex partners of drug users. Also, the data partly reflect a statistical quirk: Because the number of infections among gay men has declined, other groups—such as women—now represent a larger percentage of victims. Yet the infection rate among women not in high-risk groups appears to be holding roughly steady.

54   Meanwhile, unpublished research by the CDC itself concludes that "the most effective efforts to reduce HIV infection will target injecting drug users on the Eastern seaboard, young and minority homosexual and bisexual men, and young and minority heterosexual women and men who smoke crack cocaine and have many sexual partners."

55   Numerous studies have shown significant behavior changes in gay men who have been counseled by gay-outreach programs. Susan M. Kegeles, a behavioral scientist at UCSF's Center for AIDS Prevention Studies, reports that an eight-month program in Eugene, Oregon, reduced one of the highest-risk acts, unprotected anal intercourse, by 27% in young gay men. The program used leaders in the gay community to demonstrate and consistently reinforce safe-sex practices.

56   Other studies have shown that drug users need even more intense behavioral counseling to break their addiction. But "only 15% of active drug users are in treatment on any given day, and there are not enough treatment slots to meet the demand from drug users," according to a report by the federal Office of Technology Assessment. Further, the ban of federal funding for needle exchanges continues, even though most reports conclude that locally funded efforts to distribute sterile needles or needle-cleaning supplies have been effective in reducing the spread of infection.

57   An epidemiologist at UCSF, James G. Kahn, recently created an academic model which, he says, shows that over five years, $1 million spent in a high-risk population averts 150 infections, compared with two or three infections if the money is spent in a low-risk population. Moreover, he argues that reducing infections in high-risk groups would "almost certainly" benefit low-risk groups by reducing the pool of people who could potentially infect others.

58   Then there is the separate issue of honesty in government: Shouldn't the public hear the truth, even if there might be adverse consequences? "When the public starts mistrusting its public health officials, it takes a long time before they believe them again," says George Annas, a medical ethicist at Boston University.

59   Yet many both inside and outside the government fear that speaking more directly about AIDS transmission, and seeking federal programs to match, poses the same dangers it did nine years ago. Congress controls the purse strings, and Sen. Helms, in particular, still monitors every AIDS-related bill. Says a Helms staff member, "We would certainly have a problem" with money going to gay-activist groups or to produce materials that illustrate gay sex acts.

60   "There is a real concern that funding won't be shifted, it will be cut, that if most people in the U.S. feel they are at very low risk, there will be little support for any AIDS-prevention efforts," says Don Des Jarlais, director of research at the Chemical Dependency Institute of Beth Israel Medical Center in New York. Still, he and many others believe that prevention experts have no choice—and that it is time to fight for programs based on candor. "You can't build a good prevention program on bad epidemiology," he says.

61   Even back in the 1980s, Stephen C. Joseph, who was commissioner of public health for New York City from 1986 to 1990, blasted the notion that AIDS was making major inroads into the general population.

62   Today Dr. Joseph, who is assistant secretary of defense for health affairs at the Pentagon, says: "Political correctness has prevented us from looking at the issue squarely in the eye and dealing with it. It is the responsibility of the public-health department to tell the truth."

A Question of Odds

63   Below are rough estimates of the relative risks in the U.S. and Western Europe of various activities that can transmit AIDS. The calculations can't be used as a guide to individual behavior. Risk to any one person depends on many factors that can't be reduced to a single number. Recent research, for example, suggests that the infectiousness of the HIV virus can vary greatly over the life of an infected person; infectiousness is likely to be high both at the very outset of the infection, before symptoms have appeared, and several years later. Also, women may be several times more likely than men to be infected through vaginal intercourse, a distinction that the overall risk figure obscures.

ACTIVITY: Vaginal sexual intercourse
RISK: 1 infection per 1,000 acts with HIV-positive partner
NOTES AND SOURCES: Mean per-act risk for unprotected intercourse. Source: Isabelle de Vincenzi, European Study Group on Heterosexual Transmission of HIV, 1994

ACTIVITY: Receptive anal intercourse

RISK: 5 to 30 infections per 1,000 acts with HIV-positive partner

NOTES AND SOURCES: With no condom use. Source: Victor De-Gruttola, Harvard School of Public Health, 1989

ACTIVITY: Intravenous drug injection

RISK: 10 to 20 infections per with infected needle 1,000 needle uses

NOTES AND SOURCES: Source: Don Des Jarlais, Beth Israel Medical Center, New York

ACTIVITY: Accidental stick in medical

RISK: 3 infections per 1,000 sticks setting with infected needle

NOTES AND SOURCES: Source: Centers for Disease Control

ACTIVITY: Transfusion of screened blood

RISK: 1 infection per 450,000 to 660,000 donations

NOTES AND SOURCES: Source: Centers for Disease Control/ American National Red Cross

(4,565 words)

VOCABULARY

scourge (2)	epidemiology (8)	virologist (14)
intravenous (2)	pivotal (10)	gauge (17)

THE FACTS

1. What was the message with which health officials bombarded the public in 1987?

2. Who accounts for 83 percent of AIDS victims today?

3. Where must AIDS be fought the hardest, according to scientists quoted in the essay?

4. On what grounds did the Reagan White House object to pro-condom messages?

5. What problem did AIDS fighters worry about if only the high-risk groups were targeted for funding?

6. How did Magic Johnson contribute to fighting AIDS?

7. What was the name of the young boy who contracted AIDS through a blood transfusion used in the treatment of hemophilia?

THE STRATEGIES

1. What is the thesis of the essay? Write it in one sentence on a piece of paper.

2. What evidence do the authors use to support their thesis? How convincing is this evidence?

3. Did the opening of this essay compel you to read on? If so, why? If not, why not?

4. How are the experiences of individual people used in this essay?

5. How are poll data used in this essay?

6. What is the purpose of the addendum titled "A Question of Odds"?

THE ISSUES

1. Do you agree or disagree with the basic thesis of this argument? Explain your answer.

2. What effect did the news that people like Rock Hudson and Magic Johnson contracted AIDS have on our general population?

3. In paragraph 57, epidemiologist James G. Kahn states that "$1 million spent in a high-risk population averts 150 infections, compared with two or three infections if the money is spent in a low-risk population." If this statistic is a fact, then what should our government do about AIDS?

4. How do you answer a person who claims that AIDS is a punishment from God meted out to people who are immoral?

5. Do you believe that the public should hear the truth about AIDS even if there might be adverse consequences? (See paragraph 58.) Explain your answer.

SUGGESTIONS FOR WRITING

1. Write an essay in which you state how you think AIDS can be avoided.

2. Write an essay agreeing or disagreeing with this statement: "AIDS must be fought hardest in the places it is most prevalent."

▼▼

Donna Ferentes

AIDS IS GOD'S PUNISHMENT

DONNA FERENTES is a pseudonym derived from the Roman poet Vergil and used by this writer who, because of the painful and sensitive family situation described in this essay, does not wish to be identified.

1   When I was 17, my youngest brother was born. Thrilled, I took him to the sisters at my high school, who placed him on their chapel altar beneath Christ crucified and before the Blessed Sacrament. In the gesture was the belief and the hope that the baby's truest nature as created by God would develop with grace and in goodness, revealing his true self to himself. Today, I am 47, and my brother, now 29, is dying of AIDS. Although it is terrible to see, he will not face or admit death. The devastating disease has become a last drop into the abyss he has explored for ten years: himself. He is using the disease to deepen his rejection of the true spiritual purpose of his life. A life of use of himself and others as mere sexual objects has left him morally defenseless. The loss of his immune system is the symbol of the loss of his true spiritual center.

2   Indeed, in every way, the physical reality of AIDS finds its moral approximations: His wasted body mirrors a wasted young life. The opportunistic diseases ever at the ready to attack him reflect the unceasing efforts of the homosexual community to use the AIDS victim to the end by portraying men like my brother as innocent victims of a haphazard virus rather than as parties responsible for risking and spreading this most virulent disease. In its most macabre expressions, the disease is a twisted celebration of an immoral life. As his lover said to me, "Well, we're all going to die sometime." As I interpreted this, it means that one might as well do what one wants and if it courts and wins death, then so be it. This is an attitude antithetical to the idea that life is a gift to be treasured and which has, for its truest purpose, eventual union with God. Where this is absent, then life becomes cheap, negotiable, a trinket, a bad joke.

3   In this dreamlike reality, families are supposed to see in AIDS the final "opportunity" to accept their son's and brother's homosexuality rather than to help them to confront it as an accomplice in their murder/suicide. Those families who refuse to play this spiritual endgame and who thoroughly struggle for the repentance of these souls are made to feel intolerant, even cruel, as though they are torturing them with something extraneous, visiting upon them an extra-painful suffering

which they should not have to encounter. Worse, there is even the point of view that God himself looks kindly and tolerantly upon their "unions." At all costs, like a lurid skeleton hovering over the half-dead and ravaged AIDS victim, the homosexual death dance must be performed. Its obsessive hopes are to transfix the victim and prevent the family from struggling for the soul of one already totally weakened in spirit and morality. AIDS, because it is so devastating and debilitating, can easily become an excuse to focus on the ravages of the disease rather than on the moment of spiritual opportunity at hand.

4   Ten years ago, my brother fled the family to begin a totally selfish and sex-centered life. Fleeing the family meant he rejected finding himself in reference to it; a new identity, wound around the homosexual life, was supposed to provide his "true self." Fleeing the family was a negation of his own creation by God through the sacrament of marriage; the homosexual lifestyle was his repudiation of his roots and the center of his own being. As he lost himself and his family ties, so he lost his bond to the God of tradition and doctrine. In His place was a narcissistic god, a reflection of himself. Every lover was a compounding of this alien god as self.

5   All of his "lovers" and the "love" he experienced with them deepened his hostility to the family, and the "straight" world in general. His main contact with the family has been a fugue-like guerrilla war. Its main tactic has been emotional bribery: if the family would not underwrite his new "gay" identity, despite the breakdown of his personality that it involved, then the family was rejected. The family had to call his moral lethargy a newly found "good"; his emotional bribery had to be accepted as our own ignorance of the "fact" that homosexuality is as, or even more honest than heterosexuality, no different from marriage, etc. We watched him become less and less human, more distant from us, and also from himself. What he has never realized is that the bunker in which he has lived and defended has had all of the guns trained upon himself. One gun went off. It was AIDS.

6   He slips away from us before our efforts can prevail. The dementia, the fevers, the nausea, the disorientation, the loss of memory all seem ranged against us in our relentless struggle to restore him to himself, to us and to God. The totality of the family's love is, through the fact of AIDS, a sign to the world that only the family's love is whole and real. Even if the family universe is not perfect, as is ours, it remains the only one in which the true self as it was intended to develop by God can be found. It is the difficult threshing floor of a happy death.

7   The devastating spread of AIDS should be read as God's loving attempt to teach His children who have abandoned and rejected His love and discipline this primary, pivotal truth. For homosexuals, AIDS is an opportunity to confront the truth of their moral life. Not many diseases contain this special grace. It is the work of those who believe in

God and in natural law to set AIDS in the deepest context possible and not to give in to prejudice against or false compassion for its victims. If AIDS is not soon recognized as a way back to all that is real and whole, if we do not struggle to bring that meaning to it, then it is truly species threatening, for the family and the authentic self as created by God are basic for life in the physical world. And in turn the material world's purpose, including the body, is to reveal and obey God's will for individuals and the whole. Without this, there is no meaning or purpose to our existence or our surroundings. We are only creatures among other creatures, and the very notion of eternity is destroyed by man himself.

(1,090 words)

VOCABULARY

macabre (2)	debilitating (3)	fugue-like (5)
antithetical (2)	ravages (3)	lethargy (5)
extraneous (3)	repudiation (4)	dementia (6)
transfix (3)	narcissistic (4)	

THE FACTS

1. Into what abyss does the author accuse her stricken brother of descending?

2. What does the author accuse the homosexual community of doing to AIDS victims?

3. What does the author see as a family's duty when one of its members is dying of AIDS? In what way does she see this duty being frustrated by the homosexual community?

4. What "God" does the author accuse her brother of worshipping in place of the "God of tradition and doctrine"?

5. How did the author's brother demand that his family view his homosexuality?

THE STRATEGIES

1. What is the primary premise underlying the author's argument?

2. The essay opens with an anecdote about how the author felt when her brother was born. Aside from setting the stage for the writing that follows, how else does this anecdote help the author's argument?

3. In examining what she calls "the moral approximations" of AIDS, what rhetorical tactic does the author use?

4. In paragraph 4, what technique does the author use to achieve and maintain coherence?

5. Around what imagery is paragraph 5 developed, in which the author describes her brother's withdrawal from his family? What makes this image effective?

THE ISSUES

1. What is your attitude toward the writer's assertion that AIDS is "God's loving attempt to teach His children who have abandoned and rejected His love"?

2. What image of the author emerges from this article? Do you find this image sympathetic or repelling? Why?

3. The writer charges that the homosexual community expects society to view homosexuality as "no different from marriage." What is your attitude toward that opinion?

4. If science ever proved once and for all that homosexuals are genetically determined, what changes do you foresee taking place in the public's attitude towards homosexuality? What, if any, difference in your own point of view would that discovery make?

5. What is the author really asking of her dying brother? Why do you think this request is so difficult for him to accept? What is your attitude toward her for making this request?

SUGGESTIONS FOR WRITING

1. Write an essay attacking or defending the views of this writer on AIDS.

2. Is the writer blaming the victim? Write an essay attacking or defending her on that charge.

I

First Draft

Scott Gavorsky, DeKalb College

The Evolutionary Past and Future of AIDS

The struggle against AIDS is one of the greatest crises that humanity has faced. Caused by the human immunodeficiency virus (HIV), AIDS can take years to kill, and perhaps even years to be detected. No cure or vaccination is likely in the near future, and AIDS appears to be a problem that will affect people for a long time. Or will it? A number of immunodeficiency viruses are found among animals, *and* most exist without causing *(Better flow)* illness. One of these is simian immunodeficiency virus (SIV), the *(wordy)* likely ~~direct ancestor~~ *parent* of HIV that exists in monkeys. Another, the feline immunodeficiency virus (FIV), was the subject of ~~a July~~ *an* *Less clumsy* ~~1995 article in Discover magazine by Virginia Morrell, entitled~~ *article by Virginia Morrell, entitled "The Killer cat Virus* ~~"The Killer Cat Virus That Doesn't Kill Cats."~~ *That Doesn't Kill Cats" (Discover, July 1995).* Morrell's article examines the relationship between ~~these two~~ *animal immunodeficiency viruses* and HIV, providing both insight into the evolutionary history of immunodeficiency viruses and hope for the battle against AIDS.

Prior to discussing the evolutionary history of immunodeficiency viruses It is *first* necessary to understand how disease-causing viruses generally develop hand-in-hand with a

better wording (left margin)

Friends pointed out that the underlined section is a dangling modifier. Beats me. (right margin)

Gavorsky 2

prior to discussing the evolutionary history of immunbdeficiency viruses. species.] Typically, according to William McNeill's <u>Plagues and

<u>Peoples,</u> a species that is exposed to a new virus will suffer

severe casualties. These deaths, however, are as often as

destructive to the virus as to the infected host, since it does not

benefit from a dead host. Natural selection, therefore, usually

causes strains of the disease that are less destructive to become

dominant, for they can reproduce successfully while not killing

the host. After a time, the disease can become endemic,

occurring consistently with low mortality in a given species. A

familiar example of this phenomenon is syphilis, a disease that

killed within a week when it first appeared in Europe in the

fifteenth century, but a hundred years later took the form we

know today. ~~Interestingly enough, this selection process seems to~~

~~consistently take a set amount of time, which McNeill fixes at~~

~~five to six generations of the host species. This also appears to~~

~~have held true in the case of syphilis.~~   Interesting but not really related

completes thought   Both SIV and FIV have been studied heavily: SIV because it is

the closest relative to HIV, and FIV because it is much easier to study

disease patterns among wild populations with large animals such

as cats, as opposed to small primates. And both share the characteristics of endemic diseases.

As Arno Karlen notes in <u>Man and Microbes,</u> SIV infects African

monkeys with no apparent symptoms, although it is deadly in

Asian primates—not surprising given that immunodeficiency

viruses seem to have originated in Africa. FIV was first

discovered in 1987 after house cats in California started

developing AIDS-like symptoms, but later studies showed the

Gavorsky 3

sounds better

to be
virus quite common, and endemic, in African cats. For example,

while approximately 84% of the lions in the Serengeti harbor FIV,   *clarifies*

among lions
no cases of feline AIDS were reported between 1990 and 1995.

~~Interestingly enough, solitary cats, such a leopards, cougars, and~~

~~house-cats, seem much more likely to develop feline AIDS than~~   *Interesting, not related*

~~do communal cats, such as lions.~~

came to light
   The relationship between SIV and HIV ~~was established~~ in the   *sounds better*

early eighties. Once FIV was discovered, researchers began to

among the three viruses   *They*
Clearer look for a relationship ~~between it, SIV, and HIV. The three viruses~~   *wordy*
to each other --
are genetically similar, so similar, in fact, that they probably

the
constitute a single lineage. FIV seems to be the oldest of three,

developing between three and six million years ago. At some

point in the past, the virus was transferred to primates, probably

by a monkey escaping from a feline predator. Once in simians, the

probably
virus ~~more than likely~~ led to the development of simian AIDS.
Through
~~Over~~ time, the virus and the simians reached ~~a~~ *an* equilibrium, and
the infected   *Clarifies*
SIV became endemic in ~~certain~~ monkey populations. Sometime in

the last two centuries, humans contracted the virus, and the

process started all over again.

   One could deduce that since both FIV and SIV are endemic in

their respective host populations, the same will eventually   *Clearer*
scenario
happen with HIV and humans. While this is possible, we should
it   *, not the only one.*
remember that ~~this~~ is ~~solely~~ one possible outcome; ~~it is not a~~ *better*
HIV becomes endemic,   *be*   *from now,*   *phrasing*
~~certainty.~~ Even if ~~it does occur,~~ it will ~~take~~ years ~~to happen,~~ years

in which people will continue to suffer and die. We would do

well to remember that syphilis still kills, even if ~~it is~~ over decades

Gavorsky 4

We should still continue to encourage

as opposed to years. If, however, the evolutionary theory that

prevention and strive for a cure, not sit back and let nature take

Morrell presented is accurate, it gives hope that future its course.

generations might be spared the scourge of AIDS. And, at this

seems

time, hope is almost as valuable a commodity as facts.

Gavorsky 5

Works Cited

Karlen, Arno. <u>Man and Microbes</u>. New York: Putnam, 1995.

McNeill, William. <u>Plagues and Peoples</u>. New York: Doubleday,
    1977.

Morrell, Virginia. "The Killer Cat Virus That Doesn't Kill Cats."
    <u>Discover</u> July 1995: 62–69.

I

Final Draft

Scott Gavorsky, DeKalb College

The Evolutionary Past and Future of AIDS

The struggle against AIDS is one of the greatest crises that humanity has faced. Caused by the human immunodeficiency virus (HIV), AIDS can take years to kill, and perhaps even years to be detected. No cure or vaccination is likely in the near future, and AIDS appears to be a problem that will affect people for a long time. Or will it? A number of immunodeficiency viruses are found among animals, and most exist without causing illness. One of these is simian immunodeficiency virus (SIV), the likely parent of HIV that exists in monkeys. Another, the feline immunodeficiency virus (FIV), was the subject of an article by Virginia Morrell, entitled "The Killer Cat Virus That Doesn't Kill Cats" (Discover, July 1995). Morrell's article examines the relationship between animal immunodeficiency viruses and HIV, providing both insight into the evolutionary history of immunodeficiency viruses and hope for the battle against AIDS.

It is first necessary to understand how disease-causing viruses generally develop hand-in-hand with a species prior to discussing the evolutionary history of immunodeficiency viruses. Typically, according to William McNeill's Plagues and Peoples, a species that is exposed to a new virus will suffer severe casualties. These deaths, however, are as often as destructive to the virus as to the infected host, since it does not benefit from a dead host. Natural selection, therefore, usually causes strains of the disease that are less destructive to become dominant, for they can reproduce successfully while not killing the host. After a time, the disease can become endemic, occurring consistently with low mortality in a given species. A familiar example of this phenomenon is syphilis, a disease that killed within a week when it first appeared in Europe in the fifteenth century, but a hundred years later took the form we know today.

Both SIV and FIV have been studied heavily: SIV because it is the closest relative to HIV, and FIV because it is much easier to study disease patterns among wild populations with large animals such as cats as opposed to small primates. And both share the characteristics of endemic diseases. As Arno Karlen notes in <u>Man and Microbes,</u> SIV infects African monkeys with no apparent symptoms, although it is deadly in Asian primates—not surprising given that immunodeficiency viruses seem to have originated in Africa. FIV was first discovered in 1987 after house cats in California started developing AIDS-like symptoms, but later studies showed the virus to be quite common, and endemic, in African cats. For example, while approximately 84% of the lions in the Serengeti harbor FIV, no cases of feline AIDS were reported among lions between 1990 and 1995.

The relationship between SIV and HIV came to light in the early eighties. Once FIV was discovered, researchers began to look for a relationship among the three viruses. They are genetically similar to each other—so similar, in fact, that they probably constitute a single lineage. FIV seems to be the oldest of the three, developing between three and six million years ago. At some point in the past, the virus was transferred to primates, probably by a monkey escaping from a feline predator. Once in simians, the virus probably led to the development of simian AIDS. Through time, the virus and the simians reached an equilibrium, and SIV became endemic in the infected monkey populations. Sometime in the last two centuries, humans contracted the virus, and the process started all over again.

One could deduce that since both FIV and SIV are endemic in their respective host populations, the same will eventually happen with HIV and humans. While this scenario is possible, we should remember that it is one possible outcome—not the only one. Even if HIV becomes endemic, it will be years from now, years in which people will continue to suffer and die. We would do well to remember that syphilis still kills, even if over decades as opposed to years. We should still continue to encourage prevention and strive for a cure, not sit back and let nature take its course. If, however, the evolutionary theory that Morrell presented is accurate, it gives hope that future generations might be spared the scourge of AIDS. And, at this time, hope seems almost as valuable a commodity as facts.

Works Cited

Karlen, Arno. <u>Man and Microbes</u>. New York: Putnam, 1995.

McNeill, William. <u>Plagues and Peoples</u>. New York: Doubleday,
  1977.

Morrell, Virginia. "The Killer Cat Virus That Doesn't Kill Cats."
  <u>Discover</u> July 1995: 62–69.

How I Write

For me, the actual physical writing seems fairly easy—I sit down at the computer and type. It is the composition and revising that require the most effort. Most of my composition is done in my car, since I find myself alone in it a good bit of the time, either going to class or traveling on business. With all that time, I tend to think about my writing: mentally reviewing research, organizing the essay, composing that all-important opening paragraph. Since I am not constrained by having to jot anything down, I can just wander over the essay, changing this, dumping that, and questioning the other. After many an hour (mileage may vary), I have a fair idea of how I want the piece to look and read. All that is left is to sit down and type it.

After I have a draft done, I begin to edit and revise. I used to underestimate the importance of this step, but it has slowly dawned on me that this may be the most important part of writing. To force myself to do it, I developed a little technique. I had received a quill pen for Christmas a few years back, so I sit down with a hard copy of the piece, my quill pen, and a bottle of red ink, and I ruthlessly go through it. Besides correcting mistakes, I make comments in the margins, and often find myself adding things, re-arranging the essay, or re-evaluating my sources. Depending on the length of the writing, I may do this four or five times.

I guess that I only spend about 30 percent of the time actually writing the essay. Another 40 percent or so is thinking and composing, with the remainder doing revisions. I don't think I will ever be able to just sit down at the computer and start writing again.

How I Wrote This Essay

I am a history major, and historical epidemics are an area of interest of mine. After deciding on writing about AIDS, I turned to McNeill's *Plagues and Peoples,* a personal favorite. While the book was published before the AIDS epidemic began, I was intrigued with the endemic-disease theory, and I wondered if AIDS may fit this pattern. A visit to the school library revealed articles about the animal immunodeficiency viruses, although the Morrell article was the only one that directly tied this back to HIV.

   The most difficult part in writing this essay was condensing the information. I had two main obstacles: eliminating technical terms, and trying to avoid interesting tidbits. I wrote three rough drafts, and the first two were concerned solely with trying to find out which information I wanted in the final copy. The technical terms and theory, I finally decided, were not that important; the disease patterns could be explained without knowing the specifics of how the virus functions. The interesting tidbits, on the other hand, were a bit of a temptation. Morrell's article in particular contained a number of little facts that would add to the essay, but would not detract if left out. In the end, I left these out. *C'est la vie.*

CHAPTER WRITING ASSIGNMENTS

1. Contrast the voice of the writer of "What Is Style?" with that of the writer of "Salvation."

2. Present your own ideas on how a writer finds a voice in his or her own writing. Apply these ideas to your own work.

3. Most of us think we can recognize sincerity in a writer's work when we see it. Write an essay specifying the literary qualities you associate with sincerity. Apply your ideas to any of the selections in this chapter.

My Writing Tip

For anyone who uses a computer to write (which is most of us nowadays), I stress the importance of printing out a hard copy to read. Ideas, words, and sentences that make perfect sense on the section of a page on a screen seem ridiculous when you are looking at an entire page at once, which is exactly how the reader will see it. Even if you are one of those who never use rough drafts, print out one copy when you are done to check for grammar. A personal example may illustrate my point. I had a speech impediment when I was younger, mispronouncing 'r' as 'w', just like Elmer Fudd. I still catch myself lapsing into this from time to time. I wrote one essay for a history class in a hurry, printed it, and went directly to class to hand it in. It was in class that I discovered that, two or three times, I had written "whether" instead of "rather," and had never caught it repeating it to myself while looking at it on the computer. So print it out first!

WRITING ASSIGNMENTS FOR A SPECIFIC AUDIENCE

1. Write an essay directed at a parent or a close parental figure reminiscing about some childhood experience you shared with him or her.

2. Pretending that you're replying to an ad in the *Personals* section of your newspaper, write a letter to a prospective date about yourself.

COLLABORATIVE WRITING PROJECTS

1. About style, the Reverend Samuel Wesley (1662–1735) said, "Style is the dress of thought." On the other hand, the Comte De Buffon (1707–1788) said something that sounded just the opposite, "Style is the man." Taking these two views as opposing opinions about style, research what critics and scholars have said about style and write a paper summarizing their findings and giving the opinions of the members of your group.

2. After dividing your group into teams of two or three, each team should collaborate on writing a short piece imitating the voice used by one of the writers in this section. Meet as a group to discuss and critique whether the imitations successfully captured the voice of the particular writer.

Chapter Three

PURPOSE AND THESIS

INTRODUCTION: WHAT IS A THESIS?

The thesis of an essay is the writer's main point. It is what the essay intends to prove, assert, or argue. Some theorists claim that an essay's thesis should be as extractable as an almond from its shell, and that one should always be able to sum up the essence of any essay on a postcard. But anyone who regularly reads essays and articles knows that there is considerable variation in the way theses are used. Some essays that are otherwise perfectly clear have an indistinct thesis buried amid the prose. Other essays have a typical postcard-clear thesis. The fact is that professional writers do not write cookie-cutter theses as often as idealists would have us believe.

There are two identifiable kinds of theses that are commonly found in essays. The first is the implicit thesis. It is not plainly spelled out in any single sentence; yet it is still inferable from what the writer has written. "Once More to the Lake" by E. B. White is an example of such an essay (Chapter Six). It is unified, has focus and a definite purpose, but does not blare it out in a thesis.

The second kind of thesis explicitly states the author's position in a single sentence. Usually this sentence occurs at the end of the first paragraph. Students are encouraged and occasionally compelled to use this explicit thesis, which professional writers use only infrequently and seldom with the rigidity of the classroom practice. Virtually all the student essays in this book use an explicit thesis.

This variation between theory and the practice in the use of the thesis should not surprise us. Orthodoxy in any discipline is always demanded of the beginner, and the student writer must understandably abide by rhetorical conventions that the professional will flout. Once you have written a number of essays, you will no doubt be able to focus and follow through on a main point without first writing it down in an explicit thesis. But the hard fact is that many beginners cannot. They wander and stray from the point if they do not clearly and distinctly write it down. That is why students are encouraged to use explicit theses.

The essays in this chapter illustrate how various writers use theses to help them maintain and achieve focus. Sheridan Baker dispenses some clever advice about how a writer may derive rhetorical energy from a well-chosen thesis; Harry Crosby and George Estey tell us why the thesis is necessary and how it helps both reader and writer. Other essays in this book show us the real-world practice, in which the thesis is implied by the focus of the essay rather than trumpeted in an opening paragraph. Roxanne Roberts' experience vividly demonstrates suicide's never-ending effects; Flannery O'Connor offers a story whose theme announces that most human beings are depraved; and Edna St. Vincent Millay writes a poem about how death is the end of beauty.

Rhetorical techniques are only a means to an end, not an end in themselves. The end purpose of any written work is to communicate with an audience, and one conventional means of doing this is to make your main point crystal clear in an explicit thesis. Doing so will help you stick to the point while helping your reader follow your thinking.

A D V I C E

▼▼▼

Sheridan Baker

THE THESIS

SHERIDAN BAKER (b. 1918) is emeritus professor of English at the University of Michigan and has been a Fulbright lecturer. He has edited several works by the eighteenth-century novelist Henry Fielding, including *Joseph Andrews, Shamela,* and *Tom Jones.* Baker's two rhetorics, *The Practical Stylist* (1962) and *The Complete Stylist* (1976), have been widely used in colleges throughout the United States.

In this excerpt from The Complete Stylist, *Baker advises the student to state clearly, in a sharp-edged thesis, the controlling purpose of the essay.*

1   You can usually blame a bad essay on a bad beginning. If your essay falls apart, it probably has no primary idea to hold it together. "What's the big idea?" we used to ask. The phrase will serve as a reminder that you must find the "big idea" behind your several smaller thoughts and musings before you start to write. In the beginning was the *logos,* says the Bible—the idea, the plan, caught in a flash as if in a single word. Find your *logos,* and you are ready to round out your essay and set it spinning.

2   The big idea behind our ride in the speeding car was that in adolescence, especially, the group can have a very deadly influence on the individual. If you had not focused your big idea in a thesis, you might have begun by picking up thoughts at random, something like this:

> Everyone thinks he is a good driver. There are more accidents caused by young drivers than any other group. Driver education is a good beginning, but further practice is very necessary. People who object to driver education do not realize that modern society, with its suburban pattern of growth, is built around the automobile. The car becomes a way of life and a status symbol. When a teen-ager goes too fast he is probably only copying his own father.

3   A little reconsideration, aimed at a good thesis-sentence, could turn this into a reasonably good beginning:

> Modern society is built on the automobile. Every child looks forward to the time when he can drive; every teen-ager, to the day when his

father lets him take out the car alone. Soon he is testing his skill at higher and higher speeds, especially with a group of friends along. One final test at extreme speeds usually suffices. The teen-ager's high-speed ride, if it does not kill him, will probably open his eyes to the deadly dynamics of the group.

4   Thus the central idea, or thesis, is your essay's life and spirit. If your thesis is sufficiently firm and clear, it may tell you immediately how to organize your supporting material and so obviate elaborate planning. If you do not find a thesis, your essay will be a tour through the miscellaneous. An essay replete with scaffolds and catwalks—"We have just seen this; now let us turn to this"—is an essay in which the inherent idea is weak or nonexistent. A purely expository and descriptive essay, one simply about "Cats," for instance, will have to rely on outer scaffolding alone (some orderly progression from Persia to Siam) since it really has no idea at all. It is all subject, all cats, instead of being based on an idea *about* cats.

The Argumentative Edge

Find Your Thesis

5   The *about*-ness puts an argumentative edge on the subject. When you have something to say *about* cats, you have found your underlying idea. You have something to defend, something to fight about: not just "Cats," but "The cat is really man's best friend." Now the hackles on all dog men are rising, and you have an argument on your hands. You have something to prove. You have a thesis.

6   "What's the big idea, Mac?" Let the impudence in that time-honored demand remind you that the best thesis is a kind of affront to somebody. No one will be very much interested in listening to you deplete the thesis "The dog is man's best friend." Everyone knows that already. Even the dog lovers will be uninterested, convinced that they know better than you. But the cat . . .

7   So it is with any unpopular idea. The more unpopular the viewpoint and the stronger the push against convention, the stronger the thesis and the more energetic the essay. Compare the energy in "Democracy is good" with that in "Communism is good," for instance. The first is filled with platitudes, the second with plutonium. By the same token, if you can find the real energy in "Democracy is good," if you can get down through the sand to where the roots and water are, you will have a real essay, because the opposition against which you generate your energy is the heaviest in the world: boredom. Probably the most energetic thesis of all, the greatest inner organizer, is some tired old truth that you cause to jet with new life, making the old ground green again.

8   To find a thesis and put it into one sentence is to narrow and define your subject to a workable size. Under "Cats" you must deal with all felinity from the jungle up, carefully partitioning the eons and areas, the tigers and tabbies, the sizes and shapes. The minute you proclaim the cat the friend of man, you have pared away whole categories and chapters, and need only think up the arguments sufficient to overwhelm the opposition. So, put an argumentative edge on your subject—and you will have found your thesis.

9   Simple exposition, to be sure, has its uses. You may want to tell someone how to build a doghouse, how to can asparagus, how to follow the outlines of relativity, or even how to write an essay. Performing a few exercises in simple exposition will no doubt sharpen your insight into the problems of finding orderly sequences, of considering how best to lead your readers through the hoops, of writing clearly and accurately. It will also illustrate how much finer and surer an argument is.

10   You will see that picking an argument immediately simplifies the problems so troublesome in straight exposition: the defining, the partitioning, the narrowing of the subject. Actually, you can put an argumentative edge on the flattest of expository subjects. "How to build a doghouse" might become "Building a doghouse is a thorough introduction to the building trades, including architecture and mechanical engineering." "Canning asparagus" might become "An asparagus patch is a course in economics." "Relativity" might become "Relativity is not so inscrutable as many suppose." You have simply assumed that you have a loyal opposition consisting of the uninformed, the scornful, or both. You have given your subject its edge; you have limited and organized it at a single stroke. Pick an argument, then, and you will automatically be defining and narrowing your subject, and all the partitions you don't need will fold up. Instead of dealing with things, subjects, and pieces of subjects, you will be dealing with an idea and its consequences.

Sharpen Your Thesis

11   Come out with your subject pointed. Take a stand, make a judgment of value. Be reasonable, but don't be timid. It is helpful to think of your thesis, your main idea, as a debating question—"Resolved: Old age pensions must go"—taking out the "Resolved" when you actually write the subject down. But your resolution will be even stronger, your essay clearer and tighter, if you can sharpen your thesis even further "Resolved: Old age pensions must go because—." Fill in that blank and your worries are practically over. The main idea is to put your whole argument into one sentence.

12   Try for instance: "Old age pensions must go because they are making people irresponsible." I don't know at all if that is true, and neither

will you until you write your way into it, considering probabilities and alternatives and objections, and especially the underlying assumptions. In fact, no one, no master sociologist or future historian, can tell absolutely if it is true, so multiplex are the causes in human affairs, so endless and tangled the consequences. The basic assumption—that irresponsibility is growing—may be entirely false. No one, I repeat, can tell absolutely. But by the same token, your guess may be as good as another's. At any rate, you are now ready to write. You have found your *logos*.

13   Now you can put your well-pointed thesis-sentence on a card on the wall in front of you to keep from drifting off target. But you will now want to dress it for the public, to burnish it, and make it comely. Suppose you try:

> Old age pensions, perhaps more than anything else, are eroding our heritage of personal and familial responsibility.

But is this true? Perhaps you had better try something like:

> Despite their many advantages, old age pensions may actually be eroding our heritage of personal and familial responsibility.

This is really your thesis, and you can write that down on a scrap of paper too.

(1,415 words)

VOCABULARY

obviate (4)	inherent (4)	platitudes (7)
replete (4)	affront (6)	multiplex (12)

D I S C U S S I O N

Harry Crosby
George Estey

THE CONTROLLING CONCEPT

HARRY HERBERT CROSBY (b. 1919) is emeritus professor of American literature and rhetoric at Boston University.

GEORGE FISHER ESTEY (1924–1984) was professor of English literature and
rhetoric at the same university. They coauthored *College Writing: The Rhetorical
Imperative* (1968) and *Just Rhetoric* (1972). Estey was coeditor of two anthologies,
Non-Violence: A Reader in the Ethics of Action (1971) and *Violence: A Reader in the
Ethics of Action* (1971).

In this selection from College Writing, *the authors supply appropriate
examples and commentary to demonstrate how a thesis works.*

A speech has two parts. You must state your thesis, and you must
prove it.

—Aristotle

1   Most of the writing in serious magazines, in military, professional, political, scientific, and literary reports, in college term papers, and in
all other forms of nonfiction prose is composed of a mixture of definitive and generative sentences. Each composition has at its core a generative sentence that is the broadest or most complex idea in the work.
It is this sentence that gives unity and purpose to the total effort.

2   That prose literature has unity is easily seen by examining almost
any book or magazine article. Thomas Macaulay, in *The History of
England from the Accession of James II* (1849–1861), does not merely
present a vivid and detailed history of England from the reign of
James II to the death of William III; he tried to prove that England
under the influence of a Whig government and the Protestant religion
was the best of all possible worlds. Another famous work of history,
Frederick Jackson Turner's speech at the American Historical Association's meeting in Chicago in 1893, "The Significance of the Frontier in
American History," set out to prove that America is the product of a series of developments accompanying the new type of frontier.

3   Almost invariably the central idea is expressly stated. The monumental *Main Currents in American Thought*, by Vernon L. Parrington,
contains in its introduction this sentence:

> I have undertaken to give some account of the genesis and develop-
> ment in American letters of certain germinal ideas that have come to
> be reckoned traditionally American—how they came into being
> here, how they were exposed, and what influence they have exerted
> in determining the form and scope of our characteristic ideals and
> institutions.

4   This is Professor Parrington's purpose statement; it controls the
entire work. The work is divided into three volumes, and each volume
is broken into books. Part One of the first book in Volume I is called
"The Puritan Heritage." Preceding it is a brief introduction that ends
with the book's thesis or generative statement: "The Puritan was a
contribution of the old world, created by the rugged idealism of the
English Reformation; the Yankee was a product of native conditions,
created by practical economics."

5   Thorstein Veblen's *The Theory of the Leisure Class* (1899) attempts
to prove that the leisure class represents a continuing maladjustment
of modern institutions that causes a reversion to an archaic scheme
of life. He expresses this idea in a thesis sentence in the first chapter of
his work.

6   Shorter prose literature also has the characteristic of stating the
central idea. Francis Bacon's essay "Of Studies" begins, "Studies
serve for delight, for ornament, and for ability," thus giving the
reader cause to anticipate three reasons why study is valuable. "The
Method of Scientific Investigation," an essay by Thomas Henry Huxley, contains in its introduction the sentence, "The method of scientific investigation is nothing but the expression of the necessary
mode of working of the human mind"; the rest of the essay describes
the scientific method and shows why the human mind must use the
method to arrive at sound ideas. In an article in the *Saturday Evening
Post* (July 13, 1957), a testy English baron, Lord Conesford, put his
thesis in his title, "You Americans Are Murdering the Language," and
you can anticipate what followed. In a *New Yorker* article (December
16, 1950), John Hersey wrote, "This conference caused frightful
headlines all over the world about the possible use of the atomic
bomb in Korea and China, and it also provided a hair-raising example
of how bad news can be manufactured." Hersey's statement is another example of the generative sentence that predicts and obligates
the rest of the article.

7   This characteristic of good writing is known to skilled readers.
According to Mortimer Adler and almost every other reading expert,
the first requirement of effective reading is that you must be able to
put in a single sentence the central message or thesis of the material
you are reading. Very often, when skilled students read a book, they
underline certain passages. This is a good technique—if the proper

sections are selected. Too often, students underline only the sections they find interesting. The single sentence that should be underlined is the thesis or purpose statement of the book, its generative sentence. Almost every author, either in the introduction, the first chapter, or the final chapter, sums up his central idea. When you locate the sentence you aid comprehension. Take, for instance, the very difficult *Education of Henry Adams*. Many readers start out with Chapter 1; instead, they should begin with the preface, for in it are found these two sentences: "Except in the abandoned sphere of dead languages, no one has discussed what part of education has, in his personal experience, turned out to be useful, and what not. This volume attempts to discuss it." From these sentences the reader has a frame on which to hang all subsequent material. Reviewers frequently have misunderstood Adams's purpose; in spite of its title, they have perceived his book to be an autobiography and have criticized it because it makes no reference to such personal matters as his marriage and the suicide of his wife.

8   As Walter Pater has said, one of the delights of reading worthwhile prose is to detect the point of the composition, and then to follow an orderly mind through the content that must follow. If the thesis is not established and the content does not fulfill its obligation, we do not have effective, valuable writing.

(916 words)

VOCABULARY

definitive (1)	expressly (3)	idealism (4)
generative (1)	monumental (3)	reversion (5)
accession (2)	genesis (3)	mode (6)
Whig (2)	germinal (3)	

THE FACTS

1. What synonym do the authors use for *thesis?*

2. According to the authors, what is the purpose of a thesis?

3. What did Thomas Macaulay try to prove in *The History of England from the Accession of James II* (1849–1861)?

4. What, according to Mortimer Adler and other reading experts, is the first requirement of effective reading?

5. What mistake do student readers often make when they underline sections of a book?

THE STRATEGIES

1. What is the thesis of this essay and where is it to be found?

2. What technique do Crosby and Estey mainly use to prove their own thesis?

3. What do the authors accomplish by referring to Mortimer Adler in paragraph 7?

4. What two words in the first paragraph require defining before this essay can be understood?

THE ISSUES

1. What is a definitive sentence? What is a generative sentence?

2. The essay alludes to an article titled "You Americans Are Murdering the Language," written by an English baron. This charge has been made repeatedly against Americans by the English. What is your opinion of this charge? How can anyone murder a language?

3. What part of your own education in English so far have you found most valuable? What part least valuable?

4. Crosby and Estey quote Walter Pater on the delights of reading worthwhile prose. What delights have you discovered from your own reading?

SUGGESTIONS FOR WRITING

1. Locate and copy down the thesis of at least three books in the library. This thesis must be stated expressly in one sentence. Follow Crosby and Estey's suggestion of checking the preface or introduction in each book.

2. Using any article from this book, supply the following: (a) a thesis, (b) a controlling question as thesis, (c) a statement of purpose as thesis.

E X A M P L E S

▼▼▼

Roxanne Roberts

THE GRIEVING NEVER ENDS

ROXANNE ROBERTS is an American journalist who occasionally writes for the *Los Angeles Times.*

This essay alerts us to the truth about suicide: It is not the last word in an argument; rather, its painful results can cause lifelong, deep scars on those left behind.

1   The blood was like Jell-O. That is what blood gets like, after you die, before they tidy up. Somehow, I had expected it would be gone. The police and coroner spent more than an hour behind the closed door; surely it was someone's job to clean it up. But when they left, it still covered the kitchen floor like the glazing on a candy apple.

2   You couldn't mop it. You needed a dustpan and a bucket.

3   I got on my knees, slid the pan against the linoleum and lifted chunks to the bucket. It took hours to clean it all up.

4   It wasn't until I finally stood up that I noticed the pictures from his wallet. The wooden breadboard had been pulled out slightly, and four photographs were spilled across it. "Now what?" I thought with annoyance. "What were the police looking for?"

5   But then it hit me. The police hadn't done it. These snapshots—one of my mother, one of our dog and two of my brother and me—had been carefully set out in a row by my father.

6   It was his penultimate act, just before he knelt on the floor, put the barrel of a .22 rifle in his mouth, and squeezed the trigger.

7   He was 46 years old. I was 21. It has been 20 years since his death and I am still cleaning up.

8   By the time you finish this article, another person in the United States will have killed himself. More than 30,000 people do it every year, one every 15 minutes. My father's was a textbook case: Depressed white male with gun offs himself in May. December may be the loneliest month, April the cruelest, but May is the peak time for suicide. No one knows why, but I can guess: You've made it through another winter, but your world is no warmer.

9   This year, thousands of families will begin the process that ours began that night 20 years ago. Studies show that their grief will be

more complicated, more intense and longer lasting than for any other form of death in the family. They will receive less support and more blame from others. Some will never really get over it: Children of suicides become a higher risk for suicide themselves.

10   These are the legacies of suicide: guilt, anger, doubt, blame, fear, rejection, abandonment and profound grieving.

11   Shortly after he died, I remember thinking, "I wonder how I'll feel about this in 20 years?"

12   Twenty years later, my father's suicide is, simply, a part of me. Think of your life as a can of white paint. Each significant experience adds a tiny drop of color: pink for a birthday, yellow for a good report card. Worries are brown; setbacks, gray. Lavender—my favorite color when I was a little girl—is for a pretty new dress. Over time, a color begins to emerge. Your personality.

13   When a suicide happens, someone hurls in a huge glob of red. You can't get it out. You can't start over. The red will always be there, no matter how many drops of yellow you add.

14   The call came about 9 P.M. It was a Friday night in suburban Minneapolis; the restaurant was packed. I was racing from the bar with a tray of drinks for my customers when the manager gestured me to the phone. It's your mother, she said.

15   "Roxanne, he's got a gun. He's in the garage with a gun. You have to come."

16   There had been many, many threats. This was different. There had never been a weapon before.

17   I made many choices that night; some were smart, some stupid, some crazy. I believed my father would indeed kill himself, sooner or later. Looking back, I feel lucky to have survived the night.

18   I drove past the house. He was standing in the shadows of the frontyard; I couldn't see if he had the gun. I sped to a phone booth two blocks away and dialed.

19   She answered. "He's in the front yard," I said. "Can you get out?"

20   Five minutes later, she walked up to the car. He was quiet now, she said. She told him she was going to talk to me but would be back. Then she dropped the bombshell: He had held her at gunpoint for two hours before she called me.

21   We attempted rational conversation. We came to what seemed, at the time, a rational decision. We pulled up to the house, and my father came out the front door without the gun. He wanted to talk.

22   Give me the gun, I said. He refused. We can't talk until the gun is gone, we said. He shook his head. Come inside, he asked my mother. She shook her head.

23   He went back in, we drove to a coffee shop nearby. Frantic, we debated what to do next. To this day, I am still astonished that it never occurred to us to get help.

24   It was almost midnight; exhausted, my mother wanted to go home. She would stay the night if he let me take the gun away.

25   The house was silent; the door to the kitchen was shut. Ominous. My mother reached it first. Opened it.

26   "He did it," she whispered and slumped against the wall.

27   There was a time when suicide was considered a noble act of noble men. There was a time when corpses of suicides were dragged through the streets, refused Christian burial, and all the family's worldly goods were seized by the state. There was a time when romantics embraced suicide as a sign of their sensitivity.

28   Now we have long, impassioned debates about "assisted suicide," which pales beside the much larger issue: How do we feel about suicides when there isn't a terminal disease and a supportive family on hand? How do we feel about suicide if a 46-year-old guy just doesn't want to live anymore?

29   How do we feel about someone who's depressed but won't get help? Who blames all his problems on someone else? Who emotionally terrorizes and blackmails the people he loves? Is that OK too?

30   This is what I will tell you: Suicide is the last word in an argument, maybe an argument you never knew you were having. It is meant to be the last scene of the last act of life. Curtain down. End of story.

31   Except it isn't.

32   Tosca jumps off the parapet and I wonder who finds the shattered body. Romeo and Juliet die with a kiss, and I grieve for their parents.

33   The calls began: first to my father's only brother, who lived three blocks away, then to the police. Officers arrived, then detectives and someone from the coroner's office. Someone came into the living room to ask questions. I answered. Yes, he was depressed. Yes, he had threatened suicide. No, there wasn't a note.

34   This was the night of my brother Mike's high school senior prom. The dance was on a boat—we didn't know where—then there was an all-night party and a picnic the next day.

35   The detectives were still in the kitchen when Mike's car turned slowly onto the street and found a sea of police cars, lights flashing.

36   I watched from the front step as my mother ran to him. "Your father shot himself and he's dead," she said, guiding him to the neighbor's house. I watched as the police took the body out, dripping thick drops of blood. I watched my uncle stare blankly when I asked him to help clean up the kitchen.

37   White-lipped, he watched as I scooped up buckets of blood and flushed them down the toilet. I threw him an old sheet and told him to start wiping.

38   Years later, I learned how angry I made him, how he never forgave me for making me do that.

39   I was alone in the kitchen again when I noticed the pictures from my father's wallet. There were two portraits of his children. He loved both pictures. Everybody knew Mike Roberts loved his kids. So why ruin his son's prom night?

40   "You selfish bastard," I thought.

41   "You couldn't have waited one more night?"

42   My mother was never well liked by my father's sisters, and so they concluded that what had happened was my mother's fault. She was having an affair. That's what my father had told them before he died. The fact that she wore an aqua suit to the funeral was proof, wasn't it? (My mother swears there was no affair.)

43   And I? I was on her side. So it was my fault too.

44   After the funeral, we were simply abandoned by my father's family. My mother was still numb, but I was confused and angry. No calls, no help, no kindness. There were no invitations to dinner, not even Thanksgiving or Christmas.

45   Two years later, I found out why: They thought my mother and I killed him.

46   At one of those little get-togethers just after he died, my father's family decided that perhaps my mother and I had cleverly managed to murder my father and make it look like a suicide.

47   A cousin was so skeptical he went to the coroner and asked to see police photos. It was a suicide, the coroner assured him.

48   I vowed never, ever to speak to any of them again. When a distant member of the family—a devoted wife and mother—found her husband dead, sucking the end of an exhaust pipe, I was almost glad.

49   "Good," I thought fiercely. "Now they'll understand that suicide happens in nice families too."

50   Second-guessing is the devil's game, for there are no answers and infinite questions. But it is an inevitable, inescapable refrain, like a bad song you can't get out of your mind. What if, what if, what if. What if we had forced him to get help? Had him committed? What if we had called the police that night? Why didn't we?

51   Part of it was the natural tendency toward privacy. Part of it was arrogance, believing that we knew father best, or at least we could handle whatever he threw at us. I think I knew my father would have charmed the police, sent them away, leaving him furious with me, furious with my mother, dangerous, armed.

52   Maybe that's why. Maybe it was fear. Maybe not. Maybe I wanted him to die.

53   The police were puzzled by a wand of black mascara they found in my father's pocket. Another woman? Proof of an affair? The answer was simple: He used it to touch up the gray on his temples.

54   I don't think he ever really expected to get old. He was the baby, the youngest of five children. He was a very happy child; it was adulthood that he could never quite grasp.

55   He was charming enough to talk his way into job after job. There was the real estate phase, the radio phase, the political hanger-on phase. (In one photo, he is shaking hands with Hubert Humphrey.) No job lasted long; it never occurred to him to do heavy lifting.

56   Things started out well enough: a beautiful teenage bride, two kids and—after his mother died—his childhood home, a little bungalow, to raise his family in.

57   When did things start falling apart? Or were they ever really together?

58   I remember a night when I was 11. One of our cats streaked across the living room. In his mouth was a hamster that had somehow escaped from its cage. We all jumped to the rescue; my father caught the cat at the top of the basement stairs. He was suddenly, unaccountably livid. He shook the cat, and the hamster fell to the floor and scampered free.

59   I will never forget what came next: With all his might, he threw the cat down the stairs.

60   There was a moment of stunned silence, then tears and regret and an emergency trip to the vet. The cat lived. But I think I never fully trusted my father again.

61   The 10 years that followed were filled with sudden rages, explosions. I found out later that he first hit my mother when she was pregnant with me, and continued on and off for two decades.

62   We begged him to get help. We asked his brother and sisters to talk to him. And when, ultimately, I told my mother I thought she needed to leave for her own safety, my father saw that as a betrayal. He didn't speak to me for two months, until the night he died.

63   I lied to the police.

64   I told them there was no suicide note. In fact, there were three. Two were waiting in the living room as we walked into the house.

65   The note to my mother begged for forgiveness but said he simply could not go on the way things were. She has, to this day, no memory of reading it.

66   The note addressed to me opened with a rapprochement. "All is forgiven," read the first line. My eyes filled. No, I said silently, all is not forgiven.

67   The rest of the note instructed me to take care of things.

68   When I went to call the police, I found the third note, addressed to my brother. I cannot recall the specific words, but the short message to an 18-year-old boy was this: Son, you can't trust women.

69   My father had asked me to take care of things. And I was going to take care of things.

70   I stuffed all three notes in my purse and went back out to the living room. A week later, I ripped them to pieces and flushed them down the toilet.

71   When I recently told my brother about this, he was angry and hurt. He asked, quietly, "What made you think you could take something Dad left for me?" Fair question.

72   Here is the answer, Mike. It is simple. I hope you can live with it: I had to. The wishes of the dead do not take precedence over the needs of the living.

73   About a year after my father died, I left Minneapolis. I stumbled through my 20s, met a terrific man and got married, and spent a lot of time thinking about what I wanted to be when I grew up.

74   Nine months after the funeral, my brother moved to California. He was reckless, strong, adrift and almost died three times—once in a motorcycle accident, once in a stabbing and once in a heedless dive into a pool that split open his skull. He returned to Minnesota, subdued and gentle, and went on to a successful computer career. He was, surprisingly, never angry at my father or his family.

75   But he cannot bring himself to marry his girlfriend of 16 years. They live together, in a home they bought together, but he simply does not trust marriage.

76   Two years after the suicide, my mother remarried, changing her friends, her religion, even her first name. She was widowed again—a heart attack—and announced a year later that she was getting married again. Her fiancé was my cousin—her nephew by marriage. He was the son of the aunt who had accused us of murder.

77   "I expect you to be civil to her," my mother told me.

78   We had an ugly fight, and my mother didn't speak to me for months. I went to her wedding but fled to the other side of the room when my aunt approached me.

79   My mother tells me my aunt is very hurt by all this. The cycle continues, in ways I will never fully understand.

80   Four years ago, when my son was a month old, I took him to Minnesota to meet my family.

81   "Take me to Father's grave," I told my brother.

82   It was the first time I'd been there since the funeral. I introduced my beautiful new baby to his grandfather, and my father to his only grandchild.

83   Today, when I stare at the boy who takes my breath away, I think about how much my father missed over the past 20 years, and how much more he will miss. I've more sorrow than anger now.

84   A lot of wonderful things have happened in those years, hundreds of shimmering droplets added to the mix. When I stir the paint now, it

is a soft dusky rose. A grownup's color, with a touch of sweetness and a touch of melancholy.

(3,013 words)

VOCABULARY

coroner (1)	legacies (8)	wand (51)
penultimate (4)	Ominous (21)	rapprochement (63)

THE FACTS

1. What did the author discover from her father's wallet?

2. How many people commit suicide annually in the United States?

3. When the author drove past the house after her mother called, what did she see?

4. Where was the author's brother, Mike, when the father committed suicide?

5. Whom did the father's relatives blame for the suicide?

THE STRATEGIES

1. What is the thesis of the essay? Write it in one sentence consisting of your own words.

2. Every once in a while the author interrupts the story of the father's suicide with commentary about suicide in general. Why do you think the author does this? Does the technique appeal to you? Why or why not?

3. How important is the reference to "assisted suicide" in paragraph 26? What, if anything, does it add to the development of the author's thesis?

4. What figurative language does the author use in her essay? Point out at least one simile and one metaphor. Do you consider these images effective? Give reasons for your answer.

5. How effective is the author's strategy of relating her father's suicide from her own "I" point of view? What does it add to the essay?

THE ISSUES

1. What is the purpose of this essay on the gloomy subject of suicide? Do you agree or disagree with its purpose?

2. What does the author mean when she says, "He was 46 years old. I was 21. It has been 20 years since his death and I am still cleaning up"?

3. The author refers to the fact that in the past suicide was considered a noble act, a sinful act, or a romantic act (see paragraph 25). How do you view suicide today? Should your view be embraced by everyone? Give reasons for your answer.

4. What consequences of the father's suicide seem the worst?

5. What do you think was the basic cause of the father's suicide?

SUGGESTIONS FOR WRITING

1. Choose one of the following topics and develop a thesis-oriented essay:
   a. Suicide as an act of desperation
   b. Suicide as an act of selfishness

2. Write an essay about the consequences of a suicide with which you are familiar.

▼▼

Flannery O'Connor

A GOOD MAN IS HARD TO FIND

FLANNERY O'CONNOR (1925–1964) was a Christian humanist writer and a member of the so-called southern renaissance in American literature. She was born in Savannah, Georgia, and educated at the Woman's College of Georgia and the State University of Iowa. Her best-known stories, written from an orthodox Catholic perspective, are contained in *A Good Man Is Hard to Find and Other Stories* (1953) and *Everything That Rises Must Converge* (1956).

We do not usually think of a story as having a thesis, but we almost always think of a story as having a point. The point of this story—its thesis—is hinted at in its title, from which it proceeds with grim, irresistible logic.

1   The grandmother didn't want to go to Florida. She wanted to visit some of her connections in east Tennessee and she was seizing at every chance to change Bailey's mind. Bailey was the son she lived with, her only boy. He was sitting on the edge of his chair at the table, bent over the orange sports section of the *Journal.* "Now look here, Bailey," she

said, "see here, read this," and she stood with one hand on her thin hip and the other rattling the newspaper at his bald head. "Here this fellow that calls himself The Misfit is aloose from the Federal Pen and headed toward Florida and you read here what it says he did to these people. Just you read it. I wouldn't take my children in any direction with a criminal like that aloose in it. I couldn't answer to my conscience if I did."

2   Bailey didn't look up from his reading so she wheeled around then and faced the children's mother, a young woman in slacks, whose face was as broad and innocent as a cabbage and was tied around with a green headkerchief that had two points on the top like a rabbit's ears. She was sitting on the sofa, feeding the baby his apricots out of a jar. "The children have been to Florida before," the old lady said. "You all ought to take them somewhere else for a change so they would see different parts of the world and be broad. They never have been to east Tennessee."

3   The children's mother didn't seem to hear her but the eight-year-old boy, John Wesley, a stocky child with glasses, said, "If you don't want to go to Florida, why dontcha stay at home?" He and the little girl, June Star, were reading the funny papers on the floor.

4   "She wouldn't stay at home to be queen for a day," June Star said without raising her yellow head.

5   "Yes and what would you do if this fellow, The Misfit, caught you?" the grandmother asked.

6   "I'd smack his face," John Wesley said.

7   "She wouldn't stay at home for a million bucks," June Star said. "Afraid she'd miss something. She has to go everywhere we go."

8   "All right, Miss," the grandmother said. "Just remember that the next time you want me to curl your hair."

9   June Star said her hair was naturally curly.

10   The next morning the grandmother was the first one in the car, ready to go. She had her big black valise that looked like the head of a hippopotamus in one corner, and underneath it she was hiding a basket with Pitty Sing, the cat, in it. She didn't intend for the cat to be left alone in the house for three days because he would miss her too much and she was afraid he might brush against one of the gas burners and accidentally asphyxiate himself. Her son, Bailey, didn't like to arrive at a motel with a cat.

11   She sat in the middle of the back seat with John Wesley and June Star on either side of her. Bailey and the children's mother and the baby sat in front and they left Atlanta at eight forty-five with the mileage on the car at 55890. The grandmother wrote this down because she thought it would be interesting to say how many miles they had been when they got back. It took them twenty minutes to reach the outskirts of the city.

12   The old lady settled herself comfortably, removing her white cotton gloves and putting them up with her purse on the shelf in front of the back window. The children's mother still had on slacks and still had her head tied up in a green kerchief, but the grandmother had on a navy blue straw sailor hat with a bunch of white violets on the brim and a navy blue dress with a small white dot in the print. Her collars and cuffs were white organdy trimmed with lace and at her neckline she had pinned a purple spray of cloth violets containing a sachet. In case of an accident, anyone seeing her dead on the highway would know at once that she was a lady.

13   She said she thought it was going to be a good day for driving, neither too hot nor too cold, and she cautioned Bailey that the speed limit was fifty-five miles an hour and that the patrolmen hid themselves behind billboards and small clumps of trees and sped out after you before you had a chance to slow down. She pointed out interesting details of the scenery: Stone Mountain; the blue granite that in some places came up to both sides of the highway; the brilliant red clay banks slightly streaked with purple; and the various crops that made rows of green lace-work on the ground. The trees were full of silver-white sunlight and the meanest of them sparkled. The children were reading comic magazines and their mother had gone back to sleep.

14   "Let's go through Georgia fast so we won't have to look at it much," John Wesley said.

15   "If I were a little boy," said the grandmother, "I wouldn't talk about my native state that way. Tennessee has the mountains and Georgia has the hills."

16   "Tennessee is just a hillbilly dumping ground," John Wesley said, "and Georgia is a lousy state too."

17   "You said it," June Star said.

18   "In my time," said the grandmother, folding her thin veined fingers, "children were more respectful of their native states and their parents and everything else. People did right then. Oh look at the cute little pickaninny!" she said and pointed to a Negro child standing in the door of a shack. "Wouldn't that make a picture, now?" she asked and they all turned and looked at the little Negro out of the back window. He waved.

19   "He didn't have any britches on," June Star said.

20   "He probably didn't have any," the grandmother explained. "Little niggers in the country don't have things like we do. If I could paint, I'd paint that picture," she said.

21   The children exchanged comic books.

22   The grandmother offered to hold the baby and the children's mother passed him over the front seat to her. She sat him on her knee and bounced him and told him about the things they were passing. She

rolled her eyes and screwed up her mouth and stuck her leathery thin face into his smooth bland one. Occasionally he gave her a faraway smile. They passed a large cotton field with five or six graves fenced in the middle of it, like a small island. "Look at the graveyard!" the grandmother said, pointing it out. "That was the old family burying ground. That belonged to the plantation."

23   "Where's the plantation?" John Wesley asked.

24   "Gone With the Wind," said the grandmother. "Ha. Ha."

25   When the children finished all the comic books they had brought, they opened the lunch and ate it. The grandmother ate a peanut butter sandwich and an olive and would not let the children throw the box and the paper napkins out the window. When there was nothing else to do they played a game by choosing a cloud and making the other two guess what shape it suggested. John Wesley took one the shape of a cow and June Star guessed a cow and John Wesley said, no, an automobile, and June Star said he didn't play fair, and they began to slap each other over the grandmother.

26   The grandmother said she would tell them a story if they would keep quiet. When she told a story, she rolled her eyes and waved her head and was very dramatic. She said once when she was a maiden lady she had been courted by a Mr. Edgar Atkins Teagarden from Jasper, Georgia. She said he was a very good-looking man and a gentleman and that he brought her a watermelon every Saturday afternoon with his initials cut in it, E. A. T. Well, one Saturday, she said, Mr. Teagarden brought the watermelon and there was nobody at home and he left it on the front porch and returned in his buggy to Jasper, but she never got the watermelon, she said, because a nigger boy ate it when he saw the initials, E. A. T.! This story tickled John Wesley's funny bone and he giggled and giggled but June Star didn't think it was any good. She said she wouldn't marry a man that just brought her a watermelon on Saturday. The grandmother said she would have done well to marry Mr. Teagarden because he was a gentleman and had bought Coca-Cola stock when it first came out and that he had died only a few years ago, a very wealthy man.

27   They stopped at The Tower for barbecued sandwiches. The Tower was a part stucco and part wood filling station and dance hall set in a clearing outside of Timothy. A fat man named Red Sammy Butts ran it and there were signs stuck here and there on the building and for miles up and down the highway saying, TRY RED SAMMY'S FAMOUS BARBECUE. NONE LIKE FAMOUS RED SAMMY'S! RED SAM! THE FAT BOY WITH THE HAPPY LAUGH! A VETERAN! RED SAMMY'S YOUR MAN!

28   Red Sammy was lying on the bare ground outside The Tower with his head under a truck while a gray monkey about a foot high, chained

to a small chinaberry tree, chattered nearby. The monkey sprang back into the tree and got on the highest limb as soon as he saw the children jump out of the car and run toward him.

29   Inside, The Tower was a long dark room with a counter at one end and tables at the other and dancing space in the middle. They all sat down at a board table next to the nickelodeon and Red Sam's wife, a tall burnt-brown woman with hair and eyes lighter than her skin, came and took their order. The children's mother put a dime in the machine and played "The Tennessee Waltz," and the grandmother said that tune always made her want to dance. She asked Bailey if he would like to dance but he only glared at her. He didn't have a naturally sunny disposition like she did and trips made him nervous. The grandmother's brown eyes were very bright. She swayed her head from side to side and pretended she was dancing in her chair. June Star said play something she could tap to so the children's mother put in another dime and played a fast number and June Star stepped out onto the dance floor and did her tap routine.

30   "Ain't she cute?" Red Sam's wife said, leaning over the counter. "Would you like to come be my little girl?"

31   "No I certainly wouldn't," June Star said. "I wouldn't live in a broken-down place like this for a million bucks!" and she ran back to the table.

32   "Ain't she cute?" the woman repeated, stretching her mouth politely.

33   "Aren't you ashamed?" hissed the grandmother.

34   Red Sam came in and told his wife to quit lounging on the counter and hurry up with these people's order. His khaki trousers reached just to his hip bones and his stomach hung over them like a sack of meal swaying under his shirt. He came over and sat down at a table nearby and let out a combination sigh and yodel. "You can't win," he said. "You can't win," and he wiped his sweating red face off with a gray handkerchief. "These days you don't know who to trust," he said. "Ain't that the truth?"

35   "People are certainly not nice like they used to be," said the grandmother.

36   "Two fellers come in here last week," Red Sammy said, "driving a Chrysler. It was a old beat-up car but it was a good one and these boys looked all right to me. Said they worked at the mill and you know I let them fellers charge the gas they bought? Now why did I do that?"

37   "Because you're a good man!" the grandmother said at once.

38   "Yes'm, I suppose so," Red Sam said as if he were struck with this answer.

39   His wife brought the orders, carrying the five plates all at once without a tray, two in each hand and one balanced on her arm. "It isn't

a soul in this green world of God's that you can trust," she said. "And I don't count nobody out of that, not nobody," she repeated, looking at Red Sammy.

40   "Did you read about that criminal, The Misfit, that's escaped?" asked the grandmother.

41   "I wouldn't be a bit surprised if he didn't attact this place right here," said the woman. "If he hears about it being here, I wouldn't be none surprised to see him. If he hears it's two cent in the cash register, I wouldn't be a tall surprised if he . . . "

42   "That'll do," Red Sam said, "Go bring these people their Co'-Colas," and the woman went off to get the rest of the order.

43   "A good man is hard to find," Red Sammy said. "Everything is getting terrible. I remember the day you could go off and leave your screen door unlatched. Not no more."

44   He and the grandmother discussed better times. The old lady said that in her opinion Europe was entirely to blame for the way things were now. She said the way Europe acted you would think we were made of money and Red Sam said it was no use talking about it, she was exactly right. The children ran outside into the white sunlight and looked at the monkey in the lacy chinaberry tree. He was busy catching fleas on himself and biting each one carefully between his teeth as if it were a delicacy.

45   They drove off again into the hot afternoon. The grandmother took cat naps and woke up every few minutes with her own snoring. Outside of Toombsboro she woke up and recalled an old plantation that she had visited in this neighborhood once when she was a young lady. She said the house had six white columns across the front and that there was an avenue of oaks leading up to it and two little wooden trellis arbors on each side in front where you sat down with your suitor after a stroll in the garden. She recalled exactly which road to turn off to get to it. She knew that Bailey would not be willing to lose any time looking at an old house, but the more she talked about it, the more she wanted to see it once again and find out if the little twin arbors were still standing. "There was a secret panel in this house," she said craftily, not telling the truth but wishing that she were, "and the story went that all the family silver was hidden in it when Sherman came through but it was never found . . . "

46   "Hey!" John Wesley said. "Let's go see it! We'll find it! We'll poke all the woodwork and find it! Who lives there? Where do you turn off at? Hey Pop, can't we turn off there?"

47   "We never have seen a house with a secret panel!" June Star shrieked. "Let's go to the house with the secret panel! Hey Pop, can't we go see the house with the secret panel!"

48   "It's not far from here, I know," the grandmother said. "It wouldn't take over twenty minutes."

49   Bailey was looking straight ahead. His jaw was as rigid as a horse-shoe. "No," he said.

50   The children began to yell and scream that they wanted to see the house with the secret panel. John Wesley kicked the back of the front seat and June Star hung over her mother's shoulder and whined desperately into her ear that they never had any fun even on their vacation, that they could never do what *THEY* wanted to do. The baby began to scream and John Wesley kicked the back of the seat so hard that his father could feel the blows in his kidney.

51   "All right!" he shouted and drew the car to a stop at the side of the road. "Will you all shut up? Will you all just shut up for one second? If you don't shut up, we won't go anywhere."

52   "It would be very educational for them," the grandmother murmured.

53   "All right," Bailey said, "but get this: This is the only time we're going to stop for anything like this. This is the one and only time."

54   "The dirt road that you have to turn down is about a mile back," the grandmother directed. "I marked it when we passed."

55   "A dirt road," Bailey groaned.

56   After they had turned around and were headed toward the dirt road, the grandmother recalled other points about the house, the beautiful glass over the front doorway and the candle-lamp in the hall. John Wesley said that the secret panel was probably in the fireplace.

57   "You can't go inside this house," Bailey said. "You don't know who lives there."

58   "While you all talk to the people in front, I'll run around behind and get in a window," John Wesley suggested.

59   "We'll all stay in the car," his mother said.

60   They turned onto the dirt road and the car raced roughly along in a swirl of pink dust. The grandmother recalled the times when there were no paved roads and thirty miles was a day's journey. The dirt road was hilly and there were sudden washes in it and sharp curves on dangerous embankments. All at once they would be on a hill, looking down over the blue tops of trees for miles around, then the next minute, they would be in a red depression with the dust-coated trees looking down on them.

61   "This place had better turn up in a minute," Bailey said, "or I'm going to turn around."

62   The road looked as if no one had traveled on it in months.

63   "It's not much farther," the grandmother said and just as she said it, a horrible thought came to her. The thought was so embarrassing that she turned red in the face and her eyes dilated and her feet jumped up, upsetting her valise in the corner. The instant the valise moved, the newspaper top she had over the basket under it rose with a snarl and Pitty Sing, the cat, sprang onto Bailey's shoulder.

64   The children were thrown to the floor and their mother, clutching the baby, was thrown out the door onto the ground; the old lady was thrown into the front seat. The car turned over once and landed right-side-up in a gulch off the side of the road. Bailey remained in the driver's seat with the cat—gray-striped with a broad white face and an orange nose—clinging to his neck like a caterpillar.

65   As soon as the children saw they could move their arms and legs, they scrambled out of the car, shouting, "We've had an *ACCIDENT!*" The grandmother was curled up under the dashboard, hoping she was injured so that Bailey's wrath would not come down on her all at once. The horrible thought she had had before the accident was that the house she had remembered so vividly was not in Georgia but in Tennessee.

66   Bailey removed the cat from his neck with both hands and flung it out the window against the side of a pine tree. Then he got out of the car and started looking for the children's mother. She was sitting against the side of the red gutted ditch, holding the screaming baby, but she only had a cut down her face and a broken shoulder. "We've had an *ACCIDENT!*" the children screamed in a frenzy of delight.

67   "But nobody's killed," June Star said with disappointment as the grandmother limped out of the car, her hat still pinned to her head but the broken front brim standing up at a jaunty angle and the violet spray hanging off the side. They all sat down in the ditch, except the children, to recover from the shock. They were all shaking.

68   "Maybe a car will come along," said the children's mother hoarsely.

69   "I believe I have injured an organ," said the grandmother, pressing her side, but no one answered her. Bailey's teeth were clattering. He had on a yellow sport shirt with bright blue parrots designed in it and his face was as yellow as the shirt. The grandmother decided that she would not mention that the house was in Tennessee.

70   The road was about ten feet above and they could see only the tops of the trees on the other side of it. Behind the ditch they were sitting in there were more woods, tall and dark and deep. In a few minutes they saw a car some distance away on top of a hill, coming slowly as if the occupants were watching them. The grandmother stood up and waved both arms dramatically to attract their attention. The car continued to come on slowly, disappeared around a bend and appeared again, moving even slower, on top of the hill they had gone over. It was a big black battered hearselike automobile. There were three men in it.

71   It came to a stop just over them and for some minutes, the driver looked down with a steady expressionless gaze to where they were sitting, and didn't speak. Then he turned his head and muttered something to the other two and they got out. One was a fat boy in black trousers and a red sweat shirt with a silver stallion embossed on the front of it. He moved around on the right side of them and stood staring, his mouth partly open in a kind of loose grin. The other had on

khaki pants and a blue striped coat and a gray hat pulled down very low, hiding most of his face. He came around slowly on the left side. Neither spoke.

72   The driver got out of the car and stood by the side of it, looking down at them. He was an older man than the other two. His hair was just beginning to gray and he wore silver-rimmed spectacles that gave him a scholarly look. He had a long creased face and didn't have on any shirt or undershirt. He had on blue jeans that were too tight for him and was holding a black hat and a gun. The two boys also had guns.

73   "We've had an *ACCIDENT!*" the children screamed.

74   The grandmother had the peculiar feeling that the bespectacled man was someone she knew. His face was as familiar to her as if she had known him all her life but she could not recall who he was. He moved away from the car and began to come down the embankment, placing his feet carefully so that he wouldn't slip. He had on tan and white shoes and no socks, and his ankles were red and thin. "Good afternoon," he said. "I see you all had you a little spill."

75   "We turned over twice!" said the grandmother.

76   "Oncet," he corrected. "We seen it happen. Try their car and see will it run, Hiram," he said quietly to the boy with the gray hat.

77   "What you got that gun for?" John Wesley asked. "Whatcha gonna do with that gun?"

78   "Lady," the man said to the children's mother, "would you mind calling them children to sit down by you? Children make me nervous. I want all you all to sit down right together there where you're at."

79   "What are you telling us what to do for?" June Star asked.

80   Behind them the line of woods gaped like a dark open mouth. "Come here," said their mother.

81   "Look here now," Bailey began suddenly, "we're in a predicament! We're in . . . "

82   The grandmother shrieked. She scrambled to her feet and stood staring. "You're The Misfit!" she said, "I recognized you at once!"

83   "Yes'm," the man said, smiling slightly as if he were pleased in spite of himself to be known, "but it would have been better for all of you, lady, if you hadn't of reckernized me."

84   Bailey turned his head sharply and said something to his mother that shocked even the children. The old lady began to cry and The Misfit reddened.

85   "Lady," he said, "don't you get upset. Sometimes a man says things he don't mean. I don't reckon he meant to talk to you thataway."

86   "You wouldn't shoot a lady, would you?" the grandmother said and removed a clean handkerchief from her cuff and began to slap at her eyes with it.

87   The Misfit pointed the toe of his shoe into the ground and made a little hole and then covered it up again. "I would hate to have to," he said.

88   "Listen," the grandmother almost screamed, "I know you're a good man. You don't look a bit like you have common blood. I know you must come from nice people!"

89   "Yes mam," he said, "finest people in the world." When he smiled he showed a row of strong white teeth. "God never made a finer woman than my mother and my daddy's heart was pure gold," he said. The boy with the red sweat shirt had come around behind them and was standing with his gun at his hip. The Misfit squatted down on the ground. "Watch them children, Bobby Lee," he said. "You know they make me nervous." He looked at the six of them huddled together in front of him and he seemed to be embarrassed as if he couldn't think of anything to say. "Ain't a cloud in the sky," he remarked, looking up at it. "Don't see no sun but don't see no cloud neither."

90   "Yes, it's a beautiful day," said the grandmother. "Listen," she said, "you shouldn't call yourself The Misfit because I know you're a good man at heart. I can just look at you and tell."

91   "Hush!" Bailey yelled. "Hush! Everybody shut up and let me handle this!" He was squatting in the position of a runner about to sprint forward but he didn't move.

92   "I pre-chate that, lady," The Misfit said and drew a little circle in the ground with the butt of his gun.

93   "It'll take a half a hour to fix this here car," Hiram called, looking over the raised hood of it.

94   "Well, first you and Bobby Lee get him and that little boy to step over yonder with you," The Misfit said, pointing to Bailey and John Wesley, "The boys want to ast you something," he said to Bailey. "Would you mind stepping back in them woods there with them?"

95   "Listen," Bailey began, "we're in a terrible predicament! Nobody realizes what this is," and his voice cracked. His eyes were as blue and intense as the parrots in his shirt and he remained perfectly still.

96   The grandmother reached up to adjust her hat brim as if she were going to the woods with him but it came off in her hand. She stood staring at it and after a second she let it fall on the ground. Hiram pulled Bailey up by the arm as if he were assisting an old man. John Wesley caught hold of his father's hand and Bobby Lee followed. They went off toward the woods and just as they reached the dark edge, Bailey turned and supporting himself against a gray naked pine trunk, he shouted, "I'll be back in a minute, Mamma, wait on me!"

97   "Come back this instant!" his mother shrilled but they all disappeared into the woods.

98   "Bailey Boy!" the grandmother called in a tragic voice but she found she was looking at The Misfit squatting on the ground in front of her. "I just know you're a good man," she said desperately. "You're not a bit common!"

99   "Nome, I ain't a good man," The Misfit said after a second as if he had considered her statement carefully, "But I ain't the worst in the

world neither. My daddy said I was a different breed of dog from my brothers and sisters. 'You know,' Daddy said, 'it's some that can live their whole life out without asking about it and it's others has to know why it is, and this boy is one of the latters. He's going to be into everything!'" He put on his black hat and looked up suddenly and then away deep into the woods as if he were embarrassed again. "I'm sorry I don't have on a shirt before you ladies," he said, hunching his shoulders slightly. "We buried our clothes that we had on when we escaped and we're just making do until we can get better. We borrowed these from some folks we met," he explained.

100   "That's perfectly all right," the grandmother said. "Maybe Bailey has an extra shirt in his suitcase."

101   "I'll look and see terrectly," The Misfit said.

102   "Where are they taking him?" the children's mother screamed.

103   "Daddy was a card himself," The Misfit said. "You couldn't put anything over on him. He never got in trouble with the Authorities though. Just had the knack of handling them."

104   "You could be honest too if you'd only try," said the grandmother. "Think how wonderful it would be to settle down and live a comfortable life and not have to think about somebody chasing you all the time."

105   The Misfit kept scratching in the ground with the butt of his gun as if he were thinking about it. "Yes'm, somebody is always after you," he murmured.

106   The grandmother noticed how thin his shoulder blades were just behind his hat because she was standing up looking down on him. "Do you ever pray?" she asked.

107   He shook his head. All she saw was the black hat wiggle between his shoulder blades. "Nome," he said.

108   There was a pistol shot from the woods, followed closely by another. Then silence. The old lady's head jerked around. She could hear the wind move through the tree tops like a long satisfied insuck of breath. "Bailey Boy!" she called.

109   "I was a gospel singer for a while," The Misfit said. "I been most everything. Been in the arm service, both land and sea, at home and abroad, been twicet married, been an undertaker, been with the railroads, plowed Mother Earth, been in a tornado, seen a man burnt alive oncet," and looked up at the children's mother and the little girl who were sitting close together, their faces white and their eyes glassy; "I even seen a woman flogged," he said.

110   "Pray, pray," the grandmother began, "pray, pray . . ."

111   "I never was a bad boy that I remember of," The Misfit said in an almost dreamy voice, "but somewheres along the line I done something wrong and got sent to the penitentiary. I was buried alive," and he looked up and held her attention to him by a steady stare.

112   "That's when you should have started to pray," she said. "What did you do to get sent to the penitentiary that first time?"

113   "Turn to the right, it was a wall," The Misfit said, looking up again at the cloudless sky. "Turn to the left, it was a wall. Look up it was a ceiling, look down it was a floor. I forget what I done, lady. I set there and set there, trying to remember what it was I done and I ain't recalled it to this day. Oncet in a while, I would think it was coming to me, but it never come."

114   "Maybe they put you in by mistake," the old lady said vaguely.

115   "Nome," he said. "It wasn't no mistake. They had papers on me."

116   "You must have stolen something," she said.

117   The Misfit sneered slightly. "Nobody had nothing I wanted," he said. "It was a head-doctor at the penitentiary said what I had done was kill my daddy but I known that for a lie. My daddy died in nineteen ought nineteen of the epidemic flu and I never had a thing to do with it. He was buried in the Mount Hopewell Baptist churchyard and you can go there and see for yourself."

118   "If you would pray," the old lady said, "Jesus would help you."

119   "That's right," The Misfit said.

120   "Well then, why don't you pray?" she asked trembling with delight suddenly.

121   "I don't want no hep," he said, "I'm doing all right by myself."

122   Bobby Lee and Hiram came ambling back from the woods. Bobby Lee was dragging a yellow shirt with bright blue parrots in it.

123   "Throw me that shirt, Bobby Lee," The Misfit said. The shirt came flying at him and landed on his shoulder and he put it on. The grandmother couldn't name what the shirt reminded her of. "No, lady," The Misfit said while he was buttoning it up, "I found out the crime don't matter. You can do one thing or you can do another, kill a man or take a tire off his car, because sooner or later you're going to forget what it was you done and just be punished for it."

124   The children's mother had begun to make heaving noises as if she couldn't get her breath. "Lady," he asked, "would you and that little girl like to step off yonder with Bobby Lee and Hiram and join your husband?"

125   "Yes, thank you," the mother said faintly. Her left arm dangled helplessly and she was holding the baby, who had gone to sleep, in the other. "Hep that lady up, Hiram," The Misfit said as she struggled to climb out of the ditch, "and Bobby Lee, you hold onto that little girl's hand."

126   "I don't want to hold hands with him," June Star said. "He reminds me of a pig."

127   The fat boy blushed and laughed and caught her by the arm and pulled her off into the woods after Hiram and her mother.

128   Alone with The Misfit, the grandmother found that she had lost her voice. There was not a cloud in the sky nor any sun. There was nothing

around her but woods. She wanted to tell him that he must pray. She opened and closed her mouth several times before anything came out. Finally she found herself saying, "Jesus, Jesus," meaning, Jesus will help you, but the way she was saying it, it sounded as if she might be cursing.

129   "Yes'm," The Misfit said as if he agreed, "Jesus thrown everything off balance. It was the same case with Him as with me except He hadn't committed any crime and they could prove I had committed one because they had the papers on me. Of course," he said, "they never shown me my papers. That's why I sign myself now. I said long ago, you get you a signature and sign everything you do and keep a copy of it. Then you'll know what you done and you can hold up the crime to the punishment and see do they match and in the end you'll have something to prove you ain't been treated right. I call myself The Misfit," he said, "because I can't make what all I done wrong fit what all I gone through in punishment."

130   There was a piercing scream from the woods, followed closely by a pistol report. "Does it seem right to you, lady, that one is punished a heap and another ain't punished at all?"

131   "Jesus!" the old lady cried. "You've got good blood! I know you wouldn't shoot a lady! I know you come from nice people! Pray! Jesus, you ought not to shoot a lady, I'll give you all the money I've got!"

132   "Lady," The Misfit said, looking beyond her far into the woods, "there never was a body that give the undertaker a tip."

133   There were two more pistol reports and the grandmother raised her head like a parched old turkey hen crying for water and called, "Bailey Boy, Bailey Boy!" as if her heart would break.

134   "Jesus was the only One that ever raised the dead." The Misfit continued, "and He shouldn't have done it. He thrown everything off balance. If He did what He said, then it's nothing for you to do but throw away everything and follow Him, and if He didn't, then it's nothing for you to do but enjoy the few minutes you got left the best way you can—by killing somebody or burning down his house or doing some other meanness to him. No pleasure but meanness," he said and his voice had become almost a snarl.

135   "Maybe He didn't raise the dead," the old lady mumbled, not knowing what she was saying and feeling so dizzy that she sank down in the ditch with her legs twisted under her.

136   "I wasn't there so I can't say He didn't," The Misfit said. "I wisht I had of been there," he said, hitting the ground with his fist. "It ain't right I wasn't there because if I had of been there I would of known. Listen lady," he said in a high voice, "if I had of been there I would of known and I wouldn't be like I am now." His voice seemed about to crack and the grandmother's head cleared for an instant. She saw the man's face twisted close to her own as if he were going to cry and she

murmured, "Why you're one of my babies. You're one of my own children!" She reached out and touched him on the shoulder. The Misfit sprang back as if a snake had bitten him and shot her three times through the chest. Then he put his gun down on the ground and took off his glasses and began to clean them.

137   Hiram and Bobby Lee returned from the woods and stood over the ditch, looking down at the grandmother who half sat and half lay in a puddle of blood with her legs crossed under her like a child's and her face smiling up at the cloudless sky.

138   Without his glasses, The Misfit's eyes were red-rimmed and pale and defenseless-looking. "Take her off and throw her where you thrown the others," he said, picking up the cat that was rubbing itself against his leg.

139   "She was a talker, wasn't she?" Bobby Lee said, sliding down the ditch with a yodel.

140   "She would of been a good woman," The Misfit said, "if it had been somebody there to shoot her every minute of her life."

141   "Some fun!" Bobby Lee said.

142   "Shut up, Bobby Lee," The Misfit said. "It's no real pleasure in life."

(6,471 words)

VOCABULARY

asphyxiate (10)	dilated (63)	ambling (122)
sachet (12)	jaunty (67)	parched (133)
bland (22)	embossed (71)	

THE FACTS

1. Why didn't the grandmother want to go to Florida? Where did she want to go instead?

2. Why does the family turn off onto the lonely dirt road?

3. What caused the accident?

4. For what crime was The Misfit sent to the penitentiary?

5. Why does he call himself "The Misfit"?

THE STRATEGIES

1. The Misfit is mentioned in the first paragraph. Why does O'Connor introduce him so early?

2. What does the initial dialogue between the grandmother and the children accomplish?

3. In paragraph 70 The Misfit's automobile is described as "a big black battered hearselike automobile." What is O'Connor doing in this description?

4. At a climactic part of the story, the grandmother has a sudden dramatic recognition of responsibility. When does it occur? Whom does it involve?

5. In paragraph 80 O'Connor writes: "Behind them the line of woods gaped like a dark open mouth." What does this description accomplish? What does it signal to the reader?

THE ISSUES

1. The Misfit and his cronies commit cold-blooded murder on a family of six. What prerequisite, if any, do you think must necessarily exist before a person is capable of murder? If you think no prerequisite is necessary, do you also think anyone is capable of cold-blooded murder? Justify your answer.

2. What punishment would you regard as just and fitting for The Misfit and his henchmen?

3. Some commentators have said that the children are brats, pure and simple, while others have argued that they are rather typical. What is your opinion of the children and their behavior?

4. One interpretation argues that The Misfit is the devil and the grandmother a Christian who confronts him. What is your opinion of this interpretation?

5. What do you think the grandmother meant when she said to The Misfit, "Why you're one of my babies. You're one of my own children!" Why do you think The Misfit killed her when she said that?

SUGGESTIONS FOR WRITING

1. Write an essay analyzing the techniques used by the author to foreshadow the family's fatal encounter with The Misfit. Make specific references to scenes and images and include as many quoted passages as necessary to prove your case.

2. Write an essay interpreting this story.

▼▼

Edna St. Vincent Millay

SPRING

EDNA ST. VINCENT MILLAY (1892–1950), a graduate of Vassar and one of the most popular poets of her day, lived a Bohemian life during the 1920s in Greenwich Village, New York, writing satirical columns for *Vanity Fair* under a pseudonym. Her first volume of poetry, *Renascence*, was published in 1917 to glowing praise for its vitality. Subsequent volumes include *A Few Figs from Thistle* (1920), *The Ballad of the Hat Weaver and Other Poems* (1923; Pulitzer Prize). She also wrote verse dramas, many of which were produced by the Provincetown Players. Later volumes of her work include *Fatal Interview* (1931), *Conversation at Midnight* (1937), and *Make Bright the Arrows* (1940). Her former home, "Steepletop" in Austerlitz, New York, which she shared with husband Eugan Jan Boissevain, is a Registered Historic Landmark and the center of the Edna St. Vincent Millay National Society, founded in 1978.

It is the tone of this poem that captivates because it points out cynically how the beauty of life contrasts with the ugliness of death.

     To what purpose, April, do you return again?
     Beauty is not enough.
     You can no longer quiet me with the redness
     Of little leaves opening stickily.
5   I know what I know.
     The sun is hot on my neck as I observe
     The spikes of the crocus.
     The smell of the earth is good.
     It is apparent that there is no death.
10   But what does that signify?
     Not only under ground are the brains of men
     Eaten by maggots.

     Life in itself
     Is nothing,
15   An empty cup, a flight of uncarpeted stairs,
     It is not enough that yearly, down this hill,
     April
     Comes like an idiot, babbling and strewing flowers.

(109 words)

VOCABULARY

crocus (7)
strewing (18)

THE FACTS

1. What quality does April bring with it?
2. In what way do little red leaves open "stickily"?
3. According to the author, what is just as obvious as the fact that at death the human body is eaten by maggots?
4. What keeps the author dissatisfied with spring?

THE STRATEGIES

1. The poem begins with a question. Is the question ever answered? If so, what is the answer?
2. A sharp contrast underlies the poem. What is that contrast?
3. In what way, according to Millay, are the "brains of men eaten by maggots" symbolic?
4. What metaphors and similes are used in the poem? Explain what they mean.
5. What is the tone of the poem? Is the tone appropriate for the theme?

THE ISSUES

1. What is the theme (thesis) of Millay's poem? State it in one sentence. What do you think has caused the poem to take such a position? Do you agree with it? Why or why not?
2. What is the meaning of the expression "no longer" in line 3?
3. What concrete aspects of spring please the poet? What do these aspects have in common?
4. Why does the author stress the beautiful aspects of spring?
5. Why is it not enough to experience a beautiful spring? What is your personal answer to this poem?

SUGGESTIONS FOR WRITING

1. Write an essay on spring and what it means to you.
2. Write an essay refuting Millay's comment that "Life in itself is nothing."

ISSUE FOR CRITICAL
THINKING AND DEBATE

▼▼

AGEISM

The tendency to stereotype and discriminate against the old is called *ageism*—at least, that is the meaning our essayists implicitly give the term. In a broader sense, the term can mean any discrimination based on age, including prejudice directed against the young. However, it is the old, not the young, who most often suffer the brunt of age stereotyping and prejudice. It is the old (or the middle-aged) who are routinely denied jobs because of their age, even though the practice is illegal. It is the old who, goaded by the mass media, desperately try to look younger, annually consuming tons of creams and lotions in a futile battle against wrinkles.

The painting, *My Parents*, by Henry Koerner, symbolically sums up the issue of ageism in its portrayal of two elderly people deep in a woods. Lost in thought, the man is walking on a separate path away from the woman, who sits near a tree and stares down the narrow trail that unwinds and ominously ends ahead of her. The painting—actually a portrait of Koerner's parents who were exterminated by the Nazis— reminds us that aging also brings infirmity and befuddlement to intensify the separations that occur naturally at the end of life. Koerner wrote that he spent many days walking with his parents peacefully through the woods of Vienna before World War II and that the painting was meant to commemorate that experience. Yet in this portrayal, the painting is unrepresentative of growing old today, since many of our elderly spend their last days not in an idyllic woodland, but in a grimy apartment or cheap room.

The essayists in this section address ageism from quite different perspectives. Cowley, as the title of his essay reminds us, was past eighty when he wrote the book from which this excerpt comes, and he finds philosophical consolations in growing old. He is not embittered, but a stoical, observant elder. Food tastes wonderful when you are old, he tells us; napping drowsily in the sun is blissful. On the other hand, the view from Mayra Mannes is sharp-edged and petulant. When she wrote this essay, she was facing old age, not immersed in it, and from this perspective she rails against the pressures of growing old and the futility of trying to smother the years under creams and lotions. And she is right, too, when she reminds us that a dignified beauty awaits those who gracefully accept the battle scars of aging.

Ageism, unlike other issues, will ultimately and personally affect every reader of this book who achieves life expectancy. It is an issue that is progressively becoming not only more common, but more

Henry Koerner, My Parents. *Oil on masonite, 25 × 30 inches. Copyright © Curtis Galleries, Inc., Minneapolis, MN.*

pressing. Baby Boomers are aging in numbers unprecedented in history, making America inevitably older and grayer. The median age (the most common age of the population) in 1820 was 16.7 years; by 1980 it had jumped to 30; in the 1990 Census it was 32.9 years. Today close to 15 percent of the population is over sixty-five.

  If you die young or in your middle years, you will escape the consequences of ageism. Otherwise, ageism will surely and eventually affect your life. Indeed, how you treat the elderly today when you are young might well foreshadow how the young will treat you when you yourself are numbered among the elderly.

▼▼▼

Malcolm Cowley

THE VIEW FROM EIGHTY

MALCOLM COWLEY (1898–1989), American critic and poet, was born in Belsano, Pennsylvania, and educated at Harvard. After World War I, Cowley lived abroad for many years among the so-called lost generation of writers, eventually writing about them in *Exile's Return* (1934) and *Second Flowering* (1973). He was the literary editor of *The New Republic* from 1930 to 1940 and numbers among his published works *A Dry Season* (poems, 1942); *Blue Juanita: Collected Poems* (1964); and *The View from Eighty* (1981), from which this excerpt was taken.

> The View from Eighty *is a heartening and refreshing reminder that old age does not necessarily entail the loss of literary style, vigor, and wit. Using examples to show how the aged see the world, Cowley writes with the same freshness and liveliness that have characterized all his work.*

1   Even before he or she is 80, the aging person may undergo another identity crisis like that of adolescence. Perhaps there had also been a middle-aged crisis, the male or the female menopause, but for the rest of adult life he had taken himself for granted, with his capabilities and failings. Now, when he looks in the mirror, he asks himself, "Is this really me?"—or he avoids the mirror out of distress at what it reveals, those bags and wrinkles. In his new makeup he is called upon to play a new role in a play that must be improvised. André Gide, that long-lived man of letters, wrote in his journal, "My heart has remained so young that I have the continual feeling of playing a part, the part of the 70-year-old that I certainly am; and the infirmities and weaknesses that remind me of my age act like a prompter, reminding me of my lines when I tend to stray. Then, like the good actor I want to be, I go back into my role, and I pride myself on playing it well."

2   In his new role the old person will find that he is tempted by new vices, that he receives new compensations (not so widely known), and that he may possibly achieve new virtues. Chief among these is the heroic or merely obstinate refusal to surrender in the face of time. One admires the ships that go down with all flags flying and the captain on the bridge.

3   Among the vices of age are avarice, untidiness, and vanity, which last takes the form of a craving to be loved or simply admired. Avarice is the worst of those three. Why do so many old persons, men and women alike, insist on hoarding money when they have no prospect

of using it and even when they have no heirs? They eat the cheapest food, buy no clothes, and live in a single room when they could afford better lodging. It may be that they regard money as a form of power; there is a comfort in watching it accumulate while other powers are dwindling away. How often we read of an old person found dead in a hovel, on a mattress partly stuffed with bankbooks and stock certificates! The bankbook syndrome, we call it in our family, which has never succumbed.

4   Untidiness we call the Langley Collyer syndrome. To explain, Langley Collyer was a former concert pianist who lived alone with his 70-year-old brother in a brownstone house on upper Fifth Avenue. The once fashionable neighborhood had become part of Harlem. Homer, the brother, had been an admiralty lawyer, but was now blind and partly paralyzed; Langley played for him and fed him on buns and oranges, which he thought would restore Homer's sight. He never threw away a daily paper because Homer, he said, might want to read them all. He saved other things as well and the house became filled with rubbish from roof to basement. The halls were lined on both sides with bundled newspapers, leaving narrow passageways in which Langley had devised booby traps to catch intruders.

5   On March 21, 1947, some unnamed person telephoned the police to report that there was a dead body in the Collyer house. The police broke down the front door and found the hall impassable, then they hoisted a ladder to a second-story window. Behind it Homer was lying on the floor in a bathrobe; he had starved to death. Langley had disappeared. After some delay, the police broke into the basement, chopped a hole in the roof, and began throwing junk out of the house, top and bottom. It was 18 days before they found Langley's body, gnawed by rats. Caught in one of his own booby traps, he had died in a hallway just outside Homer's door. By that time the police had collected, and the Department of Sanitation had hauled away, 120 tons of rubbish, including besides the newspapers, 14 grand pianos and the parts of a dismantled Model T Ford.

6   Why do so many old people accumulate junk, not on the scale of Langley Collyer, but still in a dismaying fashion? Their tables are piled high with it, their bureau drawers are stuffed with it, their closet rods bend with the weight of clothes not worn for years. I suppose that the piling up is partly from lethargy and partly from the feeling that everything once useful, including their own bodies, should be preserved. Others, though not so many, have such a fear of becoming Langley Collyers that they strive to be painfully neat. Every tool they own is in its place, though it will never be used again; every scrap of paper is filed away in alphabetical order. At last their immoderate neatness becomes another vice of age, if a milder one.

7   The vanity of older people is an easier weakness to explain, and to condone. With less to look forward to, they yearn for recognition of what they have been: the reigning beauty, the athlete, the soldier, the scholar. It is the beauties who have the hardest time. A portrait of themselves at twenty hangs on the wall, and they try to resemble it by making an extravagant use of creams, powders, and dyes. Being young at heart, they think they are merely revealing their essential persons. The athletes find shelves for their silver trophies, which are polished once a year. Perhaps a letter sweater lies wrapped in a bureau drawer. I remember one evening when a no-longer athlete had guests for dinner and tried to find his sweater. "Oh, that old thing," his wife said. "The moths got into it and I threw it away." The athlete sulked and his guests went home early.

8   Often the yearning to be recognized appears in conversation as an innocent boast. Thus, a distinguished physician, retired at 94, remarks casually that a disease was named after him. A former judge bursts into chuckles as he repeats bright things that he said on the bench. Aging scholars complain in letters (or one of them does), "As I approach 70 I'm becoming avid of honors, and such things—medals, honorary degrees, etc.—are only passed around among academics on a *quid pro quo* basis (one hood capping another)." Or they say querulously, "Bill Underwood has ten honorary doctorates and I have only three. Why didn't they elect me to . . . ?" and they mention the name of some learned society. That search for honors is a harmless passion, though it may lead to jealousies and deformations of character, as with Robert Frost in his later years. Still, honors cost little. Why shouldn't the very old have more than their share of them?

9   To be admired and praised, especially by the young, is an autumnal pleasure enjoyed by the lucky ones (who are not always the most deserving). "What is more charming," Cicero observes in his famous essay *De Senectute*, "than old age surrounded by the enthusiasm of youth! . . . Attentions which seem trivial and conventional are marks of honor—the morning call, being sought after, precedence, having people rise for you, being escorted to and from the forum. . . . What pleasures of the body can be compared to the prerogatives of influence?" But there are also pleasures of the body, or the mind, that are enjoyed by a greater number of older persons.

10   Those pleasures include some that younger people find hard to appreciate. One of them is simply sitting still, like a snake on a sun-warmed stone, with a delicious feeling of indolence that was seldom attained in earlier years. A leaf flutters down; a cloud moves by inches across the horizon. At such moments the older person, completely relaxed, has become a part of nature—and a living part, with blood coursing through his veins. The future does not exist for him. He

thinks, if he thinks at all, that life for younger persons is still a battle royal of each against each, but that now he has nothing more to win or lose. He is not so much above as outside the battle, as if he had assumed the uniform of some neutral country, perhaps Liechtenstein or Andorra. From a distance he notes that some of the combatants, men or women, are jostling ahead—but why do they fight so hard when the most they can hope for is a longer obituary? He can watch the scrounging and gouging, he can hear the shouts of exultation, the moans of the gravely wounded, and meanwhile he feels secure; nobody will attack him from ambush.

11   Age has other physical compensations besides the nirvana of dozing in the sun. A few of the simplest needs become a pleasure to satisfy. When an old woman in a nursing home was asked what she really liked to do, she answered in one word: "Eat." She might have been speaking for many of her fellows. Meals in a nursing home, however badly cooked, serve as climactic moments of the day. The physical essence of the pensioners is being renewed at an appointed hour; now they can go back to meditating or to watching TV while looking forward to the next meal. They can also look forward to sleep, which has become a definite pleasure, not the mere interruption it once had been.

12   Here I am thinking of old persons under nursing care. Others ferociously guard their independence, and some of them suffer less than one might expect from being lonely and impoverished. They can be rejoiced by visits and meetings, but they also have company inside their heads. Some of them are busiest when their hands are still. What passes through the minds of many is a stream of persons, images, phrases, and familiar tunes. For some that stream has continued since childhood, but now it is deeper; it is their present and their past combined. At times they conduct silent dialogues with a vanished friend, and these are less tiring—often more rewarding—than spoken conversations. If inner resources are lacking, old persons living alone may seek comfort and a kind of companionship in the bottle. I should judge from the gossip of various neighborhoods that the outer suburbs from Boston to San Diego are full of secretly alcoholic widows. One of those widows, an old friend, was moved from her apartment into a retirement home. She left behind her a closet in which the floor was covered wall to wall with whiskey bottles. "Oh, those empty bottles!" she explained. "They were left by a former tenant."

13   Not whiskey or cooking sherry but simply giving up is the greatest temptation of age. It is something different from a stoical acceptance of infirmities, which is something to be admired. At 63, when he first recognized that his powers were failing, Emerson wrote one of his best poems, "Terminus":

It is time to be old,
To take in sail:—
The god of bounds,
Who sets to seas a shore,
Came to me in his fatal rounds,
And said: "No more!
No farther shoot
Thy broad ambitious branches, and thy root.
Fancy departs: no more invent;
Contract thy firmament
To compass of a tent."

14   Emerson lived in good health to the age of 79. Within his narrowed firmament, he continued working until his memory failed; then he consented to having younger editors and collaborators. The givers-up see no reason for working. Sometimes they lie in bed all day when moving about would still be possible, if difficult. I had a friend, a distinguished poet, who surrendered in that fashion. The doctors tried to stir him to action, but he refused to leave his room. Another friend, once a successful artist, stopped painting when his eyes began to fail. His doctor made the mistake of telling him that he suffered from a fatal disease. He then lost interest in everything except the splendid Rolls-Royce, acquired in his prosperous days, that stood in the garage. Daily he wiped the dust from its hood. He couldn't drive it on the road any longer, but he used to sit in the driver's seat, start the motor, then back the Rolls out of the garage and drive it in again, back twenty feet and forward twenty feet; that was his only distraction.

15   I haven't the right to blame those who surrender, not being able to put myself inside their minds or bodies. Often they must have compelling reasons, physical or moral. Not only do they suffer from a variety of ailments, but also they are made to feel that they no longer have a function in the community. Their families and neighbors don't ask them for advice, don't really listen when they speak, don't call on them for efforts. One notes that there are not a few recoveries from apparent senility when that situation changes. If it doesn't change, old persons may decide that efforts are useless. I sympathize with their problems, but the men and women I envy are those who accept old age as a series of challenges.

16   For such persons, every new infirmity is an enemy to be outwitted, an obstacle to be overcome by force of will. They enjoy each little victory over themselves, and sometimes they win a major success. Renoir was one of them. He continued painting, and magnificently, for years after he was crippled by arthritis; the brush had to be strapped to his arm. "You don't need your hand to paint," he said. Goya was another of

the unvanquished. At 72 he retired as an official painter of the Spanish court and decided to work only for himself. His later years were those of the famous "black paintings" in which he let his imagination run (and also of the lithographs, then a new technique). At 78 he escaped a reign of terror in Spain by fleeing to Bordeaux. He was deaf and his eyes were failing; in order to work he had to wear several pairs of spectacles, one over another, and then use a magnifying glass; but he was producing splendid work in a totally new style. At 80 he drew an ancient man propped on two sticks, with a mass of white hair and beard hiding his face and with the inscription "I am still learning."

17   Giovanni Papini said when he was nearly blind, "I prefer martyrdom to imbecility." After writing sixty books, including his famous *Life of Christ*, he was at work on two huge projects when he was stricken with a form of muscular atrophy. He lost the use of his left leg, then of his fingers, so that he couldn't hold a pen. The two big books, though never to be finished, moved forward slowly by dictation; that in itself was a triumph. Toward the end, when his voice had become incomprehensible, he spelled out a word, tapping on the table to indicate letters of the alphabet. One hopes never to be faced with the need for such heroic measures.

18   "Eighty years old!" the great Catholic poet Paul Claudel wrote in his journal. "No eyes left, no ears, no teeth, no legs, no wind! And when all is said and done, how astonishingly well one does without them!"

(2,552 words)

VOCABULARY

improvised (1)	immoderate (6)	indolence (10)
infirmities (1)	condone (7)	exultation (10)
avarice (3)	querulously (8)	nirvana (11)
succumbed (3)	deformations (8)	climactic (11)
lethargy (6)	prerogatives (9)	

THE FACTS

1. What kind of crisis does the aging person undergo?

2. What are the virtues of old age? What are its main vices?

3. What is the Langley Collyer syndrome? Why do old people suffer so often from it? What part does society's treatment of the elderly have to play in this syndrome?

4. Why are some old people so vain?

5. What pleasures do the old revel in?

THE STRATEGIES

1. Aside from examples that illustrate what it is like to be old, what kind of supporting detail does Cowley use? What does its use add to the essay?

2. What is the function of the question in paragraph 6?

3. Old people, says Cowley, suffer chronically from avarice, untidiness, and vanity. He gives extended examples of the second and third of these, but not of the first. How does he support his view that the old are often avaricious? What rhetorical logic lies behind this omission of examples?

4. What extended analogy does Cowley use to describe how the young appear to the old? How effective is this analogy?

5. In this excerpt Cowley gives anecdotes about aging in others, rather than in himself. Do you think this a better tactic than focusing on his own experiences? Why or why not?

THE ISSUES

1. Has Cowley overlooked any vices or virtues attached to old age? Make a written list of the characteristics of old age you wish to avoid and then a second list of characteristics you wish to develop.

2. What is your answer to the question posed in paragraph 3: "Why do so many old persons, men and women alike, insist on hoarding money when they have no prospect of using it and even when they have no heirs?" Do you agree with Cowley's suggestion that perhaps they regard money as a form of power, or are there other reasons for the avarice?

3. What about old age do you fear most? What do you plan to do in order to alleviate your fear?

4. In "Rabbi Ben Ezra" the famous Victorian poet, Robert Browning, wrote these lines:

> Grow old along with me!
> The best is yet to be,
> The last of life, for which the first was made:
> Our times are in His hand
> Who saith, "A whole I planned,
> Youth shows but half, trust God: see all, nor be afraid."

How do you interpret these lines? Do you agree or disagree with the poet's view? Give reasons for your answer.

5. What kind of person do you imagine yourself to be at age eighty? Describe in detail what kinds of clothes you would wear, how you would spend your time, and what philosophy would guide your existence.

SUGGESTIONS FOR WRITING

1. Some sociologists have suggested that since women outlive men, marriage laws should be relaxed to allow the elderly to practice polygyny (where a man has more than one wife or mate). Express your views on this issue in an essay in which you use examples to support your thesis.

2. Write an essay giving examples of the way age has affected an elderly friend or relative.

▼▼

Marya Mannes

STAY YOUNG

MARYA MANNES (1904–1990) was an American novelist, poet, and essayist, who worked as a staff writer for *Reporter* magazine. Her published books include *The New York I Know* (1961), *But Will It Sell* (1964), *Subverse* (poems, 1964), and *Out of My Time* (1971).

1   Like all people in the middle span, I am aware of death and saddened by its advance forces of disintegration. I do not like the signs in flesh and muscle and bone of slow decline, even if they are yet unaccompanied by pain. To one in love with physical beauty, its inevitable blurring by years is a source of melancholy.

2   Yet I feel sure that while the flesh may retreat before age, the man or woman can advance if he goes towards death rather than away from it, if he understands the excitement implicit in this progression from the part to the whole. For that is, really, what it should be: a steady ascent from personal involvement—the paths and rocks and valleys and rises of the foothills—to the ultimate height where they fuse into one grand and complex pattern, remote and yet rewarding. It is like coming into clearer air. And if that air becomes in course too rare to breathe, the final breath is one of total purity.

3   It is because of these convictions that I protest against the American tyranny of youth. There is beauty and freshness in youth (if there

is less and less innocence), but it is an accident of time and therefore ephemeral. There is no "trick" in being young: it happens to you. But the process of maturing is an art to be learned, an effort to be sustained. By the age of fifty you have made yourself what you are, and if it is good, it is better than your youth. If it is bad, it is not because you are older but because you have not grown.

4   Yet all this is obscured, daily, hourly, by the selling barrage of youth; perhaps the greatest campaign for the arrested development of the human being ever waged anywhere. Look young, be young, stay young, they call from every page and on every air wave. You must be young to be loved. And with this mandate, this threat, this pressure, millions of goods are sold and millions of hours are spent in pursuit of a youth which no longer exists and which cannot be recaptured.

5   The result of this effort is, in women, obscene; in men, pathetic. For the American woman of middle age thinks of youth only in terms of appearance and the American man of middle age thinks of youth only in terms of virility.

6   If obscene seems a strong word to use for old women who try to look young, I will be more explicit. It is quite true and quite proper that better eating habits, better care and less drudgery have made American women look ten years younger than their mothers did at the same age. One of the pleasing phenomena of our life is the naturally young and pretty grandmother, almost as lithe and active as her daughter. But I am talking of the still older woman, past her middle fifties, often alone, often idle, who has the means to spend the greater part of her leisure in beauty salons and shops and weight-reducing parlors, resisting age with desperate intensity. They do not know it, but the fact of this resistance nullifies the effects of the effort. The streets of American cities are full of these thin, massaged, made-up, corseted, tinted, overdressed women with faces that are repellent masks of frustration; hard, empty, avid. Although their ankles are slender and their feet perched on backless high-heeled slippers, they fool no one, and certainly no man. They are old legs and old feet. Although their flesh is clear and fairly firm in the visible areas, it is kneaded flesh, and fools no one. The hips are small indeed, but the girdle only emphasizes their stiff aridity. And the uplift bra, the platinum hair, the tight dress? Whom do they fool? The woman herself, alone. And the obscenity in all this is that she uses the outward techniques of sexual allure to maintain her youth when she is no longer wanted by men. And she does it because she has been told to do it by the advertising media. She has been sold a bill of goods.

7   Let me hastily say at this point that it is the solemn duty of all women to look as well as they can and to maintain through life the grooming that makes them pleasing to others. Towards this end, the advertisers have performed a signal service to Americans. But they have over-reached themselves, and us. Instead of saying "Be Yourself,"

they say, "Be Young." Instead of saying "Relax," they say "Compete!" In doing this, they deprive the maturing woman of a great joy, an astounding relief: the end, not of sex, heaven knows, but of sexual competition. By the time a woman is fifty she is either wanted as a woman of fifty or not really wanted at all. She does not have to fool her husband or her lover, and she knows that competition with women far younger than she is not only degrading but futile.

8   It is also an axiom that the more time a woman spends on herself, the less she has for others and the less desirable she is to others. If this goes for young women—and I believe it does—it goes doubly for older women, who have—if they knew it—more to give.

9   When I go to Europe and see the old people in villages in France or Italy, for instance, I am struck at once by the age of all women who are no longer young, pitying their premature withering; and at the same time startled by the occasional beauty of their old faces. Lined and grooved and puckered as they may be, their hair grizzled or lank, there is something in their eyes and in their bones that gives age austerity and makes their glossy contemporaries at a bridge table here seem parodies of women. They show that they have lived and they have not yet found the means to hide it.

10   I remember also that as a child and a young girl I never thought of my mother in terms of age. Whatever it was at any time, she looked it; and nobody then told her to lose weight or do something about her hair because she was far too interesting a human being to need such "ameliorations." It would, indeed, have been an impertinence. My mother had no illusions of beauty: she was too concerned with music and her husband and her children to be concerned, in detail, with herself. I don't doubt that, given today's aids, she could have looked younger and smarter than she did. But she would have lost something. The time and effort spent in improving her looks would have been taken from music and from love. With her unruly eyebrows plucked to a thin line, her face made-up, her plump, small body moulded into girdles, an important part of her would have vanished: her identity.

11   It is this that the older women of America are losing. At club gatherings, at hotels, at resorts, they look identical. What lives they have led have been erased from their faces along with the more obvious marks of age. They have smoothed and hardened into a mould. Their lotions have done well.

12   It could be said that if they maintain the illusion of youth to themselves only, no harm is done and some good. But I wonder if all self-deceptions do not harm, and if their price is not loss of self.

13   I wonder too whether one of the reasons for wild, intemperate, destructive youth might not be this same hard finish, this self-absorption, of the women to whom they might otherwise turn. I cannot imagine going for counsel and comfort to a mother or aunt or

grandmother tightly buttressed by lastex and heavily masked by make-up. Where is the soft wide lap, the old kind hands, the tender face of age?

14   None of us with any pride in person and any sense of aesthetics can allow ourselves to crumble into decay without trying to slow the process or at least veil its inroads. But that is not the major battle. The fight is not for what is gone but for what is coming; and for this the fortification of the spirit is paramount, the preservation of the flesh a trivial second.

15   Let the queen bee keep her royal jelly. Or so I keep telling myself.

(1,422 words)

VOCABULARY

ephemeral (3)	axiom (8)	aesthetics (14)
nullifies (6)	austerity (9)	inroads (14)
repellent (6)	ameliorations (10)	paramount (14)
allure (6)	intemperate (13)	

THE FACTS

1. According to the author, what must a man or woman do to advance with old age?

2. In what terms do American women think of youth? In what contrasting terms do American men think of youth?

3. What does the author think advertisers should be saying to women? Instead, what are they actually saying?

4. In what countries is the author often struck by the natural beauty of older women who do not try to hide their ages?

5. What price do women pay for their attempts at deceiving themselves and the world about how old they are?

THE STRATEGIES

1. The author opens her essay with a frank admission about her sadness in the face of aging. What does this admission add to the essay?

2. What evidence does the author offer to support her assertions about the obscene efforts women make to avoid looking their age? How convincing do you find this evidence?

3. Given what the author has written in paragraph 6 about American women who desperately labor to look younger, what rhetorical strategy is implicit in her description of European women in paragraph 9?

4. Why do you think the author included the anecdote about her mother in paragraph 10?

5. What does the final sentence of the essay imply about the author? Why is this an apt implication on which to end this essay?

THE ISSUES

1. What do you think is entailed in the author's advice that a person should go "towards death rather than away from it"?

2. What difference, if any, do you think the feminist movement has made in easing the unrealistic pressures on aging women?

3. From this essay, what can you infer are the causes behind what the author calls "the American tyranny of youth"?

4. What pressures, if any, are exerted upon the young by the culture of youth? Or are the young exempt from such pressures? Explain.

5. Why does it necessarily follow, as the author alleges, that there is scant comfort available from aging aunts, mothers, and grandmothers who try hard to avoid looking their age?

SUGGESTIONS FOR WRITING

1. Write an essay discussing how you would like to be treated when you are old.

2. In an essay, explore the potential benefits a successful feminist revolution could have on the present tyranny of youth.

I

First Draft

Kimberly Caitlin Wheeler, Yale University

Aging   → Title
                                     needed

There is a general perception in our society that once you

reach middle age, you are "Over the hill and going down." As   repetitive
                          their value
people get older, ~~there worth~~, unlike that of wine, is perceived to

decrease. Thus the elderly are "worthless" members of society:
                                                    explanation
They contribute nothing, but take much. This prejudice against

the elderly and even the middle aged, ~~is called~~ ageism, ~~and~~ in our

youth-oriented culture, ~~it~~ (is a big problem.) Ageism does not end
                                         There are problems with
with mere perceptions, but also begets action. Age discrimination

~~takes place~~ both in the entertainment industry and the   parallelism

workplace, but neither problem can be solved without a change

in attitude towards the elderly.
     Ageism is extremely noticeable within the entertainment
~~One aspect of society in which ageism is prevalent is the~~   more
industry.   focused
~~social arena.~~ The ~~elderly in our society are portrayed as useless,~~
                                                                  off
~~unattractive and bitter. They are bad drivers, boring company, and~~ topic

~~they contribute nothing to society. This myth is perpetrated in~~
                                        programs   cleaner
~~part by the entertainment industry.~~ Most television ~~shows~~ and

movies cater to the younger members of society. The shows ~~and~~

~~films~~ portray young characters who are facing (usually) age-specific

Wheeler 2

problems, such as starting a career or raising a family. Those who

have reached retirement and have raised their families are often

ignored or are peripheral characters. ~~This has two major~~ There are virtually

~~consequences. The first is that older actors and actresses find it~~ no shows that sympathetically portray the interests

~~more difficult to find work, and are therefore less visible to the~~ of the elderly.

~~public eye. The other~~ One consequence, ~~perhaps more significant,~~ of this focus is

that people begin to perceive the elderly through the eyes of the

media—as valueless members of society.

The entertainment industry has some economic justifications

in (only) producing shows geared towards a younger audience.

Research has shown that the 18–44 age group has more

spending money than members of older age groups. Older age   cleaner

groups are actually wealthier, but ~~their money is tied up in~~ they are less likely to spend money

~~houses, cars, and retirement accounts.~~ frivolously. They are not as receptive to advertisements and trends. Because members of the

18–44 age group are more likely to spend their money,

advertisers who pay for television shows want shows that

members of this age group are watching, and support "younger"

shows. Likewise, film studios, eager to make ~~a~~ box office ~~hit,~~ money

~~also~~ tend to produce shows designed for a more youthful   focused

audience.

Age discrimination also appears in the workplace.

~~A second area in which ageism is a serious problem is in that~~ stronger

~~of unemployment.~~ Employers are often unwilling to hire or keep

workers that have ~~exceeded~~ reached a certain age. They perceive these

workers as incompetent and lacking ambition. For example, the

European Union recently implemented a policy of not hiring   better

workers over the age of 35. This policy is ~~unjust.~~ unjustified worded For most jobs,

Wheeler 3

mature employees bring added skill and experience that can

actually improve their performance. The one exception to this

rule is in the area of technological advances. In today's

workplace, where computers are an essential means of

performing tasks, and the internet forms the hub of office   *cap*

communication, those trained in a less technological age may find

themselves at a disadvantage. In a survey done by Great Britain's

Motorola Company, 22% of people ages 16–24 had had no

internet training, compared to 78% of people over the age of 65. *cap*

Those over 65 were also less enthusiastic about technology or

comfortable using high tech equipment or online services. Thus

many older workers lack skills that are essential in a high-tech

work environment. ⊃
~~This often offsets~~ their advantages of experience and dedication.
~~There are solutions~~ to the problems that create age   *better*
do exist   *Solutions*   *implemented*   *closing*
sentence of FP
discrimination, but before they can be ~~attempted~~ it is necessary
overcome ∧   *active*
to ~~remove~~ the prejudice against older people in this country.   *voice*
better
words
The general perception of the elderly as worthless and

burdensome members of the society needs to change. Older

people should be valued for their knowledge, experience, and

successes. Once the attitude has changed, it is possible to
effect
~~implement~~ the solutions for the entertainment industry and the
repetitive   *perceived as*
workplace. If older people are ∧ valued customers and quality

shows are created for them, they are more likely to watch them
mature workers were trained
and spend their money. Likewise, if ~~an employer took the time~~
in the use of advanced technology, this skill would *add to their*
~~to train his or her more mature employees in the use of~~   *cleaner,*
other resources of experience and knowledge.   *more*
~~advanced technology, they would probably find that they were~~ *precise*

Wheeler 4

~~valuable resources in the workplace, and that their experience~~ cleaner more precise

Life doesn't have to go

~~and dedication was a valuable resource. It is never too late to~~
downhill at age 40; it should become a time to reap the rewards

~~start learning, nor it is never too early. All members of society,~~ ties into the

of previous successes, a time to enjoy maturity. opening

~~young and old, can learn from each other.~~

1

Final Draft

Kimberly Caitlin Wheeler, Yale University

Aging

There is a general perception in our society that once you reach middle age, you are "Over the hill and going down." As people get older, their value, unlike that of wine, is perceived to decrease. Thus the elderly are "worthless" members of society: They contribute nothing, but take much. This prejudice against the elderly and even the middle aged, ageism, is a big problem in our youth-oriented culture. Ageism does not end with mere perceptions, but also begets action. There are problems with age discrimination both in the entertainment industry and the workplace, but neither problem can be solved without a change in attitude towards the elderly.

Ageism is extremely noticeable within the entertainment industry. Most television programs and movies cater to the younger members of society. The shows portray young characters who are usually facing age-specific problems, such as starting a career or raising a family. Those who have reached retirement and have raised their families are often ignored or are peripheral characters. There are virtually no shows that sympathetically portray the interests of the elderly. One consequence of this is that people begin to perceive the elderly through the eyes of the media—as valueless members of society.

Wheeler 2

The entertainment industry has some economic justifications in producing only shows geared towards a younger audience. Research has shown that the 18–44 age group has more spending money than members of older age groups. Older age groups are actually wealthier, but they are less likely to spend money frivolously. They are not as receptive to advertisements and product trends. Because members of the 18–44 age group are more likely to spend their money, advertisers who pay for television shows want shows that members of this age group are watching, and support "younger" shows. Likewise, film studios, eager to make box office money, tend to produce shows designed for a more youthful audience.

Age discrimination also appears in the workplace. Employers are often unwilling to hire or keep workers that have reached a certain age. They perceive these workers as incompetent and lacking ambition. For example, the European Union recently implemented a policy of not hiring workers over the age of 35. This policy is unjustified. For most jobs, mature employees bring added skill and experience that can actually improve their performance. The one exception to this rule is in the area of technological advances. In today's workplace, where computers are an essential means of performing tasks, and the Internet forms the hub of office communication, those trained in a less technological age may find themselves at a disadvantage. In a survey done by Great Britain's Motorola Company, 22% of people ages 16–24 had had no Internet training, compared to

Wheeler 3

78% of people over the age of 65. Those over 65 were also less enthusiastic about technology or comfortable using high tech equipment or online services. Thus many older workers lack skills that are essential in a high-tech work environment. This often offsets their advantages of experience and dedication.

Solutions to the problems that create age discrimination do exist, but before they can be implemented, it is necessary to overcome the prejudice against older people in this country. The general perception of the elderly as worthless and burdensome members of the society needs to change. Older people should be valued for their knowledge, experience, and successes. Once the attitude has changed, it is possible to effect the solutions for the entertainment industry and the workplace. If older people are perceived as valued customers and quality shows are created for them, they are more likely to watch them and spend their money. Likewise, if mature workers were trained in the use of advanced technology, this skill would add to their other resources of experience and knowledge. Life doesn't have to go downhill at age 40; it should become a time to reap the rewards of previous successes, a time to enjoy maturity.

How I Write

When I first get a topic, I like to take a few days and think about it. I may do some preliminary research, but what I usually do is just think, and jot down any ideas that come to me. This is a technique known to some as "procrastination" but it really is useful. When I have thought for a few days, I do some research, to find facts and figures to support my ideas, or to derive ideas. I usually go to the library for books or periodicals. For a contemporary topic such as this, I like to turn to the Internet. Once I get books, I skim them for discussions of my topic, then take notes at my computer. I print out these notes, then sit down, away from the computer with a pencil, my notes, and a notebook, and plan my paper. My first step is to come up with a rough outline—usually two or three points to talk about. I then read through my material and find information that directly relates to the points that I may use in my paper later. I cut out my notes, divide them into piles that relate to each point, then tape them together in the order I want to use them. Once this is accomplished, I can begin writing the paper.

I always write the paper from scratch at the computer, because I type faster than I write and it is easier to make changes later. I like to listen to music while I write for several reasons. I usually listen to classical music, which is supposed to boost your IQ and focus. Music also helps when you're writing in a crowded dorm room. With headphones on, it is easier to block out the distracting conversations of my roommates. I also use earplugs sometimes. When I am typing and my fingers or brain cramp up, I take a short break and literally run around the room. Or I get a drink of water or have a short conversation with someone. When I return to writing, my brain is refreshed and ready to go. After I've finished writing, I look at the paper. If it is too short, I look for things I could explain more fully; and if it is too long, I look for things to cut. Then I print the paper out to proofread for obvious errors. At this point, I like to put it down for a while and do something else. Then I can come back to it and see what really needs to be revised and changed. Sometimes it is a few sentences, and sometimes it is the entire focus of the paper. After revising, I spell check and proofread again before printing it out and turning it in. Then I stop thinking about it until I get it back from the professor.

How I Wrote This Essay

For this paper, because I was writing at home, I used a slightly different approach. Because this topic was such a contemporary one, I turned first to the Internet for research. I typed "ageism" into several different search engines, then browsed the pages offered to see what looked interesting or relevant. I printed out the pages that appeared to be most useful, then sat down on the couch with my pencil, my notebook, and my web pages. I came up with main points, found some statistics to use in my paper, then began writing. I stopped a few times in the middle—for dinner, and to check my e-mail, but I eventually finished it. Then I printed it out to proofread. I marked my revisions, then went back to the computer and changed them.

My Writing Tip

Always write your body paragraphs first. I often don't know exactly what my thesis is until I'm done with the paper, so I always write an introduction and conclusion last. This also makes it easier to begin to write—usually the most difficult thing about writing a paper!

CHAPTER WRITING ASSIGNMENTS

1. Convert one of the following general subjects into a suitable thesis:
   a. college life
   b. parental behavior
   c. sex during the AIDS era
   d. television coverage of crime
   e. meaningful versus meaningless work
   f. youth and age
   g. nostalgia
   h. flag burning

2. Select any issue covered in your local news reports, formulate your position on it in a thesis, and explain and defend it in an essay.

WRITING ASSIGNMENTS FOR A SPECIFIC AUDIENCE

1. For an audience of third graders, explain in an essay the concept of a thesis and how you make use of it in your own writing.

2. Explain to an audience of business executives how the English education you are presently receiving will make you a better employee.

COLLABORATIVE WRITING PROJECT

Divide your group into at least three teams, each of which should research the retirement policies of some specific profession or institution of its choice. Conduct whatever interviews are necessary to learn more about the specific retirement policy. After the research is completed, the teams should meet to discuss and debate the fairness of the retirement policies. Finally, each team should write a group essay outlining what has been learned about the researched retirement policy as well as its impact on elderly employees.

▼▼▼

Chapter Four

PLANNING AND ORGANIZING

INTRODUCTION: THINKING AHEAD

To plan and organize an essay means to work it out on paper before doing the actual writing. It is an effort that all writers do not make equally. Some plan their work in exquisite detail and with complicated outlines; others do not plan at all but merely sit down and write. In between are those who occasionally jot down insights on scraps of paper and are content with that. Plainly, the need for planning and organizing an essay is likely to vary as much with the writer's personality as with the content of the subject. Absolutes are difficult to find and advice is tricky to dispense on this subject.

However, there is one well-known pitfall ahead for those who believe in advance planning of a writing project: Plans have an irritating tendency to seem ironclad once they have been made. No matter what new information you find, or what fresh breezes of inspiration blow, you feel a nagging loyalty to the plan and are loath to betray it. This is a foolish persistence and must be ignored. If you find a better way of treating your subject as you write, a way not anticipated by your plan, you must be prepared to scrap the plan and take the better way.

If you must make a plan, the next question is, What kind? In the past, planning an essay meant making a cumbersome outline of it, with branching levels more intricate than a family tree. Outlining is still recommended for complicated or difficult subjects, and especially for research papers, but it is not the only kind of plan now available to writers. You can make a jot list, which is simply a list of the order of topics you intend to cover. You can plan by writing a series of topic sentences that anticipate your paragraphs. You can plan by making a sketch of your essay's topics and showing ideas that branch off them. This sketch can be as fanciful as you like and may even resemble the flowchart of a systems analyst. The point is to get something down on paper about your subject. What format you use is less important to this generation of English teachers than it was to their ancestors.

Whether you write with or without an advance plan, the essays in this chapter will give you a glimpse into the enviable organization achieved by some writers. In the Advice section Edward T. Thompson, a former *Reader's Digest* editor, tells us how that magazine achieves its renowned simplicity. In the Discussion section we chuckle through a true-to-life story by Samuel H. Scudder that makes an important point about organizing. Then we are treated to two superbly organized essays in the Examples section—the first by E. M. Forster, the second by Donald Kagan—that demonstrate how complicated subjects can be expressed in elegant literary forms (such as the short story by James Thurber and the sonnet by Shakespeare). The Issues section focuses on drug abuse, giving us three views on this hotly debated topic.

All of us recognize a well-organized essay when we read one. What we cannot know is how the author managed to organize it so well. For some authors, organization means an advance plan and a careful plotting of topics. Other writers like to hack their way through the forest of a subject with the path ahead not too clearly lighted nor the thicket too plainly shown. The desired object in either case is the same. How you get there is a matter of temperamental difference.

A D V I C E

▼▼

Edward T. Thompson

HOW TO WRITE CLEARLY

EDWARD THORWALD THOMPSON (b. 1928) was born in Milwaukee and educated at MIT. Between 1976–1984, he was editor-in-chief of *Reader's Digest*. He is currently a consultant in publications.

> *Whatever you may think of the* Reader's Digest—*there are those who love it and those who hate it—you cannot say that its mishmash of self help, optimistic, and heartwarming articles is written in a disorganized way. In fact, the* Digest *is known above all else for its clear (some would say simplistic) style of writing. A former editor of this venerable popular publication, in the article below, offers some specific advice on how to organize your ideas and express them on paper.*

1   If you are afraid to write, don't be.

2   If you think you've got to string together big fancy words and high-flying phrases, forget it.

3   To write well, unless you aspire to be a professional poet or novelist, you only need to get your ideas across simply and clearly.

4   It's not easy. But it is easier than you might imagine.

5   There are only three basic requirements:

6   First, you must *want* to write clearly. And I believe you really do, if you've stayed this far with me.

7   Second, you must be willing to *work hard.* Thinking means work—and that's what it takes to do anything well.

8   Third, you must know and follow some *basic guidelines.*

9   If, while you're writing for clarity, some lovely, dramatic or inspired phrases or sentences come to you, fine. Put them in.

10   But then with cold, objective eyes and mind ask yourself "Do they detract from clarity?" If they do, grit your teeth and cut the frills.

Follow Some Basic Guidelines

11   I can't give you a complete list of "do's and don'ts" for every writing problem you'll ever face.

12   But I can give you some fundamental guidelines that cover the most common problems.

I. Outline What You Want to Say

13   I know that sounds grade-schoolish. But you can't write clearly until, *before you start*, you know where you will stop.

14   Ironically, that's even a problem in writing an outline (i.e., knowing the ending before you begin).

15   So try this method:

- On 3″ × 5″ cards, write—one point to a card—all the points you need to make.

- Divide the cards into piles—one pile for each group of points *closely related* to each other. (If you were describing an automobile, you'd put all the points about mileage in one pile, all the points about safety in another, and so on.)

- Arrange your piles of points in a sequence. Which are most important and should be given first or saved for last? Which must you present before others in order to make the others understandable?

- Now, *within* each pile, do the same thing—arrange the *points* in logical, understandable order.

16   There you have your outline, needing only an introduction and conclusion.

17   This is a practical way to outline. It's also flexible. You can add, delete or change the location of points easily.

2. Start Where Your Readers Are

18   How much do they know about the subject? Don't write to a level higher than your readers' knowledge of it.

19   CAUTION: Forget that old—and wrong—advice about writing to a 12 year-old mentality. That's insulting. But do remember that your prime purpose is to explain something, not prove that you're smarter than your readers.

3. Avoid Jargon

20   Don't use words, expressions, phrases known only to people with specific knowledge or interests.

21   Example: A scientist, using scientific jargon, wrote, "The biota exhibited a one hundred percent mortality response." He could have written: "All the fish died."

4. Use Familiar Combinations of Words

22   A speech writer for President Franklin D. Roosevelt wrote, "We are endeavoring to construct a more inclusive society." F. D. R. changed it to, "We're going to make a country in which no one is left out."

23   CAUTION: By familiar combinations of words, I do *not* mean incorrect grammar. *That* can be *un*clear. Example: John's father says he can't go out Friday. (Who can't go out? John or his father?)

5. Use "First-Degree" Words

24   These words immediately bring an image to your mind. Other words must be "translated" through the first-degree word before you see the image. Those are second/third-degree words.

First-degree words	Second/third-degree words
face _____	visage, countenance
stay _____	abide, remain, reside
book _____	volume, tome, publication

25   First-degree words are usually the most precise words, too.

6. Stick to the Point

26   Your outline—which was more work in the beginning—now saves you work. Because now you can ask about any sentence you write: "Does it relate to a point in the outline? If it doesn't, should I add it to the outline? If not, I'm getting off the track." Then, full steam ahead—on the main line.

7. Be as Brief as Possible

27   Whatever you write, shortening—*condensing*—almost always makes it tighter, straighter, easier to read and understand.

28   Condensing, as *Reader's Digest* does it, is in large part artistry. But it involves techniques that anyone can learn and use.

- *Present your points in logical* ABC *order:* Here again, your outline should save you work because, if you did it right, your points already stand in logical ABC order—A makes B understandable, B makes C understandable and so on. To write in a straight line is to say something clearly in the fewest possible words.

- *Don't waste words telling people what they already know:* Notice how we edited this: "Have you ever wondered how banks rate you as a credit risk? ~~You know, of course, that it's some combination of facts about your income, your job, and so on. But actually,~~ many banks have a scoring system. . . . "

- *Cut out excess evidence and unnecessary anecdotes:* Usually, one fact or example (at most, two) will support a point. More just belabor it.

- And while writing about something may remind you of a good story, ask yourself: "Does it *really help* to tell the story, or does it slow me down?"

29   (Many people think *Reader's Digest* articles are filled with anecdotes. Actually, we use them sparingly and usually for one of two reasons: either the subject is so dry it needs some "humanity" to give it life; or the subject is so hard to grasp, it needs anecdotes to help readers understand. If the subject is both lively and easy to grasp, we move right along.)

- *Look for the most common word wasters:* windy phrases.

Windy phrases	Cut to . . .
at the present time _____	now
in the event of _____	if
in the majority of instances _____	usually

- *Look for passive verbs you can make active:* Invariably, this produces a shorter sentence. "The cherry tree was chopped down by George Washington." (Passive verb and nine words.) "George Washington *chopped down* the cherry tree. (Active verb and seven words.)

- *Look for positive/negative sections from which you can cut the negative:* See how we did it here: "The answer ~~does not rest with~~ is ~~carelessness or incompetence. It lies largely in~~ having enough people to do the job."

- Finally, to write more clearly by saying it in fewer words: when you've finished, stop.

(1,078 words)

D I S C U S S I O N

▼▼

Samuel H. Scudder

TAKE THIS FISH AND LOOK AT IT

SAMUEL H. SCUDDER (1837–1911) was an American scientist who was educated at Williams College and Harvard university. His main scientific contributions were in the study of butterflies and Orthoptera (an order of insects that includes grasshoppers and crickets). He was one of the most learned and productive entomologists of his day.

> *Most of us tend to look at things without really seeing what is there. In everyday life this lack of observation may not be noticed, but in science it would be considered a serious failing. Scudder was a student of Louis Agassiz (1807–1873), the distinguished Harvard professor of natural history who used to subject his students to a rigorous but useful exercise in minute observation. The following is Scudder's account of one such exercise.*

1   It was more than fifteen years ago that I entered the laboratory of Professor Agassiz, and told him I had enrolled my name in the Scientific School as a student of natural history. He asked me a few questions about my object in coming, my antecedents generally, the mode in which I afterwards proposed to use the knowledge I might acquire, and, finally, whether I wished to study any special branch. To the latter I replied that, while I wished to be well grounded in all departments of zoology, I purposed to devote myself specially to insects.

2   "When do you wish to begin?" he asked.

3   "Now," I replied.

4   This seemed to please him, and with an energetic "Very well!" he reached from a shelf a huge jar of specimens in yellow alcohol. "Take this fish," he said, "and look at it; we call it a haemulon; by and by I will ask what you have seen."

5   With that he left me, but in a moment returned with explicit instructions as to the care of the object entrusted to me.

6   "No man is fit to be a naturalist," said he, "who does not know how to take care of specimens."

7   I was to keep the fish before me in a tin tray, and occasionally moisten the surface with alcohol from the jar, always taking care to replace the stopper tightly. Those were not the days of ground-glass stoppers and elegantly shaped exhibition jars; all the old students will

recall the huge neckless glass bottles with their leaky, wax-besmeared corks, half eaten by insects, and begrimed with cellar dust. Entomology was a cleaner science than ichthyology, but the example of the Professor, who had unhesitatingly plunged to the bottom of the jar to produce the fish, was infectious; and though this alcohol had a "very ancient and fishlike smell," I really dared not show any aversion within these sacred precincts, and treated the alcohol as though it were pure water. Still I was conscious of a passing feeling of disappointment, for gazing at a fish did not commend itself to an ardent entomologist. My friends at home, too, were annoyed when they discovered that no amount of eau-de-Cologne would drown the perfume which haunted me like a shadow.

8   In ten minutes I had seen all that could be seen in that fish, and started in search of the Professor—who had, however, left the Museum; and when I returned, after lingering over some of the odd animals stored in the upper apartment, my specimen was dry all over I dashed the fluid over the fish as if to resuscitate the beast from a fainting fit, and looked with anxiety for a return of the normal sloppy appearance. This little excitement over, nothing was to be done but to return to a steadfast gaze at my mute companion. Half an hour passed—an hour—another hour; the fish began to look loathsome. I turned it over and around; looked it in the face—ghastly; from behind, beneath, above, sideways, at a three-quarters' view—just as ghastly. I was in despair; at an early hour I concluded that lunch was necessary; so, with infinite relief, the fish was carefully replaced in the jar, and for an hour I was free.

9   On my return, I learned that Professor Agassiz had been at the Museum, but had gone, and would not return for several hours. My fellow-students were too busy to be disturbed by continued conversation. Slowly I drew forth that hideous fish, and with a feeling of desperation again looked at it. I might not use a magnifying-glass; instruments of all kinds were interdicted. My two hands, my two eyes, and the fish: it seemed a most limited field. I pushed my finger down its throat to feel how sharp the teeth were. I began to count the scales in the different rows, until I was convinced that was nonsense. At last a happy thought struck me—I would draw the fish; and now with surprise I began to discover new features in the creature. Just then the Professor returned.

10   "That is right," said he; "a pencil is one of the best of eyes. I am glad to notice, too, that you keep your specimen wet, and your bottle corked."

11   With these encouraging words, he added:

12   "Well, what is it like?"

13   He listened attentively to my brief rehearsal of the structure of parts whose names were still unknown to me: the fringed gill-arches

and movable operculum; the pores of the head, fleshy lips and lidless eyes; the lateral line, the spinous fins and forked tail; the compressed and arched body. When I finished, he waited as if expecting more, and then, with an air of disappointment:

14   "You have not looked very carefully; why," he continued more earnestly, "you haven't even seen one of the most conspicuous features of the animal, which is plainly before your eyes as the fish itself, look again, look again!" and he left me to my misery.

15   I was piqued; I was mortified. Still more of that wretched fish! But now I set myself to my task with a will, and discovered one new thing after another, until I saw how just the Professor's criticism had been. The afternoon passed quickly; and when, towards its close, the Professor inquired:

16   "Do you see it yet?"

17   "No," I replied, "I am certain I do not, but I see how little I saw before."

18   "That is next best," said he, earnestly, "but I won't hear you now; put away your fish and go home; perhaps you will be ready with a better answer in the morning. I will examine you before you look at the fish."

19   This was disconcerting. Not only must I think of my fish all night, studying, without the object before me, what this unknown but most visible feature might be; but also, without reviewing my discoveries, I must give an exact account of them the next day. I had a bad memory; so I walked home by Charles River in a distracted state, with my two perplexities.

20   The cordial greeting from the Professor the next morning was reassuring; here was a man who seemed to be quite as anxious as I that I should see for myself what he saw.

21   "Do you perhaps mean," I asked, "that the fish has symmetrical sides with paired organs?"

22   His thoroughly pleased "Of course! Of course!" repaid the wakeful hours of the previous night. After he had discoursed most happily and enthusiastically—as he always did—upon the importance of this point, I ventured to ask what I should do next.

23   "Oh, look at your fish!" he said, and left me again to my own devices. In a little more than an hour he returned, and heard my new catalogue.

24   "That is good, that is good!" he repeated; "but that is not all; go on"; and so for three long days he placed that fish before my eyes, forbidding me to look at anything else, or to use any artificial aid. "Look, look, look," was his repeated injunction.

25   This was the best entomological lesson I ever had—a lesson whose influence has extended to the details of every subsequent study; a legacy the Professor had left to me, as he has left it to so many others,

of inestimable value, which we could not buy, with which we cannot part.

26   A year afterward, some of us were amusing ourselves with chalking outlandish beasts on the Museum blackboard. We drew prancing starfishes; frogs in mortal combat; hydra-headed worms; stately crawfishes, standing on their tails, bearing aloft umbrellas; and grotesque fishes with gaping mouths and staring eyes. The Professor came in shortly after, and was as amused as any at our experiments. He looked at the fishes.

27   "Haemulons, every one of them," he said; "Mr.——drew them."

28   True; and to this day, if I attempt a fish, I can draw nothing but haemulons.

29   The fourth day, a second fish of the same group was placed beside the first, and I was bidden to point out the resemblances and differences between the two; another and another followed, until the entire family lay before me, and a whole legion of jars covered the table and surrounding shelves; the odor had become a pleasant perfume; and even now, the sight of an old, six-inch, worm-eaten cork brings fragrant memories.

30   The whole group of haemulons was thus brought in review; and, whether engaged upon the dissection of the internal organs, the preparation and examination of the bony framework, or the description of the various parts, Agassiz's training in the method of observing facts and their orderly arrangement was ever accompanied by the urgent exhortation not to be content with them.

31   "Facts are stupid things," he would say, "until brought into connection with some general law."

32   At the end of eight months, it was almost with reluctance that I left these friends and turned to insects; but what I had gained by this outside experience has been of greater value than years of later investigation in my favorite groups.

(1,529 words)

VOCABULARY

antecedents (1)	resuscitate (8)	catalogue (23)
explicit (5)	interdicted (9)	injunction (24)
entomology (7)	operculum (13)	inestimable (25)
ichthyology (7)	spinous (13)	hydra-headed (26)
aversion (7)	piqued (15)	exhortation (30)

THE FACTS

1. What kind of fish was Scudder asked to examine?

2. What did Agassiz call "one of the best of eyes"?

3. What important feature did Scudder discover about his fish after a night's rest and a second look?

4. What was the best entomological lesson that Scudder ever learned from Agassiz?

5. When, according to Agassiz, did facts cease to be stupid things?

THE STRATEGIES

1. What is the level of diction used in this essay? What kind of audience is it aimed at?

2. This is not the kind of essay that lends itself to outlining, but it does follow a pattern. What is the pattern that gives organization to the essay?

3. Despite the academic and scientific setting of this experience, humor abounds. How is this humor achieved? Point out specific examples.

4. Which passage do you consider the most descriptive in terms of details supplied? Explain your selection.

THE ISSUES

1. What relevance does Scudder's experience have to organizing an essay?

2. What characteristic do good writers and good scientists share?

3. Why would drawing the fish have helped Scudder to see it better?

4. What is a fact? What is a general law? How do they differ?

5. If drawing an object helps a science student see it more clearly, what might a student of English composition do to help him or her more clearly understand or see a certain subject?

SUGGESTIONS FOR WRITING

1. Following Scudder's example, write about an experience in which one of your teachers taught you an important lesson. Relate the experience according to an organized sequence.

2. Write an essay in which you start with the thesis, "Facts are stupid things until brought into connection with some general law." Illustrate this thesis with examples from your own experience.

E X A M P L E S

▼▼

E. M. Forster

MY WOOD

E. M. FORSTER (1879–1969) was a British novelist, essayist, and short story writer whose work first won wide recognition in 1924, with the publication of his *Passage to India*. In 1946 Forster was made an honorary fellow of King's College, Cambridge, where he lived until his death. Among his many other works are *Howard's End* (1910) and *Two Cheers for Democracy* (1951), a collection of his essays.

"My Wood," a superbly organized short essay, investigates the effect of property ownership on the individual and society.

1   A few years ago I wrote a book which dealt in part with the difficulties of the English in India. Feeling that they would have had no difficulties in India themselves, the Americans read the book freely. The more they read it the better it made them feel, and a cheque to the author was the result. I bought a wood with the cheque. It is not a large wood—it contains scarcely any trees, and it is intersected, blast it, by a public footpath. Still, it is the first property that I have owned, so it is right that other people should participate in my shame, and should ask themselves, in accents that will vary in horror, this very important question: What is the effect of property upon the character? Don't let's touch economics; the effect of private ownership upon the community as a whole is another question—a more important question, perhaps, but another one. Let's keep to psychology. If you own things, what's their effect on you? What's the effect on me of my wood?

2   In the first place, it makes me feel heavy. Property does have this effect. Property produces men of weight, and it was a man of weight who failed to get into the Kingdom of Heaven. He was not wicked, that unfortunate millionaire in the parable, he was only stout; he stuck out in front, not to mention behind, and as he wedged himself this way and that in the crystalline entrance and bruised his well-fed flanks, he saw beneath him a comparatively slim camel passing through the eye of a needle and being woven into the robe of God. The Gospels all through

couple stoutness and slowness. They point out what is perfectly obvious, yet seldom realized: that if you have a lot of things you cannot move about a lot, that furniture requires dusting, dusters require servants, servants require insurance stamps,* and the whole tangle of them makes you think twice before you accept an invitation to dinner or go for a bathe in the Jordan. Sometimes the Gospels proceed further and say with Tolstoy that property is sinful; they approach the difficult ground of asceticism here, where I cannot follow them. But as to the immediate effects of property on people, they just show straightforward logic. It produces men of weight. Men of weight cannot, by definition, move like the lightning from the East unto the West, and the ascent of a fourteen-stone bishop into a pulpit is thus the exact antithesis of the coming of the Son of Man. My wood makes me feel heavy.

3   In the second place, it makes me feel it ought to be larger.

4   The other day I heard a twig snap in it. I was annoyed at first, for I thought that someone was blackberrying, and depreciating the value of the undergrowth. On coming nearer, I saw it was not a man who had trodden on the twig and snapped it, but a bird, and I felt pleased. My bird. The bird was not equally pleased. Ignoring the relation between us, it took fright as soon as it saw the shape of my face, and flew straight over the boundary hedge into a field, the property of Mrs. Henessy, where it sat down with a loud squawk. It had become Mrs. Henessy's bird. Something seemed grossly amiss here, something that would not have occurred had the wood been larger. I could not afford to buy Mrs. Henessy out, I dared not murder her, and limitations of this sort beset me on every side. Ahab did not want that vineyard—he only needed it to round off his property, preparatory to plotting a new curve—and all the land around my wood has become necessary to me in order to round off the wood. A boundary protects. But—poor little thing—the boundary ought in its turn to be protected. Noises on the edge of it. Children throw stones. A little more, and then a little more, until we reach the sea. Happy Canute! Happier Alexander! And after all, why should even the world be the limit of possession? A rocket containing a Union Jack, will, it is hoped, be shortly fired at the moon. Mars. Sirius. Beyond which . . . But these immensities ended by saddening me. I could not suppose that my wood was the destined nucleus of universal dominion—it is so very small and contains no mineral wealth beyond the blackberries. Nor was I comforted when Mrs. Henessy's bird took alarm for the second time and flew clean away from us all, under the belief that it belonged to itself.

5   In the third place, property makes its owner feel that he ought to do something to it. Yet he isn't sure what. A restlessness comes over

---

* In England.—Ed.

him, a vague sense that he has a personality to express—the same sense which, without any vagueness, leads the artist to an act of creation. Sometimes I think I will cut down such trees as remain in the wood, at other times I want to fill up the gaps between them with new trees. Both impulses are pretentious and empty. They are not honest movements towards money-making or beauty. They spring from a foolish desire to express myself and from an inability to enjoy what I have got. Creation, property, enjoyment form a sinister trinity in the human mind. Creation and enjoyment are both very good, yet they are often unattainable without a material basis, and at such moments property pushes itself in as a substitute, saying, "Accept me instead— I'm good enough for all three." It is not enough. It is, as Shakespeare said of lust, "The expense of spirit in a waste of shame": it is "Before, a joy proposed; behind, a dream." Yet we don't know how to shun it. It is forced on us by our economic system as the alternative to starvation. It is also forced on us by an internal defect in the soul, by the feeling that in property may lie the germs of self-development and of exquisite or heroic deeds. Our life on earth is, and ought to be, material and carnal. But we have not yet learned to manage our materialism and carnality properly; they are still entangled with the desire for ownership, where (in the words of Dante) "Possession is one with loss."

6 And this brings us to our fourth and final point: the blackberries.

7 Blackberries are not plentiful in this meagre grove, but they are easily seen from the public footpath which traverses it, and all too easily gathered. Foxgloves, too—people will pull up the foxgloves, and ladies of an educational tendency even grub for toad stools to show them on the Monday in class. Other ladies, less educated, roll down the bracken in the arms of their gentlemen friends. There is a paper, there are tins. Pray, does my wood belong to me or doesn't it? And, if it does, should I not own it best by allowing no one else to walk there? There is a wood near Lyme Regis, also cursed by a public footpath, where the owner has not hesitated on this point. He has built high stone walls on each side of the path, and has spanned it by bridges, so that the public circulate like termites while he gorges on the blackberries unseen. He really does own his wood, this able chap. Dives in Hell did pretty well, but the gulf dividing him from Lazarus could be traversed by vision, and nothing traverses it here. And perhaps I shall come to this in time. I shall wall in and fence out until I really taste the sweets of property. Enormously stout, endlessly avaricious, pseudo-creative, intensely selfish, I shall weave upon my forehead the quadruple crown of possession until those nasty Bolshies come and take it off again and thrust me aside into the outer darkness.

(1,333 words)

THE FACTS

1. What intersects Forster's wood and is a source of annoyance to him?

2. What is the first effect Forster's wood had on him?

3. What or whom did Forster discover on his property when he heard a twig snap?

4. According to Forster, what does property make an owner feel he ought to do with it?

5. What does Forster think he will eventually do with his wood?

THE STRATEGIES

1. What are the obvious divisions in the topics and subtopics of this essay? Make an outline showing the thesis, main points, and subtopics of the essay.

2. Read the last sentence of paragraph 2. What is the purpose of this sentence?

3. What is the purpose of paragraph 3?

4. What tone does Forster use throughout this essay? Do you regard his tone as mocking, serious, ironic? Justify your answer.

5. In paragraph 4 Forster writes: "Happy Canute! Happier Alexander!" What is this figure of speech called? Why is Alexander happier than Canute?

THE ISSUES

1. What point does Forster make obliquely in his discussion about the bird?

2. What effect does ownership have on you? Is Forster exaggerating here or have you experienced these same effects that he describes?

3. What useful benefits, if any, do you think society gains from ownership of private property?

4. What do you think Dante meant by, "Possession is one with loss"? Interpret this statement.

5. "Our life on earth is, and ought to be, material and carnal." What is your opinion of this statement? How do you think our life on earth ought to be?

SUGGESTIONS FOR WRITING

1. Write an analysis of the tone of this essay, carefully supporting your points with quotations from the work itself.

2. Write an essay on the benefits of property ownership.

▼▼

Donald Kagan

WHY WESTERN HISTORY MATTERS

DONALD KAGAN (b. 1932), a naturalized U.S. citizen from Lithuania, is Bass professor of classics and history and Western civilization at Yale. He received his undergraduate education at the Brooklyn College of the City University of New York and his Ph.D. from Ohio State University. He authored the book *On the Origins of War and the Preservation of Peace* (1994). The essay that follows is adapted from a speech Kagan delivered to the National Association of Scholars and was reprinted in the December 28, 1994, issue of the *Wall Street Journal*.

If you have ever wondered why high schools and colleges have laid such stress on the history, civilization, and culture of Western Europe—to the exclusion of other continents—this essay will give you a well-reasoned answer. Pay attention to the author's comments about how Western civilization has influenced the human condition.

1   In 1990, I suggested to the freshmen of Yale College that they would be wise to make the study of Western civilization the center of their pursuit of a liberal education. I pointed out the devastating effects of ethnic conflict and disunity around the world and the special problems and opportunities confronting the U.S., a country that was never a nation in the sense of resting on common ancestry but one that depends on a set of beliefs and institutions deriving from Western traditions. I argued that the unity of our country and the defense of its freedom required that its citizens understand the ideas, history, and traditions that created them.

2   The debate that followed revealed a broad and deep ignorance of the historical process by which the very values that encourage current criticisms of the Western experience came into being.

3   Western civilization was not the result of some inevitable process through which other cultures will automatically pass. It emerged from a unique history in which chance and accident played a vital part. The institutions and ideas that provide for freedom and improvement in

material conditions cannot flourish without an understanding of how they came about.

Uniformity and Stability

4   The many civilizations adopted by the human race have shared basic characteristics. Most have tended toward cultural uniformity and stability. Reason, though employed for all sorts of practical and intellectual purposes, lacked independence from religion and the high status to challenge the most basic received ideas. The standard form of government has been monarchy. Religious and political institutions and beliefs have been thoroughly intertwined in a mutually supportive unified structure; government has not been subject to secular, reasoned analysis.

5   The first and sharpest break with this common experience came in ancient Greece. The Greek city-states were republics. There were no kings with the wealth to hire mercenary soldiers, so the citizens did their own fighting. As independent defenders of the common safety and interest, they demanded a role in the most important political decisions; in this way, for the first time, political life came to be shared by a relatively large portion of the people.

6   What most set the Greeks apart was their view of the world. The Greek way of looking at things requires a change from the use of faith, poetry and intuition to a reliance on reason. The Greeks exposed everything they perceived—natural, human and divine—to the searching examination of *logos*.*

7   But the Greeks combined a unique sense of mankind's possibilities with a painful understanding of its limitations. This is the tragic vision of the human condition that characterized classical Greek civilization. To cope with it, they urged human beings to restrain their over-arching ambitions. Inscribed at Apollo's temple at Delphi were the slogans "know thyself" and "nothing in excess."

8   Beyond these exhortations they relied on a good political regime to train human beings in virtue and restrain them from vice. Aristotle made the point neatly:

9   "As man is the best of the animals when perfected, so he is the worst when separated from law and justice. For injustice is most dangerous when it is armed, and man, armed by nature with good sense and virtue, may use them for entirely opposite ends. Therefore, when he is without virtue man is the most unscrupulous and savage of the animals."

10   The second great strand in the history of the West is the Judeo-Christian tradition. Christianity's main roots were in Judaism, a

---

* Reason.

religion that worships a single, all-powerful deity who is sharply separated from human beings, makes great moral demands upon them, and judges them all, even kings and emperors. Christianity began as a persecuted religion that captured the Roman Empire only after centuries of hostility, and it never entirely lost its original character as an insurgent movement, independent of the state and hostile to it.

11   The union of a universalist religion with a monarch such as the Roman emperor, who ruled a vast empire, could nevertheless have put an end to any prospect of freedom. But Christianity's inheritance of the rational, disputatious Greek philosophy led to powerfully divisive quarrels about the nature of God and other theological questions.

12   The Barbarians' destruction of the Western Empire also destroyed the power of the emperors and their efforts to impose religious and political conformity under imperial control. Here we arrive at a second sharp break with the general experience of mankind. The West of the Germanic tribes that had toppled the Roman Empire was weak and divided. Nobody sought or planned for freedom, but in the spaces left by the endless conflicts among secular rulers and between them and the church there was room for freedom to grow.

13   Into some of that space towns and cities reappeared. Taking advantage of the rivalries mentioned above, they obtained charters from the local powers establishing their right to govern themselves. In Italy some of these cities were able to gain control of the surrounding country and to become city-states resembling those of ancient Greece.

14   In these states the modern world began to take form. Although the people were Christian, their life and outlook became increasingly secular. Here, and in other cities north of the Alps, arose a world view that celebrated the greatness and dignity of mankind. Its vision is revealed with flamboyant confidence by Pico della Mirandola. He wrote that God told man:

15   "We have made thee neither of heaven nor of earth, neither mortal nor immortal, so that with freedom of choice and with honor, as though the maker and molder of thyself, thou mayest fashion thyself in whatever shape thou shalt prefer. . . . O supreme generosity of God the Father, O highest and most felicity of man! To him it is granted to have whatever he chooses, to be whatever he wills."

16   This is a remarkable leap beyond the humanism of the Greeks, something new in the world. Man is more than mortal, unlimited by nature, entirely free to shape himself and to acquire whatever he wants.

17   Another Florentine, Machiavelli, moved further in the same direction. For him "Fortune is a woman, . . . and it is necessary to hold her down and beat her and fight with her," a notion the Greeks would have regarded as dangerously arrogant and certain to produce disaster.

18   Francis Bacon, influenced by Machiavelli, urged human beings to employ their reason to force nature to give up its secrets. He assumed

that such a course would lead to progress and the general improvement of the human condition. Such thinking lay at the heart of the scientific revolution and remains the faith on which modern science and technology rest.

19   Hobbes and Locke applied a similar novelty and modernity to the sphere of politics, discovering "natural rights" that belong to man either as part of nature or as the gifts of a benevolent and reasonable God. Man's basic rights—life, liberty and property—were seen as absolute.

20   Freedom was threatened in early modern times by the emergence of monarchies, but the cause of individual liberty was enhanced by the Protestant Reformation, another upheaval within Christianity arising from its focus on individual salvation, its inheritance of a tradition of penetrating reason, and to the continuing struggle between church and state.

21   The English Revolution came about in large part because of Charles I's attempt to impose an alien religious conformity, as well as tighter political control, on his kingdom. In England the tradition of freedom and government bound by law was strong enough to produce effective resistance. From the ensuing rebellion came limited, constitutional, representative government and, ultimately, democracy. The example and the ideas it produced encouraged and informed the French and American revolutions and the entire modern constitutional tradition.

22   These ideas and institutions are the basis for modern liberal thinking about politics, the individual and society, just as the confident view of science and technology as progressive forces has been the most powerful form taken by the Western elevation of reason. In the last two centuries both these elements of Western civilization have come under heavy attack. At different times, science and technology have been blamed for the destruction of human community and the alienation of people from nature and from one another, for intensifying the gulf between rich and poor, for threatening the very existence of humanity either by producing weapons of total destruction or by destroying the environment.

23   At the same time, the foundations of freedom have also come into question. Jefferson and his colleagues could confidently proclaim their political rights as the gift of a "Creator." By now, however, the power of religion has faded, and for many the basis for a modern political and moral order has been demolished. Nietzsche announced the death of God, and Dostoevsky's Grand Inquisitor asserted that when God is dead all things are permitted. Nihilism rejects any objective basis for society and its morality, the very concept of objectivity, even the possibility of communication itself, and a vulgar form of nihilism has a remarkable influence in our educational system today.

24   The consequences of the victory of such ideas would be enormous. If both religion and reason are removed, all that remains is will and power, where the only law is that of tooth and claw. There is no protection for the freedom of weaker individuals or those who question the authority of the most powerful. There is no basis for individual rights or for a critique of existing ideas and institutions.

25   That such attacks on the greatest achievements of the West should be made by Western intellectuals is perfectly in keeping with the Western tradition, yet it seems ironic that they have gained so much currency at the height of the achievements of Western reason in the form of science, and at a moment when its concept of political freedom seems to be sweeping all before it.

26   Still, we cannot deny that there is a dark side to the Western experience. To put untrammeled reason and individual freedom at the center of a civilization is to live with the turmoil that they produce. Freedom was born and has survived in the space created by divisions and conflict within and between nations and religions. We must wonder whether the power of modern weapons will allow it and the world to survive at such a price. Individual freedom, although it greatly elevates the condition of the people who live in free societies, inevitably permits inequalities that are the more galling because each person is plainly responsible for the outcome. Freedom does permit isolation from society and an alienation of the individual at a high cost to both.

27   Nor are these the only problems posed by the Western tradition in its modern form. Whether it takes the form of the unbridled claims of Pico della Mirandola, or of the Nietzschean assertion of the power of the superior individual to shape his own nature, or of the modern totalitarian effort to change humanity by utopian social engineering, the temptation to arrogance threatens the West's traditions and achievements.

Older Traditions

28   Because of Western civilization's emergence as the exemplary civilization, it also presents problems to the whole world. The challenges presented by freedom and reason cannot be met by recourse to the experience of other cultures, where these characteristics have not been prominent. To understand and cope with our problems we all need to know and to grapple with the Western experience.

29   In my view, we need especially to examine the older traditions of the West—especially among the Greeks, who began it all. They understood the potentiality of human beings, their limitations, and the predicament in which they live. Man is potent and important, yet he is fallible and mortal, capable of the greatest achievements and the worst crimes. He is a tragic figure, powerful but limited, with freedom to choose and act but bound by his own nature, knowing that he will

never achieve perfect knowledge and understanding, justice and happiness, but determined to continue the search.

30   To me that seems an accurate description of the human condition that is meaningful not only for the Greeks and their heirs in the West but for all human beings. It is an understanding that cannot be achieved without a serious examination of the Western experience. The abandonment of such a study or its adulteration for current political purposes would be a terrible loss to all of humanity.

(2,067 words)

VOCABULARY

uniformity (4)	unscrupulous (9)	currency (25)
secular (4)	insurgent (10)	untrammeled (26)
republics (5)	universalist (11)	galling (26)
mercenary (5)	disputatious (11)	totalitarian (27)
exhortations (8)	felicity (15)	utopian (27)
regime (8)	alienation (22)	adulteration (30)

THE FACTS

1. What is the basic difference between Western civilization and other civilizations in the world?

2. What civilization caused the first and sharpest break with the common experience shared by all civilizations? What was significant about this break?

3. What did the Barbarians' destruction of the Western Empire contribute to Western history?

4. What did the Italian Pico della Mirandola say about man?

5. What was Francis Bacon's contribution to Western thought?

6. According to the author, what is the dark side to the Western experience?

THE STRATEGIES

1. How does the author convince readers of the correctness of his perspective?

2. How well is the essay organized? What organizational strategies does the author use?

3. What is the purpose of the two headings in the essay?

4. What level of English does the author use? To what kind of audience is it geared?

5. What is the thesis of the essay and where is it stated? How effective is the placement?

THE ISSUES

1. What is the author's major concern throughout the essay? What is your response to this concern?

2. What did the author suggest to the freshman of Yale College in 1990? Has he changed his opinion between that talk and the present essay? Why or why not?

3. What are the dangers, if any, of accepting the Greeks' reliance on reason as the basis for making judgments?

4. Do you agree with the author that untrammeled reason and individual freedom at the center of a civilization means we must live with turmoil? What balanced view for making decisions would you advocate today? Consider matters such as tradition, reason, faith, science, technology, and religion.

5. How prominent should Western history be in today's liberal arts curriculum? What other history, if any, do you advocate adding to the curriculum? Consider subjects such as comparative civilizations, eastern thought and history, and eastern art.

SUGGESTIONS FOR WRITING

1. Write an essay rebutting Kagan's essay and advocating the study of other histories besides Western history.

2. Write an essay in which you suggest how we can avoid the turmoil that comes from relying too heavily on reason and individual freedom.

TERM PAPER SUGGESTION

Write a research paper based on the unique contribution to Western thought made by one of the following writers: Desiderius Erasmus, Niccolo Machiavelli, Thomas More, John Colet, John Milton, Francis Bacon, Thomas Hobbes, John Locke.

▼▼

James Thurber

THE CATBIRD SEAT

JAMES THURBER (1894–1963) was an American humorist, cartoonist, and social commentator. His contributions to *The New Yorker* made him immensely popular. Among his best-known works are *My Life and Hard Times* (1933), *Fables for Our Time* (1940), and *The Thurber Carnival* (1945), from which this selection was taken.

> *A conventional, well-behaved office clerk suddenly finds his job threatened by an aggressive, loud-mouthed "special adviser to the president." To protect his job, this unobtrusive little man resorts to a most unusual crime.*

1   Mr. Martin bought the pack of Camels on Monday night in the most crowded cigar store on Broadway. It was theatre time and seven or eight men were buying cigarettes. The clerk didn't even glance at Mr. Martin, who put the pack in his overcoat pocket and went out. If any of the staff at F & S had seen him buy the cigarettes, they would have been astonished, for it was generally known that Mr. Martin did not smoke, and never had. No one saw him.

2   It was just a week to the day since Mr. Martin had decided to rub out Mrs. Ulgine Barrows. The term "rub out" pleased him because it suggested nothing more than the correction of an error—in this case an error of Mr. Fitweiler. Mr. Martin had spent each night of the past week working out his plan and examining it. As he walked home now he went over it again. For the hundredth time he resented the element of imprecision, the margin of guesswork that entered into the business. The project as he had worked it out was casual and bold, the risks were considerable. Something might go wrong anywhere along the line. And therein lay the cunning of his scheme. No one would ever see in it the cautious, painstaking hand of Erwin Martin, head of the filing department at F & S, of whom Mr. Fitweiler had once said, "Man is fallible but Martin isn't." No one would see his hand, that is, unless it were caught in the act.

3   Sitting in his apartment, drinking a glass of milk, Mr. Martin reviewed his case against Mrs. Ulgine Barrows, as he had every night for seven nights. He began at the beginning. Her quacking voice and braying laugh had first profaned the halls of F & S on March 7, 1941 (Mr. Martin had a head for dates). Old Roberts, the personnel chief, had introduced her as the newly appointed special adviser to the president of

the firm, Mr. Fitweiler. The woman had appalled Mr. Martin instantly, but he hadn't shown it. He had given her his dry hand, a look of studious concentration, and a faint smile. "Well," she had said, looking at the papers on his desk, "are you lifting the oxcart out of the ditch?" As Mr. Martin recalled that moment, over his milk, he squirmed slightly. He must keep his mind on her crimes as a special adviser, not on her peccadillos as a personality. This he found difficult to do, in spite of entering an objection and sustaining it. The faults of the woman as a woman kept chattering on in his mind like an unruly witness. She had, for almost two years now, baited him. In the halls, in the elevator, even in his own office, into which she romped now and then like a circus horse, she was constantly shouting these silly questions at him. "Are you lifting the oxcart out of the ditch? Are you tearing up the pea patch? Are you hollering down the rain barrel? Are you scraping around the bottom of the pickle barrel? Are you sitting in the catbird seat?"

4   It was Joey Hart, one of Mr. Martin's two assistants, who had explained what the gibberish meant. "She must be a Dodger fan," he had said. "Red Barber announces the Dodger games over the radio and he uses those expressions—picked 'em up down South." Joey had gone on to explain one or two. "Tearing up the pea patch" meant going on a rampage; "sitting in the catbird seat" meant sitting pretty, like a batter with three balls and no strikes on him. Mr. Martin dismissed all this with an effort. It had been annoying, it had driven him near to distraction, but he was too solid a man to be moved to murder by anything so childish. It was fortunate, he reflected as he passed on to the important charges against Mrs. Barrows, that he had stood up under it so well. He had maintained always an outward appearance of polite tolerance. "Why, I even believe you like the woman," Miss Paird, his other assistant, had once said to him. He had simply smiled.

5   A gavel rapped in Mr. Martin's mind and the case proper was resumed. Mrs. Ulgine Barrows stood charged with willful, blatant, and persistent attempts to destroy the efficiency and system of F & S. It was competent, material, and relevant to review her advent and rise to power. Mr. Martin had got the story from Miss Paird, who seemed always able to find things out. According to her, Mrs. Barrows had met Mr. Fitweiler at a party, where she had rescued him from the embraces of a powerfully built drunken man who had mistaken the president of F & S for a famous retired Middle Western football coach. She had led him to a sofa and somehow worked upon him a monstrous magic. The aging gentleman had jumped to the conclusion there and then that this was a woman of singular attainments, equipped to bring out the best in him and in the firm. A week later he had introduced her into F & S as his special adviser. On that day confusion got its foot in the door. After Miss Tyson, Mr. Brundage, and Mr. Bartlett had been fired and

Mr. Munson had taken his hat and stalked out, mailing in his resignation later, old Roberts had been emboldened to speak to Mr. Fitweiler. He mentioned that Mr. Munson's department had been "a little disrupted" and hadn't they perhaps better resume the old system there? Mr. Fitweiler had said certainly not. He had the greatest faith in Mrs. Barrows' ideas. "They require a little seasoning, a little seasoning, is all," he had added. Mr. Roberts had given it up. Mr. Martin reviewed in detail all the changes wrought by Mrs. Barrows. She had begun chipping at the cornices of the firm's edifice and now she was swinging at the foundation stones with a pickaxe.

6   Mr. Martin came now, in his summing up, to the afternoon of Monday, November 2, 1942—just one week ago. On that day, at 3 P. M., Mrs. Barrows had bounced into his office. "Boo!" she had yelled. "Are you scraping around the bottom of the pickle barrel?" Mr. Martin had looked at her from under his green eyeshade, saying nothing. She had begun to wander about the office, taking it in with her great, popping eyes. "Do you really need *all* these filing cabinets?" she had demanded suddenly. Mr. Martin's heart had jumped. "Each of these files," he had said, keeping his voice even, "plays an indispensable part in the system of F & S." She had brayed at him, "Well, don't tear up the pea patch!" and gone to the door. From there she had bawled, "But you sure have got a lot of fine scrap in here!" Mr. Martin could no longer doubt that the finger was on his beloved department. Her pickaxe was on the upswing, poised for the first blow. It had not come yet; he had received no blue memo from the enchanted Mr. Fitweiler bearing nonsensical instructions deriving from the obscene woman. But there was no doubt in Mr. Martin's mind that one would be forthcoming. He must act quickly. Already a precious week had gone by. Mr. Martin stood up in his living room, still holding his milk glass. "Gentlemen of the jury" he said to himself, "I demand the death penalty for this horrible person."

7   The next day Mr. Martin followed his routine, as usual. He polished his glasses more often and once sharpened an already sharp pencil, but not even Miss Paird noticed. Only once did he catch sight of his victim; she swept past him in the hall with a patronizing "Hi!" At five-thirty he walked home, as usual, and had a glass of milk, as usual. He had never drunk anything stronger in his life—unless you could count ginger ale. The late Sam Schlosser, the S of F & S, had praised Mr. Martin at a staff meeting several years before for his temperate habits. "Our most efficient worker neither drinks nor smokes," he had said. "The results speak for themselves." Mr. Fitweiler had sat by, nodding approval.

8   Mr. Martin was still thinking about that red-letter day as he walked over to the Schrafft's on Fifth Avenue near Forty-sixth Street. He got there, as he always did, at eight o'clock. He finished his dinner and the financial page of the *Sun* at a quarter to nine, as he always did.

It was his custom after dinner to take a walk. This time he walked down Fifth Avenue at a casual pace. His gloved hands felt moist and warm, his forehead cold. He transferred the Camels from his overcoat to a jacket pocket. He wondered, as he did so, if they did not represent an unnecessary note of strain. Mrs. Barrows smoked only Luckies. It was his idea to puff a few puffs on a Camel (after the rubbing-out), stub it out in the ashtray holding her lipstick-stained Luckies, and thus drag a small red herring across the trail. Perhaps it was not a good idea. It would take time. He might even choke, too loudly.

9   Mr. Martin had never seen the house on West Twelfth Street where Mrs. Barrows lived, but he had a clear enough picture of it. Fortunately, she had bragged to everybody about her ducky first-floor apartment in the perfectly darling three-story red-brick. There would be no doorman or other attendants; just the tenants of the second and third floors. As he walked along, Mr. Martin realized that he would get there before nine-thirty. He had considered walking north on Fifth Avenue from Schrafft's to a point from which it would take him until ten o'clock to reach the house. At that hour people were less likely to be coming in or going out. But the procedure would have made an awkward loop in the straight thread of his casualness, and he had abandoned it. It was impossible to figure when people would be entering or leaving the house, anyway. There was a great risk at any hour. If he ran into anybody, he would simply have to place the rubbing-out of Ulgine Barrows in the inactive file forever. The same thing would hold true if there were someone in her apartment. In that case he would just say that he had been passing by, recognized her charming house, and thought to drop in.

10   It was eighteen minutes after nine when Mr. Martin turned into Twelfth Street. A man passed him, and a man and a woman, talking. There was no one within fifty paces when he came to the house, halfway down the block. He was up the steps and in the small vestibule in no time, pressing the bell under the card that said "Mrs. Ulgine Barrows." When the clicking in the lock started, he jumped forward against the door. He got inside fast, closing the door behind him. A bulb in a lantern hung from the hall ceiling on a chain seemed to give a monstrously bright light. There was nobody on the stair, which went up ahead of him along the left wall. A door opened down the hall in the wall on the right. He went toward it swiftly, on tiptoe.

11   "Well, for God's sake, look who's here!" bawled Mrs. Barrows, and her braying laugh rang out like the report of a shotgun. He rushed past her like a football tackle, bumping her. "Hey, quit shoving!" she said, closing the door behind them. They were in her living room, which seemed to Mr. Martin to be lighted by a hundred lamps. "What's after you?" she said. "You're as jumpy as a goat." He found he was unable to speak. His heart was wheezing in his throat. "I—yes," he finally

brought out. She was jabbering and laughing as she started to help him off with his coat. "No, no," he said. "I'll put it here." He took it off and put in on a chair near the door. "Your hat and gloves, too," she said. "You're in a lady's house." He put his hat on top of the coat. Mrs. Barrows seemed larger than he had thought. He kept his gloves on. "I was passing by," he said. "I recognized—is there anyone here?" She laughed louder than ever. "No," she said, "we're all alone. You're as white as a sheet, you funny man. Whatever has come over you? I'll mix you a toddy." She started toward a door across the room. "Scotch-and-soda be all right? But say, you don't drink, do you?" She turned and gave him her amused look. Mr. Martin pulled himself together. "Scotch-and-soda will be all right," he heard himself say. He could hear her laughing in the kitchen.

12   Mr. Martin looked quickly around the living room for the weapon. He had counted on finding one there. There were andirons and a poker and something in a corner that looked like an Indian club. None of them would do. It couldn't be that way. He began to pace around. He came to a desk. On it lay a metal paper knife with an ornate handle. Would it be sharp enough? He reached for it and knocked over a small brass jar. Stamps spilled out of it and it fell to the floor with a clatter. "Hey," Mrs. Barrows yelled from the kitchen, "are you tearing up the pea patch?" Mr. Martin gave a strange laugh. Picking up the knife, he tried its point against his left wrist. It was blunt. It wouldn't do.

13   When Mrs. Barrows reappeared, carrying two highballs, Mr. Martin, standing there with his gloves on, became acutely conscious of the fantasy he had wrought. Cigarettes in his pocket, a drink prepared for him—it was all too grossly improbable. It was more than that; it was impossible. Somewhere in the back of his mind a vague idea stirred, sprouted. "For heaven's sake, take off those gloves," said Mrs. Barrows. "I always wear them in the house," said Mr. Martin. The idea began to bloom, strange and wonderful. She put the glasses on a coffee table in front of a sofa and sat on the sofa. "Come over here, you odd little man," she said. Mr. Martin went over and sat beside her. It was difficult getting a cigarette out of the pack of Camels, but he managed it. She held a match for him, laughing. "Well," she said, handing him a drink, "this is perfectly marvellous. You with a drink and a cigarette."

14   Mr. Martin puffed, not too awkwardly, and took a gulp of the highball. "I drink and smoke all the time," he said. He clinked his glass against hers. "Here's nuts to that old windbag, Fitweiler," he said, and gulped again. The stuff tasted awful, but he made no grimace. "Really, Mr. Martin," she said, her voice and posture changing, "you are insulting our employer." Mrs. Barrows was now all special adviser to the president. "I am preparing a bomb," said Mr. Martin, "which will blow the old goat higher than hell." He had only had a little of the drink, which was not strong. It couldn't be that. "Do you take

dope or something?" Mrs. Barrows asked coldly. "Heroin," said Mr. Martin. "I'll be coked to the gills when I bump that old buzzard off." "Mr. Martin!" she shouted, getting to her feet. "That will be all of that. You must go at once." Mr. Martin took another swallow of his drink. He tapped his cigarette out in the ashtray and put the pack of Camels on the coffee table. Then he got up. She stood glaring at him. He walked over and put on his hat and coat. "Not a word about this," he said, and laid an index finger against his lips. All Mrs. Barrows could bring out was "Really!" Mr. Martin put his hand on the doorknob. "I'm sitting in the catbird seat," he said. He stuck his tongue out at her and left. Nobody saw him go.

15   Mr. Martin got to his apartment, walking, well before eleven. No one saw him go in. He had two glasses of milk after brushing his teeth, and he felt elated. It wasn't tipsiness, because he hadn't been tipsy. Anyway, the walk had worn off all effects of the whiskey. He got in bed and read a magazine for a while. He was asleep before midnight.

16   Mr. Martin got to the office at eight-thirty the next morning, as usual. At a quarter to nine, Ulgine Barrows, who had never before arrived at work before ten, swept into his office. "I'm reporting to Mr. Fitweiler now!" she shouted. "If he turns you over to the police, it's no more than you deserve!" Mr. Martin gave her a look of shocked surprise. "I beg your pardon?" he said. Mrs. Barrows snorted and bounced out of the room, leaving Miss Paird and Joey Hart staring after her. "What's the matter with that old devil now?" asked Miss Paird. "I have no idea," said Mr. Martin, resuming his work. The other two looked at him and then at each other. Miss Paird got up and went out. She walked slowly past the closed door of Mr. Fitweiler's office. Mrs. Barrows was yelling inside, but she was not braying. Miss Paird could not hear what the woman was saying. She went back to her desk.

17   Forty-five minutes later, Mrs. Barrows left the president's office and went into her own, shutting the door. It wasn't until half an hour later that Mr. Fitweiler sent for Mr. Martin. The head of the filing department, neat, quiet, attentive, stood in front of the old man's desk. Mr. Fitweiler was pale and nervous. He took his glasses off and twiddled them. He made a small, bruffing sound in his throat. "Martin," he said, "you have been with us more than twenty years." "Twenty-two, sir," said Mr. Martin. "In that time," pursued the president, "your work and your—uh—manner have been exemplary." "I trust so, sir," said Mr. Martin. "I have understood, Martin," said Mr. Fitweiler, "that you have never taken a drink or smoked." "That is correct, sir," said Mr. Martin. "Ah, yes." Mr. Fitweiler polished his glasses. "You may describe what you did after leaving the office yesterday, Martin," he said. Mr. Martin allowed less than a second for his bewildered pause. "Certainly, sir," he said. "I walked home. Then I went to Schrafft's for dinner. Afterward I walked home again. I went to bed early, sir, and

read a magazine for a while. I was asleep before eleven." "Ah, yes," said Mr. Fitweiler again. He was silent for a moment, searching for the proper words to say to the head of the filing department. "Mrs. Barrows," he said finally, "Mrs. Barrows has worked hard, Martin, very hard. It grieves me to report that she has suffered a severe breakdown. It has taken the form of a persecution complex accompanied by distressing hallucinations." "I am very sorry, sir," said Mr. Martin. "Mrs. Barrows is under the delusion," continued Mr. Fitweiler, "that you visited her last evening and behaved yourself in an—uh—unseemly manner." He raised his hand to silence Mr. Martin's little pained outcry. "It is the nature of these psychological diseases," Mr. Fitweiler said, "to fix upon the least likely and most innocent party as the—uh—source of persecution. These matters are not for the lay mind to grasp, Martin. I've just had my psychiatrist, Dr. Fitch, on the phone. He would not, of course, commit himself, but he made enough generalizations to substantiate my suspicions. I suggested to Mrs. Barrows, when she had completed her—uh—story to me this morning, that she visit Dr. Fitch, for I suspected a condition at once. She flew, I regret to say, into a rage, and demanded—uh—requested that I call you on the carpet. You may not know, Martin, but Mrs. Barrows had planned a reorganization of your department—subject to my approval, of course, subject to my approval. This brought you, rather than anyone else, to her mind—but again that is a phenomenon for Dr. Fitch and not for us. So, Martin, I am afraid Mrs. Barrows' usefulness here is at an end." "I am dreadfully sorry, sir," said Mr. Martin.

18   It was at this point that the door to the office blew open with the suddenness of a gas-main explosion and Mrs. Barrows catapulted through it. "Is the little rat denying it?" she screamed. "He can't get away with that!" Mr. Martin got up and moved discreetly to a point beside Mr. Fitweiler's chair. "You drank and smoked at my apartment," she bawled at Mr. Martin, "and you know it! You called Mr. Fitweiler an old windbag and said you were going to blow him up when you got coked to the gills on your heroin!" She stopped yelling to catch her breath and a new glint came into her popping eyes. "If you weren't such a drab, ordinary little man," she said, "I'd think you'd planned it all. Sticking your tongue out, saying you were sitting in the catbird seat, because you thought no one would believe me when I told it! My God, it's really too perfect!" She glared at Mr. Fitweiler. "Can't you see how he has tricked us, you old fool? Can't you see his little game?" But Mr. Fitweiler had been surreptitiously pressing all the buttons under the top of his desk and employees of F & S began pouring into the room. "Stockton," said Mr. Fitweiler, "you and Fishbein will take Mrs. Barrows to her home. Mrs. Powell, you will go with them." Stockton, who had played a little football in high school, blocked Mrs. Barrows as she made for Mr. Martin. It took him and Fishbein together to

force her out of the door into the hall, crowded with stenographers and office boys. She was still screaming imprecations at Mr. Martin, tangled and contradictory imprecations. The hubbub finally died out down the corridor.

19   "I regret that this has happened," said Mr. Fitweiler. "I shall ask you to dismiss it from your mind, Martin." "Yes, sir," said Mr. Martin, anticipating his chief's "That will be all" by moving to the door. "I will dismiss it." He went out and shut the door, and his step was light and quick in the hall. When he entered his department he had slowed down to his customary gait, and he walked quietly across the room to the W20 file, wearing a look of studious concentration.

(3,827 words)

VOCABULARY

fallible (2)	patronizing (7)	exemplary (17)
appalled (3)	temperate (7)	hallucinations (17)
peccadillos (3)	red herring (8)	unseemly (17)
romped (3)	ducky (9)	catapulted (18)
gibberish (4)	monstrously (10)	surreptitiously (18)
edifice (5)	wheezing (11)	imprecations (18)
indispensable (6)	grossly (13)	
obscene (6)	bruffing (17)	

THE FACTS

1. What is the origin of the colorful expressions that Mrs. Barrows constantly uses?

2. What is Mrs. Barrows's title in the firm of F & S?

3. Why does Mr. Martin finally decide to "rub out" Mrs. Barrows?

4. What shocking disclosures does Mr. Martin reveal to Mrs. Barrows on his surprise visit to her apartment?

5. What is the outcome of Mrs. Barrows's accusations against Mr. Martin?

THE STRATEGIES

1. The organization of the story falls naturally into four divisions: (a) the trial and verdict of Mrs. Barrows, (b) preparation for the

crime, (c) change of plan and perpetration of the crime, (d) result of the crime. Summarize what happens in each of these segments.

2. Early in the story the author tells us that Mr. Martin plans to kill Mrs. Barrows. Why does this announcement not eliminate suspense from the story?

3. What is the emotional climax of the story?

4. How does Thurber prepare us for Mr. Fitweiler's incredulous reaction to Mrs. Barrows's story about Mr. Martin? Why are we amused but not surprised at Mr. Fitweiler's reaction?

THE ISSUES

1. What obvious contrasts between Mr. Martin and Mrs. Barrows does Thurber draw?

2. What is your view of the morality of Mr. Martin's actions? Was he justified in his extreme steps or not?

3. How does Mrs. Barrows's character reinforce an ancient sexual stereotype about women? How would you characterize this stereotype?

4. Would this story, if set in an office today rather than in the 1940s, be as believable? Why or why not?

5. Reverse the characters of Mrs. Barrows and Mr. Martin. She is now the fastidious head of the filing department, he the brassy opportunist who has ingratiated himself in the good graces of the boss, Fitweiler. Does the story still work? Why or why not?

SUGGESTIONS FOR WRITING

1. Choose one of your close friends and write a short caricature by exaggerating his or her traits.

2. Write an essay analyzing the humorous devices used by Thurber in the story "The Catbird Seat." Pay attention to such factors as character, plot reversal, and style.

▼▼▼

William Shakespeare

THAT TIME OF YEAR (SONNET 73)

WILLIAM SHAKESPEARE (1564–1616) is generally acknowledged as the greatest literary genius of the English language. Born in Stratford-on-Avon, England, he was the son of a prosperous businessman, and probably attended grammar schools in his native town. In 1582, Shakespeare married Anne Hathaway, who was eight years his senior, and who bore him three children. The legacy of his writing includes thirty-six plays, one hundred fifty-four sonnets, and five long poems.

The English or Shakespearean sonnet is composed of three quatrains of four lines each and a concluding couplet of two, rhyming abab cdcd efef gg. *There is usually a correspondence between the units marked off by the rhymes and the development of the thought. The three quatrains, for instance, may represent three different images or three questions from which a conclusion is drawn in the final couplet. As a result, the sonnet is one of the most tightly organized poetic forms used.*

That time of year thou mayst in me behold
When yellow leaves, or none, or few, do hang
Upon those boughs which shake against the cold,
Bare ruined choirs where late the sweet birds sang.
In me thou see'st the twilight of such day
As after sunset fadeth in the west,
Which by and by black night doth take away,
Death's second self, that seals up all in rest.
In me thou see'st the glowing of such fire,
That on the ashes of his youth doth lie
As the deathbed whereon it must expire,
Consumed with that which it was nourished by.
This thou perceivest, which makes thy love more strong,
To love that well which thou must leave ere long.

(121 words)

THE FACTS

1. In the first quatrain what image does the poet focus on? What relationship does this image have to the speaker?

2. In the second quatrain the speaker shifts to another image. What is it and what relationship does it bear to him?

3. In the third quatrain yet another image is introduced. What is the image and how does it relate to the speaker? What rather complex philosophical paradox is involved?

4. The final couplet states the poet's thesis (or theme). What is that thesis? State it in your own words.

THE STRATEGIES

1. The entire poem is organized around three analogies. State them in three succinct sentences.

2. The three images in the poem are presented in a particular order. Do you see any reason for this order?

3. In lines 3 and 4, what effect do the words "cold / Bare ruined choirs" have on the rhythm and meter?

4. In line 2, what would be the result of substituting "hang" for "do hang"?

5. What is the antecedent of "this" in line 13?

THE ISSUES

1. What can you deduce about the speaker and his frame of mind from this poem?

2. Someone once said, "Youth is wasted on the young." How might that witticism be applied to this poem?

3. Why should a student whose major is, say, business and who has no interest whatsoever in literature be forced to take classes in which poems such as this one are studied?

4. Shakespeare has been called surprisingly modern in his outlook. What about this poem would seem to justify that observation?

SUGGESTIONS FOR WRITING

1. In two or three well-developed paragraphs, answer the question, "What is the single worst aspect of old age?"

2. Write an essay in which you outline the way you plan to make your own old age as pleasant and fulfilling as possible.

I S S U E   F O R   C R I T I C A L
T H I N K I N G   A N D   D E B A T E

▼▼

DRUG ABUSE

The faces portrayed in *The Subway* by George Tooker, are gaunt, stark, and rigidly gripped with a palpable terror. In the foreground, a woman frozen in a robotic pose stares emptily into the distance. Behind her lurk men caught in the act of shuffling along with a grim, isolated detachment. Off to the side, we see a man peering timorously from around a cubicle, his visible peeping eye wary and fearful. We have selected this painting, in spite of its title, as the pictorial equivalent of the devastation of drugs, of their brutal power to wall off the individual into a private world of tormented addiction.

Ours is a society awash in a transcontinental tidal surge of drugs. We awake to the kick of caffeine, soothe our nerves with tobacco, ease our tension headaches with aspirin, wind down the day with alcohol, and swallow an antihistamine to help us sleep—all perfectly legal, respectable, and even expected. But there is a dark side to this epidemic of drug use. Over 400,000 of us annually perish from the effects of tobacco. Some 23 million of us regularly take illegal drugs, ranging from cocaine to marijuana to heroin. A causal relationship exists between drug addiction and criminal wrong-doing, with one Justice Department study showing that fully one-half to three-fourths of those arrested for serious crimes had recently used drugs. Unknown is the exact incidence of drug usage and addiction among the general population, although a National Institute on Drug Abuse survey taken in 1987 indicated that some 65 percent of people between 18 to 25 years old have tried illegal drugs.

The political response to the spreading tide of illegal drugs has been predictable: conservatives urge heightened efforts at the interdiction of illegal drugs, mandatory drug testing, stiffer prison terms for pushers, and a crack-down on recreational users. Liberals and libertarians advocate an agenda of education and rehabilitation and, probably the most controversial measure of all, the legalization of drug use. It is this last proposal that has set off the latest and most vehement round of debate.

Making the case for legalization, and doing so in his usual caustic style, is the novelist and writer Gore Vidal. His argument is not new, but it is refreshingly presented. Prohibition increases the allure of drugs, argues Vidal, and it is only because our society is so devoted to the concepts of sin and punishment that we reject out of hand this

George Tooker, The Subway. 1950. Egg tempera on composition board. Sight: 18⅛ × 36⅛ inches (46 cm × 91.8 cm). Collection of Whitney Museum of American Art. Purchase, with funds from the Juliana Force Purchase Award. 50.23. Photo by Geoffrey Clements. Photograph copyright © 1997 Whitney Museum of American Art.

simple solution. Equally emphatic in his refutation of the case of legalization is editorial writer Morton Kondracke. He makes his case with an array of statistics from which he infers the direst possible consequences of legalization. The student corner argues that only early education about the dangers can stem the tide of drug abuse.

A few countries, notably England and other European communities, have experimented with the legalization of drugs, and with some success. But no society as complex and variegated as ours has ever attempted to legalize drugs on such as vast scale as would be involved if the liberals win this argument. And what the consequences of legalization might ultimately be remains anyone's guess. Given the strong moral strain that permeates American political thinking, however, we think Vidal is right, and that unless drug abuse becomes incalculably worse than it is today, legalization will likely remain a topic for academic debate rather than be adopted as national policy by any present or future administration.

▼▼

Gore Vidal

DRUGS

GORE VIDAL (b. 1925), is a writer of novels, plays, short stories, book reviews and essays. His major novels include *The City and the Pillar* (1948), *Julian* (1964), *Myra Breckenridge* (1968), *1876* (1976), *Burr* (1980), *Creation* (1981), *Lincoln* (1984), and *Eighteen Seventy-Six* (1988).

1   It is possible to stop most drug addiction in the United States within a very short time. Simply make all drugs available and sell them at cost. Label each drug with a precise description of what effect—good and bad—the drug will have on the taker. This will require heroic honesty. Don't say that marijuana is addictive or dangerous when it is neither, as millions of people know—unlike "speed," which kills most unpleasantly, or heroin, which is addictive and difficult to kick.

2   For the record, I have tried—once—almost every drug and liked none, disproving the popular Fu Manchu theory that a single whiff of opium will enslave the mind. Nevertheless many drugs are bad for certain people to take and they should be told why in a sensible way.

3   Along with exhortation and warning, it might be good for our citizens to recall (or learn for the first time) that the United States was the creation of men who believed that each man has the right to do what he wants with his own life as long as he does not interfere with his neighbor's pursuit of happiness (that his neighbor's idea of happiness is persecuting others does confuse matters a bit).

4   This is a startling notion to the current generation of Americans. They reflect a system of public education which has made the Bill of Rights, literally, unacceptable to a majority of high school graduates (see the annual Purdue reports) who now form the "silent majority"— a phrase which that underestimated wit Richard Nixon took from Homer who used it to describe the dead.

5   Now one can hear the warning rumble begin: if everyone is allowed to take drugs everyone will and the GNP will decrease, the Commies will stop us from making everyone free, and we shall end up a race of Zombies, passively murmuring "groovie" to one another. Alarming thought. Yet it seems most unlikely that any reasonably sane person will become a drug addict if he knows in advance what addiction is going to be like.

6   Is everyone reasonably sane? No. Some people will always become drug addicts just as some people will always become alcoholics, and it is just too bad. Every man, however, has the power (and should have the legal right) to kill himself if he chooses. But since most men don't, they won't be mainliners either. Nevertheless, forbidding people things they like or think they might enjoy only makes them want those things all the more. This psychological insight is, for some mysterious reason, perennially denied our governors.

7   It is a lucky thing for the American moralist that our country has always existed in a kind of time-vacuum: we have no public memory of anything that happened before last Tuesday. No one in Washington today recalls what happened during the years Alcohol was forbidden to the people by a Congress that thought it had a divine mission to stamp out Demon Rum—launching, in the process, the greatest crime wave in the country's history, causing thousands of deaths from bad alcohol, and creating a general (and persisting) contempt among the citizenry for the laws of the United States.

8   The same thing is happening today. But the government has learned nothing from past attempts at prohibition, not to mention repression.

9   Last year when the supply of Mexican marijuana was slightly curtailed by the Feds, the pushers got the kids hooked on heroin and deaths increased dramatically, particularly in New York. Whose fault? Evil men like the Mafiosi? Permissive Dr. Spock? Wild-eyed Dr. Leary? No.

10   The Government of the United States was responsible for those deaths. The bureaucratic machine has a vested interest in playing cops and robbers. Both the Bureau of Narcotics and the Mafia want strong laws against the sale and use of drugs because if drugs are sold at cost there would be no money in it for anyone.

11   If there was no money in it for the Mafia, there would be no friendly playground pushers, and addicts would not commit crimes to

pay for the next fix. Finally, if there was no money in it, the Bureau of Narcotics would wither away, something they are not about to do without a struggle.

12   Will anything sensible be done? Of course not. The American people are as devoted to the idea of sin and its punishment as they are to making money—and fighting drugs is nearly as big a business as pushing them. Since the combination of sin and money is irresistible (particularly to the professional politician), the situation will only grow worse.

(768 words)

VOCABULARY

exhortation (3)   perennially (6)   repression (8)

THE FACTS

1. What specific proposal does Vidal make for selling drugs?

2. According to Vidal, to whom is the Bill of Rights unacceptable?

3. What lesson about repression does Vidal say the government has largely forgotten?

4. Which two groups, according to Vidal, have a vested interest in prolonging the ban against drugs?

5. What dismal prophecy does Vidal make at the conclusion of his argument? How has his prophecy stood the test of time?

THE STRATEGIES

1. Vidal opens his argument with a blunt declaration of his position and without any softening up of the opposition with statistics or background material. What do you think the reaction to this opening would be if this were an essay written by a student? Why?

2. Vidal admits to having used almost every drug and having liked none. How does this frank admission affect his argument?

3. What one word in paragraph 5 dates this essay as from another era?

4. What is the rhetorical purpose of paragraphs 5 and 6?

5. Aside from its blunt tone, what other characteristic of this essay would make it unsuitable as a student submission in a writing class?

THE ISSUES

1. What do you think is the likely effect of a governmental attitude that says all drugs are bad for you?

2. What do you think would happen if all drugs were legalized?

3. Vidal says that "forbidding people things they like or think they might enjoy only makes them want those things all the more." Do you think this a truth or a cliché? Why?

4. If the government of the United States sprays marijuana crops with a herbicide that then poisons an unknowing user, who is morally responsible?

5. Do you agree with Vidal that the American people are hooked on the idea of sin and punishment? Why or why not?

SUGGESTIONS FOR WRITING

1. Writing an essay relating any encounter you have had with, or have heard someone else tell about, drugs.

2. Attack or defend Vidal's opinions in an essay.

▼▼▼

Morton M. Kondracke

DON'T LEGALIZE DRUGS

MORTON KONDRACKE (b. 1939) is an American journalist who has worked for *Newsweek* and the *New Republic.* Kondracke is a regular commentator on the National Public Radio program "All Things Considered" and writes a monthly column for the *Wall Street Journal.* He is the author of *Gerald R. Ford* (1976), one in a series of short biographies.

1   The next time you hear that a drunk driver has slammed into a school bus full of children or that a stoned railroad engineer has killed 16 people in a train wreck, think about this: if the advocates of legalized drugs have their way, there will be more of this, a lot more. There will also be more unpublicized fatal and maiming crashes, more job accidents, more child neglect, more of almost everything associated with substance abuse: babies born addicted or retarded, teenagers zonked out of their chance for an education, careers destroyed, families wrecked, and people dead of overdoses.

2   The proponents of drug legalization are right to say that some things will get better. Organized crime will be driven out of the drug business, and there will be a sharp drop in the amount of money (currently about $10 billion per year) that society spends to enforce the drug laws. There will be some reduction in the cost in theft and injury (now about $20 billion) by addicts to get the money to buy prohibited drugs. Internationally, Latin American governments presumably will stop being menaced by drug cartels and will peaceably export cocaine as they now do coffee.

3   However, this is virtually the limit of the social benefits to be derived from legalization, and they are far outweighed by the costs, which are always underplayed by legalization advocates such as the *Economist*, Princeton scholar Ethan A. Nadelmann, economist Milton Friedman and other libertarians, columnists William F. Buckley and Richard Cohen, and Mayors Keith Schmoke of Baltimore and Marion Barry of Washington, D.C. In lives, money, and human woe, the costs are so high, in fact, that society has no alternative but to conduct a real war on the drug trade, although perhaps a smarter one than is currently being waged.

4   Advocates of legalization love to draw parallels between the drug war and Prohibition. Their point, of course, is that this crusade is as doomed to failure as the last one was, and that we ought to surrender now to the inevitable and stop wasting resources. But there are some important differences between drugs and alcohol. Alcohol has been part of Western culture for thousands of years; drugs have been the rage in America only since about 1962. Of the 115 million Americans who consume alcohol, 85 percent rarely become intoxicated; with drugs, intoxication is the whole idea. Alcohol is consistent chemically, even though it's dispensed in different strengths and forms as beer, wine, and "hard" liquor; with drugs there's no limit to the variations. Do we legalize crack along with snortable cocaine, PCPs as well as marijuana, and LSD and "Ecstasy" as well as heroin? If we don't—and almost certainly we won't—we have a black market, and some continued crime.

5   But Prohibition is a useful historical parallel for measuring the costs of legalization. Almost certainly doctors are not going to want to write prescriptions for recreational use of harmful substances, so if drugs even are legalized they will be dispensed as alcohol now is—in government-regulated stores with restrictions on the age of buyers, warnings against abuse (and, probably, with added restrictions on amounts, though this also will create a black market).

6   In the decade before Prohibition went into effect in 1920, alcohol consumption in the United States averaged 2.6 gallons per person per year. It fell to 0.73 gallons during the Prohibition decade, then doubled to 1.5 gallons in the decade after repeal, and is now back to 2.6 gallons.

So illegality suppressed usage to a third or a fourth of its former level. At the same time, incidence of cirrhosis of the liver fell by half.

7   So it seems fair to estimate that use of drugs will at least double, and possibly triple, if the price is cut, supplies are readily available, and society's sanction is lifted. It's widely accepted that there are now 16 million regular users of marijuana, six million of cocaine, a half million of heroin, and another half million of other drugs, totaling 23 million. Dr. Robert DuPont, former director of the National Institutes of Drug Abuse and an anti-legalization crusader, says that the instant pleasure afforded by drugs—superior to that available with alcohol—will increase the number of regular users of marijuana and cocaine to about 50 or 60 million and heroin users to ten million.

8   Between ten percent and 15 percent of all drinkers turn into alcoholics (ten million to 17 million), and these drinkers cost the economy an estimated $117 billion in 1983 ($15 billion for treatment, $89 billion in lost productivity, and $13 billion in accident-related costs). About 200,000 people died last year as a result of alcohol abuse, about 25,000 in auto accidents. How many drug users will turn into addicts, and what will this cost? According to President Reagan's drug abuse policy adviser, Dr. David I. McDonald, studies indicate that marijuana is about as habit-forming as alcohol, but for cocaine, 70 percent of users become addicted, as many as with nicotine.

9   So it seems reasonable to conclude that at least four to six million people will become potheads if marijuana is legal, and that coke addicts will number somewhere between 8.5 million (if regular usage doubles and 70 percent become addicted) and 42 million (if DuPont's high estimate of use is correct). An optimist would have to conclude that the number of people abusing legalized drugs will come close to those hooked on alcohol. A pessimist would figure the human damage as much greater.

10   Another way of figuring costs is this: the same study (by the Research Triangle Institute of North Carolina) that put the price of alcoholism at $117 billion in 1983 figured the cost of drug abuse then at $60 billion—$15 billion for law enforcement and crime, and $45 billion in lost productivity, damaged health, and other costs. The updated estimate for 1988 drug abuse is $100 billion. If legalizing drugs would save $30 billion now being spent on law enforcement and crime, a doubling of use and abuse means that other costs will rise to $140 billion or $210 billion. This is no bargain for society.

11   If 200,000 people die every year from alcohol abuse and 320,000 from tobacco smoking, how many will die from legal drugs?*

---

* In fact, the Centers for Disease Control estimate that 434,000 Americans died from tobacco smoking in 1988. The figure for 1985 was 188,000.—Ed.

Government estimates are that 4,000 to 5,000 people a year are killed in drug-related auto crashes, but this is surely low because accident victims are not as routinely blood-tested for drugs as for alcohol. Legalization advocates frequently cite figures of 3,600 or 4,100 as the number of drug deaths each year reported by hospitals, but this number too is certainly an understatement, based on reports from only 75 big hospitals in 27 metropolitan areas.

12   If legalization pushed the total number of drug addicts to only half the number of alcoholics, 100,000 people a year would die. That's the figure cited by McDonald. DuPont guesses that, given the potency of drugs, the debilitating effects of cocaine, the carcinogenic effects of marijuana, and the AIDS potential of injecting legalized heroin, the number of deaths actually could go as high as 500,000 a year. That's a wide range, but it's clear that legalization of drugs will not benefit human life.

13   All studies show that those most likely to try drugs, get hooked, and die—as opposed to those who suffer from cirrhosis and lung cancer—are young people, who are susceptible to the lure of quick thrills and are terribly adaptable to messages provided by adult society. Under pressure of the current prohibition, the number of kids who use illegal drugs at least once a month has fallen from 39 percent in the late 1970s to 25 percent in 1987, according to the annual survey of high school seniors conducted by the University of Michigan. The same survey shows that attitudes toward drug use have turned sharply negative. But use of legal drugs is still strong. Thirty-eight percent of high school seniors reported getting drunk within the past two weeks, and 27 percent said they smoke cigarettes every day. Drug prohibition is working with kids; legalization would do them harm.

14   And, even though legalization would lower direct costs for drug law enforcement, it's unlikely that organized crime would disappear. It might well shift to other fields—prostitution, pornography, gambling or burglaries, extortion, and murders-for-hire—much as it did in the period between the end of Prohibition and the beginning of the drug era. As DuPont puts it, "Organized crime is in the business of giving people the things that society decides in its own interest to prohibit. The only way to get rid of organized crime is to make everything legal." Even legalization advocates such as Ethan Nadelmann admit that some street crimes will continue to occur as a result of drug abuse— especially cocaine paranoia, PCP insanity, and the need of unemployable addicts to get money for drugs. Domestic crime, child abuse and neglect surely would increase.

15   Some legalization advocates suggest merely decriminalizing marijuana and retaining sanctions against other drugs. This would certainly be less costly than total legalization, but it would still be no

favor to young people, would increase traffic accidents and productivity losses—and would do nothing to curtail the major drug cartels, which make most of their money trafficking in cocaine.

16   Legalizers also argue that the government could tax legal drug sales and use the money to pay for anti-drug education programs and treatment centers. But total taxes collected right now from alcohol sales at the local, state, and federal levels come to only $13.1 billion per year—which is a pittance compared with the damage done to society as a result of alcohol abuse. The same would have to be true for drugs—and any tax that resulted in an official drug price that was higher than the street price would open the way once again for black markets and organized crime.

17   So, in the name of health, economics, and morality, there seems no alternative but to keep drugs illegal and to fight the criminals who traffic in them. Regardless of what legalization advocates say, this is now the overwhelming opinion of the public, the Reagan administration, the prospective candidates for president, and the Congress—not one of whose members has introduced legislation to decriminalize any drug. Congress is on the verge of forcing the administration to raise anti-drug spending next year from $3 billion to $5.5 billion.

18   There is, though, room to debate how best to wage this war. A consensus is developing that it has to be done both on the supply side (at overseas points of origin, through interdiction at U.S. borders and criminal prosecution of traffickers) and on the demand side (by discouraging use of drugs through education and treatment and/or by arrest and urine testing at workplaces). However, there is a disagreement about which side to emphasize and how to spend resources. Members of Congress, especially Democrats, want to blame foreigners and the Reagan administration for the fact that increasing amounts of cocaine, heroin, and marijuana are entering the country. They want to spend more money on foreign aid, use the U.S. military to seal the borders, and fund "nice" treatment and education programs, especially those that give ongoing support to professional social welfare agencies.

19   Conservatives, on the other hand, want to employ the military to help foreign countries stamp out drug laboratories, use widespread drug testing to identify—and, often, punish—drug users, and spend more on police and prisons. As Education Secretary William Bennett puts it, "How can we surrender when we've never actually fought the war?" Bennett wants to fight it across all fronts, and those who have seen drafts of a forthcoming report of the White House Conference for a Drug Free America say this will be the approach recommended by the administration, although with muted emphasis on use of the U.S. military, which is reluctant to get involved in what may be another thankless war.

20   However, DuPont and others, including Jeffrey Eisenach of the Heritage Foundation, make a strong case that primary emphasis ought to be put on the demand side—discouraging use in the United States rather than, almost literally, trying to become the world's policeman. Their argument, bolstered by a study conducted by Peter Reuter of the RAND Corporation, is that major profits in the drug trade are not made abroad (where the price of cocaine triples from farm to airstrip), but within the United States (where the markup from entry point to street corner is 12 times), and that foreign growing fields and processing laboratories are easily replaceable at low cost.

21   They say that prohibition policy should emphasize routine random urine testing in schools and places of employment, arrests for possession of drugs, and "coercive" treatment programs that compel continued enrollment as a condition of probation and employment. DuPont thinks that corporations have a right to demand that their employees be drug-free because users cause accidents and reduce productivity. He contends that urine testing is no more invasive than the use of metal detectors at airports.

22   "Liberals have a terrible time with this," says DuPont. "They want to solve every problem by giving people things. They want to love people out of their problems, while conservatives want to punish it out of them. What we want to do is take the profits out of drugs by drying up demand. You do that by raising the social cost of using them to the point where people say, 'I don't want to do this.' This isn't conservative. It's a way to save lives."

23   It is, and it's directly parallel to the way society is dealing with drunk driving and cigarette smoking—not merely through advertising campaigns and surgeon general's warnings, but through increased penalties, social strictures—and prohibitions. Random testing for every employee in America may be going too far, but testing those holding sensitive jobs or workers involved in accidents surely isn't, nor is arresting users, lifting driver's licenses, and requiring treatment. These are not nosy, moralistic intrusions on people's individual rights, but attempts by society to protect itself from danger.

24   In the end, they are also humane and moral. There is a chance, with the public and policy-makers aroused to action, that ten years from now drug abuse might be reduced to its pre-1960s levels. Were drugs to be legalized now, we would be establishing a new vice—one that, over time, would end or ruin millions of lives. Worse yet, we would be establishing a pattern of doing the easy thing, surrendering, whenever confronted with a difficult challenge.

(2,469 words)

VOCABULARY

maiming (1)

carcinogenic (12)

susceptible (13)

extortion (14)

curtail (15)

interdiction (18)

bolstered (20)

coercive (21)

invasive (21)

strictures (23)

THE FACTS

1. What parallels do advocates of drug legalization love to draw, according to the author?

2. What important differences between drugs and alcohol does the author cite?

3. According to the author, what is the addictive difference between marijuana and cocaine?

4. Which group of potential users, according to studies cited by the author, is most likely to get hooked on drugs?

5. What alternative proposals do some legalization advocates offer, and how does the author respond to them?

THE STRATEGIES

1. The author begins his argument by conceding that some things will get better if drugs are legalized. Since he is adamant against the legalization of drugs, what is the benefit of this admission to his argument?

2. The author writes: "Of the 115 million Americans who consume alcohol, 85% rarely become intoxicated; with drugs, intoxication is the whole idea." What logical objection to this statement might an advocate of drug legalization make?

3. What is the thesis of the author's argument, and where is it stated?

4. In paragraphs 6 and 7 the author deduces probable drug addiction and usage from statistics about alcohol consumption before and after prohibition. What is your opinion of the logic underlying this deduction?

5. In evaluating statistics and studies cited by the author from various agencies and institutes, what kind of questions should a cautious reader ask before accepting their validity?

THE ISSUES

1. Which of the author's arguments against the legalization of drugs do you find the most persuasive? Why?

2. The author says that tobacco smoking kills 320,000 people every year. Given this statistic, what is your opinion about the legalization of tobacco?

3. The author quotes an authority who claims that while liberals want to love people out of their problems, conservatives want to punish them. Based on your reading of these two articles, what other differences can you discern between the liberal and conservative mind-set?

4. What is your opinion about the proposed mandatory testing for drugs in schools and places of employment?

5. Which drugs would you decriminalize, given the power and opportunity? Why?

SUGGESTIONS FOR WRITING

1. Write an essay arguing for or against the banning of cigarette smoking in public places.

2. Defend or attack the proposal to decriminalize the use of marijuana.

STUDENT CORNER

First Draft

Linda Kunze, Glendale Community College

Drug Use: The Continuing Epidemic

Brakes squeal as the late model Mercury Sable speeds down the street. Onlookers stare in amazement while the driver recklessly maneuvers in and out of traffic. Suddenly, the car jumps the curb and slams head on into a power pole. Moments later, police arrive to find the young female driver dead, behind the steering wheel, of the Mercury. In her hand she clutches the six-tenths of a gram of rock cocaine she had just purchased.

not needed

No, this scenario is not the opening scene from the latest big screen action adventure. Sadly, it is a true story taken from the Sunday, November third, 1996, issue of the <u>Daily News</u> and is just another example of the death and destruction caused by the continued popularity and use of illicit drugs.

number better — *3*

Drug use is far from new. It has been a major problem in American for decades. According to Linda Villarosa, author of <u>Body & Soul</u>, heroin and cocaine (two powerfully addictive drugs) were first introduced to consumers back at the tern of the century as ingredients in many over-the-counter medical remedies and soft drinks. In time, the addictive properties of

a

u

when — *sounds better*

245

Kunze 2

these narcotics were discovered, ~~and~~ heroin, cocaine, and many [get rid of so many ands]

other harmful drugs were outlawed, but this action came far too

late. The overpowering problem of drug abuse and addiction had

already begun to spread across America.

Today, almost every adult American is aware of the dangers

involved with the use of illegal substances. However, this

knowledge has not stopped the rapid increase of drug abuse in

this nation. In the September/October 1996 issue of <u>Psychology</u>

<u>Today</u>, Owen Lipstein, Editor-in-Chief of the publication, states

that currently, "More than 5 million (adults) smoke marijuana

more than once a week; over 2 million are well acquainted with

cocaine; an estimated 750,000 use heroin." Drug dependency and

addiction are becoming far too common in this country and it is

so tempting to close our eyes and turn our backs to the drug

epidemic and just wish it away.

Unfortunately, denying the problems caused by the ever-

growing use and abuse of narcotics, will not save anyone from the

torments of drug abuse and addiction. Although there are no

easy answers to this age-old problem, early education seems to

be the only truly effective weapon the nation has against this

equal opportunity destroyer known as drug abuse.

For education to be an effective deterrent to drug abuse, it

must begin as early as grade school, because according to a

[better word] recent pamphlet ~~written~~ [published] by The United States Department of

Education, ~~entitled~~ (Schools Without Drugs,) "One out of every

six 13-year-olds has used marijuana (at least once) and fifty-four

Kunze 3

percent of high school seniors have tried some type of illicit drug

by the time they are ready to graduate." Children must be taught

the dangers of drug abuse and strategies to avoid the use of

these substances, prior to junior and senior high school where

availability and peer pressure make drug use all to acceptable and

easy too fall for.

   It is apparent that drug abuse is a problem that has grown in

leaps and bounds over the years. It will not go away overnight,

and there are no easy solutions to eliminate the stronghold drugs

have in this country. However, we must continue to educate

everyone, young and old, on the evil's of illegal drugs and remain

persistent in the fight against their use. We all deserve a drug

free future.

I

Final Draft

Linda Kunze, Glendale Community College

Drug Use: The Continuing Epidemic

Brakes squeal as the late model Mercury Sable speeds down the street. Onlookers stare in amazement while the driver recklessly maneuvers in and out of traffic. Suddenly, the car jumps the curb and slams head on into a power pole. Moments later, police arrive to find the young female driver dead behind the steering wheel. In her hand she clutches the six-tenths of a gram of rock cocaine she had just purchased.

No, this scenario is not the opening scene from the latest big screen action adventure. Sadly, it is a true story taken from the Sunday, November 3, 1996, issue of the <u>Daily News</u> and is just another example of the death and destruction caused by the continued popularity and use of illicit drugs.

Drug use is far from new. It has been a major problem in America for decades. According to Linda Villarosa, author of <u>Body & Soul</u>, heroin and cocaine (two powerfully addictive drugs) were first introduced to consumers back at the turn of the century as ingredients in many over-the-counter medical remedies and soft drinks. In time, when the addictive properties of these narcotics were discovered, heroin, cocaine, and many other harmful drugs were outlawed, but this action came far

Kunze 2

too late. The overpowering problem of drug abuse and addiction had already begun to spread across America.

Today, almost every adult American is aware of the dangers involved with the use of illegal substances. However, this knowledge has not stopped the rapid increase of drug abuse in this nation. In the September/October 1996 issue of <u>Psychology Today</u>, Owen Lipstein, Editor-in-Chief of the publication, states that currently, "More than 5 million (adults) smoke marijuana more than once a week; over 2 million are well acquainted with cocaine; an estimated 750,000 use heroin." Drug dependency and addiction are becoming far too common in this country and it is so tempting to close our eyes and turn our backs to the drug epidemic and just wish it away.

Unfortunately, denying the problems caused by the ever-growing use and abuse of narcotics, will not save anyone from the torments of drug abuse and addiction. Although there are no easy answers to this age-old problem, early education seems to be the only truly effective weapon the nation has against this equal opportunity destroyer known as drug abuse.

For education to be an effective deterrent to drug abuse, it must begin as early as grade school, because according to <u>Schools Without Drugs</u>, a recent pamphlet published by the United States Department of Education, "One out of every six 13-year-olds has used marijuana (at least once) and fifty-four percent of high school seniors have tried some type of illicit drug by the time they are ready to graduate." Children must be taught the dangers of drug abuse and strategies to avoid the use of these substances, prior to junior and senior high school where availability and peer pressure make drug use all too acceptable and easy to fall for.

It is apparent that drug abuse is a problem that has grown in leaps and bounds over the years. It will not go away overnight, and there are no easy solutions to eliminate the stronghold drugs have in this country. However, we must continue to educate everyone, young and old, on the evils of illegal drugs and remain persistent in the fight against their use. We all deserve a drug free future.

How I Write

I always sit down and brainstorm—usually alone—before I write anything. In other words, I mull over ideas to see how they might work. I have never been gifted in the art of formal outlines, but I do jot down any idea that can be developed successfully. I like to work at home, with country music playing in the background.

How I Wrote This Essay

I located as many sources on drug abuse as time permitted. I then narrowed my sources down to the amount needed. I wrote one draft and put it away for a week. After the week was up, I reread my paper, changing what I didn't like and improving what I did like. The introduction is always the hardest for me to write. Everything else flows from there.

My Writing Tip

Write what you know and develop your own style. Always give yourself enough time to do the assignment well because a shoddy assignment leads only to embarrassment.

CHAPTER WRITING ASSIGNMENTS

1. Write a well-organized essay describing your study habits and methods.

2. Write a well-organized chronological autobiography.

3. Write an essay detailing the steps you follow when you have to complete a writing assignment.

4. In a tightly organized essay, detail any particular procedure or process (e.g., how to tune a car engine) with which you are intimately familiar.

WRITING ASSIGNMENTS FOR A SPECIFIC AUDIENCE

1. Write an essay of appreciation directed at your favorite teacher—no matter from what grade—telling how he or she affected your life.

2. After doing the necessary research, write an essay telling an audience of high-school drop-outs the opportunities available to them for continuing their education.

COLLABORATIVE WRITING PROJECT

In teams of three, survey the incidence of drug use among a separate and specific segment of your college population. (For example, one group can focus on business majors, another on sociology majors, and so on.) After meeting with the group as a whole to compare the results, write a team essay on your findings.

▼▼▼

Chapter Five

DEVELOPING PARAGRAPHS

INTRODUCTION: WRITING PARAGRAPHS

Imagine a book without paragraphs. Imagine pages and pages of prose with no visual breaks to mark new ideas, no familiar indentation. Such a book would strike us as hideous to read and difficult to get through, its ideas buried in a jungle of words to be dug out only with the most persistent effort. There are a few such books around, but thankfully none that are college texts. And so we are spared grappling with them.

The paragraph is an idea whose time came almost with the dawn of writing. As Richard Weaver tells us in his essay, paragraphs were once identified with marginal marks inserted by medieval scribes who saw the usefulness of notifying the reader of the appearance of a new idea or a new twist on an old one. Since then the familiar indentation has replaced the marginal mark, and paragraphs are everywhere to be found as staple divisions of the written word.

Master the paragraph, learn to write it with style and grace and dash, and you have mastered a unit of prose rivaled in popularity only by the sentence. Although a difficult medium for many student writers, the paragraph and its writing improve with practice. Once you have written a few hundred paragraphs for teachers of various disciplines, the form will become nearly second nature to you. For there is a rhythm of the paragraph that must be learned as well as a sixth sense for inserting transitions and specific details in the right place. But these are skills that ripen with practice.

The materials in this chapter are a varied lot. First is an article by A. M. Tibbetts and Charlene Tibbetts that explains the promise paragraph writers implicitly make to readers. Then Richard Weaver gives us a glimpse into the history and evolution of the paragraph as a literary form. Following these two articles are paragraphs that demonstrate the versatility and subtlety of the form.

The chapter ends with a debate about ecology and its effects on our planet and on the workplace. For many, the ecology movement amounts to a conflict between the environment and the economy—the right to clean air and water versus the right to earn a living. This particular formula has been especially applicable to timber disputes in the Northwest, where loggers fear for their livelihoods because of federal attempts to protect endangered species such as the spotted owl. Nothing is finally settled by this debate, but the exchange between the two sides at least better acquaints us with the respective positions.

A D V I C E

▼▼

A. M. Tibbetts
Charlene Tibbetts

WRITING SUCCESSFUL PARAGRAPHS

ARNOLD M. TIBBETTS (b. 1927) has taught English at the University of Iowa, Western Illinois University, Vanderbilt University, and the University of Illinois, Urbana. His wife, CHARLENE TIBBETTS (b. 1921), has also taught parttime at the University of Illinois, Urbana. The Tibbettses are coauthors of *Strategies of Rhetoric* (1969), from which this excerpt was taken.

The proverbial warning "Don't promise more than you can give" applies to writing as well as to everyday life. The basis of a good paragraph, say the authors, is a promise that is made in the topic sentence and then carried out in the specific detail. In this excerpt, the authors demonstrate with examples how to make and keep your "paragraph promises."

1   A paragraph is a collection of sentences that helps you fulfill your thesis (theme promise). Itself a small "theme," a paragraph should be clearly

written and specific; and it should not wander or make irrelevant remarks. Each paragraph should be related in some way to the theme promise. Here are suggestions for writing successful paragraphs:

I. Get to the Point of Your Paragraph Quickly and Specifically

2   Don't waste time or words in stating your paragraph promise. Consider this good example of getting to the point—the writer is explaining the ancient Romans' technique for conquering their world:

> The technique of expansion was simple. *Divide et impera* [divide and conquer]: enter into solemn treaty with a neighbouring country, foment internal disorder, intervene in support of the weaker side on the pretense that Roman honour was involved, replace the legitimate ruler with a puppet, giving him the status of a subject ally; later, goad him into rebellion, seize and sack the country, burn down the temples, and carry off the captive gods to adorn a triumph. Conquered territories were placed under the control of a provincial governor-general, an ex-commander-in-chief who garrisoned it, levied taxes, set up courts of summary justice, and linked the new frontiers with the old by so called Roman roads—usually built by Greek engineers and native forced labour. Established social and religious practices were permitted so long as they did not threaten Roman administration or offend against the broad-minded Roman standards of good taste. The new province presently became a springboard for further aggression.
>
> —Robert Graves, "It Was a Stable World"

3   Graves makes his promise in the first nine words, in which he mentions the "simple" technique the Romans had for "dividing" and "conquering" in order to expand their empire. Suppose Graves had started his paragraph with these words:

> The technique of expansion was interesting. It was based upon a theory about human nature that the Romans practically invented. This theory had to do with how people reacted to certain political and military devices which . . .

4   Do you see what is wrong? Since the beginning sentences are so vague, the paragraph never gets going. The writer can't fulfill a promise because he hasn't made one. Another example of a poor paragraph beginning:

> The first step involves part of the golf club head. The club head has removable parts, some of which are metal. You must consider these parts when deciding how to repair the club.

5   Specify the beginning of this paragraph and get to the point quicker:

> Your first step in repairing the club head is to remove the metal plate held on by Phillips screws.

6   This solid, specific paragraph beginning gives your reader a clear promise which you can fulfill easily without wasting words. (Observe, by the way, that specifying a writer's stance—as we did in the last example—can help you write clearer paragraph beginnings.)

2. Fulfill Your Reader's Expectation Established by the Paragraph Promise

7   Do this with specific details and examples—explain as fully as you can. Example:

> The next thing is to devise a form for your essay. This, which ought to be obvious, is not. I learned it for the first time from an experienced newspaperman. When I was at college I earned extra pocket- and book-money by writing several weekly columns for a newspaper. They were usually topical, they were always carefully varied, they tried hard to be witty, and (an essential) they never missed a deadline. But once, when I brought in the product, a copy editor stopped me. He said, "Our readers seem to like your stuff all right; but we think it's a bit amateurish." With due humility I replied, "Well, I am an amateur. What should I do with it?" He said, "Your pieces are not coherent; they are only sentences and epigrams strung together; they look like a heap of clothespins in a basket. Every article ought to have a shape. Like this" (and he drew a big letter S on his pad) "or this" (he drew a descending line which turned abruptly upward again) "or this" (and he sketched a solid central core with five or six lines pushing outward from it) "or even this" (and he outlined two big arrows coming into collision). I never saw the man again, but I have never ceased to be grateful to him for his wisdom and for his kindness. Every essay must have a shape. You can ask a question in the first paragraph, discussing several different answers to it till you reach one you think is convincing. You can give a curious fact and offer an explanation of it: a man's character (as Hazlitt did with his fives champion), a building, a book, a striking adventure, a peculiar custom. There are many other shapes which essays can take; but the principle laid down by the copy editor was right. Before you start you must have a form in your mind; and it ought to be a form felt in paragraphs or sections, not in words or sentences—so that, if necessary, you could summarize each paragraph in a single line and put the entire essay on a postcard.
>
> —Gilbert Highet, "How to Write an Essay"

8   Highet makes a promise in the first three sentences, and in the remaining sentences he specifically fulfills it.

3. Avoid Fragmentary Paragraphs

9   A fragmentary paragraph does not develop its topic or fulfill its promise. A series of fragmentary paragraphs jumps from idea to idea in a jerky and unconvincing fashion:

> My freshman rhetoric class is similar in some ways to my senior English class in high school, but it is also very different.
> In my English class we usually had daily homework assignments that were discussed during the class period. If we were studying grammar, the assignments were to correct grammatical errors in the text. If we were studying literature, we were supposed to read the material and understand its ideas.
> In rhetoric class, we do basically the same things, except that in the readings we are assigned, we look much deeper into the purpose of the author.
> In my English class . . .

10   Fragmentary paragraphs are often the result of a weak writer's stance.

4. Avoid Irrelevancies in Your Paragraphs

11   The italicized sentence does not fit the development of this paragraph:

> We need a better working atmosphere at Restik Tool Company. The workers must feel that they are a working team instead of just individuals. If the men felt they were part of a team, they would not misuse the special machine tools, which now need to be resharpened twice as often as they used to be. *Management's attitude toward the union could be improved too.* The team effort is also being damaged by introduction of new products before their bugs have been worked out. Just when the men are getting used to one routine, a new one is installed, and their carefully created team effort is seriously damaged.

12   As with the fragmentary paragraph, the problem of irrelevancies in a paragraph is often the result of a vague writer's stance. The paragraph above does not seem to be written for any particular reader.

(1,271 words)

VOCABULARY

foment (2)   topical (7)   epigrams (7)

D I S C U S S I O N

▼▼▼

Richard M. Weaver

THE FUNCTION OF THE PARAGRAPH

RICHARD M. WEAVER (1910–1973) was, for many years, a professor of English at the University of Chicago. He wrote several books on rhetoric, including *A Concise Handbook of English* (1968) and *A Rhetoric and Handbook* (1967).

What follows gives a brief history of the paragraph and explains its function as a visual aid that signals the beginning of a new thought.

1   The mind naturally looks for lines of division in anything it is considering. By these it is enabled to take in, or understand, because understanding is largely a matter of perceiving parts and their relationships. The paragraph is a kind of division, and paragraphing is a way of separating out the parts of a composition. Standing between the sentence as a unit at one end of the scale and the section or chapter at the other, the paragraph has the useful role of organizing our thoughts into groups of intermediate size.

2   The usefulness of a visual aid to division was recognized long before paragraphs were set off as they are today. In medieval manuscripts, which do not have the sort of indentation that we employ now, a symbol was written in the margin to mark a turn in the thought; and the word "paragraph" means "something written beside." Where the medieval scribe used a symbol, we use indentation. But the purpose served is the same: To advise the reader that a new set of thoughts is beginning.

3   A paragraph may therefore be understood as a visible division of the subject matter. The division is initially a convenience to the reader, as it prepares him to turn his attention to something new. But beyond this, most paragraphs have an internal unity, and they can be analyzed as compositions in miniature.

4   Occasionally one finds paragraphs which are compositions in the sense that they are not parts of a larger piece of writing. These occur in the form of single-paragraph statements, themes, and even stories, which are complete and which are not related to anything outside themselves. They will naturally reflect the rules of good composition if they are successful writing. They will have unity, coherence, and emphasis. They will (1) be about something, (2) make a progression, and (3) have a major point.

5   Substantially the same may be said about paragraphs that are parts of a composition. They will have a relative self-containment, or basic unity and coherence, and they will emphasize some point or idea. Therefore what we have said about the composition in its entirety may be said with almost equal application of single paragraphs within the larger piece. Especially is it true that the subject must be reasonably definite and that the development must follow some plan, although the possible plans of development are various.

6   The point to remember is that the relative independence of the paragraph rests upon something. The paragraph is not a device marked off at mechanical intervals simply because it is felt that the reader needs a change. He does need a change, but the place of the change must be related to the course of the thought. Where that changes significantly, a new paragraph begins. It is a signal that something else is starting. This may be a different phase of the subject, an illustration, a qualification, a change of scale, or any one of a large number of things that can mark the course of systematic thinking about a subject.

(522 words)

VOCABULARY

intermediate (1)   miniature (3)   systematic (6)
scribe (2)   self-containment (5)

THE FACTS

1. Weaver describes the paragraph as an intermediary. Between what two parts does it stand?

2. What is the root meaning of the word "paragraph"?

3. What does Weaver mean when he calls the paragraph a composition in miniature?

4. The paragraph does not occur at regular intervals. When does it occur?

5. What does Weaver consider the requirements for a good paragraph?

THE STRATEGIES

1. Does Weaver follow his own rule about when paragraphs should occur? See the last half of paragraph 6.

2. In paragraph 4, through what means is coherence achieved?

3. What is the topic sentence of paragraph 6?

THE ISSUES

1. How do the paragraphs used by newspapers and popular magazines differ from those used in academic writing?

2. What do you find to be most difficult about writing coherent and complete paragraphs?

3. Aside from paragraphs, what other visual aids do you find useful in reading and understanding a written work?

E X A M P L E S

▼▼

PARAGRAPHS WITH THE TOPIC SENTENCE AT THE BEGINNING

Edith Hamilton

FROM THE LESSONS OF THE PAST

EDITH HAMILTON (1867–1963) was an American classicist, educator, and writer. Her writing career began after retirement, and at the age of eighty she started giving public addresses and lectures. When she was ninety, she was made an honorary citizen of Greece. Among her books are *The Greek Way* (1942), *The Roman Way* (1932), and *Witness to the Truth: Christ and His Interpreters* (1948).

Basic to all the Greek achievement was freedom. The Athenians were the only free people in the world. In the great empires of antiquity— Egypt, Babylon, Assyria, Persia—splendid though they were, with riches beyond reckoning and immense power, freedom was unknown. The idea of it never dawned in any of them. It was born in Greece, a poor little country, but with it able to remain unconquered no matter what manpower and what wealth were arrayed against her. At Marathon and at Salamis overwhelming numbers of Persians had been defeated by small Greek forces. It had been proved that one free man was superior to many submissively obedient subjects of a tyrant. Athens was the leader in that amazing victory, and to the Athenians freedom was their dearest possession. Demosthenes said that they would not think it worth their while to live if they could not do so as free men, and years later a great teacher said, "Athenians, if you deprive them of their liberty, will die."

(169 words)

VOCABULARY

reckoning	Salamis	Demosthenes
arrayed	submissively	
Marathon	tyrant	

THE FACTS

1. Were you convinced of the truth of the topic sentence after reading the paragraph? If so, what convinced you?

2. In what way are free men superior to those who are submissively obedient to a tyrant?

THE STRATEGIES

1. What is the topic sentence of the paragraph?

2. Who is the "great teacher" alluded to?

THE ISSUES

1. Hamilton writes that freedom was basic to the Greek achievement. What does freedom mean to you in a political context?

2. According to Hamilton, it has been proved that one free man is superior to many submissively obedient subjects. Why do you think this is so?

▼▼▼

William Somerset Maugham

PAIN

English author WILLIAM SOMERSET MAUGHAM (1874–1965) wrote short stories, novels, plays, and books of criticism. His successful plays include *The Circle* (1921), *Our Betters* (1923), and *The Constant Wife* (1927). His most famous novel is his semiautobiographical account of a young physician with a clubfoot, *Of Human Bondage* (1919).

No more stupid apology for pain has ever been devised than that it elevates. It is an explanation due to the necessity of justifying pain from the Christian point of view. Pain is nothing more than the signal given by the nerves that the organism is in circumstances hurtful to it; it would be as reasonable to assert that a danger signal elevates a train. But one would have thought that the ordinary observation of life was enough to show that in the great majority of cases, pain, far from refining, has an effect which is merely brutalising. An example in point is the case of hospital in-patients: physical pain makes them self-absorbed, selfish, querulous, impatient, unjust and greedy; I could name a score of petty vices that it generates, but not one virtue. Poverty also is pain. I have known well men who suffered from that grinding agony of poverty which befalls persons who have to live among those richer than themselves; it makes them grasping and mean, dishonest and untruthful. It teaches them all sorts of detestable tricks. With moderate means they would have been honourable men, but ground down by poverty they have lost all sense of decency.

(282 words)

VOCABULARY

querulous

THE FACTS

1. According to Maugham, why do some people think it necessary to justify pain?

2. What is Maugham's view of pain?

3. Aside from the pain of physical illness, what other cause of pain is there?

THE STRATEGIES

1. What analogy does Maugham use in refuting the view that pain elevates?

2. What example does Maugham give to support his view of pain?

3. The paragraph discusses two causes of pain. What transitional word does Maugham use to move the discussion from the one cause to the other?

THE ISSUES

1. Maugham says that he cannot name a single virtue that pain produces. What virtue is pain generally thought to produce?

2. What is the distinction between pain and suffering?

3. Maugham writes that to say pain elevates is as reasonable as asserting that "a danger signal elevates a train." What is fundamentally false about this analogy?

▼▼▼

Chief Joseph of the Nez Percé

I AM TIRED OF FIGHTING (SURRENDER SPEECH)

CHIEF JOSEPH (1840?–1904) was the leader of the Nez Percé tribe of Sahaptin Indians, who lived along the Snake River in Idaho and Oregon. In 1877, under Chief Joseph, the tribe fought the United States government in a desperate attempt to preserve their land. Eventually, the Indians lost their struggle and were forced to retreat to the border of Canada.

I am tired of fighting. Our chiefs are killed. Looking Glass is dead. Toohulsote is dead. The old men are all dead. It is the young men who say no and yes. He who led the young men is dead. It is cold and we have no blankets. The little children are freezing to death. My people, some of them, have run away to the hills and have no blankets, no food. No one knows where they are—perhaps they are freezing to death. I want to have time to look for my children and see how many of them I can find. Maybe I shall find them among the dead. Hear me, my chiefs, I am tired. My heart is sad and sick. From where the sun stands I will fight no more forever.

(135 words)

THE FACTS

1. According to this speech, what nonmilitary factor contributed most to the decision of Chief Joseph to surrender?

2. Who was left among the Nez Percé to say no and yes?

THE STRATEGIES

1. On what word do most of the sentences of this paragraph end? What is the effect of this repeated ending?

2. How would you characterize the language used in this speech? Formal? Informal? Colloquial? What effect do you think the speaker achieves in his diction?

3. What are some examples of poetic constructions that add to the stateliness and dignity of this speech? Translate them literally and say what is lost in the translation.

THE ISSUES

1. How are American Indians portrayed in popular literature and films? How has this portrayal affected your impression of them?

2. Historians agree that the Indians got short shrift at the hands of the encroaching white settlers. What responsibility, if any, do the descendants of the victors have to the descendants of the vanquished Indians?

▼▼▼

PARAGRAPHS WITH THE TOPIC SENTENCE AT THE END

W. T. Stace

MAN AGAINST DARKNESS

WALTER TERRENCE STACE (1886–1967) was an English naturalist and philosopher known for his ability to translate complex theories into terms that appealed to a general reader. An authority on Hegel, Stace was the author of numerous books, among them *A Critical History of Greek Philosophy* (1920) and *The Philosophy of Hegel* (1924).

The picture of a meaningless world, and a meaningless human life, is, I think, the basic theme of much modern art and literature. Certainly it is the basic theme of modern philosophy. According to the most characteristic philosophies of the modern period from Hume in the eighteenth century to the so-called positivists of today, the world is just what it is, and that is the end of all inquiry. There is no reason for its being what it is. Everything might just as well have been quite different, and there would have been no reason for that either. When you have stated what things are, what things the world contains, there is nothing more which could be said, even by an omniscient being. To ask any question about why things are thus, or what purpose their being so serves, is to ask a senseless question, because they serve no purpose at all. For instance, there is for modern philosophy no such thing as the ancient problem of evil. For this once famous question pre-supposes that pain and misery, though they seem so inexplicable and irrational to us, must ultimately subserve some rational purpose, must have their places in the cosmic plan. But this is nonsense. There is no such over-ruling rationality in the universe. Belief in the ultimate irrationality of everything is the quintessence of what is called the modern mind.

(233 words)

VOCABULARY

positivists	subserve	quintessence
omniscient		

THE FACTS

1. What is the basic theme of much modern art and literature?

2. How do the most characteristic philosophies of the modern era view the world?

3. Why is there in modern philosophy no such thing as the ancient problem of evil?

THE STRATEGIES

1. Stace is known for expressing complex ideas with clarity. In this example, how does he make clear the complex views of modern philosophy?

2. From whose point of view is this paragraph mainly written? How can you tell?

3. "Begging the question" is the logical name given to an argument that assumes as proved the very thing that is in dispute. Is the attitude of modern philosophy toward evil an example of begging the question? Why, or why not?

THE ISSUES

1. What is your opinion of modern philosophy, as Stace summarizes it, that ascribes everything to irrationality? How does this philosophy square with your own beliefs?

2. What is the ancient problem of evil?

3. What imaginable purpose can evil possibly serve? If evil did not exist, would it have to be invented?

▼▼

Mark Van Doren

WHAT IS A POET?

MARK VAN DOREN (1894–1973), American poet and critic, was born in Illinois and educated at Columbia University, where he later won renown as a dedicated teacher. He was the author of many books, among them *American and British Literature since 1890* (1939, written with his brother Carl); *Collected Poems, 1922–1938* (1939, Pulitzer Prize); and *The Last Days of Lincoln* (1959).

Here is the figure we have set up. A pale, lost man with long, soft hair. Tapering fingers at the ends of furtively fluttering arms. An air of abstraction in the delicate face, but more often a look of shy pain as some aspect of reality—a real man or woman, a grocer's bill, a train, a load of bricks, a newspaper, a noise from the street—makes itself manifest. He is generally incompetent. He cannot find his way in a city, he forgets where he is going, he has no aptitude for business, he is childishly gullible and so the prey of human sharks, he cares nothing for money, he is probably poor, he will sacrifice his welfare for a whim, he stops to pet homeless cats, he is especially knowing where children are concerned (being a child himself), he sighs, he sleeps, he wakes to sigh again. The one great assumption from which the foregoing portrait is drawn is an assumption which thousands of otherwise intelligent citizens go on. It is the assumption that the poet is more sensitive than any other kind of man, that he feels more than the rest of us and is more definitely the victim of his feeling.

(205 words)

VOCABULARY

gullible

THE FACTS

1. What do we expect a poet to look like?

2. What kind of personality do we expect a poet to have?

3. What one great assumption do we make about poets?

THE STRATEGIES

1. What is Van Doren attempting to do in this paragraph? What single word could you use to describe the type of portrait he is sketching?

2. Van Doren writes: "A pale, lost man with long, soft hair. Tapering fingers at the ends of furtively fluttering arms." Grammatically, what do these two assertions have in common? What effect do they contribute to the description?

3. A *catalogue* is a list of things or attributes. Where in this paragraph does the author obviously use a catalogue?

THE ISSUES

1. Given the characteristics traditionally identified as masculine and feminine, which would you expect a poet to be—more masculine than feminine, or vice versa? Why?

2. What, in your mind, is a poet? Does your definition of a poet differ substantially from the description given by Van Doren? In what way?

3. Of what use is poetry in the modern world?

▼▼

Lewis Thomas, M.D.

ON DISEASE

LEWIS THOMAS (b. 1913–1993) was born in New York and educated at Princeton and Harvard. Dr. Thomas was a former medical administrator of the Memorial Sloan-Kettering Cancer Center in New York and an essayist who has been praised for his lucid style. His essays have been published in collections such as, *The Lives of a Cell* (1974, National Book Award), *The Medusa and the Snail* (1979), *Late Night Thoughts on Listening to Mahler's Ninth Symphony* (1983), and *Etcetera Etcetera* (1990).

We were all reassured, when the first moon landing was ready to be made, that the greatest precautions would be taken to protect the life of the earth, especially human life, against infection by whatever there might be alive on the moon. And, in fact, the elaborate ceremony of lunar asepsis was performed after each of the early landings; the voyagers were masked and kept behind plate glass, quarantined away from contact with the earth until it was a certainty that we wouldn't catch something from them. The idea that germs are all around us, trying to get at us, to devour and destroy us, is so firmly rooted in modern consciousness that it made sense to think that strange germs, from the moon, would be even scarier and harder to handle.

(132 words)

VOCABULARY

asepsis

quarantined

THE FACTS

1. What were we all reassured about before the first moon landing was made?

2. What idea about germs is firmly rooted in our consciousness?

THE STRATEGIES

1. What specific detail does the author use to support his assertion that an elaborate ceremony of asepsis was performed after each of the lunar landings?

2. Assuming that the paragraph is representative of the style of the whole essay, what kind of audience do you think the essay was originally written for?

THE ISSUES

1. Do you trust medical doctors to the extent that you implicitly follow their advice? Why or why not?

2. Which disease do you fear the most? Why?

▼▼▼

Robert Frost

THE FLOOD

ROBERT FROST (1874–1963) was a lecturer, poet, and teacher. When he was nineteen and working in a mill in Lawrence, Massachusetts, the Independent accepted and published "My Butterfly, An Elegy"—the poem that began Frost's career as one of America's great poets. Rugged New England farm life was the inspiration for many of his poems.

> Blood has been harder to dam back than water.
> Just when we think we have it impounded safe
> Behind new barrier walls (and let it chafe!),
> It breaks away in some new kind of slaughter.
> 5 We choose to say it is let loose by the devil;
> But power of blood itself releases blood.
> It goes by might of being such a flood
> Held high at so unnatural a level.
> It will have outlet, brave and not so brave.
> 10 Weapons of war and implements of peace
> Are but the points at which it finds release.
> And now it is once more the tidal wave
> That when it has swept by leaves summits stained.
> Oh, blood will out. It cannot be contained.

(122 words)

VOCABULARY

impounded

chafe

THE FACTS

1. What interpretation can be given to Frost's mention of a flood of blood?

2. What is meant by the statement "power of blood itself releases blood"?

3. What is the "tidal wave" Frost refers to? Why does it leave summits stained?

THE STRATEGIES

1. In poetry, the stanza serves a similar purpose as the paragraph. That being the case, what do you consider the topic sentence of this poem? Is it stated more than once?

2. Both water and blood are mentioned in this poem. Which of these words is used literally and which symbolically?

THE ISSUES

1. What is the theme of this poem?

2. In writing about blood Frost says: " . . . implements of peace / Are but the points at which it finds release." What can this line possibly mean?

ISSUE FOR CRITICAL THINKING AND DEBATE

▼▼

ECOLOGY

The laborers in the painting, *Man and Machinery,* by Diego Rivera, are toiling with intensity, focus, and effort among a mountainous range of hulking machinery thrusting around and above them in an ugly tangle of tubes, pistons, boilers, and conveyor belts. In the background, smoke billows from what looks like a blast furnace. The painting prompts a troubling question in the viewer that the workers who are so intent on their jobs may not have had time to ask: Is this anyway to live and work? More and more, the natural adversary of the ecology movement is turning out to be the destructive manufacturing and work habits of humans. The forces being pitted against one another are the desire for a clean environment and the almost natural impulse of humans to spend their days in some productive enterprise.

Over twenty years have elapsed since April 23, 1970, a date that launched Earth Day and began the official Environmental Movement. On that memorable day, New York closed Fifth Avenue, Chicago organized ecofairs, and towns all across the country staged trash-ins and teach-ins to make people conscious of our fragile ecosystems and ecobalances. Ever since, environmentalists have sounded the alarm of a grim future if society's activities continue to outstrip its capacity to protect the environment. Such life-threatening calamities as overpopulation, pollution,

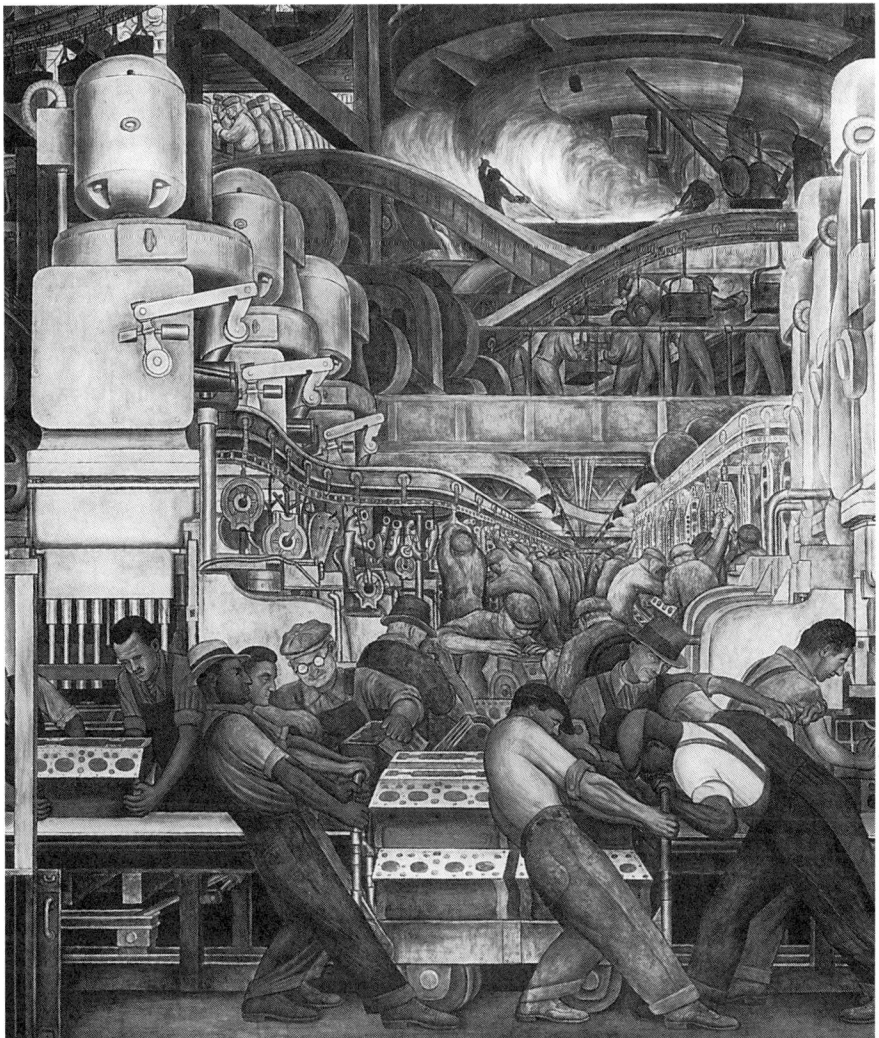

Diego M. Rivera, Detroit Industry, *North Wall (detail) 1932–1933. Fresco. Accession No. 33.10.N Photograph copyright © 1997 The Detroit Institute of Arts, Gift of Edsel B. Ford.*

global warming, desertification, and deforestation have been predicted. The most evangelical environmentalists warn that the ecological situation is hurtling toward doomsday and that quick fixes, accompanied by business-as-usual attitudes, are no longer acceptable. They insist that we must clean up this mess *now,* not tomorrow or next year. They offer two choices—either live in harmony with our environment or destroy ourselves. "Quit making demands on the environment that will diminish the lives of future generations," they plead. They preach that we must live unselfishly, viewing land as a community, not a business commodity. They admonish us to love the wilderness without violating it, to plant trees rather than chop them down, to recycle trash rather than pile it up, and to keep the air clean from pollutants. While we may never return to the pristine state of Eden, they say, we may save our planet from destruction.

Not everyone agrees with the environmentalists. Many people argue that we cannot halt technology and industrial growth without disastrous economic results, including pauperism.

The writers in this section view environmental problems from three different perspectives. First, using the disposable diaper as an example, Joseph Wood Krutch warns against creating stockpiles of refuse that cannot be reused. He suggests that industry follow nature's own example of recycling what she produces. Next, Lester C. Thurow argues that environmentalists go too far when they try to halt economic growth. He considers the problem a battle between two groups—those who wish to maintain a high standard of living and those who wish a clean environment. Thurow thinks we can have both if we remain flexible. Finally, Michèle Izzo, a college student, writes a thoughtprovoking fable in which she demonstrates what each of us can do to help the environment.

▼▼

Joseph W. Krutch

OUR VALUES HURT THE ENVIRONMENT

JOSEPH W. KRUTCH (1893–1970) was an American author, editor, naturalist, and conservationist. After receiving a PhD from Columbia University, he became much in demand as a speaker and writer on the beauty of wildlife in the desert and in national parks. In 1954, he won two prestigious awards—the Burroughs Medal for nature writing, and the National Book Award for his nonfiction work *The Measure of Man* (1954). From 1963 to 1965, he narrated and performed on NBC's "The Voice of the Desert" and "The Grand Canyon." He also served as a consultant to the Library of Congress on matters related to American culture. His most popular books include *Edgar Allen Poe: A Study of Genius* (1926), *The Voice of the Desert: A Naturalists's Interpretation* (1955), and his autobiography, *More Lives Than One* (1962). Moreover, he contributed numerous articles on natural history and on drama to various periodicals, such as the *Atlantic Monthly*, the *Saturday Evening Post*, and *Life*.

What follows is a criticism of our prevailing custom of buying more and more disposable items that clutter the environment because they can neither be fully destroyed nor recycled for some useful purpose. To prove his point, the author discusses baby diapers that are flushed down the toilet. Underlying this example is his assertion that in the battle for a happy human existence, two values, one incompatible with the other, clamor for our attention, and we must decide which to accept.

1   Flipping through the pages of a current issue of a women's magazine, I found an advertisement for Chux, a disposable diaper. Its trade name is a recognition of the fact that "produce more and more" means also "get rid of more and more." The old formula for the good citizen, "produce more and consume more," has become "produce more and chuck more." . . .

2   What we are just beginning to realize is the false implication of the word disposable. Matter is indestructible, not disposable—or at least was until Einstein came along with his $e = mc^2$, and it will remain so for practical purposes until some method is discovered for applying the magic formula to a garbage dump—although if it ever is I don't know what we will do with all the energy generated. What we manufacture we are not even in practical terms disposing of. We are merely moving it somewhere else or turning it into something different but still not disposable—even when it goes up in smoke to come down again in smog.

3   No one has really faced the fact. We are still determined to increase every day the gross national product, forgetting that increasing the gross national product means increasing the gross national junk pile, since all our products will end up ultimately in the junk piles that surround our cities, poison the water we drink and foul the air we breathe.

Our Disposable Society

4   The diaper, to take again this humble example, is flushed down the toilet and is for the moment out of sight. But it will surely turn up again, often in the untreated sewage that thousands of the smaller communities are pouring directly into the streams, clogging them with organic slime and poisoning the fish. Far from recognizing this fact, the same company that advertises the disposable diaper boasts on its television commercial that this is only the beginning. The baby's crib and ultimately all the furniture of his nursery will be disposable. You cut down trees to make more refuse and thus you keep the gross national product booming, whereas if you made something usefully durable, you would save the trees and relieve, instead of further overburden, the polluted environment. But that would cause prosperity to falter, so they say.

5   The solution, if there is one, would seem to mean one or all of the following: 1) a reduced population, which would therefore not need so

much; 2) willingness to get along with less; 3) finding some way of making our products actually, for all practical purposes, disposable; 4) developing some system of recycling the residue.

6   Nature creates no junk piles. What she herself produces is not disposable but reusable. Whatever grows also decays. The complex becomes simple again, then is raised to complexity once more, and so the eternal recycling goes on.

7   But a very large part of all that industry produces remains outside this recycling, and is neither reused nor, ultimately, disposable. Moreover, every advance in the efficiency of production along with every rise in the cost of human labor tends to diminish the extent to which anything is reused or recycled. Because it is cheaper to produce steel from newly mined ore than to reuse scrap, the abandoned automobiles threaten to engulf the cities, while the mines add to the pollution of the streams.

8   The returnable and reusable milk, soft drink or beer bottle is replaced by waxed "disposable" cartons or by metal containers which can be manufactured more cheaply than the returnable bottles can be handled and cleaned. Moreover, the so-called disposable tends to become more and more resistant to any recycling that nature can bring about—as has recently been pointed out is conspicuously the case where the tin can, which would disintegrate in ten or fifteen years, has been succeeded by the now-popular aluminum can, which can last for millenia. Ecology means literally housekeeping, but ours has been largely of the sweep-it-under-the-carpet kind, and it won't work.

The Fundamental Fact

9   The fundamental fact is that you cannot solve the problems of pollution and environmental deterioration—or adopt an ecological rather than technological view—by merely giving them some thought while still accepting prevailing values. It will often happen that the only ecologically sound procedure is economically unsound. The two philosophies meet head on. They cannot be reconciled. We must make some sort of choice between them. To put it into even simpler terms, we would just have to stop asking, "Is this the cheapest way to make something or do something?" but ask instead, "Which way will leave the least residue of one kind or another, even if (as will usually be the case) this means also a loss of convenience?" . . .

10   If you suggest, for example, that gasoline taxes should be diverted from road building (which solves no problems) to the development of public transportation, you will surely be greeted by an agonized protest from the oil companies and the auto manufacturers who will tell you, not only that they ought to get the benefit of the taxes their customers pay, but that any significant decline in the auto industry would have catastrophic effects on the total economy—which is what I

suppose it would do. Moreover, it is extremely doubtful that the public would submit to the inconvenience of the bus as opposed to the convenience of private transportation. In fact, even such public-minded citizens as you and I would object! What is to be expected of the less enlightened? Ask an economist if we can afford to do what would be necessary to reverse the current trends, and he will certainly answer "No." Ask the ecologist if we can afford not to do so, and he also will answer "No." In a sense, both are right.

11 Perhaps the time will come when we will have to abandon the whole assumption that it is the chief duty of the citizen to consume and throw away in order that prosperity will continue to increase. Perhaps we will have to return to the old philosophy that assumed that the good citizen is the one who preserves and continues to use what his grandfather had bought with the conviction that it would last for generations.

(1,055 words)

VOCABULARY

organic (4)   disintegrate (8)   diverted (10)
engulf (7)   millenia (8)   catastrophic (10)
conspicuously (8)   residue (9)

THE FACTS

1. In what magazine do you think the author might have found the advertisement for Chux? Suggest two or three possibilities.

2. To which "values," mentioned in the title of his essay, is the author referring?

3. What solutions to the problem of junk piles does the author suggest? In what paragraph? Which of the solutions seems least possible at the present time?

4. According to the author, what two philosophies are colliding head on and cannot be reconciled?

5. How does the author define the good citizen of the future?

THE STRATEGIES

1. Whom is the author addressing in his essay? Provide clues from the text for your answer.

2. How is the essay organized and what makes the organization obvious?

3. How does the author maintain coherence between paragraphs 3 and 4?

4. What is the author's thesis and where is it stated? What advantage does the position have?

5. How does the author go about defining a "disposable society"? Does he explain himself clearly? Give reasons for your answer.

THE ISSUES

1. As a "good citizen," what are you personally willing to do in order to preserve our environment? State your actions in order of importance. For instance, are you willing to car pool, use recyclable bottles instead of tin cans, preserve the wilderness, or generally get along with less?

2. What objects, not mentioned by Krutch, contribute to the junk piling of indestructible matter? What, if anything, can be done to reduce this residue?

3. Do you agree that economic growth is incompatible with environmental soundness? Think about this issue critically before providing an answer. In other words, must we stop manufacturing modern cars, computers, or weapons, and making technological advances in order to preserve our planet?

4. Of all the ecological problems presented to you, which seems the most dangerous? Give reasons for your choice.

5. What aspects of life at the turn of the century would you happily go back to? What aspects would you want to avoid? Be specific in your choices.

SUGGESTIONS FOR WRITING

1. Using one of the following statements as your thesis, write an essay using appropriate evidence to make the thesis convincing:

Trend is not necessarily destiny (even as applied to our environment) because both nature and humans have always demonstrated extraordinary abilities to change, adapt, and renew.

Because of serious threats to our environment, we are presently engaged in an elemental struggle to survive.

Overpopulation, global warming, and ecological pollution are major problems we must solve or pay a heavy price.

2. Write an essay suggesting practical steps anyone can take to help preserve our environment.

▼▼

Lester C. Thurow

ECONOMIC GROWTH REQUIRES ENVIRONMENTAL COMPROMISES

LESTER C. THUROW (b. 1938) is Dean of Faculty and Professor of Economics at Sloan School of Management for the Massachusetts Institute of Technology (MIT). He attended Williams College, Balliol College, Oxford, and Harvard (where he received his MA and PhD). In 1964 he served on the President's Council of Economic Advisers and became a consultant to government agencies and private corporations. He was awarded the David Wells Prize in 1967 by Harvard for his work *Poverty and Discrimination*. Other publications include *Thinking About Cities* (1970) and *The Impact of Taxes on the American Economy* (1971). He has also contributed articles to several edited compilations and to professional journals as well as popular magazines, including *Nation* and *Newsweek*.

Thurow takes a moderate approach to environmental problems, insisting that we do not necessarily have to give up economic growth in order to survive ecologically. He criticizes the wilderness movement for carrying its concern for the land to extreme lengths that often reveal a lack of compassion toward the needs of people. He warns that if those in favor of economic growth and those in favor of ecological reform continue their all-out war with each other, both sides are likely to fail in meeting their goals.

1   "If it were done when 'tis done, then 'twere well it were done quickly."

—Macbeth

2   Shakespeare's dictum applies to no two groups better than to environmentalists and reindustrializationists. Advocates of economic growth should agree to implement strict environmental standards without delay. Environmentalists should agree to cheap, speedy ways of determining whether a project meets environmental standards once a project is already under way.

Environmentalists Delay Industrialization

3   The environmentalists can certainly delay industrialization with lengthy court battles over each and every new factory. But the pressure

to roll back environmental standards will inevitably rise as American standards of living decline.

4   "Hungry? Eat an environmentalist for dinner," will become a political banner rather than a faintly amusing bumper sticker. If environmentalists do not bend on procedures in order to defend standards, they will ultimately be broken on both procedures and standards . . .

5   If you look at the countries that are interested in environmentalism, or at the individuals who support environmentalism within each country, one is struck by the extent to which environmentalism is an interest of the upper middle classes.

6   If you reflect upon this phenomenon, it is not surprising. As our income rises, each of us shifts our focus of demand for more goods and services. Initially, we are only interested in physiological survival. Food constitutes our main demand. As we grow even wealthier, our demand shifts toward roomier housing and higher quality food. Meat replaces grain. At still higher income levels, demands for services rise. We start to eat out more and at home less.

7   Now suppose that a family has reached an economic level where it can afford good food, fine housing, vacations, consumer durables, and most of the goods and services that represent the American dream. What is there left that can mar its economic happiness? Up to this point, the family can individually buy a rising standard of living. But now it runs into environmental pollution. If the air is dirty or noisy, the water polluted, and the land spoiled, there is a roadblock in its way to a higher standard of living. Something must be done about environmental conditions if the family is to progress.

8   Environmentalism is the demand for more goods and services (clean air, water, and land) that does not differ from other consumption demands except it can only be achieved collectively. In any geographic area, we either all breathe clean air or no one breathes clean air.

Environmentalism Is Economic

9   Environmentalism is not ethical values pitted against economic values. It is thoroughly economic. It is simply a case where a particular segment of the income distribution wants an economic good—a clean environment—that cannot be achieved without coercion. Therefore, that segment must persuade the rest of society it is important to have a clean environment, and impose rules and regulations that force others to produce a clean environment.

10   With economic growth, environmentalism is clearly the way to the future. More and more people will be moving into the income classes where a clean environment is No. 1 on their acquisitive agenda. Conversely, economic decline is a disaster from the point of view of those

interested in the environment. As the economy declines and standards of living fall, fewer and fewer people will be interested in environmentalism. The political pressure to roll back environmental standards will grow and eventually become overwhelming.

11   There is no conflict between clean air, water, and land and economic growth. Each is an economic good that does not happen to get counted in our conventional gross national product statistics. It should be counted, and whenever anyone can find a good way to evaluate a clean environment, it will be included in conventional G.N.P. measures of economic output.

Environmental Standards Not Problem

12   The lack of any fundamental conflict can be seen in West Germany and Japan. Each of these countries has environmental standards that are as high or higher than those of the United States, but each has a very successful economy. The problem is not environmental standards but the methods we use to achieve them. New plants can be built in a world of high environmental standards, but they cannot be built in a world of uncertainty, delay, and *ex post facto** alterations in standards. If business is uncertain as to what delays environmentalists will force upon them, then new factories simply do not get built. Lengthy uncertain court battles over standards for the environment just do not exist in West Germany or in Japan.

13   No one will build new factories in a world where environmental standards may change during the course of construction. One can live with standards that are known and fixed, but one cannot live with standards that change and then must be retrofitted onto a new factory.

14   It simply becomes impossible to predict whether a factory will or will not be profitable, and as a consequence, the factory is not built.

15   Environmental standards will inevitably change over time, but these new standards must apply only to new factories not yet under construction. Or, if the changes are vital, then society and not the company must pay the extra cost of retrofitting a new factory that was begun in good faith under a different set of standards.

Move Battles Out of Courts

16   To reduce delays and uncertainties, it will be necessary to move environmental battles out of the courts. One possibility would be to set up some system of compulsory arbitration similar to that now used in labor relations where disputes could be quickly and cheaply solved.

---

* Latin for "after the fact."—Ed.

17   If a consensus could not be reached within a very limited time period, then an arbitrator would be called to impose a solution.

18   Environmentalism and economic growth are not intrinsically incompatible, but poor institutional arrangements and an unwillingness to compromise can make them incompatible.

19   Under current arrangements, it is highly likely that the American economy will neither reindustrialize nor meet its environmental goals.

(981 words)

VOCABULARY

dictum (2)   acquistive (10)   compulsory (16)

phenomenon (6)   agenda (10)   arbitration (16)

physiological (6)   conversely (10)   consensus (17)

collectively (8)   retrofitted (13)

THE FACTS

1. What is the meaning of the quotation from Shakespeare's *Macbeth*? Rewrite it in your own words. How does the quotation apply to Thurow's thesis?

2. According to Thurow, the environmental battle is carried on mostly by people who can afford a high standard of living. Why is this so?

3. What two countries are held up as models for the future? Why?

4. According to the author, how should we deal with existing businesses that do not meet environmental standards?

5. What suggestions does the author make for moving environmental battles out of the courts in order to speed up the process of getting permission to build?

THE STRATEGIES

1. What is Thurow's thesis as well as proposition? Where is it explicitly stated? Could a student writing an essay for freshman English get by with this thesis? Why or why not?

2. Does the author seem to favor one side over the other? If so, which side does he favor, and how is the bias indicated?

3. How does the author achieve closeness to his readers so that they will feel involved in the cause argued?

4. For what sort of publication is this essay ideally suited? Give reasons for your choice.

5. In paragraph 8, the author offers a definition of environmentalism. How helpful is this definition?

THE ISSUES

1. Do you agree with the author's view that economic growth and environmentalism are not incompatible? What do you foresee happening in the next decade in terms of our environment?

2. What is your response to the view, often expressed by advocates of economic growth, that much of the environmental movement is a commendable concern for the land carried to extreme lengths that could cause a great deal of suffering for the poor?

3. In your view, is the government playing a positive or negative role with respect to the environment? For example, how do you feel about the National Environmental Protection Act, which requires that before undertaking any development projects involving federal lands or funds, public agencies and private entrepreneurs must look at the likely environmental consequences? (Environmental Impact Statements must be filed and are monitored by an advisory council.)

4. One possible way to move environmental battles out of the courts, the author suggests, is to set up some "system of compulsory arbitration" similar to that now used in labor relation disputes. What other suggestions do you have?

5. Is the author's outlook for the future correct (see final paragraph) or are you more optimistic? Give reasons for your view.

SUGGESTIONS FOR WRITING

1. Write a description of a typical landscape one hundred years from today.

2. Write an essay describing the major effects on the environment if environmentalists lose out to economic growth.

   Or

   Write an essay describing the major effects on the economically disadvantaged if the environmentalists curtail economic growth.

I

First Draft

Michèle Izzo, University of Maryland

Saving Life on Earth—It Doesn't Take an Education

Ecosystem, ecologically sound, biological diversity, global *[shorter and more coherent]* warming, chlorofluorocarbons, biosphere, ozone depletion . . . . It seems ~~like~~ *as if* we've added a lot of new terms to our vocabulary that are supposed to mean something to us in our everyday lives. *In fact, admitting ignorance* ~~Owning up to being ignorant~~ about their exact meaning would be very ~~gauche~~ *unfashionable*. But what do all of these *vogue words* mean? *[better word]* Everywhere we look, information is dispersed on recycling, tropical rain forests, endangered species, ~~ground~~*green*house pollution, and toxic waste. We live in an age when the Vice-President *of the United States* has authored a national bestseller, <u>Earth in the Balance</u>, summarizing the state of the world environment today and giving thoughtful and concrete *[shorter and more direct]* *solutions to* ~~strategies to solve~~ the environmental crisis. ~~On a visit to~~ *At* the *[dangling modifier]* county public library recently, an informational brochure on composting lay beside one on how to deal with the pesky white-tailed deer. ~~in the~~ (neighborhood) *[more concise in using a noun as a modifier]* Those aiming to maintain balance on the earth are at odds with those ~~who~~ wish,to change*ing* to *[make sentence parallel]* "simplify" our lives. Plastic is big business; reusing containers is not. To some it seems being environmentally conscious adds

Izzo 2

transition needed   *our*   *However, we*   *keep pronoun usage*
complexity and labor to ~~your~~ day. ~~You~~ don't have to keep abreast   *consistent in 1st person plural — we*

we
of the latest ecological crisis and political solution; ~~you~~ don't

We simply
need to know the definition of all those ecological terms. ~~You~~

unecessary
need to have common sense, ~~a desire for stewardship,~~ a sense of   *Better order to lead up to most important*

we
caring. (and) (a hate of waste.) ~~Your~~ *Our* life is simplified when ~~you~~

respect life.

clarifies pronoun reference   ~~What amazes me is~~ the sudden rise in popularity of the   *the environment and the study of ecology*
is surprising.
environment in the last ten years. Surely ~~it~~/existed before. It

takes a disruption in the climate and the atmosphere, and a

contamination of the seas to make people change old habits in

order to fend off the crises which some have called the result of

"The Earth fighting back." Are we suddenly enlightened into
a few people
making the world a better place? No. While ~~some~~ hold

themselves ~~and others~~ accountable to ensure a world fit for the
most
future, ~~others~~ contribute to environmental abuse. The

destruction we have caused should never have happened. [When

I was in high school, I always confused the word ecology with   *Time reference*
clarification
agronomy. I had a friend who was majoring in one or the other

and to this day I don't know which one his degree is in.] Few
Needs parallel structure and coherent order
fields of study can visibly be affected and changed by ordinary

people like you and me. We can't change history; ~~the English~~
and we can't create new
~~language will not adapt to the~~ sentence structures, verb
for the English language.
conjugations and spellings ~~we suggest no matter how creative,~~
the basic human anatomy
the principles of physics remain the same, and we can't suggest
does not transform.
new answers to our mathematical problems. We can ~~suggest~~
add
new titles ~~to add~~ to the literary canon, but we can't change the

(left margin, rotated) Relevant here? (Add to personal paragraph on page 5 to show dictation is for necessary conservation)

(left margin, rotated) more Simple

content of the books we read. Ecology, however, is something that you and I and the guy next door can affect. We can change its course.

Some of us feel powerless in front of the magnitude of environmental disasters. We fail to make decisions with the environment in mind because we feel one person can't make a difference. Or we join the recycling efforts because we have to or because everyone else is joining, and we don't want to trail fashion. clarity On the one hand, taking measures to preserve life on earth is trendy; on the other hand, people who recycle systematically or who crusade actively for the conservation of natural habitats and rare species are considered radical or fanatical, even miserly.

Practical handbooks and videos have emerged on how to save the planet, suggesting, for example, 750 ways you can help clean up the earth, 50 simple things you can do to save the earth, 101 easy things you can do to save the animals, and 10 ways to save life's diversity. But wonderful as these are, you and I don't have the time to read them and calculate strategies to save the earth, nor do we have the funds to make charitable contributions to the World Wildlife Fund or the Nature Conservancy to enable them to do it for us.

Without knowing that styrofoam contains Benzene (a (carcinogen) and gases which deplete the earth's vital ozone layer, Pronoun shift) common sense should keep us away from the unsightly, cumbersome white stuff. How could spraying chemicals from a

Izzo 4

can "freshen" the air? If something comes in a container labeled "hazardous," what makes it okay to toss it down the drain or to pour it onto the ground only to contaminate our drinking [pronoun consistency] water? Why would ~~you~~ *we* want to buy plastic bags when stores ~~are~~ *stores can't* ~~only too eager to place in a~~ *be eager!* *supply* *is for* bag each item purchased, no matter the size. Even so called biodegradable plastic will never completely disappear and often ends up in the ocean killing marine life. The ink on plastic bags contains the heavy metal toxic cadmium. ~~Solution:~~ *Common sense dictates* "Bring canvas bags when you shop." [pronoun consistency] While ~~they~~ *we* leave the faucet running to brush ~~their~~ *our* teeth, wash dishes, shave ~~etc. do people~~ *or* *Surely we don't* assume the sink is a magical [Recall wording of thesis] [pronoun consistency] fountain sending the same water flowing back through? ~~You~~ *We* don't need to know that a running faucet uses five gallons of water per minute to recognize the waste and instead fill a small basin and turn the faucet off. The thought of bleached coffee filters or flour should be enough to halt ~~your~~ *our* appetite without knowing that the process of bleaching produces the deadly toxic dioxin which is dumped in America's waterways. We don't need to be told that many tropical forest plants have important medicinal and commercial uses in order to desire their conservation. We don't need a list of the 500 most endangered species to want to preserve their lives.

The real life of the heroes of our fiction -- the wolves in <u>Dancing with Wolves</u>, <u>White Fang</u>, the killer whales in <u>Free Willy</u>, <u>Orca</u>, the orangutan in the Clint Eastwood movies, the gorillas, the humpback whales -- is not always a romantic ~~one~~ as ~~they~~ *these creatures* are [pronoun antecedent]

Izzo 5

threatened by habitat loss, logging, international pet or animal

parts trade, poaching, and carelessness by humans. It is
and even
unconscionable to subject animals to torture, maiming,^death in

order to find the right shade of golden blonde hair color, the

right creamy texture of wineberry lipstick, the right scent of
clarification *Yet* *are unconscionable when we*
dandruff shampoo, ~~but~~ we ~~do by~~ purchasing products from

companies who practice animal testing.

Add *Yet* In my family we always washed, saved, and reused containers.
para.
from We always enjoyed the careful unwrapping of a gift and saved the
page 2
paper for the following year. We never served our meals on

paper or plastic. We always used, washed, and reused a cloth

instead of tearing endless sheets of paper towels or wet-wipes.

We always bought large containers with little packaging rather

than individually packaged products. We did this without thought

or effort because we cared for life and despised waste. Human

selfishness and greed have resulted in ever-increasing production,

unlimited consumption, and depletion of non-renewable

resources. Leading a simple, wholesome lifestyle where people

do not step on a treadmill of unbridled overconsumption needs

to be advocated.

We don't need to be a throw-away society. Not only will

recycling and avoiding items which contain toxins save us money
Connection
individually, ~~but~~ it will save our resources, our atmosphere, and, *needed for*
coherence
most importantly, our lives. It does not take a workshop on
a visit to the local aquarium,
recycling,^or an array of ecological knowledge; it takes ~~every~~ *to*
Eventually it has^come
individual ~~demonstrating~~ common sense and caring. Albert *down to*
character.

Izzo 6

, who believed in the sanctity of life,

Schweitzer ^ wrote, "A man is truly ethical only when he obeys

the compulsion to help all life which he is able to assist, and

shrinks from injuring anything that lives." ~~(The Philosophy of~~

~~Civilization)~~.

term
"sanctity
of life"
connects
well to
essay. Adds
punch.

I

Final Draft

Michèle Izzo, University of Maryland

Saving Life on Earth—It Doesn't Take an Education

Ecosystem, ecologically sound, biological diversity, global warming, chlorofluorocarbons, biosphere, ozone depletion . . . . It seems as if we've added a lot of new terms to our vocabulary that are supposed to mean something to us in our everyday lives. In fact, admitting ignorance about their exact meaning would be very unfashionable. But what do all of these vogue words mean? Everywhere we look, information is dispersed on recycling, tropical rain forests, endangered species, greenhouse pollution, and toxic waste. We live in an age when the Vice-President of the United States has authored a national bestseller, <u>Earth in the Balance</u>, summarizing the state of the world environment today and giving thoughtful and concrete solutions to the environmental crisis. At the county public library recently, an informational brochure on composting lay beside one on how to deal with the pesky white-tailed neighborhood deer. Those aiming to maintain balance on the earth are at odds with those wishing to "simplify" our lives. Plastic is big business; reusing containers is not. To some it seems being environmentally conscious adds complexity and labor to our day. However, we don't have to keep abreast of the latest ecological crisis and

Izzo 2

political solution; we don't need to know the definition of all those ecological terms. We simply need to have common sense, a hate of waste, and a sense of caring. Our life _is_ simplified when we respect life.

The sudden rise in popularity of the environment in the last ten years is surprising. Surely the environment and the study of ecology existed before. It takes a disruption in the climate and the atmosphere, and a contamination of the seas to make people change old habits in order to fend off the crises which some have called the result of "The Earth fighting back." Are we suddenly enlightened into making the world a better place? No. While a few people hold themselves accountable to ensure a world fit for the future, most contribute to environmental abuse. The destruction we have caused should never have happened. Few fields of study can visibly be affected and changed by ordinary people like you and me. We can't change history; we can't suggest new answers to our mathematical problems; and we can't create new sentence structures, verb conjugations and spellings for the English language. The principles of physics remain the same, and the basic human anatomy does not transform. We can add new titles to the literary canon, but we can't change the content of the books we read. Ecology, however, is something that you and I and the guy next door can affect. We can change its course.

Some of us feel powerless in front of the magnitude of environmental disasters. We fail to make decisions with the environment in mind because we feel one person can't make a difference. Or we join the recycling efforts because we have to or because everyone else is joining, and we don't want to trail fashion. On the one hand, taking measures to preserve life on earth is trendy; on the other hand, people who recycle systematically or who crusade actively for the conservation of natural habitats and rare species are considered radical or fanatical, even miserly.

Practical handbooks and videos have emerged on how to save the planet, suggesting, for example, 750 ways you can help clean up the earth, 50 simple things you can do to save the earth, 101 easy things you can do to save the animals, and 10 ways to save life's diversity. But wonderful as these are, you and I don't have the time to read them and calculate strategies to save the earth, nor do we have the funds to make charitable contributions to the World Wildlife Fund or the Nature Conservancy to enable them to do it for us.

Without knowing that styrofoam contains Benzene (a carcinogen) and gases which deplete the earth's vital ozone layer, common sense should keep us away from the unsightly, cumbersome white stuff. How could spraying chemicals from a can "freshen" the air? If something comes in a container labeled "hazardous," what makes it okay to toss it down the drain or to pour it onto the ground only to contaminate our drinking water? Why would we want to buy plastic bags when stores supply bag's for each item purchased, no matter the size. Even so called biodegradable plastic will never completely disappear and often ends up in the ocean killing marine life. The ink on plastic bags contains the heavy metal toxic cadmium. Common sense dictates: "Bring canvas bags when you shop." While we leave the faucet running to brush our teeth, wash dishes, or shave, surely we don't assume the sink is a magical fountain sending the same water flowing back through? We don't need to know that a running faucet uses five gallons of water per minute to recognize the waste and instead fill a small basin and turn the faucet off. The thought of bleached coffee filters or flour should be enough to halt our appetite without knowing that the process of bleaching produces the deadly toxic dioxin which is dumped in America's waterways. We don't need to be told that many tropical forest plants have important medicinal and commercial uses in order to desire their conservation. We don't need a list of the 500 most endangered species to want to preserve their lives.

The real life of the heroes of our fiction—the wolves in Dancing with Wolves, White Fang, the killer whales in Free Willy, Orca, the orangutan in the Clint Eastwood movies, the gorillas, the humpback whales—is not always romantic as these creatures are threatened by habitat loss, logging, international pet or animal parts trade, poaching, and carelessness by humans. It is unconscionable to subject animals to torture, maiming, and even death in order to find the right shade of golden blonde hair color, the right creamy texture of wineberry lipstick, the right scent of dandruff shampoo. Yet we are unconscionable when we purchase products from companies who practice animal testing.

When I was in high school, I always confused the word ecology with agronomy. I had a friend who was majoring in one or the other and to this day I don't know which one his degree is in. Yet in my family we always washed, saved, and reused containers. We always enjoyed the careful unwrapping of a gift and saved the paper for the following year. We never served our meals on paper or plastic. We always used, washed, and reused a cloth instead of tearing endless sheets of paper towels or wet-wipes. We always bought large containers with little packaging rather than individually packaged products. We did this without thought or effort because we cared for life and despised waste. Human selfishness and greed have resulted in ever-increasing production, unlimited consumption, and depletion of non-renewable resources. Leading a simple, wholesome lifestyle where people do not step on a treadmill of unbridled overconsumption needs to be advocated.

We don't need to be a throw-away society. Not only will recycling and avoiding items which contain toxins save us money individually, it will save our resources, our atmosphere, and most importantly, our lives. It does not take a workshop on recycling, a visit to the local aquarium, or an array of ecological knowledge; it takes individual common sense and caring. Eventually it has to come down to character. Albert Schweitzer, who believed in the sanctity of life, wrote, "A man is truly ethical only when he obeys the compulsion to help all life which he is able to assist, and shrinks from injuring anything that lives."

How I Write

Because I am gregarious, I like writing with people around me. Although I am easily distracted by the sounds of television, loud music, or incidental conversation (even smells hinder my concentration), talking with friends fuels rather than cools my inspiration to write. If I have a writing project to complete, one of my most successful strategies is to call up a friend and ask him or her to have dinner with me. In the restaurant, I will explain my task and suggest several ideas I have been incubating. Rather than using friends to give me ideas or state approval or disapproval, I use them as sounding boards. I suppose one could say that I am using their presence as an opportunity to run my ideas by *me.* Not only does this strategy serve as a brainstorming technique, but I actually do some of the writing right there on the spot—on a napkin if I neglected to bring paper.

Other times the setting is more spontaneous: I'm not planning to write nor am I seeking inspiration, but the situation—usually a room with several people in it talking—spurs me on, and I jot down words and sentences that I later merge into a written piece. The topic may or may not be related to the conversation at hand.

How I Wrote This Essay

I brainstormed in my usual manner, talking aloud in the presence of people—although this time it didn't help. (My favorite dinner friend has moved to California.) Then I turned on my laptop and between baby cries and baby feedings (I am a new mother), I typed in phrases and ideas as they popped into my head. I made a quick trip to my local library to get a list of titles that are out there to advise the general public on ecological matters. Then I sat and typed for a couple of hours. With a multitude of ideas bouncing around in my head, I had the hardest time with choosing a definite purpose. Should I define all of the ecosystems and list every possible area of crisis? Should I preach recycling and conservation? Should I list ways to save life on earth? In the end, I focused on what has always amazed me about all the environmental talk—people's indifference. If people only cared and used common sense, most of our environmental crisis would not exist. We should not have needed to be educated in the first place. I hope this approach comes across as the thesis of my essay. I tried to show that *ecology* is a very simple matter and that we don't even need to know what the word means. The easy part of completing this assignment was that the topic is one about which I had strong feelings; I cared about it. That is important when writing.

My Writing Tip

People often do not know how to end an essay or a report. I find it helpful to ask, "So what?" at the end of the essay. Now that you've proven what you set out to do as stated in your thesis, so what? What difference does it make to the big picture? Why is it so important? For instance, if you are writing about two characters in a novel, how do your ideas affect the work as a whole? You've proven that the two characters are in sharp contrast with each other—so what? The answer is likely to make a forceful conclusion. Asking "So what?" helps you end your essay with a bang rather than a whimper.

CHAPTER WRITING ASSIGNMENTS

1. Select one of the following topics and develop it into a unified, coherent, and complete paragraph:
   a. Carelessness can do more harm than lack of knowledge.
   b. Today the prevailing mood on the campus is one of . . . . (Fill in
the words you think apply.)
   c. Many cars are still not designed for safety.
   d. Kissing is an odd, overly romanticized act.
   e. A plagiarized paper has several bad effects.
   f. Buying term papers from a commercial source is an unethical
act.

2. List the particular details that you would use to write a convincing
paragraph on the following topic sentences:
   a. Sarcastic people are unpleasant to be around.
   b. I like the security of dating the same person (or, I like the freedom of dating different persons).
   c. Yuppies have gotten bad press and a bad name.
   d. Children and fools speak the truth.
   e. Common sense is . . . (define it).

WRITING ASSIGNMENTS FOR A SPECIFIC AUDIENCE

1. Write an essay aimed at an audience of unemployed loggers arguing
the importance of preserving the habitat of the spotted owl even at
the cost of logging jobs.

   Or

2. Write an essay aimed at an audience of environmentalists arguing
the importance of preserving jobs even at the cost of the spotted
owls' habitat.

COLLABORATIVE WRITING PROJECT

Divide your group into four teams. Assign each team to investigate and
report on the paragraph writing techniques practiced by such publications as *Reader's Digest, Atlantic, Consumer Reports,* and the editorial
page of your local newspaper. Consider the relationship between the
audience of the publication and the kinds of paragraphs used in it.
Meet to discuss your findings and then team write an essay outlining
what you have learned.

▼▼▼

Introduction to the Patterns of Development

Behind the rhetorical modes or patterns in composition is this simple idea: To write about a subject, you must first have thought about it, and this systematic thinking can be translated into an idealized pattern. For example, you might choose to tell a story about your subject **(narration)**; to describe it **(description)**; to say how it happened **(process analysis)**; to give examples of it **(example)**; to define it **(definition)**; to compare it to something else **(comparison and contrast)**; to break it down into its constituent parts **(division and classification)**; or to say what its known causes or effects are **(causal analysis)**. Superimposing one of these seven abstract modes or patterns on your subject will make writing about it easier.

Each of these rhetorical modes is a composite of specific writing and organizing techniques that can be isolated and taught. All narrations are alike, whether they tell a story about aliens from Mars or about facing up to a bully. All descriptions draw on common organizing and focusing techniques, no matter what they describe. If you are writing a comparison and contrast, for example, you know that you must alternate back and forth between the compared items and that you must insert suitable transitions so your reader can follow this movement. If you are defining, you know that there are specific techniques to be used in a definition. Knowing that a subject is to be approached a certain way also endows a writer's purpose with a refreshing narrowness. For what is especially bedeviling to the writer is not necessarily the complexity of a subject, but the infinity of possible approaches suggested by the blank sheet of paper.

The advice that instructors often give beginning writers is, "Narrow your subject." Writing by rhetorical modes allows you to limit and narrow your *approach* to a subject. You say, "I'm going to divide and classify this subject," and you have an abstract pattern in mind that you can follow. You say, "I'm going to analyze cause," and you also have an abstract pattern to follow. In either case, you are not left dangling between "What shall I say?" and "How shall I say it?" You know how to say it in the abstract. What's left is the application of the ideal pattern to your particular subject.

Here is an example, the subject of guilt as developed in the eight most widely used rhetorical patterns. Notice how the writer's focus shifts with the use of each new pattern.

▼▼

The Editors

PATTERNS OF DEVELOPMENT FOR THE SUBJECT "GUILT"

I. Narration

I was seven years old when I first became aware of the terrible power of guilt. For piling our toys into the toy box, Mother had rewarded my brother and me with five shiny pennies each. If I had had ten pennies instead of just five, I could have bought a gingerbread man with raisin eyes and sugarfrosted hair. The image danced in my head all day, until, finally, I crept into my brother's room and stole his five pennies. The next morning, as my brother and I were dressing to go to school, I hid all ten pennies in the pocket of my coat, cramming one of my father's handkerchiefs on top of them. As my brother and I lined up in front of Mother to be kissed goodbye, she looked at my bulging pocket with amazement. "What on earth do you have in your pocket?" she asked. "It's nothing," I said as offhandedly as I could. "It's nothing at all." Bewildered, but too busy to investigate any further, Mother kissed me goodbye. I ran out the door and down our gravel path as fast as my feet could carry me. But the farther from home I got, the more miserable I became. The shiny pennies in my pocket felt oppressively like one-ton boulders. And I was haunted by the idea that I had become a thief. Forgotten was the gingerbread man, for whose sake I had stolen my brother's pennies. Finally, unable to bear my horrible feeling of guilt, I ran back home to blurt out my crime to my mother.

2. Description

Never before had Pedro experienced such a depth of despair and such a sense of isolation. He began to avoid those nearest to him, returning their friendly greetings with rough and indifferent replies. Often he sat in his room staring vacantly into space with hollow eyes. His hands were cold and clammy most of the time; yet his forehead burned hot with a mysterious fever. Terrible nightmares haunted his sleep, causing him to rise out of bed in the middle of the night, overcome with terror. When strangers at the store asked him a simple question such as "Where is the thread?" or "Have you any molasses?" he would read silent accusations in their eyes and his hands would tremble. He had become a man tormented by guilt.

3. Process Analysis

Do you know the most effective way to handle a friend turned a debtor? Make the person feel guilty. Let us say that you lent your friend Tom $500.00 to buy a motorcycle, but he refuses to repay the loan. Your first step is to place him in a category of bogus moral superiority. Say, "Tom, you have always been a person of honor. Why do you refuse to pay what you owe me?" If that doesn't work, your second step is to take the behavior personally, indicating that it is causing you emotional pain. Say, "I can't tell you how disappointed I am that you are treating me worse than a total stranger. You would pay back your bank, your credit cards, but you ignore me, your best friend, who needs the money." Unless your present debtor and former friend is a sociopath, he will feel bad about hurting you. Finally, you can threaten to cut off the relationship, making the threat look as if it were the debtor's doing. Say, "Look, Tom, unless I get the money you owe me within a week, I will take your refusal to repay me as a sign that you don't care any more about our friendship." With that, you have really turned up the guilt barometer. Indeed, inducing guilt can be a powerful tool in the process of debt collection.

4. Example

Seneca once said, "Every guilty person is his own hangman." The truth of this observation can be illustrated by the lives of countless villains. One such is Macbeth, from Shakespeare's tragedy of the same name. At the instigation of his wife, Macbeth kills the king of Scotland and usurps his throne—an act of treachery for which Macbeth and his wife suffer torments of guilt. Lady Macbeth develops an obsession that her hands are stained with blood, and she wanders somnambulistically through the castle trying vainly to cleanse them. Before he murders the king, Macbeth hallucinates a dagger floating in the air. Later, after his assassins murder Banquo, Macbeth is tormented by hallucinations of Banquo's ghost. Eventually, Lady Macbeth commits suicide. Macbeth is killed during a rebellion of his noblemen, which is brought about—in the main—by the excesses to which his guilt has driven him.

5. Definition

Guilt is the remorse that comes from an awareness of having done something wrong. The origin of guilt is psychological. From childhood, we have all been conditioned by family and society to act within defined standards of reasonableness and decency. Gradually, over a period of years, these standards are internalized and modified to become the core of what is called "conscience." When we do something that violates these internalized standards, we feel guilty. If we have been brought up in a religious environment, we feel an added measure of guilt when we break what we think is a divine commandment. Whenever we don't play according to our internalized rules, we feel miserable, and this misery is what guilt is all about.

6. Comparison and Contrast

Although the two words may seem to share some connotations, *guilt* is not a synonym for *blame*. Guilt must be felt; blame must be assessed. Guilt implies self-reproach that comes from an internal consciousness of wrong. Blame hints at fault that has been externally assessed. A man may suffer guilt yet be entirely exonerated of blame; conversely, he may be blamed and yet feel no guilt. In short, while guilt is a feeling, blame is a judgment—and that is the chief distinction between the two.

7. Division and Classification

The Bible identifies three kinds of guilt: guilt of the unpardonable sin, redeemable guilt, and guilt of innocence. First, the guilt of the unpardonable sin belongs to any being who has become so steeped in evil that a change for good is no longer possible. Lucifer is said to have committed this sin by which he cut himself off eternally from Yahweh, the source of all good. Second, redeemable guilt is guilt that can be erased because it belongs to one whose heart is not incorrigibly corrupt, but which has weakened temporarily under the pressure of temptation. King David, for instance, murdered Uriah in order to marry Bathsheba, Uriah's wife. But despite this sin, David was a noble king with a thirst for righteousness; he was redeemable. Finally, the guilt of innocence is the guilt that Jesus bore when he decided to be crucified for the collective wrong of mankind even though he was, of all men, most innocent. In other words, Jesus died as if he were guilty when, in fact, his character was free from any trace of evil.

8. Causal Analysis

Guilt is caused by the failure of the will. The human mind, according to Freudian theory, is delicately balanced between the drive for instant gratification that comes from the id, and the desire for regulation and postponement that originates in the superego, which is sometimes identified with what we call the conscience. The function of the will is to mediate between these two desires. When the individual succumbs to temptation, the forces of the id have triumphed over the repression of the superego. But the superego fights back by tormenting the self with regret—in short, by evoking feelings of guilt. The stricter the superego, or conscience, the harsher the toll in guilt and the greater the person suffers. Whoever allows the will to fail must therefore pay for the gratification of the libido's urges in the coin of guilt.

These eight rhetorical modes allow us to teach idealized writing forms and techniques. You will not always use them, and you will most likely use them less and less consciously as your writing skills mature. But, in the beginning, you will find it easier to approach a writing assignment from the viewpoint of a specific mode rather than to invent a wholly original form for every essay.

vvvvvvvvvvvvvvvvvvvvvvvvvvvvvvvvvvvvvv

REPORTING

*Narration, Description, and
Process Analysis*

ADVICE

vvvvvvvvvvvvvvvvvvvvvvvvvvvvvvvvvvvvvvvvvvvvvvvvvvvvvvvvvvvvvvvvvvvvvvvvvvvvvvv

HOW TO WRITE A NARRATION

If there is a rhetorical mode that can be said to be inborn in some people, it is narration. Most of us think we can tell a good story, and almost all of us have tried our hand at narration. Granted our stories may have been oral and told on the front porch to family and friends, but a story is a story and the techniques for telling one orally or in writing are essentially similar. Briefly and in order of importance, they are as follows:

Have a Point

The point of a story is what endows it with movement—with a beginning, a middle, and an end. If your story has no point, it will also seem to have no movement, to go nowhere, to become bogged down and stagnant. Good storytellers always begin with a point in mind. They want to show how absent-minded Uncle Mickey has become; they wish to prove that "haste makes waste." From this beginning, the story should proceed without pause or slip. Sometimes a storyteller will even begin by telling us the point of the story, an admission that is often helpful to both writer and reader. A classic example of a story that begins by telling us its point is George Orwell's "Shooting an Elephant."

> One day something happened which in a roundabout way was enlightening. It was a tiny incident in itself, but it gave me a better glimpse than I had had before of the real nature of imperialism—the real motives for which despotic governments act.

This tells us what to expect. As we read on, we expect the author to deliver what he or she has advertised.

Have a point and stick to it—that age-old advice often given by writing teachers definitely applies to narration.

Pace Your Story

Fiction tells lies about time. It has to. Real time is not always action-packed, does not always carry us to the dizzying brink or make us feel the throb of life. In fact, time is usually humdrum and dull in real life. But no reader wants a story to trudge through uneventful hours. What the reader wants is for the dull and humdrum to disappear in the puff of a sentence, and for the focus of the story always to be on time that is eventful and exciting. The technique of doing this is known as **pacing.**

All storytellers pace their materials to focus only on eventful periods and to ignore all inconsequential stretches in between. In the following example, taken from a story titled "We're Poor," an entire season disappears in a single paragraph:

> I didn't go back to school that fall. My mother said it was because I was sick. I did have a cold the week that school opened; I had been playing in the gutters and had got my feet wet, because there were holes in my shoes. . . . As long as I had to stay in the house anyway, they were all right.
>
> I stayed cooped up in the house, without any companionship. . . .

In "We're Poor" the author, Floyd Dell, learns from a Christmas experience that his family is destitute. The story consequently spends a good deal of time and attention on that climactic Christmas Eve during which the narrator makes this discovery. But the inconsequential months of the preceding fall are quickly dismissed in a paragraph.

Tell the Story from a Consistent Point of View

The point of view of a story is the angle from which it is told. This angle may be personal and intimate, a narrator being referred to by the pronoun *I*. Or it may be an omniscient point of view, in which the narrator is like a supernatural video camera sweeping over the scene and pausing briefly to focus on selective characters—describing how they look, what they say, and how they feel. Often this omniscient observer will select one central character, setting the person in relief so that he or she will catch the reader's intense and undivided attention. In any case, you must always stay in character when telling a story, and you must always remain consistent to the viewpoint from which you are telling it.

Here is an example of the omniscient point of view in a narration. Telling the story of a troubled teacher–student relationship as an omniscient narrator, Joyce Carol Oates, the writer, moves deftly from character to character as if seeing everything clearly and truthfully. About the main female character, the narrator observes:

> Sister Irene was a tall, deft woman in her early thirties. What one could see of her face made a striking impression—serious, hard gray eyes, a long slender nose, a face waxen with thought. Seen at the right time, from the right angle, she was almost handsome. In her past teaching positions she had drawn a little upon the fact of her being young and brilliant and also a nun, but she was beginning to grow out of that.

A little further into the story, the narrator moves from Sister Irene to the male lead character, a student, seeing him just as clearly as she sees Sister Irene:

> About two weeks after the semester began, Sister Irene noticed a new student in her class. He was slight and fair-haired, and his face was blank, but not blank by accident, blank on purpose, suppressed and restricted into a dumbness that looked hysterical.

The story continues to develop both characters, the teacher and the student. Although Sister Irene is the central consciousness of the story, Allen Weinstein, the student, becomes a crucial part of the total narrative conflict—with the author recording faithfully all he does, says, and feels, just as she also records the comings and goings of Sister Irene. In fact, in this story the narrator records even the actions and words of minor characters, which makes her a typical omniscient narrator.

Now consider the following excerpt from a vivid childhood memory by Beryl Markham, "Praise God for the Blood of the Bull":

I lean for a moment on my spear peering outward at what is nothing, and then turn toward my thorn tree.

"Are you here, Lakwani?"

Arap Maina's voice is cool as water on shaded rocks.

"I am here, Maina."

He is tall and naked and very dark beside me. His shuka is tied around his left forearm to allow his body freedom to run.

"You are alone, and you have suffered, my child."

"I am all right, Maina, but I fear for Buller. I think he may die."

Arap Maina kneels on the earth and runs his hand over Buller's body.

"He has been seriously and perhaps mortally wounded, Lakwani, but do not permit your mind to be too obsessed with any imaginary deficiencies or self-recriminations on your part. I conjecture that your lance has rescued him from a certain death, and God will recompense you for that . . . . "

If the final paragraph sounds bizarre to you in the context of the excerpt, it should. We have altered the dialogue (and added italics to clearly distinguish it from Markham's words) to dramatize what we mean by a lapse in consistency. In the final paragraph, Maina suddenly and inexplicably shifts from the simple speech of a native African to the pompous, long-winded speech of a British magistrate. A character in a narrative must always speak more or less the same way throughout and cannot lurch from one style of talk to another as we have made Maina do. Make your characters consistent and your narrative will seem believable.

Insert Appropriate Details

Details are indispensable to narrative writing and can make the difference between boredom and delight in a reader. No one can teach you the art of including captivating details, but common sense tells us that you are more likely to include the absolutely right details if you write your narrations about what you truly know. Here, for example, in Beryl Markham's description of a warthog, we get the feeling that the writer has had personal experience with the animals:

I know animals more gallant than the African warthog, but none more courageous. He is the peasant of the plains—the drab and dowdy digger in the earth. He is the uncomely but intrepid defender of family, home, and bourgeois convention, and he will fight anything of any size that intrudes upon his smug existence. Even his weapons are plebeian—curved tusks, sharp, deadly, but not beautiful, used inelegantly for rooting as well as for fighting.

If you cannot write about what you know, the next best thing is to know about what you write. The advice to always research your subject before writing about it cannot be imparted too strongly. Even veteran fiction writers do not simply plunge into their narrations without doing the spadework necessary to make their scenes authentic. And while personal experience is probably the best basis for a narration, adequate and detailed research can be every bit as good.

E X A M P L E S

▼▼

George Orwell

SHOOTING AN ELEPHANT

GEORGE ORWELL (1903–1950) was the pseudonym of Eric Arthur Blair. Born in India and educated at Eton, he served with the imperial police in Burma and fought on the republican side in the Spanish civil war. Orwell published two influential novels, *Animal Farm* (1945) and *Nineteen Eighty-four* (1949). He is widely admired for the crisp, lucid prose style of his essays.

> *George Orwell writes in a style that has been described as having "singular directness and honesty." In this selection he relates an incident that occurred while he was with the imperial police in Burma.*

1   In Moulmein, in Lower Burma, I was hated by large numbers of people—the only time in my life that I have been important enough for this to happen to me. I was sub-divisional police officer of the town, and in an aimless, petty kind of way anti-European feeling was very bitter. No one had the guts to raise a riot, but if a European woman went through the bazaars alone somebody would probably spit betel juice over her dress. As a police officer I was an obvious target and was baited whenever it seemed safe to do so. When a nimble Burman tripped me up on the football field and the referee (another Burman) looked the other way, the crowd yelled with hideous laughter. This happened more than once. In the end the sneering yellow faces of young men that met me everywhere, the insults hooted after me when I was at a safe distance, got badly on my nerves. The young Buddhist priests were the worst of all. There were several thousand of them in

the town and none of them seemed to have anything to do except stand on the street corners and jeer at Europeans.

2   All this was perplexing and upsetting. For at that time I had already made up my mind that imperialism was an evil thing and the sooner I chucked up my job and got out of it the better. Theoretically—and secretly, of course—I was all for the Burmese and all against their oppressors, the British. As for the job I was doing, I hated it more bitterly than I can perhaps make clear. In a job like that you see the dirty work of Empire at close quarters. The wretched prisoners huddling in the stinking cages of the lock-ups, the grey, cowed faces of the long-term convicts, the scarred buttocks of the men who had been flogged with bamboos—all these oppressed me with an intolerable sense of guilt. But I could get nothing into perspective. I was young and ill-educated and I had had to think out my problems in the utter silence that is imposed on every Englishman in the East. I did not even know that the British Empire is dying, still less did I know that it is a great deal better than the younger empires that are going to supplant it. All I knew was that I was stuck between my hatred of the empire I served and my rage against the evil-spirited little beasts who tried to make my job impossible. With one part of my mind I thought of the British Raj as an unbreakable tyranny, as something clamped down, in *saecula saeculorum*,[1] upon the will of prostrate peoples; with another part I thought that the greatest joy in the world would be to drive a bayonet into a Buddhist priest's guts. Feelings like these are the normal by-products of imperialism; ask any Anglo-Indian official, if you can catch him off duty.

3   One day something happened which in a roundabout way was enlightening. It was a tiny incident in itself, but it gave me a better glimpse than I had had before of the real nature of imperialism—the real motives for which despotic governments act. Early one morning the sub-inspector at a police station the other end of the town rang me up on the 'phone and said that an elephant was ravaging the bazaar. Would I please come and do something about it? I did not know what I could do, but I wanted to see what was happening and I got on to a pony and started out. I took my rifle, an old .44 Winchester and much too small to kill an elephant, but I thought the noise might be useful *in terrorem*.[2] Various Burmans stopped me on the way and told me about the elephant's doings. It was not, of course, a wild elephant, but a tame one which had gone "must." It had been chained up, as tame elephants always are when their attack of "must" is due, but on the previous night it had broken its chain and escaped. Its mahout, the only person who

---

[1] Latin, "for ever and ever."—Ed.

[2] Latin, "as a warning."—Ed.

could manage it when it was in that state, had set out in pursuit, but had taken the wrong direction and was now twelve hours' journey away, and in the morning the elephant had suddenly reappeared in the town. The Burmese population had no weapons and were quite helpless against it. It had already destroyed somebody's bamboo hut, killed a cow and raided some fruit-stalls and devoured the stock; also it had met the municipal rubbish van and, when the driver jumped out and took to his heels, had turned the van over and inflicted violences upon it.

4   The Burmese sub-inspector and some Indian constables were waiting for me in the quarter where the elephant had been seen. It was a very poor quarter, a labyrinth of squalid bamboo huts, thatched with palm-leaf, winding all over a steep hillside. I remember that it was a cloudy, stuffy morning at the beginning of the rains. We began questioning the people as to where the elephant had gone and, as usual, failed to get any definite information. That is invariably the case in the East; a story always sounds clear enough at a distance, but the nearer you get to the scene of events the vaguer it becomes. Some of the people said that the elephant had gone in one direction, some said that he had gone in another, some professed not even to have heard of any elephant. I had almost made up my mind that the whole story was a pack of lies, when we heard yells a little distance away. There was a loud, scandalized cry of "Go away, child! Go away this instant!" and an old woman with a switch in her hand came round the corner of a hut, violently shooing away a crowd of naked children. Some more women followed, clicking their tongues and exclaiming; evidently there was something that the children ought not to have seen. I rounded the hut and saw a man's dead body sprawling in the mud. He was an Indian, a black Dravidian coolie, almost naked, and he could not have been dead many minutes. The people said that the elephant had come suddenly upon him round the corner of the hut, caught him with its trunk, put its foot on his back and ground him into the earth. This was the rainy season and the ground was soft, and his face had scored a trench a foot deep and a couple of yards long. He was lying on his belly with arms crucified and head sharply twisted to one side. His face was coated with mud, the eyes wide open, the teeth bared and grinning with an expression of unendurable agony. (Never tell me, by the way, that the dead look peaceful. Most of the corpses I have seen looked devilish.) The friction of the great beast's foot had stripped the skin from his back as neatly as one skins a rabbit. As soon as I saw the dead man I sent an orderly to a friend's house nearby to borrow an elephant rifle. I had already sent back the pony, not wanting it to go mad with fright and throw me if it smelt the elephant.

5   The orderly came back in a few minutes with a rifle and five cartridges, and meanwhile some Burmans had arrived and told us that the elephant was in the paddy fields below, only a few hundred yards

away. As I started forward practically the whole population of the quarter flocked out of the houses and followed me. They had seen the rifle and were all shouting excitedly that I was going to shoot the elephant. They had not shown much interest in the elephant when he was merely ravaging their homes, but it was different now that he was going to be shot. It was a bit of fun to them, as it would be to an English crowd; besides they wanted the meat. It made me vaguely uneasy. I had no intention of shooting the elephant—I had merely sent for the rifle to defend myself if necessary—and it is always unnerving to have a crowd following you. I marched down the hill, looking and feeling a fool, with the rifle over my shoulder and an ever-growing army of people jostling at my heels. At the bottom, when you got away from the huts, there was a metalled road and beyond that a miry waste of paddy fields a thousand yards across, not yet ploughed but soggy from the first rains and dotted with coarse grass. The elephant was standing eight yards from the road, his left side towards us. He took not the slightest notice of the crowd's approach. He was tearing up bunches of grass, beating them against his knees to clean them and stuffing them into his mouth.

6   I had halted on the road. As soon as I saw the elephant I knew with perfect certainty that I ought not to shoot him. It is a serious matter to shoot a working elephant—it is comparable to destroying a huge and costly piece of machinery—and obviously one ought not to do it if it can possibly be avoided. And at that distance, peacefully eating, the elephant looked no more dangerous than a cow. I thought then and I think now that his attack of "must" was already passing off; in which case he would merely wander harmlessly about until the mahout came back and caught him. Moreover, I did not in the least want to shoot him. I decided that I would watch him for a little while to make sure that he did not turn savage again, and then go home.

7   But at that moment I glanced round at the crowd that had followed me. It was an immense crowd, two thousand at the least and growing every minute. It blocked the road for a long distance on either side. I looked at the sea of yellow faces above the garish clothes—faces all happy and excited over this bit of fun, all certain that the elephant was going to be shot. They were watching me as they would watch a conjurer about to perform a trick. They did not like me, but with the magical rifle in my hands I was momentarily worth watching. And suddenly I realized that I should have to shoot the elephant after all. The people expected it of me and I had got to do it; I could feel their two thousand wills pressing me forward, irresistibly. And it was at this moment, as I stood there with the rifle in my hands, that I first grasped the hollowness, the futility of the white man's dominion in the East. Here was I, the white man with his gun, standing in front of the unarmed native crowd—seemingly the leading actor of the piece; but

in reality I was only an absurd puppet pushed to and fro by the will of those yellow faces behind. I perceived in this moment that when the white man turns tyrant it is his own freedom that he destroys. He becomes a sort of hollow, posing dummy, the conventionalized figure of a sahib. For it is the condition of his rule that he shall spend his life in trying to impress the "natives," and so in every crisis he has got to do what the "natives" expect of him. He wears a mask, and his face grows to fit it. I had got to shoot the elephant. I had committed myself to doing it when I sent for the rifle. A sahib has got to act like a sahib; he has got to appear resolute, to know his own mind and do definite things. To come all that way, rifle in hand, with two thousand people marching at my heels, and then to trail feebly away, having done nothing—no, that was impossible. The crowd would laugh at me. And my whole life, every white man's life in the East, was one long struggle not to be laughed at.

8   But I did not want to shoot the elephant. I watched him beating his bunch of grass against his knees, with that preoccupied grandmotherly air that elephants have. It seemed to me that it would be murder to shoot him. At that age I was not squeamish about killing animals, but I had never shot an elephant and never wanted to. (Somehow it always seems worse to kill a *large* animal.) Besides, there was the beast's owner to be considered. Alive, the elephant was worth at least a hundred pounds; dead, he would only be worth the value of his tusks, five pounds, possibly. But I had got to act quickly. I turned to some experienced-looking Burmans who had been there when we arrived, and asked them how the elephant had been behaving. They all said the same thing: he took no notice of you if you left him alone, but he might charge if you went too close to him.

9   It was perfectly clear to me what I ought to do. I ought to walk up to within, say, twenty-five yards of the elephant and test his behavior. If he charged, I could shoot; if he took no notice of me, it would be safe to leave him until the mahout came back. But also I knew that I was going to do no such thing. I was a poor shot with a rifle and the ground was soft mud into which one would sink at every step. If the elephant charged and I missed him, I should have about as much chance as a toad under a steam-roller. But even then I was not thinking particularly of my own skin, only of the watchful yellow faces behind. For at that moment, with the crowd watching me, I was not afraid in the ordinary sense, as I would have been if I had been alone. A white man mustn't be frightened in front of "natives"; and so, in general, he isn't frightened. The sole thought in my mind was that if anything went wrong those two thousand Burmans would see me pursued, caught, trampled on and reduced to a grinning corpse like that Indian up the hill. And if that happened it was quite probable that some of them would laugh. That would never do. There was only one alternative. I

shoved the cartridges into the magazine and lay down on the road to get a better aim.

10   The crowd grew very still, and a deep, low, happy sigh, as of people who see the theatre curtain go up at last, breathed from innumerable throats. They were going to have their bit of fun after all. The rifle was a beautiful German thing with cross-hair sights. I did not then know that in shooting an elephant one would shoot to cut an imaginary bar running from ear-hole to ear-hole. I ought, therefore, as the elephant was sideway on, to have aimed straight at his ear-hole; actually I aimed several inches in front of this, thinking the brain would be further forward.

11   When I pulled the trigger I did not hear the bang or feel the kick—one never does when a shot goes home—but I heard the devilish roar of glee that went up from the crowd. In that instant, in too short a time, one would have thought, even for the bullet to get there, a mysterious, terrible change had come over the elephant. He neither stirred nor fell, but every line of his body had altered. He looked suddenly stricken, shrunken, immensely old, as though the frightful impact of the bullet had paralyzed him without knocking him down. At last, after what seemed a long time—it might have been five seconds, I dare say he sagged flabbily to his knees. His mouth slobbered. An enormous senility seemed to have settled upon him. One could have imagined him thousands of years old. I fired again into the same spot. At the second shot he did not collapse but climbed with desperate slowness to his feet and stood weakly upright, with legs sagging and head drooping. I fired a third time. That was the shot that did for him. You could see the agony of it jolt his whole body and knock the last remnant of strength from his legs. But in falling he seemed for a moment to rise, for as his hind legs collapsed beneath him he seemed to tower upward like a huge rock toppling, his trunk reaching skywards like a tree. He trumpeted, for the first and only time. And then down he came, his belly towards me, with a crash that seemed to shake the ground even where I lay.

12   I got up. The Burmans were already racing past me across the mud. It was obvious that the elephant would never rise again, but he was not dead. He was breathing very rhythmically with long rattling gasps, his great mound of a side painfully rising and falling. His mouth was wide open—I could see far down into caverns of pale pink throat. I waited for a long time for him to die, but his breathing did not weaken. Finally I fired my two remaining shots into the spot where I thought his heart must be. The thick blood welled out of him like red velvet, but still he did not die. His body did not even jerk when the shots hit him, the tortured breathing continued without a pause. He was dying, very slowly and in great agony, but in some world remote from me where not even a bullet could damage him further. I felt that

I had got to put an end to that dreadful noise. It seemed dreadful to see the great beast lying there, powerless to move and yet powerless to die, and not even to be able to finish him. I sent back for my small rifle and poured shot after shot into his heart and down his throat. They seemed to make no impression. The tortured gasps continued as steadily as the ticking of a clock.

13   In the end I could not stand it any longer and went away. I heard later that it took him half an hour to die. Burmans were bringing dahs and baskets even before I left, and I was told they had stripped his body almost to the bones by the afternoon.

14   Afterwards, of course, there were endless discussions about the shooting of the elephant. The owner was furious, but he was only an Indian and could do nothing. Besides, legally I had done the right thing, for a mad elephant has to be killed, like a mad dog, if its owner fails to control it. Among the Europeans opinion was divided. The older men said I was right, the younger men said it was a damn shame to shoot an elephant for killing a coolie, because an elephant was worth more than any damn Coringhee coolie. And afterwards I was very glad that the coolie had been killed; it put me legally in the right and it gave me a sufficient pretext for shooting the elephant. I often wondered whether any of the others grasped that I had done it solely to avoid looking a fool.

(3,305 words)

VOCABULARY

supplant (2)	labyrinth (4)	conventionalized (7)
prostrate (2)	squalid (4)	resolute (7)
despotic (3)	garish (7)	pretext (14)

THE FACTS

1. Which class of Burmese did Orwell despise most of all?

2. What would likely happen to a white woman who went through the bazaars alone?

3. What is Orwell's opinion of the younger empires that were going to supplant the British Empire?

4. What is invariably the case with stories set in the East?

5. According to Orwell, what is a condition of white rule over the empire?

THE STRATEGIES

1. Orwell writes: "They had not shown much interest in the elephant when he was merely ravaging their homes, but it was different now that he was going to be shot." What tone is he using here?

2. Why does Orwell use Latin phrases? What purpose do they have in the story?

3. The story is told in two tenses: the past and the present. What effect does this have on its telling?

4. Orwell encloses some remarks in parentheses in paragraphs 4 and 8. Why are these remarks set off in this way?

5. What analogy does Orwell use in paragraph 10 to describe his feelings about the crowd gathered to see him kill the elephant? Is this an appropriate analogy? Explain.

THE ISSUES

1. What is the value of a role and of role playing in the relationships of everyday life?

2. What are the obvious disadvantages of role playing?

3. How would you characterize Orwell's attitude toward the empire he serves?

4. How do you think the author might have behaved, and what do you think he might have done, if he had had other Europeans with him when he met the elephant?

5. What circumstances of today's life might similarly make someone, say a student, feel impelled to behave in a way contrary to his or her better judgment?

SUGGESTIONS FOR WRITING

1. Analyze and discuss "Shooting an Elephant" as a story about the abstract versus the concrete, the general versus the particular.

2. Write an essay entitled "I Wore a Mask, and My Face Grew to Fit It."

▼▼

Amy Tan

THE RED CANDLE

AMY TAN (b. 1951) is an American novelist who was born in Oakland, California, two years after her parents immigrated to the United States from China. Although her parents expected her to become a physician by trade and concert pianist by hobby, she chose to work with disabled children and to write fiction. Her novels quickly achieved wide popularity and made the *New York Times* best-seller list. Among her best-known works are *The Joy Luck Club* (1989)—from which the essay below is excerpted—*The Kitchen God's Wife* (1991), *The Moon Lady* (1992), and *The Hundred Secret Senses* (1996). Tan's novels deal with the cultural differences between the East and West, often stressing the relationship between mothers and daughters.

> *A sensitive reader will empathize with the narrator's deep desire to be her own person instead of the little puppet of a domineering mother-in-law and husband. As you read, follow the inner life of the narrator and try to understand her emotions.*

1   I once sacrificed my life to keep my parents' promise. This means nothing to you, because to you promises mean nothing. A daughter can promise to come to dinner, but if she has a headache, if she has a traffic jam, if she wants to watch a favorite movie on TV, she no longer has a promise.

2   I watched this same movie when you did not come. The American soldier promises to come back and marry the girl. She is crying with a genuine feeling and he says, "Promise! Promise! Honey-sweetheart, my promise is as good as gold." Then he pushed her onto the bed. But he doesn't come back. His gold is like yours, it is only fourteen carats.

3   To Chinese people, fourteen carats isn't real gold. Feel my bracelets. They must be twenty-four carats, pure inside and out.

4   It's too late to change you, but I'm telling you this because I worry about your baby. I worry that someday she will say, "Thank you, Grandmother, for the gold bracelet. I'll never forget you." But later, she will forget her promise. She will forget she had a grandmother.

5   In this same war movie, the American soldier goes home and he falls to his knees asking another girl to marry him. And the girl's eyes run back and forth, so shy, as if she had never considered this before. And suddenly!—her eyes look straight down and she knows now she loves

him, so much she wants to cry. "Yes," she says at last, and they marry forever.

6   This was not my case. Instead, the village matchmaker came to my family when I was just two years old. No, nobody told me this, I remember it all. It was summertime, very hot and dusty outside, and I could hear cicadas crying in the yard. We were under some trees in our orchard. The servants and my brothers were picking pears high above me. And I was sitting in my mother's hot sticky arms. I was waving my hand this way and that, because in front of me floated a small bird with horns and colorful paper-thin wings. And then the paper bird flew away and in front of me were two ladies. I remember them because one lady made watery "shrrhh, shrrhh" sounds. When I was older, I came to recognize this as a Peking accent, which sounds quite strange to Taiyuan people's ears.

7   The two ladies were looking at my face without talking. The lady with the watery voice had a painted face that was melting. The other lady had the dry face of an old tree trunk. She looked first at me, then at the painted lady.

8   Of course, now I know the tree-trunk lady was the old village matchmaker, and the other was Huang Taitai, the mother of the boy I would be forced to marry. No, it's not true what some Chinese say about girl babies being worthless. It depends on what kind of girl baby you are. In my case, people could see my value. I looked and smelled like a precious buncake, sweet with a good clean color.

9   The matchmaker bragged about me: "An earth horse for an earth sheep. This is the best marriage combination." She patted my arm and I pushed her hand away. Huang Taitai whispered in her shrrhh-shrrhh voice that perhaps I had an unusually bad *pichi*, a bad temper. But the matchmaker laughed and said, "Not so, not so. She is a strong horse. She will grow up to be a hard worker who serves you well in your old age."

10   And this is when Huang Taitai looked down at me with a cloudy face as though she could penetrate my thoughts and see my future intentions. I will never forget her look. Her eyes opened wide, she searched my face carefully and then she smiled. I could see a large gold tooth staring at me like the blinding sun and then the rest of her teeth opened wide as if she were going to swallow me down in one piece.

11   This is how I became betrothed to Huang Taitai's son, who I later discovered was just a baby, one year younger than I. His name was Tyan-yu—*tyan* for "sky," because he was so important, and *yu*, meaning "leftovers," because when he was born his father was very sick and his family thought he might die. Tyan-yu would be the leftover of his father's spirit. But his father lived and his grandmother was scared

the ghosts would turn their attention to this baby boy and take him instead. So they watched him carefully, made all his decisions, and he became very spoiled.

12   But even if I had known I was getting such a bad husband, I had no choice, now or later. That was how backward families in the country were. We were always the last to give up stupid old-fashioned customs. In other cities already, a man could choose his own wife, with his parents' permission of course. But we were cut off from this type of new thought. You never heard if ideas were better in another city, only if they were worse. We were told stories of sons who were so influenced by bad wives that they threw their old, crying parents out into the street. So, Taiyuanese mothers continued to choose their daughters-in-law, ones who would raise proper sons, care for the old people, and faithfully sweep the family burial grounds long after the old ladies had gone to their graves.

13   Because I was promised to the Huangs' son for marriage, my own family began treating me as if I belonged to somebody else. My mother would say to me when the rice bowl went up to my face too many times, "Look how much Huang Taitai's daughter can eat."

14   My mother did not treat me this way because she didn't love me. She would say this biting back her tongue, so she wouldn't wish for something that was no longer hers.

15   I was actually a very obedient child, but sometimes I had a sour look on my face—only because I was hot or tired or very ill. This is when my mother would say, "Such an ugly face. The Huangs won't want you and our whole family will be disgraced." And I would cry more to make my face uglier.

16   "It's no use," my mother would say. "We have made a contract. It cannot be broken." And I would cry even harder.

17   I didn't see my future husband until I was eight or nine. The world that I knew was our family compound in the village outside of Taiyuan. My family lived in a modest two-story house with a smaller house in the same compound, which was really just two side-by-side rooms for our cook, an everyday servant, and their families. Our house sat on a little hill. We called this hill Three Steps to Heaven, but it was really just centuries of hardened layers of mud washed up by the Fen River. On the east wall of our compound was the river, which my father said liked to swallow little children. He said it had once swallowed the whole town of Taiyuan. The river ran brown in the summer. In the winter, the river was blue-green in the narrow fast-moving spots. In the wider places, it was frozen still, white with cold.

18   Oh, I can remember the new year when my family went to the river and caught many fish—giant slippery creatures plucked while they were still sleeping in their frozen riverbeds—so fresh that even after

they were gutted they would dance on their tails when thrown into the hot pan.

19   That was also the year I first saw my husband as a little boy. When the firecrackers went off, he cried loud—wah!—with a big open mouth even though he was not a baby.

20   Later I would see him at red-egg ceremonies when one-month-old boy babies were given their real names. He would sit on his grandmother's old knees, almost cracking them with his weight. And he would refuse to eat everything offered to him, always turning his nose away as though someone were offering him a stinky pickle and not a sweet cake.

21   So I didn't have instant love for my future husband the way you see on television today. I thought of this boy more like a troublesome cousin. I learned to be polite to the Huangs and especially to Huang Taitai. My mother would push me toward Huang Taitai and say, "What do you say to your mother?" And I would be confused, not knowing which mother she meant. So I would turn to my real mother and say, "Excuse me, Ma," and then I would turn to Huang Taitai and present her with a little goodie to eat, saying, "For you, Mother." I remember it was once a lump of *syaumei*, a little dumpling I loved to eat. My mother told Huang Taitai I had made this dumpling especially for her, even though I had only poked its steamy sides with my finger when the cook poured it onto the serving plate.

22   My life changed completely when I was twelve, the summer the heavy rains came. The Fen River which ran through the middle of my family's land flooded the plains. It destroyed all the wheat my family had planted that year and made the land useless for years to come. Even our house on top of the little hill became unlivable. When we came down from the second story, we saw the floors and furniture were covered with sticky mud. The courtyards were littered with uprooted trees, broken bits of walls, and dead chickens. We were so poor in all this mess.

23   You couldn't go to an insurance company back then and say, Somebody did this damage, pay me a million dollars. In those days, you were unlucky if you had exhausted your own possibilities. My father said we had no choice but to move the family to Wushi, to the south near Shanghai, where my mother's brother owned a small flour mill. My father explained that the whole family, except for me, would leave immediately. I was twelve years old, old enough to separate from my family and live with the Huangs.

24   The roads were so muddy and filled with giant potholes that no truck was willing to come to the house. All the heavy furniture and bedding had to be left behind, and these were promised to the Huangs as my dowry. In this way, my family was quite practical. The dowry

was enough, more than enough, said my father. But he could not stop my mother from giving me her *chang*, a necklace made out of a tablet of red jade. When she put it around my neck, she acted very stern, so I knew she was very sad. "Obey your family. Do not disgrace us," she said. "Act happy when you arrive. Really, you're very lucky."

25   The Huangs' house also sat next to the river. While our house had been flooded, their house was untouched. This is because their house sat higher up in the valley. And this was the first time I realized the Huangs had a much better position than my family. They looked down on us, which made me understand why Huang Taitai and Tyan-yu had such long noses.

26   When I passed under the Huangs' stone-and-wood gateway arch, I saw a large courtyard with three or four rows of small, low buildings. Some were for storing supplies, others for servants and their families. Behind these modest buildings stood the main house.

27   I walked closer and stared at the house that would be my home for the rest of my life. The house had been in the family for many genera-tions. It was not really so old or remarkable, but I could see it had grown up along with the family. There were four stories, one for each generation: great-grandparents, grandparents, parents, and children. The house had a confused look. It had been hastily built and then rooms and floors and wings and decorations had been added on in every which manner, reflecting too many opinions. The first level was built of river rocks held together by straw-filled mud. The second and third levels were made of smooth bricks with an exposed walkway to give it the look of a palace tower. And the top level had gray slab walls topped with a red tile roof. To make the house seem important, there were two large round pillars holding up a veranda entrance to the front door. These pillars were painted red, as were the wooden window borders. Someone, probably Huang Taitai, had added imperial dragon heads at the corners of the roof.

28   Inside, the house held a different kind of pretense. The only nice room was a parlor on the first floor, which the Huangs used to receive guests. This room contained tables and chairs carved out of red lac-quer, fine pillows embroidered with the Huang family name in the an-cient style, and many precious things that gave the look of wealth and old prestige. The rest of the house was plain and uncomfortable and noisy with the complaints of twenty relatives. I think with each gener-ation the house had grown smaller inside, more crowded. Each room had been cut in half to make two.

29   No big celebration was held when I arrived. Huang Taitai didn't have red banners greeting me in the fancy room on the first floor. Tyan-yu was not there to greet me. Instead, Huang Taitai hurried me

upstairs to the second floor and into the kitchen, which was a place where family children didn't usually go. This was a place for cooks and servants. So I knew my standing.

30   That first day, I stood in my best padded dress at the low wooden table and began to chop vegetables. I could not keep my hands steady. I missed my family and my stomach felt bad, knowing I had finally arrived where my life said I belonged. But I was also determined to honor my parents' words, so Huang Taitai could never accuse my mother of losing face. She would not win that from our family.

31   As I was thinking this I saw an old servant woman stooping over the same low table gutting a fish, looking at me from the corner of her eye. I was crying and I was afraid she would tell Huang Taitai. So I gave a big smile and shouted, "What a lucky girl I am. I'm going to have the best life." And in this quick-thinking way I must have waved my knife too close to her nose because she cried angrily, *"Shemma bende ren!"*—What kind of fool are you? And I knew right away this was a warning, because when I shouted that declaration of happiness, I almost tricked myself into thinking it might come true.

32   I saw Tyan-yu at the evening meal. I was still a few inches taller than he, but he acted like a big warlord. I knew what kind of husband he would be, because he made special efforts to make me cry. He complained the soup was not hot enough and then spilled the bowl as if it were an accident. He waited until I had sat down to eat and then would demand another bowl of rice. He asked why I had such an unpleasant face when looking at him.

33   Over the next few years, Huang Taitai instructed the other servants to teach me how to sew sharp corners on pillowcases and to embroider my future family's name. How can a wife keep her husband's household in order if she has never dirtied her own hands, Huang Taitai used to say as she introduced me to a new task. I don't think Huang Taitai ever soiled her hands, but she was very good at calling out orders and criticism.

34   "Teach her to wash rice properly so that the water runs clear. Her husband cannot eat muddy rice," she'd say to a cook servant.

35   Another time, she told a servant to show me how to clean a chamber pot: "Make her put her own nose to the barrel to make sure it's clean." That was how I learned to be an obedient wife. I learned to cook so well that I could smell if the meat stuffing was too salty before I even tasted it. I could sew such small stitches it looked as if the embroidery had been painted on. And even Huang Taitai complained in a pretend manner that she could scarcely throw a dirty blouse on the floor before it was cleaned and on her back once again, causing her to wear the same clothes every day.

36   After a while I didn't think it was a terrible life, no, not really. After a while, I hurt so much I didn't feel any difference. What was

happier than seeing everybody gobble down the shiny mushrooms and bamboo shoots I had helped to prepare that day? What was more satisfying than having Huang Taitai nod and pat my head when I had finished combing her hair one hundred strokes? How much happier could I be after seeing Tyan-yu eat a whole bowl of noodles without once complaining about its taste or my looks? It's like those ladies you see on American TV these days, the ones who are so happy they have washed out a stain so the clothes look better than new.

37   Can you see how the Huangs almost washed their thinking into my skin? I came to think of Tyan-yu as a god, someone whose opinions were worth much more than my own life. I came to think of Huang Taitai as my real mother, someone I wanted to please, someone I should follow and obey without question.

38   When I turned sixteen on the lunar new year, Huang Taitai told me she was ready to welcome a grandson by next spring. Even if I had not wanted to marry, where would I go live instead? Even though I was strong as a horse, how could I run away? The Japanese were in every corner of China.

39   "The Japanese showed up as uninvited guests," said Tyan-yu's grand-mother, "and that's why nobody else came." Huang Taitai had made elaborate plans, but our wedding was very small.

40   She had asked the entire village and friends and family from other cities as well. In those days, you didn't do RSVP. It was not polite not to come. Huang Taitai didn't think the war would change people's good manners. So the cook and her helpers prepared hundreds of dishes. My family's old furniture had been shined up into an impressive dowry and placed in the front parlor. Huang Taitai had taken care to remove all the water and mud marks. She had even commissioned someone to write felicitous messages on red banners, as if my parents themselves had draped these decorations to congratulate me on my good luck. And she had arranged to rent a red palanquin to carry me from her neighbor's house to the wedding ceremony.

41   A lot of bad luck fell on our wedding day, even though the match-maker had chosen a lucky day, the fifteenth day of the eighth moon, when the moon is perfectly round and bigger than any other time of the year. But the week before the moon arrived, the Japanese came. They invaded Shansi province, as well as the provinces bordering us. People were nervous. And the morning of the fifteenth, on the day of the wedding celebration, it began to rain, a very bad sign. When the thunder and lightening began, people confused it with Japanese bombs and would not leave their houses.

42   I heard later that poor Huang Taitai waited many hours for more people to come, and finally, when she could not wring any more guests

out of her hands, she decided to start the ceremony. What could she do? She could not change the war.

43   I was at the neighbor's house. When they called me to come down and ride the red palanquin, I was sitting at a small dressing table by an open window. I began to cry and thought bitterly about my parents' promise. I wondered why my destiny had been decided, why I should have an unhappy life so someone else could have a happy one. From my seat by the window I could see the Fen River with its muddy brown waters. I thought about throwing my body into this river that had destroyed my family's happiness. A person has very strange thoughts when it seems that life is about to end.

44   It started to rain again, just a light rain. The people from downstairs called up to me once again to hurry. And my thoughts became more urgent, more strange.

45   I asked myself, What is true about a person? Would I change in the same way the river changes color but still be the same person? And then I saw the curtains blowing wildly, and outside rain was falling harder, causing everyone to scurry and shout. I smiled. And then I realized it was the first time I could see the power of the wind. I couldn't see the wind itself, but I could see it carried the water that filled the rivers and shaped the countryside. It caused men to yelp and dance.

46   I wiped my eyes and looked in the mirror. I was surprised at what I saw. I had on a beautiful red dress, but what I saw was even more valuable. I was strong. I was pure. I had genuine thoughts inside that no one could see, that no one could ever take away from me. I was like the wind.

47   I threw my head back and smiled proudly to myself. And then I draped the large embroidered red scarf over my face and covered these thoughts up. But underneath the scarf I still knew who I was. I made a promise to myself: I would always remember my parents' wishes, but I would never forget myself.

48   When I arrived at the wedding, I had the red scarf over my face and couldn't see anything in front of me. But when I bent my head forward, I could see out the sides. Very few people had come. I saw the Huangs, the same old complaining relatives now embarrassed by this poor showing, the entertainers with their violins and flutes. And there were a few village people who had been brave enough to come out for a free meal. I even saw servants and their children, who must have been added to make the party look bigger.

49   Someone took my hands and guided me down a path. I was like a blind person walking to my fate. But I was no longer scared. I could see what was inside me.

50   A high official conducted the ceremony and he talked too long about philosophers and models of virtue. Then I heard the matchmaker speak

about our birthdates and harmony and fertility. I tipped my veiled head forward and I could see her hands unfolding a red silk scarf and holding up a red candle for everyone to see.

51   The candle had two ends for lighting. One length had carved gold characters with Tyan-yu's name, the other with mine. The matchmaker lighted both ends and announced, "The marriage had begun." Tyan yanked the scarf off my face and smiled at his friends and family, never even looking at me. He reminded me of a young peacock I once saw that acted as if he had just claimed the entire courtyard by fanning his still-short tail.

52   I saw the matchmaker place the lighted red candle in a gold holder and then hand it to a nervous-looking servant. This servant was supposed to watch the candle during the banquet and all night to make sure neither end went out. In the morning the matchmaker was supposed to show the result, a little piece of black ash, and then declare, "This candle burned continuously at both ends without going out. This is a marriage that can never be broken."

53   I still can remember. That candle was a marriage bond that was worth more than a Catholic promise not to divorce. It meant I couldn't divorce and I couldn't ever remarry, even if Tyan-yu died. That red candle was supposed to seal me forever with my husband and his family, no excuses afterward.

54   And sure enough, the matchmaker made her declaration the next morning and showed she had done her job. But I know what really happened, because I stayed up all night crying about my marriage.

55   After the banquet, our small wedding party pushed us and half carried us up to the third floor to our small bedroom. People were shouting jokes and pulling boys from underneath the bed. The matchmaker helped small children pull red eggs that had been hidden between the blankets. The boys who were about Tyan-yu's age made us sit on the bed side by side and everybody made us kiss so our faces would turn red with passion. Firecrackers exploded on the walkway outside our open window and someone said this was a good excuse for me to jump into my husband's arms.

56   After everyone left, we sat there side by side without words for many minutes, still listening to the laughing outside. When it grew quiet, Tyan-yu said, "This is my bed. You sleep on the sofa." He threw a pillow and a thin blanket to me. I was so glad! I waited until he fell asleep and then I got up quietly and went outside, down the stairs and into the dark courtyard.

57   Outside it smelled as if it would soon rain again. I was crying, walking in my bare feet and feeling the wet heat still inside the bricks. Across the courtyard I could see the matchmaker's servant through a yellow-lit open window. She was sitting at a table, looking very sleepy

as the red candle burned in its special gold holder. I sat down by a tree to watch my fate being decided for me.

58   I must have fallen asleep because I remember being startled awake by the sound of loud cracking thunder. That's when I saw the matchmaker's servant running from the room, scared as a chicken about to lose its head. Oh, she was asleep too, I thought, and now she thinks it's the Japanese. I laughed. The whole sky became light and then more thunder came, and she ran out of the courtyard and down the road, going so fast and hard I could see pebbles kicking up behind her. Where does she think she's running to, I wondered, still laughing. And then I saw the red candle flickering just a little with the breeze.

59   I was not thinking when my legs lifted me up and my feet ran me across the courtyard to the yellow-lit room. But I was hoping—I was praying to Buddha, the goddess of mercy, and the full moon—to make that candle go out. It fluttered a little and the flame bent down low, but still both ends burned strong. My throat filled with so much hope that it finally burst and blew out my husband's end of the candle.

60   I immediately shivered with fear. I thought a knife would appear and cut me down dead. Or the sky would open up and blow me away. But nothing happened, and when my senses came back, I walked back to my room with fast guilty steps.

61   The next morning the matchmaker made her proud declaration in front of Tyan-yu, his parents, and myself. "My job is done," she announced, pouring the remaining black ash onto the red cloth. I saw her servant's shame-faced, mournful look.

62   I learned to love Tyan-yu, but it is not how you think. From the beginning, I would always become sick thinking he would someday climb on top of me and do his business. Every time I went into our bedroom, my hair would already be standing up. But during the first months, he never touched me. He slept in his bed, I slept on my sofa.

63   In front of his parents, I was an obedient wife, just as they taught me. I instructed the cook to kill a fresh young chicken every morning and cook it until pure juice came out. I would strain this juice myself into a bowl, never adding any water. I gave this to him for breakfast, murmuring good wishes about his health. And every night I would cook a special tonic soup called *tounau*, which was not only very delicious but has eight ingredients that guarantee long life for mothers. This pleased my mother-in-law very much.

64   But it was not enough to keep her happy. One morning, Huang Taitai and I were sitting in the same room, working on our embroidery. I was dreaming about my childhood, about a pet frog I once kept named Big Wind. Huang Taitai seemed restless, as if she had an itch in the bottom of her shoe. I heard her huffing and then all of a sudden she stood up from her chair, walked over to me, and slapped my face.

65   "Bad wife!" she cried. "If you refuse to sleep with my son, I refuse to feed you or clothe you." So that's how I knew what my husband had said to avoid his mother's anger. I was also boiling with anger, but I said nothing, remembering my promise to my parents to be an obedient wife.

66   That night I sat on Tyan-yu's bed and waited for him to touch me. But he didn't. I was relieved. The next night, I lay straight down on the bed next to him. And still he didn't touch me. So the next night, I took off my gown.

67   That's when I could see what was underneath Tyan-yu. He was scared and turned his face. He had no desire for me, but it was his fear that made me think he had no desire for any woman. He was like a little boy who had never grown up. After a while I was no longer afraid. I even began to think differently toward Tyan-yu. It was not like the way a wife loves a husband, but more like the way a sister protects a younger brother. I put my gown back on and lay down next to him and rubbed his back. I knew I no longer had to be afraid. I was sleeping with Tyan-yu. He would never touch me and I had a comfortable bed to sleep on.

68   After more months had passed and my stomach and breasts remained small and flat, Huang Taitai flew into another kind of rage. "My son says he's planted enough seeds for thousands of grandchildren. Where are they? It must be you are doing something wrong." And after that she confined me to the bed so that her grandchildren's seeds would not spill out so easily.

69   Oh, you think it is so much fun to lie in bed all day, never getting up. But I tell you it was worse than a prison. I think Huang Taitai became a little crazy.

70   She told the servants to take all sharp things out of the room, thinking scissors and knives were cutting off her next generation. She forbade me from sewing. She said I must concentrate and think of nothing but having babies. And four times a day, a very nice servant girl would come into my room, apologizing the whole time while making me drink a terrible-tasting medicine.

71   I envied this girl, the way she could walk out the door. Sometimes as I watched her from my window, I would imagine I was that girl, standing in the courtyard, bargaining with the traveling shoe mender, gossiping with other servant girls, scolding a handsome delivery man in her high teasing voice.

72   One day, after two months had gone by without any results, Huang Taitai called the old matchmaker to the house. The matchmaker examined me closely, looked up my birthdate and the hour of my birth, and then asked Huang Taitai about my nature. Finally, the matchmaker gave her conclusions: "It's clear what has happened. A woman can have sons only if she is deficient in one of the elements. Your daughter-in-law was

born with enough wood, fire, water, and earth, and she was deficient in metal, which was a good sign. But when she was married, you loaded her down with gold bracelets and decorations and now she has all the elements, including metal. She's too balanced to have babies."

73   This turned out to be joyous news for Huang Taitai, for she liked nothing better than to reclaim all her gold and jewelry to help me become fertile. And it was good news for me too. Because after the gold was removed from my body, I felt lighter, more free. They say this is what happens if you lack metal. You begin to think as an independent person. That day I started to think about how I would escape this marriage without breaking my promise to my family.

74   It was really quite simple. I made the Huangs think it was their idea to get rid of me, that they would be the ones to say the marriage contract was not valid.

75   I thought about my plan for many days. I observed everyone around me, the thoughts they showed in their faces, and then I was ready. I chose an auspicious day, the third day of the third month. That's the day of the Festival of Pure Brightness. On this day, your thoughts must be clear as you prepare to think about your ancestors. That's the day when everyone goes to the family graves. They bring hoes to clear the weeds and brooms to sweep the stones and they offer dumplings and oranges as spiritual food. Oh, it's not a somber day, more like a picnic, but it has special meaning to someone looking for grandsons.

76   On the morning of that day, I woke up Tyan-yu and the entire house with my wailing. It took Huang Taitai a long time to come into my room. "What's wrong with her now," she cried from her room. "Go make her be quiet." But finally, after my wailing didn't stop, she rushed into my room, scolding me at the top of her voice.

77   I was clutching my mouth with one hand and my eyes with another. My body was writhing as if I were seized by a terrible pain. I was quite convincing, because Huang Taitai drew back and grew small like a scared animal.

78   "What's wrong, little daughter? Tell me quickly," she cried.

79   "Oh, it's too terrible to think, too terrible to say," I said between gasps and more wailing.

80   After enough wailing, I said what was so unthinkable. "I had a dream," I reported. "Our ancestors came to me and said they wanted to see our wedding. So Tyan-yu and I held the same ceremony for our ancestors. We saw the matchmaker light the candle and give it to the servant to watch. Our ancestors were so pleased, so pleased. . . ."

81   Huang Taitai looked impatient as I began to cry softly again. "But then the servant left the room with our candle and a big wind came and blew the candle out. And our ancestors became very angry. They shouted that the marriage was doomed! They said that Tyan-yu's end

of the candle had blown out! Our ancestors said Tyan-yu would die if he stayed in this marriage!"

82   Tyan-yu's face turned white. But Huang Taitai only frowned. "What a stupid girl to have such bad dreams!" And then she scolded everybody to go back to bed.

83   "Mother," I called to her in a hoarse whisper. "Please don't leave me! I am afraid! Our ancestors said if the matter is not settled, they would begin the cycle of destruction."

84   "What is this nonsense!" cried Huang Taitai, turning back toward me. Tyan-yu followed her, wearing his mother's same frowning face. And I knew they were almost caught, two ducks leaning into the pot.

85   "They knew you would not believe me," I said in a remorseful tone, "because they know I do not want to leave the comforts of my marriage. So our ancestors said they would plant the signs, to show our marriage is now rotting."

86   "What nonsense from your stupid head," said Huang Taitai, sighing. But she could not resist. "What signs?"

87   "In my dream, I saw a man with a long beard and a mole on his cheek."

88   "Tyan-yu's grandfather?" asked Huang Taitai. I nodded, remembering the painting I had observed on the wall.

89   "He said there are three signs. First, he has drawn a black spot on Tyan-yu's back, and this spot will grow and eat away Tyan-yu's flesh just as it ate away our ancestor's face before he died."

90   Huang Taitai quickly turned to Tyan-yu and pulled his shirt up. "Ai-ya!" she cried, because there it was, the same black mole, the size of a fingertip, just as I had always seen it these past five months of sleeping as sister and brother.

91   "And then our ancestor touched my mouth," and I patted my cheek as if it already hurt. "He said my teeth would start to fall out one by one, until I could no longer protest leaving this marriage."

92   Huang Taitai pried open my mouth and gasped upon seeing the open spot in the back of my mouth where a rotted tooth fell out four years ago.

93   "And finally, I saw him plant a seed in a servant girl's womb. He said this girl only pretends to come from a bad family. But she is really from imperial blood, and . . ."

94   I lay my head down on the pillow as if too tired to go on. Huang Taitai pushed my shoulder, "What does he say?"

95   "He said the servant girl is Tyan-yu's true spiritual wife. And the seed he has planted will grow into Tyan-yu's child."

96   By mid-morning they had dragged the matchmaker's servant over to our house and extracted her terrible confession.

97   And after much searching they found the servant girl I liked so much, the one I had watched from my window every day. I had seen her eyes grow bigger and her teasing voice become smaller whenever the

handsome delivery man arrived. And later, I had watched her stomach grow rounder and her face become longer with fear and worry.

98   So you can imagine how happy she was when they forced her to tell the truth about her imperial ancestry. I heard later she was so struck with this miracle of marrying Tyan-yu she became a very religious person who ordered servants to sweep the ancestors' graves not just once a year, but once a day.

99   There's no more to the story. They didn't blame me so much. Huang Taitai got her grandson. I got my clothes, a rail ticket to Peking, and enough money to go to America. The Huangs asked only that I never tell anybody of any importance about the story of my doomed marriage.

100   It's a true story, how I kept my promise, how I sacrificed my life. See the gold metal I can now wear. I gave birth to your brothers and then your father gave me these two bracelets. Then I had you. And every few years, when I have a little extra money, I buy another bracelet. I know what I'm worth. They're always twenty-four carats, all genuine.

101   But I'll never forget. On the day of the Festival of Pure Brightness, I take off all my bracelets. I remember the day when I finally knew a genuine thought and could follow where it went. That was the day I was a young girl with my face under a red marriage scarf. I promised not to forget myself.

102   How nice it is to be that girl again, to take off my scarf, to see what is underneath and feel the lightness come back into my body!

(6,807 words)

VOCABULARY

cicadas (6)	dumpling (20)	palanquin (42)
matchmaker (8)	warlord (31)	elements (70)
compound (17)	lunar (37)	auspicious (73)

THE FACTS

1. What is the difference between Chinese and American gold?

2. At what age and under what circumstances was the narrator engaged?

3. What kind of reception did the narrator receive when she moved to the Huangs' house after her family home was flooded?

4. What kind of husband was Tyan-yu? Describe his personality, using specific details.

5. What two facts ruined the narrator's wedding, which had been elaborately planned by the Huangs?

6. On her wedding night, where did the narrator sleep? Why?

7. How did Tyan-yu hide the fact that he was afraid of having sex?

8. How did the narrator finally force the breakup of her unhappy marriage?

THE STRATEGIES

1. What is the relationship of the title to the story? Explain it in detail.

2. How does the narrator cover so many years in a few pages? Does the narration suffer from too many gaps or is the story paced so that it focuses on enough important events to satisfy the reader?

3. What is the main conflict in the story? How is the conflict resolved? Are you satisfied with the resolution? Why or why not?

4. Which character is more important in this story—the husband or his mother? Give reasons for your answer.

5. To whom is the narrator telling her story? How do you know who it is? What effect does this create?

THE ISSUES

1. What is your reaction to the way the families treated the narrator? What kind of society does such treatment naturally create? What are the advantages of such a society? What are the disadvantages?

2. In our society, a newly-wed couple is usually left to work out their own family life, without a mother-in-law's constant intervention. Does our system have some disadvantages that the old Chinese system does not have? If so, what are they?

3. The narrator repeatedly states that she learned to love her husband. Why, then, does the story end the way it does? Could the Huang family have prevented this ending?

4. In what way was the wedding celebration symbolic of the entire marriage between the narrator and Tyan-yu?

5. What lessons about cultural traditions does this story teach?

SUGGESTIONS FOR WRITING

1. Write an essay expressing your views concerning the requirements of a Chinese marriage relationship.

2. Narrate an incident that reveals an ideal love relationship between two people.

▼▼

Dick Gregory

SHAME

DICK GREGORY (b. 1932) is a Black political activist, comedian, and writer. He attended Southern Illinois University, where he was named Outstanding Athlete in 1953. Gregory has been much admired for his interest in social issues, such as world famine, and for his outstanding ability as a stand-up comedian. In 1966, he ran for Mayor of Chicago, and in 1968, he was the presidential candidate of the Freedom and Peace Party. Gregory has written several books, including *From the Back of the Bus* (1962), *What's Happening?* (1965), *The Shadow That Scares Me* (1968), *Dick Gregory's Bible Tales* (1974), and his autobiography, *Up from Nigger* (1976). Gregory was one of the first comedians to break the "color barrier" and perform for white audiences. His popularity is based on his ability to satirize race relations without being derogatory.

> *Even if you have never felt the poverty described by the narrator in the story that follows, you can probably remember someone from your childhood or adolescence who somehow represented all of the romance and beauty for which you longed. Ponder the details that make the narrator's experience so heartbreaking.*

1   I never learned hate at home, or shame. I had to go to school for that. I was about seven years old when I got my first big lesson. I was in love with a little girl named Helene Tucker, a light-complected little girl with pigtails and nice manners. She was always clean and she was smart in school. I think I went to school mostly to look at her. I brushed my hair and even got me a little old handkerchief. It was a lady's handkerchief, but I didn't want Helene to see me wipe my nose on my hand. The pipes were frozen again, there was no water in the house, but I washed my socks and shirt every night. I'd get a pot, and go over to Mr. Ben's grocery store, and stick my pot down into his soda machine. Scoop out some chopped ice. By evening the ice melted to water for washing. I got sick a lot that winter because the fire would go out at night before the clothes were dry. In the morning I'd put them on, wet or dry, because they were the only clothes I had.

2   Everybody's got a Helene Tucker, a symbol of everything you want. I loved her for her goodness, her cleanliness, her popularity. She'd walk down my street and my brothers and sisters would yell, "Here comes Helene," and I'd rub my tennis sneakers on the back of my pants and wish my hair wasn't so nappy and the white folks' shirt fit me better. I'd run out on the street. If I knew my place and didn't come too close, she'd wink at me and say hello. That was a good feeling. Sometimes I'd follow her all the way home, and shovel the snow off her walk and try to make friends with her Momma and her aunts. I'd drop money on her stoop late at night on my way back from shining shoes in the taverns. And she had a Daddy, and he had a good job. He was a paper hanger.

3   I guess I would have gotten over Helene by summertime, but something happened in that classroom that made her face hang in front of me for the next twenty-two years. When I played the drums in high school it was for Helene and when I broke track records in college it was for Helene and when I started standing behind microphones and heard applause I wished Helene could hear it, too. It wasn't until I was twenty-nine years old and married and making money that I really got her out of my system. Helene was sitting in that classroom when I learned to be ashamed of myself.

4   It was on a Thursday. I was sitting in the back of the room, in a seat with a chalk circle drawn around it. The idiot's seat, the trouble-maker's seat.

5   The teacher thought I was stupid. Couldn't spell, couldn't read, couldn't do arithmetic. Just stupid. Teachers were never interested in finding out that you couldn't concentrate because you were so hungry, because you hadn't had any breakfast. All you could think about was noontime, would it ever come? Maybe you could sneak into the cloak-room and steal a bit of some kid's lunch out of a coat pocket. A bit of something. Paste. You can't really make a meal out of paste, or put it on bread for a sandwich, but sometimes I'd scoop a few spoonfuls out of the paste jar in the back of the room. Pregnant people get strange tastes. I was pregnant with poverty. Pregnant with dirt and pregnant with smells that made people turn away, pregnant with cold and pregnant with shoes that were never bought for me, pregnant with five other people in my bed and no Daddy in the next room, and pregnant with hunger. Paste doesn't taste too bad when you're hungry.

6   The teacher thought I was a troublemaker. All she saw from the front of the room was a little black boy who squirmed in his idiot's seat and made noises and poked the kids around him. I guess she couldn't see a kid who made noises because he wanted someone to know he was there.

7   It was on a Thursday, the day before the Negro payday. The eagle always flew on Friday. The teacher was asking each student how much his father would give to the Community Chest. On Friday night, each

kid would get the money from his father, and on Monday he would bring it to the school. I decided I was going to buy me a Daddy right then. I had money in my pocket from shining shoes and selling papers and whatever Helene Tucker pledged for her Daddy I was going to top it. And I'd hand the money right in. I wasn't going to wait until Monday to buy me a Daddy.

8   I was shaking, scared to death. The teacher opened her book and started calling our names alphabetically.

9   "Helene Tucker?"

10   "My Daddy said he'd give two dollars and fifty cents."

11   "That's very nice, Helene. Very, very nice indeed."

12   That made me feel pretty good. It wouldn't take too much to top that. I had almost three dollars in dimes and quarters in my pocket. I stuck my hand in my pocket and held onto the money, waiting for her to call my name. But the teacher closed her book after she called everybody else in the class.

13   I stood up and raised my hand.

14   "What is it now?"

15   "You forgot me."

16   She turned toward the blackboard. "I don't have time to be playing with you, Richard."

17   "My Daddy said he'd . . ."

18   "Sit down, Richard, you're disturbing the class."

19   "My Daddy said he'd give . . . fifteen dollars."

20   She turned around and looked mad. "We are collecting this money for you and your kind, Richard Gregory. If your Daddy can give fifteen dollars you have no business being on relief."

21   "I got it right now, I got it right now, my Daddy gave it to me to turn in today, my Daddy said . . ."

22   "And furthermore," she said, looking right at me, her nostrils getting big and her lips getting thin and her eyes opening wide, "we know you don't have a Daddy."

23   Helene Tucker turned around, her eyes full of tears. She felt sorry for me. Then I couldn't see her too well because I was crying, too.

24   "Sit down, Richard."

25   And I always thought the teacher kind of liked me. She always picked me to wash the blackboard on Friday, after school. That was a big thrill, it made me feel important. If I didn't wash it, come Monday the school might not function right.

26   "Where are you going, Richard?"

27   I walked out of school that day, and for a long time I didn't go back very often. There was shame there.

28   Now there was shame everywhere. It seemed like the whole world had been inside that classroom, everyone had heard what the teacher had said, everyone had turned around and felt sorry for me. There was

shame in going to the Worthy Boys Annual Christmas Dinner for you and your kind, because everybody knew what a worthy boy was. Why couldn't they just call it the Boys Annual Dinner, why'd they have to give it a name? There was shame in wearing the brown and orange and white plaid mackinaw the welfare gave to 3,000 boys. Why'd it have to be the same for everybody so when you walked down the street the people could see you were on relief? It was a nice warm mackinaw and it had a hood, and my Momma beat me and called me a little rat when she found out I stuffed it in the bottom of a pail full of garbage way over on Cottage Street. There was shame in running over to Mister Ben's at the end of the day and asking for his rotten peaches, there was shame in asking Mrs. Simmons for a spoonful of sugar, there was shame in running out to meet the relief truck. I hated that truck, full of food for you and your kind. I ran into the house and hid when it came. And then I started to sneak through alleys, to take the long way home so people going into White's Eat Shop wouldn't see me. Yeah, the whole world heard the teacher that day, we all know you don't have a Daddy.

(1,423 words)

VOCABULARY

mackinaw (28)

THE FACTS

1. Where did the narrator learn shame?

2. What did the narrator do for Helene Tucker? How important was she in his life?

3. Why, according to the narrator, could he not do well in school? What did the teachers think?

4. What event at school caused shame to control the narrator's life for a long time? Briefly summarize what happened.

5. Why did the narrator dislike the Worthy Boys Annual Christmas Dinner?

THE STRATEGIES

1. The narration begins in paragraph 3, following two paragraphs of commentary about Helene Tucker, a girl on whom the narrator had a crush. What is the purpose of the preliminary paragraphs?

2. What dominant impression is always in the background of the narration? Why?

3. Beginning with paragraph 9, the narrator uses conversation to boost the narration. What is the effect of this technique?

4. What is the main theme (lesson about life) revealed in this story? Is it implied or stated?

5. In paragraph 5, what is the purpose of repeating the word *pregnant?* What does the author mean?

THE ISSUES

1. Do you agree with the narrator's comment that "everybody's got a Helene Tucker"? What does Helene Tucker symbolize? From your own experience, give an example of a Helene Tucker.

2. The teacher thought that the narrator was a troublemaker. Was he really, or was there another reason for drawing attention to himself?

3. Why did the teacher humiliate the narrator when he announced that his father would donate fifteen dollars? Do you think the teacher should have handled the situation differently? If so, how should she have reacted?

4. The narrator states that he thought the teacher liked him because she always picked him to clean the blackboard on Friday. Why do *you* think she picked him?

5. Did the narrator do the right thing by not going back to the school often after the shame incident? What kept him away? Do you empathize or do you think the narrator was excessively pouty?

SUGGESTIONS FOR WRITING

1. Write about an incident in which you or someone you love experienced shame. Use the techniques of pacing, using vivid details, and making a point.

2. Write an essay in which you examine the psychological effects of poverty on children in elementary school.

▼▼

Jerome K. Jerome

THE ODOUR OF CHEESE

JEROME KLAPKA JEROME (1859–1927) was an English writer known for his genial humor. Among his works are *Idle Thoughts of an Idle Fellow* (1886); his best known and still read *Three Men in a Boat* (1889); and a morality play, *The Passing of the Third Floor Back* (1907).

In 1889, when the author was only 30, Three Men in a Boat *was published to overnight success. It has been translated in every European language and several Asian ones as well. This excerpt, a hilarious narrative about the author's misadventures with smelly cheese, contains one of its funniest stories.*

1   Cheese, like oil, makes too much of itself. It wants the whole boat to itself. It goes through the hamper, and gives a cheesy flavour to everything else there. You can't tell whether you are eating apple-pie or German sausage, or strawberries and cream. It all seems cheese. There is too much odour about cheese.

2   I remember a friend of mine buying a couple of cheeses at Liverpool. Splendid cheeses they were, ripe and mellow, and with a two hundred horse-power scent about them that might have been warranted to carry three miles, and knock a man over at two hundred years. I was in Liverpool at the time, and my friend said that if I didn't mind he would get me to take them back with me to London, as he should not be coming up for a day or two himself, and he did not think the cheeses ought to be kept much longer.

3   "Oh, with pleasure, dear boy," I replied, "with pleasure."

4   I called for the cheeses, and took them away in a cab. It was a ramshackle affair, dragged along by a knock-kneed, broken-winded somnambulist, which his owner, in a moment of enthusiasm, during conversation, referred to as a horse. I put the cheeses on the top, and we started off at a shamble that would have done credit to the swiftest steam-roller ever built, and all went merry as a funeral bell, until we turned the corner. There, the wind carried a whiff from the cheeses full on to our steed. It woke him up, and, with a snort of terror, he dashed off at three miles an hour. The wind still blew in his direction, and before we reached the end of the street he was laying himself out at the rate of nearly four miles an hour, leaving the cripples and stout old ladies simply nowhere.

5   It took two porters as well as the driver to hold him in at the station; and I do not think they would have done it, even then, had not one of the men had the presence of mind to put a handkerchief over his nose, and to light a bit of brown paper.

6   I took my ticket, and marched proudly up the platform, with my cheeses, the people falling back respectfully on either side. The train was crowded, and I had to get into a carriage where there were already seven other people. One crusty old gentleman objected, but I got in, notwithstanding; and putting my cheeses upon the rack, squeezed down with a pleasant smile, and said it was a warm day. A few moments passed, and then the old gentleman began to fidget.

7   "Very close in here," he said.

"Quite oppressive," said the man next him.

8   And then they both began sniffing, and, at the third sniff, they caught it right on the chest, and rose up without another word and went out. And then a stout lady got up, and said it was disgraceful that a respectable married woman should be harried about in this way, and gathered up a bag and eight parcels and went. The remaining four passengers sat on for a while, until a solemn-looking man in the corner who, from his dress and general appearance, seemed to belong to the undertaker class, said it put him in mind of a dead baby; and the other three passengers tried to get out of the door at the same time, and hurt themselves.

9   I smiled at the black gentleman, and said I thought we were going to have the carriage to ourselves; and he laughed pleasantly and said that some people made such a fuss over a little thing. But even he grew strangely depressed after we had started, and so, when we reached Crewe, I asked him to come and have a drink. He accepted, and we forced our way into the buffet, where we yelled, and stamped, and waved our umbrellas for a quarter of an hour; and then a young lady came and asked us if we wanted anything.

10   "What's yours?" I said, turning to my friend.

"I'll have a half a crown's worth of brandy, neat, if you please, miss," he responded.

11   And he went off quietly after he had drunk it and got into another carriage, which I thought mean.

12   From Crewe I had the compartment to myself, though the train was crowded. As we drew up at the different stations, the people, seeing my empty carriage, would rush for it. "Here y'are, Maria; come along, plenty of room." "All right, Tom; we'll get in here," they would shout. And they would run along, carrying heavy bags, and fight around the door to get in first. And one would open the door and mount the steps and stagger back into the arms of the man behind him; and they would all come and have a sniff, and then droop off and squeeze into other carriages, or pay the difference and go first.

13   From Euston I took the cheeses down to my friend's house. When his wife came into the room she smelt round for an instant. Then she said:

14   "What is it? Tell me the worst."

I said: "It's cheeses. Tom bought them in Liverpool, and asked me to bring them up with me."

15   And I added that I hoped she understood that it had nothing to do with me; and she said that she was sure of that, but that she would speak to Tom about it when he came back.

16   My friend was detained in Liverpool longer than he expected; and three days later, as he hadn't returned home, his wife called on me. She said:

17   "What did Tom say about those cheeses?"

I replied that he had directed they were to be kept in a moist place, and that nobody was to touch them.

She said: "Nobody's likely to touch them. Had he smelt them?"

I thought he had, and added that he seemed greatly attached to them.

"You think he would be upset," she queried, "if I gave a man a sovereign to take them away and bury them?"

I answered that I thought he would never smile again.

An idea struck her. She said:

18   "Do you mind keeping them for him? Let me send them round to you."

19   "Madam," I replied, "for myself I like the smell of cheese, and the journey the other day with them from Liverpool I shall ever look back upon as a happy ending to a pleasant holiday. But, in this world, we must consider others. The lady under whose roof I have the honour of residing is a widow, and, for all I know, possibly an orphan too. She has a strong, I may say an eloquent, objection to being what she terms 'put upon.' The presence of your husband's cheeses in her house she would, I instinctively feel, regard as a 'put upon'; and it shall never be said that I put upon the widow and the orphan."

20   "Very well, then," said my friend's wife, rising, "all I have to say is, that I shall take the children and go to an hotel until those cheeses are eaten. I decline to live any longer in the same house with them."

21   She kept her word, leaving the place in charge of the charwoman, who, when asked if she could stand the smell, replied, "What smell?" and who, when taken close to the cheeses and told to sniff hard, said she could detect a faint odour of melons. It was argued from this that little injury could result to the woman from the atmosphere, and she was left.

22   The hotel bill came to fifteen guineas; and my friend, after reckoning everything up, found that the cheeses had cost him eight-and-sixpence a pound. He said he dearly loved a bit of cheese, but it was

beyond his means; so he determined to get rid of them. He threw them into the canal; but had to fish them out again, as the bargemen complained. They said it made them feel quite faint. And, after that, he took them one dark night and left them in the parish mortuary. But the coroner discovered them, and made a fearful fuss.

23   He said it was a plot to deprive him of his living by waking up the corpses.

24   My friend got rid of them, at last, by taking them down to a seaside town, and burying them on the beach. It gained the place quite a reputation. Visitors said they have never noticed before how strong the air was, and weak-chested and consumptive people used to throng there for years afterwards.

(1,460 words)

VOCABULARY

ramshackle (4)   somnambulist (4)   harried (8)

THE FACTS

1. What happened when the horse drawing the cab caught a whiff of the cheese?

2. What effect did the odor of the cheese have on the passengers in the train compartment?

3. What did the wife do when the cheeses were delivered to her?

4. Upon whom did the cheeses have no effect at all? What did the smell remind that person of?

5. How were the cheeses finally disposed of?

THE STRATEGIES

1. What is the thesis of this short piece and where is it stated?

2. What is the author's main technique for achieving humor?

3. The excerpt comes from an immensely popular Victorian book. What characteristics of its writing tell you that it was intended for a popular audience?

4. Paragraphs 21 and 22 contain an example of how this narrative is paced. In what way is the narrative paced in these paragraphs?

5. The author writes: "I took my ticket, and marched proudly up the platform, with my cheeses, and people falling respectfully on either side." What word in that sentence gives rise to subtle humor?

THE ISSUES

1. How does the humor of this piece differ from the written humor we are likely to find today?

2. Deducing the narrator's lifestyle from this piece, what social type would we likely call him today?

3. What modern convenience is obviously missing from the author's life, and how did it seem to affect him and his relationship with others around him?

4. What did the people aboard the train, in response to the stink of the cheeses, not do that they would likely do in America today?

5. How do you think people today would react to a similar situation of a conspicuous stink in public transportation?

SUGGESTIONS FOR WRITING

1. Narrate a humorous incident that you had happen to you or witnessed in a public place.

2. Rewrite this story in a modern time and setting, placing it in a large urban area today. Be sure that your characters are realistically drawn to conform to modern types.

▼▼▼

Robert Hayden

THOSE WINTER SUNDAYS

ROBERT HAYDEN (1913–1980) was born in Detroit, attended the University of Michigan, and taught at Fisk University. His *Ballad of Remembrance* was awarded a prize at the 1966 World Festival of Negro Arts held in Dakar, Senegal.

The following poem recounts a childhood memory.

> Sundays too my father got up early
> and put his clothes on in the blueblack cold,
> then with cracked hands that ached

from labor in the weekday weather made

5   banked fires blaze. No one ever thanked him.
I'd wake and hear the cold splintering, breaking.
When the rooms were warm, he'd call,
and slowly I would rise and dress,
fearing the chronic angers of that house,

10 Speaking indifferently to him,
who had driven out the cold
and polished my good shoes as well.
What did I know, what did I know
of love's austere and lonely offices?

(100 words)

THE FACTS

1. What did the narrator's father do on Sundays?

2. How did the narrator react to his father in the morning?

3. How would you characterize the narrator's attitude as he looks back on this time with his father?

THE STRATEGIES

1. What poetic form is this narration framed in? (Hint: Count the number of lines.)

2. The author writes about his father: "No one ever thanked him." Why do you think he chose to put it this way? Why not simply say "I never thanked him"?

3. The poet writes: "I'd wake and hear the cold splintering, breaking." What kind of figure of speech is this?

4. Examine the sentences in the poem. How many are there? What is the technique of running a sentence into several lines without an end-stop or break called?

THE ISSUES

1. What kind of work do you suppose the speaker's father did? How can his probable occupation be deduced from the poem?

2. What are "love's austere and lonely offices"? What other examples can you give of them?

SUGGESTIONS FOR WRITING

1. Write an analysis of this poem.

2. Narrate an incident from your own childhood that involved your relationship with a parent.

A D V I C E

▾▾▾

HOW TO WRITE A DESCRIPTION

Focus and concentration contribute more to a vivid description than either the size of the writer's vocabulary or the heedless splattering of the page with adjectives. Here is an example of what we mean. The author, Charles Reade, in this excerpt from *The Cloister and the Hearth*, is describing a medieval inn partly through the eyes, but mainly through the nose, of a weary traveler:

> In one corner was a travelling family, a large one; thence flowed into the common stock the peculiar sickly smell of neglected brats. Garlic filled up the interstices of the air. And all this with closed window, and intense heat of the central furnace, and the breath of at least forty persons.
>
> They had just supped.
>
> Now Gerard, like most artists, had sensitive organs, and the potent effluvia struck dismay into him. But the rain lashed him outside, and the light and the fire tempted him in.
>
> He could not force his way all at once through the palpable perfumes, but he returned to the light again and again like a singed moth. At last he discovered that the various smells did not entirely mix, no fiend being there to stir them around. Odor of family predominated in two corners; stewed rustic reigned supreme in the center; and garlic in the noisy group by the window. He found, too, by hasty analysis, that of these the garlic described the smallest aerial orbit, and the scent of reeking rustic darted farthest—a flavor as if ancient goats, or the fathers of all foxes, had been drawn through a river, and were here dried by Nebuchadnezzar.

What is characteristic about this vivid description is its focus. Instead of trying to give us a sweeping view of the dingy inn, the writer zooms in on how bad it smells. The stink of the inn is the *dominant impression* of this description, and the writer's every word, image, and metaphor aims only to serve up this stench to our nostrils.

Focus on a Dominant Impression

Vivid descriptions invariably focus on a single dominant impression and unremittingly deliver it. Nothing distracts from the dominant impression; every word and image is devoted to rendering it keener and sharper. By *dominant impression* we mean a feature of the scene that is characteristic of it. Not all scenes have strikingly characteristic features, and writers must often steep themselves in the aura of a place before they can sum it up in a dominant impression. But some scenes will give off a dominant impression that leaps out at you. For example, a freeway at rush hour is anything but a scene of placidity. Usually it is a tangled skein of cars jockeying for position or trying to nose from one lane into another. To describe a freeway scene at rush hour, you should word your dominant impression to take in the madcap antics of the drivers, the choking fumes of the cars, the background grind and roar of traffic. You might write, as your dominant impression, "The San Diego Freeway at rush hour is a bedlam of traffic noise, choking fumes, and aggressive drivers." Then you would support that dominant impression with specific images and details.

The dominant impression of your description should be the heart of the person, place, or scene you are attempting to describe. If you are describing an elderly aunt who is dull, use her dullness as your dominant impression. If you are writing a description of a Christmas shopping scene, word your dominant impression to show the frazzled throng of weary shoppers, the harried sales clerks, the dazzling glitter of Christmas lights. What you must not try to do in your dominant impression is to account for every speck in the scene you are describing. For example, among the streaming throngs in the department store at Christmas, there are bound to be a few souls who are calm and composed and seemingly immune to the shopping frenzy. But since these lucky few are not at all representative of the overall scene, you should leave them out lest they water down the description. So, if your sister is mainly a bundle of nerves, that is how you should paint her on the page, even if you have glimpsed her occasionally in rare moments of serenity.

Use Images in Your Descriptions

Most of us know the basics about imagery, especially the simile and the metaphor. We know that the simile is an image based on an explicit comparison. For example, in "The King of the Birds," Flannery O'Connor describes the crest of a peabiddy with this simile: "This looks at first like a bug's antennae and later like the head feathers of an Indian." On the other hand, we also know that the metaphor is an image based on an indirect comparison with no obvious linking word such as "as" or "like" used to cement it. For example, in "Once More to the Lake," E. B. White uses metaphors to describe a thunderstorm: "Then the kettle drum, then the snare, then the bass drum and cymbals, then crackling light against the dark, and the gods grinning and licking their chops in the hills." This is how a thunderstorm seems to the writer—it makes noises *like* many drums and flashes wicked lights against the hills that look *like* gods licking their chops. Even though the writer omits the "like" that might have made the comparison explicit, we still get the picture.

Aside from these basic images, which every writer occasionally uses, there are some other hard-won lessons about descriptive imagery that can be imparted. The first is this: Vivid images do not miraculously drip off the pen but are usually the result of the writer's reworking the material repeatedly. If nothing original or fresh occurs to you after you've sat at your desk for a scant few minutes trying to write a description, all it means is that you have not sat long enough or worked hard enough. Reread what you have written. Try to picture in your mind the person, place, or thing you are struggling to describe. Cut a word here; replace another there; persistently scratch away at what you have written and you'll soon be astonished at how much better it begins to sound.

The second lesson to impart about writing vivid images is summed up in the adage, "Less is more." Overdoing a descriptive passage is not only possible, it is very likely. If you are unhappy with a description you have written, instead of stuffing it with more adjectives, try taking some out. Here is an example of a bloated and overdone description; it is from *Delina Delaney* by Amanda McKittrick Ros. The speaker is trying his utmost to describe his feelings as he says goodbye to his sweetheart:

> I am just in time to hear the toll of a parting bell strike its heavy weight of appalling softness against the weakest fibers of a heart of love, arousing and tickling its dormant action, thrusting the dart of evident separation deeper into its tubes of tenderness, and fanning the flame, already unextinguishable, into volumes of blaze.

This is, of course, wretched stuff. One can see the writer huffing and puffing at the pen as she tries desperately to infuse her hero's words with passion. She fails awfully from too much effort.

Appeal to All the Reader's Senses

Most of us are so unabashedly visual that we are tempted to deliver only looks in our descriptions. But there is usually much more to a scene than its looks. You could also write about how it sounds, smells, or feels to the touch. The best descriptions draw on all kinds of images and appeal to as many senses as are appropriate. Here is an example from Elspeth Huxley's *The Flame Trees of Thika*. The writer is describing a World War I troop train leaving an African station at night carrying soldiers to the front:

> The men began to sing the jingle then that was so popular then—"Marching to Tabora"; and the shouts and cheers, the whistles, the hissing and chugging of the engine, filled the station as a kettle fills with steam. Everything seemed to bubble over; men waved from windows; Dick gave a hunting cry; the red hair of Pioneer Mary flared under a lamp; the guard jumped into his moving van; and we watched the rear light of the last coach vanish, and heard the chugging die away. A plume of sparks, a long coil of dancing fireflies, spread across the black ancient shoulder of the crater Menegai; and gradually the vast digesting dark of Africa swallowed up all traces of that audacious grub, the hurrying train.

This description is a mixture of appeals to our senses of sight and sound. The men sing and cheer, and the engine chugs and hisses. We see Pioneer Mary's red hair and the sparks from the train's engine. We are regaled with a clever simile, "filled the station as a kettle fills with steam"; and treated to a riveting image, "the vast digesting dark of Africa swallowed up all traces of that audacious grub, the hurrying train." And did the author really just sit down and calmly mine this rich descriptive vein without effort? We do not know for certain, but most likely not. If her experience is at all typical, she hit this motherlode of imagery only after persistent and labored digging.

EXAMPLES

Albert Speer

THE DECEPTION OF HITLER

ALBERT SPEER (1905–1981) was a German architect and National Socialist (Nazi) leader. When Hitler came to power, he became Germany's official architect. His grandiose designs included the stadium at Nuremberg (1934). Because of his exceptional ability to organize, Speer was made minister for armaments in 1942. In 1943 he also took over part of Hermann Goering's responsibilities as planner of the German war economy. Speer used forced labor to complete his construction of public roads and other defenses. In 1946, after the end of World

War II, when Hitler's entourage was under moral scrutiny, it was this use of forced labor that caused the Nuremberg war crimes tribunal to sentence Speer to 20 years of imprisonment. He was released from Spandau Prison in 1966. His memoir *Inside the Third Reich* (tr. 1970) is invaluable for its insights into Hitler's personality and political organization. The excerpt that follows is taken from Speer's *Spandau—the Secret Diaries* (1976).

In this excerpt from a diary by Hitler's trusted architect, you will catch a glimpse of an emotionally disturbed human being. Unlike the bigger-than-life image of Hitler as described in history books, we here observe a pathetic man watching his dreams for the future of his country crumble. As you read, try to analyze your own reaction to Speer as well as Hitler.

1   *November 20, 1952* Hitler. Suddenly he has again become present to my mind. I had almost driven him from my thoughts. How long it is since I have written about him. Almost nothing for years, I imagine, aside from anecdotes and an odd remark here and there. I have no way of checking on that. If I look searchingly into myself, I must say that this is scarcely due to my having rid myself of him. Rather, it seems to me that I have been evading him because he still has too strong a hold on me. Whatever turn my life takes in the future, whenever my name is mentioned, people will think of Hitler. I shall never have an independent existence. And sometimes I see myself as a man of seventy, children long since adult and grandchildren growing up, and wherever I go people will not ask about me but about Hitler.

2   What would I reply? I saw Hitler in moments of triumph and moments of despondency, in his headquarters and stooped over the drawing board, in Montmartre in Paris and deep underground in the bunker. But if I were to describe a single scene in which he was everything at once and his many faces really merged into one, I think of a relatively minor incident, nothing more than a walk in the snow.

3   It was probably during the second half of November 1942. Matters at Stalingrad were going very badly. In view of the depressing news, Hitler left his East Prussian headquarters and sought refuge at Obersalzberg. Dr. Morell had urged him, as he so often did, to take a few days' rest. Surprisingly, this time Hitler complied. He had his adjutant telephone my office and ask me to come to Berchtesgaden. At the Berghof he liked to gather his old cronies around him. Their familiar faces and innocuous jokes could free him from his gloomy moods. His military entourage, meanwhile, was quartered in the village down below.

4   When I arrived at the Berghof in the evening, we exchanged only brief greetings. As was his habit these days, Hitler sat in silence in

front of the big fireplace, staring for hours into the flames. The following day, too, he was tired and dispirited. Toward noon he asked us to join the daily walk to the Teahouse farther down the mountain.* It was one of those dismal Obersalzberg days, with west winds driving low-lying clouds from the plateau of Upper Bavaria down into the valley. These clouds piled up against the surrounding mountain slopes, producing steady falls of snow. In spite of the noon hour, it was dark, but at least the gusts of snow had let up. Hitler came down from the upper floor in his shabby field-gray windbreaker. His valet handed him his worn velours hat and a cane. Pleasantly, with a somewhat remote cordiality and as though he were seeking my tacit understanding, he turned to me. "You come. I'd like to talk a bit." Turning to Bormann, he went on, "Stay behind with the others." We walked down the path, which had been newly cleared of snow. To the right and left were low walls of snow; in the background the Untersberg. The clouds had dissipated; the sun was already low in the sky, casting long shadows, and the Alsatian dashed barking through the snow.

5   After we had walked in silence side by side for a few minutes, Hitler suddenly said, "How I hate the East! The snow alone depresses me. Sometimes I think I'll even stop coming to this mountain in winter. I can't stand seeing snow any longer."

6   I said nothing; what reply could I have made? Subdued, I walked along at his side. He went on talking without inflection about his antipathy to the East, the winter, the war. Lately he had been complaining, to persuade himself and others, of how he was suffering because fate was forever forcing him to do nothing but wage war. Abruptly he stopped, thrust his cane into the ground, and turned to face me. "Speer, you are my architect. You know that I always wanted to be an architect myself." His voice low, sounding as through all strength had been drained from him, he went on: "The World War and the criminal November Revolution prevented that. Otherwise I might today be Germany's foremost architect, as you are now. But the Jews! November ninth was the consequence of their systematic sedition." Hitler grew excited. One could practically see the gears beginning to mesh as he wound himself up into his old rage. His voice gained strength too; it became louder, passing after a while into a hoarse staccato. An old man, a man who was really already defeated, stood there in the snow impotently squeezing out his stored-up bitterness, his toxic resentments. "The Jews were doing it even then. They organized the munitions strike too! In my regiment alone hundreds of soldiers lost their lives. The Jews made me go into politics."

---

* Hitler would walk down to this Teahouse below the Berghof almost every day. On the other hand he very rarely turned his steps toward the higher Eagle's Nest, or Eyrie, often wrongly called the Teahouse.

7   Often before, he had declared that the defeat of the Reich, the humiliation of the nation, and the dishonorable Revolution of 1918 had made him a politician; but he had never put it this way. Yet I distinctly had the feeling that he had started on this walk solely for the sake of a little distraction, so that he could forget the depressing news from the battlefronts. When we set out he had probably not even thought of the Jews. But the snow evidently brought the wintry plains of the East to his mind, and to escape these odious images he had taken refuge in thoughts of that old adversary who from the outset had stood behind all the failures and threats of his life. Never before had I felt so clearly how absolutely essential the figure of the Jew was for Hitler—as an object of hatred and at the same time an escape. For now he had found what the landscape of his beloved mountain and this winter walk could not give him. The tightening noose around the armies at Stalingrad, the intensifying air war, Montgomery's breakthrough at El Alamein— obviously he had forgotten all that, and his dawning recognition that the war was already lost.

8   As though the outburst had exhausted him, he went on talking without excitement, in the same weary manner as before, drained of energy. "You know, Speer, I have never really lived like other people. In the last thirty years I have sacrificed my health. Before the First World War I often did not know what I was going to live on next day. In the war I was an ordinary frontline soldier. Then came the Revolution and my mission, and with that the difficulties began, for ten long years. Anyone else would have given up. But fate wanted it so; Providence helped me."

9   We began walking somewhat faster. "Then when I was called to head the nation, I wanted to create Germany anew—with you, Speer— erecting buildings and more buildings. Germany was going to become the most beautiful country in the world. Just think of what we would have made of Berlin! Paris would have been nothing by comparison. But they've spoiled everything for me. They always read my offers as signs of weakness. They thought I was easily frightened. They thought that of *me!* What does that crew know about the Führer of National Socialist Germany! But we'll get hold of them! And then we'll settle accounts. They'll find out who I am! This time not one will escape. I've always been too lenient. But no more. Now we'll settle accounts." He called Blondi, the Alsatian, who had run on ahead.

10   At the time I often wondered whether Hitler still believed in victory. It is indicative of the atmosphere in the top leadership that I never candidly discussed this question with the few higher-ranking military men with whom I had a personal friendship that went beyond official relations, such as General Guderian and Grand Admiral Dônitz, or with whom I even used the pronoun of intimacy, the *Du*, like Field Marshal Milch. At most I tried to sound them out with a few anxious

hints. Today it seems to me that in spite of all his invocations of Providence, even Hitler was uncertain. This walk, with its continual shifts of mood from depression to aggression, from self-pity to delusory projects for the future, was typical of Hitler's unstable state not only on this day, but in general. During the war such shifts could be observed almost daily.

11   As though to bolster his confidence, he began citing examples from history. "Now I know," he said, "why Frederick the Great decided he had at last had enough after the Third Silesian War. I've had enough for a lifetime too. This war is robbing me of the best years of my life. I wanted to make history not with won battles but with the buildings you and I designed together. Those barbarians almost conquered the empire once before; they were at the gates of Vienna. But there, too, a great man opposed them and drove the Asiatics back. How our old empire flourished then, after Prince Eugene's victory. Remember that beautiful baroque Vienna sprang up immediately after the hour of gravest danger. It will be like that for us, too, after we have won. In the same way we will build palaces and glorious buildings. They will be the monuments of our victory over the Bolshevists."

12   Have I reproduced that more or less accurately? Has the character been made plausible? I must remember that, after all, I am always listening to his voice, hearing him clear his throat, seeing his slightly stooped figure before my eyes. After my release I must listen to records and look at films to see whether he has shifted in my memory, and whether the sinister or repulsive features have been thrust too much into the foreground. For if that were the whole Hitler, how is it possible that he captivated me so, and for more than a decade?

(1,697 words)

VOCABULARY

despondency (2)	inflection (6)	impotently (6)
adjutant (3)	antipathy (6)	odious (7)
innocuous (3)	sedition (6)	invocations (10)
plateau (4)	staccato (6)	delusory (10)
velours (4)	toxic (6)	

THE FACTS

1. What particular scene, according to the author, allows all of Hitler's characteristics to merge into one?

2. Why had Hitler left his East Prussian headquarters to seek respite at his mountain home at Obersalzberg?

3. Why did Hitler ask the author to join him on his walk in the snowy landscape?

4. According to Speer, whom did Hitler blame for all of his troubles, even the war? On what basis is the blame assigned?

5. What did Hitler say was his real ambition for Germany?

6. What kind of personality does Hitler reveal during his walk with the author?

THE STRATEGIES

1. What advantage is there in having Speer describe a simple walk in the snow with Hitler?

2. To what literary genre does this essay belong? How do you know? How enjoyable do you consider it?

3. What effect do the passages quoting Hitler have? Would the essay suffer in quality if these quotations were removed? Why or why not?

4. What details are included to make Hitler seem human? Name at least three.

5. In paragraph 12, Speer worries about whether he has represented Hitler as a plausible person. What is your view of this worry? Is Hitler represented as plausible or not?

THE ISSUES

1. What does knowing that Speer was in prison when he wrote his recollections add or subtract in your mind?

2. Do you believe Speer is right when he speculates that for the rest of his life people will not ask about him but about Hitler? Why or why not?

3. What, in your view, is the most revealing aspect of Hitler's conversation with Speer?

4. Why was the figure of the Jew so important to Hitler's view of himself? What is your reaction to his obsession with the Jews?

5. In the final paragraph, the author muses about why Hitler had captivated him so strongly for over a decade. What answer might one give?

SUGGESTIONS FOR WRITING

1. Think of a person in your life who has captivated your mind and heart. Write an essay in which you examine this captivation.

2. Write an essay describing Hitler as he is revealed in Speer's memoir. Then compare this description with what you have read or heard about Hitler from other sources.

▼▼

H. L. Mencken

THE LIBIDO FOR THE UGLY

HENRY LOUIS MENCKEN (1880–1956) was an editor, author, and critic. He began his journalism career on the *Baltimore Morning Herald* and later became editor of the *Baltimore Evening Herald*. From 1906 until his death, he was on the staff of the *Baltimore Sun* (or *Evening Sun*). In 1924, with George Jean Nathan, Mencken founded the *American Mercury* and served as its editor from 1925 to 1933. Mencken's writing was chiefly devoted to lambasting the smug, conventional attitudes of the middle class. Among his numerous works is *The American Language*, Mencken's monumental study of the American idiom, first published in 1919.

Few writers have such an eye for colorful detail as the incomparable Mencken, at his best when he's railing against physical ugliness or storming against a tradition he dislikes. In the essay that follows, Mencken turns his literary wrath against the ugliness of the industrial heartland of America.

1   On a Winter day some years ago, coming out of Pittsburgh on one of the expresses of the Pennsylvania Railroad, I rolled eastward for an hour through the coal and steel towns of Westmoreland county. It was familiar ground; boy and man, I had been through it often before. But somehow I had never quite sensed its appalling desolation. Here was the very heart of industrial America, the center of its most lucrative and characteristic activity, the boast and pride of the richest and grandest nation ever seen on earth—and here was a scene so dreadfully hideous, so intolerably bleak and forlorn that it reduced the whole aspiration of man to a macabre and depressing joke. Here was wealth beyond computation, almost beyond imagination—and here were human habitations so abominable that they would have disgraced a race of alley cats.

2   I am not speaking of mere filth. One expects steel towns to be dirty. What I allude to is the unbroken and agonizing ugliness, the sheer revolting monstrousness, of every house in sight. From East Liberty to Greensburg, a distance of twenty-five miles, there was not one in sight from the train that did not insult and lacerate the eye. Some were so bad, and they were among the most pretentious—churches, stores, warehouses, and the like—that they were downright startling; one blinked before them as one blinks before a man with his face shot away. A few linger in memory, horrible even there: a crazy little church just west of Jeannette, set like a dormer-window on the side of a bare, leprous hill; the headquarters of the Veterans of Foreign Wars at another forlorn town, a steel stadium like a huge rat-trap somewhere further down the line. But most of all I recall the general effect—of hideousness without a break. There was not a single decent house within eye-range from the Pittsburgh suburbs to the Greensburg yards. There was not one that was not misshapen, and there was not one that was not shabby.

3   The country itself is not uncomely, despite the grime of the endless mills. It is, in form, a narrow river valley, with deep gullies running up into the hills. It is thickly settled, but not noticeably overcrowded. There is still plenty of room for building, even in the larger towns, and there are very few solid blocks. Nearly every house, big and little, has space on all four sides. Obviously, if there were architects of any professional sense or dignity in the region, they would have perfected a chalet to hug the hillsides—a chalet with a high-pitched roof, to throw off the heavy Winter snows, but still essentially a low and clinging building, wider than it was tall. But what have they done? They have taken as their model a brick set on end. This they have converted into a thing of dingy clapboards, with a narrow, low-pitched roof. And the whole they have set upon thin, preposterous brick piers. By the hundreds and thousands these abominable houses cover the bare hillsides, like gravestones in some gigantic and decaying cemetery. On their deep sides they are three, four and even five stories high; on their low sides they bury themselves swinishly in the mud. Not a fifth of them are perpendicular. They lean this way and that, hanging on to their bases precariously. And one and all they are streaked in grime, with dead and eczematous patches of paint peeping through the streaks.

4   Now and then there is a house of brick. But what brick! When it is new it is the color of a fried egg. When it has taken on the patina of the mills it is the color of an egg long past all hope or caring. Was it necessary to adopt that shocking color? No more than it was necessary to set all of the houses on end. Red brick, even in a steel town, ages with some dignity. Let it become downright black, and it is still sightly, especially if its trimmings are of white stone, with soot in the depths and

the high spots washed by the rain. But in Westmoreland they prefer that uremic yellow, and so they have the most loathsome towns and villages ever seen by mortal eye.

5   I award this championship only after laborious research and incessant prayer. I have seen, I believe, all of the most unlovely towns of the world; they are all to be found in the United States. I have seen the mill towns of decomposing New England and the desert towns of Utah, Arizona and Texas. I am familiar with the back streets of Newark, Brooklyn and Chicago, and have made scientific explorations to Camden, N.J. and Newport News, Va. Safe in a Pullman, I have whirled through the gloomy, God-forsaken villages of Iowa and Kansas, and the malarious tide-water hamlets of Georgia. I have been to Bridgeport, Conn., and to Los Angeles. But nowhere on this earth, at home or abroad, have I seen anything to compare to the villages that huddle along the line of the Pennsylvania from the Pittsburgh yards to Greensburg. They are incomparable in color, and they are incomparable in design. It is as if some titanic and aberrant genius, uncompromisingly inimical to man, had devoted all the ingenuity of Hell to the making of them. They show grotesqueries of ugliness that, in retrospect, become almost diabolical. One cannot imagine mere human beings concocting such dreadful things, and one can scarcely imagine human beings bearing life in them.

6   Are they so frightful because the valley is full of foreigners—dull, insensate brutes, with no love of beauty in them? Then why didn't these foreigners set up similar abominations in the countries that they came from? You will, in fact, find nothing of the sort in Europe—save perhaps in the more putrid parts of England. There is scarcely an ugly village on the whole Continent. The peasants, however poor, somehow manage to make themselves graceful and charming habitations, even in Spain. But in the American village and small town the pull is always toward ugliness, and in that Westmoreland valley it has been yielded to with an eagerness bordering upon passion. It is incredible that mere ignorance should have achieved such masterpieces of horror.

7   On certain levels of the American race, indeed, there seems to be a positive libido for the ugly, as on other and less Christian levels there is a libido for the beautiful. It is impossible to put down the wallpaper that defaces the average American home of the lower middle class to mere inadvertence, or to the obscene humor of the manufacturers. Such ghastly designs, it must be obvious, give a genuine delight to a certain type of mind. They meet, in some unfathomable way, its obscure and unintelligible demands. They caress it as "The Palms" caresses it, or the art of the movie, or jazz. The taste for them is as enigmatical and yet as common as the taste for dogmatic theology and the poetry of Edgar A. Guest.

8   Thus I suspect (though confessedly without knowing) that the vast majority of the honest folk of Westmoreland county, and especially the 100% Americans among them, actually admire the houses they live in, and are proud of them. For the same money they could get vastly better ones, but they prefer what they have got. Certainly there was no pressure upon the Veterans of Foreign Wars to choose the dreadful edifice that bears their banner, for there are plenty of vacant buildings along the track-side, and some of them are appreciably better. They might, indeed, have built a better one of their own. But they chose that clapboarded horror with their eyes open, and having chosen it, they let it mellow into its present shocking depravity. They like it as it is: beside it, the Parthenon would no doubt offend them. In precisely the same way the authors of the rat-trap stadium that I have mentioned made a deliberate choice. After painfully designing and erecting it, they made it perfect in their own sight by putting a completely impossible penthouse, painted a staring yellow, on top of it. The effect is that of a fat woman with a black eye. It is that of a Presbyterian grinning. But they like it.

9   Here is something that the psychologists have so far neglected: the love of ugliness for its own sake, the lust to make the world intolerable. Its habitat is the United States. Out of the melting pot emerges a race which hates beauty as it hates truth. The etiology of this madness deserves a great deal more study than it has got. There must be causes behind it; it arises and flourishes in obedience to biological laws, and not as a mere act of God. What, precisely, are the terms of those laws? And why do they run stronger in America than elsewhere? Let some honest *Privat Dozent* in pathological sociology apply himself to the problem.

(1,531 words)

VOCABULARY

lucrative (1)

aspiration (1)

macabre (1)

lacerate (2)

dormer-window (2)

clapboards (3)

eczematous (3)

patina (4)

uremic (4)

malarious (5)

aberrant (5)

inimical (5)

grotesqueries (5)

insensate (6)

libido (7)

inadvertence (7)

enigmatical (7)

dogmatic (7)

Parthenon (8)

etiology (9)

Privat Dozent (9)

pathological (9)

THE FACTS

1. What area of the country does this essay describe?

2. What is the principal occupation of the region?

3. Mencken not only criticizes the architecture of the region, but he also suggests an alternative. What sort of architecture does he think suited to this region?

4. On what does Mencken blame the ugliness he describes?

5. What are Mencken's views of the villages in Europe? In his view, how do they compare with American towns?

THE STRATEGIES

1. A good description focuses on a dominant impression, and develops it. Examine the second paragraph. What is the dominant impression here?

2. Examine the third paragraph. What dominant impression does Mencken focus on in his description of the buildings?

3. What aspect of the ugliness does paragraph 4 deal with?

4. "I have seen, I believe, all of the most unlovely towns of the world; they are all to be found in the United States." Why does he say *unlovely* rather than *ugly?* Which is more effective? Why?

5. "And one and all they are streaked in grime, with dead and eczematous patches of paint peeping through the streaks." What comparison is implied in this metaphor?

THE ISSUES

1. One of the most vigilant civic groups in the United States today is that of the environmentalists—men and women determined to preserve historical buildings, wilderness areas, sea coasts, and public parks. What importance do you attribute to the efforts of these people? What do you think would happen if they no longer cared?

2. Mencken seems to feel that while architectural ugliness on any scale is lamentable, it is especially insulting when the edifice is pretentious. Do you agree with Mencken's view? Why or why not?

3. What stretch of highway in the United States is charmingly beautiful and stands in total contrast to Mencken's description of the houses in Westmoreland County? Describe such a stretch in detail, focusing on architectural characteristics.

4. Do you agree with Mencken that Americans are psychologically obsessed with ugliness? If you agree, try to find reasons for this obsession. If you disagree, prove that Mencken is wrong by citing instances in which typical Americans have promoted beauty and good taste.

5. If you were to oversee a development of beautiful homes, what aesthetic requirements would you insist on? Describe the development in concrete terms.

SUGGESTIONS FOR WRITING

1. Write an essay describing the town or city you live in.

2. Write an analysis of Mencken's diction in this essay, paying particular attention to his use of adjectives.

▼▼▼

E. B. White

ONCE MORE TO THE LAKE

ELWYN BROOKS WHITE (1899–1985) was one of the wittiest and most admired observers of contemporary American society. As a member of *The New Yorker* magazine staff he wrote a number of essays for the section called "Talk of the Town," and some of these essays have been collected in *The Wild Flag* (1946) and a new book, *Writings from The New Yorker*. With James Thurber, he wrote *Is Sex Necessary?* (1929). Some of his other well-known works include *One Man's Meat* (1942), *Here Is New York* (1949), and two beloved children books, *Stuart Little* (1945) and *Charlotte's Web* (1952).

This is an essay that ends with a bang, not a whimper. The writer tackles what might seem at first glance a humdrum subject—an annual vacation trip to a lake—and describes in evocative and lovely prose the carefree summer days he spent hiking and fishing with his son. Then, at the very end, the trap is sprung.

August 1941

1   One summer, along about 1904, my father rented a camp on a lake in Maine and took us all there for the month of August. We all got ringworm from some kittens and had to rub Pond's Extract on our arms and legs night and morning, and my father rolled over in a canoe with all his clothes on; but outside of that the vacation was a success and

from then on none of us ever thought there was any place in the world like that lake in Maine. We returned summer after summer—always on August 1 for one month. I have since become a salt-water man, but sometimes in summer there are days when the restlessness of the tides and the fearful cold of the sea water and the incessant wind that blows across the afternoon and into the evening make me wish for the placidity of a lake in the woods. A few weeks ago this feeling got so strong I bought myself a couple of bass hooks and a spinner and returned to the lake where we used to go, for a week's fishing and to revisit old haunts.

2   I took along my son, who had never had any fresh water up his nose and who had seen lily pads only from train windows. On the journey over to the lake I began to wonder what it would be like. I wondered how time would have marred this unique, this holy spot—the coves and streams, the hills that the sun set behind, the camps and the paths behind the camps. I was sure that the tarred road would have found it out, and I wondered in what other ways it would be desolated. It is strange how much you can remember about places like that once you allow your mind to return into the grooves that lead back. You remember one thing, and that suddenly reminds you of another thing. I guess I remembered clearest of all the early mornings, when the lake was cool and motionless, remembered how the bedroom smelled of the lumber it was made of and of the wet woods whose scent entered through the screen. The partitions in the camp were thin and did not extend clear to the top of the rooms, and as I was always the first up I would dress softly so as not to wake the others, and sneak out into the sweet outdoors and start out in the canoe, keeping close along the shore in the long shadows of the pines. I remembered being very careful never to rub my paddle against the gunwale for fear of disturbing the stillness of the cathedral.

3   The lake had never been what you would call a wild lake. There were cottages sprinkled around the shores, and it was in farming country although the shores of the lake were quite heavily wooded. Some of the cottages were owned by nearby farmers, and you would live at the shore and eat your meals at the farmhouse. That's what our family did. But although it wasn't wild, it was a fairly large and undisturbed lake and there were places in it that, to a child at least, seemed infinitely remote and primeval.

4   I was right about the tar: it led to within half a mile of the shore. But when I got back there, with my boy, and we settled into a camp near a farmhouse and into the kind of summertime I had known, I could tell that it was going to be pretty much the same as it had been before—I knew it, lying in bed the first morning smelling the bedroom and hearing the boy sneak quietly out and go off along the shore in a boat. I began to sustain the illusion that he was I, and therefore, by

simple transposition, that I was my father. This sensation persisted, kept cropping up all the time we were there. It was not an entirely new feeling, but in this setting it grew much stronger. I seemed to be living a dual existence. I would be in the middle of some simple act, I would be picking up a bait box or laying down a table fork, or I would be saying something and suddenly it would be not I but my father who was saying the words or making the gesture. It gave me a creepy sensation.

5   We went fishing the first morning. I felt the same damp moss covering the worms in the bait can, and saw the dragonfly alight on the tip of my rod as it hovered a few inches from the surface of the water. It was the arrival of this fly that convinced me beyond any doubt that everything was as it always had been, that the years were a mirage and that there had been no years. The small waves were the same, chucking the rowboat under the chin as we fished at anchor, and the boat was the same boat, the same color green and the ribs broken in the same places, and under the floorboards the same fresh water leavings and débris—the dead helgramite, the wisps of moss, the rusty discarded fishhook, the dried blood from yesterday's catch. We stared silently at the tips of our rods, at the dragonflies that came and went. I lowered the tip of mine into the water, tentatively, pensively dislodging the fly, which darted two feet away, poised, darted two feet back, and came to rest again a little farther up the rod. There had been no years between the ducking of this dragonfly and the other one—the one that was part of memory. I looked at the boy, who was silently watching his fly, and it was my hands that held his rod, my eyes watching. I felt dizzy and didn't know which rod I was at the end of.

6   We caught two bass, hauling them in briskly as though they were mackerel, pulling them over the side of the boat in a businesslike manner without any landing net, and stunning them with a blow on the back of the head. When we got back for a swim before lunch, the lake was exactly where we had left it, the same number of inches from the dock, and there was only the merest suggestion of a breeze. This seemed an utterly enchanted sea, this lake you could leave to its own devices for a few hours and come back to, and find that it had not stirred, this constant and trustworthy body of water. In the shallows, the dark, water-soaked sticks and twigs, smooth and old, were undulating in clusters on the bottom against the clean ribbed sand, and the track of the mussel was plain. A school of minnows swam by, each minnow with its small individual shadow, doubling the attendance, so clear and sharp in the sunlight. Some of the other campers were in swimming, along the shore, one of them with a cake of soap, and the water felt thin and clear and unsubstantial. Over the years there had been this person with the cake of soap, this cultist, and here he was. There had been no years.

7   Up to the farmhouse to dinner through the teeming dusty field, the road under our sneakers was only a two-track road. The middle track was missing, the one with the marks of the hooves and the splotches of dried, flaky manure. There had always been three tracks to choose from in choosing which track to walk in; now the choice was narrowed down to two. For a moment I missed terribly the middle alternative. But the way led past the tennis court, and something about the way it lay there in the sun reassured me; the tape had loosened along the backline, the alleys were green with plantains and other weeds, and the net (installed in June and removed in September) sagged in the dry noon, and the whole place steamed with midday heat and hunger and emptiness. There was a choice of pie for dessert, and one was blueberry and one was apple, and the waitresses were the same country girls, there having been no passage of time, only the illusion of it as in a dropped curtain—the waitresses were still fifteen; their hair had been washed, that was the only difference—they had been to the movies and seen the pretty girls with the clean hair.

8   Summertime, oh, summertime, pattern of life indelible with fadeproof lake, the wood unshatterable, the pasture with the sweetfern and the juniper forever and ever, summer without end; this was the background, and the life along the shore was the design, the cottages with their innocent and tranquil design, their tiny docks with the flagpole and the American flag floating against the white clouds in the blue sky, the little paths over the roots of the trees leading from camp to camp and the paths leading back to the outhouses and the can of lime for sprinkling, and at the souvenir counters at the store the miniature birch-bark canoes and the postcards that showed things looking a little better than they looked. This was the American family at play, escaping the city heat, wondering whether the newcomers in the camp at the head of the cove were "common" or "nice," wondering whether it was true that the people who drove up for Sunday dinner at the farmhouse were turned away because there wasn't enough chicken.

9   It seemed to me, as I kept remembering all this, that those times and those summers had been infinitely precious and worth saving. There had been jollity and peace and goodness. The arriving (at the beginning of August) had been so big a business in itself, at the railway station the farm wagon drawn up, the first smell of the pine-laden air, the first glimpse of the smiling farmer, and the great importance of the trunks and your father's enormous authority in such matters and the feel of the wagon under you for the long ten-mile haul, and at the top of the last long hill catching the first view of the lake after eleven months of not seeing this cherished body of water. The shouts and cries of the other campers when they saw you, and the trunks to be unpacked, to give up their rich burden. (Arriving was less exciting nowadays, when you sneaked up in your car and parked it under a tree

near the camp and took out the bags and in five minutes it was all over, no fuss, no loud wonderful fuss about trunks.)

10   Peace and goodness and jollity. The only thing that was wrong now, really, was the sound of the place, an unfamiliar nervous sound of the outboard motors. This was the note that jarred, the one thing that would sometimes break the illusion and set the years moving. In those other summertimes all motors were inboard; and when they were at a little distance, the noise they made was a sedative, an ingredient of summer sleep. They were one-cylinder and two-cylinder engines, and some were make-and-break and some were jump-spark, but they all made a sleepy sound across the lake. The one-lungers throbbed and fluttered, and the twin-cylinder ones purred and purred, and that was a quiet sound, too. But now the campers all had outboards. In the daytime, in the hot mornings, these motors made a petulant, irritable sound; at night in the still evening when the afterglow lit the water, they whined about one's ears like mosquitoes. My boy loved our rented outboard, and his great desire was to achieve single-handed mastery over it, and authority, and he soon learned the trick of choking it a little (but not too much), and the adjustment of the needle valve. Watching him I would remember the things you could do with the old one-cylinder engine with the heavy flywheel, how you could have it eating out of your hand if you got really close to it spiritually. Motorboats in those days didn't have clutches, and you would make a landing by shutting off the motor at the proper time and coasting in with a dead rudder. But there was a way of reversing them, if you learned the trick, by cutting the switch and putting it on again exactly on the final dying revolution of the flywheel, so that it would kick back against compression and begin reversing. Approaching a dock in a strong following breeze, it was difficult to slow up sufficiently by the ordinary coasting method, and if a boy felt he had complete mastery over his motor, he was tempted to keep it running beyond its time and then reverse it a few feet from the dock. It took a cool nerve, because if you threw the switch a twentieth of a second too soon you would catch the flywheel when it still had speed enough to go up past center, and the boat would leap ahead, charging bull-fashion at the dock.

11   We had a good week at the camp. The bass were biting well and the sun shone endlessly, day after day. We would be tired at night and lie down in the accumulated heat of the little bedrooms after the long hot day and the breeze would stir almost imperceptibly outside and the smell of the swamp drift in through the rusty screens. Sleep would come easily and in the morning the red squirrel would be on the roof, tapping out his gay routine. I kept remembering everything, lying in bed in the mornings—the small steamboat that had a long rounded stern like the lip of a Ubangi, and how quietly she ran on the moonlight sails, when the older boys played their mandolins and the girls

sang and we ate doughnuts dipped in sugar, and how sweet the music was on the water in the shining night, and what it had felt like to think about girls then. After breakfast we would go up to the store and the things were in the same place—the minnows in a bottle, the plugs and spinners disarranged and pawed over by the youngsters from the boys' camp, the Fig Newtons and the Beeman's gum. Outside, the road was tarred and cars stood in front of the store. Inside, all was just as it had always been, except there was more Coca-Cola and not so much Moxie and root beer and birch beer and sarsaparilla. We would walk out with the bottle of pop apiece and sometimes the pop would backfire up our noses and hurt. We explored the streams, quietly, where the turtles slid off the sunny logs and dug their way into the soft bottom; and we lay on the town wharf and fed worms to the tame bass. Everywhere we went I had trouble making out which was I, the one walking at my side, the one walking in my pants.

12   One afternoon while we were at that lake a thunderstorm came up. It was like the revival of an old melodrama that I had seen long ago with childish awe. The second-act climax of the drama of the electrical disturbance over a lake in America had not changed in any important respect. This was the big scene, still the big scene. The whole thing was so familiar, the first feeling of oppression and heat and a general air around camp of not wanting to go very far away. In midafternoon (it was all the same) a curious darkening of the sky, and a lull in everything that had made life tick; and then the way the boats suddenly swung the other way at their moorings with the coming of a breeze out of the new quarter, and the premonitory rumble. Then the kettle drum, then the snare, then the bass drum and cymbals, then crackling light against the dark, and the gods grinning and licking their chops in the hills. Afterward the calm, the rain steadily rustling in the calm lake, the return of light and hope and spirits, and the campers running out in joy and relief to go swimming in the rain, their bright cries perpetuating the deathless joke about how they were getting simply drenched, and the children screaming with delight at the new sensation of bathing in the rain, and the joke about getting drenched linking the generations in a strong indestructible chain. And the comedian who waded in carrying an umbrella.

13   When the others went swimming my son said he was going in, too. He pulled his dripping trunks from the line where they had hung all through the shower and wrung them out. Languidly, and with no thought of going in, I watched him, his hard little body, skinny and bare, saw him wince slightly as he pulled up around his vitals the small, soggy, icy garment. As he buckled the swollen belt, suddenly my groin felt the chill of death.

(2,884 words)

VOCABULARY

incessant (1)	pensively (5)	sedative (10)
desolated (2)	undulating (6)	imperceptibly (11)
primeval (3)	unsubstantial (6)	premonitory (12)
transposition (4)	cultist (6)	
tentatively (5)	indelible (8)	

THE FACTS

1. How old was White when he first went to the lake with his father? How old was he when he took his own son there?

2. What illusion did White begin to sustain on hearing his own son sneaking out to go down to the boat on the lake?

3. What changes did the author notice in the road leading from the lake to the farmhouse? What did this change say about the passing of time?

4. What difference did the author note between the way guests arrived at the lake in his own boyhood days and their arrival now?

5. What experience precipitated White's realization that time had passed, that he was no longer young, that he was mortal?

THE STRATEGIES

1. Aside from description, what other mode of development is implicitly part of the structure of this essay?

2. In paragraph 2, White writes that he "was sure that the tarred road would have found it [the lake] out." What is odd about the phrasing of this sentence? What do you think White was trying to achieve in phrasing it that way?

3. Examine the author's boyhood recollections of the lake (paragraph 2). To which of our senses do his detail and images appeal?

4. Examine the description of the fishing boat in paragraph 5. How does White manage to convey such a vivid picture of the boat?

5. In what part of his body did White feel the chill of death? In the context of the essay, why is this such an appropriate place?

THE ISSUES

1. In paragraph 2, why does White refer to the lake as a "holy spot"? What is the connotation of this term, since the place was not a

religious shrine? What, in your life, would be a similar spot? Give reasons for your choice.

2. The author states that he missed the "middle track" of the road leading up to the farmhouse for dinner. Try to imagine yourself in a similar situation forty years hence. What vehicles of transportation, not yet commonly used, might invade your road then?

3. What is the social implication of the words *common* or *nice* in paragraph 8? Have times changed or are these distinctions still made?

4. Not everyone would have reacted the way the author describes himself in the final sentence of the essay. What might be another realistic reaction?

5. What are some clear signs in your life to indicate that you are not immortal? What are your feelings about these signs?

SUGGESTIONS FOR WRITING

1. Write an essay about any favorite vacation spot or a favorite relative. Be specific in your description, providing details that evoke the feeling of the place or person.

2. Write an essay in which you contrast the descriptive styles of "Libido for the Ugly" and "Once More to the Lake." Pinpoint how each author evokes a mood.

▼▼

James Joyce

HELL

JAMES JOYCE (1882–1941) is considered by many to be among the most significant novelists of this century. He was born in Dublin, Ireland, and educated at University College, Dublin. A writer who pushed language to its outer limit of comprehensibility, Joyce wrote poetry, short stories, and novels. His major novels include *A Portrait of the Artist as a Young Man* (1916), *Ulysses* (written between 1914 and 1921 and published in the United States in 1933), and *Finnegans Wake* (1939).

Joyce, in this selection from A Portrait of the Artist *as a Young Man, shows us the wreathing fires of hell and persuades us to smell its stench of brimstone and sin. The description below is so graphic, so detailed, filled with such shuddering imagery, that we almost believe that someone has returned from this dreadful place to tell the tale.*

1   Hell is a strait and dark and foulsmelling prison, an abode of demons and lost souls, filled with fire and smoke. The straitness of this prison-house is expressly designed by God to punish those who refused to be bound by His laws. In earthly prisons the poor captive has at least some liberty of movement, were it only within the four walls of his cell or in the gloomy yard of his prison. Not so in hell. There, by reason of the great number of the damned, the prisoners are heaped together in their awful prison, the walls of which are said to be four thousand miles thick: and the damned are so utterly bound and helpless that, as a blessed saint, saint Anselm, writes in his book on similitudes, they are not even able to remove from the eye a worm that gnaws it.

2   —They lie in exterior darkness. For, remember, the fire of hell gives forth no light. As, at the command of God, the fire of the Babylonian furnace lost its heat but not its light so, at the command of God, the fire of hell, while retaining the intensity of its heat, burns eternally in darkness. It is a neverending storm of darkness, dark flames and dark smoke of burning brimstone, amid which the bodies are heaped one upon another without even a glimpse of air. Of all the plagues with which the land of the Pharaohs was smitten one plague alone, that of darkness, was called horrible. What name, then, shall we give to the darkness of hell which is to last not for three days alone but for all eternity?

3   —The horror of this strait and dark prison is increased by its awful stench. All the filth of the world, all the offal and scum of the world, we are told, shall run there as to a vast reeking sewer when the terrible conflagration of the last day has purged the world. The brimstone too which burns there in such prodigious quantity fills all hell with its intolerable stench; and the bodies of the damned themselves exhale such a pestilential odour that as saint Bonaventure says, one of them alone would suffice to infect the whole world. The very air of this world, that pure element, becomes foul and unbreathable when it has been long enclosed. Consider then what must be the foulness of the air of hell. Imagine some foul and putrid corpse that has lain rotting and decomposing in the grave, a jellylike mass of liquid corruption. Imagine such a corpse a prey to flames, devoured by the fire of burning brimstone and giving off dense choking fumes of nauseous loathsome decomposition. And then imagine this sickening stench, multiplied a millionfold and a millionfold again from the millions upon millions of fetid carcasses massed together in the reeking darkness, a huge and rotting human fungus. Imagine all this and you will have some idea of the horror of the stench of hell.

4   —But this stench is not, horrible though it is, the greatest physical torment to which the damned are subjected. The torment of fire is the greatest torment to which the tyrant has ever subjected his fellowcreatures. Place your finger for a moment in the flame of a candle and you

will feel the pain of fire. But our earthly fire was created by God for the benefit of man, to maintain in him the spark of life and to help him in the useful arts whereas the fire of hell is of another quality and was created by God to torture and punish the unrepentant sinner. Our earthly fire also consumes more or less rapidly according as the object which it attacks is more or less combustible so that human ingenuity has even succeeded in inventing chemical preparations to check or frustrate its action. But the sulphurous brimstone which burns in hell is a substance which is specially designed to burn for ever and for ever with unspeakable fury. Moreover our earthly fire destroys at the same time as it burns so that the more intense it is the shorter is its duration: but the fire of hell has this property that it preserves that which it burns and though it rages with incredible intensity it rages for ever.

5   —Our earthly fire again, no matter how fierce or widespread it may be, is always of a limited extent: but the lake of fire in hell is boundless, shoreless and bottomless. It is on record that the devil himself, when asked the question by a certain soldier, was obliged to confess that if a whole mountain were thrown into the burning ocean of hell it would be burned up in an instant like a piece of wax. And this terrible fire will not afflict the bodies of the damned only from without but each lost soul will be a hell unto itself, the boundless fire raging in its very vitals. O, how terrible is the lot of those wretched beings! The blood seethes and boils in the veins, the brains are boiling in the skull, the heart in the breast glowing and bursting, the bowels a redhot mass of burning pulp, the tender eyes flaming like molten balls.

6   —And yet what I have said as to the strength and quality and boundlessness of this fire is as nothing when compared to its intensity, an intensity which it has as being the instrument chosen by divine design for the punishment of soul and body alike. It is a fire which proceeds directly from the ire of God, working not of its own activity but as an instrument of divine vengeance. As the waters of baptism cleanse the soul with the body so do the fires of punishment torture the spirit with the flesh. Every sense of the flesh is tortured and every faculty of the soul therewith: the eyes with impenetrable utter darkness, the nose with noisome odours, the ears with yells and howls and execrations, the taste with foul matter, leprous corruption, nameless suffocating filth, the touch with redhot goads and spikes, with cruel tongues of flame. And through the several torments of the senses the immortal soul is tortured eternally in its very essence amid the leagues upon leagues of glowing fires kindled in the abyss by the offended majesty of the Omnipotent God and fanned into everlasting and ever increasing fury by the breath of the anger of the Godhead.

7   Consider finally that the torment of this infernal prison is increased by the company of the damned themselves. Evil company on earth is so noxious that even the plants, as if by instinct, withdraw

from the company of whatsoever is deadly or hurtful to them. In hell all laws are overturned: there is no thought of family or country, of ties, of relationships. The damned howl and scream at one another, their torture and rage intensified by the presence of beings tortured and raging like themselves. All sense of humanity is forgotten. The yells of the suffering sinners fill the remotest corners of the vast abyss. The mouths of the damned are full of blasphemies against God and of hatred for their fellow sufferers and of curses against those souls which were their accomplices in sin. In olden times it was the custom to punish the parricide, the man who had raised his murderous hand against his father, by casting him into the depths of the sea in a sack in which were placed a cock, a monkey and a serpent. The intention of those lawgivers who framed such a law, which seems cruel in our times, was to punish the criminal by the company of hateful and hurtful beasts. But what is the fury of those dumb beasts compared with the fury of execration which bursts from the parched lips and aching throats of the damned in hell when they behold in their companions in misery those who aided and abetted them in sin, those whose words sowed the first seeds of evil thinking and evil living in their minds, those whose immodest suggestions led them on to sin, those whose eyes tempted and allured them from the path of virtue. They turn upon those accomplices and upbraid them and curse them. But they are helpless and hopeless: it is too late now for repentance.

(1,406 words)

VOCABULARY

strait (1)	prodigious (3)	execrations (6)
similitudes (1)	pestilential (3)	parricide (7)
offal (3)	fetid (3)	allured (7)
conflagration (3)	noisome (6)	upbraid (7)

THE FACTS

1. How thick are the walls of hell?

2. What peculiar characteristics does the fire of hell have?

3. What is the greatest physical torment that the damned of hell suffer?

4. What is the source of the fire in hell?

5. How were parricides punished in olden times?

THE STRATEGIES

1. Examine carefully this description of hell. What is its overall structure? How are its paragraphs deployed?

2. Examine paragraph 4. How is it developed? What is its purpose?

3. What is the purpose of mentioning the "earthly prisons" in paragraph 1?

4. Examine paragraph 5. How is this paragraph structured? What technique does the writer use to make his description so vivid?

5. In the novel *A Portrait of the Artist as a Young Man,* this description of hell is delivered in a sermon. Identify at least one technique that the preacher uses to involve his listeners in the description.

THE ISSUES

1. Modern minds have, for the most part, rejected the medieval view of a physical hell, where the damned suffer such tortures as heat, cold, foul smell, laceration, and persecution from demons. What, if anything, has replaced this notion of hell?

2. In your view, why do many people believe in paradise and hell? What disadvantage or advantage does the *lack* of belief in these places provide?

3. What effect do you think this sermon on hell might have on young boys listening to it? What is your opinion of the technique used?

4. Is torture as a means of punishment ever justified in a civilized society? Why or why not?

5. A portion of Dante's hell was reserved for those who encouraged others to sin. Where in this excerpt does Joyce express a similar idea? Why do both Dante and Joyce call down a harsh judgment on those who aid and abet evil?

SUGGESTIONS FOR WRITING

1. Write an essay on hell as it is described here, arguing for or against a belief in its existence.

2. Following the example of this selection, write a brief description of heaven.

▼▼▼

Eudora Welty

A WORN PATH

EUDORA WELTY (b. 1909) is an American novelist and short-story writer whose tales about eccentric but charming characters from small Mississippi towns have won her a large audience. The best-known of her stories have been collected in *A Curtain of Green* (1941), *The Wide Net* (1943), and *The Golden Apples* (1949). Among her novels are *Delta Wedding* (1946), *The Ponder Heart* (1954), and *The Optimist's Daughter* (1972). In 1983 she delivered the William E. Massey Sr. Lectures in American Civilization at Harvard, which were published as *One Writer's Beginnings* (1984).

In this story, a woman, undaunted by age and hardships, presses on toward her goal—to get the medicine her sick grandchild must have in order to survive.

1   It was December—a bright frozen day in the early morning. Far out in the country there was an old Negro woman with her head tied in a red rag, coming along a path through the pinewoods. Her name was Phoenix Jackson. She was very old and small and she walked slowly in the dark pine shadows, moving a little from side to side in her steps, with the balanced heaviness and lightness of a pendulum in a grandfather clock. She carried a thin, small cane made from an umbrella, and with this she kept tagging the frozen earth in front of her. This made a grave and persistent noise in the still air, that seemed meditative, like the chirping of a solitary little bird.

2   She wore a dark striped dress reaching down to her shoetops, and an equally long apron of bleached sugar sacks, with a full pocket; all neat and tidy, but every time she took a step she might have fallen over her shoelaces, which dragged from her unlaced shoes. She looked straight ahead. Her eyes were blue with age. Her skin had a pattern all its own of numberless branching wrinkles and as though a whole little tree stood in the middle of her forehead, but a golden color ran underneath, and the two knobs of her cheeks were illuminated by a yellow burning under the dark. Under the red rag her hair came down on her neck in the frailest of ringlets, still black, and with an odor like copper.

3   Now and then there was a quivering in the thicket. Old Phoenix said, "Out of my way, all you foxes, owls, beetles, jack rabbits, coons, and wild animals! . . . Keep out from under these feet, little bobwhites. . . . Keep the big wild hogs out of my path. Don't let none of

those come running my direction. I got a long way." Under her small black-freckled hand her cane, limber as a buggy whip, would switch at the brush as if to rouse up any hiding things.

4   On she went. The woods were deep and still. The sun made the pine needles almost too bright to look at, up where the wind rocked. The cones dropped as light as feathers. Down in the hollow was the mourning dove—it was not too late for him.

5   The path ran up a hill. "Seem like there is chains about my feet, time I get this far," she said, in the voice of argument old people keep to use with themselves. "Something always take a hold on this hill—pleads I should stay."

6   After she got to the top she turned and gave a full, severe look behind where she had come. "Up through pines," she said at length. "Now down through oaks."

7   Her eyes opened their widest and she started down gently. But before she got to the bottom of the hill a bush caught her dress.

8   Her fingers were busy and intent, but her skirts were full and long, so that before she could pull them free in one place they were caught in another. It was not possible to allow the dress to tear. "I in the thorny bush," she said. "Thorns, you doing your appointed work. Never want to let folks past—no sir. Old eyes thought you was a pretty little *green* bush."

9   Finally, trembling all over, she stood free, and after a moment dared to stoop for her cane.

10   "Sun so high!" she cried, leaning back and looking, while the thick tears went over her eyes. "The time getting all gone here."

11   At the foot of this hill was a place where a log was laid across the creek.

12   "Now comes the trial," said Phoenix.

13   Putting her right foot out, she mounted the log and shut her eyes. Lifting her skirt, leveling her cane fiercely before her, like a festival figure in some parade, she began to march across. Then she opened her eyes and she was safe on the other side.

14   "I wasn't as old as I thought," she said.

15   But she sat down to rest. She spread her skirts on the bank around her and folded her hands over her knees. Up above her was a tree in a pearly cloud of mistletoe. She did not dare to close her eyes, and when a little boy brought her a little plate with a slice of marble-cake on it she spoke to him. "That would be acceptable," she said. But when she went to take it there was just her own hand in the air.

16   So she left that tree, and had to go through a barbed-wire fence. There she had to creep and crawl, spreading her knees and stretching her fingers like a baby trying to climb the steps. But she talked loudly to herself: she could not let her dress be torn now, so late in the day,

and she could not pay for having her arm or her leg sawed off if she got caught fast where she was.

17   At last she was safe through the fence and risen up out in the clearing. Big dead trees, like black men with one arm, were standing in the purple stalks of the withered cotton field. There sat a buzzard.

18   "Who you watching?"

19   In the furrow she made her way along.

20   "Glad this not the season for bulls," she said, looking sideways, "and the good Lord made his snakes to curl up and sleep in the winter. A pleasure I don't see no two-headed snake coming around that tree, where it come once. It took a while to get by him, back in the summer."

21   She passed through the old cotton and went into a field of dead corn. It whispered and shook, and was taller than her head. "Through the maze now, she said, for there was no path.

22   Then there was something tall, black, and skinny there, moving before her.

23   At first she took it for a man. It could have been a man dancing in the field. But she stood still and listened, and it did not make a sound. It was as silent as a ghost.

24   "Ghost," she said sharply, "who be you the ghost of? For I have heard of nary death close by."

25   But there was no answer, only the ragged dancing in the wind.

26   She shut her eyes, reached out her hand, and touched a sleeve. She found a coat and inside that an emptiness, cold as ice.

27   "You scarecrow," she said. Her face lighted. "I ought to be shut up for good," she said with laughter. "My senses is gone. I too old. I the oldest people I ever know. Dance, old scarecrow," she said, "while I dancing with you."

28   She kicked her foot over the furrow, and with mouth drawn down shook her head once or twice in a little strutting way. Some husks blew down and whirled in streamers about her skirts.

29   Then she went on, parting her way from side to side with the cane, through the whispering field. At last she came to the end, to a wagon track, where the silver grass blew between the red ruts. The quail were walking around like pullets, seeming all dainty and unseen.

30   "Walk pretty," she said. "This is the easy place. This is the easy going."

31   She followed the track, swaying through the quiet bare fields, through the little strings of trees silver in their dead leaves, past cabins silver from weather, with the doors and windows boarded shut, all like old women under a spell sitting there. "I walking in their sleep," she said, nodding her head vigorously.

32   In a ravine she went where a spring was silently flowing through a hollow log. Old Phoenix bent and drank. "Sweetgum makes the water

sweet," she said, and drank more. "Nobody know who made this well, for it was here when I was born."

33   The track crossed a swampy part where the moss hung as white as lace from every limb. "Sleep on, alligators, and blow your bubbles." Then the track went into the road.

34   Deep, deep the road went down between the high green-colored banks. Overhead the live-oaks met, and it was as dark as a cave.

35   A black dog with a lolling tongue came up out of the weeds by the ditch. She was meditating, and not ready, and when he came at her she only hit him a little with her cane. Over she went in the ditch, like a little puff of milkweed.

36   Down there, her senses drifted away. A dream visited her, and she reached her hand up, but nothing reached down and gave her a pull. So she lay there and presently went to talking. "Old woman," she said to herself, "that black dog come up out of the weeds to stall you off, and now there he sitting on his fine tail, smiling at you."

37   A white man finally came along and found her—a hunter, a young man, with his dog on a chain.

38   "Well, Granny!" he laughed. "What are you doing there?"

39   "Lying on my back like a June-bug waiting to be turned over, mister," she said, reaching up her hand.

40   He lifted her up, gave her a swing in the air, and set her down, "Anything broken, Granny?"

41   "No sir, them old dead weeds is springy enough," said Phoenix, when she had got her breath. "I thank you for your trouble."

42   "Where do you live, Granny?" he asked, while the two dogs were growling at each other.

43   "Away back yonder, sir, behind the ridge. You can't even see it from here."

44   "On your way home?"

45   "No sir, I going to town."

46   "Why, that's too far! That's as far as I walk when I come out myself, and I get something for my trouble." He patted the stuffed bag he carried, and there hung down a little closed claw. It was one of the bobwhites, with its beak hooked bitterly to show it was dead. "Now you go on home, Granny!"

47   "I bound to go to town, mister," said Phoenix. "The time come around."

48   He gave another laugh, filling the whole landscape. "I know you colored people! Wouldn't miss going to town to see Santa Claus!"

49   But something held Old Phoenix very still. The deep lines in her face went into a fierce and different radiation. Without warning she had seen with her own eyes a flashing nickel fall out of the man's pocket on to the ground.

50   "How old are you, Granny?" he was saying.

51   "There is no telling, mister," she said, "no telling."

52   Then she gave a little cry and clapped her hands, and said, "Git on away from here, dog! Look! Look at that dog!" She laughed as if in admiration. "He ain't scared of nobody. He a big black dog." She whispered, "Sick him!"

53   "Watch me get rid of that cur," said the man. "Sick him, Pete! Sick him!"

54   Phoenix heard the dogs fighting and heard the man running and throwing sticks. She even heard a gunshot. But she was slowly bending forward by that time, further and further forward, the lids stretched down over her eyes, as if she were doing this in her sleep. Her chin was lowered almost to her knees. The yellow palm of her hand came out from the fold of her apron. Her fingers slid down and along the ground under the piece of money with the grace and care they would have in lifting an egg from under a sitting hen. Then she slowly straightened up, she stood erect, and the nickel was in her apron pocket. A bird flew by. Her lips moved. "God watching me the whole time. I come to stealing."

55   The man came back, and his own dog panted about them. "Well, I scared him off that time," he said, and then he laughed and lifted his gun and pointed it at Phoenix.

56   She stood straight and faced him.

57   "Doesn't the gun scare you?" he said, still pointing it.

58   "No sir, I seen plenty go off closer by, in my day, and for less than what I done," she said, holding utterly still.

59   He smiled, and shouldered the gun. "Well, Granny," he said, "you must be a hundred years old, and scared of nothing. I'd give you a dime if I had any money with me. But you take my advice and stay home, and nothing will happen to you."

60   "I bound to go on my way, mister," said Phoenix. She inclined her head in the red rag. Then they went in different directions, but she could hear the gun shooting again and again over the hill.

61   She walked on. The shadows hung from the oak trees to the road like curtains. Then she smelled wood-smoke, and smelled the river, and she saw a steeple and the cabins on their steep steps. Dozens of little black children whirled around her. There ahead was Natchez shining. Bells were ringing. She walked on.

62   In the paved city it was Christmas time. There were red and green electric lights strung and crisscrossed everywhere, and all turned on in the day time. Old Phoenix would have been lost if she had not distrusted her eyesight and depended on her feet to know where to take her.

63   She paused quietly on the sidewalk, where people were passing by. A lady came along in the crowd, carrying an armful of red-, green-, and silver-wrapped presents; she gave off perfume like the red roses in hot summer, and Phoenix stopped her.

64   "Please, missy, will you lace up my shoe?" She held up her foot.

65   "What do you want, Grandma?"

66   "See my shoe," said Phoenix. "Do all right for out in the country, but wouldn't look right to go in a big building."

67   "Stand still then, Grandma," said the lady. She put her packages down carefully on the sidewalk beside her and laced and tied both shoes tightly.

68   "Can't lace 'em with a cane," said Phoenix. "Thank you, missy. I doesn't mind asking a nice lady to tie up my shoes when I gets out on the street."

69   Moving slowly and from side to side, she went into the stone building and into a tower of steps, where she walked up and around and around until her feet knew to stop.

70   She entered a door, and there she saw nailed up on the wall the document that had been stamped with the gold seal and framed in the gold frame which matched the dream that was hung up in her head.

71   "Here I be," she said. There was a fixed and ceremonial stiffness over her body.

72   "A charity case, I suppose," said an attendant who sat at the desk before her.

73   But Phoenix only looked above her head. There was sweat on her face; the wrinkles shone like a bright net.

74   "Speak, up, Grandma," the woman said. "What's your name? We must have your history, you know. Have you been here before? What seems to be the trouble with you?"

75   Old Phoenix only gave a twitch to her face as if a fly were bothering her.

76   "Are you deaf?" cried the attendant.

77   But then the nurse came in.

78   "Oh, that's just old Aunt Phoenix," she said. "She doesn't come for herself—she has a little grandson. She makes these trips just as regular as clockwork. She lives away back off the Old Natchez Trace." She bent down. "Well, Aunt Phoenix, why don't you just take a seat? We won't keep you standing after your long trip." She pointed.

79   The old woman sat down, bolt upright in the chair.

80   "Now how is the boy?" asked the nurse.

81   Old Phoenix did not speak.

82   "I said, how is the boy?"

83   But Phoenix only waited and stared straight ahead, her face very solemn and withdrawn into rigidity.

84   "Is his throat any better?" asked the nurse. "Aunt Phoenix, don't you hear me? Is your grandson's throat any better since the last time you came for the medicine?"

85   With her hand on her knees, the old woman waited, silent, erect and motionless, just as if she were in armor.

86   "You mustn't take up our time this way, Aunt Phoenix," the nurse said. "Tell us quickly about your grandson, and get it over. He isn't dead, is he?"

87   At last there came a flicker and then a flame of comprehension across her face, and she spoke.

88   "My grandson. It was my memory had left me. There I sat and forgot why I made my long trip."

89   "Forgot?" The nurse frowned. "After you came so far?"

90   Then Phoenix was like an old woman begging a dignified forgiveness for waking up frightened in the night. "I never did go to school— I was too old at the Surrender," she said in a soft voice. "I'm an old woman without an education. It was my memory fail me. My little grandson, he is just the same, and I forgot it in the coming."

91   "Throat never heals, does it?" said the nurse, speaking in a loud, sure voice to Old Phoenix. By now she had a card with something written on it, a little list. "Yes. Swallowed lye. When was it—January— two—three years ago—"

92   Phoenix spoke unasked now. "No, missy, he not dead, he just the same. Every little while his throat begin to close up again, and he not able to swallow. He not get his breath. He not able to help himself. So the time come around, and I go on another trip for the soothing medicine."

93   "All right. The doctor said as long as you came to get it you could have it," said the nurse. "But it's an obstinate case."

94   "My little grandson, he sit up there in the house all wrapped up, waiting by himself," Phoenix went on. "We is the only two left in the world. He suffer and it don't seem to put him back at all. He got a sweet look. He going to last. He wear a little patch quilt and peep out, holding his mouth open like a little bird. I remembers so plain now. I not going to forget him again, no, the whole enduring time. I could tell him from all the others in creation."

95   "All right." The nurse was trying to hush her now. She brought her a bottle of medicine. "Charity," she said, making a check mark in a book.

96   Old Phoenix held the bottle close to her eyes and then carefully put in into her pocket.

97   "I thank you," she said.

98   "It's Christmas time, Grandma," said the attendant. "Could I give you a few pennies out of my purse?"

99   "Five pennies is a nickel," said Phoenix stiffly.

100   "Here's a nickel," said the attendant.

101   Phoenix rose carefully and held out her hand. She received the nickel and then fished the other nickel out of her pocket and laid it beside the new one. She stared at her palm closely, with her head on one side.

102   Then she gave a tap with her cane on the floor.

103   "This is what come to me to do," she said. "I going to the store and buy my child a little windmill they sells, made out of paper. He going to find it hard to believe there such a thing in the world. I'll march myself back where he waiting, holding it straight up in this hand."

104   She lifted her free hand, gave a little nod, turned round, and walked out of the doctor's office. Then her slow step began on the stairs, going down.

(3,382 words)

VOCABULARY

meditative (1)	maze (21)	lolling (35)
illuminated (2)	nary (24)	radiation (49)
bobwhites (3)	strutting (28)	ceremonial (71)
limber (3)	husks (28)	lye (91)
appointed (8)	pullets (29)	
furrow (19)	sweetgum (32)	

THE FACTS

1. In paragraph 1, to what piece of antique furniture is Phoenix Jackson's walk compared? What characteristic is Welty trying to get across? Where, later on in the narrative, is the same piece of furniture alluded to again? Why?

2. What is the purpose of the old woman's journey?

3. Essentially this is the story of a courageous woman. What part of the trip is especially difficult for her? How does she manage this obstacle?

4. What details indicate that Phoenix Jackson is slightly senile and therefore not always in touch with reality?

5. What excuse does the old woman offer for not remembering what errand she was on?

THE STRATEGIES

1. What kind of plot structure is the story based on? What is the conflict in the plot? When is the conflict resolved?

2. Analyze Phoenix's language. What is conveyed through her speech?

3. Point out some specific instances of humor. What kind of humor is it?

4. During what decade would you judge this story to have taken place? What clues to your answer are given in the story?

5. In paragraph 85 we read: "With her hand on her knees, the old woman waited, silent, erect and motionless, just as if she were in armor." What meaning do you attribute to this passage?

THE ISSUES

1. In Egyptian mythology the phoenix was a bird of great splendor that every five hundred years consumed itself by fire and rose renewed from its own ashes. In what way is Phoenix Jackson like this bird?

2. The narrative abounds in descriptive passages. What is the dominant impression in paragraph 2? Are any details included that do not support this impression? What other descriptive passages can you identify?

3. Why does Phoenix keep talking to herself? What do her monologues add to the total portrait of her?

4. What is the meaning of the episode in which Phoenix steals the nickel? Does the act offend our sense of honesty? Explain your answer.

5. What significance can you attach to the fact that the journey takes place at Christmas time?

6. Phoenix Jackson's journey is in the literary tradition of the mythological quest. What aspects of the story place it in that tradition?

SUGGESTIONS FOR WRITING

1. Using your imagination, describe Phoenix's journey home. Make your scenes descriptive by selecting details that support a dominant impression.

2. Write an essay comparing and contrasting Phoenix Jackson with the Pigeon Woman in the poem that follows.

▼▼▼

May Swenson

PIGEON WOMAN

MAY SWENSON (1919–1989) poet, playwright, and lecturer, was born in Logan, Utah, and educated at Utah State University. She resided in New York City until her death. She has published a number of collections of poetry including her latest, *New and Selected Things Taking Place* (1978).

The meaning of "Pigeon Woman" emerges from the irony contained in a strange old lady's fantasy.

Slate, or dirty-marble-colored,
or rusty-iron-colored, the pigeons
on the flagstones in front of the
Public Library make a sharp lake

5   into which the pigeon woman wades
at exactly 1:30. She wears a
plastic pink raincoat with a round
collar (looking like a little

girl, so gay) and flat gym shoes,
10   her hair square-cut, orange.
Wide-apart feet carefully enter
the spinning, crooning waves

(as if she'd just learned how
to walk, each step conscious,
15   an accomplishment); blue knots in the
calves of her bare legs (uglied marble),

age in angled cords of jaw
and neck, her pimento-colored hair,
hanging in thin tassels, is gray
20   around a balding crown.

The day-old bread drops down
from her veined hand dipping out
of a paper sack. Choppy, shadowy ripples
the pigeons strike around her legs.

25   Sack empty, she squats and seems to rinse
her hands in them—the rainy greens and
oily purples of their necks. Almost
they let her wet her thirsty fingertips—

30   but drain away in an untouchable tide.
A make-believe trade
she has come to, in her lostness
or illness or age—to treat the motley

35   city pigeons at 1:30 every day, in all
weathers. It is for them she colors
her own feathers. Ruddy-footed
on the lime-stained paving,

40   purling to meet her when she comes,
they are a lake of love. Retreating
from her hands as soon as empty,
they are the flints of love.

(266 words)

VOCABULARY

crooning	motley	flints
pimento	purling	

THE FACTS

1. What is the dominant impression conveyed by this "pigeon woman"? In terms of her looks, what role could she play in a fairy tale?

2. As the poem develops, how do our feelings change about the woman?

3. What is the fantasy that gives purpose to the woman's life? Describe it.

4. What is the meaning of the final stanza?

5. Is this woman an impossible figment of the poet's imagination, or does she represent a kind of reality? Comment.

THE STRATEGIES

1. How does the level of language used contribute to the description of the woman?

2. How do you explain the image of the pigeons as a lake?

3. What are the "blue knots in the/calves of her bare legs"? Comment on the effectiveness of this image.

4. What is the meaning of the metaphor "her own feathers" in the next-to-last stanza?

5. Interpret the metaphor "the flints of love" in the final line.

THE ISSUES

1. Various public, as well as private, agencies have been concerned with the plight of the poor, especially women who have been labeled "bag ladies," "crazy drifters," or "old female transients." What suggestions do you have for dealing with this alienated group of our population? Are we doing enough or should we do more?

2. What is it that keeps this woman from giving up on life? What do you consider the single most important driving force that keeps most people who lead desperate lives from committing suicide?

3. The woman in the poem chooses to feed a flock of pigeons. What other activities could give meaning to such a person's life?

4. How would you describe the male counterpart of the Pigeon Woman? Include the details of his appearance.

5. What measures do you suggest for reducing the number of street vagrants in our major cities?

SUGGESTIONS FOR WRITING

1. As vividly as possible, describe the relationship between a human being and an animal.

2. Imagine the loneliness that comes from being old and alone. Describe this loneliness in terms of specific, concrete details.

ADVICE

HOW TO WRITE A PROCESS ANALYSIS

An essay written to give instructions on how to do something or to describe how something was done is developed by process analysis. Many bestsellers have been written in this mode, all bearing such telltale how-to titles as *How to Make a Million in Real Estate* or *How to Learn Spanish the Easy Way.* Historians such as Will Durant also use process analysis to tell us how Spartan warriors were trained, how Christianity became the dominant religion of Western civilization, and how the Battle of Normandy was won.

Although process analysis is a simple rhetorical mode and fairly straightforward to write, it is often done badly and with irksome consequences. Anyone who has ever struggled to understand an inept manual meant to explain some necessary but practical chore can attest to the importance of clear process writing.

Select an Appropriate Subject

The first and most important step in writing a process essay is to select an appropriate subject. Decide whether your overall purpose is to give instructions or to inform. If you intend, say, to instruct readers in how to organize a volunteer team to nab graffiti writers or how to study for the new SAT exam, your purpose is to give instructions. On the other hand, if you want to describe the steps that led to the 1993 riots in Los Angeles or the pressures that forced Richard Nixon's resignation from the U.S. presidency, your purpose is to inform. In writing either kind of essay, you must know and be able to cite appropriate details.

State Your Purpose in a Clear Thesis

The second step in writing your process essay is to begin with a thesis that plainly states your overall aim. "It is possible for you to acquire a competitive spirit" is an example of a thesis that leaves your reader in the dark and is singularly unhelpful to you, the writer. On the other hand, the thesis, "You can acquire a competitive spirit by practicing five personality traits," establishes an agenda for the writer and tells the reader what to expect—a recital and description of five personality traits. Similarly, "I want to inform you how Juveniles are imprisoned," tells your reader practically nothing. Contrast it with this more helpful thesis, "Juveniles face four legal steps before they can be imprisoned."

Logically Organize the Sequence of Steps

Next, you should arrange the sequence of steps in the most logical order. Essays that cover simple how-to tasks such as changing a tire or baking a cake are best organized chronologically. On the other hand, essays on broader topics, such as how to build self-esteem in a child, make a marriage work, or how Stalin rose to power, are best organized in order of importance.

Regardless of which arrangement you use, you should single out and explain each step clearly. It often helps to sketch out the steps exactly as they will occur in your chosen order. For example, let us say that your parents won a court case against a landlord for discriminating against them because of their ethnic origin. Using your familiarity with their case, combined with further research, you decide to write a paper on how to file an anti-discrimination housing suit. Here are your steps, outlined chronologically:

1. File the complaint with the local Fair Housing Council.

2. Explain your reasons for filing to the investigator who hears your complaint.

3. If the investigation uncovers evidence of discrimination, state or federal authorities will formally accuse the landlord of discrimination. (If your case has no merit, the matter will probably fizzle out here.)

4. Choose between appearing before an administrative hearing officer or hiring an attorney to file a lawsuit in civil court.

5. The case will either be solved through a settlement or the state may impose a punitive fine to compensate for damages.

Once these steps have been clearly outlined, all you have to do is flesh out the essay with necessary facts and details.

Explain Everything

The devil is said to be in the details, and that is clearly where he (or she) lives in process essays. Always assume that your reader is completely dense about your subject. Explain everything. Don't call the same part a "thingamabob" here and a "thingamajig" there as is often done in maddeningly unhelpful manuals. If your essay is giving specific directions about how to do something, simply address the reader directly, as in a command: "Next, [you] take the paper and fold it along the dotted line. . . . Then, [you] write your personal number in the upper left-hand corner," and so on.

It also helps to carefully signal the succession of described steps through the use of words such as "first," second," "next," "then," "finally." Within each step, using words such as "before," "after," and "while" can help the reader keep track of the discussion. It might even be helpful to mention a previous step before going on to the next. For example, in a process essay about how juveniles are imprisoned, the first step might be for the police to bring the youth to a screening office. If so, you might introduce the second step this way, "If after the screening has taken place the case still cannot be informally resolved, the second step is to arrange a date for a court hearing."

As we said, process essays are usually straightforward and relatively simple to write. Most require no poetic or metaphoric language—a manual so written would drive consumers over the brink—and generally demand nothing more of a writer than a sensible grasp of facts and the ability to explain them in understandable sequence.

E X A M P L E S

Sir Arthur Grimble

SHARKS

SIR ARTHUR GRIMBLE (1888–1956) was a British Colonial government official and writer. After receiving an education from Magdalene College at Cambridge, he joined the Colonial Service in the Pacific and was posted to the Gilbert and Ellice Islands, where he remained in various positions until 1933. From 1933 to 1948 he worked as Administrator and then Governor of the Windward Islands, retiring from the Colonial service in 1948. It is while in retirement that he developed a talent for narrating his island experiences on radio for the British Broadcasting Corporation. The result was a series of talks that became so popular that they were brought out in published form under the title of *A Pattern of Islands* (1952)—from which the following excerpt was taken.

The narrative that follows is clearly autobiographical and should engross anyone who likes adventure. The descriptive scenes are so visual that it is no wonder the author's work was turned into a highly popular film in 1956. The best way to read the essay is to pretend you are on the scene when the fishermen are hunting for sharks. You will then experience what it means to outsmart one of nature's fiercest sea creatures.

1   There is a four-fathom bank of Tarawa lagoon where the tiger-shark muster in hundreds for a day or two every month. If you let your canoe drift offshore at rising tide, you can watch their great striped bodies sliding and swooping with arrogant ease not six feet under your keel. They range in length from nine to fourteen feet, with an occasional giant of seventeen or eighteen feet among them. There is nightmare in

the contrast between their hideous size and the slack grace of their movements in the glassy water. Their explosions out of quietude into action are even more atrocious. An evil shape comes gliding below you, smoothly, negligently, as if tranced in idleness; the next instant, one monstrous convulsion has flung it hurtling into attack.

2   In my earliest days at Tarawa, I spent a good deal of time watching the tigers there. I wanted to find out why, for a couple of days each month, they preferred that particular hunting-ground to a dozen others that seemed as good. Tigers always do cruise around banks where the smaller fish swarm, but not usually in hundreds. Any village fisherman could have told me the whole story in a few seconds, but I was new to the place, and the Gilbertese do not render up their knowledge easily to strangers. It was only by chance that I stumbled on the first clue. I happened to tell my cook-boy that I wanted to go trolling for trevally over the shark-grounds.

3   He smiled: "When the *rereba* (trevally) are there, the *tababa* (tiger-shark) also are there. If you hook a rereba you will end with a hot bottom, for the tababa will take it from you."

4   I paused to wonder what a hot bottom might be. "Sir," he replied, "it is the fisherman's word for the state of one who sits, and sits, and catches nothing, and behold! as it were, his bottom burns."

5   "And say now—if the tababa are there for the rereba, what are the rereba there for?"

6   "*Kai ngkam*," he replied, meaning anything from "I really couldn't say" to "I'm not sure I ought to tell you that."

7   But I had my clue. The inquiry that followed led me right back from the trevally in the four-fathom water, down through a gradually diminishing series of ravenous mouths to the shoreline.

8   The land in that part of Tarawa is cut by a tidal passage between lagoon and ocean. When the springs flood high through the passage, they bring riding in with them from outside a minute marine organism, which settles along the shallows. The weed, or animalcule, or plankton (I do not know which it is) makes tempting food for millions of tiny soft crabs that live on the water's edge. Great hosts of these, none much bigger than a sequin, are lured by the bait an inch or so deeper into the sea than they usually venture.

9   The next scene belongs to the teeming sardines. Perhaps they too have mustered in their millions because of the tide-borne food; or perhaps they know that the coming of the food spells crabs in the shallows. Whichever enticed them first, they remain for only one purpose. Their battalions, massed like silver clouds in the two-foot shoals, charge wave upon wave to the lip of the tide bent upon nothing but the massacre of crabs.

10   But sardines make just the food the grey mullet love best. The mullet have been massing for their own purposes a little farther out. If these

again are initially attracted by the floating food, they soon forget it. They plunge in among the sardines, a ravening army of one-pounders. The small fish twist and scatter wildly into open water, the bigger ones after them.

11   And that is why the vivid, blue backed trevally have come so close inshore. Their meat is mullet. They sweep to landward of their quarry and hunt them out to sea, devouring as they go. But alas for their strength and beauty! Engrossed in their chase, they drive straight for the bank where the tiger-shark are mustered. A sixty-pound trevally is a streak of azure lightning over the shining bottom. He can zig-zag in a flash and leap a man's height sheer from the sea to escape a close pursuer. No heavy-barrelled tiger-shark, hunting alone, is a match for his dazzling tactics. But for all his desperate twists and turns, his breachings and his soundings, he is lost where a hundred rushing jaws are above and below and around him.

12   Yet, in the last act, it is not the tigers that triumph. The ultimate destroyer in that chain of hungry bellies and ravening jaws is no creature of the sea but man himself, out after shark-flesh in those innocently smiling waters.

13   Thirty-five years ago, the Gilbertese were beginning to use steel hooks for shark-fishing; but there were many who still claimed that the old-style twelve-inch ironwood hook, trained to the right shape on the living tree, was the only thing for tiger-shark. A twig of the tree *(pemphis acidula)* was bent so that it recurved upon itself, and left to grow lashed in that position for a year or two. When it was rather more than half an inch thick, it was cut and fashioned for service. The outstanding virtue of this gigantic instrument was that it could be grown with magic, trained with magic, cut with magic, and trimmed with magic. Good luck for the fisherman and bad luck for the shark could be poured into it at every stage of its manufacture, whereas a steel hook bought from a trade-store could only be magicked once, as a finished article. According to the old men, nobody but folk ignorant of the proper spells would ever dream of using anything but ironwood.

14   A three-foot length of plaited hair from the head of the fisher's wife or daughter made the trace for an old-style hook, and the line was a coconut-fibre rope as thick as a man's forefinger. The shark-hunter was not out for sport; he wanted nothing but dead shark. His gaff was not a gaff, but a glorious club with a ten-pound rock for its head. And it was not for simple fun that he did his fishing from a canoe not much longer than a man; the basic reason was that he could not handle the line himself; if he did, the bite of any sizeable shark would snatch him flying into the sea. He had to make the line fast to the middle of his craft; and that spelt a small canoe, because the resistance of a big one to the first furious jerks of his catch would tear the hull apart.

15   I imagine the broad technique of it is still very much as it used to be in those days. The fisher paddles out in his cockleshell, baits his hook, whether ironwood or steel, with a couple of pounds of almost any kind of offal, lets it hang from amidships on two or three fathoms of line, and drifts waiting for a bite, his club beside him. A big one takes the hook. The quiet canoe gives a sudden lurch and starts careering round in mad little circles; or it bounces insanely up and down; or it zig-zags like a misdirected rocket; or it rushes off in a straight line, forwards or backwards as the case may be, at sizzling speed, the fisherman holding on grimly whatever it does. Half a dozen small craft milling around like that all at the same time, without visible means of propulsion, make a wildly eccentric sight from the shore. But the fury of a tiger-shark's struggles soon exhausts it. It floats limply to the surface and then comes the high moment of the fisherman's day. He hauls the spent brute cautiously alongside and, letting out one piercing howl of pleasure, cracks it on the nose with his trusty club. That is the only part of the business, I think, that affords him anything like the savage thrill that civilized sportsmen get out of killing things.

16   But although safety first is the rule when tiger-shark are about in numbers, plenty of Gilbertese are ready to fight a lone prowler in its own element. Owing to his great girth, a tiger cannot turn quickly; once launched on its attack, it thunders straight forward like a bull; there lies the hunter's advantage in single combat. Out sailing with a Tarawa friend one day, I pointed out a cruising dorsal fin. "That's a tababa," he said, "watch me kill him."

17   We lowered sail and drifted. He slid overboard with his knife and paddled around waiting to be noticed. He soon was. The fin began to circle him, and he knew he was being stalked; he trod water; it closed in gradually, lazily to fifteen yards.

18   He held his knife right-handed, blade down, the handle just above the water, his crooked right elbow pointed always towards the gliding fin. He would have a split second to act in when the charge came. It came from ten yards' range. There was a frothing swirl; the fin shot forward like an arrow; the head and shoulders of the brute broke surface, rolling as they lunged. My friend flicked aside in the last blink of time and shot his knife into the upswinging belly as it surged by. His enemy's momentum did the rest. I saw the belly rip itself open like a zip-fastener, discharging blood and guts. The tiger disappeared for a while, to float up dead a hundred yards off.

19   That kind of single combat used to be fairly common. It was rather like a nice score of fifty at cricket in England; the villagers applauded but did not make a great song about it. But the feat of Teriakai, another Tarawa man, became a matter of official record. Teriakai was a guest of His Majesty's at the time, having got himself into trouble for a rather too carefree interpretation of the marriage laws. He was an

exceptionally welcome guest; his vital, stocky frame was the equal of a giant's for work, and the bubbling of his unquenchable humour kept his warders as well as his fellow-prisoners laughing and labouring from morning to night. A happy prison is a tremendous asset to any Government Station. Whenever there was a special job to be done, he was the man we always chose to do it. It followed naturally that, when the captain and chief engineer of S.S. *Tokelau*—lying beached for cleaning in Tarawa lagoon —wanted to go out for a sail in weather that threatened to turn nasty, Teriakai went also to look after them.

20   The south-east trades* have their treacheries on the Equator. Though they breathe steady at twenty-five miles an hour for months on end, you can never afford to forget how suddenly the wind can slam round to the north and blow a forty-mile gale. If the northerly buster brakes your mainsail aback close-hauled to the south-easter you are capsized before you know what has hit you. The Tarawans call that particular wind Nei Bairara, the Long-armed Woman. She caught Teriakai and his friends just after they had put about for the homeward run. They were spilled into the lagoon ten miles from their starting point and eight miles from the nearest land on Tarawa's northern arm.

21   Two chief dangers threatened them then: tiger-shark were all around them, and they were near enough to the ocean reef to be sucked out to sea when the tide began to fall. Teriakai attended to the sharks first of all. He started by hacking the mainsail adrift with gaff and boom complete (His Majesty's guests are not supposed to carry sheath-knives, but he had one, bless his impertinence). The canvas, buoyed at head and foot by its spars, made a fine bag under water, into which he ushered the captain and engineer: "Stay inside this," he said, bridling their refuge by a length of halyard to the upturned boat, "and the tababa won't smell you." Then he looked for the anchor. The chain had fortunately been made fast to a thwart, but it took him an hour of diving and groping to get everything unsnarled so that the anchor reached bottom. "I'll go and get help now," he said when that was done: "If I can get past those tababa, we shall perhaps be meeting again."

22   He swam straight at the ring of tigers—the captain and engineer watched him—and the devils let him through. I asked him afterwards if he had any notion why. He replied, "If you stay still in the sea, the tababa will charge you. If you swim away from them in fear, they will smell your fear and chase you. If you swim without fear towards them, they will be afraid and leave you in peace." So he chose his shark, swam full speed towards it, and lo! the line melted away before him. There was absolutely nothing to it except a courage that passes belief.

---

* Trade winds.

23   He had gone about four miles before anything else happened. I have an idea it need not have happened at all unless he had wanted it to. He said the next tababa just attacked him, but he never could explain for laughing why he trod water and waited for this one instead of trying to shoo it off like the others. It is a good guess that he was overcome by the thrill of wearing a sheath-knife again and the delight of feeling himself, after months of prison, alone and free for a little in his loved lagoon. Then again, the tababa was a male. I do not know how males and females are distinguished from a distance, but the Gilbertese fishermen knew, and they valued the genital organ of a bull-tiger very highly. They said a man who had the right magic could appropriate its virile qualities to his own unspeakable advantage as a squire of dames. Teriakai made a nice job of the tababa, extracted the priceless organ from its ventral slot, tucked it into his belt, and swam on.

24   The swift night of the equator fell on him in the next half-hour. The moon was not yet up, repeated busters from the north were whipping the water to fury. In the welter of waves about his head, he missed his direction and swam into a maze of reefs off the coast to left of his objective. The breaking seas flung him on cruel edges, rolled him over splintering coral branches, sucked him into clefts bristling with barbs, spewed him out again stabbed and torn until more than a quarter of the skin (so the doctor reported) was flayed from his body. But he got through still conscious, swam a mile to shore, waded and walked two more to a white trader's house, and collapsed on his verandah. The trader brought him around with a tot of rum, but refused to take his boat out to the rescue on a night like that.

25   Teriakai's answer was better than words. He grabbed the bottle of rum (forbidden by law to natives) from the man's hand and ran with it out into the night. He had another five miles to struggle to the next trader's house; I doubt if even his gay courage could have made it but for the liquor. In any case, it would be pettifogging to carp at the good cheer of his arrival. He awoke Jimmy Anton with a stentorian song about tababa, and himself, and girls, and capsized white men, beating time for himself on the front door with whangs of the thing he had cut from the shark. In his left hand was an empty rum bottle. He streamed blood from head to ankles, but a smile of pure rapture shone through the torn mask of his face.

26   Jimmy Anton, the son of an Austrian father and a Gilbertese mother, was not the man to refuse a risk either for himself or his boat. He called out his Gilbertese wife, and between the three of them they got the boat launched at once. His wife brought coconut oil for Teriakai's wounds, blankets and brandy for the rescued. They set out together. The moon had risen by then. They found the capsized boat just before dawn. The captain and engineer had been in the water twelve

hours, but they were still safe inside their canvas bag. Teriakai was awarded the bronze medal of the Royal Humane Society. Before that arrived he had acquired a uniform to wear it on, for we discharged him from prison at once and made a colony policeman of him. Nobody ever found out what he did with the trophy the shark gave him. It disappeared from official ken the moment we got him into hospital.

(2,864 words)

VOCABULARY

fathom (1)	breachings (11)	thwart (21)
muster (1)	soundings (11)	flayed (24)
atrocious (1)	gaff (14)	pettifogging (25)
trolling (2)	offal (15)	stentorian (25)
battalions (9)	careering (15)	ken (26)
ravening (10)	dorsal (16)	

THE FACTS

1. What is the Gilbertese name for tiger shark?

2. While the sharks kill the trevally, who triumphs over the shark?

3. What is the traditional Gilbertese instrument for catching tiger sharks? What reputation of superiority did this traditional instrument have?

4. What technique did the Gilbertese fishermen use to kill the tiger shark?

5. What does the author mean when he says that Teriakai was "a guest of His Majesty"? Why was he a guest?

6. What strategy did Teriakai use to avoid being attacked by the tiger sharks in the lagoon? What was the result?

THE STRATEGIES

1. To what kind of reader would this essay about tiger sharks appeal most? Why?

2. How does the author keep his readers from getting bored?

3. What is the effect of the many Gilbertese words used in the essay?

4. From what point of view is the narration told? What does this point of view contribute to the essay?

5. Why do you think the author included the incident in which Teriakai cut off the bull tiger shark's genital organ and tucked it into his belt?

THE ISSUES

1. Why does the author allude to "the nightmare" that comes from the contrast between the shark's graceful movements and its monstrous size? What is the nightmare?

2. What would happen in the United States if the adventures described in this essay were to be publicized?

3. What does the way Teriakai was treated after his swim among the tigers tell us about the Gilbertese sense of heroism? What kind of male do they admire?

4. According to this essay, how is the balance of nature preserved in the ocean? What do you believe to be humanity's role in this matter?

5. In paragraph 15, the author refers to "the savage thrill that civilized sportsmen get out of killing things." Do you agree with this comment? What should society do about the thrill human beings get out of killing things?

SUGGESTIONS FOR WRITING

1. Describe any process that deals with catching animals. Be sure to proceed step by step.

2. Write an essay in which you either attack or defend the killing of sharks.

▼▼▼

Consumer Reports

USED CARS: FINDING A GOOD BUY

This article, which appeared in April 1993, was written by the editors of *Consumer Reports.*

At one time or another, most of us have shopped for a used car, sometimes with good luck, sometimes with woeful consequences. Using the step-by-step method characteristic of a process essay, this article systematically tells us how to buy a used car—what to look for, where to shop, and how to bargain with the seller.

1   In a perfect world, all of us would drive out of the showroom in the car of our dreams, spanking new and outfitted with an ironclad guarantee. But in this imperfect world, where a driver with a merely modest dream can spend $20,000, many of us opt for a used model. If it's not the car of our dreams, we hope at least that it's not the car of our nightmares.

2   Buying a used car can make economic sense even when you look beyond the saving in price. New cars depreciate fairly rapidly, losing half or more of their value during their first three years. Thus, a 1990 model that sold originally for $18,000 might be worth less than $9000 today, if it's in reasonably good condition. If the car stays in decent shape, its future rate of depreciation should slow markedly, so it will hold its value.

3   On the other hand, used-car buyers lack some of the assurances enjoyed by new-car buyers. Warranties are skimpy, if available at all. The goods themselves may have been abused, not merely used. Finding out how much a car has suffered usually entails a good bit more than the proverbial kick in the tires.

What to Consider

4   Conservative models—small and midsized sedans, in particular—generally provide the best used-car values. Station wagons, especially those in the lower trim lines, may also be a sensible buy. Such practical styles are most likely to have been driven responsibly and maintained prudently during their first tour of ownership.

5   Luxury and sporty models, on the other hand, may not deliver value commensurate with their cachet. Part of the high price of luxury models covers appointments that may lose appeal as they age. When

power windows, mirrors, antennas, and door locks fail, they can be expensive to fix. Sporty cars often command premium prices, chiefly for the fun of driving them hard. But by the time a second owner gets behind the wheel, the days of carefree, repair-free fun may be numbered.

6   Whatever your taste in vehicles, you can increase your chances of satisfaction by choosing a model that has proved reliable in the past. We've analyzed our readers' experiences with more than a half-million cars, trucks, and vans to create the lists of good and bad bets for 1987 to 1991 models.

Where to Shop

7 Among the most trustworthy sources of younger used cars are franchised new-car dealers. Typically, they draw a fair portion of their used stock from late-model tradeins—some of which they sold originally and then maintained. Dealerships often provide a warranty on the used cars they sell, and they have the service facilities to back it up. Further, they usually have a reputation to protect, and want to stay in your good graces. Although those are all good reasons to buy from a new-car dealer, they also explain why such dealers are apt to charge more for used cars than other sellers do.

8   You'll probably find lower prices at independent used-car lots, especially low-overhead operations without repair facilities. But their inventory is likely to be less savory, perhaps consisting of rejects from new-car dealers or weary specimens from wholesale auctions or from police or taxi fleets. The most responsible independent dealers may be established neighborhood service stations that sell used cars as a sideline. Like new-car dealers, they can draw from stock they've serviced, and they have a reputation to preserve. In any case, choose an independent dealer that has been at the same location for a while; shady operators tend to move often.

9   The Federal Trade Commission requires that every used car sold by a dealer have a "Buyer's Guide" label, containing warranty information, on one of its windows. Examine the label closely for the words "as is." They constitute a denial of warranty coverage, except in Connecticut, Massachusetts, Minnesota, New York, and Rhode Island, where dealers must warrant all but their oldest and cheapest cars.

10   Banks and other lenders may enter the used-car business from time to time, but their repossessed goods can't be counted on to have received the best of care.

11   Consider, finally, a private sale.

12   Because private sellers needn't worry about markup and have essentially no overhead, their prices should be lower than a dealer's. However, they're not going to give you a written guarantee, and you can't expect help from them if the car goes on the fritz. You may be on

slightly surer ground if you buy the car from a relative, friend, or neighbor and know its history. But then you have to be careful that the transaction doesn't strain a valued relationship. And, as with any private-car purchase, you'll have to handle the registration paperwork yourself.

What to Examine First

13   To assess the basic condition of a used car, you don't have to be a mechanic, but it helps to bring along a knowledgeable friend. Before you begin your inspection, ask the seller to show you service and repair bills. At the very least, look for a sticker on a door jamb or look in the warranty booklet, to see if the car has been maintained regularly. Our Frequency-of-Repair charts, beginning on page xxx, can give you an idea of the kinds of problems that owners have reported in the past.

14   Start looking at the car, piece by piece, for potential trouble spots.

15   Fluid levels and leaks. If the car has an automatic transmission, check the transmission fluid. It should be a healthy pink, not brown, and it shouldn't have a burnt smell. With the engine cold, examine the coolant in the radiator to make sure it isn't rusty. Look for greenish stains on the radiator, a sign of pinhole-sized leaks, and for oil spots around the engine, which can indicate leaks in the valve-cover gaskets and other engine parts.

16   Examine the pavement under the car for fresh stains or puddles. Try also to look at the car's undercarriage. Although wet, oily residue originating from above could indicate merely a loose gasket, it could also foretell engine or transmission problems.

17   Body integrity. Rust lurking beneath blistered or peeling paint can not only destroy a car's looks; if allowed to eat through the car or trunk floor, it can let in lethal exhaust fumes. (Ideally, a state inspection would catch the damage before it reached that stage, however.) If left unchecked elsewhere, rust can eventually compromise the structural integrity of the car's body and suspension. The wheel wells and the rocker panels under the doors are especially vulnerable to rust.

18   If you suspect that a car may have been in an accident, check the underbody for new welds and surfaces discolored by heat. Other signs of accident repair are ripply body work, panels whose color doesn't quite match the paint on the rest of the car, and doors that sag or don't close properly. On older vehicles, a fresh undercoating or paint job may hint of something to hide.

19   Tires. A car with fewer than 25,000 miles on its odometer should have its original tires, with some useful tread still on them. If the tires are bald—or new, for that matter—it may mean that the odometer has been turned back (a violation of Federal law, if it can be proved). Uneven tire wear may signal accident damage or simply improper wheel

alignment (something, in any event, to investigate further). Look at the spare tire and make sure that it comes with a decent jack and lug wrench. And while you're rooting around in the trunk, check for water stains and musty odors that can signify water leakage.

20   Suspension. Grab the top of each front tire and try to tug it back and forth. If you feel play in it or hear a clunking sound, the wheel bearings or suspension joints may be nearly shot. Next, try to bounce the car by pushing down hard on each corner and letting go suddenly. If the car keeps bouncing instead of leveling, the shock absorbers or struts could be badly worn. Finally, on level ground, stand about 10 feet behind the car and then 10 feet to the side, to see whether one part of the car is lower than the rest. A lopsided car may need new springs.

21   Interior. Test the seats for comfort. They should be firm, not saggy, and free of rips. Again, a musty odor may indicate leaks. Examine the pedals. Badly worn pedal pads—or brand-new ones—may cast doubt on the odometer's reading.

22   Check out the safety belts and all the controls and accessories. Have your helper, if you have one, stand outside to verify that exterior lights work properly.

What to Check on the Road

23   If you're still interested in the car, ask to take it for a test drive. Spend at least half an hour driving at various speeds on various roads. Along the way, check out all the important systems.

24   Steering. Before you turn on the ignition, unlock the steering wheel and start turning it. You should feel no more than two inches of play. During the course of the drive, be aware of the steering characteristics. The car should hold the road nicely, and steering should be smooth and precise, without much vibration. If the car constantly tends to pull to one side, the wheels may need aligning or a tire may be underinflated or defective. Fixing those problems is no big deal. On the other hand, the car may have been in an accident. Fixing that kind of problem is a very big deal.

25   If a friend is with you, there's a simple way to determine whether the car's waywardness results from a serious problem. Stop in an untraveled area and have your friend kneel behind the car as you drive it slowly straight ahead—through a puddle, if possible—to mark the path of the tires. If the car's path looks normal, it's likely that the wheels aren't properly aligned. But if the car seems to move sideways, like a crab, and its rear tires don't follow in the track of its front tires, the body or frame has been bent. Start looking for another car.

26   Engine. How easily does the car start? Does it accelerate without bucking or other complaint? Can it keep up with traffic, without pinging, when it's going up grades in top gear? An engine that pings when

you accelerate may simply need higher-octane fuel or a tune-up. But if you hear knocking even when the car is idling, the problem may lie elsewhere and may be more expensive to fix.

27   After driving awhile at highway speeds, take your foot off the accelerator for a few seconds and glance at the rear-view mirror for a reaction from the car's exhaust. Blue smoke indicates burning oil, a warning of expensive engine repairs. Billowy white smoke, especially on a warm day, may indicate that coolant is getting into the combustion chambers, possibly through a blown head gasket or cracks in the engine block or cylinder heads. The remedy in those cases is also very expensive. Note, though, that it's normal for white vapor to puff from the exhaust pipe when a car is started in cold weather. And black smoke usually means only that the fuel system needs adjustment.

28   Transmission. With an automatic transmission, you want the shifting to work smoothly and quietly. But you don't want to confuse smoothness with slippage, indicated by a hesitation between the engine's acceleration and the car's. That's an almost sure sign of transmission wear. Similar impressions apply in evaluating a manual transmission. The car should shift easily, without bucking or jerking, but the shifting shouldn't be so smooth that the clutch doesn't engage fully until the pedal is nearly all the way up. If the pedal doesn't have at least an inch or so of play at the top of its travel, the car may soon need a new clutch.

29   Brakes. On an empty stretch of road, at a speed of about 45 mph, apply the brakes firmly but without locking the wheels. Repeat that exercise twice. The car should continue to stop quickly, evenly, and in a straight line. Unless the car is equipped with antilock brakes, you shouldn't feel the pedal vibrate underfoot.

30   Now stop at the side of the road and, with the engine idling, step firmly on the brake pedal for about 30 seconds. If it feels spongy or keeps sinking to the floor, there may be a leak in the brake system.

31   Exhaust. When the car is stopped and idling, get out and listen. Sputtering or rumbling sounds from underneath the car may serve notice of leaks in the exhaust pipe, manifold, muffler, or catalytic converter. Replacing any of those components, especially the catalytic converter, can be costly.

32   Comfort and quiet. Drive at 30 to 40 mph over a bumpy road. If the car seems to bounce more than it should or hop from side to side, there may be suspension problems. Rattles and squeaks are annoyances you'll probably have to tolerate; they're notoriously hard to trace and fix.

Closing Advice

33   If you're still impressed with the car, ask a trustworthy mechanic to check it, too. Get a written estimate of projected repairs, which can

give you a bargaining point in discussions over price. And in those discussions, try to quell your enthusiasm and impatience.

34   When it's time to talk price, there are several used-car guides available in most libraries. However, their prices may represent simply a starting point for dealers. A convenient source for prices at which cars are actually selling in your part of the country is the Consumer Reports Used Car Price Service, which quotes prices over the phone. You'll need basic facts about the car you want: mileage, model name or number, year, number of cylinders, options, and condition. Given those facts, the service will state a purchase price and, for many models, will provide information on the model's reliability. The number is 900 446–0500. Each call costs $1.75 a minute and is likely to take at least five minutes.

(2,422 words)

VOCABULARY

commensurate (5)   savory (8)   quell (33)
cachet (5)   waywardness (25)

THE FACTS

1. Why does buying a used car make good economic sense?

2. What models of used cars are generally the best buys? Why?

3. Why are new-car dealers likely to charge higher prices for used cars than are other sellers?

4. Aside from a new-car dealer and an independent used car lot, what outlet is likely to be a responsible source of used cars? Why?

5. What are the benefits of buying a used car from a private seller? What are the risks?

THE STRATEGIES

1. What logic underlies the suggested sequence of actions for checking the road-worthiness of a used car?

2. What transition technique do the authors use that is not available to the student writer? How could a student writer compensate for the lack of this technique?

3. What major assumption about buying a used car is an implicit premise behind the practical advice given in this article?

4. The authors write in paragraph 12, "However, they're not going to give you a written guarantee, and you can't expect help from them if the car goes on the fritz." What is the meaning of that phrase, "goes on the fritz"? Why would such a phrase generally be regarded as unsuitable for a freshman essay?

5. What function in the article do paragraphs 11 and 14 have in common?

THE ISSUES

1. What common stereotypes is a shopper likely to encounter when he or she inquires about the ownership history of a used car?

2. What image does the phrase "used-car salesman" usually conjure up in the popular consciousness? How true have you found this image to be?

3. What, in your opinion, should an ethical person be prepared to disclose about the history and condition of a used car he or she is trying to sell?

4. What part, if any, should government regulation play in the private sale of used cars?

5. In negotiating to buy a used car from a private seller, aside from assessing the condition of the car itself, what other assessment should the smart buyer be making?

SUGGESTIONS FOR WRITING

1. Write an essay describing the process you personally used in buying a used car and the kind of vehicle you ended up with.

2. Write an essay on the common popular stereotypes attached to used car salespeople.

▼▼

Jane Elizabeth Lemke

AN OPEN WINDOW ON MY PRIVATE WORLD

JANE ELIZABETH LEMKE is a short story writer who, for the last fifteen years, has chosen to live in a remote area on one of the gulf islands off the coast of British Columbia. She believes that this kind of isolation is necessary for the renewal of her spirit and to inspire creative thoughts.

The breath-taking beauty of the view from the author's little cottage is vividly described in terms of billowy clouds, rippling waterways, and intensely green flora. Her day is filled with the simple chores required by her reclusive life.

1   This morning it was a fresh ocean breeze that woke me, blowing softly through the lace curtains on the half-opened window. Occasionally, in the winter, it's barking sea lions. But generally, nothing in particular wakes me. Most sounds here are no louder than the soft cry of a sea gull or the rain pelting its monotonous lullaby onto the shingled roof. And so I slip into consciousness gently, stretching, turning over in my warm, down nest, letting my dreams slowly disperse to make way for another day of reality. Out of bed I put on my robe, open the curtains to see what kind of day Gaia[1] has given us, and then, always slightly amazed to see that the world is still here and everything still in its place, I go to the kitchen and begin my day.

2   As an impecunious writer who will do just about anything, anywhere, to be able to write, I have made my home in a 17-foot-square converted summer cottage on one of the gulf islands off the coast of British Columbia. I have an outhouse for a toilet, a wood-burning stove, and a rain-collecting cistern to provide me with water.

3   My cottage sits at the end of a mile-long dirt road and faces a tiny cove whose waters lap not 30 feet from my typewriter. The cove mostly empties at low tide, exposing a sandbar; at high tide it fills completely, like a fjord, leaving no beach at all. Surrounding everything is a thick, tranquil forest of evergreen conifers. Below, the ground is covered by a lush tangle of bushes, berries, and wildflowers.

4   My tiny home has three rooms: a living room and office combined in a glass-enclosed porch, a kitchen, and a bedroom. Pale-green carpet

---

[1] Greek goddess of the earth.

covers the floor, and periwinkle-blue curtains set off the Victorian wallpaper. There are books everywhere. And oil lamps for light when the power goes.

5   At first I didn't think I could ever get used to this small place. Or to an outhouse. And no bathtub. I wasn't raised like this. But by spending mornings at my desk, surrounded by windowpane, my office expands by hundreds of feet and I forget how cramped it is behind me.

6   In May, spring fills my picture windows with the pastel greens of mosses and new growth, with the pink of wild tulips and the lavender of lilac, with the blues of the ocean and the sky, with billowing white clouds that hover above the trees just as they did in the hot Minnesota summers of my childhood. On sunny days there are brushstrokes of diamond dust painted right across the rippling water that just about knock my eyes out.

7   Some might assume this magnificent view would prove far too distracting for work. But the contrary is true: Such intense beauty is my buffer against the distractions of the outside world.

8   With the exception of the one day a week that I trek by bicycle and ferry to the big island for supplies (I don't have a car), I work every morning until about noon. Afternoons are a mix of play and chores. I might explore one of the beaches, read, write letters, sew. And spend time looking at it all. The island is full of wildlife, and I feel compelled to pay close attention. It is a breeding ground for bald eagles. Sometimes as many as a few dozen will be fishing or gliding or resting in the trees. Killer whales, sea lions, and river otters also pay the occasional visit.

9   Some afternoons I bike through the woods to the general store for butter, day-old bread, or a newspaper. And on rainy afternoons a walk through the forest is like stepping into an Eliot Porter[2] photograph: close and gray, filled with the intense green and dark brown of soaked trees, smelling of fresh, potent earth, and glistening with raindrops clinging to wildrose leaves.

10   One of the delights of living in a place like this is that you get to know so many of the locals. Occasionally the three little girls who live up the road come for a visit. I give them a drawing lesson, or we have a tea party, or they try on all my jewelry. Often we wade into the bay to turn over stones and look for crabs, or go on expeditions along the wooded paths.

11   During the rainless summer months I must buy water; the man who delivers it is a lusty, bearded German. One day, sitting in the sun drinking tea, we discussed why neither of us had yet married. "Most women are looking for Prince Charming, wanting men to do everything for them," he said. "Most men," I replied, "are looking for

---

[2] Contemporary American landscape photographer.

Princess Charming, wanting women who will let them do everything." He grinned: "That makes us pretty equal." "Yes," I said, "it does." We have become lovely friends.

12   Not the least of my afternoon activities is the omnipresent task of cutting firewood. My stove consumes more than half a cord each month. At first I relied on others to cut it for me, but that proved too unreliable. So I bought myself a chain saw. And it wasn't long before I realized how good it felt to be so self-sufficient. Cutting is heavy, dirty, tiring work, so after a few hours it is with welcome relief that I wash up, pick out splinters, nestle into my velour bathrobe, make a cup of Earl Grey tea, collapse onto the sofa, and listen to the wind rustle through the trees. If it is summer, I often go for a swim in the cove, where mostly I am alone. Floating aimlessly on my air mattress, I often wonder if, as I approach mid-life, my existence ought to be somewhat more luxurious. But then I remember my favorite Buddhist saying: "Before enlightenment, chop wood and carry water. After enlightenment, chop wood and carry water."

13   I try to finish with chores and people and dinner by 6:30 so I can get back to my writing. But during summers here there are incredibly sensuous sunsets, so work gives way to a wonderful light show as I sit at water's edge to watch. The sky and ocean merge into a shimmering quilt of lilac, carnelian, turquoise, indigo, and jade-black satin until the star-flecked curtain of deepest navy moves in from the east.

14   On the hottest nights I often play Gregorian chants on the stereo, move one of the speakers to the porch, and listen while I lie on a blanket in the yard and look up past the black velvet cutouts of treetops, past the 600-odd orbiting satellites and pieces of garbage, past our own solar system, and peer right out into the middle of the galaxy. I watch tiny bat wings flutter across the moon, listen to the tinkling bell buoy a mile offshore, and smell the incoming sea as it laps thickly against the rocks. And all the while, swirling around me as I lie there like a rooted plant, are my travels, my writings, my romances, and my dreams. I feel so whole living here.

15   During cozy nights when the rain is pouring noisily onto the roof like so many tap-dancing night creatures, I'll snuggle under my afghan on the sofa and read mysteries. Sometimes I make popcorn or chocolate chip cookies. I write in my diary, play Handel's Coronation Anthems at full volume, dance to jazz.

16   Then about midnight, when the picture windows have turned to glass blackboards scrubbed clean and ready for my upcoming night's dreams, I take my sponge bath at the kitchen sink and go to bed. But not before I make one last trip to the outhouse. And this, like so much else of my life here, is often touched by the unexpected.

17   Last New Year's Eve, for example. Moonbeams bathed the yard in an ethereal glow as I made my way out to look at the sky for the last

time that day. I checked for supernovas and UFOs and kept track of Venus. Then I sat in that little nook—leaving the door open so I could watch the shadows—thinking about the primevalness of my life. And as I sat, midnight occurred. In the distance I could hear clanging bells and a few gunshots—and suddenly, right out of the dark, the sound of bagpipes from the cliff across the cove. "Amazing Grace" filled the night air. I knew it was Neil, doing what he does every New Year's Eve. He is a Scot and takes such tradition very seriously. I envisioned him standing there, facing the slumbering ocean, proudly piping in a new year, leading us into our future, into yet another revolution around the sun.

18   The ancient sound of those pipes stopped time as I sat there in the forest, in the midst of the whole of human history, there with all the others who have passed this way, looking up at those same stars, keeping their eyes on Venus.

19   The moment passed. It grew quiet again, and I went back to the cottage. Then, with one last look around, I shut down the stove, slipped under my quilt, reached over and turned off the light.

20   And thus ended another of my days—my very beautiful, whole days—here at the beach, living in the country.

(1,598 words)

VOCABULARY

impecunious (2)	carnelian (13)	UFO's (17)
fjord (3)	indigo (13)	primevalness (17)
conifers (3)	Gregorian (14)	
sensuous (13)	supernovas (17)	

THE FACTS

1. Where does the author live? Why did she decide to make her home there?

2. At the beginning of her move, why was the author fearful that she might not be able to adjust to her new surroundings?

3. How does the author make up for her cramped living quarters?

4. Who are some of the people who keep the author company in her isolated environment?

5. What feeling does cutting her own firewood give the author? Why?

THE STRATEGIES

1. How is the title of this essay relevant to its content?

2. In what way is this a process analysis? How are the steps divided? List them all. Is the purpose directional or informational?

3. What characteristics, if any, of the author's style appeal to you? Why?

4. What figure of speech does the author use in paragraph 9? What is its effect?

5. What role does the final sentence play in the essay? How effective is it? Use your imagination to compose a different ending and share it with the class. How is your ending different from that of the author?

THE ISSUES

1. To be truly great, is it important that writers be poor and live in isolation? Or should they be rich so that they need not worry about money and can freely concentrate on their art? Give reasons for your answer.

2. What is your opinion of the author's cutting her own firewood? Do you believe she was being environmentally responsible, or do you believe she should not have contributed to the deforestation danger? What alternative for heating, if any, can you suggest?

3. What are the advantages of writing in an environment of complete solitude? What are the advantages of writing in an environment where company is available? Which of the two environments would work best for you? Give reasons for your choice.

4. What philosophic musings might the episode about Neil, the Scottish bagpiper, engender? If they caused some in you, what were they?

5. What is your interpretation of the Buddhist saying "Before enlightenment, chop wood and carry water. After enlightenment, chop wood and carry water" (see paragraph 12)?

SUGGESTIONS FOR WRITING

1. Write a process analysis of one of the best days of your life, starting in the morning when you got up and leading the reader step-by-step through the day until you retired for sleep. Using Lemke as a model, try to divide your day into major steps, avoiding silly or insignificant details.

2. Imagining yourself in some kind of job ten years from now, write a process analysis of a typical day in your life. The process should provide your reader with a genuine feeling of how your day passes.

▼▼▼

Donald Barthelme

SOME OF US HAD BEEN THREATENING
OUR FRIEND COLBY

DONALD BARTHELME (1933–1990) was an American fiction writer who belongs to that modern group who, like Kafka, could no longer reflect society in realistic stories, but reached beyond realism to fantasy and surrealistic situations to capture the absurdity of society and its values. His stories are packed with parodies of advertising jargon, cocktail talk, and plain silliness. Born in Texas, Barthelme lived for several years in New York City, but later moved back to Texas, where he taught at the University of Houston. Among his best-known works are the novel *Snow White* (1967), and the following short story collections: *Unspeakable Practices, Unnatural Acts* (1968), *City Life* (1970), and *Sadness* (1972).

> *The story that follows receives its quixotic sense and mood from the fact that we never find out how Colby had "gone too far" nor what he did to be punished so severely. Yet, as we puzzle over the events that unfold, we also begin to realize in horror that many common American values and traditions are threaded throughout the acts this community contemplates and performs.*

1   Some of us had been threatening our friend Colby for a long time, because of the way he had been behaving. And now he'd gone too far, so we decided to hang him. Colby argued that just because he had gone too far (he did not deny that he had gone too far) did not mean that he should be subjected to hanging. Going too far, he said, was something everybody did sometimes. We didn't pay much attention to this argument. We asked him what sort of music he would like played at the hanging. He said he'd think about it but it would take him a while to decide. I pointed out that we'd have to know soon, because Howard, who is a conductor, would have to hire and rehearse the musicians and he couldn't begin until he knew what the music was going to be. Colby said he'd always been fond of Ives' Fourth Symphony. Howard said that this was a "delaying tactic" and that everybody knew that Ives was almost impossible to perform and would involve weeks of rehearsal, and

that the size of the orchestra and chorus would put us way over the music budget. "Be reasonable," he said to Colby. Colby said he'd try to think of something a little less exacting.

2   Hugh was worried about the wording of the invitations. What if one of them fell into the hands of the authorities? Hanging Colby was doubtless against the law, and if the authorities learned in advance what the plan was they would very likely come in and try to mess everything up. I said that although hanging Colby was almost certainly against the law, we had a perfect *moral* right to do so because he was *our* friend, *belonged* to us in various important senses, and he had after all gone too far. We agreed that the invitations would be worded in such a way that the person invited could not know for sure what he was being invited to. We decided to refer to the event as "An Event Involving Mr. Colby Williams." A handsome script was selected from a catalogue and we picked a cream-colored paper. Magnus said he'd see to having the invitations printed, and wondered whether we should serve drinks. Colby said he thought drinks would be nice but was worried about the expense. We told him kindly that the expense didn't matter, that we were after all his dear friends and if a group of his dear friends couldn't get together and do the thing with a little bit of *éclat,** why, what was the world coming to? Colby asked if he would be able to have drinks, too, before the event. We said, "Certainly."

3   The next item of business was the gibbet. None of us knew too much about gibbet design, but Tomás, who is an architect, said he'd look it up in old books and draw the plans. The important thing, as far as he recollected, was that the trapdoor function perfectly. He said that just roughly, counting labor and materials, it shouldn't run us more than four hundred dollars. "Good God!" Howard said. He said what was Tomás figuring on, rosewood? No, just a good grade of pine, Tomás said. Victor asked if unpainted pine wouldn't look kind of "raw," and Tomás replied that he thought it could be stained a dark walnut without too much trouble.

4   I said that although I thought the whole thing ought to be done really well, and all, I also thought four hundred dollars for a gibbet, on top of the expense for the drinks, invitations, musicians and everything, was a bit steep, and why didn't we just use a tree—a nice-looking oak, or something? I pointed out that since it was going to be a June hanging the trees would be in glorious leaf and that not only would a tree add a kind of "natural" feeling but it was also strictly traditional, especially in the West. Tomás, who had been sketching gibbets on the backs of envelopes, reminded us that an outdoor hanging always had to contend with the threat of rain. Victor said he liked the idea of doing it

---

* French—pomp or glitter.

outdoors, possibly on the bank of a river, but noted that we would have to hold it some distance from the city, which presented the problem of getting the guests, musicians, etc., to the site and then back to town.

5   At this point everybody looked at Harry, who runs a car-and-truck-rental business. Harry said he thought he could round up enough limousines to take care of that end but that the drivers would have to be paid. The drivers, he pointed out, wouldn't be friends of Colby's and couldn't be expected to donate their services, any more than the bartender or the musicians. He said that he had about ten limousines, which he used mostly for funerals, and that he could probably obtain another dozen by calling around to friends of his in the trade. He said also that if we did it outside, in the open air, we'd better figure on a tent or awning of some kind to cover at least the principals and the orchestra, because if the hanging was being rained on he thought it would look kind of dismal. As between gibbet and tree, he said, he had no particular preferences, and he really thought that the choice ought to be left up to Colby, since it was his hanging. Colby said that everybody went too far, sometimes, and weren't we being a little Draconian. Howard said rather sharply that all that had already been discussed, and which did he want, gibbet or tree? Colby asked if he could have a firing squad. No, Howard said, he could not. Howard said a firing squad would just be an ego trip for Colby, the blindfold and last-cigarette bit, and that Colby was in enough hot water already without trying to "upstage" everyone with unnecessary theatrics. Colby said he was sorry, he hadn't meant it that way, he'd take the tree. Tomás crumpled up the gibbet sketches he'd been making, in disgust.

6   Then the question of the hangman came up. Paul said did we really need a hangman? Because if we used a tree, the noose could be adjusted to the appropriate level and Colby could just jump off something—a chair or stool or something. Besides, Paul said, he very much doubted if there were any free-lance hangmen wandering around the country, now that capital punishment has been done away with absolutely, temporarily, and that we'd probably have to fly one in from England or Spain or one of the South American countries, and even if we did that how could we know in advance that the man was a professional, a real hangman, and not just some moneyhungry amateur who might bungle the job and shame us all, in front of everybody? We all agreed that Colby should just jump off something and that a chair was not what he should jump off of, because that would look, we felt, extremely tacky—some old kitchen chair sitting out there under our beautiful tree. Tomás, who is quite modern in outlook and not afraid of innovation, proposed that Colby be standing on a large round rubber ball ten feet in diameter. This, he said, would afford a sufficient "drop" and would also roll out of the way if Colby suddenly changed

his mind after jumping off. He reminded us that by not using a regular hangman we were placing an awful lot of the responsibility for the success of the affair on Colby himself, and that although he was sure Colby would perform creditably and not disgrace his friends at the last minute, still, men have been known to get a little irresolute at times like that, and the ten-foot-rubber ball, which could probably be fabricated rather cheaply, would ensure a "bang-up" production right down to the wire.

7   At the mention of "wire," Hank, who had been silent all this time, suddenly spoke up and said he wondered if it wouldn't be better if we used wire instead of rope—more efficient and in the end kinder to Colby, he suggested. Colby began looking a little green, and I didn't blame him, because there is something extremely distasteful in thinking about being hanged with wire instead of rope—it gives you sort of a revulsion, when you think about it. I thought it was really quite unpleasant of Hank to be sitting there talking about wire, just when we had solved the problem of what Colby was going to jump off of so neatly, with Tomás's idea about the rubber ball, so I hastily said that wire was out of the question, because it would injure the tree—cut into the branch it was tied to when Colby's full weight hit it—and that in these days of increased respect for environment, we didn't want that, did we? Colby gave me a grateful look, and the meeting broke up.

8   Everything went off very smoothly on the day of the event (the music Colby finally picked was standard stuff, Elgar, and it was played very well by Howard and his boys). It didn't rain, the event was well attended, and we didn't run out of Scotch, or anything. The ten-foot rubber ball had been painted a deep green and blended in well with the bucolic setting. The two things I remember best about the whole episode are the grateful look Colby gave me when I said what I said about the wire, and the fact that nobody has ever gone too far again.

(1,659 words)

VOCABULARY

gibbet (3)	creditably (6)	bucolic (8)
principals (5)	irresolute (6)	
Draconian (5)	revulsion (7)	

THE FACTS

1. How many persons are gathered to plan Colby's hanging? Name as many as you can remember. Why do you think the author created so many characters?

2. For what crime is Colby to be punished by being hanged? Is the crime fully explained or does it leave the reader wondering?

3. Why does Hugh worry about the wording of the invitations? How does the narrator reassure Hugh?

4. What are the major steps involved in this hanging? Who decides on the process?

5. What aspect of the hanging made the most lasting impression on the narrator?

THE STRATEGIES

1. What is the tone of this story? How long did it take for you to figure out this tone? Why is this particular tone used? Could another tone have served as well?

2. How does the author tie together the beginning and the ending of the story? What is the effect?

3. How does the author indicate the passing of time?

4. Some readers of this story have suggested that many of the concerns fit a wedding better than a hanging. What details support such a view?

5. How does the author handle dialogue in this story? What characteristics does the dialogue have? Why do you suppose the author chose to handle dialogue as he did?

THE ISSUES

1. What view of the world does this story convey? Is it optimistic or pessimistic? What is your reaction to this view?

2. What do you suppose Colby might have done that caused the narrator to state that he had "gone too far"? Is it a realistic appraisal of some humans?

3. Does the ending of the story square with your knowledge of hanging? Is it likely that when you hang someone for a crime, no one else will commit that same crime?

4. What message does the author convey by having the characters in the story discuss the hanging of one of their friends as if it were an item on a business agenda or a social occasion to be planned?

5. What attitude toward tradition does the story show? What danger, if any, lies in this attitude?

SUGGESTIONS FOR WRITING

1. Write an essay in which you defend (or reject) the tradition of hanging as a punishment for a capital crime.

2. Focusing on the event and characters in this story, write an essay in which you analyze the language used. Consider such matters as trite phrases, dialogue, and dimensions of the characters involved.

▼▼

Kenneth Patchen

HOW TO BE AN ARMY

KENNETH PATCHEN (1911–1972) was an American poet and graphic artist who became famous in poetry circles for pioneering the technique of reading his poetry to the accompaniment of jazz music. During his career as a poet he received many literary awards, including a Guggenheim fellowship in 1936 and a National Foundation on Arts and Humanities Award in 1967. Collections of his works include *Poems of Humor and Protest* (1960) and *The Collected Poems of Kenneth Patchen* (1969). He also wrote a novel, *Sleepers Awake* (1946). His paintings have been exhibited in various cities and at university galleries.

The unusual amalgamation of figures on page 409 is a concrete poem. Concrete poetry emerged as a form during the 1950s to protest against the aridness of a tradition demanding that poets follow certain stanza, meter, and rhyme forms. Concrete poetry depends on visual effects instead of mere words to deliver its message, suggesting meaning through iconographic pictures and word arrangements.

THE FACTS

1. How would you summarize the content of this poem in one complete sentence?

2. Why does the poet choose shoes as the first element necessary to the process of waging war?

3. What is the meaning of the equation presented?

THE STRATEGIES

1. The art work in the poem resembles the drawings of elementary school children. Why do you suppose the author did not choose more sophisticated drawings?

HOW TO BE AN ARMY

 MANY SHOES    POTATOES    FLAGS & FLEAS

 RIFLES   TRENCHES    DETERMINATION

>>>>>>>>>>>>>>>>>>>>>>>>
KNOWLEDGE OF MARCHING

$$\frac{58207}{27850} = BLOOD$$

+(GENERALS)

AND A FAITH IN THE RIGHT

✝✝✝✝✝✝✝✝✝✝✝✝✝✝✝✝✝✝✝✝✝✝✝
✝✝✝ ✝ ✝✝✝✝✝✝ ✝✝✝ ✝ ✝✝✝✝✝✝ ✝✝✝✝
✝✝✝ ✝ ✝✝✝✝ ✝✝ ✝✝ ✝ ✝✝✝✝✝ ✝ ✝✝ ✝✝✝
✝✝✝✝ ✝✝✝✝ ✝✝ ✝✝✝ ✝ ✝✝✝✝✝✝✝ ✝ ✝ ✝✝
✝✝✝✝ ✝✝✝✝✝✝✝✝ ✝✝✝✝✝✝ ✝✝✝✝✝
✝✝✝✝ ✝✝✝✝✝✝ ✝✝ ✝✝ ✝✝✝✝✝✝✝ ✝ ✝✝✝

82

2. What irony exists between the words "and a faith in the right" and the drawings that follow those words?

3. What technique does the author use to stress certain concepts more than others? How effective is this technique?

THE ISSUES

1. Under what circumstances would you be willing to go to war and possibly lose your life in battle?

2. Of all the ingredients listed in the poem, which one do you consider the most important to waging a successful war?

3. What ingredient seems to be missing from the poem when dealing with a third world war?

SUGGESTIONS FOR WRITING

1. Write an essay in which you describe, as best you can, the steps involved in training one soldier to serve in an old-fashioned war such as the Civil War.

2. Write a process analysis of how an army leader could boost troop morale before heading into combat.

ISSUE FOR CRITICAL THINKING AND DEBATE

▼▼

EDUCATION

We introduce the debate about education with a painting by William H. Johnson, titled *Booker T. Washington Legend* (1942–1943). In the foreground we glimpse rows of stick-like African-American figures, sitting on stools beneath the looming form of Booker T. Washington teaching them the agricultural and industrial arts. A large poster depicting tools the students will need for their work is hanging behind Washington, who is touching an open book with his left hand while his huge right hand is raised in a gesture of blessing or preaching. The tools—saw, shovel, ruler, rake, wheel, and even a small book and bottle of ink with a pen in it—symbolize the new jobs for which the recently emancipated African Americans could now strive.

Who should receive a college education? Everyone, or just a small group of students who are presumed sophisticated and cultured enough to appreciate one? Do women have the same right to an advanced education as do men? What subjects should form the required core of a general education? The classics as defined by Western civilization, including the writings of such greats as Plato, Aristotle, Shakespeare, Descartes, and Dante? Or should we respond to the call for global competence by including outstanding works by and about Asians, African Americans, Native Americans, and Hispanics?

Some argue that pressuring students to attend college accomplishes nothing but resistance and resentment. Others contend that

William H. Johnson, Booker T. Washington Legend, *c. 1944–1945. Oil on ply-wood, 32⅝ × 25¼ inches (82.9 × 64.1 cm). National Museum of American Art, Washington, DC/Art Resource, NY.*

only an advanced education can teach the habit of attention, the art of expression, the ability to see through intellectual poses, the sensitivity to enter into another person's thoughts, and the courage to think independently, all of which are necessary to save us from decline into barbarism. In past decades, universities and colleges in our country agreed without much dissent on what courses should be required for a college degree. They believed in a core that combined the Western classical liberal arts with the sciences, to create a balanced set of knowledge. But recently some professors have insisted that we must widen our scope to encompass ideas from every part of the world, especially developing nations.

All of these issues are worth debating; however, the three essays that follow focus on three aspects of the debate: Lynn Z. Bloom tells us what it is like to pursue a career in teaching at the university. William Zinsser, a college professor of English, insists that young people who seek success by following paths other than those leading through college should not be branded as failures or misfits. Rebecca Schlafer, a drama student, describes an unusual but rewarding class in theater arts.

▼▼▼

Lynn Z. Bloom

TEACHING COLLEGE ENGLISH AS A WOMAN

LYNN Z. BLOOM (b. 1934) is a professor of English and Aetna Chair of Writing at the University of Connecticut, Storrs. She has been Chair of the MLA Division of Teaching Writing and has also served as President of the Council of Writing Program Administrators.

> *Bloom's great love for teaching did not assure her an assignment free from gender bias or free from feeling like a second-class citizen. Often forced to settle for part-time jobs, poor parking assignments, and few benefits, Bloom continued to teach because this was the work she loved and had carved out for herself. In the essay that follows, she outlines the many humiliations to which she, as a woman teacher, was subjected.*

Prologue

1   During my first year of doctoral work I spent all my savings on a lifetime membership in NCTE.[1] Already, in my first year as a TA,[2] I knew

---

[1] National Council of Teachers of English.

[2] Teacher Assistant.

I loved to teach. Nothing less than a lifetime commitment to the profession I was preparing to join could express that love.

2   It has taken thirty years to find the voice, the place in the profession, to tell the stories that follow. When the events occurred, I would never discuss them, silenced by guilt, shame, anger, and embarrassment. Like discussing childbirth (which for the same reasons I never did either until a recent reunion with college roommates), it would not have been ladylike. But two years ago at a summer conference, a one-hour session on "gender and teaching," attended by women and men alike, metamorphosed into two nights of telling life-saving stories.[3] And so I tell you what it has been like to teach college English as a woman, to become a member of the profession I now and ever embrace anew. Call me Lynn.

I. My Job as Ventriloquist's Dummy

3   Once upon a time, as a newly-minted PhD with a newly-minted baby, I got the best part-time job I've ever had, a half-time assistant professorship at a distinguished midwestern university. Unusual for the early 60s, and unique to that institution, my job was created in response to the dean's estimate of an impending shortage of faculty. "It's going to be hell on wheels facultywise around here for the next five years," he said. So I was hired for exactly half of a full-time job: half the teaching load, half the advising and committee work, half the regular benefits. Our second child was born, conveniently, during my second summer vacation. Though not on a tenure track, I did have a parking space; it seemed a fair exchange. I taught freshman composition, of course, and sometimes sophomore lit surveys. I even taught in a room that overlooked the playground of our children's nursery school.

4   During the whole five years I taught there, I never expressed an original opinion about literature, either in class or out. In the course of my very fine education at one of our nation's very finest universities, taught entirely by men except for women's phys. ed. where they allowed a woman to teach us how to develop graceful "posture, figure, and carriage," I learned, among other things, that only real professors had the right to say what they thought. Anyway, in the 50s there were no concepts, no language, to say what I, as a nascent feminist critic, wanted to say. I tried, in a fifteen-page junior year honors paper, "Milton's Eve did too have some redeeming virtues." The paper was returned, next day, in virgin condition, save a small mark in the margin on page two where the professor had apparently stopped reading, and

---

[3] See also my essay "Hearing Our Own Voices: Life-saving Stories" in *Writing Ourselves into the Story: Unheard Voices from Composition Studies*, ed. Sheryl I. Fontaine and Susan Hunter (Carbondale: Southern Illinois UP, 1992), 89–102.

a tiny scarlet C discreetly tattooed at the end. In shame and horror at getting less than my usual A, I went to see the professor. "Why did I get a C?" I was near tears. "Because," he said in measured tones, drawing on his pipe, "you simply can't say that." End of discussion. I did not sin again.

5   I had majored in English because I loved to read and to write, and I continued to love reading and writing all the way through graduate school. But somewhere along the line, perhaps through the examples of my professors, measured, judicious, self-controlled, I had come to believe that my job as a teacher was to present the material in a neutral manner, even-handedly citing a range of Prominent Male Critics, and let the students make up their own minds. It would have been embarrassing, unprofessional, to express the passion I felt, so I taught every class in my ventriloquist's dummy voice. Indifferent student evaluations reflected the disengagement this approach provoked—"although she's a nice lady," some students added.

6   Editing textbooks didn't count. Only the other women who taught freshman composition part-time took this work seriously. (Collectively we were known to the male full-time faculty as the "Heights Housewives," as we learned from the captions on the witchlike cartoons that would occasionally appear on the bulletin board in the English Department office.) I had collaboratively edited a collection of critical essays on Faulkner intended for freshman writing courses, signing the book contract in the hospital the day after the birth of my first child. I was working on two other collaborative texts. The English Department invited my Faulkner collaborator, a gracious scholar of international renown, to come to campus to lecture on the subject of our book, but they did not invite me to either the lecture or the dinner for him. The university's public relations spokesman nevertheless called and asked if I'd be willing to give a cocktail party for him, at my expense. That may have been the only time I ever said "no" during the whole five years I taught there.

7   Freshman composition didn't count. I was so apprehensive about publishing original writing in my own name that when my husband Martin, a social psychologist, and I collaborated on an article about a student's writing process, I insisted that we submit it in Martin's name only. Only real professors with full-time jobs could publish academic articles, and I knew I wasn't one. *College English* accepted it by return mail. "Now do you want your name on it?" Martin asked, "you should be first author." "Yes," I said, "Yes."

8   My work in nonfiction didn't count. I proudly told the department chair that I was beginning research on a biography of Dr. Benjamin Spock, soon to retire from his faculty position at the same university. I had access to all the primary sources I needed, including Spock himself. "Why don't you write a series of biographical articles on major

literary figures?" asked our leader, whose customary advice to faculty requests for raises was "Diversify your portfolio." "Once you've established your reputation you can afford to throw it away by writing about a popular figure." I thanked him politely and continued my research, a logical extension of my dissertation study of biographical method. I could learn a lot about how people wrote biographies, I reasoned, if I wrote one myself. And because I couldn't say to the children, "Go away, don't bother me, I'm writing about Doctor Spock," I learned to write with them in the room.

9   Ultimately, I didn't count either. A new department chairman arrived soon after I began the biography. His first official act, prior to making a concerted but unsuccessful effort to abolish Freshman English, was to fire all the part-time faculty, everyone (except TAs) who taught the lowly subject. All women but one. He told me privately, in person; a doctorate, after all, has some privileges, though my office mate learned of her status when the chairman showed a job candidate the office, announcing, "This will be vacant next year." He was kind enough to write me a letter of recommendation, a single sentence that said, "Mrs. Bloom would be a good teacher of freshman composition." I actually submitted that letter along with a job application. Once.

II. On the Floor with the Kitty Litter

10   One of the textbooks so scorned during my first part-time job actually got me my first full-time job, two years later. The department had adopted it for the freshman honors course, and the chair had written an enthusiastic review. Then, dear reader, he hired me! This welcoming work enabled me to find my voice. After ten years of part-time teaching, as bland as vanilla pudding, I felt free to spice up the menu. Being a full-time faculty member gave me the freedom to express my opinions about what we read and wrote, and to argue and joke with my students. My classes became noisy, personal, and fun. Two years later, I received tenure, promotion, and an award for good teaching. But after four years in Indiana, my husband was offered a job in St. Louis too good to turn down. I resigned to move.

11   My voice was reduced to a whisper. I could find no full-time job in St. Louis in that inhospitable year of 1974 when there were several hundred applicants for every job. In hopes of ingratiating myself with one or another of the local universities, I taught part-time at three, marginal combinations of writing and women's studies. I taught early in the morning, in mid-afternoon, at night, coming and going under cover of lightness and darkness. It didn't matter, for no one except my students knew I was there anyway. Department chairmen wouldn't see me; with insulated indifference faculty—even some I'd known in graduate school—walked past my invisible self in the halls.

For administrative convenience, I was paid once a semester, after Thanksgiving, $400. Fringe benefits, retirement, the possibility of raises or continuity of employment were nonexistent. At none of the three schools did I have any stationery, mailing privileges, secretarial help, telephone, or other amenities—not even an ID or a library card. I was treated as an illegal alien. Nowhere did I have an office, until I finally begged for one at the plushest school, frustrated and embarrassed at having to confer with my students in the halls on the run. After several weeks, the word trickled down that I could share space with a TA—and, as it turned out, her cat, which she kept confined there. This office symbolized my status on all three jobs. It was in a building across campus from the English Department, where no one could see us. It was under a stairwell, so we couldn't stand up. It had no windows, so we couldn't see out, but it did have a Satanic poster on the wall—shades of the underworld. The TA had the desk, so I got to sit on the floor next to the kitty litter. I stayed there, in the redolent dark, for a full thirty seconds.

12   Then my voice returned, inside my head this time. Its message was powerful and clear, "If I ever do this again, I deserve what I get." I did finish the semester. But I never went back to that office. And I never again took another job that supported such an exploitative system, even though that meant commuting two thousand miles a week to my next job, a real job, in New Mexico. "Go for it," said Martin, and took care of the children while I was away.

III. Poison in the Public Ivy

13   Four years later we moved again to eliminate my cross-country commute. Through research support, graduate teaching, directing a writing program, and supervising some sixty TAs and part-time faculty, my New Mexico job had given me a grownup voice. I was beginning to talk to colleagues throughout the country, at meetings, through my own publications and those of my students, and I was looking forward to continuing the dialogue on the new job as Associate Professor and Writing Director at a Southern, and therefore by definition gracious, Public Ivy.

14   As I entered the mellowed, red-brick building on the first day of class, a colleague blocked the door. "We expected to get a beginning Assistant Professor and wash *him* out after three years," he sneered. "Instead, we got *you*, and *you'll* probably get tenure." I took a deep breath and replied in a firm voice, "You bet."

15   "We" contains multitudes; one never knows at the outset how many. Although the delegated greeter never spoke to me again, it soon became clear that *we* meant a gang of four equal opportunity harassers, all men, all tenured faculty of long standing, all eager to stifle my voice. Their voices, loud and long, dominated all department and

committee meetings and, word had it, the weekly poker games where the decisions were really made. I could do no right. I was too nice to my students; everybody knows that undergraduates can't write. I was merely flattering the students by encouraging them to publish; that they did indeed publish showed they were pandering to the public. My writing project work with schoolteachers was—aha!—proof that I was more interested in teaching than in literary criticism; misplaced priorities. My own publications, ever increasing, were evidence of blatant careerism. I received a number of grants and fellowships; just a way to get out of teaching. The attendant newspaper publicity, though good for the school, reflected badly on my femininity.

16   Although I was heard in class and, increasingly, in the profession at large, I had no voice in the departmental power structure. The gang of four and, by extrapolation, the rest of the faculty, already knew everything they needed to know about teaching writing, they'd learned it long ago as TAs. Faculty development workshops were a waste of time. The college didn't need a Writing Director anyway; the students all wrote well, the faculty all taught well, and Southern Public Ivy had gotten along for two hundred years without a Writing Director. Why start now? As a way to forestall my imminent tenure review, this hospitable group initiated a review of the position of Writing Director. If they could demonstrate that there was no need for the job, despite the thousand students enrolled every semester in required Freshman English, not to mention the upper-division writing courses, oversubscribed and with waiting lists, and the initiative in other departments for a writing-across-the-curriculum program, I would not have the opportunity to come up for tenure. Because the review was, of course, of the job and not of the person in it, I, of course, could not be consulted; that would compromise the impartiality of the process. Nor could I discuss the ongoing review with colleagues; ditto. Or the department chair; ditto. Or the dean; ditto, ditto.

17   The review began in September of my second year. Nobody identified its criteria; nobody told me what it covered; I could not ask. Occasionally a friendly colleague would sneak into my office during that very long fall semester and tell me that he was so anguished by the proceedings he wanted to resign from the review committee; *sotto voce*[4] I urged him to stay on it. A borrowed voice was better than none. Rumor had it, I heard, that I was talking to a lawyer. How unprofessional. Or was I? I whispered. The campus AAUP[5] president heard about the review; write me a letter he said, outlining what's going on, and I'll send it to the national office. So I did. And he did.

---

[4] In a soft voice (Italian).

[5] Association of American University Professors.

18   Then, on a clear crisp evening in January, tenure became irrelevant. Our family dinner was interrupted by the phone call that every parent dreads. Come right away.

19   We saw the car first, on a curve in the highway near the high school, crushed in to a concrete telephone pole. Next was the rescue squad ambulance, lights revolving red and white, halted amidst shattered glass. Then the figure on the stretcher, only a familiar chin emerging from the bandages that swathed the head. "He was thrown out of the back seat. The hatchback door smashed his face as if he'd been hit with an axe," said the medic. "I'm fine," said our son, and we responded with terror's invariable lie, "You're going to be all right."

20   After six hours of ambiguous X-rays, clear pictures finally emerged long after midnight, explaining why Laird's eyes were no longer parallel—one socket had simply been pulverized. The line of jagged-lightning stitches, sixty in all, that bolted across his face would be re-opened the next day for reconstructive surgery. "Don't go out in a full moon," sick-joked the doctor, howling like a banshee, "People will mistake you for a zombie."

21   Laird had to remain upright for a month so his head would drain, and our family spent every February evening on the couch in front of the wood stove, propping each other up. Every day the Writing Directorship review committee asked by memo for more information; every day I replied, automatically. I do not know, now, what they asked; I do not know, now, what I answered; or what I wrote on student papers; or what we ate, or read, or wrote checks for during that long month.

22   But I do know that in early March the AAUP's lawyer called me and his message was simple: "A university has every right to eliminate a position, or a program, if there is no academic need, if there are no students in it, for example. But it cannot eliminate a position just to get rid of the person holding the job. If Southern Ivy does this, they'll be blacklisted." He repeated this to the department chair. When the department voted, in its new wisdom, in late April to table the review of the Writing Directorship until after I had been reviewed for tenure, a friend, safely tenured, whispered to me, "You just got tenure." The thick copies of the committee's review were never distributed; I was awarded tenure the next year—and left immediately to become department chair at Urban State University, tenured, promoted to Professor, with authority to have an emphatic voice. The review was never reinstated, says a faculty friend still at Southern Ivy; for six years the Writing Directorship went unfilled.

IV. Escaping the Rapist

23   Fortunately, even as department chair I could continue to teach, and I often taught Women Writers. One day my class, not only writing-

intensive but discussion-intensive, began arguing about Joyce Carol Oates's "Where Are You Going, Where Have You Been?" Some claimed that Arnold Friend, "thirty, maybe," who invades Connie's driveway in "an open jalopy, painted a bright gold," his eyes hidden behind mirrored, metallic sunglasses, is in love with the pubescent teenager about whom "everything has two sides to it, one for home and one for anywhere that was not home." Others asserted that from the moment they met, Arnold's "Gonna get you, baby," signalled the abduction with which the story concludes. Though he does not lay a finger on his victim, Friend does, they pointed out, threaten to burn down her house and kill her parents—scarcely acts of love. After screaming for help into a disconnected phone until she loses her breath, Connie has no more voice and walks sacrificially out into the sunlight and Friend's mockingly waiting arms. "What else is there for a girl like you but to be sweet and pretty and give in? . . . You don't want [your family] to get hurt. . . . You're better than them because not a one of them would have done this for you."

24   Such compelling evidence clinched the debate, and I decided to reaffirm the students' interpretation with a life-saving story of my own. "A decade earlier," I began, taking a deep breath. I had never thought I would tell this story to my students. "My husband, adolescent sons, and I were camping in Scandinavia. But it was a dark and stormy night in Stockholm, so we decided to spend the night in a university dorm converted to a youth hostel for the summer. At 10 P.M., the boys tucked in, Martin and I headed for the showers down the hall. He dropped me off in front of the door decorated with a large, hand-lettered sign—Damar. Women. Frauen. Dames.—and went to the men's shower at the other end of the long corridor. As I groped for a light switch in the pitch black room, it struck me as odd that the lights were off at night in a public building. The room was dead silent, not even a faucet dripping. I walked past a row of sinks to the curtained shower stall closest to the window, where I could leave my clothes and towel on the sill.

25   "As I turned, naked, to step into the shower, a man wearing a bright blue track suit and blue running shoes shoved aside the curtain of a shower stall across the aisle and headed toward me. I began to scream in impeccable English, 'Get out! You're in the women's shower.' He kept on coming. My voice had the wrong words, the wrong language. I screamed again, now into his face, looming over mine as he hit me on the mouth. I screamed again, 'Get out!' as he hit me on the cheek. My mouth was cut, I could taste the salty blood as he hit me again in the head. I began to lose my balance. 'If he knocks me down on the tile,' I thought, 'he'll kill me.' Then I thought, still screaming, 'I don't want my children to hear this.'

26   "Then time slowed down, inside my head, the way it does just before you think your car is going to crash when it goes into a skid, and

the voices, all mine, took over. One voice could say nothing at all for terror. I had never been hit before in my life. How could I know what to do? The man in blue, silent, continued to pummel my head, his face suffused with hatred, his eyes vacant. Another voice reasoned, 'I need to get my clothes and get out.' 'But to get my clothes I'll have to go past him twice.' 'I should just get out.' Still I couldn't move, the whirling blue arms continued to pound me, I was off balance now and afraid of falling. Then the angry message came, etched in adrenaline, 'I didn't ask for this, I don't deserve it, and I'm not going to take it.' I ran naked into the corridor."

27   The bell rang. "You're right," I said. "Oates's story is about violence, not love." The students, whose effervescent conversation usually bubbled out into the corridor as they dispersed, filed out in silence.

28   That was on a Thursday. The following Tuesday, an hour before our next class meeting, a student, svelte and usually poised, came into my office, crying. "What's the matter?" I asked. "Saturday night," she said, "I was walking home alone—I live alone—and heard the phone ringing in my apartment. When I rushed in to answer it I must have left the door open. Because after I'd hung up, when I went into the kitchen a man stepped out from behind the curtain, grabbed me from behind, and shoved a gasoline-soaked rag over my face. As he began to wrestle with me, he ripped my shirt trying to throw me down. Suddenly I heard your voice in my head, repeating the words you'd said in class, 'I didn't ask for this, I don't deserve it, and I'm not going to take it.' I ran, screaming, into the street and flagged a passing policeman. You saved my life."

29   "No," I said, "you saved your own life."

Coda

30   The computerized NCTE membership card says that my lifetime membership expires in 1999. As the date draws closer, I write headquarters about this. Several times, and still no answer.

31   I will have to raise my voice. My commitment to teaching English is, after all, for life.

(3,925 words)

VOCABULARY

metamorphosed (2)	judicious (5)	Diversify (8)
tenure (3)	disengagement (5)	portfolio (8)
nascent (4)	collaboratively (6)	ingratiating (11)

insulated (11)

amenities (11)

redolent (11)

exploitative (12)

pandering(15)

careerism (15)

extrapolation (16)

criteria (17)

swathed (19)

ambiguous (20)

pubescent (23)

impeccable (25)

suffused (26)

effervescent (27)

svelte (28)

coda (heading)

THE FACTS

1. Why does the author claim to have had a job as a ventriloquist's dummy?

2. What criticism does the author level against the professor who graded her paper about Milton's Eve?

3. Why was the author so incensed at having no office of her own?

4. Who were the gang of four? What role did they play in the author's professional life?

5. What was the author's point in telling her students about an incident in which she barely escaped being raped?

THE STRATEGIES

1. How does the title of this essay contrast with the headings within the text? What is the purpose of this contrast?

2. What purpose is served by repeating four times that something "didn't count"(at the beginning of paragraphs 6, 7, 8, and 9)?

3. How effective is the section entitled "On the Floor with the Kitty Litter"? What purpose does it serve?

4. What connotation is attached to the term "gang of four"? Why did the author use this term?

5. What principles of good narration does the author use in telling her experience with a rapist in Scandinavia? How did the story affect you?

THE ISSUES

1. Does the author's rendition of her personal experience as a college teacher of English square with your knowledge of how your female English teachers are treated by their peers or by the college administration?

2. Judging from this essay, what kind of teacher is the author? What characteristics would she bring to the classroom?

3. In your view, what should be the tenure process for college teachers? What criteria should be used for granting an instructor tenure?

4. What is your opinion of TAs at the university? How useful are they? Do you think they should continued to have a role? Why or why not?

5. What do you think the references to the accident of the author's son and to the attempted rape of the author contribute to the essay's thesis?

SUGGESTIONS FOR WRITING

1. Write a 500-word essay in which you deplore the politics of universities and colleges, using examples from your own experience or from your reading to bolster your argument.

   Or

   Write a 500-word essay in which you take the position that politics on university and college campuses plays a minor role compared with the emphasis on academic standards in the classroom and on curriculum development by the various departments.

2. Write an essay in which you describe an incident that required courage and strength on your part and which later on stood you in good stead.

▼▼▼

William Zinsser

THE RIGHT TO FAIL

WILLIAM K. ZINSSER (b. 1922), American critic and writer, was born in New York and educated at Princeton. A former columnist for *Look* and *Life*, he has been on the faculty of Yale University since 1970. His books include *Pop Goes America* (1966), *The Lunacy Boom* (1970), *On Writing Well* (1980), and *Writing with a Word Processor* (1983).

> *Zinsser opposes the common view of the college dropout as someone who at best will emerge as a "late bloomer" and at worst will be stuck on the sidelines of success. In fact, he points out, dropping out may be the prelude to greater awareness and more purposeful ambition. It may simply be the sign of a ruggedly individualistic nature.*

1   I like "dropout" as an addition to the American language because it's brief and it's clear. What I don't like is that we use it almost entirely as a dirty word.

2   We only apply it to people under twenty-one. Yet an adult who spends his days and nights watching mindless TV programs is more of a dropout than an eighteen-year-old who quits college, with its frequently mindless courses, to become, say, a VISTA volunteer. For the young, dropping out is often a way of dropping in.

3   To hold this opinion, however, is little short of treason in America. A boy or girl who leaves college is branded a failure—and the right to fail is one of the few freedoms that this country does not grant its citizens. The American dream is a dream of "getting ahead," painted in strokes of gold wherever we look. Our advertisements and TV commercials are a hymn to material success, our magazine articles a toast to people who made it to the top. Smoke the right cigarette or drive the right car—so the ads imply—and girls will be swooning into your deodorized arms or caressing your expensive lapels. Happiness goes to the man who has the sweet smell of achievement. He is our national idol, and everybody else is our national fink.

4   I want to put in a word for the fink, especially the teen-age fink, because if we give him time to get through his finkdom—if we release him from the pressure of attaining certain goals by a certain age—he has a good chance of becoming our national idol, a Jefferson or a Thoreau, a Buckminster Fuller or an Adlai Stevenson, a man with a mind of his own. We need mavericks and dissenters and dreamers far more than we need junior vice-presidents, but we paralyze them by insisting that every step be a step up to the next rung of the ladder. Yet in the fluid years of youth, the only way for boys and girls to find their proper road is often to take a hundred side trips, poking out in different directions, faltering, drawing back, and starting again.

5   "But what if we fail?" they ask, whispering the dreadful word across the Generation Gap to their parents, who are back home at the Establishment nursing their "middle-class values" and cultivating their "goal-oriented society." The parents whisper back: "Don't!"

6   What they should say is "Don't be afraid to fail!" Failure isn't fatal. Countless people have had a bout with it and come out stronger as a result. Many have even come out famous. History is strewn with eminent dropouts, "loners" who followed their own trail, not worrying about its odd twists and turns because they had faith in their own sense of direction. To read their biographies is always exhilarating, not only because they beat the system, but because their system was better than the one that they beat.

7   Luckily, such rebels still turn up often enough to prove that individualism, though badly threatened, is not extinct. Much has been written, for instance, about the fitful scholastic career of Thomas P. F.

Hoving, New York's former Parks Commissioner and now director of the Metropolitan Museum of Art. Hoving was a dropout's dropout, entering and leaving schools as if they were motels, often at the request of the management. Still, he must have learned something during those unorthodox years, for he dropped in again at the top of his profession.

8   His case reminds me of another boyhood—that of Holden Caulfield in J. D. Salinger's *The Catcher in the Rye*, the most popular literary hero of the postwar period. There is nothing accidental about the grip that this dropout continues to hold on the affections of an entire American generation. Nobody else, real or invented, has made such an engaging shambles of our "goal-oriented society," so gratified our secret belief that the "phonies" are in power and the good guys up the creek. Whether Holden has also reached the top of his chosen field today is one of those speculations that delight fanciers of good fiction. I speculate that he has. Holden Caulfield, incidentally, is now thirty-six.

9   I'm not urging everyone to go out and fail just for the sheer therapy of it, or to quit college just to coddle some vague discontent. Obviously it's better to succeed than to flop, and in general a long education is more helpful than a short one. (Thanks to my own education, for example, I can tell George Eliot from T. S. Eliot, I can handle the pluperfect tense in French, and I know that Caesar beat the Helvetii because he had enough frumentum.) I only mean that failure isn't bad in itself, or success automatically good.

10   Fred Zinnemann, who has directed some of Hollywood's most honored movies, was asked by a reporter, when *A Man for All Seasons* won every prize, about his previous film, *Behold a Pale Horse*, which was a box-office disaster. "I don't feel any obligation to be successful," Zinnemann replied. "Success can be dangerous—you feel you know it all. I've learned a great deal from my failures." A similar point was made by Richard Brooks about his ambitious money loser, *Lord Jim*. Recalling the three years of his life that went into it, talking almost with elation about the troubles that befell his unit in Cambodia, Brooks told me that he learned more about his craft from this considerable failure than from his many earlier hits.

11   It's a point, of course, that applies throughout the arts. Writers, playwrights, painters and composers work in the expectation of periodic defeat, but they wouldn't keep going back into the arena if they thought it was the end of the world. It isn't the end of the world. For an artist—and perhaps for anybody—it is the only way to grow.

12   Today's younger generation seems to know that this is true, seems willing to take the risks in life that artists take in art. "Society," needless to say, still has the upper hand—it sets the goals and condemns as a failure everybody who won't play. But the dropouts and the hippies are not as afraid of failure as their parents and grandparents. This

could mean, as their elders might say, that they are just plumb lazy, secure in the comforts of an affluent state. It could also mean, however, that they just don't buy the old standards of success and are rapidly writing new ones.

13   Recently it was announced, for instance, that more than two hundred thousand Americans have inquired about service in VISTA (the domestic Peace Corps) and that, according to a Gallup survey, "more than 3 million American college students would serve VISTA in some capacity if given the opportunity." This is hardly the road to riches or to an executive suite. Yet I have met many of these young volunteers, and they are not pining for traditional success. On the contrary, they appear more fulfilled than the average vice-president with a swimming pool.

14   Who is to say, then, if there is any right path to the top, or even to say what the top consists of? Obviously the colleges don't have more than a partial answer—otherwise the young would not be so disaffected with an education that they consider vapid. Obviously business does not have the answer—otherwise the young would not be so scornful of its call to be an organization man.

15   The fact is, nobody has the answer, and the dawning awareness of this fact seems to me one of the best things happening in America today. Success and failure are again becoming individual visions, as they were when the country was younger, not rigid categories. Maybe we are learning again to cherish this right of every person to succeed on his own terms and to fail as often as necessary along the way.

(1,349 words)

VOCABULARY

VISTA (2)
unorthodox (7)

pluperfect (9)
frumentum (9)

disaffected (14)
vapid (14)

THE FACTS

1. Which sentence in the opening paragraphs of Zinsser's argument best states his thesis?

2. What two sides of society are pitted against each other in the essay? On whose side is Zinsser?

3. How does Zinsser go about defending a young person's right to fail? What advantage does this method have?

4. In what paragraph does the author explain that he does not consider failure a goal in itself? Why is this qualification necessary?

THE STRATEGIES

1. What makes Zinsser's title catchy?

2. As he develops his argument, the author often qualifies his meaning and sets limits for interpretation. What purpose do these techniques serve? Point to specific examples as you answer this question.

3. What is the author's purpose in alluding to Holden Caulfield, hero of *Catcher in the Rye* (see paragraph 8)? What is your response to the allusion?

4. What is Zinsser's definition of *dropout?* How does it differ from the Establishment's definition?

THE ISSUES

1. Do you agree with Zinsser's view that society as a whole distrusts mavericks, loners, or rebels because they do not live up to the rigid standards of success espoused by the Establishment? Or do you believe that history has often chronicled an admiration for such men and women, calling them "rugged individualists" and accepting them as a colorful part of the human heritage? Support your view with examples from history or literature.

2. What advice would you give a friend with high intellect who wanted to drop out of college?

3. What disadvantages can be cited as a warning against dropping out of college?

4. Reread paragraph 9. What list of specific facts, similar to that of the author, can you make thanks to *your* own education?

5. Do you agree with Zinsser that parents and society provide teenagers with rigid standards of success? Give examples to support your view.

SUGGESTIONS FOR WRITING

1. Write an essay in which you argue either for or against Zinsser's view that some college courses are mindless.

2. Write an essay in which you argue, as does Zinsser, that failure can be a step toward success. Provide appropriate evidence to support your thesis.

STUDENT CORNER

▼▼▼

Draws in education more

The first experience of my theatre education began as a tedious and trying project, but looking back on those beginnings, I realized how I was learning without being fully aware, and had joined a long and proud past of artists. I also discovered a truth about education: it happens even when you don't know it.

First Draft

Rebecca Schlafer, Indiana University

helps orient audience,

Finding the Force (*past titles include Mrs. Noodles and Her Flock of Sheep*)

On my first day,

I nervously gripped my schedule and shuffled into room 21A. It was expansive, with floor to ceiling mirrors to my right and chalkboards on the opposite walls. The wooden floor was newly waxed and seemed like *a* treacherous crossing. In the middle of the

too vague to simplify

floor on a large red pillow sat a ~~small woman with long dark hair~~ *waif-like woman.* ~~and delicate features.~~ "Oh come in, come in, I'm Mari Matteis!" she exclaimed, gesturing wildly. "Make room for our new rug

simpler

rat." Seven teenagers, looking ~~as~~ confused and nervous ~~as me~~, made a space in the circle they had formed around this strange pixy-like woman. "Welcome to Theater One, I am so happy to

new paragraph

Refers back to intro for better reinforcement

have you guys!" my teacher bubbled. I couldn't follow the rest of her speech closely because I was too busy wondering when we

better tense

could start acting. All summer long I had *had* an image in my head of *the first year in my education as a performer* what ~~my first year at the Youth Performing Arts School~~ would be like. We would spend hours pouring over plays, discussing and performing monologues and scenes, like "real" artists. "Okay,

comma

since you guys are in your first year here, we are going to begin

comma needed

by spending both hours on Monday, Wednesday, and Friday

427

Schlafer 2

concentrating on mime isolation and body strengthening." My

eyes wandered around the circle in surprise. body strengthening?

I thought this was a theater class, not gym. Before anyone could

protest Ms. Matteis was up and prancing around the room trying

to coax our sluggish bodies into action.

She had us stagger ourselves around the room, and got a giant

stereo out of a nearby cabinet. The whole time she was

blathering on about how much she loved to do these exercises to

music from Buffalo Springfield. "It's almost like Zen meditation,"

she ~~confided to us.~~ chirped Then she zipped up to the front to lead us in

mime isolation, (a grammar type thing) which she described as a way to isolate certain [this is more directly related to physical aspects]

muscles of the body. "Actors must have very powerful bodies so

that they can ~~convey strong emotions~~," create strong and well-formed characters Ms. Matteis told us as she comma needed

stood perfectly still, shifting all her weight forward from her unnecessary work

ankles, putting her body at a very unnatural angle. Then she

whipped around and contorted her very limber arms into painful

looking forms. This woman was a human pretzel. I knew I could

never keep up. During body strengthening, ~~when~~ Ms. Matteis comma needed

could keep her legs up at a forty five degree angle, ~~the rest of us~~ extraneous

~~were groaning in pain.~~ I was thankful when class ended, and I to emphasize how different this class seemed

could hobble back to regular school. commas

Over the next few weeks, I grudgingly went to class, still unable

to see how Ms. Matteis's exercise were going to benefit me as an

~~actor.~~ actress The physical ~~aches and~~ extraneous pains that I woke up with had wordy

subsided, but I just hated the monotony ~~of repeating this routine~~.

During class, Ms. Matteis would scamper around the room

Schlafer 3

correcting the position of our arms and encouraging us to push

ourselves further. She could see that our drooping arms and stiff

legs were a sign of lagging interest. "One day, my little rug rats,

you will get up to speak and have beautiful posture and good

projection from a strong diaphragm. It just takes practice," she

said with the solemnity of Obi-wan Kenobi, the Jedi master. →

At one time this reference was related to Mrs. Matteis being our shephard. I felt like the Star Wars reference was better suited for a student audience

After two months of slaving, we had our first chance to

wordy perform, ~~After an endless wait~~ *and* I made my journey up to the front

to avoid repeating "perform" of the class to ~~perform~~ *speak* my monologue. I began to speak and

became very conscious of the rising and falling of the muscles in

my stomach pushing out my breath to create ~~the~~ *a* clear tone of

~~my~~ voice. The muscles in my legs were taut, and I could feel my

vertebrae stacked one on top of the other in proper alignment.

What a wonderful feeling! After my performance, I sat down,

feeling energized with the realization ~~that the seemingly pointless~~ *that the*

exercises had made me a better actress. *This was one of my first*

experiences with an unconscious education.

wordy (~~With my new found realization,~~ our class felt more peaceful,

not clear *Not only were we strengthening ourselves, but our sense of ensemble.* ~~we had grown stronger as a group, and helped to motivate each~~

~~other.~~ It was ~~during this time~~ *then that* Ms. Matteis announced to us that it

was time to begin rehearsals for the Theater One Workshop.

She told us we ~~c~~ould be performing adaptations of fairy tales, ~~but~~

the catch was there would be no sets or props, ~~we were going to~~ *other than our bodies.*

~~be the sets and props.~~ We all broke up into groups and began to

better as a separate sentence

try to mold our bodies into shapes. The job came easy to us

because, much like Ms. Matteis at the beginning of the year, we

were able to contort our bodies into strange shapes and have the

Schlafer 4

stamina to stay frozen. Finally, we all had a chance to showcase our hard work.

Comma needed   On opening night, everyone was giddy with excitement.

~~Together~~ we had spent the mornings usually reserved for mime   *wordy* isolation creating convincing adaptations. When we went out on stage, our bodies became Oak trees for Red Riding Hood to hide behind, or tables and chairs for the three bears to eat their porridge from. The bright lights reflected the smiles from the audience, and made me realize the value of discipline and faith, I and the wonder of a stealth education. ~~had put my full trust in Ms. Matteis, and tried to be open to new ideas and ways of learning. As a result I could sense a change in my body. The end products of discipline showed through in my monologue work in class and in our successful performance.~~   *Wordy* ~~Because I was able to compromise my vision of the perfect class, I was able to find even more surprise and pleasure in my Theater I movement class.~~

1

Final Draft

Rebecca Schlafer, Indiana University

Finding the Force

The first experience of my theater education began as a tedious and trying project, but looking back on those beginnings, I realized how I was learning without being fully aware, and had joined a long and proud past of artists. I also discovered a truth about education: it happens even when you don't know it.

On my first day, I nervously gripped my schedule and shuffled into room 21A. It was expansive, with floor to ceiling mirrors to my right and chalkboards on the opposite walls. The wooden floor was newly waxed and seemed like a treacherous crossing. In the middle of the floor on a large red pillow sat a waif-like woman. "Oh come in, come in, I'm Mari Matteis!" she exclaimed, gesturing wildly. "Make room for our new rug rat." Seven teenagers, looking confused and nervous, made a space in the circle they had formed around this strange pixy-like woman. "Welcome to Theater One, I am so happy to have you guys!" my teacher bubbled. I couldn't follow the rest of her speech closely because I was too busy wondering when we could start acting.

All summer long I had had an image in my head of what the first year in my education as a performer would be like. We would spend hours pouring over plays, discussing and performing monologues and scenes, like "real" artists. "Okay, since you guys are in your first year here, we are going to begin by spending both hours on Monday, Wednesday, and Friday concentrating on mime isolation and body strengthening." My eyes wandered around the circle in surprise. Body strengthening? I thought this was a theater class, not gym. Before anyone could protest, Ms. Matteis was up and prancing around the room trying to coax our sluggish bodies into action.

She had us stagger ourselves around the room, and got a giant stereo out of a nearby cabinet. The whole time she was blathering on about how much she loved to do these exercises to music from Buffalo Springfield. "It's almost like Zen meditation," she chirped. Then she zipped up to the front to lead us in mime isolation, which she described as a way to isolate certain muscles of the body. "Actors must have very powerful bodies so that they can create strong and well formed characters," Ms. Matteis told us as she stood perfectly still, shifting all her weight forward from her ankles, putting her body at a very unnatural angle. Then she whipped around and contorted her very limber arms into painful looking forms. This woman was a human pretzel. I knew I could never keep up. During body strengthening, Ms. Matteis could keep her legs up at a forty five degree angle. I was thankful when class ended, and I could hobble back to regular school.

Over the next few weeks, I grudgingly went to class, still unable to see how Ms. Matteis's exercises were going to benefit me as an actress. The physical pains that I woke up with had subsided, but I just hated the monotony. During class, Ms. Matteis

Schlafer 3

would scamper around the room correcting the position of our arms and encouraging us to push ourselves further. She could see that our drooping arms and stiff legs were a sign of lagging interest. "One day, my little rug rats, you will get up to speak and have beautiful posture and good projection from a strong diaphragm. It just takes practice," she said with the solemnity of Obi-wan Kenobi, the Jedi master.

After two months of slaving, we had our first chance to perform, and I made my journey up to the front of the class to speak my monologue. I began to speak and became very conscious of the rising and falling of the muscles in my stomach pushing out my breath to create a clear tone of voice. The muscles in my legs were taut, and I could feel my vertebrae stacked one on top of the other in proper alignment. What a wonderful feeling! After my performance, I sat down, feeling energized with the realization that the exercises had made me a better actress.

This was one of my first experiences with an unconscious education. With my new found realization, our class was more peaceful. Not only were we strengthening ourselves, but our sense of ensemble. It was then that Ms. Matteis announced to us that it was time to begin rehearsals for the Theater One Workshop. She told us we would be performing adaptations of fairy tales. The catch was there would be no sets or props other than our bodies. We all broke up into groups and began to try to mold our bodies into shapes. The job came easy to us because,

Schlafer 4

much like Ms. Matteis at the beginning of the year, we were able to contort our bodies into strange shapes and have the stamina to stay frozen. Finally, we all had a chance to showcase our hard work.

On opening night, everyone was giddy with excitement. We had spent the mornings usually reserved for mime isolation creating convincing adaptations. When we went out on stage, our bodies became oak trees for Red Riding Hood to hide behind, or tables and chairs for the three bears to eat their porridge from. The bright lights reflected the smiles from the audience, and made me realize the value of discipline and faith, and the wonder of a stealth education.

How I Write

When I write I usually have to lock the door and strap myself to the chair. Music is another important need, but nothing classical or soothing, or I just end up taking a nap. For me, the best music is whatever I listened to while driving around over the summer. That way I know the words and can keep myself awake by singing. Another thing I do is spend most of my time on the rough draft. The most satisfying part of writing an essay, especially when research is involved, is taking all the information I have gathered and giving it my own voice and point of view.

How I Wrote This Essay

With this essay, I tried to focus on not overdoing the nostalgia and sentimentality. I wanted it to move quickly and not get bogged down in detail. I tried to keep the language clean and simple to avoid flowery pontificating.

My Writing Tip

I think it is very important to pay special attention to transitions. Don't be afraid of the one sentence paragraphs; many times, they give a paper its flow.

CHAPTER WRITING ASSIGNMENTS

1. Write an essay in which you narrate an incident that proves one of the following:
   a. That people are often bigoted
   b. That having good neighbors is important
   c. That pets are often astoundingly loyal
   d. That difficulties can be stepping stones to success

2. Write a vivid description by following this procedure:
   a. With a notebook in hand, go to the scene of some activity such as an airport, a restaurant, a park, a supermarket, or an employment office.
   b. Observe until you can formulate a general impression of the place.
   c. Take notes that support your general impression. (Leave out the details that do not support that impression.)
   d. Organize your notes and write the description.

3. Write an essay explaining one of the following processes:
   a. How to cook a gourmet meal
   b. How to study for a major test
   c. How to meet members of the opposite sex
   d. How to develop the habit of being courteous

WRITING ASSIGNMENTS FOR A SPECIFIC AUDIENCE

1. Write a diary entry, listing chronologically the major events of your day. Treat your diary as a confidential, intimate friend to whom you can trust your innermost feelings.

2. Write to your parents, describing to them your college living quarters.

COLLABORATIVE WRITING PROJECT

Joining three other students in the class, go—pen and notebook in hand—to some specific place on campus. Sit and observe your environment for five minutes, trying to absorb details you normally would not notice. Then spend another ten to fifteen minutes writing a list of these details into your notebook. Exchange your list with that of the other three students in your group. Since we can assume that four pairs of eyes are better than one, you should now have enough details to develop an essay vividly describing the spot you observed, beginning with a dominant impression and supporting that impression with the right details. Once you have completed your essay, compare it with the essays of the other members in your group.

Chapter Seven

▼▼▼

EXPLAINING

Illustration and Definition

ADVICE

▼▼▼

HOW TO WRITE WITH EXAMPLES

A writer should support all generalizations with examples. Prose that generalizes without examples can be tedious and vague. For instance, consider this extract from an essay in which the writer is trying to define courage:

> Courage is the willingness to take risk when the outcome is uncertain, and when the risk taken may involve harm, loss, or danger to the one taking it. The courageous person fears no one and no thing. He or she is undaunted by danger or peril. He or she will venture boldly into an uncertain situation, hardly giving a thought to the harm or consequences which may result to his or her person.

The writer generalizes throughout the paragraph; one assertion about courage merely sums up and restates another. The paragraph is cloyed with vague, stultifying writing about courage. Without specific

437

examples, twenty volumes of this sort of writing will still not convey to the reader what the writer means by courage. Compare this rewritten version:

> Courage is the willingness to take risk when the outcome is uncertain, and when the risk taken may involve harm, loss, or danger to the one taking it. For example, in a Los Angeles suburb, a twelve-year-old girl ran into a burning house to rescue her baby brother, pulled him unconscious out of the burning bedroom, and dragged him down the stairs and outside to safety. This was a rousing display of courage. The girl had been safe outside the flaming house when she remembered her sleeping brother. Disregarding her personal safety, she plunged into the flaming house to save him.

It is easier to understand here what the writer means by courage. First, she generalizes about courage; then she gives an example. The definition of courage is still incomplete—more examples are needed—but at least the writer's meaning is clearer. Notice that an example is always more narrow or specific than the generalization it tries to prove.

The use of examples in writing is necessary because language is ambiguous and circular. Words are defined by other words. The dictionary, for instance, defines courage as "the quality of being fearless or brave; spirit, temper"—in effect, it refers the reader from the one word *courage* to several words: *fearless, brave, spirit, temper.* By giving an example, the writer creates a context specifying more exactly what is meant by *courage* and avoids the circularity inherent in language.

As an instance of how examples are used, consider the selection, "Mirror, Mirror, on the Wall . . ." by John Leo. The author generalizes that ideas of beauty vary from one era to another. This generalization is then supported with examples from the Stone Age, Greece, Rome, Egypt, Victorian England, and the twentieth century. In this article, moreover, the writer introduces his examples without the use of prefatory transitions such as "my first example is" or "my second example is." Instead, he devotes a separate paragraph to each era and aligns every example with the era to which it belongs. His presentation is logical and smooth, even without the use of mechanical transitions.

The most common accusation made against freshman writing is this: students generalize without giving examples. Movies, a student will write, are wretched things: they distort, they warp, they impose improbable endings on their material. Fine and good. The instructor waits for the examples. Instead, he or she is barraged by more generalities: movies are not only wretched, they are also horrid; they are dishonest; how they end is dictated more by box office probabilities than by dramatic necessities. The resulting essay is inconclusive and vague. Only an example could have demonstrated to the instructor what the student meant.

For instance, in the *Sands of Iwo Jima*, John Wayne . . .

or:

The movie *China Syndrome* furnishes an example of this . . .

Each should be followed by a discussion of the example.

Our advice, therefore, is to give many examples of what you mean when you write. Bear in mind that the best writing is specific and concrete; the worst is general and vague.

Select Appropriate Examples

The example you cite must appropriately support your generalization. If you are writing an essay about the dangers of having a handgun in the house, your example must representatively specify this danger. One danger certainly is that someone will accidentally shoot someone else. A more remote danger is that the gun owner's pet orangutan will find the gun and deliberately shoot its master. Since most people do not own pet orangutans, this doleful story would be an unrepresentative example of the dangers of owning a handgun. Far better to cite the typical case of a man whose son thought the gun was unloaded and accidentally shot a friend.

Make It Clear What Your Examples Are Illustrating

Having generalized, most writers will introduce the example with a phrase such as "for example." Other phrases commonly used to introduce examples are:

As an example, consider

For instance

To illustrate

A case in point is

Thus

Hence

An illustration of this

Sometimes a writer will omit the introductory phrase if it is clear from the context of the writing what the example is intended to illustrate. For instance, in John Leo's "Mirror, Mirror, on the Wall . . ." the examples from ancient cultures such as the Greeks, Romans, and Egyptians are so obvious that no prefacing phrases are necessary.

Do Not Overuse Examples

Too many examples can be interpreted as padding. If, for instance, a writer declaims against immorality in movies in two sentences, then lists one hundred immoral movies, the instructor will justifiably feel shortchanged. Examples are, after all, subsidiary to generalizations. Essay assignments are intended to give a student practice in original thinking and writing, not in cataloguing. Use examples; but use them judiciously to support a generalization, not to usurp it.

E X A M P L E S

▼▼▼

Barry Parr

THE BUCK STOPS WHERE?

BARRY PARR is a freelance journalist who lives and writes in the San Francisco Bay Area.

You will enjoy the humor in Parr's recital of anecdotes involving many of our best-loved presidents. One way to approach this essay is to note what past leaders of our nation got by with compared to the more recent occupants of the White House. Have we become more scrutinizing or have the media become more invasive?

1   "It's been my experience," observed Honest Abe, "that people who have no vices have very few virtues."

2   Such a wise and tolerant perception would make a fine sound bite in an election year. But rest assured, no one will touch it, for the sad truth is that a little dab of vice makes for a more interesting campaign than a whole vat of virtue. An unflattering image, a well-delivered sound bite, a silly gaffe or a youthful indiscretion raked through the muck all attract far more attention than a lifetime of honest public service.

3   Doubtless, voters in the early days of the republic were no less hungry for all the sottish details—and, indeed, our public leaders were no less inclined to provide them. But for better or worse—probably for better—our forefathers (and foremothers) simply didn't have the technology that we have today for efficiently disseminating a public figure's flaws, shenanigans and peccadilloes to an eager and expectant nation.

4   Could George Washington—who was totally toothless by age 57—have weathered the merciless barrage of jokes on late-night TV? Would daytime television talk-show hosts have ever allowed Lincoln to get beyond his early career as a stripped-down, frontier wrestler?

5   And what would the news media—which have shown more than a passing interest in Bill Clinton's jogging shorts and pale thighs—have made of John Quincy Adams's daily constitutional of skinny-dipping in the Potomac River? When on one occasion a rascal stole his clothes, our sixth president was forced to hail a passing boy, requesting him to ring at the White House to obtain a change of clothes from the first lady.

6   The news media have not played the game on an equal footing with all the presidents. They could tiptoe around the White House with utmost discretion during the sometimes ribald Kennedy tenure, and yet quail with shock when Jimmy Carter fessed up, with boy-like candor, that he had known lust in his heart.

7   Protest trumpeted mightily across the land when Lyndon Johnson lifted his pet beagle by the ears, but the gentlemen of the press were more bemused than outraged when visitors plucked bald spots on Zachary Taylor's old war horse, Whitey, in an effort to collect souvenirs. (Taylor had pastured poor Whitey on the White House lawn.)

8   No one batted an eye while President Grant smoked up the Oval Office with his daily allotment of 20 cigars, and yet, Andrew Jackson's wife, Rachel, was driven to despair (and Old Hickory believed even unto death) by gleefully mean-spirited rumors that she smoked a pipe.

9   We are all too familiar with hullabaloos that arise over completely trivial matters—the hole in presidential candidate Adlai Stevenson's shoe, for instance, or Richard Nixon's 5 o'clock shadow in his famous Kennedy debate (both of which have been blamed for costing their election bids). But the reverse is also true: The most stupendous of presidential stunts has sometimes gone almost totally unnoticed. Somewhat less than obscure is the tale of when Harry S. Truman buzzed the White House. After taking off from Washington, D.C., in May 1946, Truman reportedly bid his pilot to detour through the no-fly zone that surrounds the presidential mansion. After spotting his family and friends gathered on the roof—where he'd apparently summoned them for a surprise—"Give 'em Hell" Harry ordered his pilot to dive. As the plane nosed down and accelerated into a steep descent, Truman was delighted to see their excited waves of recognition suddenly dissolve into a wild scramble for cover. Truman apparently enjoyed the prank so much that he ordered a second round, before proceeding onward to Independence, Missouri.

10   Decidedly less spectacular are some of the incidental diversions of Thomas Jefferson, probably our most intellectually accomplished president. A cultured violinist, superb architect and successful lawyer, Jefferson spoke six languages and held his own with the best philosophers of his day, but he still found time for puttering around with other pursuits of a more practical nature. Not only did he invent the chaise lounge, the swivel chair and a successful prototype of an indoor toilet—all considered essential fixtures in the White House to this day—but he also introduced his country to waffles and ice cream, and was reputed to be the first man in America to grow a tomato. (JFK once remarked at one of his famous state dinners—glittering events that garnered cultivated crowds of poets, novelists, musicians, Nobel laureates, Harvard lecturers and heads of states—that the last time so much brilliance had gathered in the White House was when Jefferson ate his supper there, alone.)

11   "Public opinion in this country is everything," Abe Lincoln once noted, indicating that the primal force we now know as "spin" was operating full tilt even in the 19th century. Spin doctors made hay out of Lincoln's humble birth by celebrating him as "The Log Cabin President." Yet, the same "Washington insiders" dealt a dirty hand to his successor, Andrew Johnson, and for much the same humble origins. A tailor and the son of a tailor, Johnson never received a formal education, and first learned to write as a young man, tutored by his patient and sterling wife, Eliza McArdle Johnson. The contempt that fueled his impeachment charges was to no small degree inspired by the vicious snobbery rampant in Washington's higher society. (It bears noting, too, that the egalitarian 1960s never did warm up to Richard Nixon, even after it was revealed that the supreme commander of the United States of America, when a youth, had taken a summer job at the Slippery Gulch Rodeo in Prescott, Arizona, where he worked as a barker for the wheel of chance.)

12   Spin doctors are an ingenious bunch, and even can score points—or deduct them—from something so trivial as a presidential snack. The public was charmed by Gerald Ford's habit of toasting his own muffin for breakfast. We feel somewhat closer to Grover Cleveland to learn that his favorite meal was a plate of corned beef and cabbage. Ronald Reagan's fondness for jelly beans sparked a nationwide run on that commodity. And who can resist smiling with benign indulgence upon learning that U.S. Grant enjoyed nothing better for breakfast than a cucumber in vinegar? On the other hand, Nixon seems to have inspired almost universal condemnation for enjoying a luncheon of cottage cheese with ketchup. Nixon's advisers seem to have been particularly inept at the science of managing spin. The nation expressed almost universal shock and displeasure at the saltiness of his language on the Watergate

tapes. Yet, we are almost universally inclined to view the "oaths" of the Jackson era as, well, something rather quaint. (At Jackson's funeral, his pet parrot had to be removed from the room for peppering the solemnities with a barrage of fine 19th century cusses.) And, of course, "Give 'em Hell" Harry Truman is actually venerated for the pungency of his discourse. ("I never did give anybody hell," Truman once snapped. "I just told the truth, and they thought it was hell.")

13   Some presidents have survived public-relations disasters that would ring the death knell with today's voters. Warren Harding routinely parted with pieces of White House china, which he used as chips in friendly poker games. Probably the second most famous act of William Howard Taft—who stood 6 feet 2 inches and weighed up to 350 pounds during his presidential tenure—was becoming stuck in the White House bathtub. (His most famous act? Starting the presidential custom of throwing out the first pitch of the baseball season.) And, of course, we could never stand for a modern president to be as cavalier as Andrew Jackson over matters of security. At his inaugural reception, a rowdy crowd of thousands poured into the White House on open invitation, gobbling and drinking the refreshments in record speed and heatedly demanding more, while Old Hickory himself was forced to escape to a local hotel for the night. On another occasion, the Hero of New Orleans invited the public to enjoy a gigantic cheese, which measured 4 feet in diameter and 2 feet thick, and weighed 1,400 pounds. Milling throngs pressed with knives through the White House entry and ravenously hacked it to pieces, devouring some on the spot and carrying away hunks wrapped in newspapers. The hallowed halls stunk of cheese for weeks thereafter.

14   Despite the all-too-human behavior of many of our leaders, there is indeed something almost shiningly virtuous in any man or woman who has the courage to survive the toss and gore of a presidential campaign amid the fickle court of public opinion. Our next president, whoever that might be, could do worse than take heart from the wry, but wise, observations of Harry Truman, who knew firsthand the glory, and the thankless strain, of life at the top.

15   "A politician," said he, "is a man who understands government, and it takes a politician to run a government. A statesman is a politician who's been dead 10 or 15 years."

16   I believe it also was Truman who noted, "If you want a friend in this life, get a dog."

(1,541 words)

VOCABULARY

sound bite (2)	gaffe (2)	pungency (12)
dab (2)	sottish (3)	
vat (2)	peccadilloes (3)	

THE FACTS

1. Who made the following observation: "It's been my experience that people who have no vices have very few virtues"?

2. What kept our forebears from hearing about the indiscretions of their leaders?

3. Which American president had his clothes stolen while skinny dipping in the Potomac?

4. What prank did President Truman organize while his friends and family gathered on the roof of the White House, where he had summoned them?

5. Which president spoke six languages, played the violin, and was an architect as well as a lawyer?

6. Who said, "A statesman is a politician who's been dead 10 or 15 years"?

THE STRATEGIES

1. What pre-writing strategy do you think the author used in order to develop this essay?

2. In addition to comparing contemporary presidents with those of the past, what other rhetorical strategy does the author use? How important is it to his subject?

3. The author seems to poke fun at U.S. presidents. Does his attitude make you respect these presidents less? Why or why not?

4. How does the author portray the presidents he mentions? Are they well-rounded, three-dimensional people, or is his description superficial? State how his descriptions relate to the purpose of the essay.

5. What is the meaning of the title? Explain how it fits the essay.

THE ISSUES

1. What kind of president would you prefer—one who is exemplary and virtuous in every respect or one who has a few vices? Describe the morality of your ideal president.

2. People are intrigued by the vices of public figures. Why is this so?

3. Are the news media excessive in their quest for scandalous news about public figures? Why should Americans have the right to know all the details of the lives of important people, especially those who lead our country?

4. Do public figures have a duty to curb their tongues and to behave like gentlemen or gentlewomen so long as they hold public office?

5. What does the author mean when he states that "spin doctors are an ingenious bunch, and even can score points—or deduct them—from something so trivial as a presidential snack"? Give an example from recent news where this kind of spin was created.

SUGGESTIONS FOR WRITING

1. Write an essay describing an important trait you admire in your favorite American president. Give examples of the trait you have chosen.

2. Write an essay in which you deplore the way the news media intrude into the private lives of public figures. Give examples of this kind of intrusion.

▼▼▼

John Leo

"MIRROR, MIRROR, ON THE WALL . . ."

JOHN LEO (b. 1935), associate editor of *Time*, was born in Hoboken, New Jersey, and educated at the University of Toronto. He has been associated with *Commonweal*, *The New York Times*, and the *Village Voice*.

In the following brief essay from Time, *Leo discusses and gives examples of the relativity of beauty.*

1   The poet may insist that beauty is in the eye of the beholder; the historian might argue that societies create the image of female perfection that they want. There has always been plenty of evidence to support both views. Martin Luther thought long, beautiful hair was essential. Edmund Burke recommended delicate, fragile women. Goethe insisted on "the proper breadth of the pelvis and the necessary fullness of the breasts." Hottentot men look for sharply projecting buttocks. Rubens favored a full posterior, and Papuans require a big nose. The Mangaians of Polynesia care nothing of fat or thin and never seem to notice

face, breasts or buttocks. To the tribesmen, the only standard of sexiness is well-shaped female genitals.

2   An anthropologized world now knows that notions of what is most attractive do vary with each age and culture. One era's flower is another's frump. Primitive man, understandably concerned with fertility, idealized ample women. One of the earliest surviving sculptures, the Stone Age Venus of Willendorf, depicts a squat woman whose vital statistics—in inches—would amount to 96-89-96. This adipose standard stubbornly recurs in later eras. A 14th-century treatise on beauty calls for "narrow shoulders, small breasts, large belly, broad hips, fat thighs, short legs and a small head." Some Oriental cultures today are turned on by what Simone de Beauvoir calls the "unnecessary, gratuitous blooming" of wrap-around fat.

3   The Greeks were so concerned with working out precise proportions for beauty that the sculptor Praxiteles insisted that the female navel be exactly midway between the breasts and genitals. The dark-haired Greeks considered fair-haired women exotic, perhaps the start of the notion that blondes have more fun. They also offered early evidence of the rewards that go to magnificent mammaries. When Phryne, Praxiteles' famous model and mistress, was on trial for treason, the orator defending her pulled aside her veil, baring her legendary breasts. The awed judges acquitted her on the spot.

4   Romans favored more independent, articulate women than the Greeks. Still, there were limits. Juvenal complains of ladies who "discourse on poets and poetry, comparing Vergil with Homer. . . . Wives shouldn't read all the classics—there ought to be some things women don't understand."

5   In ancient Egypt, women spent hours primping: fixing hair, applying lipstick, eye shadow and fingernail polish, grinding away body and genital hair with pumice stones. It worked: Nefertiti could make the cover of *Vogue* any month she wanted. For Cleopatra, the most famous bombshell of the ancient world, eroticism was plain hard work. Not a natural beauty, she labored diligently to learn coquettishness and flattery and reportedly polished her amatory techniques by practicing on slaves.

6   If Cleopatra had to work so hard at being desirable, can the average woman do less? Apparently not. In the long history of images of beauty, one staple is the male tendency to spot new flaws in women, and the female tendency to work and suffer to remedy them. In the Middle Ages, large women rubbed themselves with cow dung dissolved in wine. When whiter skin was demanded, women applied leeches to take the red out. Breasts have been strapped down, cantilevered up, pushed together or apart, oiled and siliconed and, in 16th-century Venice, fitted with wool or hair padding for a sexy "duck breast" look, curving from bodice to groin. In the long run, argues feminist Elizabeth Gould Davis, flat-chested women are evolutionary losers. Says

she: "The female of the species owes her modern mammary magnificence to male sexual preference."

7   Still, a well-endowed woman can suddenly find herself out of favor when cultural winds change. The flapper era in America is one example. So is Europe's Romantic Age, which favored the wan, cadaverous look. In the 1820s, women sometimes drank vinegar or stayed up all night to look pale and interesting. Fragility was all. Wrote Keats: "God! she is like a milkwhite lamb that bleats/For man's protection."

8   Victorians took this ideal of the shy, clinging vine, decorously de-sexed it, and assigned it to the wife. According to one well-known Victorian doctor, it was a "vile aspersion" to suggest that women were capable of sexual impulses. Inevitably that straitlaced era controlled women's shapes by severe compression of the waistline, without accenting breasts or hips.

9   Those womanly curves reasserted themselves at the turn of the century. During the hourglass craze, Lillie Langtry seemed perfection incarnate at 38-18-38. Since then, the ideal woman in Western culture has gradually slimmed down. Psyche, the White Rock girl,* was 5 ft. 4 in. tall and weighed in at a hippy 140 lbs. when she first appeared on beverage bottles in 1893. Now, *sans* cellulite, she is 4 in. taller and 22 lbs. lighter.

10   In psychological terms, the current slim-hipped look amounts to a rebellion against male domination: waist-trimming corsets are associated with male control of the female body, and narrow hips with a reluctance to bear children. Says Madge Garland, a former editor of British *Vogue:* "The natural shape of the female body has not been revealed and free as it is today for 1,500 years." W. H. Auden once complained that for most of Western history, the sexy beautiful women have seemed "fictionalized," set apart from real life. In the age of the natural look, a beauty now has to seem as though she just strolled in from the beach at Malibu. Like Cheryl Tiegs.

(918 words)

VOCABULARY

frump (2)	amatory (5)	incarnate (9)
adipose (2)	cantilevered (6)	cellulite (9)
gratuitous (2)	decorously (8)	
coquettishness (5)	aspersion (8)	

---

* Psyche has been the emblem of White Rock brand soft drinks and mixes since the nineteenth century.—Ed.

THE FACTS

1. What kinds of women did primitive man idealize?

2. What was the Greeks' standard of beauty?

3. According to feminist Elizabeth Gould Davis, to what do women owe their "modern mammary magnificence"?

4. What kind of feminine beauty was favored during Europe's Romantic Age?

5. What does the modern, slim-hipped look signify in psychological terms?

THE STRATEGIES

1. What notion do most of the examples in this essay support? Where is this notion stated?

2. Much of the detail about beauty is given not in full-blown examples, but in sketchy references to the opinions of famous people. What are such references called?

3. In paragraph 3, what does the anecdote about Phryne exemplify?

4. The author quotes Goethe, Simone de Beauvoir, Juvenal, Elizabeth Gould Davis, John Keats, Madge Garland, and W. H. Auden. What effect does all this opinion-sampling have on the tone of the essay?

5. In paragraph 6, the author writes: "In the long history of images of beauty, one staple is the male tendency to spot new flaws in women, and the female tendency to work and suffer to remedy them." How does the author then proceed to support and document this view?

THE ISSUES

1. Paragraph 2 alludes to an "anthropologized world." How would you define this world? What significance lies in this label?

2. What, for you, constitutes a beautiful female? A beautiful male? Refer to specific examples from history, the current scene, or from your personal encounters.

3. How do you feel about the present emphasis on an athletic female body? Is it justified, or does it diminish some other innately feminine characteristic? Give reasons for your answer.

4. Even if you agree with the poet that beauty is in the eye of the beholder, argue against this proposition and for an objective standard of beauty in art.

5. In paragraph 8, the author describes the typical Victorian wife as a woman who must never be perceived as having sexual impulses. How would you compare today's American wife with this English woman of the nineteenth century?

SUGGESTIONS FOR WRITING

1. Write an essay that specifies your idea of human beauty. Give convincing examples to illustrate your point.

2. Follow the instructions above, but make the subject of your essay human ugliness. Be sure to give examples.

▾▾

Gail Godwin

A DIARIST ON DIARISTS

GAIL GODWIN (1937–   ), a teacher and writer, was born in Birmingham, Alabama, and educated at the University of North Carolina and the University of Iowa. She is a regular contributor to periodicals such as *Atlantic, Harper's,* and *Ms.* Her books include *The Perfectionists* (1970), and *A Mother and Two Daughters* (1981).

In "A Diarist on Diarists," Godwin takes us into the private world of that most solitary of writer, the diarist. She speculates on why diarists write, what kind of people they are, and how their chosen form differs from other writing such as fiction. Along the way she treats us to examples from a wide range of diaries kept throughout the years by known and unknown writers.

This inescapable duty to observe oneself: if someone else is observing me, naturally I have to observe myself too; if none observes me, I have to observe myself all the closer.

—Kafka, November 7, 1921

I fall back on this journal just as some other poor devil takes to drink.

—Barbellion

I am enamoured of my journal.

—Sir Walter Scott

1   Diarists: that shrewdly innocent breed, those secret exhibitionists and incomparable purveyors of sequential, self-conscious life: how

they fascinate me and endear themselves to me by what they say and do not say. If my friends kept diaries, and if I read them, would I know them as well as I know Kafka, standing in front of his mirror, playing with his hair? And Virginia Woolf, languishing because of a snide remark made about her novels by an undergraduate. And poor Dorothy Wordsworth, trying valiantly to stick to descriptions of sunsets while losing all her teeth. And Pepys, giving a colorful account of his latest fight with his wife. And Camus, coolly observing, "Whatever does not kill me strengthens me." Or plantation owner William Byrd, "dancing his dances" and "rogering his wife" (code words for bowel movements and sexual intercourse). Or the anonymous Irish scribe driven to confide into the margin of a medieval text: "I am very cold without fire or covering . . . the robin is singing gloriously, but though its red breast is beautiful I am all alone. Oh God be gracious to my soul and grant me a better handwriting."

2   In the old days everybody kept diaries. That's how we know that "Carlyle wandered down to tea looking dusky and aggrieved at having to live in such a generation": from Caroline Fox's diary; and that Henry James "kept up a perpetual vocal search for words even when he wasn't saying anything": from his nineteen-year-old nephew's diary; and that when Liszt played, he compressed his lips, dilated his nostrils and, when the music expressed quiet rapture, "a sweet smile flitted over his features": from George Eliot's diary. People came home from their dinners and visits and wrote down what others said and how the great men looked and who wore what and who made an ass or a pig of himself ("A little swinish at dinner," the diligent Dr. Rutty wrote of himself in his eighteenth-century diary). Those who stayed home alone also documented their evenings. ("I dined by myself and read an execrably stupid novel called 'Tylney Hall.' Why do I read such stuff?" wrote Macaulay.) Even a literate body snatcher gave an account of himself before he turned in at night: "March 16, 1812, Went to Harps got 3 Large and 1 Large Small, 1 Small & 1 Foetus, took 2 Large to St. Thomas's, 1 Large to Guy's."

3   Are there fewer diarists now? It seems so, to me, but perhaps I'm unusual in that I have not one friend who keeps a diary—or at least who admits to it. Sometimes I'll happen upon a diarist and we greet each other like lonely explorers. Last spring I discovered a fellow diarist over lunch, and what a time we had discussing the intricacies of our venture-in-common, our avocation . . . specialty . . . compulsion? We confessed eccentricities (he has a pseudonymn for the self that gambles; I often reread old journals and make notes to my former selves in the margin). We examined our motives: why keep these records, year after year? What would happen if we stopped? *Could* we stop? We indulged in shoptalk: hardbound or softcover? lined or unlined? about how many pages a night? proportion of external events to

internal? Did one write more on bad days than on good? More or less on quiet days? (More, we both decided.) Did we feel honor-bound to report in at night, even when exhausted—or intoxicated? Ah, it was a good lunch we had.

4   "I should live no more than I can record, as one should not have more corn growing than one can get at. There is a waste of good if it be not preserved." This, from Boswell, expresses the aspect of duty that many diarists typically feel. Queen Victoria continued her diary strictly as a duty from the age of thirteen to eighty-two. Unfortunately, much of it reads like it. Many diaries, left by long-forgotten owners in attic trunks, describe neither affairs of state nor the table talk of great geniuses nor the growing pains of profound souls. But a sense of *accountability* emanates from these old books. ("Went with Maud to Chok's for a soda. J.L. lost two heifers from shipping disease . . . nothing of interest to record today.") Man and woman were beholden to the *recording* of God's hours, be they interesting or not.

> No mighty deeds, just common things,
> The tasks and pleasures each day brings.
> And yet I hope that when I look
> Over the pages of this book,
> Twill be (and, if so, I'm content)
> The record of five years well spent.

5   This, from the title page of my mother's college diary, offers captured memory as incentive to daily diligence. *Nulla dies sine linea,** it orders, and my mother obeyed, detailing in tiny handwriting, in a variety of inks, the social and mental highlights of 1932–36. People seemed to go to the movies every day, sometimes twice in one day. They ate a lot of spaghetti—but, of course, there was a Depression. No longer a diarist, my mother offered the little blue and gold book to me (we had to pick the lock—she had no idea it was even hers until we opened it). Her parents had given her the five-year diary as a going-away present for college, and she felt she owed it to them to write in it. I'm glad she did. How many daughters can read—in purple ink—about the night they were conceived?

6   Now I'm the only practicing diarist in my family. Not one of my friends keeps a diary, as I've mentioned. "To tell the truth, I've never thought I was that interesting," says one. "I'm not a *writer*," says another. A third writes letters, sometimes three or four every evening, and says this serves the purpose of a diary. Another person who is a very prolific writer has advised me to "put all that material into stories

* There will be no days without writing.—Ed.

rather than hide it in your journals. When you feel haunted or sad, write a story about a person, not necessarily yourself, who feels haunted or sad. Because, you see, *it's the feelings that are universal, not the person.*"

7   Art, fiction, if it is to be public, must tap the universal. A diary by its very nature is the unfolding of the private, personal story—whether that story be told from a distance (the "I" in a political diary, observing affairs of state; the "I" in the captain's log, marking latitude, longitude, and the moods of the sea) or with the subjectivity of a person whose politics and moods and sea-changes exist inside his own head. I need to write a diary, just as I need to write fiction, but the two needs come from very different sources. I write fiction because I need to organize the clutter of too many details into some meaning, because I enjoy turning something promising into something marvelous; I keep a diary because it keeps my mind fresh and open. Once the details of being me are safely stored away every night, I can get on with what isn't just me. So, as I explained to my friend, the fictional and the diary-making processes are not interchangeable. I had to keep a diary for many years before I could begin writing fiction.

8   Like Victoria, I, too, began keeping track of my days at the age of thirteen. But it was not because I felt the young queen, whose comings and goings would one day be read by the world. Nor did anyone make me a present of a sumptuous diary with a lock and key that cried out to be made the repository of secrets. I made my first diary, with half-sheets of notebook paper, cardboard, and yarn, and I wrote in it passionately, because I felt there was nobody else like me and I had to know why—or why not. "I don't believe people exist whose inner plight resembles mine; still, it is possible for me to imagine such people—but that the secret raven forever flaps about their head as it does about mine, even to imagine that is impossible." That is Kafka at thirty-eight, speaking for me at thirteen—and for diarists not yet born.

9   There are many books about diarists, and some of them make fascinating reading. What is odd, however, is that many of the authors do not seem to be diarists themselves: they write with the air of scientists, observing this peculiar organism called a "diarist" from the other side of a polished lens. F. A. Spalding states in *Self-Harvest, a Study of Diaries and Diarists* that we seldom if ever find development within the individual diary, either in what is recorded or in the manner of recording it. Also that "diarists who hope to aid memory continue to the end to complain of the lack of it." Also that diaries do not seem to teach diarists "how the better to spend my time for the future," even if they read over their diaries, "and few do so." Spalding also says that, except for Scott and Byron, "there is hardly an example of a diary written out of a first-class creative mind." "We cannot imagine a Shakespeare keeping a diary," he says. In fairness to Mr. Spalding, he wrote his book before access to the Kafka diaries was possible—or Virginia

Woolf's—though maybe he wouldn't have considered these writers first-class creative minds. As for Shakespeare, that enigma, who can say with certainty whether he did not jot down his moods and plots for plays into a little book that lies crumbling in the earth or awaiting its finder in some forgotten cranny?

10   Every true diarist knows that having a relationship with a diary is like having a relationship with anyone or anything else: the longer it lasts, the more it is bound to change. When I began my diary, at age thirteen, I traversed that naked space between my mind and my little book's pages as hesitantly as a virgin approaching a man who may or may not prove trustworthy. Now, two-and-a-half decades later, my diary and I have an old marriage. The space between us is gone. I hardly *see* my diary anymore. And yet, there is a confident sense that we are working together. We have been down many roads together, my diary and I (I use the singular, but what I call "my diary" resides in many separate books—some of them lost, others maimed or destroyed [more on this later]), and I have been neglectful and insincere and offhand and have not always shown consideration for this fellow traveler of mine. In adolescence, I weighed him down with feelings of gloom and doom; in late teens, I wasted his pages cataloguing the boys who fell into, or eluded, my snare; in my twenties, I drove him to near death-from-boredom with my lists of resolutions, budgets, and abortive plans for "the future." Sometimes I shunned the sight of him, and I wrote my secrets on sheets of loose paper—not wanting to be bound by him—and, of course, those pages are now lost. In my thirties, as my craft of fiction was consolidated and I felt I had "something of my own," I returned to him with new respect. I told him when good things happened, and shared ideas for future work. As I became less trapped in my universe of moods and recognized my likeness to other people and other things in the universe-at-large, my entries began to include more space. Now there are animals and flowers and sunsets in my diary, as well as other people's problems. As a rule, I complain less and describe more; even my complaints I try to lace with memorable description, because . . . yes, Mr. Spalding, diarists do reread their diaries, and how many times I have exclaimed aloud with rage when I looked up a year or a day, hoping to catch the fever or the flavor of the past, and found only a meager, grudging, "I feel awful today." So now I write for my future self, as well as my present mood. And sometimes, to set the record straight, I jot down a word or two in old diaries to my former self—to encourage, to scold, to correct, or to set things in perspective.

11   As for memory, I don't complain of the lack of it or use my diary to improve it, as Mr. S. would have me do. It is rather that I know one of us has it—my diary or me—and so, if I can't remember something, I look it up. (Though, as I've said, sometimes nothing's there except a mood nobody wants anymore.) Yet, though I frequently look things up, or

sometimes browse through a year, I have never read my diaries straight through, and possibly never will. I have tried, a couple of times, but there are simply too many of them, and, after a while, I get the peculiar dizziness that comes from watching a moving train while on another moving train. One cannot live two lives at once, for long periods of time.

12   Early or late, there comes a time in every diarist's life when he asks himself: "What if someone should read this?" If he truly recoils at the thought, he might take measures to prevent it, writing in cipher, like Pepys, or in mirror-writing (da Vinci's notebooks) or in a mixture of foreign languages. One seventeenth-century schoolmaster wrote his diary in a notebook so small as to be illegible without a magnifying glass, the whole in abbreviated Latin. (The diary was four inches by two and a half inches; and there were seventy lines to the page!)

13   But far, far more prevalent, I think, is the breed of diarist who writes for *some* form of audience. This audience may be God, it may be a friendly (or unfriendly) spirit (witness the way some diarists must justify their self-contradictions and shortcomings); or it may be one's future self (at thirty-eight, Virginia Woolf wrote in her journal that she was hoping to entertain herself at fifty) or . . . in many cases, more often than we may care to admit . . . we write for some form of posterity. How many diarists can honestly say they have never once imagined their diaries being "discovered," either before or after their deaths? Many of us hope we will make good reading. (I occasionally catch myself "explaining," in my diary: putting in that extra bit of information that I know quite well but cannot expect a stranger to know.)

14   In *The Golden Notebook* Doris Lessing writes about a pair of lovers, each of whom keeps two diaries. It is understood tacitly between them that one diary may be "secretly read" but the second diary, the really private one, may not. Of course, one of the partners cheats and the couple is sundered forever because of this unpardonable breach. I know perfectly well that if I had a partner who kept a diary (or two diaries) I would probably cheat. Several times over my diary-keeping years, people have read my journals. Some sneaked and were caught (perhaps others sneaked and were not); a few let me know about it, in a variety of ways. One left a cheerful note: "Enjoy the halcyon days!" Another tore out a handful of pages. Another tossed the whole book into the Atlantic Ocean. On several occasions I have actually read parts of my diary aloud to someone. But too much "publicity" is destructive to a diary, because the diarist begins, unconsciously perhaps, to leave out, to tone down, to pep up, to falsify experience, and the reason for the undertaking becomes buried beneath posings.

15   The prospect of people reading my diaries after I am dead does not disturb me in the least. I like to think of pooling myself with other introspective hearts: madmen (and women), prudes, profligates, celebrities, outcasts, heroes, artists, saints, the lovelorn and the lucky, the

foolish and the proud. I have found so many sides of myself in the diaries of others. I would like it if I someday reflect future readers to themselves, provide them with examples, warnings, courage, and amusement. In these unedited glimpses of the self in others, of others in the self, is another of the covenants posterity makes with the day-to-day.

(2,770 words)

VOCABULARY

exhibitionists (1)	pseudonym (3)	prevalent (13)
purveyors (1)	accountability (4)	tacitly (14)
languishing (1)	emanates (4)	sundered (14)
snide (1)	prolific (6)	halcyon (14)
dilated (2)	sumptuous (8)	introspective (15)
rapture (2)	repository (8)	profligates (15)
execrably (2)	enigma (9)	lovelorn (15)
intricacies (3)	traversed (10)	covenants (15)
avocation (3)	maimed (10)	posterity (15)
eccentricities (3)	consolidated (10)	

THE FACTS

1. According to the author, when did everyone used to keep diaries?

2. What happens when the author meets someone who is also a fellow diarist?

3. What famous personality began a diary at age thirteen and kept it faithfully until she was eighty-two? What happens usually to diaries that are so compulsively kept?

4. From whose family-member's diary does the author quote? What unusual information did she get from it?

5. The author quotes one F. A. Spalding, who writes about diaries and diarists. What remark does he make about diarists that seems to annoy her? How does she refute this remark?

THE STRATEGIES

1. The author makes it clear in the title that she herself is a diarist. What effect does this acknowledgment have on her treatment of the subject?

2. What is different about the evidence used to support the topic sentences of paragraphs 2 and 3? How do you account for this difference?

3. In paragraph 4, the author quotes from a diary without identifying its writer. Why do you think she omits the writer's identification?

4. The author quotes many excerpts from diaries but uses no formal introduction of them as examples. How do you think she's able to get away with no introductions?

5. The author writes, "Early or late, there comes a time in every diarist's life when he asks himself: 'What if someone should read this?'" What might some readers find objectionable about this sentence?

THE ISSUES

1. The author remarks that in the old days everybody kept diaries. Given the evidence she cites to back up this assertion, do you believe it. Why or why not?

2. If you think there are fewer diarists today than in the old days, how do you explain the decline in diary keeping?

3. Do you keep a diary or know anyone who does? What reasons can you give for diary-keeping?

4. What does F. A. Spalding seem to imply about diary-keeping?

5. Many writing teachers urge their students to keep a diary. How do you think diary-keeping might help a beginning writer?

SUGGESTIONS FOR WRITING

1. Just for fun, chronicle the events of yesterday in a diary entry.

2. If you keep a diary or know someone who does, write an essay explaining why.

▼▼▼

Adrienne Rich

LIVING IN SIN

ADRIENNE RICH (b. 1929) is an award-winning poet, critic, and translator. She graduated from Radcliff College in 1951 and has since held many academic positions, including Adjunct Professor teaching writing at Columbia University, and

Visiting Poet at Swarthmore College. She won the National Institute of Arts and Letters Award for poetry in 1961. Her works are represented in many anthologies, such as *New Poets of England and America* (1961) and *A Little Treasure of Modern Poetry, English and American* (1970). Rich's other works include *Diving Into the Wreck* (1973) and *The Dream of a Common Language* (1979).

The poem that follows points out the unrealistic outlook of lovers caught in the grip of sexual passion, providing graphic examples of what these lovers do not foresee.

       She had thought the studio would keep itself;
       no dust upon the furniture of love.
       Half heresy, to wish the taps less vocal,
       the panes relieved of grime. A plate of pears,
5   a piano with a Persian shawl, a cat
       stalking the picturesque amusing mouse
       had risen at his urging.
       Not that at five each separate stair would writhe
       under the milkman's tramp; that morning light
10   so coldly would delineate the scraps
       of last night's cheese and three sepulchral bottles;
       that on the kitchen shelf among the saucers
       a pair of beetle-eyes would fix her own—
       envoy from some black village in the mouldings . . .
15   Meanwhile, he, with a yawn,
       sounded a dozen notes upon the keyboard,
       declared it out of tune, shrugged at the mirror,
       rubbed at his beard, went out for cigarettes;
       while she, jeered by the minor demons,
20   pulled back the sheets and made the bed and found
       a towel to dust the table-top,
       and let the coffee-pot boil over on the stove.
       By evening she was back in love again,
       though not so wholly but throughout the night
25   she woke sometimes to feel the daylight coming
       like a relentless milkman up the stairs.

                                                    (205 words)

VOCABULARY

heresy (3)   delineate (10)   envoy (14)
picturesque (6)   sepulchral (11)

THE FACTS

1. What is the meaning of the first line?

2. What happens at five in the morning?

3. What difference is there between the activity of the male and the activity of the female in the poem?

THE STRATEGIES

1. What words are omitted in front of the "Not" of line 8? What effect is created by the omission?

2. Whose point of view dominates the poem? Why?

3. What two different roles does the milkman play in the poem?

4. What does the word "sepulchral" in line 11 contribute?

THE ISSUES

1. What is the theme (the lesson about life) of this poem? Try to express it in one complete sentence.

2. Through the many vivid examples provided, what contrast is clearly drawn?

3. What does the author mean by the lines "By evening she was back in love again,/though not so wholly . . . "?

4. How does this poem relate to real love?

SUGGESTIONS FOR WRITING

1. Write an essay using examples to describe a feeling of disappointment you have experienced or observed.

2. In an essay about the dangers of pure romance and passion in a relationship, supply vivid examples to support your thesis.

ADVICE

▼▼▼

HOW TO WRITE A DEFINITION

A definition answers the question "What is it?" Law students must know
what a *brief* is before they can compile one; likewise, medical interns ro-
tating through the obstetrics floor of a hospital must know what a
breech is before they can perform a breech delivery. In the first instance,
the law textbook might define *brief* as "a summary of the essential
points of a decision." In the second instance, the medical text might tell
the interns that "a breech is the lower rear portion of the human trunk"
and that a breech birth is, therefore, one in which the buttocks of the
baby emerge before its head. No matter what discipline the student is in
the definition will be an indispensable source of information.

Various strategies can be employed to define any word, phrase, or
term. How much detail the student must give will vary with how abstract, fuzzy, or controversial the word, phrase, or term is. The following is a thumbnail sketch of how a definition may be constructed.

Begin with a Formal Definition

A formal definition first places a word in a general class and then
shows how that word differs from others in the same class. The following definitions illustrate this simple system:

Word	General Class	How Word Differs
miracle	an event or action	that contradicts natural laws
pedant	a person	who exhibits scholarship ostentatiously
to succor	to render help	in times of distress

The formal definition is implicit in most good defining essays. In
this section, for example, Gilbert Highet defines *kitsch* by identifying
it as a kind of art that is junky; Frank Deford tells us that *cystic fibrosis* is a disease of the lungs. Kitsch is placed in the general class of art,
cystic fibrosis in the class of lung diseases. Both are then differenti-
ated from other items in their respective classes—kitsch by its junki-
ness, cystic fibrosis by its lethal effect on the lungs.

Sometimes it is also useful to define a word by discussing its
etymology or origin. In the example below, science writer Isaac Asimov
defines *botulism* by referring to its etymology:

Pride of place, however, must be taken by the product of a bacterium which is to be found everywhere and which harms no one—ordinarily. It is Clostridium botulinum. "Clostridium" is Latin for "little spindle," which describes its shape, and "botulinum" is from the Latin word *botulus*, which means "sausage," where it has sometimes been detected.

Expand the Definition by Description, Example, or Comparison/Contrast

In a defining essay more than a simple dictionary definition is required. Further explanation must be given to make the meaning of the term crystal-clear to the reader.

Description

The meanings of some words may be clarified or elaborated on by a description. In the example below, a student extends the definition of *milksop* with a rather detailed description:

> A milksop is a boy or a man who lacks courage and manliness. Usually he is of small stature, with a voice that peeps and squeaks rather than roars. He speaks so timidly that people always ask, "What did you say?" or comment, "I beg your pardon." He is further distinguished by a rather limp and squishy handshake. He merely proffers five appendages dangling uselessly from a wrist. Moreover, the milksop prefers to cock his head and dart his eyes here and there rather than look another in the eye. Wherever you see him, he seems incapable of standing straight, and is either slumping like an understuffed pillow or sagging like a falling doorpost.

Example

Ambiguous or difficult terms can usually be clarified by examples. In his essay "Kitsch," Gilbert Highet expands on his definition by citing numerous examples of kitsch in art and literature. The following passage, written by a student, extends the definition of *deduction* by supplying an example:

> Deduction is the process of drawing conclusions by reasoning from the general to the specific. Consider, for instance, the statement "Johnny cannot read because he was taught by the Montessori method." The reasoning proceeds from a vast generalization:
> All children taught by the Montessori method are nonreaders.
> Then the reasoning moves to a specific assertion:
> Johnny was taught by the Montessori method.

And to a specific conclusion:
> Therefore, Johnny cannot read.

The above equation, known as a syllogism, is the most common process of reasoning used in deductions.

Comparison/Contrast

Sometimes it is useful to define a term by contrasting it with what it is not, or by comparing the term to something similar. For instance, a Spanish poet once defined death as follows: "Death is like a black camel that kneels at the gates of all." This comparison was the poet's way of graphically defining death. But comparisons do not have to be so metaphorical or farfetched. On a plainer level, one might define a pharmacist by comparing/contrasting him or her to a cook. Here is an example of the use of contrast in furthering a definition. The writer, Carl Becker, has just asserted that *democracy* means "government by the people as opposed to government by a tyrant, a dictator, or an absolute monarch." He then proceeds to some contrasting examples:

> Peisistratus, for example, was supported by a majority of the people, but his government was never regarded as a democracy for all that. Caesar's power derived from a popular mandate, conveyed through established republican forms, but that did not make his government any the less a dictatorship. Napoleon called his government a democratic empire, but no one, least of all Napoleon himself, doubted that he had destroyed the last vestiges of the democratic empire. Since the Greeks first used the term, the essential test of democratic government has always been this: the source of political authority must be and remain in the people and not in the ruler.

All the instances cited by Becker help to make clear the definition of democracy by asserting what it is not.

As you write your defining essays, beware of the most common student error—the circular definition. To say that "taxation is the act of imposing taxes" is repetitious. Better to say "Taxation is the principle of levying fees to support basic government services." Examples and details can then be provided until you have answered the question "What is it?"

E X A M P L E S

▼▼

Ellen Goodman

PUTTING IN A GOOD WORD FOR GUILT

ELLEN GOODMAN (1941–   ) is a popular newspaper columnist whose work is widely syndicated. Born in Newton, Massachusetts, and educated at Radcliffe College, Goodman won the Pulitzer Prize for distinguished commentary in 1980. Her books include two collections of her columns, *Close to Home* (1979) and *At Large* (1981), and *Turning Points* (1979), a study of how various men and women have been changed by the feminist movement.

> *The trend nowadays is to regard guilt as useless mental baggage that should be uprooted from the psyche through group therapy and psychological counseling. Overlooked in all this modern analysis is the moral dimension of guilt—the fact that often it is guilt that makes us toe the line and live up to our obligations. In this timely essay, Goodman points out that guilt, as long as it is properly directed, does have some valuable uses.*

1   Feeling guilty is nothing to feel guilty about. Yes, guilt can be the excess baggage that keeps us paralyzed unless we dump it. But it can also be the engine that fuels us. Yes, it can be a self-punishing activity, but it can also be the conscience that keeps us civilized.

2   Not too long ago I wrote a story about that amusing couple Guilt and the Working Mother. I'll tell you more about that later. Through the mail someone sent me a gift coffee mug carrying the message "I gave up guilt for Lent."

3   My first reaction was to giggle. But then it occurred to me that this particular Lent has been too lengthy. For the past decade or more, the pop psychologists who use book jackets rather than couches all were busy telling us that I am okay, you are okay and whatever we do is okay.

4   In most of their books, guilt was given a bad name—or rather, an assortment of bad names. It was a (1) Puritan (2) Jewish (3) Catholic hangover from our (1) parents (2) culture (3) religion. To be truly liberated was to be free of guilt about being rich, powerful, number one, bad to your mother, thoughtless, late, a smoker or about cheating on your spouse.

5   There was a popular notion, in fact, that self-love began by slaying one's guilt. People all around us spent a great portion of the last decade trying to tune out guilt instead of decoding its message and learning what it was trying to tell us.

6   With that sort of success, guilt was ripe for revival. Somewhere along the I'm-okay-you're-okay way, many of us realized that, in fact, I am not always okay and neither are you. Furthermore, we did not want to join the legions who conquered their guilt en route to new depths of narcissistic rottenness.

7   At the deepest, most devastating level, guilt is the criminal in us that longs to be caught. It is the horrible, pit-of-the-stomach sense of having done wrong. It is, as Lady Macbeth obsessively knew, the spot that no one else may see . . . and we can't see around.

8   To be without guilt is to be without a conscience. Guilt-free people don't feel bad when they cause pain to others, and so they go on guilt-freely causing more pain. The last thing we need more of is less conscience.

9   Freud once said, "As regards conscience, God has done an uneven and careless piece of work, for a large majority of men have brought along with them only a modest amount of it, or scarcely enough to be worth mentioning."

10   Now, I am not suggesting that we all sign up for a new guilt trip. But there has to be some line between the accusation that we all should feel guilty for, say, poverty or racism and the assertion that the oppressed have "chosen" their lot in life.

11   There has to be something between puritanism and hedonism. There has to be something between the parents who guilt-trip their children across every stage of life and those who offer no guidance, no—gulp—moral or ethical point of view.

12   At quite regular intervals, for example, my daughter looks up at me in the midst of a discussion (she would call it a lecture) and says: "You're making me feel guilty." For a long time this made me, in turn, feel guilty. But now I realize that I am doing precisely what I am supposed to be doing: instilling in her a sense of right and wrong so that she will feel uncomfortable if she behaves in hurtful ways.

13   This is, of course, a very tricky business. Guilt is ultimately the way we judge ourselves. It is the part of us that says, "I deserve to be punished." But we all know people who feel guilty just for being alive. We know people who are paralyzed by irrational guilt. And we certainly don't want to be among them, or to shepherd our children into their flock.

14   But it seems to me that the trick isn't to become flaccidly nonjudgmental, but to figure out whether we are being fair judges of ourselves. Karl Menninger once wrote that one aim of psychiatric treatment isn't to get rid of guilt but "to get people's guilt feelings attached to the 'right' things."

15   In his book *Feelings*, Willard Gaylin quotes a Reverend Tillotson's definition of guilt as "nothing else but trouble arising in our mind from our consciousness of having done contrary to what we are verily perswaded [sic] was our Duty."

16   We may, however, have wildly different senses of duty. I had lunch with two friends a month ago when they both started talking about feeling guilty for neglecting their mothers. One, it turned out, worried that she didn't call "home" every day; the other hadn't even chatted with her mother since Christmas.

17   We are also particularly vulnerable to feelings of duty in a time of change. Today an older and ingrained sense of what we should do may conflict with a new one. In the gaps that open between what we once were taught and what we now believe grows a rich crop of guilt.

18   Mothers now often tell me that they feel guilty if they are working and guilty if they aren't. One set of older expectations, to be a perfect milk-and-cookies supermom, conflicts with another, to be an independent woman or an economic helpmate.

19   But duty has its uses. It sets us down at the typewriter, hustles us to the job on a morning when everything has gone wrong, pushes us toward the crying baby at 3 A.M.

20   If guilt is a struggle between our acceptance of shoulds and should nots, it is a powerful and intensely human one. Gaylin writes, "Guilt represents the noblest and most painful of struggles. It is between us and ourselves." It is better to struggle with ourselves than give up on ourselves.

21   This worst emotion, in a sense, helps bring out the best in us. The desire to avoid feeling guilty makes us avoid the worst sort of behavior. The early guilt of a child who has hurt a younger sister or brother, even when no one else knows, is a message. The adult who has inflicted pain on an innocent, who has cheated, lied, stolen, to get ahead of another—each of us has a list—wakes up in the middle of the night and remembers it.

22   In that sense guilt is the great civilizer, the internal commandment that helps us choose to be kind to each other rather than to join in a stampede of me-firsts. "If guilt is coming back," said Harvard Professor David Riesman, who wrote *The Lonely Crowd*, "one reason is that a tremendous surge of young people overpowered the adults in the sixties. You might say the barbarians took Rome. Now there are more adults around who are trying to restore some stability."

23   Guilt is the adult in each of us, the parent, the one who upholds the standards. It is the internal guide against which we argue in vain that "everybody else is doing it."

24   We even wrestle with ethical dilemmas and conflicts of conscience so that we can live with ourselves more comfortably. I know two people who were faced with a crisis about their infidelities. One woman resolved the triangle she was in by ending her marriage. The other ended her affair. In both cases, it was the pain that had motivated them to change.

25   It is not easy to attach our guilt to the right things. It is never easy to separate right from wrong, rational guilt from neurotic guilt. We

may resolve one by changing our view of it and another by changing our behavior.

26   In my own life as a working mother, I have done both half a dozen times. When my daughter was small and I was working, I worried that I was not following the pattern of the good mother, my mother. Only through time and perspective and reality did I change that view; I realized that my daughter clearly did not feel neglected and I clearly was not uncaring. Good child care, love, luck and support helped me to resolve my early guilt feelings.

27   Then again, last winter I found myself out of town more than I was comfortable with. This time I changed my schedule instead of my mind.

28   For all of us, in the dozens of daily decisions we make, guilt is one of the many proper motivations. I am not saying our lives are ruled by guilt. Hardly. But guilt is inherent in the underlying question: "If I do that, can I live with myself?"

29   People who don't ask themselves that question, people who never get no for an answer, may seem lucky. They can, we think, be self-centered without self-punishment, hedonistic without qualms. They can worry about me-first and forget about the others.

30   It is easy to be jealous of those who go through life without a moment of wrenching guilt. But envying the guiltless is like envying a house pet. Striving to follow their lead is like accepting a catatonic as your role model. They are not the free but the antisocial. In a world in which guilt is one of the few emotions experienced only by human beings, they are, even, unhuman.

31   Guilt is one of the most human of dilemmas. It is the claim of others on the self, the recognition both of our flaws and of our desire to be the people we want to be.

(1,620 words)

VOCABULARY

narcissistic (6)	flaccidly (13)	inherent (28)
hedonism (11)	ingrained (17)	qualms (29)
instilling (12)	dilemmas (24)	catatonic (30)

THE FACTS

1. What gift did the author receive after writing a story about guilt and the working mother?

2. According to the author, to be without guilt is to be without what?

3. In her relationship with her daughter, the author says she realizes that she was doing "precisely what she was supposed to be doing." What is that?

4. What, according to Karl Menninger, should be the aim of psychiatric treatment when it comes to dealing with guilt?

5. Why, according to the author, should we not envy those who have no feelings of guilt?

THE STRATEGIES

1. What assumptions does the writer make about her audience? What are some of the stylistic characteristics that show that this essay is written for a particular audience?

2. What does the opening paragraph of this essay immediately establish? Why do you think it was necessary for the writer to strike this note at the very outset?

3. What are some of the challenges faced by the column writer, and how does this essay seem to respond to them?

4. The author quotes from Lady Macbeth (paragraph 7), Freud (paragraph 9), and Karl Menninger (paragraph 14). What does her handling of these quotations say about her audience?

5. Given that the author is a popular columnist, what reasons do you think she has for quoting her own daughter (paragraph 12)?

THE ISSUES

1. What is your own feeling about guilt? How do you cope with guilt when it strikes?

2. What do you think the writer means by "narcissistic rottenness?" What example can you give that might amplify on the meaning of that phrase?

3. The author quotes Karl Menninger as saying that psychiatry should make sure that people's guilt is attached to the "right things." What do you think are the right things for guilt?

4. What do you think of someone who does his or her duty merely because he or she wishes not to feel guilty?

5. What does guilt imply about free will and choice? If we had no free will and choice, how would guilt likely affect us?

SUGGESTIONS FOR WRITING

1. In an essay, relate an episode that made you feel guilty and analyze why.

2. Write an essay that defines guilt.

▼▼

Pico Iyer

IN PRAISE OF THE HUMBLE COMMA

PICO IYER is a freelance writer and contributing editorial writer for *Time* magazine.

> *This essay appeared as the featured essay on the back page of* Time *magazine. Its purpose is to define punctuation in general and the comma in specific. Iyer suggests that punctuation marks are highly underrated, since they give writing elegance as well as clarity, often keeping it from becoming a jumble of words strung along on a page.*

1 The gods, they say, give breath, and they take it away. But the same could be said—could it not?—of the humble comma. Add it to the present clause, and, of a sudden, the mind is, quite literally, given pause to think; take it out if you wish or forget it and the mind is deprived of a resting place. Yet still the comma gets no respect. It seems just a slip of a thing, a pedant's tick, a blip on the edge of our consciousness, a kind of printer's smudge almost. Small, we claim, is beautiful (especially in the age of the microchip). Yet what is so often used, and so rarely recalled, as the comma—unless it be breath itself?

2 Punctuation, one is taught, has a point: to keep up law and order. Punctuation marks are the road signs placed along the highway of our communication—to control speeds, provide directions and prevent head-on collisions. A period has the unblinking finality of a red light; the comma is a flashing yellow light that asks us only to slow down; and the semicolon is a stop sign that tells us to ease gradually to a halt, before gradually starting up again. By establishing the relations between words, punctuation establishes the relations between the people using words. That may be one reason why schoolteachers exalt it and lovers defy it ("We love each other and belong to each other let's don't ever hurt each other Nicole let's don't ever hurt each other," wrote Gary Gilmore to his girlfriend). A comma, he must have known, "separates inseparables," in the clinching words of H. W. Fowler, King of English Usage.

3   Punctuation, then, is a civic prop, a pillar that holds society up-right. (A run-on sentence, its phrases piling up without division, is as unsightly as a sink piled high with dirty dishes.) Small wonder, then, that punctuation was one of the first proprieties of the Victorian age, the age of the corset, that the modernists threw off: the sexual revolution might be said to have begun when Joyce's Molly Bloom spilled out all her private thoughts in 36 pages of unbridled, almost unperioded and officially censored prose; and another rebellion was surely marked when E. E. Cummings first felt free to commit "God" to the lower case.

4   Punctuation thus becomes the signature of cultures. The hot-blooded Spaniard seems to be revealed in the passion and urgency of his doubled exclamation points and question marks *("¡Caramba! ¿Quien sabe?"),* while the impassive Chinese traditionally added to his so-called inscrutability by omitting directions from his ideograms. The anarchy and commotion of the '60s were given voice in the explod-ing exclamation marks, riotous capital letters and Day-Glo italics of Tom Wolfe's spray-paint prose; and in Communist societies, where the State is absolute, the dignity—and divinity—of capital letters is re-served for Ministries, Sub-Committees and Secretariats.

5   Yet punctuation is something more than a culture's birthmark; it scores the music in our minds, gets our thoughts moving to the rhythm of our hearts. Punctuation is the notation in the sheet music of our words, telling us when to rest, or when to raise our voices; it acknowl-edges that the meaning of our discourse, as of any symphonic com-position, lies not in the units but in the pauses, the pacing and the phrasing. Punctuation is the way one bats one's eyes, lowers one's voice or blushes demurely. Punctuation adjusts the tone and color and volume till the feeling comes into perfect focus: not disgust exactly, but distaste; not lust, or like, but love.

6   Punctuation, in short, gives us the human voice, and all the mean-ings that lie between the words. "You aren't young, are you?" loses its innocence when it loses the question mark. Every child knows the menace of a dropped apostrophe (the parent's "Don't do that" shifting into the more slowly enunciated "Do not do that"), and every believer, the ignominy of having his faith reduced to "faith." Add an exclama-tion point to "To be or not to be . . ." and the gloomy Dane has all the resolve he needs; add a comma, and the noble sobriety of "God save the Queen" becomes a cry of desperation bordering on double sacrilege.

7   Sometimes, of course, our markings may be simply a matter of aes-thetics. Popping in a comma can be like slipping on the necklace that gives an outfit quiet elegance, or like catching the sound of running water that complements, as it completes, the silence of a Japanese landscape. When V. S. Naipaul, in his latest novel, writes, "He was a middle-aged man, with glasses," the first comma can seem a little precious. Yet it gives the description a spin, as well as a subtlety, that

it otherwise lacks, and it shows that the glasses are not part of the middle-agedness, but something else.

8   Thus all these tiny scratches give us breadth and heft and depth. A world that has only periods is a world without inflections. It is a world without shade. It has a music without sharps and flats. It is a martial music. It has a jackboot rhythm. Words cannot bend and curve. A comma, by comparison, catches the gentle drift of the mind in thought, turning in on itself and back on itself, reversing, redoubling and returning along the course of its own sweet river music; while the semicolon brings clauses and thoughts together with all the silent discretion of a hostess arranging guests around her dinner table.

9   Punctuation, then, is a matter of care. Care for words, yes, but also, and more important, for what the words imply. Only a lover notices the small things: the way the afternoon light catches the nape of a neck, or how a strand of hair slips out from behind an ear, or the way a finger curls around a cup. And no one scans a letter so closely as a lover, searching for its small print, straining to hear its nuances, its gasps, its sighs and hesitations, poring over the secret messages that lie in every cadence. The difference between "Jane (whom I adore)" and "Jane, whom I adore," and the difference between them both and "Jane—whom I adore—" marks all the distance between ecstasy and heartache. "No iron can pierce the heart with such force as a period put at just the right place," in Isaac Babel's lovely words; a comma can let us hear a voice break, or a heart. Punctuation, in fact, is a labor of love. Which brings us back, in a way, to gods.

(1,115 words)

VOCABULARY

pedant (1)	enunciated (6)	inflections (8)
proprieties (3)	ignominy (6)	martial (8)
inscrutability (4)	aesthetics (7)	nuances (9)
ideograms (4)	heft (8)	

THE FACTS

1. How does Iyer define punctuation? Which definition seems most helpful and which least? Give reasons for your answers.

2. The author never gives a formal definition of the comma. What reason can you offer for this omission?

3. What does the author mean when he suggests that punctuation is the "signature of cultures"?

4. In the author's view, how is punctuation related to music?

5. According to the author, what would writing be like if it were deprived of the comma?

THE STRATEGIES

1. Why does the author entitle his essay "In Praise of the Humble Comma" when most of the essay deals with punctuation in general?

2. What is the author's own style in this essay? How effective do you consider it?

3. What is the author's tone when he uses the word "humble" in connection with the comma?

4. What technique does the author use in closing his essay? How effective is it?

5. How does the author establish coherence between paragraphs 5 and 6?

THE ISSUES

1. If the author is correct and punctuation truly is "the signature of cultures," then how would you define our culture in terms of the way we use punctuation?

2. In your own writing, which punctuation mark gives you the most trouble? Which do you find the most helpful?

3. Review paragraph 3. What is your reaction to the author's view that our modern age has thrown off the Victorian restrictions of punctuation? If the author's view is true, has our new freedom improved writing? Why or why not?

4. How important is it for students to learn how to write with care? Support your answer with reasons.

5. What examples can you provide to support Isaac Babel's opinion that "[n]o iron can pierce the heart with such force as a period put at just the right place"? Use your imagination to create appropriate sentences.

SUGGESTIONS FOR WRITING

1. Write an essay in which you create your own definition of punctuation.

2. Write an essay in which you either support or attack the author's view that punctuation is a matter of care for what words imply.

3. Write an essay in which you assign responsibility for teaching punctuation to the proper educational institution.

▼▼

Gilbert Highet

KITSCH

GILBERT HIGHET (1906–1978) was born in Glasgow, Scotland, educated at the University of Glasgow and at Oxford, and became a naturalized American citizen in 1951. A classicist, Highet was known for his scholarly and critical writing, including *The Classical Tradition* (1949) and *The Anatomy of Satire* (1962).

You probably have had some experience with kitsch even if you do not know what the word means. You may have friends or relatives whose furniture, curios, or even favorite books are clearly kitschy. Gilbert Highet draws mainly on literary examples to define kitsch; but as you shall see, the concept applies to nearly all matters of bad taste.

1   If you have ever passed an hour wandering through an antique shop (not looking for anything exactly, but simply looking), you must have noticed how your taste gradually grows numb, and then—if you stay—becomes perverted. You begin to see unsuspected charm in those hideous pictures of plump girls fondling pigeons, you develop a psychopathic desire for spinning wheels and cobblers' benches, you are apt to pay out good money for a bronze statuette of Otto von Bismarck, with a metal hand inside a metal frock coat and metal pouches under his metallic eyes. As soon as you take the things home, you realize that they are revolting. And yet they have a sort of horrible authority; you don't like them; you know how awful they are; but it is a tremendous effort to drop them in the garbage, where they belong.

2   To walk along a whole street of antique shops—that is an experience which shakes the very soul. Here is a window full of bulbous Chinese deities; here is another littered with Zulu assagais, Indian canoe paddles, and horse pistols which won't fire; the next shopfront is stuffed with gaudy Italian majolica vases, and the next, even worse, with Austrian pottery—tiny ladies and gentlemen sitting on lace cushions and wearing lace ruffles, with every frill, every wrinkle and reticulation translated into porcelain: pink; stiff; but fortunately not unbreakable. The nineteenth century produced an appalling amount of junky art like this, and sometimes I imagine that clandestine underground factories are continuing to pour it out like illicit drugs.

3   There is a name for such stuff in the trade, a word apparently of Russian origin, kitsch:[1] it means vulgar showoff, and it is applied to anything that took a lot of trouble to make and is quite hideous.

4   It is paradoxical stuff, kitsch:[1] It is obviously bad: so bad that you can scarcely understand how any human being would spend days and weeks making it, and how anybody else would buy it and take it home and keep it and dust it and leave it to her heirs. It is terribly ingenious, and terribly ugly, and utterly useless; and yet it has one of the qualities of good art—which is that, once seen, it is not easily forgotten. Of course it is found in all the arts: think of Milan Cathedral, or the statues in Westminster Abbey, or Liszt's settings of Schubert songs. There is a lot of it in the United States—for instance, the architecture of Miami, Florida, and Forest Lawn Cemetery in Los Angeles. Many of Hollywood's most ambitious historical films are superb kitsch. Most Tin Pan Alley love songs are perfect 100 per cent kitsch.

5   There is kitsch in the world of books also. I collect it. It is horrible, but I enjoy it.

6   The gem of my collection is the work of the Irish novelist Mrs. Amanda McKittrick Ros, whose masterpiece, *Delina Delaney*, was published about 1900. It is a stirringly romantic tale, telling how Delina, a fisherman's daughter from Erin Cottage, was beloved by Lord Gifford, the heir of Columbia Castle, and—after many trials and even imprisonment—married him. The story is dramatic, not to say impossible; but it is almost lost to view under the luxuriant style. Here, for example, is a sentence in which Mrs. Ros explains that her heroine used to earn extra cash by doing needlework:

> She tried hard to assist in keeping herself a stranger to her poor old father's slight income by the use of the finest production of steel, whose blunt edge eyed the reely covering with marked greed, and offered its sharp dart to faultless fabrics of flaxen fineness.

Revolting, but distinctive: what Mr. Polly called "rockockyo" in manner. For the baroque vein, here is Lord Gifford saying goodby to his sweetheart:

> My darling virgin! my queen! my Delina! I am just in time to hear the toll of a parting bell strike its heavy weight of appalling softness against the weakest fibers of a heart of love, arousing and tickling its dormant action, thrusting the dart of evident separation deeper into its tubes of tenderness, and fanning the flame, already unextinguishable, into volumes of blaze.

---

[1] The Russian verb *keetcheetsya* means "to be haughty and puffed up."

Mrs. Ros had a remarkable command of rhetoric, and could coin an unforgettable phrase. She described her hero's black eyes as "glittering jet revolvers." When he became ill, she said he fell "into a state of lofty fever"—doubtless because commoners have high fever, but lords have lofty fever. And her reflections on the moral degeneracy of society have rarely been equaled, in power and penetration:

> Days of humanity, whither hast thou fled? When bows of compulsion, smiles for the deceitful, handshakes for the dogmatic, and welcome for the tool of power live under your objectionable, unambitious beat, not daring to be checked by the tongue of candour because the selfish world refuses to dispense with her rotten policies. The legacy of your forefathers, which involved equity, charity, reason, and godliness, is beyond the reach of their frivolous, mushroom offspring—deceit, injustice, malice and unkindness—and is not likely to be codiciled with traits of harmony so long as these degrading vices of mock ambition fester the human heart.

Perhaps one reason I enjoy this stuff is because it so closely resembles a typical undergraduate translation of one of Cicero's finest perorations: sound and fury, signifying nothing. I regret only that I have never seen Mrs. Ros's poetry. One volume was called *Poems of Puncture* and another *Bayonets of Bastard Sheen:* alas, jewels now almost unprocurable. But at least I know the opening of her lyric written on first visiting St. Paul's Cathedral:

> Holy Moses, take a look,
> Brain and brawn in every nook!

7   Such genius is indestructible. Soon, soon now, some earnest researcher will be writing a Ph.D. thesis on Mrs. Amanda McKittrick Ros, and thus (as she herself might put it) conferring upon her dewy brow the laurels of concrete immortality.

8   Next to Mrs. Ros in my collection of kitsch is the work of the Scottish poet William McGonagall. This genius was born in 1830, but did not find his vocation until 1877. Poor and inadequate poets pullulate in every tongue, but (as the *Times Literary Supplement* observes) McGonagall "is the only truly memorable bad poet in our language." In his command of platitude and his disregard of melody, he was the true heir of William Wordsworth as a descriptive poet.

9   In one way his talents, or at least his aspirations, exceeded those of Wordsworth. He was at his best in describing events he had never witnessed, such as train disasters, shipwrecks, and sanguinary battles, and in picturing magnificent scenery he had never beheld except with the eye of the imagination. Here is his unforgettable Arctic landscape:

Greenland's icy mountains are fascinating and grand,
And wondrously created by the Almighty's command;
And the works of the Almighty there's few can understand:
Who knows but it might be a part of Fairyland?

Because there are churches of ice, and houses glittering
     like glass,
And for scenic grandeur there's nothing can it surpass,
Besides there's monuments and spires, also ruins,
Which serve for a safe retreat from the wild bruins.

The icy mountains they're higher than a brig's topmast,
And the stranger in amazement stands aghast
As he beholds the water flowing off the melted ice
Adown the mountain sides, that he cries out, Oh! how nice!

10   McGonagall also had a strong dramatic sense. He loved to tell of
agonizing adventures, more drastic perhaps but not less moving than
that related in Wordsworth's "Vaudracour and Julia." The happy ending of one of his "Gothic" ballads is surely unforgettable:

So thus ends the story of Hanchen, a heroine brave,
That tried hard her master's gold to save,
And for her bravery she got married to the miller's eldest
     son,
And Hanchen on her marriage night cried Heaven's will be
     done.

11   These scanty selections do not do justice to McGonagall's ingenuity as a rhymester. His sound effects show unusual talent. Most poets
would be baffled by the problem of producing rhymes for the proper
names *General Graham* and *Osman Digna*, but McGonagall gets them
into a single stanza, with dazzling effect:

Ye sons of Great Britain, I think no shame
To write in praise of brave General Graham!
Whose name will be handed down to posterity without any
     stigma,
Because, at the battle of El-Tab, he defeated Osman Digna.

12   One of McGonagall's most intense personal experiences was his
visit to New York. Financially, it was not a success. In one of his vivid
autobiographical sketches, he says, "I tried occasionally to get an
engagement from theatrical proprietors and music-hall proprietors,
but alas! 'twas all in vain, for they all told me they didn't encourage

rivalry." However, he was deeply impressed by the architecture of Manhattan. In eloquent verses he expressed what many others have felt, although without adequate words to voice their emotion:

> Oh! Mighty City of New York, you are wonderful to
>   behold,
> Your buildings are magnificent, the truth be it told;
> They were the only thing that seemed to arrest my eye,
> Because many of them are thirteen stories high.
>
> And the tops of the houses are all flat,
> And in the warm weather the people gather to chat;
> Besides on the house-tops they dry their clothes,
> And also many people all night on the house-tops repose.

13   Yet McGonagall felt himself a stranger in the United States. And here again his close kinship with Wordsworth appears. The Poet Laureate, in a powerful sonnet written at Calais, once reproached the English Channel for delaying his return by one of those too frequent storms in which (reckless tyrant!) it will indulge itself:

> Why cast ye back upon the Gallic shore,
> Ye furious waves! a patriotic Son
> Of England?

14   In the same vein McGonagall sings with rapture of his return to his "ain countree":

> And with regard to New York, and the sights I did see,
> One street in Dundee is more worth to me,
> And, believe me, the morning I sailed from New York,
> For bonnie Dundee—my heart it felt as light as a cork.

15   Indeed, New York is a challenging subject for ambitious poets. Here, from the same shelf, is a delicious poem on the same theme, by Ezra Pound:

> My City, my beloved
> Thou art a maid with no breasts
> Thou art slender as a silver reed.
> Listen to me, attend me!
> And I will breathe into thee a soul,
> And thou shalt live for ever.

16   The essence of this kind of trash is incongruity. The kitsch writer is always sincere. He really means to say something important. He

feels he has a lofty spiritual message to bring to an unawakened world, or else he has had a powerful experience which he must communicate to the public. But either his message turns out to be a majestic platitude, or else he chooses the wrong form in which to convey it—or, most delightful of all, there is a fundamental discrepancy between the writer and his subject, as when Ezra Pound, born in Idaho, addresses the largest city in the world as a maid with no breasts, and enjoins it to achieve inspiration and immortality by listening to him. This is like climbing Mount Everest in order to carve a head of Mickey Mouse in the east face.

17   Bad love poetry, bad religious poetry, bad mystical prose, bad novels both autobiographical and historical—one can form a superb collection of kitsch simply by reading with a lively and awakened eye. College songs bristle with it. The works of Father Divine[2] are full of it—all the more delightful because in him it is usually incomprehensible. One of the Indian mystics, Sri Ramakrishna, charmed connoisseurs by describing the Indian scriptures (in a phrase which almost sets itself to kitsch-music) as

> fried in the butter of knowledge and steeped in the honey of love.

Bad funeral poetry is a rich mine of the stuff. Here, for example, is the opening of a jolly little lament, "The Funeral" by Stephen Spender, apparently written during his pink period:

> Death is another milestone on their way,
> With laughter on their lips and with winds blowing round
>   them
> They record simply
> How this one excelled all others in making driving belts.

Observe the change from humanism to communism. Spender simply took Browning's "Grammarian's Funeral," threw away the humor and the marching rhythm, and substituted wind and the Stakhanovist[3] speed-up. Such also is a delicious couplet from Archibald MacLeish's elegy on the late Harry Crosby:

> He walks with Ernest in the streets in Saragossa
> They are drunk their mouths are hard they saw *qué cosa*.

18   From an earlier romantic period, here is a splendid specimen. Coleridge attempted to express the profound truth that men and animals

---

[2] A black evangelist of New York.—Ed.

[3] Alexei Stakhanov, a Russian miner who devised a worker incentive system.—Ed.

are neighbors in a hard world; but he made the fundamental mistake
of putting it into a monologue address to a donkey:

> Poor Ass! Thy master should have learnt to show
> Pity—best taught by fellowship of Woe!
> Innocent foal! thou poor despised forlorn!
> I hail thee brother. . . .

19   Once you get the taste for this kind of thing it is possible to find
pleasure in hundreds of experiences which you might otherwise have
thought either anesthetic or tedious: bad translations, abstract painting, grand opera . . . Dr. Johnson, with his strong sense of humor, had
a fancy for kitsch, and used to repeat a poem in celebration of the marriage of the Duke of Leeds, composed by "an inferiour domestick . . . in
such homely rhimes as he could make":

> When the Duke of Leeds shall married be
> To a fine young lady of high quality,
> How happy will that gentlewoman be
> In his Grace of Leed's good company.
>
> She shall have all that's fine and fair,
> And the best of silk and sattin shall wear;
> And ride in a coach to take the air,
> And have a house in St. James's Square.

20   Folk poetry is full of such jewels. Here is the epitaph on an old gentleman from Vermont who died in a sawmill accident:

> How shocking to the human mind
> The log did him to powder grind.
> God did command his soul away
> His summings we must all obey.

21   Kitsch is well known in drama, although (except for motion pictures) it does not usually last long. One palmary instance was a play
extolling the virtues of the Boy Scout movement, called *Young England*. It ran for a matter of years during the 1930's, to audiences
almost wholly composed of kitsch-fanciers, who eventually came to
know the text quite as well as the unfortunate actors. I can still remember the opening of one magnificent episode. Scene: a woodland
glade. Enter the hero, a Scoutmaster, riding a bicycle, and followed by
the youthful members of his troop. They pile bicycles in silence. Then
the Scoutmaster raises his finger, and says (accompanied fortissimo
by most of the members of the audience):

Fresh water must be our first consideration

22   In the decorative arts kitsch flourishes, and is particularly wide-spread in sculpture. One of my favorite pieces of bad art is a statue in Rockefeller Center, New York. It is supposed to represent Atlas, the Titan condemned to carry the sky on his shoulders. That is an ideal of somber, massive tragedy: greatness and suffering combined as in Hercules or Prometheus. But this version displays Atlas as a powerful moron, with a tiny little head, rather like the pan-fried young men who appear in the health magazines. Instead of supporting the heavens, he is lifting a spherical metal balloon: it is transparent, and quite empty; yet he is balancing insecurely on one foot like a furniture mover walking upstairs with a beach ball; and he is scowling like a mad baboon. If he ever gets the thing up, he will drop it; or else heave it onto a Fifth Avenue bus. It is a supremely ridiculous statue, and delights me every time I see it.

23   Perhaps you think this is a depraved taste. But really it is an extension of experience. At one end, Homer. At the other, Amanda McKittrick Ros. At one end, *Hamlet*. At the other, McGonagall, who is best praised in his own inimitable words:

> The poetry is moral and sublime
> And in my opinion nothing could be more fine.
> True genius there does shine so bright
> Like unto the stars of night.

(2,816 words)

VOCABULARY

psychopathic (1)	ingenious (4)	mystical (17)
frock coat (1)	luxuriant (6)	incomprehensible (17)
bulbous (2)	perorations (6)	connoisseurs (17)
Zulu (2)	unprocurable (6)	anesthetic (19)
assagais (2)	pullulate (8)	palmary (21)
majolica (2)	platitude (8)	extolling (21)
reticulation (2)	sanguinary (9)	fortissimo (21)
appalling (2)	rapture (14)	spherical (22)
illicit (2)	incongruity (16)	depraved (23)
paradoxical (4)	enjoins (16)	inimitable (23)

THE FACTS

1. Where in his essay does Highet give a succinct definition of *kitsch?* After reading the essay, how would you explain this term to a friend who has never heard it?

2. What examples of kitsch does Highet provide? Name the three that impressed you most. Give reasons for your choice.

3. What metaphor does Mrs. Ros use to describe her hero's black eyes? Provide a metaphor or simile that would not be kitsch.

4. What characteristics of William McGonagall's poetry make it kitsch? Give a brief critique of two or three excerpts reprinted by Highet.

5. What is the essence of *kitsch,* according to the author? In what paragraph is this essence revealed?

THE STRATEGIES

1. What is the predominant tone of the essay? Supply appropriate examples of this tone.

2. Point out some examples of striking figurative language in the essay. Are they serious or humorous?

3. What mode of development does Highet use more than any other? How does this method help his definition?

4. In the final paragraph, what is the irony of using McGonagall's own words to praise him?

THE ISSUES

1. Can you think of some well-known examples of kitsch in the United States, not cited by Highet? What makes them kitsch?

2. Highet admits that certain kitsch items delight him. Explain how a person of taste might feel such delight.

3. How do you explain the overwhelming popularity of kitsch?

4. Popular lyrics are always a good source of kitsch. What lines from one of today's well-known songs can you quote as an example of kitsch? Do you still like the song despite the fact that it is kitsch? Give reasons for your answer.

5. Following are excerpts from two different love poems (A and B). Which of them might be considered kitsch? Why?

A.

The time was long and long ago,
  And we were young, my dear;
The place stands fair in memory's glow,
  But it is far from here.

The springtimes fade, the summers come,
  Autumn is here once more;
The voice of ecstasy is dumb,
  The world goes forth to war.

But though the flowers and birds were dead,
  And all the hours we knew,
And though a hundred years had fled,
  I'd still come back to you.

B.

Ah, love, let us be true
To one another! for the world, which seems
To lie before us like a land of dreams,
So various, so beautiful, so new,
Hath really neither joy, nor love, nor light,
Nor certitude, nor peace, nor help for pain;
And we are here as on a darkling plain
Swept with confused alarms of struggle and flight,
Where ignorant armies clash by night.

SUGGESTIONS FOR WRITING

1. Using Gilbert Highet's definition of *kitsch*, choose one area of popular taste today and show how it fits the definition.

2. Write a paragraph in which you compare or contrast the meaning of *camp* with that of *kitsch*.

▼▼

Frank Deford

CYSTIC FIBROSIS

Journalist and author FRANK DEFORD (b. 1938) was born in Baltimore and educated at Princeton University. Since 1962 he has been a senior writer for *Sports Illustrated*. He is also a commentator on sports for radio and television. Among his many published books are *There She Is: The Life and Times of Miss America* (1971), *The Owner* (1976), and *Alex: The Life of a Child* (1983), a tribute to his daughter who died of cystic fibrosis. Deford is vice-president of the Cystic Fibrosis Foundation.

Alexandra Deford, daughter of Frank and Carol Deford, was born in 1971 with the grim genetic inheritance of cystic fibrosis. Eight years later she was dead. This excerpt, taken from her grieving father's loving and moving account of his daughter's brief life, defines this deadly disease by describing its symptoms and showing the brutal and primitive treatment its victims must suffer daily to breathe.

1   Cystic fibrosis is, notwithstanding its name, a disease primarily of the lungs. It has nothing to do with cysts. It was not identified as a distinct clinical entity until the midthirties, and not until some years later was the full pathology comprehended. Inexplicably, the disease attacks not only the lungs but other disparate parts of the body: the pancreas, the major digestive organ; and, in males, the testes. So it undermines breathing, eating, reproduction—all of life itself.

2   The common agent in all cases is mucus. The cystic fibrosis victim's body manufactures too much mucus, or the mucus is too thick, or both. So baffling is the disease that nobody knows for sure which basic factor is the issue. Whatever, the mucus obstructs the airflow in the lungs and clogs the pancreas and the testes. Adding to the perplexity is the fact that no two patients have the same history, except in the sense that CF is always progressive, always terminal.

3   The luckiest patients are those born without lung involvement. Others have such mild cases that they go undetected for years; quite possibly there are even some CF patients who never know they have the disease, but die relatively young of some misunderstood pulmonary involvement. At the other end of the spectrum, some infants are essentially born dead, their tiny bodies so ravaged by the disease that they cannot even begin to draw breath.

4   As events proved, Alex was toward the worse end of the spectrum. While she died at eight, half of the children now born in the United States with cystic fibrosis who are diagnosed and treated live to the age of eighteen. Be grateful for small favors. Back in the midfifties, when the Cystic Fibrosis Foundation was started, a child with CF could not even expect to live to kindergarten. Regrettably, early steady advances stopped just about the time Alex was born. Until the early seventies almost every passing year saw another year of life expectancy added for a CF kid, but these advances were somewhat illusory. They were largely prophylactic, stemming almost entirely from

better maintenance and more powerful antibiotics. The longer life span in no way indicated an approaching cure, nor even a control (as, for example, insulin keeps diabetes under control). In a sense, it isn't accurate to say that we kept Alex alive—we merely postponed her dying.

5   Alex's day would start with an inhalation treatment that took several minutes. This was a powerful decongestant mist that she drew in from an inhaler to loosen the mucus that had settled in her lungs. Then, for a half hour or more, we would give her postural drainage treatment to accomplish the same ends physically. It is quite primitive, really, but all we had, the most effective weapon against the disease. Alex had to endure eleven different positions, each corresponding to a section of the lung, and Carol or I would pound away at her, thumping her chest, her back, her sides, palms cupped to better "catch" the mucus. Then, after each position, we would press hard about the lungs with our fingers, rolling them as we pushed on her in ways that were often more uncomfortable than the pounding.

6   Some positions Alex could do sitting up, others lying flat on our laps. But a full four of the eleven she had to endure nearly upside down, the blood rushing to her head, as I banged away on her little chest, pounding her, rattling her, trying somehow to shake loose that vile mucus that was trying to take her life away. One of her first full sentences was, "No, not the down ones now, Daddy."

7   Psychologists have found that almost any child with a chronic disease assumes that the illness is a punishment. Soon, the treatment itself blurs with the disease and becomes more punishment. Sick children have highly ambivalent feelings about their doctors, on the one hand hating them for the pain and suffering they inflict, on the other admiring them, wanting to grow up and be doctors. Wendy Braun and Aimee Spengler, Alex's best friends, told me after Alex died that whenever the three of them played doctors and nurses, Alex participated with enthusiasm, but when she played the doctor, it was always cancer she was seeking to cure. She could not bring herself to be a cystic fibrosis doctor. As much as she adored and trusted her specialist, Tom Dolan, she must have associated too much pain with him ever to want to *be* him.

8   In cystic fibrosis a child must transfer this attitude toward the parents, as well, for we were intimately and daily involved in the medical process. Imagine, if you will, that every day of your child's life you forced medicines upon her, although they never seemed to do any good; you required her to participate in uncomfortable regimens, which you supervised; and then, for thirty minutes or more, twice a day, you turned her upside down and pounded on her. And this never seemed to help either. I have been told that parents let their self-conscious resentment of the illness surface during the

treatments, and I must face the fact that this was sometimes surely true of me too. In some moments I must have thought that I was also being punished.

9   And say what you will, explain to me intellectually all you want about how much the postural drainage helped Alex—still, when every day I had to thump my little girl, pound away on her body, sometimes when she was pleading with me, crying out in pain to stop, something came over me, changed me. I guess, over eight years, I did therapy two thousand times, and Carol many more, probably three thousand, having to manage both times each day when I was traveling. I never understood how she managed. But still, me: Two thousand times I had to beat my sick child, make her hurt and cry and plead—"No, not the down ones, Daddy"—and in the end, for what?

10   After the therapy was finished, we had to start on the medicines. I recall how exciting it was during one period—Alex was two and a half—when she *only* had to take one antibiotic. How glorious that was, just one antibiotic every day. Usually it was two, and Dr. Dolan had to keep changing them, as Alex's body built up immunities.

11   She had to take many other medications, too, including, relentlessly, an enzyme preparation named Viokase. The bulk of Viokase is animal enzyme, which Alex needed because her pancreas couldn't produce sufficient enzymes of its own. Relative to the medicines that dealt primarily with her lung problems, Viokase was pretty effective. The minority of CF patients who don't have lung involvement initially can get by with the pancreas problem as long as they diligently take their enzyme substitutes. Alex had to take Viokase every time she ate anything. Of course, considering her lung condition, this seemed like small potatoes. Carol and I didn't even think about it much.

12   For most of her life, before she learned to swallow pills, Alex took the Viokase as a powder, mixed into apple sauce, which was an inexpensive carrying agent that could transport the drug into the system without its breaking down. And so, before every meal she ever ate, Alex had a plate of apple sauce with the enzyme powder mixed in. It was foul-tasting stuff, a bitter ordeal to endure at every meal. "Oh, my appasaws," she would moan, "my appasaws," always pronouncing it as if it were a cousin to chain saws or buzz saws.

13   "Come on Alex, eat your Viokase," I would say, and rather impatiently, too. After all, she had already been through an inhalation treatment, a half hour of physical therapy, several liquid medications—so what was the big deal with the apple sauce. *Come on, let's go.* Alex had had a great appetite when she was younger, but a few years later she'd just pick at her food. It occurred to me then that if all your life eating was a project, and you couldn't eat a lot of the delicious things everybody else enjoyed, eventually eating would bore you.

Imagine having to start off with apple sauce every time you ate anything—and not getting much sympathy for it, either.

14   Later, doctors and nurses or other people would say, "Alex seems to have lost her appetite," and I would nod gravely, being pretty sure by then that it was psychological. Eating, like everything else for Alex, had become strictly a matter of staying alive.

15   When she was very young, before she began to comprehend how pointless it all was, Alex was wonderfully accepting of all that was demanded of her. At first, like any baby, she wasn't in any position to quibble; she just seemed to go along, assuming that inhalation, apple sauce, and all that were things all babies endured. When she played with her dolls, she would give them therapy, putting off the down ones if the dolls behaved. After a time Alex began to notice that her brother was not required to endure what she did every day, but that didn't bother her too much either. Since she was the only baby girl around, she simply assumed that therapy was something that all babies and/or all girls must go through.

16   Only slowly did the recognition come that she was singled out for these things. Then she began to grope for the implications. One spring day when she was four, Alex came into my office and said she had a question. Just one was all she would bother me with. All right, I asked, what was it. And Alex said, "I won't have to do therapy when I'm a lady, will I?"

17   It was a leading question; she knew exactly where she was taking me.

18   As directly as I could I said, "No, Alex"—not because I would lie outright about it, but because I knew the score by then. I knew that she would not grow up to be a lady unless a cure was found.

(1,712 words)

VOCABULARY

disparate (1)	prophylactic (4)	regimens (8)
illusory (4)	ambivalent (7)	

THE FACTS

1. What is cystic fibrosis? What parts of the organ system does it attack?

2. What is the life expectancy of half the children now born in the United States with cystic fibrosis?

3. What is the attitude of children born with chronic diseases toward the doctors who treat them?

4. What kinds of treatment was Deford's daughter forced to suffer many years before she died in the end at age eight?

5. What question that Alex asked her father indicates that she was searching for the long-term implications of her disease?

THE STRATEGIES

1. Most definitions place the term to be defined in a certain class and then distinguish it from all others within that class. How and where does Deford use this technique?

2. Examine the first five paragraphs of this excerpt. What logical sequence does Deford follow in his order of topics?

3. What does the description of Alex's daily treatment add to your understanding of *cystic fibrosis?*

4. Deford repeatedly addresses the reader as "you." What effect does this have on you?

THE ISSUES

1. Do you agree with those who say that babies diagnosed in the womb as suffering from a terminal disease such as cystic fibrosis should be aborted? Why or why not?

2. How should parents treat children who suffer from painful diseases? Should they treat them as they would any other child? Should they give them extra sympathy? Should they be more protective?

3. What personal experience have you had with a young person suffering from some terminal disease or some incurable handicap? Describe the quality of life led by this person.

4. What more, if anything, should be done by our government or society to help families with offspring like the little girl described?

5. Why is it that children tend to think of chronic diseases as punishment?

SUGGESTIONS FOR WRITING

1. Some time ago, a child born with Down syndrome was not fed and allowed to die. The famous case of "Baby Doe" raised the issue of whether children born with terminal or incapacitating illnesses

should be given any treatment necessary to keep them alive. Write an essay expressing your views on this issue.

2. Write an essay defining the common cold, explaining its effects on you.

▼▼

Archibald MacLeish

ARS POETICA

ARCHIBALD MACLEISH (1892–1982), poet and playwright, was born in Glencoe, Illinois, and educated at Yale University. Trained as a lawyer, MacLeish served as librarian of Congress and as an adviser to President Franklin D. Roosevelt. A recurrent theme in his poetry was his deep apprehension about the rise of fascism. MacLeish won a Pulitzer Prize for a poetry collection, *Conquistador* (1932), and another for his play *J. B.* (1958).

In this famous poem, MacLeish proposes a succinct definition of poetry.

> A poem should be palpable and mute
> As a globed fruit,
>
> Dumb
> As old medallions to the thumb,
>
> 5 Silent as the sleeve-worn stone
> Of casement ledges where the moss has grown—
>
> A poem should be wordless
> As the flight of birds.
>
> A poem should be motionless in time
> 10 As the moon climbs,
>
> Leaving, as the moon releases
> Twig by twig the night-entangled trees,
>
> Leaving, as the moon behind the winter leaves,
> Memory by memory the mind—
>
> 15 A poem should be motionless in time
> As the moon climbs.

A poem should be equal to:
Not true.

For all the history of grief
An empty doorway and a maple leaf.

For love
The leaning grasses and two lights above the sea—

A poem should not mean
But be.

(144 words)

VOCABULARY

palpable   medallions   casement

THE FACTS

1. Translated, the poem's Latin title means "the art of poetry." Why is the title in Latin? How does the title relate to the poem?

2. Where does MacLeish give an explicit definition of poetry? How does he convey to the reader what poetry is?

3. In lines 17–18, what does MacLeish mean by the words "equal to: / Not true"?

4. The final stanza contains MacLeish's summarized view of poetry. What is your interpretation of the stanza?

THE STRATEGIES

1. "Ars Poetica" is developed through a series of paradoxes. Analyze and interpret each.

2. MacLeish suggests that all the history of grief could be summarized by "an empty doorway and a maple leaf." Do you consider this an appropriate image? Can you suggest another equally appropriate image?

3. What image does MacLeish suggest for love? Do you find this appropriate? Explain.

4. What synonyms for *mute* does the poet use? Cite them all.

5. What is the significance of repeating the fifth stanza in the eighth stanza?

THE ISSUES

1. What are some other definitions of poetry? What is your own definition? How does it compare or contrast with that of MacLeish?

2. MacLeish states that in a poem all of the history of grief can become "an empty doorway and a maple leaf." What other effective expressions or embodiments of grief can you suggest?

3. What does the author mean when he writes, in stanza 4, that "A poem should be wordless/As the flight of birds"? How does this statement relate to Highet's notion of kitsch? (See Highet's essay on pages 471–78)

4. Find a short poem that, in your view, perfectly exemplifies MacLeish's view that a poem should "not mean/But be." Do you like this poem? Why or why not?

SUGGESTIONS FOR WRITING

1. Consulting a collection of their works, find a definition of poetry by Wordsworth, Coleridge, Keats, or Shelley. Contrast that definition with "Ars Poetica." State which definition you like best and why.

2. Write a paragraph in which you give a definition of *love*, and support that definition with appropriate images. Then write another paragraph in which you do the same thing for *hate*.

ISSUES FOR CRITICAL THINKING AND DEBATE

RACISM

Even to the casual observer, racism in America remains a festering problem. Its toxic influence ranges from blatant discrimination in the housing market, where minorities are deliberately steered to specific neighborhoods, to subtle hiring practices where promotions are denied qualified applicants because of skin color. Blacks live shorter lives than whites, earn less money, and make up over half of U.S. murder

Rupert Garcia, Mexico, Chile, Soweto . . . , 1977. Pastel on paper 51 × 35 inches. Courtesy of the artist and Rena Bransten Gallery, San Francisco and Galerie Glaude Samvel, Paris, France.

victims (94% of whom are killed by other blacks). Compared to whites, blacks are also imprisoned more often and are more likely to be executed.

To remedy the inequality between whites and blacks, the Civil Rights Act was passed over twenty-five years ago and laws promoting affirmative action were firmly set in place. Although the effect of these measures was to narrow the educational gap between blacks and whites, nearly one-third of all black families and nearly one-half of all black children still live in poverty. Indeed, black married couples still earn about three-quarters the income of their white counterparts and are more than twice as likely to be poor. (Shulman, Steven, "The causes of black poverty: Evidence and interpretation," *Journal of Economic Issues*, December 1990).

How this inequality is viewed depends as much on the viewer's race as on any objective facts. The stark differences between whites and blacks in racial perception burst into the public consciousness with the October 1995, not-guilty verdict in the O.J. Simpson trial. Whites generally thought Simpson guilty and believed that a murderer had been set free; blacks typically thought him innocent and celebrated. There was an odder response exemplified by some blacks intellectuals who thought Simpson guilty, yet still gloated over his acquittal. One black professor who had been a federal prosecutor in the Bush administration even praised the defense tactic of encouraging jurors to forget the facts and, instead, render a verdict based on race (*Commentary*, December 1995). The prosecutor went on to argue in the *Yale Law Review* that "jury nullification," or playing the "race card" in high stakes trials, is "morally as well as legally right," because "African-Americans live in a police state."

The inequality between the races is so plain and stark that statistics do no more than confirm what the eye already sees. And predictably, the explanations for the causes of the inequality are divided along liberal/conservative fault lines. Liberals blame white racism and its poisonous legacy, arguing that the remedy for racial inequality is more government intervention. Conservatives argue that the time has come for racially neutral laws, with no affirmative action boost for minorities. Neither side denies the historical effects of racism. But while conservatives emphasize that the past is past and the playing field now level, liberals insist that the damage that has been done to black consciousness by past injustices cannot be so casually dismissed.

These two themes are implicit in the pieces we have chosen for this debate. The first is a wrenching chapter from a book, *Warriors Don't Cry*, by an African-American woman who helped desegregate Central High School in Little Rock, Arkansas, in 1954. For daring to want an education equal to that white Americans regard as their birthright, she was hounded with obscene phone calls, pelted with rocks, threatened by mobs, and tormented by her fellow students. The second is paradoxically by an Indian immigrant, himself a minority, who argues that black adaptation cultural patterns, used in the past to combat and resist racism, have now become hindrances to their full participation in the general society.

The turmoil caused by racism is as unsettling as it is unsettled. But the liberal/conservative argument over race boils down to the question: How much is the past really past? And what can we do to ensure that the ugly legacy of racism won't continue to poison the efforts of those men and women who try to make race relations better?

▼▼

Melba Patillo Beals

WARRIORS DON'T CRY

MELBA PATILLO BEALS (1941–   ) earned a B.A. degree from San Francisco State and a graduate degree from Columbia. She has worked as a reporter for NBC. Today she works as a communication consultant and has written books on public relations and marketing. In 1954, she was one of nine students chosen to integrated Central High School in Little Rock, Arkansas, in the wake of the Supreme Court Decision, *Brown vs. Board of Education of Topeka, Kansas*, that declared segregated schools illegal. The reading that follows is the opening chapter from her memoir of that traumatic experience, *Warriors Don't Cry* (1994).

1   In 1957, while most teenage girls were listening to Buddy Holly's "Peggy Sue," watching Elvis gyrate, and collecting crinoline slips, I was escaping the hanging rope of a lynch mob, dodging lighted sticks of dynamite, and washing away burning acid sprayed into my eyes.

2   During my junior year in high school, I lived at the center of a violent civil rights conflict. In 1954, the Supreme Court had decreed an end to segregated schools. Arkansas Governor Orval Faubus and states' rights segregationists defied that ruling. President Eisenhower was compelled to confront Faubus—to use U.S. soldiers to force him to obey the law of the land. It was a historic confrontation that generated worldwide attention. At the center of the controversy were nine black children who wanted only to have the opportunity for a better education.

3   On our first day at Central High, Governor Faubus dispatched gun-toting Arkansas National Guard soldiers to prevent us from entering. Mother and I got separated from the others. The two of us narrowly escaped a rope-carrying lynch mob of men and women shouting that they'd kill us rather than see me go to school with their children.

4   Three weeks later, having won a federal court order, we black children maneuvered our way past an angry mob to enter the side door of Central High. But by eleven that morning, hundreds of people outside were running wild, crashing through police barriers to get us out of school. Some of the police sent to control the mob threw down their badges and joined the rampage. But a few other brave members of the Little Rock police force saved our lives by spiriting us past the mob to safety.

5   To uphold the law and protect lives, President Eisenhower sent soldiers of the 101st Airborne Division, the elite "Screaming Eagles"— Korean War heroes.

6   On my third trip to Central High, I rode with the 101st in an army station wagon guarded by jeeps with turret guns mounted on their hoods and helicopters roaring overhead. With the protection of our 101st bodyguards, we black students walked through the front door of the school and completed a full day of classes.

7   But I quickly learned from those who opposed integration that the soldiers' presence meant a declaration of war. Segregationists mounted a brutal campaign against us, both inside and out of school.

8   My eight friends and I paid for the integration of Central High with our innocence. During those years when we desperately needed approval from our peers, we were victims of the most harsh rejection imaginable. The physical and psychological punishment we endured profoundly affected all our lives. It transformed us into warriors who dared not cry even when we suffered intolerable pain.

9   I became an instant adult, forced to take stock of what I believed and what I was willing to sacrifice to back up my beliefs. The experience endowed me with an indestructible faith in God.

10   I am proud to report that the Little Rock experience also gave us courage, strength, and hope. We nine grew up to become productive citizens, with special insights about how important it is to respect the value of every human life.

11   I am often asked, in view of the state of race relations today, if our effort was in vain. Would I integrate Central if I had it to do over again? My answer is yes, unequivocally yes. I take pride in the fact that, although the fight for equality must continue, our 1957 effort catapulted the civil rights movement forward a giant step and shifted the fight to a more dignified battlefield. For the first time in history, a President took a very bold step to defend civil rights—our civil rights.

12   Back then, I naively believed that if we could end segregation in the schools, all barriers of inequality would fall. If you had asked me in 1957 what I expected, I would have told you that by this time our struggle for human rights would have been won. Not so. But I am consoled by the words my grandmother spoke: "Even when the battle is long and the path is steep, a true warrior does not give up. If each one

of us does not step forward to claim our rights, we are doomed to an eternal wait in hopes those who would usurp them will become benevolent. The Bible says, WATCH, FIGHT, and PRAY."

13   Although I am perplexed by the state of race relations in this country today, I am at the same time very hopeful because I have ample evidence that what Grandmother promised me is true. With time and love, God solves all our problems. When we returned to Central High School for our first reunion in 1987, many Little Rock residents, white and black, greeted the nine of us as heroines and heroes. Hometown white folk in the mall smiled and said hello and offered directions even when they did not recognize us from our newspaper photos.

14   During all the fancy ceremonies, some of Arkansas's highest officials and businessmen came from far and wide to welcome us. And perhaps the most astounding evidence that things have indeed changed for the better was the attitude of Governor Bill Clinton.

15   "Call me Bill," he said, extending his hand, looking me in the eye. "You'all come on up to the house and sit a while." He flashed that charming grin of his. A few minutes of conversation assured me that his warm invitation was genuine. He is, after all, a man my brother refers to as "good people," based on their working relationship over the years.

16   So my eight friends and I found ourselves hanging out at the governor's mansion, the one Faubus built. Governor Clinton sauntered about serving soft drinks and peanuts. He and his wife, Hillary, were the kind of host and hostess who could make me feel at home even in the place where Faubus had hatched his devilish strategies to get the nine of us out of Central High School by any means possible.

17   "You'all ought to think about coming on back home now. Things are different," Governor Clinton said. He had been eleven years old when Faubus waged his segregationist battle against us. He displayed genuine respect for our contribution to the civil rights struggle. That visit was to become an evening I shall always treasure. As Chelsea played the piano and Bill and Hillary talked to me as though we'd known each other always, I found myself thinking, "Oh, Mr. Faubus, if only you and your friends could see us now."

18   My grandmother India always said God had pointed a finger at our family, asking for just a bit more discipline, more praying, and more hard work because He had blessed us with good health and good brains. My mother was one of the first few blacks to integrate the University of Arkansas, graduating in 1954. Three years later, when Grandma discovered I would be one of the first blacks to attend Central High School, she said the nightmare that had surrounded my birth was proof positive that destiny had assigned me a special task.

19   First off, I was born on Pearl Harbor Day, December 7, 1941. Mother says while she was giving birth to me, there was a big uproar, with the announcement that the Japanese had bombed Pearl Harbor. She remembers how astonished she was, and yet her focus was necessarily on the task at hand. There was trouble with my delivery because Mom was tiny and I was nine pounds. The doctor used forceps to deliver me and injured my scalp. A few days later, I fell ill with a massive infection. Mother took me to the white hospital, which reluctantly treated the families of black men who worked on the railroad. A doctor operated to save my life by inserting a drainage system beneath my scalp.

20   Twenty-four hours later I wasn't getting better. Whenever Mother sought help, neither nurses nor doctors would take her seriously enough to examine me. Instead, they said, "Just give it time."

21   Two days after my operation, my temperature soared to 106 and I started convulsing. Mother sent for the minister to give me the last rites, and relatives were gathering to say farewell.

22   That evening, while Grandmother sat in my hospital room, rocking me back and forth as she hummed her favorite hymn, "On the Battlefield for My Lord," Mother paced the floor weeping aloud in her despair. A black janitor who was sweeping the hallway asked why she was crying. She explained that I was dying because the infection in my head had grown worse.

23   The man extended his sympathy. As he turned to walk away, dragging his broom behind him, he mumbled that he guessed the Epsom salts hadn't worked after all. Mother ran after him asking what he meant. He explained that a couple of days before, he had been cleaning the operating room as they finished up with my surgery. He had heard the doctor tell the white nurse to irrigate my head with Epsom salts and warm water every two or three hours or I wouldn't make it.

24   Mother shouted the words "Epsom salts and water" as she raced down the hall, desperately searching for a nurse. The woman was indignant, saying, yes, come to think of it, the doctor had said something about Epsom salts. "But we don't coddle niggers," she growled.

25   Mother didn't talk back to the nurse. She knew Daddy's job was at stake. Instead, she sent for Epsom salts and began the treatment right away. Within two days, I was remarkably better. The minister went home, and the sisters from the church abandoned their death watch, declaring they had witnessed a miracle.

26   So fifteen years later, when I was selected to integrate Central High, Grandmother said, "Now you see, that's the reason God spared your life. You're supposed to carry this banner for our people."

(1,669 words)

VOCABULARY

decreed (2)   usurp (12)   sauntered (16)
endowed (9)   benevolent (12)   convulsing (21)
unequivocally (11)

THE FACTS

1. What president ordered the troops in to ensure the integration of the high school that the author attended?

2. What does the author admit she naively believed would happen if the segregation of schools could be ended?

3. Who was governor of Arkansas when the author returned to her former high school to be greeted as a heroine?

4. What happened to the author when she was born?

5. Whose muttered remark resulted in the author getting the treatment that saved her life?

THE STRATEGIES

1. The author wrote her memoir some forty years after the actual event. What kind of problems do you think she encountered in writing this piece so many years after it actually happened?

2. How would you characterize the person who seems to be telling the story? How old a person do you think she is? What characteristics of her language help project her onto the page?

3. What technique does the writer use in the opening paragraph to grab our interest?

4. The author tells the story of how she almost died when she was a baby, but does so with little or no editorial comment. Why is this an effective technique?

5. What else, other than the author's religious convictions, does the story about her early childhood illness dramatically illustrate?

THE ISSUES

1. What effect do you think living through such a traumatic experience is likely to have on someone? How does it seem to have affected the author?

2. The author says that she is perplexed by the state of race relations today. How do you feel about the relationship between the races in the United States today?

3. What do you regard as the most pressing issue in race relations today? What solution do you have for that issue?

4. The author says that the experience of desegregating Central High made her an "instant adult." What do you think she meant by that? What is an instant adult?

5. What, in your opinion, is necessary to end racism in the United States once and for all?

SUGGESTIONS FOR WRITING

1. Write an essay about an encounter with prejudice.

2. Write an essay about any side of racism.

▼▼▼

Dinesh D'Souza

THE END OF RACISM

DINESH D'SOUZA (1961–   ), writer and editor, was born in Bombay, India, and educated at Dartmouth College. He regularly writes for periodicals such as the *New York Times, Los Angeles Times,* and *Washington Post.* His books include *Falwell: Before the Millennium* (1985) and *Catholic Classics* (1986).

1   The affirmative action dilemma in the United States arises out of a conflict between two important social goals: equality of rights of individuals and equality of results for groups. The first, which Martin Luther King articulated when he called for us to be judged by our character rather than skin color, is probably the most widely shared tenet of the American Political creed. But if we wish to live in a pluralistic and inclusive nation, we will have to strive to avoid a social system in which some groups are durably ensconced at the top while others remained at the bottom; we cannot be indifferent to concerns about group equality of results.

2   Yet equality of rights for persons and equality of outcomes for groups are in conflict. An example from the University of California at Berkeley illustrates the point. I asked an admissions officer there to estimate the chances of acceptance for a black or Hispanic student with

a high school grade average of A-minus and a Scholastic Assessment Test (SAT) score of 1,200 out of 1,600. He said they were virtually 100 percent; the student would be guaranteed admission. I then asked him what were the acceptance odds for a student with the same grades, test scores, and extracurricular background who happened to be white or Asian. He said they would be about five percent.

3   So Berkeley, like most other universities, has established some racial preference in its admissions policies. Some conservatives have charged that Berkeley is getting rid of merit in its applications process, but this is not strictly true. Berkeley is considering merit, but within a given racial group. Berkeley admits the best white applicants, the best Hispanic applicants, and so on. But there seems to be no direct competition across racial lines; each applicant competes, in a sense, by running in his or her own ethnic lane.

4   Why do universities like Berkeley act in this manner? The public pretense is that university officials are deploying affirmative action remedies to fight racial discrimination. But the main obstacle to higher rates of black enrollment at Berkeley is not bigots in the admissions office; it is the merit principle. Studies have shown that under a strictly meritocratic admissions policy, the student body at the Berkeley campus would be more than 90 percent white and Asian (majority Asian). Black enrollment would be down in the 1 to 2 percent range. These ratios generate such intense liberal embarrassment that the pressure becomes irresistible to manipulate the admissions standards to produce a result more hospitable to group equality.

5   The effects of such proportional representation are now evident throughout higher education. Both in student admissions and faculty hiring, universities have institutionalized the practice of combating historical discrimination by practicing it. Blacks from middle-class and affluent families are routinely granted preference at the expense of poor whites with stronger academic credentials. Hispanics who have historically been classified as white in this country now get preferential treatment at the expense of Asians who are themselves a minority, who have suffered both *de facto* and *de jure* discrimination, and who have played no part in America's history of racial oppression. It is difficult to understand how these consequences of affirmative action help to promote social justice.

6   Even for groups who are intended as beneficiaries, the effect of affirmative action is mixed. Some students graduate from prestigious schools like Berkeley and are better off; but over the past decade more than 50 percent of blacks have dropped out, some for financial reasons surely, but many because they were outmatched in the extremely demanding atmosphere of Berkeley. Yet these are students whose level of preparation suggests that at another California campus, they would be evenly matched against their peers and would graduate in comparable

numbers. These minority students are worse off as a consequence of the "ratcheting up" effect of affirmative action.

7   Where does the concept of proportional representation come from? It developed over the past generation as the logical and common-sense expression of cultural relativism. As anthropologist Renato Rosaldo puts it, all cultures are equally legitimate and "no one of them is higher or lower, greater or lesser than any other."

8   In the early part of this century, cultural relativism became the best way for a new generation of American intellectuals and activists to defeat the old racism. The racism of the 19th century was not based on simple ignorance, fear, and hate as is often supposed; rather, it grew out of a rational attempt to account for the large differences of civilizational development between the West and other cultures—specifically sub-Saharan Africa—that emerged beginning in the 16th century and that could not be explained by environment. The old racists erected a hierarchy stretching from savagery to barbarism to civilization; only whites, they argued, were capable of civilization, while other groups occupied lower rungs on the totem pole of human achievement.

9   Led by the immigrant anthropologist Franz Boas and his famous students—Margaret Mead, Ruth Benedict, Melville Herskovits, and others—a newly ascendant group of American scholars challenged the old racist hierarchy by asserting that civilizational superiority was entirely in the eye of the beholder, that all human customs represented equally valid adaptations to local environments. The Boasians used a leveling vocabulary that replaced the 19th-century term "civilization" with the 20th-century term "culture."

10   A tremendous battle erupted between the old racists and the new antiracists. According to the civil rights morality tale, the good guys prevailed through logic and force of argument. In fact, neither side had a clear edge; it was Hitler who settled the argument. Hitler discredited the old *racism* not by proving it false but by showing it could have genocidal consequences. After World War II, the cultural relativists had established themselves as the only ethical alternative to Nazism.

11   Cultural relativism is very much alive today; indeed, it is the hidden rudder for the movement that we know as multiculturalism. What is wrong, its advocates ask, with students studying other cultures and employing diverse perspectives in thinking about issues? Indeed, if multiculturalism represented nothing more than an upsurge of interest in other cultures, it would be uncontroversial. Who can possibly be against studying the Analects of Confucius or the writings of Al Farabi and Ibn Sina?

12   The debate about multiculturalism, however, is not about whether to study other cultures but about how to study the West and other

cultures. Multiculturalism is based on a denial of Western cultural superiority.

13   But the doctrine that all cultures are equal does not square with our everyday observation of the world. Most of the developed world today is white and European. Asian countries are progressing rapidly, Latin and South America are gaining more slowly, while much of southern Africa remains mired in economic and political chaos. This pattern is repeated within the United States: on many important measures of academic and economic performance—from the SAT to the firefighters' test to rates of small business formation—whites and Asians come out on top, Hispanics fall in the middle, and blacks do least well.

14   Advocates of multiculturalism attribute these differences entirely to externally imposed factors such as a history of racist oppression. This is not to protest the moral legitimacy of the multicultural assault against slavery. Yet slavery was historically a universal practice; it is the abolition of slavery that is distinctively Western. Ironically, multiculturalism has come to suppress systematically the liberal tradition of the West that produced the abolition of slavery, the liberation of women, and other advances in civilization, even as it camouflages the illiberal traditions of non-Western cultures.

15   These classroom abuses are being increasingly exposed and recognized for what they are. Western civilization is proving more attractive than non-Western cultures, even to people who live in non-Western cultures. The deservedly neglected figures of Third World cultures who are now being forced into the academic canon cannot survive comparison with the greatest thinkers and creative minds of the West. In the long term, Shakespeare will survive Stanley Fish, one of today's leading literary deconstructionists.

16   How liberalism metamorphosed from an attack on *racism* to an attack on merit makes an interesting story. Cultural relativism supplied the premises for the civil rights movement that emerged in the 1950s and 1960s. Since racial groups were presumed equal in endowments and potential, civil rights leaders like Martin Luther King took it for granted that inequality was the consequence of whites at the top oppressing blacks at the bottom. They expected that outlawing racial discrimination would produce group equality. Martin Luther King himself predicted that equality of rights for individuals would lead, within a reasonably short period of time, to equality of results for groups, to "privilege and property widely distributed."

17   Over the past few decades, we have discovered that this premise is false. Merit, no less than the old *racism*, produces inequality—not just inequality between individuals but inequality among groups. Consequently, many civil rights organizations, and intellectuals such as black legal scholar Derrick Bell and white political scientist Andrew

Hacker, now attack merit standards as a camouflaged form of *racism*. Stanley Fish argues that tests like the SAT measure little more than "accidents of birth, social position . . . the opportunities to take vacations or tennis lessons."

18   Yet put aside the verbal section of the SAT, which conceivably includes terms like sonnet and sonata that are more familiar to young people who grow up in the suburbs, and concentrate only on the math section. Would anyone with a straight face maintain that equations are racially biased or that algebra is rigged against African Americans? Yet data from the College Board, which administers the SAT, show that year after year the racial gaps apparent on the verbal section of the test are equaled or exceeded on the math section.

19   This is the heart of America's race problem, which today is less a race problem than a black problem. The hard fact is that blacks are basically uncompetitive with other groups on many important measures of academic achievement and economic potential, so that equality of rights typically produces scandalous inequality of results. The liberal explanation is that black under-performance is the product of white *racism*, now expressed in increasingly subtle and exotic institutional forms. Richard Herrnstein and Charles Murray in *The Bell Curve* suggest that the problem may be due partly to genetic differences. If either of these views is correct, then it is very difficult to conceive of a way out of our present racial dilemma.

20   Yet there is an alternative theory that had greater explanatory power than either the liberal view or the genetic view. According to this view, group differences of academic achievement, economic performance, and social stability can be attributed to differences in culture. For instance, studies by psychologist James Flynn and sociologist Sanford Dombusch show that little separates the IQ test scores of whites and Asian Americans at the early age. Yet Asians on average do better on tests of academic performance in later years. The reason: Asian American students study harder. Cultural factors such as intact families and an orientation toward hard work and deferred gratification undoubtedly contribute to greater academic diligence among Asian American youngsters.

21   African Americans in this country are held back by aspects of black culture that developed as adaptations to historical circumstances, including racial opposition, but that have become outdated and dysfunctional today. Among these cultural traits are a reflexive racial paranoia that blames *racism* for every problem, even those that are intensely personal; a heavy reliance on government, both for jobs and welfare; a neglect of entrepreneurship; a hostility to homework and academic success, which are viewed as "acting white"; the valorization of the outlaw or "bad Negro," whose incivility and irresponsibility are viewed as

forms of courageous resistance to white oppression; and the normalization of illegitimacy and single-parent families.

22   These problems are not the result of genetic deficiency and they are not caused by contemporary white *racism*. Indeed the most serious of them did not exist in their present form a generation ago. For the first half of the 20th century, African Americans had an illegitimacy rate of around 20 to 25 percent, considerably higher than the white rate but vastly lower than the current rate, which is approaching 70 percent. Similarly, black crime rates have soared over the past generation. A generation ago the gene pool for blacks was roughly the same as it is today, and *racism* was far more overt and pervasive.

23   Some critics have pointed out that the African American cultural problems are really American problems, and to some degree this is true. The illegitimacy rate for whites today, for example, is not far from the black rate that Daniel Patrick Moynihan wrote about in his famous report on the black family in the 1960s, leading my colleague Charles Murray to warn of a "coming white underclass." The glamorization of violence and promiscuity pervades all of American popular culture today. Yet, even controlling for socioeconomic status, blacks are far more likely to bear children out of wedlock than other groups. Similarly, although crime rates for young people have risen nationwide, young black males are several times more likely to be arrested and convicted of burglary, rape, or homicide than their white counterparts.

24   The results of tests of academic achievement show that while there has been a decline in standards across the board, its effects are especially severe when it comes to the performance of African Americans. Data from the College Board, for example, show that whites and Asians who come from families earning less than $20,000 a year consistently score higher on the SAT than blacks who come from families earning more than $60,000 a year. These are ethnic, not merely socioeconomic, differences in academic skills.

25   Now there is much in African American culture that is both distinctively black and distinctively admirable; the black middle class has produced many notable leaders in education, religion, and the professions and is generally beset by many fewer problems than poor blacks. Yet there are some problems that the two groups share. One is a high degree of reliance on government, and there is a historical reason for it. While whites in America have historically viewed the government as the enemy of rights, for African Americans the federal government has been a deliverer and guarantor of rights. It was the federal government that abolished slavery, abolished Jim Crow and segregation, and that was employer of last resort (and in many cases first resort) for many blacks for much of this century.

26   Yet this cultural orientation, which made sense for a long time, is problematical today because government resources are more limited, because its record of solving complex social problems has proved to be poor, and because public confidence in government is at an all-time low. Other ethnic groups are finding that entrepreneurship is today a much quicker and more reliable route to prosperity and security.

27   Describing the contemporary black problem as largely a cultural problem is a tough message because nobody likes to hear that his culture is in any way less than perfect. Yet it is also a hopeful message, because if cultural deficiencies are recognized and confronted, they can be corrected. Unfortunately, I have found among many prominent intellectuals, both liberal and conservative, a ferocious aversion to acknowledging cultural breakdown in the black community. All criticism of black culture is dismissed as a form of *racism* or "racialism" or a callous way of "blaming the victim."

28   Now no one is to blame for being victim. Yet if as a reaction to being victimized, a group develops patterns of behavior that perpetuate poverty, dependency, and violence, then continuing to inveigh against the historical oppressor cannot offer the victim group much relief. Indeed, if white *racism* were to disappear overnight, many of the most serious problems plaguing the black community would remain.

29   Regarding pathologies like illegitimacy and violent crime, the victim may be in the best position to address the problem even though he was not entirely responsible for causing it. This does not absolve society of a responsibility to help, but in a free society the tentacles of government do not reach far enough to reform socialization practices. Blacks, then, must take primary responsibility even for cultural traits they did not freely choose, but which were to some extent imposed on them.

30   Mainstream black intellectuals and civil rights activists are not inclined to see matters this way; they are committed to a philosophy in which black problems are the fault of white oppression. Similarly, many white liberals refuse to support social policies that treat blacks as fully responsible citizens because they view black failures as the product of socially imposed deprivation. Raising the question of "why so many young men are engaged in what amounts to self-inflicted genocide," Andrew Hacker provides the prescribed answer: "It is white American that has made being black so disconsolate an estate."

31   This brings us to the ultimate irony: cultural relativism, once an effective weapon against the old *racism*, has now become the main obstacle to improving the civilizational standards of African Americans. Committed to a doctrine of cultural parity, relativism refuses to recognize the cultural dysfunctionalities in the black community. The black anthropologist Elijah Anderson identifies two cultures in the inner

city: a besieged culture of decency, characterized by people who work hard, maintain steady jobs, and keep their families together, and a hegemonic culture of incivility, promiscuity, and violence. Cultural relativism prevents many political and intellectual leaders from saying that one is better than the other.

32   *Racism* need not always be with us; it had a historical beginning, and it may have a historical end. But to achieve a society of true racial harmony in the United States, we need to adopt a new strategy, very different from the one that served so well in the civil rights era. We need, in my view, a twofold strategy: first, a public policy that is strictly race neutral; second, a program of cultural restoration. The University of California regents took an admirable step recently by outlawing racial preferences.

33   Yet color-blindness cannot succeed unless it is accompanied by a vigorous program of cultural restoration, so that blacks will become competitive with other groups on a wide range of measures of social achievement. Only then can African Americans dispel suspicions of inferiority, win the earned respect of other citizens, and full access to the fruits of the American dream.

(3,091 words)

VOCABULARY

articulated (1)	metamorphosed (16)	overt (22)
tenet (1)	endowments (16)	pervasive (22)
durably (1)	sonnet (18)	promiscuity (23)
ensconced (1)	sonata (18)	guarantor (25)
meritocratic (2)	deferred	aversion (27)
deploying (4)	gratification (20)	inveigh (28)
de facto (5)	dysfunctional (21)	socialization (29)
de jure (5)	entrepreneurship	disconsolate (30)
hierarchy (8)	(21)	hegemonic (31)
illiberal (14)	valorization (21)	dispel (33)
canon (15)	incivility (21)	

THE FACTS

1. According to the author, what did an admissions officer tell him about the chances of different groups being accepted for admission at the University of California at Berkeley?

2. What have studies shown would be the ethnic breakdown of students in the university system if affirmative action quotas were abolished?

3. Why, according to the author, have more than 50 percent of the black students dropped out of Berkeley?

4. What does the author mean by "cultural relativism?"

5. To what factor does the writer attribute what he alleges is black underachievement in academics and business?

THE STRATEGIES

1. What level audience do you think this essay is written for? What are some of its characteristics that identify it as being meant for a specific level of audience?

2. Early in the essay, the author alleges that Berkeley practices some kind of ethnic preference in its admissions policy. How would you evaluate his evidence for that particular claim?

3. What is the writer's evidence for his claims made in paragraph 5 that proportional minority representation, based on ethnicity rather than merit, is now widely evident throughout the educational system?

4. Read paragraph 18. In it the author uses a common rhetorical technique to advance his argument. What is it, and how effective do you rate this technique?

5. Examine the claims the author makes in paragraph 26. What counterargument might an opponent legitimately make against the author's claims?

THE ISSUES

1. What is your opinion of affirmative action programs? Do you think they do more harm than good, or more good than harm?

2. The author says that the old racial hierarchy derived not from fear and ignorance but from a rational attempt to account for differences in "civilizational development." What was irrational about this hierarchy from the very outset?

3. What about the author's argument may be identified as characteristic of a conservative point of view?

4. What, if anything, about white culture might also be subjected to the cultural restoration the author proposes for black culture?

5. What is your opinion of the future of race relations in the United States?

SUGGESTIONS FOR WRITING

1. Write an essay on race relations, taking any point of view that you prefer.

2. Do you think you could be a close friend with someone of another race? Write an essay saying why or why not.

STUDENT CORNER

▾▾

1

First Draft

Nancey Phillips, California State University at Long Beach

Racism: How Far Have We Come?

Add MLK Quote, "I have a dream..."
Dr. King had great hopes for
racial harmony in this country.

Intro needs attention, getter The 1960's saw many advancements towards ~~racial harmony.~~ *that end;*
The destruction of segregation and the passage of the Civil Rights

Amendment were giant steps toward equality. But today, as the
Twenty-first
~~21st~~ century approaches, one sensational crime has split the

country along racial lines and revealed the continuing problem of

deep-seated racism in the U.S. The arrest and trial of O.J. Simpson
in every level of American
for double murder has sparked heated debate ~~that proves~~ that *Society*
~~ing~~
there still remains a great divide between black and white.

On June 12, 1994, Nicole Brown Simpson and Ronald
California
Goldman were stabbed to death outside of Brown's ~~Brentwood~~

condominium. In the days that followed the murders, famous

football hero O.J. Simpson was arrested for the crime. The case

soon became a national obsession as millions tuned in to watch

the notorious slow-speed Bronco chase. The fact that Simpson, a

convicted spousal abuser, was thought to have killed his ex-wife

could have set off hostility between genders. The fact that

Simpson was an extremely wealthy celebrity, capable of

Phillips 2

assembling a virtual ^{\\}dream team["]of defense attorneys, could have

sparked controversy among opposed socio-economic classes. But

the O.J. Simpson trial did not pit men against women or rich

against poor; instead the country divided by race with black

America crying "innocent" and white America crying "guilty."

   After the lengthy and highly publicized trial, a predominately

black jury found Simpson not guilty, triggering ~~(one of the worst)~~ *the worst*   *too general*

wave~~s~~ of racial tension, *since the beating of Rodney King.* The evidence against Simpson was

considerable: his blood was found at the murder scene, the

victim's blood was found in his car, he had a history of violence

against Ms. Brown, and he had no alibi. Despite this mountain of

evidence, Simpson went home a free man. Prosecut~~er~~ *o sp* Marcia

Clark sharply criticized jurors and implied that race was the

paramount factor in their decision. <u>USA Today</u> quoted her as

saying, "Liberals don't want to admit it, but a majority black jury *under-line*

won't convict in a case like this. They won't bring justice."

   Simpson's supporters seem to fall into two distinct categories.

There are those who believe that he is guilty of the crime, but

deserves to go free to make up for the injustices that African

Americans have suffered through the years. Many black men have

been wrongly prosecuted and imprisoned due to the ~~the~~ color of

their skin. In addition, many white men have gone free simply

because their victims were black. The Medgar Evers murder case

is one example where a white jury would not convict a white

defend~~en~~t *a sp* for killing the civil rights leader. The black community

longs for atonement from the justice system, and O.J. is it.

Although this theory of making up for the past is flawed, the sentiment behind it is understandable to blacks and whites alike.

The second group of Simpson advocates truly believe in his innocence. It is here that black and white divide. The difference in opinion goes far beyond basic prejudice, although it is a contributing factor. The main issue here seems to be differing experiences with the criminal justice system. A large majority of African Americans distrust the police force, whereas most white Americans have nothing but confidence in ~~the police force.~~ these officers When the defense team suggested that much of the evidence in the case was planted by racist cops, the prosecutors balked at such a preposterous notion. The jurors had quite an opposite reaction. Psychologist Craig Haney, an expert on the role of race in the courtroom, states, "My guess is they went into the jury room and someone voiced concern about racism and a police conspiracy, and then there was widespread agreement that they couldn't trust the evidence." Quoted by USA Today, he continues, "That's a seemingly far-fetched idea to white folks underline who don't distrust the system, but in the African American community, it's not a hard sell at all."

Therefore, the seemingly overwhelming mountain of evidence is nullified in the mind of anyone who is suspicious of police work; the fact that most of those distrusting the police are black indicates a problem far more serious than the guilt or innocence of a football star. Black Americans are not receiving equal treatment at the hands of police or there would not be

Phillips 4

such wide-spread doubt regarding the validity of evidence. If

racist behavior [SP] is present on the police force, it is surely

present in others fractions of society.

too choppy move to Conclusion

And so, Americans find themselves still in the midst of racial

crisis. One must surmise that O.J. simpson has illuminated the

on-going problem of racism in this country, not because of his

guilt/innocence, but because of America's polarized reaction to

the case.

More than thirty years after Dr. King's landmark speech,

Positions on the Simpson case are not chosen randomly; different opinions are based on different experiences. Blacks and whites are simply not experiencing the same America.

I

Final Draft

Nancey Phillips, California State University at Long Beach

Racism: How Far Have We Come?

> "I have a dream my four little children will one day live in
> a nation where they will not be judged by the color of their
> skin but by the content of their character"
>
> —Martin Luther King, Jr.

Dr. Martin Luther King, Jr. had great hopes for racial harmony in this country. The 1960s saw many advancements towards that end; the destruction of segregation and the passage of the Civil Rights Amendment were giant steps toward equality. But today, as the Twenty-First Century approaches, one sensational crime has split the country along racial lines and revealed the continuing problem of deep-seated racism in the U.S. The arrest and trial of O.J. Simpson for double murder has sparked heated debate in every level of American society, proving that there still remains a great divide between black and white.

On June 12, 1994, Nicole Brown Simpson and Ronald Goldman were stabbed to death outside of Brown's California condominium. In the days that followed the murders, famous football hero O.J. Simpson was arrested for the crime. The case soon became a national obsession as millions tuned in to watch the notorious slow-speed Bronco chase. The fact that Simpson, a convicted spousal abuser, was thought to have killed his ex-wife could have set off hostility between genders. The fact that Simpson was an extremely wealthy celebrity, capable of assembling a virtual "dream team" of defense attorneys, could have sparked controversy among opposed socio-economic classes. But the O.J. Simpson trial did not pit men against women or rich against poor; instead the country divided by race with black America crying "innocent" and white America crying "guilty."

After the lengthy and highly publicized trial, a predominately black jury found Simpson not guilty, triggering the worst wave of racial tension since the beating of Rodney King. The evidence against Simpson was considerable: his blood was found at the murder scene, the victim's blood was found in his car, he had a history of violence against Ms. Brown, and he had no alibi. Despite this mountain of evidence, Simpson went home a free man. Prosecutor Marcia Clark sharply criticized jurors and implied that race was the paramount factor in their decision. USA Today quoted her as saying, "Liberals don't want to admit it, but a majority black jury won't convict in a case like this. They won't bring justice."

Simpson's supporters seem to fall into two distinct categories. There are those who believe that he is guilty of the crime, but deserves to go free to make up for the injustices that African Americans have suffered through the years. Many black men have been wrongly prosecuted and imprisoned due to the color of their skin. In addition, many white men have gone free simply because their victims were black. The Medgar Evers murder case is one example where a white jury would not convict a white defendant for killing the civil rights leader. The black community longs for atonement from the justice system, and O.J. is it. Although this theory of making up for the past is flawed, the sentiment behind it is understandable to blacks and whites alike.

The second group of Simpson advocates truly believe in his innocence. It is here that black and white divide. The difference in opinion goes far beyond basic prejudice, although it is a contributing factor. The main issue here seems to be differing experiences with the criminal justice system. A large majority of African Americans distrust the police force, whereas most white Americans have nothing but confidence in these officers. When the defense team suggested that much of the evidence in the case was planted by racist cops, the prosecutors balked at such a preposterous notion. The jurors had quite the opposite reaction. Psychologist Craig Haney, an expert on the role of race in the courtroom, states, "My guess is they went into the jury room and someone voiced concern about racism and a police conspiracy, and then there was widespread agreement that they couldn't trust the evidence." Quoted by <u>USA Today</u>, he continues, "That's a seemingly far-fetched idea to white folks who don't distrust the system, but in the African American community, it's not a hard sell at all."

Therefore, the seemingly overwhelming mountain of evidence is nullified in the mind of anyone who is suspicious of police work; the fact that most of those distrusting the police are black indicates a problem far more serious than the guilt or innocence of a football star. Black Americans are not receiving equal treatment at the hands of police or there would not be such wide-spread doubt regarding the validity of evidence. Positions on the Simpson case are not chosen randomly; different opinions are based on different experiences. Blacks and whites are simply not experiencing the same America.

And so, more than thirty years after Dr. King's landmark speech, Americans find themselves still in the midst of racial crisis. One must surmise that if racist behavior is present on the police force, it is surely present in other factions of society. O.J. Simpson has illuminated the on-going problem of racism in this country, not because of his guilt or innocence, but because of America's polarized reaction to the case.

How I Write

I need absolute quiet when I write, so I usually lock myself away in my bedroom to work. My list of necessary tools is quite succinct: my powerbook and a strong cup of tea. Inspiration tends to strike late at night . . . and very often the night before the assignment is due. (I suppose that would be desperation rather than inspiration.) Nevertheless, you can now understand my need for the tea; the powerbook, of course, is self-explanatory. My writing tends to be highly structured, and so I simply cannot begin a paper without having a clear outline in my head. I rarely write down a formal outline, but I will jot down on paper my main points and the order in which I will use them. Once I know where I'm going with a paper, I sometimes write the body paragraphs first, and go back to construct the introduction later. I find it difficult to give my reader a preview of coming attractions when I'm not even sure what's ahead; once the body is done, the introduction practically writes itself. I compose very slowly, agonizing over each sentence as I go, instead of simply getting the basic idea down and rewriting later. As a result, my first draft is generally pretty close to the final product. I know plenty of people who can breeze through their first draft and then spend time perfecting their work; but I simply cannot write that way. My time on a project is spent mentally categorizing and organizing my points, and then physically sitting at the computer, choosing the best words to express my ideas. Once I start writing, I don't like to stop until I'm finished with the project or until I run out of tea . . . and actually it appears that my cup is now empty.

How I Wrote This Essay

The most difficult part of writing this essay was narrowing down the topic. Volumes and volumes have been written on the topic of racism, and so I had to find the one small area that I could manage in an essay of this length. I must admit that I was absolutely addicted to the Simpson trial, and with the issue of race being so prominent in the case, it seemed natural to write about it. I did my research on the Internet. I searched under "Racism in the Simpson Case" and came up with over one thousand matches; there was no shortage of information to sift through. I found using the Internet quick and easy compared to digging through microfiche at the library. After compiling my information, I jotted down a few main points and went to work on writing the essay. I spent about four hours writing the first draft and another hour revising it.

My Writing Tip

My best writing tip is to have someone else read your paper before you print the final draft. I mean ANYONE! It doesn't have to be a tutor or an English major; even your Mom or Dad will suffice. I find that after writing a paper, I am too used to looking at the words to be objective, and I often miss simple spelling or punctuation errors. An outsider will give you a fresh perspective and often find errors that you missed.

CHAPTER WRITING ASSIGNMENTS

1. Write an essay in which you provide illustrations from history, physics, biology, psychology, or literature to prove one of the following maxims:
   a. "Every man is the architect of his own fortune." (Seneca)
   b. "The injury of prodigality leads to this, that he who will not economize will have to agonize." (Confucius)
   c. "The foundation of every state is the education of its youth." (Diogenes)
   d. "The pull of gravity exerts far more influence than one might think." (Anonymous)
   e. "Satire is the guerrilla weapon of political warfare." (Horace Greeley)

2. Choose one of the following terms and write an essay in which you first define the term as a dictionary would. Then give an extended definition, using the development most suitable for answering the question, "What is it?"
   a. romance
   b. tyranny
   c. adolescence
   d. education
   e. humility
   f. prejudice
   g. law
   h. *glasnost*

WRITING ASSIGNMENTS FOR A SPECIFIC AUDIENCE

1. Addressing yourself to a group of high school dropouts, write an essay about racism using examples from your own experience or that of acquaintances and friends.

2. Define the term authority for a seven-year-old child.

COLLABORATIVE WRITING PROJECT

Join a group of six other students. Brainstorm on the topic of race relations and racism. Ask yourself these questions: have you ever been the victim of a racial snub or slur? Have race relations gotten better or worse? How do you feel about the present state of race relations? What can be done to improve relations between the races? After gathering opinions and making notes, write an essay on one of the following topics:

1. What are the personal effects of racism?

2. What can be done to improve race relations?

3. Inter-racial relations?

4. The impact of the past on today's race relations.

Chapter Eight

ANALYZING

*Comparison/Contrast,
Division/Classification,
and Causal Analysis*

ADVICE
▼▼

HOW TO WRITE A COMPARISON OR CONTRAST

Comparisons and contrasts clarify a situation by pointing out similarities and differences. *Comparing* means to point out similarities; *contrasting* means to point out differences. Students today are often compared or contrasted with students of yesterday. A Cadillac is contrasted with a Rolls-Royce, or détente with peaceful coexistence. The effects of marijuana are compared with the effects of alcohol. In a special kind of comparison called *analogy,* conditions are compared that on surface view seem completely unlike: for instance, giving aid to Third World nations is compared to helping shipwrecked persons into a lifeboat, or the functions of the brain are compared to the functions of a computer. Analogies are useful for illustration but rarely for proving an argument, because sooner or later the analogy breaks down and becomes illogical.

Clarify the Bases of Your Comparison or Contrast

In writing a comparison/contrast, your first step is to identify the basis of it. Notice, for example, how Emerson's essay "Conservatism and Liberalism" contrasts on the basis of people's attitude toward change and reform. Suzanne Jordan's contrast of fat people and thin people focuses on differences in their personalities, outlooks, and temperaments.

Organize Your Comparison or Contrast

Let us assume that you wish to contrast the usefulness of a motorcycle with that of an automobile. First, you must establish the bases on which your contrast will rest—perhaps expense, upkeep, and safety. Once these have been established, you can develop your paragraphs in two ways. One approach is to use the *alternating method;* that is, you write about the difference between a motorcycle and a car insofar as expense is concerned, then move to the difference as far as upkeep is concerned, and finally to the difference as far as safety is concerned. This system would yield the following outline:

   I. Expense
      A. Motorcycle
      B. Automobile

  II. Upkeep
      A. Motorcycle
      B. Automobile

III. Safety
      A. Motorcycle
      B. Automobile

Another approach is the *block method* of dividing the essay into two parts, one dealing with the motorcycle and its expense, upkeep, and safety, the other dealing similarly with the automobile. This system would be outlined as follows:

   I. Motorcycle
      A. Expense
      B. Upkeep
      C. Safety

  II. Automobile
      A. Expense
      B. Upkeep
      C. Safety

The second system has the advantage of allowing you to deal with one item at a time (the motorcycle, without mentioning the automobile), but has the disadvantage of forcing your reader to wait until the end of the essay to draw a conclusive contrast between the two sides. The first system is more clearly a contrast because it requires the reader to move back and forth between the motorcycle and the automobile, continuously contrasting the two.

Use Verbal Indicators to Maintain Coherence

A good writer will sprinkle contrast paragraphs with indicators such as "on the other hand," "whereas," "but," "in contrast to," and "unlike." When comparing, the writer will use indicators such as "like," "as," "likewise," "similarly," and "also." These indicators help the coherence of the development.

E X A M P L E S

Ralph Waldo Emerson

FROM CONSERVATISM AND LIBERALISM

RALPH WALDO EMERSON (1803–1882), American poet, essayist, and lecturer, was born in Boston and educated at Harvard University. Publication of his essay "Nature" in 1836 established him as a leading spokesman for transcendentalism. This philosophy was based on a belief in the intuitive and spiritual nature of humankind that transcends physical experience. Though he considered himself primarily a poet, Emerson is better known for his essays and lectures.

Conservatism and liberalism are nowadays used almost exclusively as political labels. In this essay, however, Emerson contrasts the two philosophies as fundamentally opposing views—not only of politics but of life itself. His essay exemplifies the alternating method of comparing and contrasting.

1   The two parties which divide the state, the party of Conservatism and that of Innovation, are very old, and have disputed the possession of the world ever since it was made. This quarrel is the subject of civil history. The conservative party established the reverend hierarchies and monarchies of the most ancient world. The battle of patrician and

plebeian, of parent state and colony, of old usage and accommodation to new facts, of the rich and the poor, reappears in all countries and times. The war rages not only in battlefields, in national councils, and ecclesiastical synods, but agitates every man's bosom with opposing advantages every hour. On rolls the old world meantime, and now one, now the other gets the day, and still the fight renews itself as if for the first time, under new names and hot personalities.

2   Such an irreconcilable antagonism, of course, must have a correspondent depth of seat in the human constitution. It is the opposition of Past and Future, of Memory and Hope, of the Understanding and the Reason. It is the primal antagonism, the appearance in trifles of the two poles of nature. . . .

3   There is always a certain meanness in the argument of conservatism, joined with a certain superiority in its fact. It affirms because it holds. Its fingers clutch the fact, and it will not open its eyes to see a better fact. The castle, which conservatism is set to defend, is the actual state of things, good and bad. The project of innovation is the best possible state of things. Of course, conservatism always has the worst of the argument, is always apologizing, pleading a necessity, pleading that to change would be to deteriorate; it must saddle itself with the mountainous load of the violence and vice of society, must deny the possibility of good, deny ideas, and suspect and stone the prophet; whilst innovation is always in the right, triumphant, attacking, and sure of final success. Conservatism stands on man's confessed limitations; reform, on his indisputable infinitude; conservatism, on circumstance; liberalism, on power; one goes to make an adroit member of the social frame; the other to postpone all things to the man himself; conservatism is debonair and social; reform is individual and imperious. We are reformers in spring and summer; in autumn and winter we stand by the old; reformers in the morning, conservers at night. Reform is affirmative, conservatism negative; conservatism goes for comfort, reform for truth. Conservatism is more candid to behold another's worth; reform more disposed to maintain and increase its own. Conservatism makes no poetry, breathes no prayer, has no invention; it is all memory. Reform has no gratitude, no prudence, no husbandry. It makes a great difference to your figure and to your thought, whether your foot is advancing or receding. Conservatism never puts the foot forward; in the hour when it does that, it is not establishment, but reform. Conservatism tends to universal seeming and treachery, believes in a negative fate; believes that men's temper governs them; that for me, it avails not to trust in principles; they will fail me; I must bend a little; it distrusts nature; it thinks there is a general law without a particular application,—law for all that does not include any one. Reform in its antagonism inclines to asinine resistance, to kick with hoofs; it runs to egotism and bloated self-conceit; it runs to a bodiless

pretension, to unnatural refining and elevation, which ends in hypocrisy and sensual reaction.

4   And so whilst we do not go beyond general statements, it may be safely affirmed of these two metaphysical antagonists, that each is a good half, but an impossible whole. Each exposes the abuses of the other, but in a true society, in a true man, both must combine. Nature does not give the crown of its approbation, namely, beauty, to any action or emblem or actor, but to one which combines both these elements; not to the rock which resists the waves from age to age, nor to the wave which lashes incessantly the rock, but the superior beauty is with the oak which stands with its hundred arms against the storms of a century, and grows every year like a sapling; or the river which ever flowing, yet is found in the same bed from age to age; or, greatest of all, the man who has subsisted for years amid the changes of nature, yet has distanced himself, so that when you remember what he was, and see what he is, you say, what strides! what a disparity is here!

(765 words)

VOCABULARY

hierarchies (1)	agitates (1)	asinine (3)
patrician (1)	primal (2)	sensual (3)
plebeian (1)	infinitude (3)	approbation (4)
ecclesiastical (1)	debonair (3)	disparity (4)
synods (1)	imperious (3)	

THE FACTS

1. Emerson writes: "Such an irreconcilable antagonism, of course, must have a correspondent depth of seat in the human constitution" (paragraph 2). What does he mean by that?

2. Which of the two attitudes contrasted has the worst of the argument? Why is the other sure of final success?

3. Emerson says that conservatism is "all memory." What does he mean by that?

4. What are the weaknesses of conservatism? What are the weaknesses of liberalism? Why is it necessary that conservatism and liberalism be combined in a person?

5. Emerson says that either conservatism or liberalism makes a "good half, but an impossible whole." What does he mean by that?

THE STRATEGIES

1. Reread the final sentence in the first paragraph. Is this the natural wording of this sentence? Why is the sentence worded this way?

2. "The battle of patrician and plebeian, of parent state and colony, of old usage and accommodation to new facts, of the rich and the poor, reappears in all countries and times." What characteristic of style marks the sentence? Which sentences in paragraph 3 show similar construction?

3. "The castle, which conservatism is set to defend, is the actual state of things, good and bad." Does Emerson mean "castle" literally or figuratively? If the latter, what figure of speech is this, and what does "castle" mean?

4. "It makes a great difference to your figure and to your thought, whether your foot is advancing or receding." What figure of speech is this?

5. The contrast between liberalism and conservatism is developed within paragraphs. What technique of sentence construction makes this possible?

THE ISSUES

1. What issues—political, religious, or social—have recently revealed the antagonism between liberals and conservatives as discussed by Emerson?

2. Most of us are combinations of liberalism and conservatism, being conservative in some matters but liberal in others. Discuss where you stand on the following matters: spending your own money, premarital sex, joining the army, voting for a U.S. president, criminal punishment, ecology.

3. Emerson insists that in an ideal person, the two forces of liberalism and conservatism must combine. Do you agree? Why or why not?

4. What important world figure embodies the ideal of combined conservatism and liberalism? Do you admire this person? Why or why not?

5. Emerson uses the symbols of an oak tree and a river to embody the balance between conservatism and liberalism. Would the following symbols work? Why or why not? Analyze each in turn.

   fire

   rose

   bridge

   mountain

SUGGESTIONS FOR WRITING

1. Contrast your own political beliefs with those of a conservative or a liberal.

2. Analyze and discuss Emerson's characterization of conservatism. What are its most important elements?

▼▼

Suzanne Britt

THAT LEAN AND HUNGRY LOOK

SUZANNE BRITT (b. 1946), formerly a university teacher of English, is now a feature writer for the Raleigh, North Carolina, *News and Observer.*

Flying in the face of today's admiration for slimly elegant people, Britt gives the winning edge to the chubbies, favorably comparing them point by point with "that lean and hungry look" so mistrusted by Shakespeare.

1   Caesar was right. Thin people need watching. I've been watching them for most of my adult life, and I don't like what I see. When these narrow fellows spring at me, I quiver to my toes. Thin people come in all personalities, most of them menacing. You've got your "together" thin person, your mechanical thin person, your condescending thin person, your tsk-tsk thin person, your efficiency-expert thin person. All of them are dangerous.

2   In the first place, thin people aren't fun. They don't know how to goof off, at least in the best, fat sense of the word. They've always got to be adoing. Give them a coffee break, and they'll jog around the block. Supply them with a quiet evening at home, and they'll fix the screen door and lick S&H green stamps. They say things like "there aren't enough hours in the day." Fat people never say that. Fat people think the day is too damn long already.

3   Thin people make me tired. They've got speedy little metabolisms that cause them to bustle briskly. They're forever rubbing their bony hands together and eying new problems to "tackle." I like to surround myself with sluggish, inert, easygoing fat people, the kind who believe that if you clean it up today, it'll just get dirty again tomorrow.

4   Some people say the business about the jolly fat person is a myth, that all of us chubbies are neurotic, sick, sad people. I disagree. Fat people may not be chortling all day long, but they're a hell of a lot *nicer* than the wizened and shriveled. Thin people turn surly, mean and hard at a young age because they never learn the value of a hot-fudge sundae

for easing tension. Thin people don't like gooey soft things because they themselves are neither gooey nor soft. They are crunchy and dull, like carrots. They go straight to the heart of the matter while fat people let things stay all blurry and hazy and vague, the way things actually are. Thin people want to face the truth. Fat people know there is no truth. One of my thin friends is always staring at complex, unsolvable problems and saying, "The key thing is . . . " Fat people never say that. They know there isn't any such thing as the key thing about anything.

5   Thin people believe in logic. Fat people see all sides. The sides fat people see are rounded blobs, usually gray, always nebulous and truly not worth worrying about. But the thin person persists. "If you consume more calories than you burn," says one of my thin friends, "you will gain weight. It's that simple." Fat people always grin when they hear statements like that. They know better.

6   Fat people realize that life is illogical and unfair. They know very well that God is not in his heaven and all is not right with the world. If God was up there, fat people could have two doughnuts and a big orange drink anytime they wanted it.

7   Thin people have a long list of logical things they are always spouting off to me. They hold up one finger at a time as they reel off these things, so I won't lose track. They speak slowly as if to a young child. The list is long and full of holes. It contains tidbits like "get a grip on yourself," "cigarettes kill," "cholesterol clogs," "fit as a fiddle," "ducks in a row," "organize" and "sound fiscal management." Phrases like that.

8   They think these 2,000-point plans lead to happiness. Fat people know happiness is elusive at best and even if they could get the kind thin people talk about, they wouldn't want it. Wisely, fat people see that such programs are too dull, too hard, too off the mark. They are never better than a whole cheesecake.

9   Fat people know all about the mystery of life. They are the ones acquainted with the night, with luck, with fate, with playing it by ear. One thin person I know once suggested that we arrange all the parts of a jigsaw puzzle into groups according to size, shape and color. He figured this would cut the time needed to complete the puzzle by at least 50 per cent. I said I wouldn't do it. One, I like to muddle through. Two, what good would it do to finish early? Three, the jigsaw puzzle isn't the important thing. The important thing is the fun of four people (one thin person included) sitting around a card table, working a jigsaw puzzle. My thin friend had no use for my list. Instead of joining us, he went outside and mulched the boxwoods. The three remaining fat people finished the puzzle and made chocolate, double-fudged brownies to celebrate.

10   The main problem with thin people is they oppress. Their good intentions, bony torsos, tight ships, neat corners, cerebral machinations

and pat solutions loom like dark clouds over the loose, comfortable, spread-out, soft world of the fat. Long after fat people have removed their coats and shoes and put their feet up on the coffee table, thin people are still sitting on the edge of the sofa, looking neat as a pin, discussing rutabagas. Fat people are heavily into fits of laughter, slapping their thighs and whooping it up, while thin people are still politely waiting for the punch line.

11   Thin people are downers. They like math and morality and reasoned evaluation of the limitations of human beings. They have their skinny little acts together. They expound, prognose, probe and prick.

12   Fat people are convivial. They will like you even if you're irregular and have acne. They will come up with a good reason why you never wrote the great American novel. They will cry in your beer with you. They will put your name in the pot. They will let you off the hook. Fat people will gab, giggle, guffaw, gallumph, gyrate and gossip. They are generous, giving and gallant. They are gluttonous and goodly and great. What you want when you're down is soft and jiggly, not muscled and stable. Fat people know this. Fat people have plenty of room. Fat people will take you in.

(1,035 words)

VOCABULARY

metabolisms (3)	mulched (9)	guffaw (12)
inert (3)	boxwoods (9)	gallumph (12)
wizened (4)	machinations (10)	gyrate (12)
surly (4)	rutabagas (10)	gluttonous (12)
nebulous (5)	prognose (11)	
elusive (8)	convivial (12)	

THE FACTS

1. In a nutshell, what bothers the author most about thin people?

2. What is your view of the myth about the "jolly fat person" mentioned in paragraph 4? What evidence is there for your view?

3. In paragraph 9, what is the "list" objected to by the thin person? What is ironic about this objection?

4. The thesis of Britt's essay is obvious, but what is her underlying purpose? Since the essay is humorous, you might say that she simply wants to entertain the reader; but what more serious purpose is revealed?

5. In paragraph 10, Britt claims that thin people "oppress." What evidence does she cite to support this claim?

THE STRATEGIES

1. The title of the essay is a literary allusion that is echoed in the opening sentence. What is the origin of the allusion? What other allusion can you identify in the essay?

2. What rhetorical organization does the author use to develop her essay? What advantage does her organization present? What other type of organization could be used to contrast thin and fat people?

3. Paragraph 5 and other paragraphs open with short declarative sentences. What is the effect?

4. Here and there throughout the essay, Britt uses figurative language. Find three examples and label the kind of figure of speech used in each.

5. How does the author achieve humor in her essay? Cite appropriate examples of her techniques.

THE ISSUES

1. "Thin is in" is irrefutably one of the maxims of today. Why have we placed such emphasis on the slim look?

2. Reread John Leo's essay "Mirror, Mirror, on the Wall . . ." on pages 445–47. What does Leo say about the slim-hipped look of today? Does your answer to question one fit in with his view? Why or why not?

3. Are you convinced by Britt's logic about the superiority of fat people? How does it strike you? Be specific in your answer.

4. If you were to play devil's advocate, how would you describe the thin person as desirable and the fat person as undesirable? Give specific examples as does Britt.

5. How much or how little should a person's appearance affect his or her success on the job?

SUGGESTIONS FOR WRITING

1. Write a 500-word essay in which you prove the superiority of thin people over fat. Follow Suzanne Britt's style of using vivid details, but remain serious in your approach.

2. Using Britt's piece as a model, write a 500-word essay in which you contrast tall and short people.

▼▼

Gilbert Highet

DIOGENES AND ALEXANDER

GILBERT HIGHET (1906–1978) was born in Glasgow, Scotland, educated at the University of Glasgow and at Oxford, and became a naturalized American citizen in 1951. A classicist, Highet was known for his scholarly and critical writing, including *The Classical Tradition* (1949) and *The Anatomy of Satire* (1962).

This essay describes a meeting between two sharply contrasting personalities in Greek history—the Greek Cynic philosopher Diogenes (c. 412–323 B.C.) and Alexander the Great (356–323 B.C.), King of Macedonia. As Highet shows, although the two men occupied strikingly different positions in Greek society, they shared at least one quality that made them unique among the people of their time.

1   Lying on the bare earth, shoeless, bearded, half-naked, he looked like a beggar or a lunatic. He was one, but not the other. He had opened his eyes with the sun at dawn, scratched, done his business like a dog at the roadside, washed at the public fountain, begged a piece of breakfast bread and a few olives, eaten them squatting on the ground, and washed them down with a few handfuls of water scooped from the spring. (Long ago he had owned a rough wooden cup, but he threw it away when he saw a boy drinking out of his hollowed hands.) Having no work to go to and no family to provide for, he was free. As the market place filled up with shoppers and merchants and gossipers and sharpers and slaves and foreigners, he had strolled through it for an hour or two. Everybody knew him, or knew of him. They would throw sharp questions at him and get sharper answers. Sometimes they threw jeers, and got jibes; sometimes bits of food, and got scant thanks; sometimes a mischievous pebble, and got a shower of stones and abuse. They were not quite sure whether he was mad or not. He knew they were mad, each in a different way; they amused him. Now he was back at his home.

2   It was not a house, not even a squatter's hut. He thought everybody lived far too elaborately, expensively, anxiously. What good is a house? No one needs privacy; natural acts are not shameful; we all do the same things, and need not hide them. No one needs beds and chairs and such furniture: the animals live healthy lives and sleep on the

ground. All we require, since nature did not dress us properly, is one garment to keep us warm, and some shelter from rain and wind. So he had one blanket—to dress him in the daytime and cover him at night— and he slept in a cask. His name was Diogenes. He was the founder of the creed called Cynicism (the word means "doggishness"); he spent much of his life in the rich, lazy, corrupt Greek city of Corinth, mocking and satirizing its people, and occasionally converting one of them.

3   His home was not a barrel made of wood: too expensive. It was a storage jar made of earthenware, something like a modern fuel tank— no doubt discarded because a break had made it useless. He was not the first to inhabit such a thing: the refugees driven into Athens by the Spartan invasion had been forced to sleep in casks. But he was the first who ever did so by choice, out of principle.

4   Diogenes was not a degenerate or a maniac. He was a philosopher who wrote plays and poems and essays expounding his doctrine; he talked to those who cared to listen; he had pupils who admired him. But he taught chiefly by example. All should live naturally, he said, for what is natural is normal and cannot possibly be evil or shameful. Live without conventions, which are artificial and false; escape complexities and superfluities and extravagances: only so can you live a free life. The rich man believes he possesses his big house with its many rooms and its elaborate furniture, his pictures and his expensive clothes, his horses and his servants and his bank accounts. He does not. He depends on them, he worries about them, he spends most of his life's energy looking after them; the thought of losing them makes him sick with anxiety. They possess him. He is their slave. In order to procure a quantity of false, perishable goods he has sold the only true, lasting good, his own independence.

5   There have been many men who grew tired of human society with its complications, and went away to live simply—on a small farm, in a quiet village, in a hermit's cave, or in the darkness of anonymity. Not so Diogenes. He was not a recluse, or a stylite, or a beatnik. He was a missionary. His life's aim was clear to him: it was "to restamp the currency." (He and his father had once been convicted for counterfeiting, long before he turned to philosophy, and this phrase was Diogenes' bold, unembarrassed joke on the subject.) To restamp the currency: to take the clean metal of human life, to erase the old false conventional markings, and to imprint it with its true values.

6   The other great philosophers of the fourth century before Christ taught mainly their own private pupils. In the shady groves and cool sanctuaries of the Academy, Plato discoursed to a chosen few on the unreality of this contingent existence. Aristotle, among the books and instruments and specimens and archives and research-workers of his Lyceum, pursued investigations and gave lectures that were rightly named *esoteric* "for those within the walls." But for Diogenes,

laboratory and specimens and lecture halls and pupils were all to be found in a crowd of ordinary people. Therefore he chose to live in Athens or in the rich city of Corinth, where travelers from all over the Mediterranean world constantly came and went. And, by design, he publicly behaved in such ways as to show people what real life was. He would constantly take up their spiritual coin, ring it on a stone, and laugh at its false superscription.

7   He thought most people were only half-alive, most men only half-men. At bright noonday he walked through the market place carrying a lighted lamp and inspecting the face of everyone he met. They asked him why. Diogenes answered, "I am trying to find a *man.*"

8   To a gentleman whose servant was putting on his shoes for him, Diogenes said, "You won't be really happy until he wipes your nose for you: that will come after you lose the use of your hands."

9   Once there was a war scare so serious that it stirred even the lazy, profit-happy Corinthians. They began to drill, clean their weapons, and rebuild their neglected fortifications. Diogenes took his old cask and began to roll it up and down, back and forward. "When you are all so busy," he said, "I felt I ought to do *something!*"

10   And so he lived—like a dog, some said, because he cared nothing for privacy and other human conventions, and because he showed his teeth and barked at those whom he disliked. Now he was lying in the sunlight, as contented as a dog on the warm ground, happier (he himself used to boast) than the Shah of Persia. Although he knew he was going to have an important visitor, he would not move.

11   The little square began to fill with people. Page boys elegantly dressed, spearmen speaking a rough foreign dialect, discreet secretaries, hard-browed officers, suave diplomats, they all gradually formed a circle centered on Diogenes. He looked them over, as a sober man looks at a crowd of tottering drunks, and shook his head. He knew who they were. They were the attendants of the conqueror of Greece, the servants of Alexander, the Macedonian king, who was visiting his newly subdued realm.

12   Only twenty, Alexander was far older and wiser than his years. Like all Macedonians he loved drinking, but he could usually handle it; and toward women he was nobly restrained and chivalrous. Like all Macedonians he loved fighting; he was a magnificent commander, but he was not merely a military automaton. He could think. At thirteen he had become a pupil of the greatest mind in Greece, Aristotle. No exact record of his schooling survives. It is clear, though, that Aristotle took the passionate, half-barbarous boy and gave him the best of Greek culture. He taught Alexander poetry: the young prince slept with the *Iliad* under his pillow and longed to emulate Achilles, who brought the mighty power of Asia to ruin. He taught him philosophy, in particular the shapes and uses of political power: a few years later Alexander was

to create a supranational empire that was not merely a power system but a vehicle for the exchange of Greek and Middle Eastern cultures.

13   Aristotle taught him the principles of scientific research: during his invasion of the Persian domains Alexander took with him a large corps of scientists, and shipped hundreds of zoological specimens back to Greece for study. Indeed, it was from Aristotle that Alexander learned to seek out everything strange which might be instructive. Jugglers and stunt artists and virtuosos of the absurd he dismissed with a shrug; but on reaching India he was to spend hours discussing the problems of life and death with naked Hindu mystics, and later to see one demonstrate Yoga self-command by burning himself impassively to death.

14   Now, Alexander was in Corinth to take command of the League of Greek States which, after conquering them, his father Philip had created as a disguise for the New Macedonian Order. He was welcomed and honored and flattered. He was the man of the hour, of the century: he was unanimously appointed commander-in-chief of a new expedition against old, rich, corrupt Asia. Nearly everyone crowded to Corinth in order to congratulate him, to seek employment with him, even simply to see him: soldiers and statesmen, artists and merchants, poets and philosophers. He received their compliments graciously. Only Diogenes, although he lived in Corinth, did not visit the new monarch. With that generosity which Aristotle had taught him was a quality of the truly magnanimous man, Alexander determined to call upon Diogenes. Surely Dio-genes, the God-born, would acknowledge the conqueror's power by some gift of hoarded wisdom.

15   With his handsome face, his fiery glance, his strong supple body, his purple and gold cloak, and his air of destiny, he moved through the parting crowd, toward the Dog's kennel. When a king approaches, all rise in respect. Diogenes did not rise, he merely sat up on one elbow. When a monarch enters a precinct, all greet him with a bow or an acclamation. Diogenes said nothing.

16   There was a silence. Some years later Alexander speared his best friend to the wall, for objecting to the exaggerated honors paid to His Majesty; but now he was still young and civil. He spoke first, with a kindly greeting. Looking at the poor broken cask, the single ragged garment, and the rough figure lying on the ground, he said: "Is there anything I can do for you, Diogenes?"

17   "Yes," said the Dog, "Stand to one side. You're blocking the sunlight."

18   There was silence, not the ominous silence preceding a burst of fury, but a hush of amazement. Slowly, Alexander turned away. A titter broke out from the elegant Greeks, who were already beginning to make jokes about the Cur that looked at the King. The Macedonian officers, after deciding that Diogenes was not worth the trouble of kicking, were starting to guffaw and nudge one another. Alexander was

still silent. To those nearest him he said quietly, "If I were not Alexander, I should be Diogenes." They took it as a paradox, designed to close the awkward little scene with a polite curtain line. But Alexander meant it. He understood Cynicism as the others could not. Later he took one of Diogenes' pupils with him to India as a philosophical interpreter (it was he who spoke to the naked *saddhus*). He was what Diogenes called himself, a *cosmopolitēs*, "citizen of the world." Like Diogenes, he admired the heroic figure of Hercules, the mighty conqueror who labors to help mankind while all others toil and sweat only for themselves. He knew that of all men then alive in the world only Alexander the conqueror and Diogenes the beggar were truly free.

(1,960 words)

VOCABULARY

expounding (4)	discoursed (6)	suave (11)
conventions (4)	contingent (6)	supranational (12)
superfluities (4)	archives (6)	virtuosos (13)
stylite (5)	superscription (6)	

Professor Highet explains the meanings of several words used in the essay. How does he interpret the following?

Cynicism (2)	Diogenes (14)	cosmopolitēs (18)
esoteric (6)		

THE FACTS

1. What characteristics do Diogenes and Alexander share?

2. In what ways are Diogenes and Alexander different?

3. What is Diogenes's rationale for living so humbly?

4. According to Diogenes, the richer a man is, the more enslaved he becomes. How does he explain this statement?

5. How did the teaching method of Diogenes differ from that of Plato or Aristotle?

6. Paragraph 12 states that Alexander was far older and wiser than his twenty years. How is this maturity indicated?

7. According to the essay, Alexander "understood Cynicism as the others could not." What is Cynicism? Why did Alexander understand it better than others?

THE STRATEGIES

1. In what paragraph does the focus shift from Diogenes to Alexander?

2. Does Highet draw his contrast by alternating back and forth between Diogenes and Alexander, or does he first draw a full portrait of Diogenes and then a full portrait of Alexander? What does Highet's method require of the reader?

3. How do you explain the paradox "If I were not Alexander, I should be Diogenes"?

4. The opening paragraph contains a sentence characterized by balance and parallelism. What are the opening words of this sentence?

5. What is the literary term for the phrase "to restamp the currency"? What is the meaning?

6. What is the topic sentence for paragraphs 7, 8, and 9? How is it developed?

THE ISSUES

1. Which of the two men—Alexander or Diogenes—had a better chance for leading a contented life? Give reasons for your answer.

2. Reread the essay "My Wood" by E. M. Forster, pages 210–12. Then make a connection between Alexander's and Diogenes's lives and the essay. Ask yourself which of the two world figures most closely resembles the owner of the wood. Why?

3. Respond to paragraph 2. Do you agree with the idea that man should live naturally and that we have become far too elaborate? Give reasons for your answer.

4. How important are philosophy, poetry, and the principles of scientific investigation—all subjects taught Alexander by Aristotle—to a modern curriculum? What other subjects, if any, would you add to a balanced curriculum?

5. Which would you prefer being, a person of power or a person of influence? Be specific in describing yourself, later in life, as having achieved either of these characteristics. What job would you be holding? What kind of family life would you lead?

SUGGESTIONS FOR WRITING

1. Write a 500-word essay in which you state why you admire Alexander more than Diogenes, or vice versa. Base your essay on the portraits of the two men as drawn by Highet.

2. Choosing one of the pairs listed below, write an essay developed by contrast. Begin with a thesis that summarizes the contrast. Keep in mind the basis of your contrast.
   a. jealousy/envy
   b. Thoreau/Gandhi
   c. wisdom/knowledge
   d. statesman/politician
   e. old age/youth

▼▼

Bruce Catton

GRANT AND LEE: A STUDY IN CONTRASTS

BRUCE CATTON (1899–1978) is regarded as one of the most outstanding Civil War historians of the twentieth century. His books include *Mr. Lincoln's Army* (1951), *Glory Road* (1952), *A Stillness at Appomattox* (1953, Pulitzer Prize), and *This Hallowed Ground* (1956).

The following essay contrasts two famous personalities in American Civil War history: Ulysses S. Grant (1822–1885), commander in chief of the Union army and, later, eighteenth president of the United States (1869–1877); and his principal foe, Robert E. Lee (1807–1870), general in chief of the Confederate armies, who surrendered his forces to Grant in April of 1865. The essay illustrates the development of a comparison/contrast between paragraphs, rather than within a paragraph.

1   When Ulysses S. Grant and Robert E. Lee met in the parlor of a modest house at Appomattox Court House, Virginia, on April 9, 1865, to work out the terms for the surrender of Lee's Army of Northern Virginia, a great chapter in American life came to a close, and a great new chapter began.

2   These men were bringing the Civil War to its virtual finish. To be sure, other armies had yet to surrender, and for a few days the fugitive Confederate government would struggle desperately and vainly, trying to find some way to go on living now that its chief support was gone. But in effect it was all over when Grant and Lee signed the papers. And the little room where they wrote out the terms was the scene of one of the poignant, dramatic contrasts in American history.

3   They were two strong men, these oddly different generals, and they represented the strengths of two conflicting currents that, through them, had come into final collision.

4   Back of Robert E. Lee was the notion that the old aristocratic concept might somehow survive and be dominant in American life.

5   Lee was tidewater Virginia, and in his background were family, culture, and tradition . . . the age of chivalry transplanted to a New World which was making its own legends and its own myths. He embodied a way of life that had come down through the age of knighthood and the English country squire. America was a land that was beginning all over again, dedicated to nothing much more complicated than the rather hazy belief that all men had equal rights and should have an equal chance in the world. In such a land Lee stood for the feeling that it was somehow of advantage to human society to have a pronounced inequality in the social structure. There should be a leisure class, backed by ownership of land; in turn, society itself should be keyed to the land as the chief source of wealth and influence. It would bring forth (according to this ideal) a class of men with a strong sense of obligation to the community; men who lived not to gain advantage for themselves, but to meet the solemn obligations which had been laid on them by the very fact that they were privileged. From them the country would get its leadership; to them it could look for the higher values—of thought, of conduct, of personal deportment—to give it strength and virtue.

6   Lee embodied the noblest elements of this aristocratic ideal. Through him, the landed nobility justified itself. For four years, the Southern states had fought a desperate war to uphold the ideals for which Lee stood. In the end, it almost seemed as if the Confederacy fought for Lee; as if he himself was the Confederacy . . . the best thing that the way of life for which the Confederacy stood could ever have to offer. He had passed into legend before Appomattox. Thousands of tired, underfed, poorly clothed Confederate soldiers, long since past the simple enthusiasm of the early days of the struggle, somehow considered Lee the symbol of everything for which they had been willing to die. But they could not quite put this feeling into words. If the Lost Cause, sanctified by so much heroism and so many deaths, had a living justification, its justification was General Lee.

7   Grant, the son of a tanner on the Western frontier, was everything Lee was not. He had come up the hard way and embodied nothing in particular except the eternal toughness and sinewy fiber of the men who grew up beyond the mountains. He was one of a body of men who owed reverence and obeisance to no one, who were self-reliant to a fault, who cared hardly anything for the past but who had a sharp eye for the future.

8   These frontier men were the precise opposites of the tidewater aristocrats. Back of them, in the great surge that had taken people over the Alleghenies and into the opening Western country, there was a deep, implicit dissatisfaction with a past that had settled into grooves.

They stood for democracy, not from any reasoned conclusion about the proper ordering of human society, but simply because they had grown up in the middle of democracy and knew how it worked. Their society might have privileges, but they would be privileges each man had won for himself. Forms and patterns meant nothing. No man was born to anything, except perhaps to a chance to show how far he could rise. Life was competition.

9   Yet along with this feeling had come a deep sense of belonging to a national community. The Westerner who developed a farm, opened a shop, or set up in business as a trader, could hope to prosper only as his own community prospered—and his community ran from the Atlantic to the Pacific and from Canada down to Mexico. If the land was settled, with towns and highways and accessible markets, he could better himself. He saw his fate in terms of the nation's own destiny. As its horizons expanded, so did his. He had, in other words, an acute dollars-and-cents stake in the continued growth and development of his country.

10   And that, perhaps, is where the contrast between Grant and Lee becomes most striking. The Virginia aristocrat, inevitably, saw himself in relation to his own region. He lived in a static society which could endure almost anything except change. Instinctively, his first loyalty would go to the locality in which that society existed. He would fight to the limit of endurance to defend it, because in defending it he was defending everything that gave his own life its deepest meaning.

11   The Westerner, on the other hand, would fight with an equal tenacity for the broader concept of society. He fought so because everything he lived by was tied to growth, expansion, and a constantly widening horizon. What he lived by would survive or fall with the nation itself. He could not possibly stand by unmoved in the face of an attempt to destroy the Union. He would combat it with everything he had, because he could only see it as an effort to cut the ground out from under his feet.

12   So Grant and Lee were in complete contrast, representing two diametrically opposed elements in American life. Grant was the modern man emerging; beyond him, ready to come on the stage, was the great age of steel and machinery, of crowded cities and a restless, burgeoning vitality. Lee might have ridden down from the old age of chivalry, lance in hand, silken banner fluttering over his head. Each man was the perfect champion of his cause, drawing both his strengths and his weaknesses from the people he led.

13   Yet it was not all contrast, after all. Different as they were—in background, in personality, in underlying aspiration—these two great soldiers had much in common. Under everything else, they were marvelous fighters. Furthermore, their fighting qualities were really very much alike.

14   Each man had, to begin with, the great virtue of utter tenacity and fidelity. Grant fought his way down the Mississippi Valley in spite of acute personal discouragement and profound military handicaps. Lee hung on in the trenches at Petersburg after hope itself had died. In each man there was an indomitable quality . . . the born fighter's refusal to give up as long as he can still remain on his feet and lift his two fists.

15   Daring and resourcefulness they had, too; the ability to think faster and move faster than the enemy. These were the qualities which gave Lee the dazzling campaigns of Second Manassas and Chancellorsville and won Vicksburg for Grant.

16   Lastly, and perhaps greatest of all, there was the ability, at the end, to turn quickly from war to peace once the fighting was over. Out of the way these two men behaved at Appomattox came the possibility of a peace of reconciliation. It was a possibility not wholly realized, in the years to come, but which did, in the end, help the two sections to become one nation again . . . after a war whose bitterness might have seemed to make such a reunion wholly impossible. No part of either man's life became him more than the part he played in their brief meeting in the McLean house at Appomattox. Their behavior there put all succeeding generations of Americans in their debt. Two great Americans, Grant and Lee—very different, yet under everything very much alike. Their encounter at Appomattox was one of the great moments of American history.

(1,438 words)

VOCABULARY

poignant (2)	sanctified (6)	diametrically (12)
deportment (5)	obeisance (7)	burgeoning (12)
embodied (6)	tenacity (11)	

THE FACTS

1. What was Lee's background? What ideal did he represent?

2. What was Grant's background? What did he represent?

3. What was Grant's view of the past? What was his attitude toward society and democracy?

4. What was the most striking contrast between Grant and Lee?

5. Catton writes that the behavior of Grant and Lee at Appomattox "put all succeeding generations of Americans in their debt." Why?

THE STRATEGIES

1. Although the article is entitled "Grant and Lee: A Study in Contrasts," Catton begins by examining what Lee represented. Why? What logic is there to his order?

2. What function does paragraph 4 serve? Why is this one sentence set off by itself in a separate paragraph?

3. What common contrast phrase does paragraph 11 use?

4. In paragraph 8, the author writes: "These frontier men were the precise opposites of the tidewater aristocrats." What do these types have to do with a contrast between Grant and Lee?

5. What function does paragraph 8 serve?

THE ISSUES

1. Does an aristocracy still survive in our multicultural United States? If you believe it has survived, describe where and what it is. If you believe it has vanished, then describe what has taken its place.

2. Which kind of citizen do you admire most—the aristocrat or the frontiersman? Which do you believe is needed most for the betterment of our society today? Give reasons for your answers.

3. The aristocrat believes in form and tradition. How important are these in your view? Which traditions would you be willing to part with? Which would you want to keep?

4. What two women from history present an interesting contrast in two cultures? Describe both women and describe their contrasting cultures.

5. Which U.S. president, besides Ulysses S. Grant, is known for his support of economic growth and expansion? Do you favor continued growth and expansion, or are there other values you cherish more?

SUGGESTIONS FOR WRITING

1. Examine and analyze the organization of the contrast in this essay. In what various respects are Grant and Lee contrasted? How does Catton order and structure his contrast?

2. Discuss the idea that a society can benefit from the presence of a privileged class.

▼▼▼

Alfred Lubrano

BRICKLAYER'S BOY

ALFRED LUBRANO is a writer on the staff of the *Philadelphia Inquirer*. He has written articles for magazines such as *GQ* and regularly contributes commentaries on *National Public Radio*.

What happens when a son, through the labors and sacrifices of his blue-collar father, becomes an educated white-collar professional? How will his newly acquired white-collar values affect his relationship with his father? This situation, which is really quite common in opportunity-laden America, occurred to the author of this essay. In telling his appealing story, the author also develops a touching contrast between blue-collar father and white-collar son.

1   My father and I were college buddies back in the mid 1970s. While I was in class at Columbia, struggling with the esoterica du jour, he was on a bricklayer's scaffold not far up the street, working on a campus building.

2   Sometimes we'd hook up on the subway going home, he with his tools, I with my books. We didn't chat much about what went on during the day. My father wasn't interested in Dante, I wasn't up on arches. We'd share a *New York Post* and talk about the Mets.

3   My dad has built lots of places in New York City he can't get into: colleges, condos, office towers. He makes his living on the outside. Once the walls are up, a place takes on a different feel for him, as if he's not welcome anymore. It doesn't bother him, though. For my father, earning the dough that paid for my entrée into a fancy, bricked-in institution was satisfaction enough, a vicarious access.

4   We didn't know it then, but those days were the start of a branching off, a redefining of what it means to be a workingman in our family. Related by blood, we're separated by class, my father and I. Being the white-collar son of a blue-collar man means being the hinge on the door between two ways of life.

5   It's not so smooth jumping from Italian old-world style to U.S. yuppie in a single generation. Despite the myth of mobility in America, the true rule, experts say, is rags to rags, riches to riches. According to Bucknell University economist and author Charles Sackrey, maybe 10 percent climb from the working to the professional class. My father has had a tough time accepting my decision to become a mere newspaper

reporter, a field that pays just a little more than construction does. He wonders why I haven't cashed in on that multi-brick education and taken on some lawyer-lucrative job. After bricklaying for thirty years, my father promised himself I'd never pile bricks and blocks into walls for a living. He figured an education—genielike and benevolent—would somehow rocket me into the consecrated trajectory of the upwardly mobile, and load some serious loot into my pockets. What he didn't count on was his eldest son breaking blue-collar rule No. 1: Make as much money as you can, to pay for as good a life as you can get.

6   He'd tell me about it when I was nineteen, my collar already fading to white. I was the college boy who handed him the wrong wrench on help-around-the-house Saturdays. "You better make a lot of money," my blue-collar handy dad wryly warned me as we huddled in front of a disassembled dishwasher I had neither the inclination nor the aptitude to fix. "You're gonna need to hire someone to hammer a nail into a wall for you."

7   In 1980, after college and graduate school, I was offered my first job, on a now-dead daily paper in Columbus, Ohio. I broke the news in the kitchen, where all the family business is discussed. My mother wept as if it were Vietnam. My father had a few questions: "Ohio? Where the hell is Ohio?"

8   I said it's somewhere west of New York City, that it was like Pennsylvania, only more so. I told him I wanted to write, and these were the only people who'd take me.

9   "Why can't you get a good job that pays something, like in advertising in the city, and write on the side?"

10   "Advertising is lying," I said, smug and sanctimonious, ever the unctuous undergraduate. "I wanna tell the truth."

11   "The truth?" the old man exploded, his face reddening as it does when he's up twenty stories in high wind. "What's truth?" I said it's real life, and writing about it would make me happy. "You're happy with your family," my father said, spilling blue-collar rule No. 2. "That's what makes you happy. After that, it all comes down to dollars and cents. What gives you comfort besides your family? Money, only money."

12   During the two weeks before I moved, he reminded me that newspaper journalism is a dying field, and I could do better. Then he pressed advertising again, though neither of us knew anything about it, except that you could work in Manhattan, the borough with the water-beading high gloss, the island polished clean by money. I couldn't explain myself, so I packed, unpopular and confused. No longer was I the good son who studied hard and fumbled endearingly with tools. I was hacking people off.

13   One night, though, my father brought home some heavy tape and that clear, plastic bubble stuff you pack your mother's second-string

dishes in. "You probably couldn't do this right," my father said to me before he sealed the boxes and helped me take them to UPS. "This is what he wants," my father told my mother the day I left for Columbus in my grandfather's eleven-year-old gray Cadillac. "What are you gonna do?" After I said my good-byes, my father took me aside and pressed five $100 bills into my hands. "It's okay," he said over my weak protests. "Don't tell your mother."

14   When I broke the news about what the paper was paying me, my father suggested I get a part-time job to augment the income. "Maybe you could drive a cab." Once, after I was chewed out by the city editor for something trivial, I made the mistake of telling my father during a visit home. "They pay you nothin', and they push you around too much in that business," he told me, the rage building. "Next time, you gotta grab the guy by the throat and tell him he's a big jerk."

15   "Dad, I can't talk to the boss like that."

16   "Tell him. You get results that way. Never take any shit." A few years before, a guy didn't like the retaining wall my father and his partner had built. They tore it down and did it again, but the guy still bitched. My father's partner shoved the guy into the freshly laid bricks. "Pay me off," my father said, and he and his partner took the money and walked. Blue-collar guys have no patience for office politics and corporate bile-swallowing. Just pay me off and I'm gone. Eventually, I moved on to a job in Cleveland, on a paper my father has heard of. I think he looks on it as a sign of progress, because he hasn't mentioned advertising for a while.

17   When he was my age, my father was already dug in with a trade, a wife, two sons and a house in a neighborhood in Brooklyn not far from where he was born. His workaday, family-centered life has been very much in step with his immigrant father's. I sublet what the real-estate people call a junior one-bedroom in a dormlike condo in a Cleveland suburb. Unmarried and unconnected in an insouciant, perpetual-student kind of way, I rent movies during the week and feed single women in restaurants on Saturday nights. My dad asks me about my dates, but he goes crazy over the word "woman." "A girl," he corrects. "You went out with a girl. Don't say 'woman.' It sounds like you're takin' out your grandmother."

18   I've often believed blue-collaring is the more genuine of lives, in greater proximity to primordial manhood. My father is provider and protector, concerned only with the basics: food and home, love and progeny. He's also a generation closer to the heritage, a warmer spot nearer the fire that forged and defined us. Does heat dissipate and light fade further from the source? I live for my career, and frequently feel lost and codeless, devoid of the blue-collar rules my father grew up with. With no baby-boomer groomer to show me the way, I've been

choreographing my own tentative shuffle across the wax-shined dance floor on the edge of the Great Middle Class, a different rhythm in a whole new ballroom.

19   I'm sure it's tough on my father, too, because I don't know much about bricklaying, either, except that it's hell on the body, a daily sacrifice. I idealized my dad as a kind of dawn-rising priest of labor, engaged in holy ritual. Up at five every day, my father has made a religion of responsibility. My younger brother, a Wall Street white-collar guy with the sense to make a decent salary, says he always felt safe when he heard Dad stir before him, as if Pop were taming the day for us. My father, fifty-five years old, but expected to put out as if he were three decades stronger, slips on machine-washable vestments of khaki cotton without waking my mother. He goes into the kitchen and turns on the radio to catch the temperature. Bricklayers have an occupational need to know the weather. And because I am my father's son, I can recite the five-day forecast at any given moment.

20   My father isn't crazy about this life. He wanted to be a singer and actor when he was young, but that was frivolous doodling to his Italian family, who expected money to be coming in, stoking the stove that kept hearth fires ablaze. Dreams simply were not energy-efficient. My dad learned a trade, as he was supposed to, and settled into a life of pre-scripted routing. He says he can't find the black-and-white publicity glossies he once had made.

21   Although I see my dad infrequently, my brother, who lives at home, is with the old man every day. Chris has a lot more blue-collar in him than I do, despite his management-level career; for a short time, he wanted to be a construction worker, but my parents persuaded him to go to Columbia. Once in a while he'll bag a lunch and, in a nice wool suit, meet my father at a construction site and share sandwiches of egg salad and semolina bread.

22   It was Chris who helped my dad most when my father tried to change his life several months ago. My dad wanted a civil-service bricklayer foreman's job that wouldn't be so physically demanding. There was a written test that included essay questions about construction work. My father hadn't done anything like it in forty years. Why the hell they needed bricklayers to write essays I have no idea, but my father sweated it out. Every morning before sunrise, Chris would be ironing a shirt, bleary-eyed, and my father would sit at the kitchen table and read aloud his practice essays on how to wash down a wall, or how to build a tricky corner. Chris would suggest words and approaches.

23   It was so hard for my dad. He had to take a Stanley Kaplan-like prep course in a junior high school three nights a week after work for six weeks. At class time, the outside men would come in, twenty-five

construction workers squeezing themselves into little desks. Tough blue-collar guys armed with No. 2 pencils leaning over and scratching out their practice essays, cement in their hair, tar on their pants, their work boots too big and clumsy to fit under the desks.

24   "Is this what finals felt like?" my father would ask me on the phone when I pitched in to help long-distance. "Were you always this nervous?" I told him yes. I told him writing's always difficult. He thanked Chris and me for the coaching, for putting him through school this time. My father thinks he did okay, but he's still awaiting the test results. In the meantime, he takes life the blue-collar way, one brick at a time.

25   When we see each other these days, my father still asks how the money is. Sometimes he reads my stories; usually he likes them, although he recently criticized one piece as being a bit sentimental: "Too schmaltzy," he said. Some psychologists say that the blue-white-collar gap between fathers and sons leads to alienation, but I tend to agree with Dr. Al Baraff, a clinical psychologist and director of the Men-Center in Washington, D.C. "The core of the relationship is based on emotional and hereditary traits," Baraff says. "Class [distinctions] just get added on. If it's a healthful relationship from when you're a kid, there's a respect back and forth that'll continue."

26   Nice of the doctor to explain, but I suppose I already knew that. Whatever is between my father and me, whatever keeps us talking and keeps us close, has nothing to do with work and economic class.

27   During one of my visits to Brooklyn not long ago, he and I were in the car, on our way to buy toiletries, one of my father's weekly routines. "You know, you're not as successful as you could be," he began, blue-collar blunt as usual. "You paid your dues in school. You deserve better restaurants, better clothes." Here we go, I thought, the same old stuff. I'm sure every family has five or six similar big issues that are replayed like well-worn videotapes. I wanted to fast-forward this thing when we stopped at a red light.

28   Just then my father turned to me, solemn and intense. His knees were aching and his back muscles were throbbing in clockable intervals that registered in his eyes. It was the end of a week of lifting fifty-pound blocks. "I envy you," he said quietly. "For a man to do something he likes and get paid for it—that's fantastic." He smiled at me before the light changed, and we drove on. To thank him for the understanding, I sprang for the deodorant and shampoo. For once, my father let me pay.

(2,332 words)

VOCABULARY

esoterica (1)

vicarious (3)

lawyer-lucrative (5)

consecrated (5)

sanctimonious (10)

unctuous (10)

insouciant (17)

proximity (18)

primordial (18)

progeny (18)

dissipate (18)

choreographing (18)

THE FACTS

1. Despite the America dream, what does the author say the rule really is about mobility in American society?

2. The author says he broke blue-collar rule number 1. What is that rule?

3. Where was the author's first newspaper job?

4. What ambition did the author's father have but never fulfilled?

5. What was the outcome of the civil service test the author's father took?

THE STRATEGIES

1. In paragraph 1, the author says he was in class, struggling with "esoterica du jour." What is the meaning of this phrase? Where does it come from?

2. Although this is not formally structured as a contrasting essay, it still draws many contrasts between father and son. What are some of these contrasts, and how are they presented?

3. Throughout, the author occasionally peppers his language with slang phrases, such as, "I wasn't up on arches," or "I was hacking people off." Why do you think he does this?

4. Which paragraph sums up the thesis of this essay? What is its thesis?

5. Which of the two contrast patterns, interparagraph or intraparagraph, does the author chiefly use? Which pattern do you think better suits his purpose? Why?

THE ISSUES

1. How do you think a college education is likely to affect your relationship with your own family?

2. The author talks about the implicit rules of blue-collar life. What rule or rules can you think of that apply to white-collar life?

3. If blue-collar people work primarily for money, what do you think white-collar people primarily work for?

4. Which of the two lifestyles do you personally prefer, blue-collar or white-collar? Why?

5. The author reports being scolded by his father for saying "women" instead of "girls." What does this say about the relative sexism between of the two classes?

SUGGESTIONS FOR WRITING

1. Write an essay about any class conflict you've had with your own family.

2. Write a contrast between you and one of your parents.

▼▼

Alastair Reid

CURIOSITY

ALASTAIR REID (b. 1926) is a contemporary poet. He has translated the works of Jorge L. Borges, Pablo Neruda, and José E. Pacheo.

The poem that follows ostensibly draws a contrast between cats and dogs, but careful reading reveals that the animals are symbolic of certain types of people.

CURIOSITY

may have killed the cat. More likely,
the cat was just unlucky, or else curious
to see what death was like, having no cause
to go on licking paws, or fathering
litter on litter of kittens, predictably.

Nevertheless, to be curious
is dangerous enough. To distrust
what is always said, what seems,
to ask odd questions, interfere in dreams,
smell rats, leave home, have hunches,

does not endear cats to those doggy circles
where well-smelt baskets, suitable wives, good lunches
are the order of things, and where prevails
much wagging of incurious heads and tails.

15 Face it. Curiosity
will not cause us to die—
only lack of it will.

Never to want to see
the other side of the hill
20 or that improbable country
where living is an idyll
(although a probable hell)
would kill us all.
Only the curious
25 have if they live a tale
worth telling at all.

Dogs say cats love too much, are irresponsible,
are dangerous, marry too many wives,
desert their children, chill all dinner tables
30 with tales of their nine lives.

Well, they are lucky. Let them be
nine-lived and contradictory,
curious enough to change, prepared to pay
the cat-price, which is to die
35 and die again and again,
each time with no less pain.
A cat-minority of one
is all that can be counted on
to tell the truth; and what cats have to tell
40 on each return from hell
is this: that dying is what the living do,
that dying is what the loving do,
and that dead dogs are those who never know
that dying is what, to live, each has to do.

(276 words)

VOCABULARY

incurious

idyll

THE FACTS

1. On the surface, this poem is about cats and dogs. What deeper meaning does the poem have?

2. According to the author, what are the advantages of being a cat? What are the disadvantages?

3. Why are cats not loved by the "doggy circles"?

4. Who tells the real truth, cats or dogs?

THE STRATEGIES

1. The idea of death or dying is used repeatedly throughout the poem. In what different senses are *death, die,* and *dying* used?

2. What is the meaning of the parenthetical words in line 22?

3. What do the "doggy circles" of the second stanza symbolize?

4. What kind of person is "nine-lived"?

5. In what way are *living* and *loving* related in the fifth stanza?

THE ISSUES

1. As portrayed in Reid's poem, which would you rather be, a cat or a dog? Give reasons for your preference.

2. What famous characters from history would you align with cats, which with dogs? Why?

3. In favor of which species, if any, is the poem slanted? How can you tell?

4. Which would you rather be married to, a "cat" or a "dog"? Give reasons for your preference.

5. In an ideal society, what kind of balance or imbalance would you want between the number of "cats" and "dogs"?

SUGGESTIONS FOR WRITING

1. Using Alastair Reid's poem as a model, write a 500-word essay in which you compare and contrast two kinds of animals symbolic of people. For instance, you could contrast larks and owls, larks being people who rise early and owls people who love to stay up at night.

2. Write a 300-word essay in praise of "dogs" (cautious, conventional people).

A D V I C E

▼▼

HOW TO WRITE A DIVISION AND CLASSIFICATION

The term *division* refers to any piece of writing that intends to break a subject down into smaller units. For instance, an essay on types of automobiles that analyzes and classifies automobiles according to their sizes is developed by division; similarly, an essay on American personality types is also developed by division.

Division and classification are common to the way we think. We divide and classify the plant and animal kingdoms into phyla, genera, families, and species; we divide the military into the Army, Navy, Air Force, Marines, and Coast Guard. We divide and classify people into kinds and types. When we ask, "What kind of person is he?" we are asking for information developed by division and classification. An assignment asking for an essay developed by division is therefore an exercise in this common mode of thinking.

In developing an essay by division, it is useful to make this intent immediately clear. For instance, the essay by William Golding, "Thinking as a Hobby," which is anthologized in this section, makes it clear in the first paragraph what the writer intends to do:

> While I was still a boy, I came to the conclusion that there were three grades of thinking; and since I was later to claim thinking as my hobby, I came to an even stranger conclusion—namely, that I myself could not think at all.

We are therefore prepared for this division of thinking into three types, and for his anecdotes about why he has decided that he cannot think. Likewise, in John Holt's essay, "Kinds of Discipline," the opening sentence announces that "a child, in growing up, may meet and learn from three different kinds of discipline."

Having promised a division, both essays deliver it.

Divide Your Subject by a Single Principle

Once the division is made, stick to it. In the example below, the writer has violated this:

> Mating between man and woman takes place in four stages: the courtship, commitment, marriage, and deciding who will be responsible for household chores.

Courtship, commitment, and marriage are all part of mating; assigning responsibilities for household chores is not. Even if well executed, this essay contains a gross flaw by failing to subdivide its subjects according to the promised single principle—stages of mating.

Make Your Categories Mutually Exclusive

If you are dividing a subject into smaller categories, these must mutually exclude each other. This proposed division fails to develop mutually exclusive categories:

> College students may be divided into three groups: the so-called athletic "jock"; the scholarly "egghead"; and the student working his way through college.

Both the "jock" and the "egghead" could also be working their way through college. The categories are therefore not mutually exclusive.

Make the Division Complete

A division is useless if its categories are incomplete. For instance:

> The dialogue and the recitation are the primary ways in which information can be passed from teacher to student.

This division omits the lecture method and is therefore faulty.

Students sometimes wonder why essays are assigned to conform to specific types of development such as division and classification—why a student is not allowed to simply meander over a subject freely. The answer is that writing by strict means of development also trains the student to think. A pattern such as division forces the student to submit meanderings to the discipline of structure. Moreover, the pattern itself is not only a writing pattern but a thought pattern. Division and classification are a necessary part of logical thinking; assignments on them force a student to think on paper.

E X A M P L E S

▼▼

William Golding

THINKING AS A HOBBY

English novelist WILLIAM GOLDING (1911–1993) was educated at Oxford. Golding once described his hobbies as "thinking, classical Greek, sailing, and archaeology." His recent works include *The Pyramid* (1964), *The Scorpion God* (1971), and *Paper Work* (1984), but he is best known for his novel *Lord of the Flies* (1954). In 1983, Golding won the Nobel Prize for Literature.

Division and classification are often creative thinking exercises in which the essayist tries to find patterns and relationships that are not immediately obvious. In this essay, for example, William Golding concludes that there are three grades of thinking, which he explains with examples and anecdotes. Are there really only three grades of thinking? That is beside the point. The essayist is not a scientific researcher, but an expresser and shaper of opinion. Golding does here what any essayist should do: He makes us think.

1   While I was still a boy, I came to the conclusion that there were three grades of thinking; and since I was later to claim thinking as my hobby, I came to an even stranger conclusion—namely, that I myself could not think at all.

2   I must have been an unsatisfactory child for grownups to deal with. I remember how incomprehensible they appeared to me at first, but not, of course, how I appeared to them. It was the headmaster of my grammar school who first brought the subject of thinking before me—though neither in the way, nor with the result he intended. He had some statuettes in his study. They stood on a high cupboard behind his desk. One was a lady wearing nothing but a bath towel. She seemed frozen in an eternal panic lest the bath towel slip down any farther, and since she had no arms, she was in an unfortunate position to pull the towel up again. Next to her, crouched the statuette of a leopard, ready to spring down at the top drawer of a filing cabinet labeled A-AH. My innocence interpreted this as the victim's last, despairing cry. Beyond the leopard was a naked, muscular gentleman, who sat, looking down, with his chin on his fist and his elbow on his knee. He seemed utterly miserable.

3   Some time later, I learned about these statuettes. The headmaster had placed them where they would face delinquent children, because they symbolized to him the whole of life. The naked lady was the Venus

of Milo. She was Love. She was not worried about the towel. She was just busy being beautiful. The leopard was Nature, and he was being natural. The naked, muscular gentleman was not miserable. He was Rodin's Thinker, an image of pure thought. It is easy to buy small plaster models of what you think life is like.

4   I had better explain that I was a frequent visitor to the headmaster's study, because of the latest thing I had done or left undone. As we now say, I was not integrated. I was, if anything, disintegrated; and I was puzzled. Grownups never made sense. Whenever I found myself in a penal position before the headmaster's desk, with the statuettes glimmering whitely above him, I would sink my head, clasp my hands behind my back and writhe one shoe over the other.

5   The headmaster would look opaquely at me through flashing spectacles. "What are we going to do with you?"

6   Well, what *were* they going to do with me? I would writhe my shoe some more and stare down at the worn rug.

7   "Look up, boy! Can't you look up?"

8   Then I would look up at the cupboard, where the naked lady was frozen in her panic and the muscular gentleman contemplated the hindquarters of the leopard in endless gloom. I had nothing to say to the headmaster. His spectacles caught the light so that you could see nothing human behind them. There was no possibility of communication.

9   "Don't you ever think at all?"

10   No, I didn't think, wasn't thinking, couldn't think—I was simply waiting in anguish for the interview to stop.

11   "Then you'd better learn—hadn't you?"

12   On one occasion the headmaster leaped to his feet, reached up and plonked Rodin's masterpiece on the desk before me.

13   "That's what a man looks like when he's really thinking."

14   I surveyed the gentleman without interest or comprehension.

15   "Go back to your class."

16   Clearly there was something missing in me. Nature had endowed the rest of the human race with a sixth sense and left me out. This must be so, I mused, on my way back to the class, since whether I had broken a window, or failed to remember Boyle's Law, or been late for school, my teachers produced me one, adult answer: "Why can't you think?"

17   As I saw the case, I had broken the window because I had tried to hit Jack Arney with a cricket ball and missed him; I could not remember Boyle's Law because I had never bothered to learn it; and I was late for school because I preferred looking over the bridge into the river. In fact, I was wicked. Were my teachers, perhaps, so good that they could not understand the depths of my depravity? Were they clear, untormented people who could direct their every action by this mysterious

business of thinking? The whole thing was incomprehensible. In my earlier years, I found even the statuette of the Thinker confusing. I did not believe any of my teachers were naked, ever. Like someone born deaf, but bitterly determined to find out about sound, I watched my teachers to find out about thought.

18   There was Mr. Houghton. He was always telling me to think. With a modest satisfaction, he would tell me that he had thought a bit himself. Then why did he spend so much time drinking? Or was there more sense in drinking than there appeared to be? But if not, and if drinking were in fact ruinous to health—and Mr. Houghton was ruined, there was no doubt about that—why was he always talking about the clean life and the virtues of fresh air? He would spread his arms wide with the action of a man who habitually spent his time striding along mountain ridges.

19   "Open air does me good, boys—I know it!"

20   Sometimes, exalted by his own oratory, he would leap from his desk and hustle us outside into a hideous wind.

21   "Now, boys! Deep breaths! Feel it right down inside you—huge draughts of God's good air!"

22   He would stand before us, rejoicing in his perfect health, an open-air man. He would put his hands on his waist and take a tremendous breath. You could hear the wind, trapped in the cavern of his chest and struggling with all the unnatural impediments. His body would reel with shock and his ruined face go white at the unaccustomed visitation. He would stagger back to his desk and collapse there, useless for the rest of the morning.

23   Mr. Houghton was given to high-minded monologues about the good life, sexless and full of duty. Yet in the middle of one of these monologues, if a girl passed the window, tapping along on her neat little feet, he would interrupt his discourse, his neck would turn of itself and he would watch her out of sight. In this instance, he seemed to me ruled not by thought but by an invisible and irresistible spring in his nape.

24   His neck was an object of great interest to me. Normally it bulged a bit over his collar. But Mr. Houghton had fought in the First World War alongside both Americans and French, and had come—by who knows what illogic?—to a settled detestation of both countries. If either country happened to be prominent in current affairs, no argument could make Mr. Houghton think well of it. He would bang the desk, his neck would bulge still further and go red. "You can say what you like," he would cry, "but I've thought about this—and I know what I think!"

25   Mr. Houghton thought with his neck.

26   There was Miss Parsons. She assured us that her dearest wish was our welfare, but I knew even then, with the mysterious clairvoyance of

childhood, that what she wanted most was the husband she never got. There was Mr. Hands—and so on.

27   I have dealt at length with my teachers because this was my introduction to the nature of what is commonly called thought. Through them I discovered that thought is often full of unconscious prejudice, ignorance and hypocrisy. It will lecture on disinterested purity while its neck is being remorselessly twisted toward a skirt. Technically, it is about as proficient as most businessmen's golf, as honest as most politicians' intentions, or—to come near my own preoccupation—as coherent as most books that get written. It is what I came to call grade-three thinking, though more properly, it is feeling, rather than thought.

28   True, often there is a kind of innocence in prejudices, but in those days I viewed grade-three thinking with an intolerant contempt and an incautious mockery. I delighted to confront a pious lady who hated the Germans with the proposition that we should love our enemies. She taught me a great truth in dealing with grade-three thinkers; because of her, I no longer dismiss lightly a mental process which for nine-tenths of the population is the nearest they will ever get to thought. They have immense solidarity. We had better respect them, for we are outnumbered and surrounded. A crowd of grade-three thinkers, all shouting the same thing, all warming their hands at the fire of their own prejudices, will not thank you for pointing out the contradictions in their beliefs. Man is a gregarious animal, and enjoys agreement as cows will graze all the same way on the side of a hill.

29   Grade-two thinking is the detection of contradictions. I reached grade two when I trapped the poor, pious lady. Grade-two thinkers do not stampede easily, though often they fall into the other fault and lag behind. Grade-two thinking is a withdrawal, with eyes and ears open. It became my hobby and brought satisfaction and loneliness in either hand. For grade-two thinking destroys without having the power to create. It set me watching the crowds cheering His Majesty the King and asking myself what all the fuss was about, without giving me anything positive to put in the place of that heady patriotism. But there were compensations. To hear people justify their habit of hunting foxes and tearing them to pieces by claiming that the foxes like it. To hear our Prime Minister talk about the great benefit we conferred on India by jailing people like Pandit Nehru and Gandhi. To hear American politicians talk about peace in one sentence and refuse to join the League of Nations in the next. Yes, there were moments of delight.

30   But I was growing toward adolescence and had to admit that Mr. Houghton was not the only one with an irresistible spring in his neck. I, too, felt the compulsive hand of nature and began to find that pointing out contradiction could be costly as well as fun. There was

Ruth, for example, a serious and attractive girl. I was an atheist at the time. Grade-two thinking is a menace to religion and knocks down sects like skittles. I put myself in a position to be converted by her with an hypocrisy worthy of grade three. She was a Methodist—or at least, her parents were, and Ruth had to follow suit. But, alas, instead of relying on the Holy Spirit to convert me, Ruth was foolish enough to open her pretty mouth in argument. She claimed that the Bible (King James Version) was literally inspired. I countered by saying that the Catholics believed in the literal inspiration of Saint Jerome's *Vulgate*, and the two books were different. Argument flagged.

31   At last she remarked that there were an awful lot of Methodists, and they couldn't be wrong, could they—not all those millions? That was too easy, said I restively (for the nearer you were to Ruth, the nicer she was to be near to) since there were more Roman Catholics than Methodists anyway; and they couldn't be wrong, could they—not all those hundreds of millions? An awful flicker of doubt appeared in her eyes. I slid my arm round her waist and murmured breathlessly that if we were counting heads, the Buddhists were the boys for my money. But Ruth had *really* wanted to do me good, because I was so nice. She fled. The combination of my arm and those countless Buddhists was too much for her.

32   That night her father visited my father and left, red-cheeked and indignant. I was given the third degree to find out what had happened. It was lucky we were both of us only fourteen. I lost Ruth and gained an undeserved reputation as a potential libertine.

33   So grade-two thinking could be dangerous. It was in this knowledge, at the age of fifteen, that I remember making a comment from the heights of grade two, on the limitations of grade three. One evening I found myself alone in the school hall, preparing it for a party. The door of the headmaster's study was open. I went in. The headmaster had ceased to thump Rodin's Thinker down on the desk as an example to the young. Perhaps he had not found any more candidates, but the statuettes were still there, glimmering and gathering dust on top of the cupboard. I stood on a chair and rearranged them. I stood Venus in her bath towel on the filing cabinet, so that now the top drawer caught its breath in a gasp of sexy excitement. "A-ah!" The portentous Thinker I placed on the edge of the cupboard so that he looked down at the bath towel and waited for it to slip.

34   Grade-two thinking, though it filled life with fun and excitement, did not make for content. To find out the deficiencies of our elders bolsters the young ego but does not make for personal security. I found that grade two was not only the power to point out contradictions. It took the swimmer some distance from the shore and left him there, out of his depth. I decided that Pontius Pilate was a typical grade-two

thinker. "What is truth?" he said, a very common grade-two thought, but one that is used always as the end of an argument instead of the beginning. There is a still higher grade of thought which says, "What is truth?" and sets out to find it.

35   But these grade-one thinkers were few and far between. They did not visit my grammar school in the flesh though they were there in books. I aspired to them, partly because I was ambitious and partly because I now saw my hobby as an unsatisfactory thing if it went no further. If you set out to climb a mountain, however high you climb, you have failed if you cannot reach the top.

36   I *did* meet an undeniably grade-one thinker in my first year at Oxford. I was looking over a small bridge in Magdalen Deer Park, and a tiny mustached and hatted figure came and stood by my side. He was a German who had just fled from the Nazis to Oxford as a temporary refuge. His name was Einstein.

37   But Professor Einstein knew no English at that time and I knew only two words of German. I beamed at him, trying wordlessly to convey by my bearing all the affection and respect that the English felt for him. It is possible—and I have to make the admission—that I felt here were two grade-one thinkers standing side by side; yet I doubt if my face conveyed more than a formless awe. I would have given my Greek and Latin and French and a good slice of my English for enough German to communicate. But we were divided; he was as inscrutable as my headmaster. For perhaps five minutes we stood together on the bridge, undeniable grade-one thinker and breathless aspirant. With true greatness, Professor Einstein realized that any contact was better than none. He pointed to a trout wavering in midstream.

38   He spoke: "Fisch."

39   My brain reeled. Here I was, mingling with the great, and yet helpless as the veriest grade-three thinker. Desperately I sought for some sign by which I might convey that I, too, revered pure reason. I nodded vehemently. In a brilliant flash I used up half of my German vocabulary. "*Fisch. Ja. Ja.*"

40   For perhaps another five minutes we stood side by side. Then Professor Einstein, his whole figure still conveying good will and amiability, drifted away out of sight.

41   I, too, would be a grade-one thinker. I was irreverent at the best of times. Political and religious systems, social customs, loyalties and traditions, they all came tumbling down like so many rotten apples off a tree. This was a fine hobby and a sensible substitute for cricket, since you could play it all the year round. I came up in the end with what must always remain the justification for grade-one thinking, its sign, seal and charter. I devised a coherent system for living. It was a moral system, which was wholly logical. Of course, as I readily admitted, conversion of the world to my way of thinking might be difficult, since

my system did away with a number of trifles, such as big business, centralized government, armies, marriage . . .

42   It was Ruth all over again. I had some very good friends who stood by me, and still do. But my acquaintances vanished, taking the girls with them. Young women seemed oddly contented with the world as it was. They valued the meaningless ceremony with a ring. Young men, while willing to concede the chaining sordidness of marriage, were hesitant about abandoning the organizations which they hoped would give them a career. A young man on the first rung of the Royal Navy, while perfectly agreeable to doing away with big business and marriage, got as red-necked as Mr. Houghton when I proposed a world without any battleships in it.

43   Had the game gone too far? Was it a game any longer? In those prewar days, I stood to lose a great deal, for the sake of a hobby.

44   Now you are expecting me to describe how I saw the folly of my ways and came back to the warm nest, where prejudices are so often called loyalties, where pointless actions are hallowed into custom by repetition, where we are content to say we think when all we do is feel.

45   But you would be wrong. I dropped my hobby and turned professional.

46   If I were to go back to the headmaster's study and find the dusty statuettes still there, I would arrange them differently. I would dust Venus and put her aside, for I have come to love her and know her for the fair thing she is. But I would put the Thinker, sunk in his desperate thought, where there were shadows before him—and at his back, I would put the leopard, crouched and ready to spring.

(3,084 words)

VOCABULARY

incomprehensible (2)	detestation (24)	restively (31)
statuettes (2)	clairvoyance (26)	libertine (32)
integrated (4)	disinterested (27)	inscrutable (37)
penal (4)	proficient (27)	veriest (39)
opaquely (5)	proposition (28)	revered (39)
ruinous (18)	solidarity (28)	amiability (40)
draughts (21)	Pandit (29)	coherent (41)
impediments (22)	skittles (30)	
monologues (23)	flagged (30)	

THE FACTS

1. Into what three types does Golding divide all thinking? Describe each type in your own words. Is there a value judgment implied in the division?

2. Why does Golding take up so much time describing some of his grade-school teachers? How are they related to the purpose of the essay?

3. Why is it so difficult to find grade-one thinkers? Describe someone whom you consider a grade-one thinker.

4. How do you interpret Golding's last two paragraphs? Has the author reverted to grade-three or grade-two thinking, or has he become a grade-one thinker? Comment.

5. What does the encounter between Golding and Albert Einstein indicate?

THE STRATEGIES

1. In paragraph 2, the author describes three statuettes on a cupboard behind the headmaster's desk. In what paragraph is each of the statuettes explained? Why is the explanation necessary?

2. Much of the article reflects a young boy's point of view. How is this point of view achieved? Point to some specific passages.

3. Paragraphs 24, 25, and 27 allude to the word *neck* repeatedly. What has the neck come to symbolize in this context?

4. What is the analogy used in paragraph 28 to describe grade-three thinkers? Is the analogy effective? Explain.

5. What is Golding's purpose in alluding to the jailing of Nehru and Gandhi, and to the Americans' refusal to join the League of Nations?

THE ISSUES

1. To be a grade-one thinker, must one do away with big business, centralized government, armies, marriages, and so on? How could one be a grade-one thinker without wanting to destroy these?

2. Golding seems to indicate that his teachers were either conformists, hypocrites, or men of prejudice. Here is a loaded question: What kinds of thinkers do you remember your grade-school teachers to have been? Give examples of their thinking.

3. What groups in our society reveal typical grade-three thinking? Give reasons for your choices.

4. What, if anything, is important about grade-two thinking? Does one need to be a grade-two thinker before going on to grade-one?

5. How does nature assist or resist grade-one thinking?

SUGGESTIONS FOR WRITING

1. Write an essay in which you answer the question, "Does a college education help to get rid of prejudice and hypocrisy?" Support your answer with examples from your own experience.

2. Write an essay in which you divide your acquaintances into types according to the kinds of behavior they project. Be sure that your categories are mutually exclusive and that they take in all your acquaintances.

▼▼▼

John Holt

KINDS OF DISCIPLINE

JOHN HOLT (b. 1923), education theorist, was born in New York. He has taught at Harvard University and the University of California, Berkeley. His works include *How Children Fail* (1964), *How Children Learn* (1967), and *Freedom and Beyond* (1972), from which this selection was taken, *Escape from Childhood* (1974), *Instead of Eduction* (1976), and *Teach Your Own* (1981).

Because discipline is an ambiguous and often misunderstood word, the author attempts to give it a clearer meaning by focusing on three specific kinds of discipline.

1   A child, in growing up, may meet and learn from three different kinds of disciplines. The first and most important is what we might call the Discipline of Nature or of Reality. When he is trying to do something real, if he does the wrong thing or doesn't do the right one, he doesn't get the result he wants. If he doesn't pile one block right on top of another, or tries to build on a slanting surface, his tower falls down. If he hits the wrong key, he hears the wrong note. If he doesn't hit the nail squarely on the head, it bends, and he has to pull it out and start with another. If he doesn't measure properly what he is trying to build, it won't open, close, fit, stand up, fly, float, whistle, or do whatever he wants it to do. If he closes his eyes when he swings, he doesn't hit the ball. A child meets this kind of discipline every time he tries to *do* something, which is why it is so important in school to give children more chances to do things, instead of just reading or listening to

someone talk (or pretending to). This discipline is a great teacher. The learner never has to wait long for his answer; it usually comes quickly, often instantly. Also it is clear, and very often points toward the needed correction; from what happened he can not only see that what he did was wrong, but also why, and what he needs to do instead. Finally, and most important, the giver of the answer, call it Nature, is impersonal, impartial, and indifferent. She does not give opinions, or make judgments; she cannot be wheedled, bullied, or fooled; she does not get angry or disappointed; she does not praise or blame; she does not remember past failures or hold grudges; with her one always gets a fresh start, this time is the one that counts.

2   The next discipline we might call the Discipline of Culture, of Society, of What People Really Do. Man is a social, a cultural animal. Children sense around them this culture, this network of agreements, customs, habits, and rules binding the adults together. They want to understand it and be a part of it. They watch very carefully what people around them are doing and want to do the same. They want to do right, unless they become convinced they can't do right. Thus children rarely misbehave seriously in church, but sit as quietly as they can. The example of all those grownups is contagious. Some mysterious ritual is going on, and children, who like rituals, want to be part of it. In the same way, the little children that I see at concerts or operas, though they may fidget a little, or perhaps take a nap now and then, rarely make any disturbance. With all those grownups sitting there, neither moving nor talking, it is the most natural thing in the world to imitate them. Children who live among adults who are habitually courteous to each other, and to them, will soon learn to be courteous. Children who live surrounded by people who speak a certain way will speak that way, however much we may try to tell them that speaking that way is bad or wrong.

3   The third discipline is the one most people mean when they speak of discipline—the Discipline of Superior Force, of sergeant to private, of "you do what I tell you or I'll make you wish you had." There is bound to be some of this in a child's life. Living as we do surrounded by things that can hurt children, or that children can hurt, we cannot avoid it. We can't afford to let a small child find out from experience the danger of playing in a busy street, or of fooling with the pots on the top of a stove, or of eating up the pills in the medicine cabinet. So, along with other precautions, we say to him, "Don't play in the street, or touch things on the stove, or go into the medicine cabinet, or I'll punish you." Between him and the danger too great for him to imagine we put a lesser danger, but one he can imagine and maybe therefore wants to avoid. He can have no idea of what it would be like to be hit by a car, but he can imagine being shouted at, or spanked, or sent to his room. He avoids these substitutes for the greater danger until he can

understand it and avoid it for its own sake. But we ought to use this discipline only when it is necessary to protect the life, health, safety, or well-being of people or other living creatures, or to prevent destruction of things that people care about. We ought not to assume too long, as we usually do, that a child cannot understand the real nature of the danger from which we want to protect him. The sooner he avoids the danger, not to escape our punishment, but as a matter of good sense, the better. He can learn that faster than we think. In Mexico, for example, where people drive their cars with a good deal of spirit, I saw many children no older than five or four walking unattended on the streets. They understood about cars, they knew what to do. A child whose life is full of the threat and fear of punishment is locked into babyhood. There is no way for him to grow up, to learn to take responsibility for his life and acts. Most important of all, we should not assume that having to yield to the threat of our superior force is good for the child's character. It is never good for *anyone's* character. To bow to superior force makes us feel impotent and cowardly for not having had the strength or courage to resist. Worse, it makes us resentful and vengeful. We can hardly wait to make someone pay for our humiliation, yield to us as we were once made to yield. No, if we cannot always avoid using the Discipline of Superior Force, we should at least use it as seldom as we can.

4   There are places where all three disciplines overlap. Any very demanding human activity combines in it the disciplines of Superior Force, of Culture, and of Nature. The novice will be told, "Do it this way, never mind asking why, just do it that way, that is the way we always do it." But it probably *is* just the way they always do it, and usually for the very good reason that it is a way that has been found to work. Think, for example, of ballet training. The student in a class is told to do this exercise, or that; to stand so; to do this or that with his head, arms, shoulders, abdomen, hips, legs, feet. He is constantly corrected. There is no argument. But behind these seemingly autocratic demands by the teacher lie many decades of custom and tradition, and behind that, the necessities of dancing itself. You cannot make the moves of classical ballet unless over many years you have acquired, and renewed every day, the needed strength and suppleness in scores of muscles and joints. Nor can you do the difficult motions, making them look easy, unless you have learned hundreds of easier ones first. Dance teachers may not always agree on all the details of teaching these strengths and skills. But no novice could learn them all by himself. You could not go for a night or two to watch the ballet and then, without any other knowledge at all, teach yourself how to do it. In the same way, you would be unlikely to learn any complicated and difficult human activity without drawing heavily on the experience of those who know it better. But the point is that the authority of these experts

or teachers stems from, grows out of their greater competence and experience, the fact that what they do *works,* not the fact that they happen to be the teacher and as such have the power to kick a student out of the class. And the further point is that children are always and everywhere attracted to that competence, and ready and eager to submit themselves to a discipline that grows out of it. We hear constantly that children will never do anything unless compelled to by bribes or threats. But in their private lives, or in extracurricular activities in school, in sports, music, drama, art, running a newspaper, and so on, they often submit themselves willingly and wholeheartedly to very intense disciplines, simply because they want to learn to do a given thing well. Our Little-Napoleon football coaches, of whom we have too many and hear far too much, blind us to the fact that millions of children work hard every year getting better at sports and games without coaches barking and yelling at them.

(1,512 words)

VOCABULARY

wheedled (1)   impotent (3)   autocratic (4)
ritual (2)   novice (4)

THE FACTS

1. What principle or basis of division does Holt use?

2. How does Holt clarify for the reader what he means by "Discipline of Nature or of Reality"? Is this method of clarification effective? Why?

3. What are the advantages of learning from nature or reality?

4. What additional examples can you supply of the ways in which children submit to the discipline of culture or society?

5. According to the author, when should the discipline of superior force be used? Do you agree?

6. At the end of his essay Holt identifies the most successful motivation for discipline. What is it?

THE STRATEGIES

1. In the last sentence of paragraph 1, the author uses the feminine pronouns *she* and *her* in referring to nature. What is his purpose?

2. What transitional guideposts does the author use in order to gain coherence and organization?

3. What is the effect of labeling certain football coaches "Little Napoleons"?

THE ISSUES

1. What additional examples can you supply of the ways in which children submit to the discipline of culture or society?

2. What tips can you provide for someone who has no discipline in studying college courses? What method has worked best for you personally?

3. Holt warns adults that the use of superior force in order to punish children is never good for the children's characters (see paragraph 3) and should therefore be used as little as possible. What, in your opinion, is the result of never using this superior force in the training of children? Give examples to support your point.

4. Our society is witnessing the self-destruction of many young people due to chemical abuse of one kind or another. How is this abuse tied to Holt's idea of discipline?

5. How important is discipline in your life? Do you choose friends who are strongly disciplined, or do you prefer those who are more "laid back" and like to "hang loose"? Give reasons for your answers.

SUGGESTIONS FOR WRITING

1. Write a 500-word essay in which you divide discipline according to the kinds of effects it produces. Example: discipline that results in strong study habits.

2. Develop the following topic sentence into a three-paragraph essay: "To be successful, a person must have three kinds of discipline: of the intellect, of the emotions, and of the body." Use Holt's essay as a model for your organization.

▼▼

Francis Bacon

THE IDOLS

FRANCIS BACON (1561–1626) was born in London and educated at Trinity College, Cambridge, and Gray's Inn. Bacon is generally credited with applying the inductive method of logic to scientific investigation. His essays, which are notable for their aphoristic style, are his best-known works.

> *This excerpt comes from* Novum Organum *(1620), possibly Bacon's most famous work. Bacon was struggling against the traditions of medieval scholasticism, which assumed a given and unchangeable set of premises from which, by deductive logic, one could infer truths about the world. Our way of thinking today, especially in science, is just the opposite, thanks in part to Bacon. We begin not with givens but with questions. We proceed by gathering data and using induction to draw conclusions. (See the discussion of logic in Chapter 9.) This method of thinking does not completely safeguard us from Bacon's* Idols, *but it does help keep them at bay.*

1   The *Idols* and false notions which have already preoccupied the human understanding, and are deeply rooted in it, not only so beset men's minds, that they become difficult to access, but even when access is obtained, will again meet and trouble us in the instauration of the sciences, unless mankind, when forewarned, guard themselves with all possible care against them.

2   Four species of *Idols* beset the human mind: to which (for distinction's sake) we have assigned names: calling the first *Idols of the Tribe;* the second *Idols of the Den;* the third *Idols of the Market;* the fourth *Idols of the Theater.*

3   The formation of notions and axioms on the foundations of true *induction,* is the only fitting remedy, by which we can ward off and expel these *Idols.* It is however of great service to point them out. For the doctrine of *Idols* bears the same relation to the *interpretation of nature,* as that of the confutation of sophisms does to common logic.

4   The *Idols of the Tribe* are inherent in human nature, and the very tribe or race of man. For man's sense is falsely asserted to be the standard of things. On the contrary, all the perceptions, both of the senses and the mind, bear reference to man, and not to the universe, and the human mind resembles those uneven mirrors, which impart their own

properties to different objects, from which rays are emitted, and distort and disfigure them.

5   The *Idols of the Den* are those of each individual. For every body (in addition to the errors common to the race of man) has his own individual den or cavern, which intercepts and corrupts the light of nature; either from his own peculiar and singular disposition, or from his education and intercourse with others, or from his reading, and the authority acquired by those whom he reverences and admires, or from a different impression produced on the mind, as it happens to be preoccupied and predisposed, or equable and tranquil, and the like: so that the spirit of man (according to its several dispositions) is variable, confused, and as it were actuated by chance; and Heraclitus* said well that men search for knowledge in lesser worlds and not in the greater or common world.

6   There are also *Idols* formed by the reciprocal intercourse and society of man with man, which we call *Idols of the Market*, from the commerce and association of men with each other. For men converse by means of language; but words are formed at the will of the generality; and there arises from a bad and unapt formation of words a wonderful obstruction to the mind. Nor can the definitions and explanations, with which learned men are wont to guard and protect themselves in some instances, afford a complete remedy: words still manifestly force the understanding, throw everything into confusion, and lead mankind into vain and innumerable controversies and fallacies.

7   Lastly there are *Idols* which have crept into men's minds from the various dogmas of peculiar systems of philosophy, and also from the perverted rules of demonstration, and these we denominate *Idols of the Theater*. For we regard all the systems of philosophy hitherto received or imagined, as so many plays brought out and performed, creating fictitious and theatrical worlds. Nor do we speak only of the present systems, or of the philosophy and sects of the ancients, since numerous other plays of a similar nature can be still composed and made to agree with each other, the causes of the most opposite errors being generally the same. Nor, again, do we allude merely to the general systems, but also to many elements and axioms of sciences, which have become inveterate by tradition, implicit credence and neglect. We must, however, discuss each species of *Idols* more fully and distinctly in order to guard the human understanding against them.

(645 words)

---

* Greek philosopher of the sixth century B.C.—Ed.

VOCABULARY

beset (1)	inherent (4)	denominate (7)
instauration (1)	predisposed (5)	sects (7)
axioms (3)	equable (5)	inveterate (7)
induction (3)	reciprocal (6)	implicit (7)
confutation (3)	wont (6)	credence (7)
sophisms (3)	dogmas (7)	

THE FACTS

1. Exactly what is being divided in this essay? Why does Bacon use the term *idols?*

2. Using your own words, describe each idol in the order listed by Bacon. Supply an example for each from your own experience.

3. According to Bacon, what is the remedy for all these idols? How will this remedy work?

THE STRATEGIES

1. What connection is there between Bacon's thought and his style?

2. Point out specific words or phrases to show that Bacon's style is archaic.

3. What method of thinking does Bacon use in order to conclude that idols preoccupy the human understanding? Trace his use of the method in the essay.

4. What is the analogy used to illustrate the last idol? Explain how this analogy helps clarify the idol.

THE ISSUES

1. Compare Bacon's division with some more contemporary ideas on the same subject. Is his essay still valid, or is it out of date? Give reasons for your answer.

2. What specific examples can you cite to illuminate Bacon's "idols of the tribe"?

3. How dangerous to present society are "idols of the market"? Give reasons for your opinion.

4. What examples can you cite from your own upbringing to indicate that you have bowed to "idols of the den"?

5. In your view, what ideas marketed publicly today are dangerous but highly seductive—especially for the naïve?

SUGGESTIONS FOR WRITING

1. Write an essay in which you divide your bad habits into three or four categories. Make sure that these categories are mutually exclusive and that they include the entire range of your bad habits.

2. Write a brief report on Francis Bacon's major contributions to society. In the report, organize these contributions into separate divisions.

▼▼▼

Bart Edelman

ENGLISH 101

BART EDELMAN (b. 1951) is a contemporary American poet who spent his childhood in Teaneck, New Jersey, the subject or stage for many of his poems. Today he lives in Southern California, where he frequently reads his poetry on college campuses and in coffee houses. He has been the recipient of numerous grants and fellowships to study literature in India, Egypt, Nigeria, and Poland. He is presently a professor of English at Glendale College in California. His poetry collections include *Crossing the Hackensack* (1993) and *Under Damaris' Dress* (1996).

This poem conjures up familiar memories in anyone who has taken freshman composition and remembers the opening session when students are first introduced to the requirements and goals of the course. The poet uses concrete language to convey vivid portraits of three kinds of students in class on opening day.

ENGLISH 101

They appear-
Always-
That first day,
Astray;
Some wait to fall,
Others to rise:

Here rests the tired boy,
The hour long,

10
He drops his brain
Upon the desk
And thinks he'd be better off dead,
Five worlds away
From Frost and Twain . . .
(He'll have no part of 101).

15
A fair-haired girl in knots
Twists her braids so tight
They make her ache;
She takes good notes,
Does what she's told,
20
If asked a quote
She knows it cold . . .
(But could a smile unclench those lips?)

Then the hand,
One resolute voice
25
Speaks through the bell
And the great stampede-
Engaged in speculation
We turn wheat to notion,
Sifting through each tiny grain . . .
30
(The composition now complete).

(118 words)

VOCABULARY

Astray (1)   resolute (4)   stampede (4)

THE FACTS

1. Where does the action of the poem take place? How do you know?

2. Who are the "They" of the first stanza? Why are they described as "astray"?

3. What is meant by "He drops his brain/Upon the desk" in the second stanza? Explain the figure of speech.

4. What kind of student is described in stanza 3? Describe her in your own words.

5. What is the meaning of the phrase "one resolute voice/Speaks through the bell"?

THE STRATEGIES

1. In what sense is this poem a classification? What is being classified? How many items belong to the classification? List them.

2. After listing the first two students as a boy and a girl, why does the poet then refer to a "hand" and "voice" as the third student?

3. Why do you suppose the author chose the title "English 101" rather than, say, "Math 220" or "Economics 300"?

4. What comparison does the poet draw in stanza 4? What other simile might be used? Use your poetic imagination to find one.

THE ISSUES

1. What is the theme (thesis) of this poem? State it in one complete sentence.

2. According to the poem, wherein lies a teacher's greatest challenge while in the classroom?

3. If you were a teacher, which student would bother you more—the student of stanza 2 or the student of stanza 3? Give reasons for your answer.

4. What is your opinion on the basic importance of freshman composition? Should it be a requirement? Why or why not?

5. In stanza 2, the poet refers to Frost and Twain. How are these two literary figures related to the theme of the poem?

SUGGESTIONS FOR WRITING

1. Write an essay in which you classify the various kinds of teachers who have taught you in the past. For your bases of classification, consider such aspects as ability to communicate, personality, values, and attitude toward the subject matter.

2. Using Edelman's poem as a springboard, choose three or four friends that serve as representative types to classify your most intimate friends. Try to make each type come to life by using vivid details in describing him or her.

A D V I C E

▼▼

HOW TO WRITE A CAUSAL ANALYSIS

Some essays have as their dominant purpose the analysis of cause or effect. *Cause* refers to events that have occurred in the past; *effect* refers to consequences that will occur in the future. An essay on why some students get poor grades, which points to the failure to study, is analyzing cause. However, an essay on the consequences of failing to study for a test is analyzing effect. Both essays are said to be rhetorically developed by causal analysis, even though one focuses on cause and the other on effect. Generally, the essay asking for the analysis of cause or for the prediction of effect requires the most abstract thinking and gives students the most trouble. Causes do not parade around wearing identity tags. Moreover, even simple effects can be said to be produced by a complex of multiple causes, which the student must sift out and analyze.

Take, for instance, the straightforward enough incident of a student getting a poor grade on a test. Why did the student get a poor grade? Possibly, because he failed to study. On the other hand, perhaps the student failed to study because he thought he was doomed to failure anyway, and didn't see any point in a meaningless exertion. Why did he feel that way? Possibly, because the instructor impressed upon the class how high her standards were, and how impossible it was for anyone to pass. The instructor, in turn, may have been reacting to pressure brought by the Regents against her and her department, for having in the past given out too many high grades. The Regents, on the other hand, may have been set upon by the community because of a newspaper article that accused the university of wasting taxpayers' money by giving out cheap grades. The possibilities are virtually endless. Every cause, if traced back patiently enough, will lead through infinite regression to the Creator.

It is useful, therefore, to bear in mind that there are three kinds of causes: necessary, contributory, and sufficient. A necessary cause is one that *must* be present for an effect to occur, but by itself cannot cause the occurrence of the effect. For instance, irrigation is necessary for a good crop of corn, but irrigation alone will not result in a good crop. Other factors such as adequate sunshine, good soil, and correct planting must also be present.

A contributory cause is one that *may* produce an effect, but cannot produce the effect by itself. For instance, good training may help a fighter win a bout, but that alone is not enough. The fighter also has to have sharper reflexes, more skill, and more strength than his opponent.

A sufficient cause is one that *can* produce an effect by itself. For instance, a heart attack alone can kill, even though the person may have other problems such as an ulcer, a toothache, or a weak back.

Most causes are not sufficient; they are either contributory or necessary. Bearing this in mind will restrain you from dogmatizing about cause. For instance, the following assertions mistake a contributory cause for a sufficient one:

> Crime in America is caused by a breakdown of discipline in the family structure. In the farming days, both the father and the mother were around to supervise the upbringing and disciplining of the children. Nowadays, however, the father is away working, as is the mother, and the children are left to the schools for rearing. This breakdown of the family structure is the cause of crime.

The fragmentation of the family is probably a contributory cause of crime, but it is hardly a sufficient one. Many children reared in families where both parents work have not succumbed to crime. Simplistic thinking and writing about cause usually come from mistaking a contributory for a sufficient cause.

Make Your Purpose Initially Clear

The excerpt from Jim Corbett's book opens with this clear statement, "As many of the stories in this book are about man-eating tigers, it is perhaps desirable to explain why these animals develop man-eating tendencies." It then proceeds to explain exactly that. This sort of definiteness early in the piece adds a guiding focus to any explanation of cause.

Be Modest in Your Choice of a Subject

It is difficult enough to analyze the causes of simple effects without compounding your problem through the choice of a monstrously large subject. The student who tries to write an essay on the causes of war is already in deep trouble. Such a complex phenomenon bristles with thousands of causes. Selecting a more manageable subject for causal analysis will make your task a lot easier.

Concentrate on Proximate, as Opposed to Remote, Causes

As we pointed out earlier, it is easy in analysis of cause to become entangled in the infinite. In a series of causations, the proximate cause is the nearest cause. For instance, in the case of the student who received poor grades, the proximate cause for the poor grade was failure to study. The remote cause was the dissatisfaction of the community with the university. Common sense should guide you in this sort of analysis; but since infinity can be unraveled out of the reason why someone purchases a popsicle, it is, as a rule of thumb, safer to stay with the proximate cause and ignore the remote.

Do Not Dogmatize About Cause

Institutions of learning rigorously demand that students analyze cause with caution and prudence. The reasoning is simple enough: colleges and universities are quite determined to impress their students with the complexity of the world. It is advisable, therefore, that you be modest in your claims of causation. You can easily temper a dogmatic statement by interjecting qualifiers into your claims. Instead of

> The divorce rate in America is caused by the sexual revolution, with its promiscuity and ideas on free love.

you could more prudently write:

> The divorce rate in America is probably influenced by the sexual revolution, with its promiscuity and ideas on free love.

This paragraph, for instance, had it been written by a student, would no doubt draw criticism from the instructor:

> This brings me to the major cause of unhappiness, which is that most people in America act not on impulse but on some principle, and that principles upon which people act are usually based upon a false psychology and a false ethic. There is a general theory as to what makes for happiness and this theory is false. Life is conceived as a competitive struggle in which felicity consists in getting ahead of your neighbor. The joys which are not competitive are forgotten.

Yet this paragraph is from a Bertrand Russell article, "The Unhappy American Way," which we will read with much sagacious head-nodding. Bertrand Russell was a Nobel laureate, a mathematician, and a noted philosopher when he wrote this. No doubt it is unfair, but his obvious accomplishments gain for him a temporary suspension of the rules against dogmatizing. Students, however, are not readily granted such license. For the time being, anyway, we advise that you generalize about cause prudently.

E X A M P L E S

▼▼

Jim Corbett

WHY TIGERS BECOME MAN-EATERS

JAMES EDWARD CORBETT (1875–1955) was born in Nainital, India, and worked with a railroad company for 20 years. He served first as a captain then as major during World War II. From 1907 to 1938, he was a tiger hunter in the remote regions of India, where he was often summoned to destroy man-eaters preying on villagers. His memoirs, *Man-Eaters of Kumaon*, was first published in 1944 in India.

The big-game hunter has dwindled into something of a movie spoof. But not so many years ago, such a figure was a godsend to helpless remote villagers being preyed upon by rogue animals. Yet though he has hunted many such predators, the author tells us in an opening note to his famed book, Man-Eaters of Kumaon *(1944), that when an animal becomes a man-eater, the transformation is rare, unnatural, and never without cause. In this, his opening chapter, the author explains why tigers change suddenly into man-eaters, giving us a sympathetic view of the tiger, who has today been hunted by humans to the brink of extinction.*

1   As many of the stories in this book are about man-eating tigers, it is perhaps desirable to explain why these animals develop man-eating tendencies.

2   A man-eating tiger is a tiger that has been compelled, through stress of circumstances beyond its control, to adopt a diet alien to it. The stress of circumstances is, in nine cases out of ten, wounds, and in the tenth case old age. The wound that has caused a particular tiger to take to man-eating might be the result of a carelessly fired shot and failure to follow up and recover the wounded animal, or be the result of the tiger having lost his temper when killing a porcupine. Human beings are not the natural prey of tigers, and it is only when tigers have been incapacitated through wounds or old age that, in order to live, they are compelled to take to a diet of human flesh.

3   A tiger when killing its natural prey, which it does either by stalking or lying in wait for it, depends for the success of its attack on its speed and, to a lesser extent, on the condition of its teeth and claws. When, therefore, a tiger is suffering from one or more painful wounds, or when its teeth are missing or defective and its claws worn down,

and it is unable to catch the animals it has been accustomed to eating, it is driven by necessity to killing human beings. The change-over from animal to human flesh is, I believe, in most cases accidental. As an illustration of what I mean by "accidental" I quote the case of the Muktesar man-eating tigress. This tigress, a comparatively young animal, in an encounter with a porcupine lost an eye and got some fifty quills, varying in length from one to nine inches, embedded in the arm and under the pad of her right foreleg. Several of these quills after striking a bone had doubled back in the form of a U, the point and the broken-off end being quite close together. Suppurating sores formed where she endeavored to extract the quills with her teeth, and while she was lying up in a thick patch of grass, starving and licking her wounds, a woman selected this particular patch of grass to cut as fodder for her cattle. At first the tigress took no notice, but when the woman had cut the grass right up to where she was lying the tigress struck once, the blow crushing in the woman's skull. Death was instantaneous, for, when found the following day, she was grasping her sickle with one hand and holding a tuft of grass, which she was about to cut when struck, with the other. Leaving the woman lying where she had fallen, the tigress limped off for a distance of over a mile and took refuge in a little hollow under a fallen tree. Two days later a man came to chip firewood off this fallen tree, and the tigress who was lying on the far side killed him. The man fell across the tree and, as he had removed his coat and shirt and the tigress had clawed his back when killing him, it is possible that the smell of the blood trickling down his body as he hung across the bole of the tree first gave her the idea that he was something that she could satisfy her hunger with. However that may be, before leaving him she ate a small portion from his back. A day later she killed her third victim deliberately, and without having received any provocation. Thereafter she became an established man-eater and had killed twenty-four people before she was finally accounted for.

4   A tiger on a fresh kill, or a wounded tiger, or a tigress with small cubs will occasionally kill human beings who disturb them; but these tigers cannot, by any stretch of imagination, be called man-eaters, though they are often so called. Personally I would give a tiger the benefit of the doubt once, and once again, before classing it as a man-eater, and whenever possible I would subject the alleged victim to a post-mortem before letting the kill go down on the records as the kill of a tiger or a leopard, as the case might be. This subject of post-mortems of human beings alleged to have been killed by either tigers or leopards or, in the plains, by wolves or hyenas, is of great importance, for, though I refrain from giving instances, I know of cases where deaths have wrongly been ascribed to carnivora.

5   It is a popular fallacy that *all* man-eaters are old and mangy, the mange being attributed to the excess of salt in human flesh. I am not competent to give any opinion on the relative quantity of salt in human

or animal flesh; but I can, and I do, assert that a diet of human flesh, so far from having an injurious effect on the coat of man-eaters, has quite the opposite effect, for all the man-eaters I have seen have had remarkably fine coats.

6   Another popular belief in connection with man-eaters is that the cubs of these animals automatically become man-eaters. This is quite a reasonable supposition; but it is not borne out by actual facts, and the reason why the cubs of a man-eater do not themselves become man-eaters is that human beings are not the natural prey of tigers, or of leopards.

7   A cub will eat whatever its mother provides, and I have even known of tiger cubs' assisting their mothers to kill human beings; but I do not know of a single instance of a cub, after it had left the protection of its parent, or after that parent had been killed, taking to killing human beings.

8   In the case of human beings killed by carnivora, the doubt is often expressed as to whether the animal responsible for the kill is a tiger or leopard. As a general rule—to which I have seen no exceptions—tigers are responsible for all kills that take place in daylight, and leopards are responsible for all kills that take place in the dark. Both animals are semi-nocturnal forest-dwellers, have much the same habits, employ similar methods of killing, and both are capable of carrying their human victims for long distances. It would be natural, therefore, to expect them to hunt at the same hours; and that they do not do so is due to the difference in courage of the two animals. When a tiger becomes a man-eater it loses all fear of human beings and, as human beings move about more freely in the day than they do at night, it is able to secure its victims during daylight hours and there is no necessity for it to visit their habitations at night. A leopard on the other hand, even after it has killed scores of human beings, never loses its fear of man; and, as it is unwilling to face up to human beings in daylight, it secures its victims when they are moving about at night, or by breaking into their houses at night. Owing to those characteristics of the two animals, namely, that one loses its fear of human beings and kills in the daylight, while the other retains its fear and kills in the dark, man-eating tigers are easier to shoot than man-eating leopards.

9   The frequency with which a man-eating tiger kills depends on (a) the supply of natural food in the area in which it is operating; (b) the nature of the disability which has caused it to become a man-eater; and (c) whether it is a male or a female with cubs.

10   Those of us who lack the opportunity of forming our own opinion on any particular subject are apt to accept the opinions of others, and in no case is this more apparent than in the case of tigers—here I do not refer to man-eaters in particular, but to tigers in general. The author who first used the words "as cruel as a tiger" and "as bloodthirsty as a tiger," when attempting to emphasize the evil character

of the villain of his piece, not only showed a lamentable ignorance of the animal he defamed, but coined phrases which have come into universal circulation, and which are mainly responsible for the wrong opinion of tigers held by all except that very small proportion of the public who have the opportunity of forming their own opinions.

11   When I see the expression "as cruel as a tiger" and "as bloodthirsty as a tiger" in print, I think of a small boy armed with an old muzzle-loading gun—the right barrel of which was split for six inches of its length, and the stock and barrels of which were kept from falling apart by lashings of brass wire—wandering through the jungles of the terai and *bhabar* in the days when there were ten tigers to every one that now survives; sleeping anywhere he happened to be when night came on, with a small fire to give him company and warmth, wakened at intervals by the calling of tigers, sometimes in the distance, at other times near at hand; throwing another stick on the fire and turning over and continuing his interrupted sleep without one thought of unease; knowing from his own short experience and from what others, who like himself had spent their days in the jungles, had told him, that a tiger, unless molested, would do him no harm; or during daylight hours avoiding any tiger he saw, and when that was not possible, standing perfectly still until it had passed and gone, before continuing on his way. And I think of him on one occasion stalking half-a-dozen jungle fowl that were feeding in the open, and, on creeping up to a plum bush and standing up to peer over, the bush heaving and a tiger walking out on the far side and, on clearing the bush, turning round and looking at the boy with an expression on its face which said as clearly as any words, "Hello, kid, what the hell are you doing here?" and, receiving no answer, turning round and walking away very slowly without once looking back. And then again I think of the tens of thousands of men, women, and children who, while working in the forests or cutting grass or collecting dry sticks, pass day after day close to where tigers are lying up and who, when they return safely to their homes, do not even know that they have been under the observation of this so-called "cruel" and "bloodthirsty" animal.

12   Half a century has rolled by since the day the tiger walked out of the plum bush, the latter thirty-two years of which have been spent in the more or less regular pursuit of man-eaters, and though sights have been seen which would have caused a stone to weep, I have not seen a case where a tiger has been deliberately cruel or where it has been bloodthirsty to the extent that it has killed, without provocation, more than it has needed to satisfy its hunger or the hunger of its cubs.

13   A tiger's function in the scheme of things is to help maintain the balance in nature and if, on rare occasions when driven by dire necessity, he kills a human being, or when his natural food has been ruthlessly exterminated by man he kills two percent of the cattle he is

alleged to have killed, it is not fair that for these acts a whole species should be branded as being cruel and bloodthirsty.

14   Sportsmen are admittedly conservative, the reason being that it has taken them years to form their opinions, and as each individual has a different point of view, it is only natural that opinions should differ on minor, or even in some cases on major, points, and for this reason I do not flatter myself that all the opinions I have expressed will meet with universal agreement.

15   There is, however, one point on which I am convinced that all sportsmen—no matter whether their point of view has been a platform on a tree, the back of an elephant, or their own feet—will agree with me, and that is, that a tiger is a largehearted gentleman with boundless courage and that when he is exterminated—as exterminated he will be unless public opinion rallies to his support—India will be the poorer by having lost the finest of her fauna.

16   Leopards, unlike tigers, are to a certain extent scavengers and become man-eaters by acquiring a taste for human flesh when unrestricted slaughter of game has deprived them of their natural food.

17   The dwellers in our hills are predominantly Hindu, and as such cremate their dead. The cremation invariably takes place on the bank of a stream or river in order that the ashes may be washed down into the Ganges and eventually into the sea. As most of the villages are situated high up on the hills, while the streams or rivers are in many cases miles away down in the valleys, it will be realized that a funeral entails a considerable tax on the man-power of a small community when, in addition to the carrying party, labor has to be provided to collect and carry the fuel needed for the cremation. In normal times these rites are carried out very effectively; but when disease in epidemic form sweeps through the hills and the inhabitants die faster than they can be disposed of, a very simple rite, which consists of placing a live coal in the mouth of the deceased, is performed in the village and the body is then carried to the edge of the hill and cast into the valley below.

18   A leopard, in an area in which his natural food is scarce, finding these bodies very soon acquires a taste for human flesh, and when the disease dies down and normal conditions are established, he very naturally, on finding his food supply cut off, takes to killing human beings.

19   Of the two man-eating leopards of Kumaon, which between them killed five hundred and twenty-five human beings, one followed on the heels of a very severe outbreak of cholera, while the other followed the mysterious disease which swept through India in 1918 and was called "war fever."

(2,443 words)

VOCABULARY

incapacitated (2)   fallacy (5)   terai and bhabar (11)

suppurating (3)   semi-nocturnal (8)   fauna (15)

ascribed (4)   habitations (8)   entails (17)

carnivora (4)   defamed (10)

THE FACTS

1. In nine cases out of ten, what is the cause of a tiger suddenly becoming a man-eater? What is the cause in the tenth case?

2. What animal was responsible for wounding the Muktesar tigress, making her incapable of hunting her natural prey?

3. What popular fallacy does the author cite about the condition of man-eaters?

4. In the author's opinion, what are the chances of a tiger cub, whose mother has become a man-eater, also preying on humans?

5. What phrases often applied to the tiger does the author find untrue and objectionable? Why?

THE STRATEGIES

1. Aside from explaining why tigers become man-eaters, what else do the early paragraphs do? Why is this task necessary to the author's purpose?

2. What kinds of support does the author offer for most of his assertions about tigers?

3. In paragraph 11, the author relates his boyhood experiences with tigers, using the third-person singular rather than the first-person. Why do you think he makes this odd choice of pronouns? What effect does this usage have on the story?

4. The author is a big-game hunter, not a writer, and his style reflects an expected roughness. What example of this roughness can you cite from paragraph 12?

5. Throughout the explanation of why tigers become man-eaters, the author subtly contrasts the tiger with the leopard. Why? What effect does that contrast have on his explanation?

THE ISSUES

1. What can you infer from the author's writing about his childhood?

2. What would you imagine would be the author's initial reaction if he were asked to hunt down a tiger that had allegedly become a man-eater?

3. Given the fact that by the author's own admissions, tigers and leopards have killed hundreds of humans, why should these animals be saved from extinction?

4. The author says in paragraph 14 that sportsmen are conservative. What is your opinion of sportsmen?

5. Of the two animals, tigers and leopards, which has the greater claim on the public imagination? How do you account for this difference?

SUGGESTIONS FOR WRITING

1. Find a poem or short work about the tiger and write an essay on the way the animal is depicted in it.

2. Write an essay for or against hunting as a sport.

▼▼▼

Allan Bloom

BOOKS

ALLAN BLOOM (1920–   ) is an American philosopher, educator, editor, and author. He was born in Indianapolis, Indiana, and has been a professor of Political Science at the University of Chicago since 1979. His books include *The Political Philosophy of Isocrates* (1955), *Shakespeare's Politics* (1964), and *The Closing of the American Mind: How Higher Education Has Failed Democracy and Impoverished the Souls of Today's Students* (1987), from which this excerpt is taken.

It has become something of a cottage industry among critics to blast the deficiencies of the young, and this excerpt is from a popular book that does exactly that. It is useful, however, to recall that there is scant record of any generation thinking that its children are its betters. The Roman writer Horace (65–8 BC) put the universal sentiment this way: "Our parents, worse than our grandparents, gave birth to us who are worse than they, and we shall in our turn bear offspring still more evil." As you read ask yourself, is this generation as bad as

Bloom contends, or is he merely rehashing, in modern terms, the sentiment of Horace?

1   I have begun to wonder whether the experience of the greatest texts from early childhood is not a prerequisite for a concern throughout life for them and for lesser but important literature. The soul's longing, its intolerable irritation under the constraints of the conditional and limited, may very well require encouragement at the outset. At all events, whatever the cause, our students have lost the practice of and the taste for reading. They have not learned how to read, nor do they have the expectation of delight or improvement from reading: They are "authentic," as against the immediately preceding university generations, in having few cultural pretensions and in refusing hypocritical ritual bows to high culture.

2   When I first noticed the decline in reading during the late sixties, I began asking my large introductory classes, and any other group of younger students to which I spoke, what books really count for them. Most are silent, puzzled by the question. The notion of books as companions is foreign to them. Justice Black with his tattered copy of the Constitution in his pocket at all times is not an example that would mean much to them. There is no printed word to which they look for counsel, inspiration or joy. Sometimes one student will say "the Bible." (He learned it at home, and his Biblical studies are not usually continued at the university.) There is always a girl who mentions Ayn Rand's *The Fountainhead*, a book, although hardly literature, which, with its sub-Nietzschean assertiveness, excites somewhat eccentric youngsters to a new way of life. A few students mention recent books that struck them and supported their own self-interpretation, like *The Catcher in the Rye*. (Theirs is usually the most genuine response and also shows a felt need for help in self-interpretation. But it is an uneducated response. Teachers should take advantage of the need expressed in it to show such students that better writers can help them more.) After such sessions I am pursued by a student or two who wants to make it clear that he or she is really influenced by books, not just by one or two but by many. Then he recites a list of classics he may have grazed in high school.

3   Imagine such a young person walking through the Louvre or the Uffizi, and you can immediately grasp the condition of his soul. In his innocence of the stories of Biblical and Greek or Roman antiquity, Raphael, Leonardo, Michelangelo, Rembrandt and all the others can say nothing to him. All he sees are colors and forms—modern art. In short, like almost everything else in his spiritual life, the paintings and statues are abstract. No matter what much of modern wisdom asserts, these artists counted on immediate recognition of their subjects and, what is more, on their having a powerful meaning for their viewers. The works were the fulfillment of those meanings, giving them a sensuous reality

and hence completing them. Without those meanings, and without their being something essential to the viewer as a moral, political and religious being, the works lose their essence. It is not merely the tradition that is lost when the voice of civilization elaborated over millennia has been stilled in this way. It is being itself that vanishes beyond the dissolving horizon. One of the most flattering things that ever happened to me as a teacher occurred when I received a postcard from a very good student on his first visit to Italy, who wrote, "You are not a professor of political philosophy but a travel agent." Nothing could have better expressed my intention as an educator. He thought I had prepared him to see. Then he could begin thinking for himself with something to think about. The real sensation of the Florence in which Machiavelli is believable is worth all the formulas of metaphysics ten times over. Education in our times must try to find whatever there is in students that might yearn for completion, and to reconstruct the learning that would enable them autonomously to seek that completion.

4   In a less grandiose vein, students today have nothing like the Dickens who gave so many of us the unforgettable Pecksniffs, Micawbers, Pips, with which we sharpened our vision, allowing us some subtlety in our distinction of human types. It is a complex set of experiences that enables one to say so simply, "He is a Scrooge." Without literature, no such observations are possible and the fine art of comparison is lost. The psychological obtuseness of our students is appalling, because they have only pop psychology to tell them what people are like, and the range of their motives. As the awareness that we owed almost exclusively to literary genius falters, people become more alike, for want of knowing they can be otherwise. What poor substitutes for real diversity are the wild rainbows of dyed hair and other external differences that tell the observer nothing about what is inside.

5   Lack of education simply results in students' seeking for enlightenment wherever it is readily available, without being able to distinguish between the sublime and trash, insight and propaganda. For the most part students turn to the movies, ready prey to interested moralisms such as the depictions of Gandhi or Thomas More—largely designed to further passing political movements and to appeal to simplistic needs for greatness—or to insinuating flattery of their secret aspirations and vices, giving them a sense of significance. *Kramer vs. Kramer* may be up-to-date about divorces and sex roles, but anyone who does not have *Anna Karenina* or *The Red and the Black* as part of his viewing equipment cannot sense what might be lacking, or the difference between an honest presentation and an exercise in consciousness-raising, trashy sentimentality and elevated sentiment. As films have emancipated themselves from the literary tyranny under which they suffered and which gave them a bad conscience, the ones with serious pretensions have become intolerably ignorant and manipulative. The distance

from the contemporary and its high seriousness that students most need in order not to indulge their petty desires and to discover what is most serious about themselves cannot be found in the cinema, which now only knows the present. Thus, the failure to read good books both enfeebles the vision and strengthens our most fatal tendency—the belief that the here and now is all there is.

6   The only way to counteract this tendency is to intervene most vigorously in the education of those few who come to the university with a strong urge for *un je ne sais quoi,** who fear that they may fail to discover it, and that the cultivation of their minds is required for the success of their quest. We are long past the age when a whole tradition could be stored up in all students, to be fruitfully used later by some. Only those who are willing to take risks and are ready to believe the implausible are now fit for a bookish adventure. The desire must come from within. People do what they want, and now the most needful things appear so implausible to them that it is hopeless to attempt universal reform. Teachers of writing in state universities, among the noblest and most despised laborers in the academy, have told me that they cannot teach writing to students who do not read, and that it is practically impossible to get them to read, let alone like it. This is where high schools have failed most, filled with teachers who are products of the sixties and reflecting the pallor of university-level humanities. The old teachers who loved Shakespeare or Austen or Donne, and whose only reward for teaching was the perpetuation of their taste, have all but disappeared.

7   The latest enemy of the vitality of classic texts is feminism. The struggles against elitism and racism in the sixties and seventies had little direct effect on students' relations to books. The democratization of the university helped dismantle its structure and caused it to lose its focus. But the activists had no special quarrel with the classic texts, and they were even a bit infected by their Frankfurt School masters' habit of parading their intimacy with high culture. Radicals had at an earlier stage of egalitarianism already dealt with the monarchic, aristocratic and antidemocratic character of most literary classics by no longer paying attention to their manifest political content. Literary criticism concentrated on the private, the intimate, the feelings, thoughts and relations of individuals, while reducing to the status of a literary convention of the past the fact that the heroes of many classic works were soldiers and statesmen engaged in ruling and faced with political problems. Shakespeare, as he has been read for most of this century, does not constitute a threat to egalitarian right thinking. And as for racism, it just did not play a role in the classic literature, at least in the forms in which we are concerned about it today, and no great work of literature is ordinarily considered racist.

---

* Something indefinable.—Ed.

8   But *all* literature up to today is sexist. The Muses never sang to the poets about liberated women. It's the same old *chanson* from the Bible and Homer through Joyce and Proust. And this is particularly grave for literature, since the love interest was most of what remained in the classics after politics was purged in the academy, and was also what drew students to reading them. These books appealed to eros while educating it. So activism has been directed against the content of books. The latest translation of Biblical text—sponsored by the National Council of the Churches of Christ—suppresses gender references to God, so that future generations will not have to grapple with the fact that God was once a sexist. But this technique has only limited applicability. Another tactic is to expunge the most offensive authors—for example, Rousseau—from the education of the young or to include feminist responses in college courses, pointing out the distorting prejudices, and using the books only as evidence of the misunderstanding of woman's nature and the history of injustice to it. Moreover, the great female characters can be used as examples of the various ways women have coped with their enslavement to the sexual role. But never, never, must a student be attracted to those old ways and take them as models for him or herself. However, all this effort is wasted. Students cannot imagine that the old literature could teach them anything about the relations they want to have or will be permitted to have. So they are indifferent.

9   Having heard over a period of years the same kinds of responses to my question about favorite books, I began to ask students who their heroes are. Again, there is usually silence, and most frequently nothing follows. Why should anyone have heroes? One should be oneself and not form oneself in an alien mold. Here positive ideology supports them: their lack of hero-worship is a sign of maturity. They posit their own values. They have turned into a channel first established in the *Republic* by Socrates, who liberated himself from Achilles, and picked up in earnest by Rousseau in *Emile.* Following on Rousseau, Tolstoy depicts Prince Andrei in *War and Peace,* who was educated in Plutarch and is alienated from himself by his admiration for Napoleon. But we tend to forget that Andrei is a very noble man indeed and that his heroic longings give him a splendor of soul that dwarfs the petty, vain, self-regarding concerns of the bourgeoisie that surrounds him. Only a combination of natural sentiment and unity with the spirit of Russia and its history can, for Tolstoy, produce human beings superior to Andrei, and even they are only ambiguously superior. But in America we have only the bourgeoisie, and the love of the heroic is one of the few counterpoises available to us. In us the contempt for the heroic is only an extension of the perversion of the democratic principle that denies greatness and wants everyone to feel comfortable in his skin without having to suffer unpleasant comparisons. Students have not the slightest notion of what an achievement it is to free oneself from

public guidance and find resources for guidance within oneself. From what source within themselves would they draw the goals they think they set for themselves? Liberation from the heroic only means that they have no resource whatsoever against conformity to the current "role models." They are constantly thinking of themselves in terms of fixed standards that they did not make. Instead of being overwhelmed by Cyrus, Theseus, Moses or Romulus, they unconsciously act out the roles of the doctors, lawyers, businessmen or TV personalities around them. One can only pity young people without admirations they can respect or avow, who are artificially restrained from the enthusiasm for great virtue.

10   In encouraging this deformity, democratic relativism joins a branch of conservatism that is impressed by the dangerous political consequences of idealism. These conservatives want young people to know that this tawdry old world cannot respond to their demands for perfection. In the choice between the somewhat arbitrarily distinguished realism and idealism, a sensible person would want to be both, or neither. But, momentarily accepting a distinction I reject, idealism as it is commonly conceived should have primacy in an education, for man is a being who must take his orientation by his possible perfection. To attempt to suppress this most natural of all inclinations because of possible abuses is, almost literally, to throw out the baby with the bath. Utopianism is, as Plato taught us at the outset, the fire with which we must play because it is the only way we can find out what we are. We need to criticize false understandings of Utopia, but the easy way out provided by realism is deadly. As it now stands, students have powerful images of what a perfect body is and pursue it incessantly. But deprived of literary guidance, they no longer have any image of a perfect soul, and hence do not long to have one. They do not even imagine that there is such a thing.

11   Following on what I learned from this second question, I began asking a third: Who do you think is evil? To this one there is an immediate response: Hitler. (Stalin is hardly mentioned.) After him, who else? Up until a couple of years ago, a few students said Nixon, but he has been forgotten and at the same time is being rehabilitated. And there it stops. They have no idea of evil; they doubt its existence. Hitler is just another abstraction, an item to fill up an empty category. Although they live in a world in which the most terrible deeds are being performed and they see brutal crime in the streets, they turn aside. Perhaps they believe that evil deeds are performed by persons who, if they got the proper therapy, would not do them again—that there are evil deeds, not evil people. There is no *Inferno* in this comedy. Thus, the most common student view lacks an awareness of the depths as well as the heights, and hence lacks gravity.

(2,550 words)

VOCABULARY

prerequisite (1)
constraints (1)
conditional (1)
preceding (1)
Nietzschean (2)
sensuous (3)
millennia (3)
autonomously (3)
grandiose (4)

obtuseness (4)
sublime (5)
moralisms (5)
sentimentality (5)
implausible (6)
perpetuation (6)
egalitarianism (7)
chanson (8)
expunge (8)

posit (9)
bourgeoisie (9)
counterpoises (9)
democratic
    relativism (10)
tawdry (10)
Utopianism (10)
incessantly (10)

THE FACTS

1. What does the author claim students have lost?

2. What did a former student write to the author on a postcard?

3. What does the author say films have lately become?

4. What did writing teachers tell the author about students today?

5. What does the author say about all literature up to today?

THE STRATEGIES

1. What is the overall aim of this excerpt?

2. How would you characterize the author's writing style? What examples can you give to support your characterization?

3. What evidence does the author cite to support his conclusions about today's students? What logical fallacy might a logician accuse him of making?

4. The author writes, "The Muses never sang to the poets about liberated women." What does he mean by that?

5. The author says that literature enables us to say, "He's a Scrooge," and be understood. What does the allusion mean? Why is this a good or bad example?

THE ISSUES

1. What is your opinion of Bloom's charges against this generation?

2. The author writes in paragraph 8 that the muses never sang to the poets about liberated women. What other explanation can be offered to this glib opinion?

3. How much do you read? Would Bloom's attack on this generation apply to you? Why or why not?

4. What should be done with ancient texts, considered classics, that are sexist? How would you approach teaching such texts to the present young generation?

5. How do you feel about the attempts to suppress gender references to God?

SUGGESTIONS FOR WRITING

1. Write an essay replying to Bloom's attacks on the younger generation.

2. Write an essay about a favorite book.

▼▼▼

Henry David Thoreau

WHY I WENT TO THE WOODS

HENRY DAVID THOREAU (1817–1862), essayist, lecturer, and moralist, was born in Concord, Massachusetts, and educated at Harvard University. He is regarded as one of the seminal influences on American thought and literature. His most famous work is *Walden* (1854), which grew out of the journal recording his solitary existence in a cabin beside Walden Pond, near Concord. His essay, "Civil Disobedience" (1849), has been enormously influential since it was first published and has affected the actions and thoughts of such men as Mahatma Gandhi and Martin Luther King, Jr.

In this excerpt from Walden, *Thoreau explains why he went to the woods to live by himself. Unlike many of the writers in this section, Thoreau writes in a voice rich with metaphors, allusions, and images.*

1   I went to the woods because I wished to live deliberately, to front only the essential facts of life, and see if I could not learn what it had to teach, and not, when I came to die, discover that I had not lived. I did not wish to live what was not life, living is so dear; nor did I wish to practise resignation, unless it was quite necessary. I wanted to live deep and suck out all the marrow of life, to live so sturdily and Spartanlike as to put to rout all that was not life, to cut a broad swath and shave close, to drive life into a corner, and reduce it to its lowest terms, and, if it proved to be mean, why then to get the whole and genuine meanness of it, and publish its meanness to the world; or if it

were sublime, to know it by experience, and be able to give a true account of it in my next excursion. For most men, it appears to me, are in a strange uncertainty about it, whether it is of the devil or of God, and have *somewhat hastily* concluded that it is the chief end of man here to "glorify God and enjoy him forever."

2   Still we live meanly, like ants; though the fable tells us that we were long ago changed into men; like pygmies we fight with cranes; it is error upon error, and clout upon clout, and our best virtue has for its occasion a superfluous and evitable wretchedness. Our life is frittered away by detail. An honest man has hardly need to count more than his ten fingers, or in extreme cases he may add his ten toes, and lump the rest. Simplicity, simplicity, simplicity! I say, let your affairs be as two or three, and not a hundred or a thousand; instead of a million count half a dozen, and keep your accounts on your thumb-nail. In the midst of this chopping sea of civilized life, such are the clouds and storms and quicksands and thousand-and-one items to be allowed for, that a man has to live, if he would not founder and go to the bottom and not make his port at all, by dead reckoning, and he must be a great calculator indeed who succeeds. Simplify, simplify. Instead of three meals a day, if it be necessary eat but one; instead of a hundred dishes, five; and reduce other things in proportion. Our life is like a German Confederacy, made up of petty states, with its boundary forever fluctuating, so that even a German cannot tell you how it is bounded at any moment. The nation itself, with all its so-called internal improvements, which, by the way are all external and superficial, is just such an unwieldy and overgrown establishment, cluttered with furniture and tripped up by its own traps, ruined by luxury and heedless expense, by want of calculation and a worthy aim, as the million households in the lands; and the only cure for it, as for them, is in a rigid economy, a stern and more than Spartan simplicity of life and elevation of purpose. It lives too fast. Men think that it is essential that the *Nation* have commerce, and export ice, and talk through a telegraph, and ride thirty miles an hour, without a doubt, whether *they* do or not; but whether we should live like baboons or like men, is a little uncertain. If we do not get our sleepers, and forge rails, and devote days and nights to the work, but go to tinkering upon our *lives* to improve *them*, who will build railroads? And if railroads are not built, how shall we get to heaven in season? But if we stay at home and mind our business, who will want railroads? We do not ride on the railroad; it rides upon us. Did you ever think what those sleepers[1] are that underlie the railroad? Each one is a man, an Irishman, or a Yankee man. The rails are laid on them, and they are covered with sand, and the cars run

---

[1] Crossties. Thoreau is playing on the word.—Ed.

smoothly over them. They are sound sleepers, I assure you. And every few years a new lot is laid down and run over; so that, if some have the pleasure of riding on a rail, others have the misfortune to be ridden upon. And when they run over a man that is walking in his sleep, a supernumerary sleeper in the wrong position, and wake him up, they suddenly stop the cars, and make a hue and cry about it, as if this were an exception. I am glad to know that it takes a gang of men for every five miles to keep the sleepers down and level in their beds as it is, for this is a sign that they may sometimes get up again.

3   Why should we live with such hurry and waste of life? We are determined to be starved before we are hungry. Men say that a stitch in time saves nine, and so they take a thousand stitches to-day to save nine to-morrow. As for *work*, we haven't any of any consequence. We have the Saint Vitus' dance, and cannot possibly keep our heads still. If I should only give a few pulls at the parish bell-rope, as for a fire, that is, without setting the bell, there is hardly a man on his farm in the outskirts of Concord, notwithstanding that press of engagements which was his excuse so many times this morning, nor a boy, nor a woman, I might almost say, but would foresake all and follow that sound, not mainly to save property from the flames, but, if we will confess the truth, much more to see it burn, since burn it must, and we, be it known, did not set it on fire,—or to see it put out, and have a hand in it, if that is done as handsomely; yes, even if it were the parish church itself. Hardly a man takes a half-hour's nap after dinner, but when he wakes he holds up his head and asks, "What's the news?" as if the rest of mankind had stood his sentinels. Some give directions to be waked every half-hour, doubtless for no other purpose; and then, to pay for it, they tell what they have dreamed. After a night's sleep the news is as indispensable as the breakfast. "Pray tell me anything new that has happened to a man anywhere on this globe,"—and he reads it over his coffee and rolls, that a man has had his eyes gouged out this morning on the Wachito River; never dreaming the while that he lives in the dark unfathomed mammoth cave of this world, and has but the rudiment of an eye himself.

4   For my part, I could easily do without the post-office. I think that there are very few important communications made through it. To speak critically, I never received more than one or two letters in my life—I wrote this some years ago—that were worth the postage. The penny-post is, commonly, an institution through which you seriously offer a man that penny for his thoughts which is so often safely offered in jest. And I am sure that I never read any memorable news in a newspaper. If we read of one man robbed, or murdered, or killed by accident, or one house burned, or one vessel wrecked, or one steamboat blown up, or one cow run over on the Western Railroad, or one mad dog killed, or one lot of grasshoppers in the winter,—we never need read of another. One is enough. If you are acquainted with the principle, what do you care for a myriad instances and applications? To a philosopher all *news*, as it is

called, is gossip, and they who edit and read it are old women over their tea. Yet not a few are greedy after this gossip. There was such a rush, as I hear, the other day at one of the offices to learn the foreign news by the last arrival, that several large squares of plate glass belonging to the establishment were broken by the pressure,—news which I seriously think a ready wit might write a twelvemonth, or twelve years, beforehand with sufficient accuracy. As for Spain, for instance, if you know how to throw in Don Carlos and the Infanta, and Don Pedro and Seville and Granada, from time to time in the right proportions,—they may have changed the names a little since I saw the papers,—and serve up a bullfight when other entertainments fail, it will be true to the letter, and give us as good an idea of the exact state or ruin of things in Spain as the most succinct and lucid reports under this head in the newspapers: and as for England, almost the last significant scrap of news from that quarter was the revolution of 1649; and if you have learned the history of her crops for an average year, you never need attend to that thing again, unless your speculations are of a merely pecuniary character. If one may judge who rarely looks into the newspapers, nothing new does ever happen in foreign parts, a French revolution not excepted.

5   What news! how much more important to know what that is which was never old! "Kieou-he-yu (great dignitary of the state of Wei) sent a man to Khoung-tseu to know his news. Khoung-tseu caused the messenger to be seated near him, and questioned him in these tens: What is your master doing? The messenger answered with respect: My master desires to diminish the number of his faults, but he cannot come to the end of them. The messenger being gone, the philosopher remarked: What a worthy messenger! What a worthy messenger!" The preacher, instead of vexing the ears of drowsy farmers on their day of rest at the end of the week,—for Sunday is the fit conclusion of an ill-spent week, and not the fresh and brave beginning of a new one,—with this one other draggle-tail of a sermon, should shout with thundering voice, "Pause! Avast! Why so seeming fast, but deadly slow?"

6   Shams and delusions are esteemed for soundless truths, while reality is fabulous. If men would steadily observe realities only, and not allow themselves to be deluded, life, to compare it with such things as we know, would be like a fairy tale and the Arabian Nights' Entertainments. If we respected only what is inevitable and has a right to be, music and poetry would resound along the streets. When we are unhurried and wise, we perceive that only great and worthy things have any permanent and absolute existence, that petty fears and petty pleasures are but the shadow of the reality. This is always exhilarating and sublime. By closing the eyes and slumbering, and consenting to be deceived by shows, men establish and confirm their daily life of routine and habit everywhere, which still is built on purely illusory foundations. Children, who play life, discern its true law and relations more clearly

than men, who fail to live it worthily, but who think that they are wiser by experience, that is, by failure. I have read in a Hindoo book, that "there was a king's son, who, being expelled in infancy from his native city, was brought up by a forester, and, growing up to maturity in that state, imagined himself to belong to the barbarous race with which he lived. One of his father's ministers having discovered him, revealed to him what he was, and the misconception of his character was removed, and he knew himself to be a prince. So soul," continues the Hindoo philosopher, "from the circumstances in which it is placed, mistakes its own character, until the truth is revealed to it by some holy teacher, and then it knows itself to be *Brahme.*" I perceive that we inhabitants of New England live this mean life that we do because our vision does not penetrate the surface of things. We think that that *is* which *appears* to be. If a man should walk through this town and see only the reality, where, think you, would the "Mill-dam" go to? If he should give us an account of the realities he beheld there, we should not recognize the place in his description. Look at the meetinghouse, or a court-house, or a jail, or a shop, or a dwelling-house, and say what that thing really is before a true gaze, and they would all go to pieces in your account of them. Men esteem truth remote, in the outskirts of the system, behind the farthest star, before Adam and after the last man. In eternity there is indeed something true and sublime. But all these times and places and occasions are now and here. God himself culminates in the present moment, and will never be more divine in the lapse of all the ages. And we are enabled to apprehend at all what is sublime and noble only by the perpetual instilling and drenching of the reality that surrounds us. The universe constantly and obediently answers to our conceptions; whether we travel fast or slow, the track is laid for us. Let us spend our lives in conceiving then. The poet or the artist never yet had so fair and noble a design but some of his posterity at least could accomplish it.

7   Let us spend one day as deliberately as Nature, and not be thrown off the track by every nutshell and mosquito's wing that falls on the rails. Let us rise early and fast, or breakfast, gently and without perturbation; let company come and let company go, let the bells ring and the children cry,—determined to make a day of it. Why should we knock under and go with the stream? Let us not be upset and overwhelmed in that terrible rapid and whirlpool called a dinner, situated in the meridian shallows. Weather this danger and you are safe, for the rest of the way is down hill. With unrelaxed nerves, with morning vigor, sail by it, looking another way, tied to the mast like Ulysses.[2] If the engine whistles, let it whistle till it is hoarse for its pains. If the bell

---

[2] tied . . . Ulysses: In Homer's *Odyssey*, Ulysses had himself tied to the mast of his boat so that he could listen, but not respond, to the irresistible songs of the Sirens, who were believed to lure ships to their doom.—Ed.

rings, why should we run? We will consider what kind of music they are like. Let us settle ourselves, and work and wedge our feet downward through the mud and slush of opinion, and prejudice, and tradition, and delusion, and appearance, that alluvion which covers the globe, through Paris and London, through New York and Boston and Concord, through Church and State, through poetry and philosophy and religion, till we come to a hard bottom and rocks in place, which we can call *reality*, and say, This is, and no mistake; and then begin, having a *point d'appui*,[3] below freshet and frost and fire, a place where you might found a wall or a state, or set a lamp-post safely, or perhaps a gauge, not a Nilometer, but a Realometer, that future ages might know how deep a freshet of shams and appearances had gathered from time to time. If you stand right fronting and face to face to a fact, you will see the sun glimmer on both its surfaces, as if it were a cimeter, and feel its sweet edge dividing you through the heart and marrow, and so you will happily conclude your mortal career. Be it life or death, we crave only reality. If we are really dying, let us hear the rattle in our throats and feel cold in the extremities; if we are alive, let us go about our business.

8   Time is but the stream I go a-fishing in. I drink at it; but while I drink I see the sandy bottom and detect how shallow it is. Its thin current slides away, but eternity remains. I would drink deeper; fish in the sky, whose bottom is pebbly with stars. I cannot count one. I know not the first letter of the alphabet. I have always been regretting that I was not as wise as the day I was born. The intellect is a cleaver; it discerns and rifts its way into the secret of things. I do not wish to be any more busy with my hands than is necessary. My head is hands and feet. I feel all my best faculties concentrated on it. My instinct tells me that my head is an organ for burrowing, as some creatures use their snout and fore paws, and with it I would mine and burrow my way through these hills. I think that the richest vein is somewhere hereabouts; so by the divining-rod and thin rising vapors, I judge; and here I will begin to mine.

(2,857 words)

VOCABULARY

superfluous (2)	succinct (4)	freshet (7)
evitable (2)	pecuniary (4)	meridian (7)
supernumerary (2)	posterity (6)	alluvion (7)
rudiment (3)	culminates (6)	
myriad (4)	perturbation (7)	

---

[3] *point d'appui:* point of stability.—Ed.

THE FACTS

1. Why did Thoreau go to the woods? What, in his opinion, is wrong with the nation?

2. Thoreau writes: "We do not ride on the railroad; it rides upon us." What does he mean?

3. What is Thoreau's definition of "news"? What is his definition of gossip? According to Thoreau, how does news differ from gossip?

4. What does Thoreau mean when he says that the "universe constantly and obediently answers to our conceptions"? How, then, is truth possible?

5. Where, according to Thoreau, is truth to be found? What prevents us from finding it?

THE STRATEGIES

1. Reread the final sentence of paragraph 1. What tone is Thoreau using?

2. Thoreau uses two anecdotes in this excerpt (paragraphs 5 and 6). What do these have in common? What do they indicate about the writer's philosophy?

3. "We have the Saint Vitus' dance, and cannot possibly keep our heads still" (paragraph 3). What figure of speech is this? Can you find other examples of this same figure of speech in the text? What effect do they have on Thoreau's writing?

4. "Our life is like a German Confederacy, made up of petty states, with its boundary forever fluctuating, so that even a German cannot tell you how it is bounded at any moment" (paragraph 2). What figure of speech is this? How does it differ from the example in the preceding question?

5. An allusion is a figure of speech in which some famous historical or literary figure or event is casually mentioned. Can you find an allusion in Thoreau's text? (Hint: examine paragraph 7.) What effect does the allusion have on the writer's style?

THE ISSUES

1. Reread the essay "Diogenes and Alexander," on pages 529–33. What views about society do Diogenes and Thoreau share? Do you agree with these views? Why or why not?

2. Thoreau witnessed the creation of the railroad and felt that it was an intrusion on life. In paragraph 2 he states, "We do not ride on

the railroad; it rides upon us." What new industrial creation of your time might evoke a similar statement from some social commentator like Thoreau?

3. Do you agree with Thoreau that few important communications reach you through the post office? Why or why not?

4. In paragraph 6, Thoreau follows in Plato's footsteps when he tells us that only great and worthy things have absolute existence, but that petty things are a mere shadow of reality. Imagine yourself to be like Thoreau, living alone out in the woods. What would be essential to your life? What would seem petty? Give examples.

5. What memorable experience, if any, have you had of being alone in nature? How did this experience affect you? What did you learn from it?

SUGGESTIONS FOR WRITING

1. Write an essay describing the clutter of petty affairs in an average person's life. Suggest some ways of simplifying life.

2. Pretend that you are Thoreau and that you have just been brought back to life and introduced to twentieth-century America. Write a diary putting down your first impressions.

TERM PAPER SUGGESTION

Thoreau was once sent to jail for refusing to pay his taxes. Research this episode and write about it.

▼▼▼

Kate Chopin

THE STORM

KATE O'FLAHERTY CHOPIN (1851–1904) was an American author, born in St. Louis of Creole-Irish descent. In 1870 she married a Louisiana businessman and lived with him in Natchitoches parish and New Orleans, where she acquired an intimate knowledge of Creole and Cajun life, on which she based most of her best stories. After her husband's death in 1883, she returned with their six children to St. Louis and began to write seriously. Her novel, *The Awakening* (1899), caused a furor among readers because of its treatment of feminine sexuality that seemed to ignore the mores of the time. For the next sixty years, Chopin was virtually ignored. But today her work is praised for its regional flavor and for its remarkable independence of mind and feeling. Among her works are two collections of short stories, *Bayou Folk* (1894), and *A Night in Acadie* (1897).

The plot of the story that follows is based on a single event, but this event evokes a multitude of questions concerning why it happened. The reader cannot help but wonder what motivated two people to act so impulsively under the circumstances described.

I

1   The leaves were so still that even Bibi thought it was going to rain. Bobinôt, who was accustomed to converse on terms of perfect equality with his little son, called the child's attention to certain sombre clouds that were rolling with sinister intention from the west, accompanied by a sullen, threatening roar. They were at Friedheimer's store and decided to remain there till the storm had passed. They sat within the door on two empty kegs. Bibi was four years old and looked very wise.

2   "Mama'll be 'fraid, yes," he suggested with blinking eyes.

3   "She'll shut the house. Maybe she got Sylvie helpin' her this evenin'," Bobinôt responded reassuringly.

4   "No; she ent got Sylvie. Sylvie was helpin' her yistiday," piped Bibi.

5   Bobinôt arose and going across to the counter purchased a can of shrimps, of which Calixta was very fond. Then he returned to his perch on the keg and sat stolidly holding the can of shrimps while the storm burst. It shook the wooden store and seemed to be ripping great furrows in the distant field. Bibi laid his little hand on his father's knee and was not afraid.

II

6   Calixta, at home, felt no uneasiness for their safety. She sat at a side window sewing furiously on a sewing machine. She was greatly occupied and did not notice the approaching storm. But she felt very warm and often stopped to mop her face on which the perspiration gathered in beads. She unfastened her white sacque[1] at the throat. It began to grow dark, and suddenly realizing the situation she got up hurriedly and went about closing windows and doors.

7   Out on the small front gallery she had hung Bobinôt's Sunday clothes to air and she hastened out to gather them before the rain fell. As she stepped outside, Alcée Laballière rode in at the gate. She had not seen him very often since her marriage, and never alone. She stood there with Bobinôt's coat in her hands, and the big rain drops began to fall. Alcée rode his horse under the shelter of a side projection where the chickens had huddled and there were plows and a harrow piled up in the corner.

---

[1] Work dress, house dress.—Ed.

8   "May I come and wait on your gallery till the storm is over, Calixta?" he asked.

9   "Come 'long in, M'sieur Alcée."

10   His voice and her own startled her as if from a trance, and she seized Bobinôt's vest. Alcée, mounting to the porch, grabbed the trousers and snatched Bibi's braided jacket that was about to be carried away by a sudden gust of wind. He expressed an intention to remain outside, but it was soon apparent that he might as well have been out in the open: the water beat in upon the boards in driving sheets, and he went inside, closing the door after him. It was even necessary to put something beneath the door to keep the water out.

11   "My! what a rain! It's good two years since it rain' like that," exclaimed Calixta as she rolled up a piece of bagging and Alcée helped her to thrust it beneath the crack.

12   She was a little fuller of figure than five years before when she married; but she had lost nothing of her vivacity. Her blue eyes still retained their melting quality; and her yellow hair, dishevelled by the wind and rain, kinked more stubbornly than ever about her ears and temples.

13   The rain beat upon the low, shingled roof with a force and clatter that threatened to break an entrance and deluge them there. They were in the dining room—the sitting room—the general utility room. Adjoining was her bed room, with Bibi's couch along side her own. The door stood open, and the room with its white, monumental bed, its closed shutters, looked dim and mysterious.

14   Alcée flung himself into a rocker and Calixta nervously began to gather up from the floor the lengths of a cotton sheet which she had been sewing.

15   "If this keeps up, *Dieu sait*[2] if the levees goin' to stan' it!" she exclaimed.

16   "What have you got to do with the levees?"

17   "I got enough to do! An' there's Bobinôt with Bibi out in that storm—if he only didn' left Friedheimer's!"

18   "Let us hope, Calixta, that Bobinôt's got sense enough to come in out of a cyclone."

19   She went and stood at the window with a greatly disturbed look on her face. She wiped the frame that was clouded with moisture. It was stiflingly hot. Alcée got up and joined her at the window, looking over her shoulder. The rain was coming down in sheets obscuring the view of far-off cabins and enveloping the distant wood in a gray mist. The playing of the lightning was incessant. A bolt struck a tall chinaberry tree at the edge of the field. It filled all visible space with a blinding glare and the crash seemed to invade the very boards they stood upon.

---

[2] French for "God knows."—Ed.

20   Calixta put her hands to her eyes, and with a cry, staggered backward. Alcée's arm encircled her, and for an instant he drew her close and spasmodically to him.

21   "Bonté!"[3] she cried, releasing herself from his encircling arm and retreating from the window, "the house'll go next! If I only knew w'ere Bibi was!" She would not compose herself; she would not be seated. Alcée clasped her shoulders and looked into her face. The contact of her warm, palpitating body when he had unthinkingly drawn her into his arms, had aroused all the old-time infatuation and desire for her flesh.

22   "Calixta," he said, "don't be frightened. Nothing can happen. The house is too low to be struck, with so many tall trees standing about. There! aren't you going to be quiet? say, aren't you?" He pushed her hair back from her face that was warm and steaming. Her lips were as red and moist as pomegranate seed. Her white neck and a glimpse of her full, firm bosom disturbed him powerfully. As she glanced up at him the fear in her liquid blue eyes had given place to a drowsy gleam that unconsciously betrayed a sensuous desire. He looked down into her eyes and there was nothing for him to do but to gather her lips in a kiss. It reminded him of Assumption.

23   "Do you remember—in Assumption, Calixta?" he asked in a low voice broken by passion. Oh! she remembered; for in Assumption he had kissed her and kissed and kissed her; until his senses would well nigh fail, and to save her he would resort to a desperate flight. If she was not an immaculate dove in those days, she was still inviolate; a passionate creature whose very defenselessness had made her defense, against which his honor forbade him to prevail. Now—well, now—her lips seemed in a manner free to be tasted, as well as her round, white throat and her whiter breasts.

24   They did not heed the crashing torrents, and the roar of the elements made her laugh as she lay in his arms. She was a revelation in that dim, mysterious chamber; as white as the couch she lay upon. Her firm, elastic flesh that was knowing for the first time its birthright, was like a creamy lily that the sun invites to contribute its breath and perfume to the undying life of the world.

25   The generous abundance of her passion, without guile or trickery, was like a white flame which penetrated and found response in depths of his own sensuous nature that had never yet been reached.

26   When he touched her breasts they gave themselves up in quivering ecstasy, inviting his lips. Her mouth was a fountain of delight. And when he possessed her, they seemed to swoon together at the very borderland of life's mystery.

------

[3] French for "Goodness!"—Ed.

27   He stayed cushioned upon her, breathless, dazed, enervated, with his heart beating like a hammer upon her. With one hand she clasped his head, her lips lightly touching his forehead. The other hand stroked with a soothing rhythm his muscular shoulders.

28   The growl of the thunder was distant and passing away. The rain beat softly upon the shingles, inviting them to drowsiness and sleep. But they dared not yield.

29   The rain was over; and the sun was turning the glistening green world into a palace of gems. Calixta, on the gallery, watched Alcée ride away. He turned and smiled at her with a beaming face; and she lifted her pretty chin in the air and laughed aloud.

III

30   Bobinôt and Bibi, trudging home, stopped without at the cistern to make themselves presentable.

31   "My! Bibi, w'at will yo' mama say! You ought to be ashame'. You oughtn' put on those good pants. Look at 'em! An' that mud on yo' collar! How you got that mud on yo' collar, Bibi? I never saw such a boy!" Bibi was the picture of pathetic resignation. Bobinôt was the embodiment of serious solicitude as he strove to remove from his own person and his son's the signs of their tramp over heavy roads and through wet fields. He scraped the mud off Bibi's bare legs and feet with a stick and carefully removed all traces from his heavy brogans. Then, prepared for the worst—the meeting with an overscrupulous housewife, they entered cautiously at the back door.

32   Calixta was preparing supper. She had set the table and was dripping coffee at the hearth. She sprang up as they came in.

33   "Oh, Bobinôt! You back! My! but I was uneasy. W'ere you been during the rain? An' Bibi? he ain't wet? he ain't hurt?" She had clasped Bibi and was kissing him effusively. Bobinôt's explanations and apologies which he had been composing all along the way, died on his lips as Calixta felt him to see if he were dry, and seemed to express nothing but satisfaction at their safe return.

34   "I brought you some shrimps, Calixta," offered Bobinôt, hauling the can from his ample side pocket and laying it on the table.

35   "Shrimps! Oh, Bobinôt! you too good fo' anything!" and she gave him a smacking kiss on the cheek that resounded. *"J'vous réponds,*[4] we'll have a feas' to night! umph-umph!"

36   Bobinôt and Bibi began to relax and enjoy themselves, and when the three seated themselves at table they laughed much and so loud that anyone might have heard them as far away as Laballière's.

---

[4] French for "I answer you."—Ed.

IV

37 Alcée Laballìere wrote to his wife, Clarisse, that night. It was a loving letter, full of tender solicitude. He told her not to hurry back, but if she and the babies liked it at Biloxi, to stay a month longer. He was getting on nicely; and though he missed them, he was willing to bear the separation a while longer—realizing that their health and pleasure were the first things to be considered.

V

38 As for Clarisse, she was charmed upon receiving her husband's letter. She and the babies were doing well. The society was agreeable; many of her old friends and acquaintances were at the bay. And the first free breath since her marriage seemed to restore the pleasant liberty of her maiden days. Devoted as she was to her husband, their intimate conjugal life was something which she was more than willing to forego for a while.

39   So the storm passed and every one was happy.

(1,895 words)

VOCABULARY

sombre (1)	spasmodically (20)	resignation (31)
projection (7)	palpitating (21)	embodiment (31)
harrow (7)	sensuous (22)	solicitude (31)
gallery (8)	immaculate (23)	brogans (31)
deluge (13)	inviolate (23)	effusively (33)
monumental (13)	revelation (24)	conjugal (38)
levees (15)	enervated (27)	
incessant (19)	cistern (30)	

THE FACTS

1. What relationship exists between Calixta and Alcée? What do you infer from their past?

2. How does the storm contribute to the love tryst that takes place?

3. What caused the lovers to act so impetuously? Do you consider the cause valid and acceptable?

4. How do the lovers react to their mates after the love affair? Does the reaction seem plausible? Give reasons for your answer.

5. In paragraph 13, what is the significance in describing Calixta's bedroom as "dim and mysterious"? Explain the reference.

THE STRATEGIES

1. What setting forms the backdrop for this story? What does the setting contribute?

2. What is the purpose of the Roman numerals dividing the story?

3. What kind of language does the author resort to in describing the passion of the two lovers? Point to specific examples.

4. What do you think of the title of this story? Is the story really about a storm? Explain your answer.

5. Where does the climax of the story take place? Explain your answer.

THE ISSUES

1. In your opinion, did the lovers handle the situation as morally as possible, given that they yielded to the temptation of the situation? If you disagree with their reactions, what should they have done?

2. The narrator tells us that Calixta's flesh "was knowing for the first time its birthright." What is meant by this statement? What similar comment is made about Alcée?

3. As indicated in the biographical headnote about Kate Chopin, the author's work was criticized for its "feminine sexuality." What do you think readers of her day thought about a story like "The Storm"? How does your view of the story compare with the view of Chopin's contemporaries?

4. What kind of conjugal life do the couples described seem to share? What, if anything, is good about it?

5. What is the theme (main point) of the story? Express it in one sentence.

SUGGESTIONS FOR WRITING

1. Write an analysis of what happens when people lose control of their passions. Use examples to prove your point.

2. Write an essay probing the causes of the widespread marital infidelity so common in our society today.

▼▼

Robert Frost

DESIGN

ROBERT FROST (1874–1963) was a lecturer, poet, and teacher. When he was nineteen and working in a mill in Lawrence, Massachusetts, the *Independent* accepted and published "My Butterfly, an Elegy"—the poem that began Frost's career as one of America's great poets. Rugged New England farm life was the inspiration for many of his poems.

Like much of Frost's poetry, "Design" appears on the surface to be simple and plain. But a closer study will reveal subtleties and depth. The speaker observes nature with a philosophic mind.

> I found a dimpled spider, fat and white,
> On a white heal-all, holding up a moth
> Like a white piece of rigid satin cloth—
> Assorted characters of death and blight
5
> Mixed ready to begin the morning right,
> Like the ingredients of a witches' broth—
> A snow-drop spider, a flower like a froth,
> And dead wings carried like a paper kite.
>
> What had that flower to do with being white,
10
> The wayside blue and innocent heal-all?
> What brought the kindred spider to that height,
> Then steered the white moth thither in the night?
> What but design of darkness to appall?—
> If design govern in a thing so small.

(110 words)

VOCABULARY

characters	kindred	appall
blight		

THE FACTS

1. The heal-all is a wildflower, usually blue or violet, but occasionally white, commonly found blooming along footpaths and roads. The

name derives from the belief that this flower possessed healing qualities. As described in the first stanza, what do the spider, the heal-all, and the moth have in common?

2. Three questions are asked in the second stanza. How can these be condensed into one question? And what answer is implied in the poem?

3. The "argument from design" was a well-known eighteenth-century argument for the existence of God. It proposed a broad view of history and the cosmos, which revealed that some divine intelligence fashioned and then sustained existence. What twist does Frost give this argument?

4. Is the poem probing a sufficient, a necessary, or a contributory cause?

THE STRATEGIES

1. What five examples of figurative language are used in the first stanza? Tell what effect each has.

2. In the second stanza, why does the poet use the adjective *kindred* in connection with the spider?

3. In the second stanza, what synonyms does the poet use to repeat the concept of design?

THE ISSUES

1. The problem of whether or not our destinies are controlled by some higher intelligence concerns most thinking persons. Why do you suppose human beings wrestle so often with this problem?

2. How would you argue against Frost's theme? Use an example from nature to take the opposite viewpoint.

3. Judging from past experience, which of your intimate acquaintances are better able to cope with life, those with a strong belief in a God who controls human destiny, or those with the belief that existence is simply experience and that no god controls any aspect of the universe?

SUGGESTIONS FOR WRITING

1. Using an example from nature, write a brief essay showing how an incontrovertible harmony seems to regulate the activities of the world as a whole.

2. Write a brief essay in which you explain what in the poem causes you to like or dislike it.

ISSUE FOR CRITICAL
THINKING AND DEBATE

THE VALUES OF THE NEW GENERATION

The idea that an entire generation can be presumed to share a common set of values is, on the face of it, ridiculous. Equally ridiculous is the business of carving up generations under various nicknames. Generally, the *Baby Boomers* represent the one clear-cut generation to have emerged since World War II. Experts agree that this is the group born between 1946 to 1964, years of an especially high birthrate. And even though it is obvious that another generation followed the Boomers, no widespread agreement exists about its defining birth years, values, or habits.

Some experts peg as *Generation X* those born after the Boomers and into a world defined by MTV, Game Boy, and divorced parents. Others arbitrarily lump into the Generation X bucket anyone between the ages of 15 and 35, a group said to number about 80 million, ranging from the president's daughter, Chelsea Clinton, to the basketball rebounder Dennis Rodman. This group is also sometimes referred to as the Baby Busters, Twenty-somethings, Slackers, and Generation X. It is this last term, Generation X, that has stuck.

But what is Generation X, and what are its values? Here we are greeted with disclaimers and mystery. The name is said to come from the 1991 novel, *Generation X: Tales for an Accelerated Culture*, by Canadian writer Douglas Coupland. But even Coupland himself shrugs off this responsibility, telling *USA Today*, "I speak for myself, not for a generation. I never have. I seem to travel through life with that one disclaimer." (March 7, 1994). As for the actual existence of such a generation, a spokesman for the Census Bureau declared flatly to *USA Today*, "There is no document in the Census Bureau I know of that mentions Generation X" (September 23, 1996).

What do we know for sure about Generation X? Not much, if hard facts are what we're after. It exists, if only by chronological definition. Otherwise, its defining traits seem to have been dreamed up mainly by marketeers desperate to craft sales pitches for a group whose spending power is estimated to range from $100 billion to $600 billion. Beyond that, Generation X, as a definable group, is mainly a fiction.

Yet commentators continue the drumbeat of criticism aimed at Generation X. They are said to be slackers, self-absorbed, lazy, and cynical. One think-tank issued a report styling them "IDI's," for their presumed credo, "I deserve it" ("Missed Manners," Jack Smith, *Los*

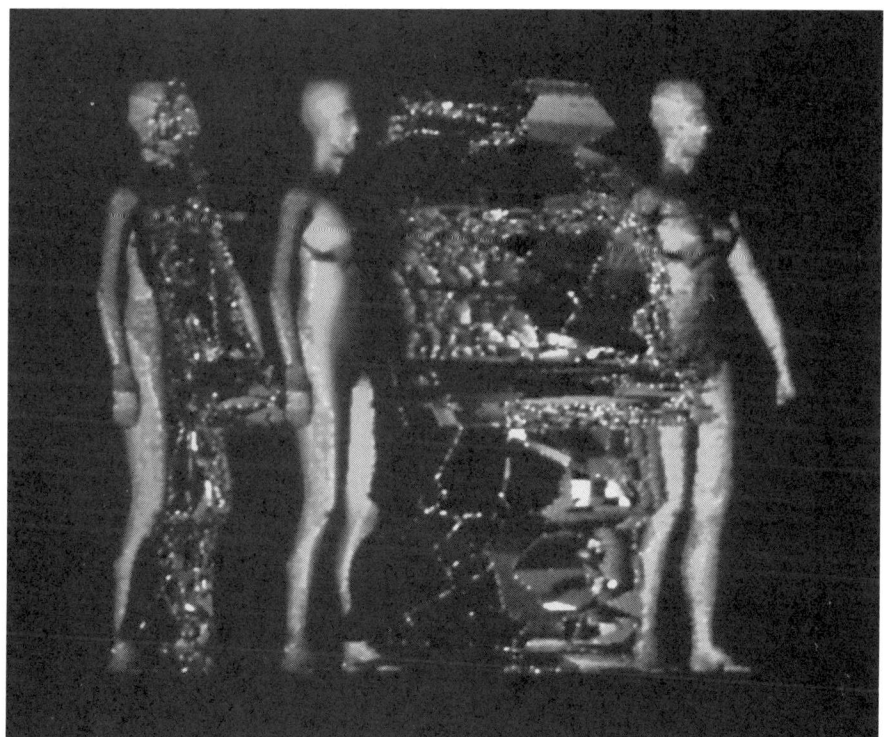

Duane Palyka, Picasso 2, *1979. Computer art, New York Institute of Technology.*

Angeles Times Magazine, December 2, 1990.) Behind all these charges and countercharges is the false assumption that Generation X is a definable group with shared traits, values, and habits.

The ambiguity about this new generation is reflected in the two essays of this section. Leading off the discussion is a satirical essay from a member of so-called Generation X who whines for a defining war. His ironic piece is followed by a faintly damning commentary by a Canadian journalist who professes delight in meeting members of the younger generation while bemoaning the moral vacuum in which they were allegedly raised.

Conflict between the generations is nothing new. Nor is the condescension of an older generation towards a younger unexpected. As it declines, the older generation always thinks itself better raised and more stout-hearted than the one emerging. Predictably, when the younger generation replaces the present older one, it will feel exactly the same about its own children.

▼▼▼

Brian Gabriel

A GOOD WAR WILL SET GEN X STRAIGHT

BRIAN GABRIEL is a self-confessed member of Generation X and a writer who lives in Los Angeles.

1   It has been said that Generation X, or is it the MTV Generation? or is that the Slacker Generation or maybe the Baby Busters, or whatever it's called, it's been said that this generation of which I, being 27, am part is aimless, apathetic, unmotivated. These twentysomething Americans, it's been said, are spoiled, don't know how good they have it, are nothing but crybabies, whiners with degrees. Naturally, all this is said by our elders who, no matter the era, always feel it their duty to disparage the younger generation.

2   But while this younger generation may be apathetic, spoiled, lacking purpose, etc. (just look how many different names it's called and then tell me it doesn't have an identity problem), let me add one more whine and say: It's not our fault. Throughout this century, the older generation has consistently supplied the younger generation with a cause that conferred an identity: the Lost Generation of World War I, in which the older generation thoughtfully supplied its offspring with a catastrophic war to scar their remaining years; the Depression/World War II Generation, in which the older generation supplied the younger with two catastrophes for the price of one; the Baby Boomer Generation, in which the older generation supplied the young with an unpopular jungle war, causing them to take drugs and protest and drop out.

3   Which brings us to the present younger generation. The preceding generations' identities were forged mostly in response to war. And therein lies our problem. Our elders have failed to provide us with a suitable war to forge an identity around.

4   Oh, sure, our noble leaders have done their best to get us one. Ever since the mid-80s they have tried and tried again with no luck: Panama, Grenada, El Salvador, Somalia, Haiti, the Persian Gulf. Unfortunately, all these efforts failed, either through bungled leadership (Haiti, Somalia) or, worst of all, excessive success—wars that have lasted only a matter of hours or days. How are we supposed to forge an identity around Operation Desert Storm?

5   That one, by the way, was the great hope. Over the course of a couple of months, while President Bush (God bless him) assembled our

military might in the heart of Arabia, I could feel a generation bursting forth: Nirvana played incessantly on the radio, "Slacker" was fast approaching status as an official cult movie and the Clash's "Rock the Casbah" was the first song to be blasted on the armed forces radio in the liberation of Kuwait. I remember being in Santa Cruz in January of '91 as students and others took to the park for a protest against the encroaching war—a real antiwar protest!—and then, right there on CNN, there it was, a generation forming on the tip of a missile as it pierced the roof of an Iraqi building and blew to pieces everything and everyone inside. What a glorious moment that was.

6   And then it was over. American troops defeated Iraq in what—six days? Give me a break. World War I lasted about a year and a half after America entered the fray. World War II took almost four. And Vietnam ran somewhere in the neighborhood of 10 years. Six days? What is that?

7   And so my generation continues to drift here and then there, whining every so often and turning on MTV (but not really watching) and falling asleep and waking up, not knowing really what to do with ourselves, waiting for our fearless leaders to give us a cause, something to care about. The Soviet Union is no more, the Eastern Bloc is being swallowed by NATO and Central America is safely capitalist again. Nelson Mandela is president of his country and Manuel Noriega isn't. Sure, there are issues, there always are issues, but that's not good enough. We need a war.

8   Where exactly is Bosnia?

(647 words)

VOCABULARY

apathetic (1)   conferred (2)   encroaching (5)
disparage (1)

THE FACTS

1. According to the writer, what do elders always feel it their duty to do?

2. What, according to the author, does his generation lack?

3. What two catastrophes did one generation inherit?

4. What was the defining event for the Baby Boomer generation?

5. What event gave the author's generation hope?

THE STRATEGIES

1. What is the overall tone of this essay? How do you know?

2. How does the writer use parentheses throughout the essay?

3. Satire is said to fall into two main types, *Horatian satire,* which is gentle and smiling, and *Juvenalian satire,* which is biting and angry. Which type would this fall under?

4. Satire always aims an underlying criticism at its target. What valid criticism does the writer seem to make of his elders?

5. Reread paragraph 2. What technique does the author use in it to drive home his point?

THE ISSUES

1. The writer says that elders "always feel it their duty to disparage the younger generation." Do you believe this? Why do you think elders always have this need?

2. What is your opinion of the Baby Boomer generation?

3. What are the values of the present generation? How would you define these values?

4. One writer elsewhere claimed that Generation X has no heroes. What is your opinion of this assertion?

5. Writers in America are always harping on generational differences. What differences do you see between yours and your father's generation?

SUGGESTIONS FOR WRITING

1. Write an essay of any type, whether serious or funny, about your generation.

2. Write an essay about your personal values and the values of your generation.

▼▼▼

Ted Byfield

ONE DELIGHTFUL HOUR SPENT WITH THE GENERATION WE HAVE BETRAYED

TED BYFIELD is president of United Western Communications Ltd., which publishes three weekly news magazines in Canada, *Alberta Report, Western Report,* and *BC Report*. He was educated at George Washington University and has worked at the *Washington Post, Ottawa Journal,* and the *Sudbury Star.* In 1957, he won the National Newspaper Award for political reporting.

1   There were about 60 of them, about 30 men and 30 women, aged maybe 18 to 25 with some a little older, and they constituted the first-year journalism class which Bill Sass, a reporter on the *Edmonton Journal,* is conducting at Grant MacEwan Community College. Mr. Sass had invited me to talk to them about the news business. We spent half an hour discussing what you had to know, how unglamorous things like spelling and geography (that "cemetery" has three e's and Pittsburgh carries the "h") are far more significant than they may have been led to believe.

2   How about an "inquiring mind?" somebody asked. Very important. No doubt about it. So okay. Nearly everybody there had crossed the North Saskatchewan River one or two thousand times. Where does it flow to? Nobody knew. So much for the "inquiring mind." (An exception, notably, was Mr. Sass himself who did know it eventually gets to Lake Winnipeg, thus demonstrating that perhaps you actually do learn something practicing journalism.)

3   We spent the next half hour discussing this magazine, whether it is a good thing, and why it isn't. Most of the women, the ones who did the talking anyhow, were pretty well agreed it's awful. Yes it is generally well written, and yes it does cover important topics the other media tend to ignore, but it has a very antiquated attitude towards women. It wants them all back in the kitchen raising children, and women today have more essential things to do. Like study journalism.

4   Through it all I had two impressions. One was that these were delightful people and I would have enjoyed arguing with them all day. The other was the chilling realization, present like an ache in the gut, that many of these kids—and at 67 you start to think of nearly everybody as "kids"—will never be journalists. Indeed, they may not have a full-time job of any kind ever. For that is the economic fact of it, and it is a very unacceptable fact.

5   I read about a decade ago that there were ten times as many students in journalism as there were total jobs in the business. I doubt things have changed. Last week we learned that although the Canadian unemployment rate has hit a five-year low, jobs for 18- to 24-year-olds continue to decline. The proportion of young people in the labor market is at a 20-year low of 62 percent. In 1990 it was 72 percent. Job prospects are so poor that people in their 20s are actually dropping out of the labor market, probably to return to school. Unemployment among young women is at depression levels of 25 percent; among young men it's 20 percent.

6   According to the *Globe and Mail,* only 59 percent of Canadians between 25 and 29 whose education ended with high school have a full-year, full-time job. Only 46 percent of women in that category have one. It is also reported that only 35 percent of kids go to university and one third of these drop out after the first year. Those without a university education face the abysmal prospect of part-time, largely unskilled, transient work for the rest of their lives. And even university graduates have no assurance of work in their chosen professions.

7   This is the lot of the unfortunate Generation X, the first beneficiaries of the New Era of freedom and emancipation built on the hallucinations of the 'sixties. In other words, it is probably the most ill-served, ill-educated, ill-raised generation ever. Sound exaggerated? Consider this:

8   They were raised by a society which prided itself on its "tolerance." But what it really meant by this word was that no moral principal must be considered universal or objectively true, because that would make anything incompatible with it objectively false. There could be no ultimate right and wrong, because the assertion of such a claim would constitute "intolerance." It sounded so altogether liberal, so all-inclusive, so open-minded. But what we in fact taught was that everybody can make up his own rules. If nobody could ever be "really right," neither could anybody be "really wrong." Good conduct was anything you could get away with. That was the message.

9   They were led to believe there could be no real standards of performance. The idea of "failing a grade" in school had been abolished. No one failed; everyone passed. For the same reason, determinate examinations were discontinued. There might be "tests," yes, but these rarely decided what would happen to you. Because, after all, there is no "good, better and best" among people. We're all equal, aren't we?

10   They were given little sense of belonging to anything. History had long been supplanted by "social studies," so they had no secure notion that they had emerged from a tradition, or were part of a culture, or were expected to sustain any discernible heritage. All such things were considered passé, and many of their educators believed it their responsibility to divorce young people from the "shackles" of the past. Like

the educator so approvingly quoted this year in a newsletter of the British Columbia Teachers' Federation: "The process of education is intended to free the mind from certainty, to liberate children and adolescents so that they can consider options not entertained by their parents. Indeed the purpose of education in the broadest sense, and particularly given the characteristics of our world today, is to succeed at the paradoxical activity of helping children become what we are not." Who could say it better?

11   Many were raised by a single parent, or more usually by Mom and her latest boyfriend. The concept of domestic permanence, like any other sort of permanence, was something they never really experienced. Home and family were subject to change with little notice.

12   Finally, the society that had stripped them of every other permanence took away from them the possibility of permanent work. We can very easily explain this. We were building what Mr. Trudeau called "the Just Society," you see. And the Just Society meant that everyone had to be comfortable. We couldn't actually afford this, of course. So we borrowed more than half a trillion dollars, and in the pursuit of "Justice" we have piled the debt on this generation. Meanwhile, with the government absorbing all surplus capital to service the debt, nothing is available to start new businesses and inaugurate new ideas. So there are no new jobs for the new generation.

13   This, then, is our bequest to the young people I met in Mr. Sass's class: We have assured them that nothing is true; nothing is real; nothing is certain; nothing lasts; and sorry, there are no jobs. In short, we have left them impoverished economically, culturally, spiritually. We have created a disaster, and when they realize what we've done to them, they will be angry, and they will be right.

(1,159 words)

VOCABULARY

antiquated (3)	beneficiaries (7)	discernible (10)
abysmal (6)	incompatible (8)	paradoxical (10)
transient (6)	supplanted (10)	inaugurate (12)

THE FACTS

1. In what kind of class did the author visit the new generation?

2. What complaint did the women have about the author's magazine?

3. What "chilling realization" did the author have about the students in the class?

4. Among which group does the author claim that unemployment is at depression levels?

5. What subject does the author say has supplanted history in the high schools?

THE STRATEGIES

1. How would you characterize the author's tone in this essay?

2. Why do you think the author makes a point of telling us his age?

3. Read the end of paragraph 3. What is odd about the final construction?

4. How does the author prepare us for his angry comments about what we have done to the new generation?

5. In paragraph 8, the author puts quotation marks around his use of the word "tolerance." What does he intend those quotation marks to mean?

THE ISSUES

1. The essay focuses on Canadian students. How applicable do you think its criticisms are to Generation X Americans?

2. What political perspective does the author seem to cling to in his criticisms of the younger generation?

3. The author claims that this generation was raised to believe that good conduct was anything you could get away with. What is your opinion of this assertion?

4. What does the author find so offensive about the quotation in paragraph 10 from the Teachers' Federation? What is your opinion of it?

5. What is your opinion of the author's belief that the younger generation, sooner or later, will be angry at what has been done to them?

SUGGESTIONS FOR WRITING

1. Do you think your generation is as badly raised as the author claims? Write an essay arguing for or against that assertion.

2. Write an essay about one incident in your upbringing that taught you an important lesson.

STUDENT CORNER

▼▼

I

First Draft

Sean Cotton, New York University

Generation X

As a baby-boomer generation grew older and began ~more specific~ to procreate, they spawned what is now known as "Generation X," ~They were~ *a group of young adults* raised by aging flower children, corporate rat-runners, and the new church of television. ~What~ ~came out of this was~ *They are* a mixture of apathetic, self-oriented ~parallelism~ realists and *fervent* anti-establishment idealists. As these two extremes enter "the real world," it ~will as~ *is* yet to be seen whether the actions of Generation X will be dominated by ~the~ realis**m**~ts~ or ~same letters~ idealis**m**~ts~.

The great social upheaval committed by our parents in the ~set off with dashes~ 60's was a mixture of idealism and realism. The goals of many *idealistic* leaders of this time‸ *–* Martin Luther King, Bobby Kennedy, and ‸*P* John Kennedy,‸ *–* were backed up by realistic movements such as ~sentence needs better balance~ King's social changes for Blacks in America~, advertised by~ *finding implementation in* the March on Washington; or, President Kennedy's many idealistic ~outlooks on~ *hopes for* civil rights~, realistically implemented~ *being turned into actuality* by the brute force used when the National Guard was sent into the South to abolish Jim Crow laws.

611

Cotton 2

P   These ideas and actions were a rebellion against the old guard

of the 50's and 40's, who had come to power in a U.S. that had
     World War II
suddenly, after ~~WW II~~, found itself one of the two major world
                                        were
agr   powers. The children of the 60's ~~was~~ a backlash against the

P   conservatism that pervaded thought in the generation before
                                    children,
slang   them. Yet, as they brought up their ~~kids~~ they let the pendulum
P
show   swing too far in the opposite direction of the way they had been
contrast   reared. Youngsters
           ~~raised. Kids~~ were not made to work for ~~whaqt~~ what they earned; ~~as~~ instead,

P   they were given everything and denied nothing. A materialistic
P | tighten
     consciousness, not seen since the 1920's, shaped the outlook on
          shared by   ers
     life ~~that~~ most ~~of those in~~ Generation X ~~share~~.

     The idea of living the good life without earning it became the
                                                              that
P   ~~d~~driving force of a lackadaisical generation, A generation ~~with~~
pronoun   depended for   on   son
ref   ~~such~~ cultural stimulation ~~as~~ Michael Jack~~son~~ and Beavis and Butthead.
        Generation X
        ~~They~~ grew up learning that experimentation with drugs was all
                                                     aspect of the
     right; just as long as it was experimentation. The worst ~~of it~~ was situation
              Generation X's
     that the rebellion of ~~their~~ parents against their parents was so underline

     much part of raising a child that none of this was seen to be

     wrong because the flower children remembered, their own   misplaced
                                                                phrase
     wavy gravy days of peace, (with fondness) Even though the drugs
     of the 60s   been dangerous,   users
     had ~~gotten harder,~~ causing many ~~in the 60's~~ to drop out of   tense
                                                                   better
     society, little was done to stop the rampant use of drugs, uch as placement
                                                                   of phrase
     cocaine, (in the 80's) ~~It is becaue of~~ all these factors ~~put~~ added together
          make   A segment of society with Summary
     ~~that~~ Generation X ~~is~~ what it is today. ~~One that has~~ no real   paragraph

     driving force and no ideals that keep them dreaming of
                    or revolution.
     reformation ~~for the better.~~

Cotton 3

In the next ten years Generation X will be taking over
governmental positions, high corporate jobs, and various ~~other~~
influential offices in the United States. For twenty to forty years
after that they will be the decision makers ~~for~~ our country. It   better word

whether

may~~y~~ not even matter ~~if~~ the realists or the idealists take control,   agr

because both are flawed in many ways. Maybe a happy medium

it

between the two will arise and ~~they~~ will be able to get something

In the meantime,

done. ~~W~~hat Gen*e*ration X need*s* *now* is something almost all other

have

generations before them ~~has~~ had: they need to rally behind a

cause, even if it brings them to the brink of revolution. It will be

earns a good name in the future

interesting to see if Generation X ~~makes a name for themselves~~

or simply gets lost in the foggy annals of history.

I

Final Draft

Sean Cotton, New York University

Generation X

As the baby-boomer generation grew older and began to procreate, they spawned what is now known as "Generation X," a group of young adults raised by aging flower children, corporate rat-runners, and the new church of television. They are a mixture of apathetic self-oriented realists and fervent anti-establishment idealists. As these two extremes enter "the real world," it is yet to be seen whether the actions of Generation X will be dominated by realism or idealism.

The great social upheaval committed by our parents in the 60s was a mixture of idealism and realism. The idealistic goals of many leaders of this time—Martin Luther King, Bobby Kennedy, and John Kennedy—were backed up by realistic movements, such as King's social changes for Blacks in America finding implementation in the March on Washington; or, President Kennedy's many idealistic hopes for civil rights being turned into actuality by the brute force used when the National Guard was sent into the South to abolish Jim Crow laws.

These ideas and actions were a rebellion against the old guard of the 40s and 50s, who had come to power in a U.S. that had suddenly, after World War II, found itself one of the two major world powers. The children of the 60s were a backlash against the conservatism that pervaded thought in the generation before them. Yet, as they brought up <u>their</u> children, they let the pendulum swing too far in the opposite direction of the way they had been reared. Youngsters were not made to work for what they earned; instead, they were given everything and denied nothing. A materialistic consciousness, not seen since the 1920s, shaped the outlook on life shared by most Generation Xers.

The idea of living the good life without earning it became the driving force of a lackadaisical generation—a generation that depended for cultural stimulation on Michael Jackson and Beavis and Butthead. Generation X grew up learning that experimentation with drugs was all right, just as long as it was experimentation. The worst aspect of the situation was that the rebellion of Generation X's parents against <u>their</u> parents was so much part of raising a child that none of this was seen to be wrong because the flower children remembered with fondness their own wavy-gravy days of peace. Even though the drugs of the 60s had been dangerous, causing many users to drop out of society, little was done in the 80s to stop the rampant use of drugs, such as cocaine.

All of these factors added together make Generation X what it is today—a segment of society with no real driving force and no ideals that keep them dreaming of reformation or revolution.

In the next ten years Generation X will be taking over governmental positions, high corporate jobs, and various other influential offices in the United States. For twenty to forty years after that, they will be the decision makers of our country. It may not even matter whether the realists or the idealists take control, because both are flawed in many ways. Maybe a happy medium between the two will arise and it will be able to get something done. In the meantime, what Generation Xers need now is something almost all other generations before them have had: They need to rally behind a cause, even if it brings them to the brink of revolution. It will be interesting to see if Generation X earns a good name in the future or simply gets lost in the foggy annals of history.

How I Write

Basically I don't like to write because writing is lonely, difficult work. But when I have an assignment heaped on me—usually by an instructor—I put off the task as long as possible—with a constant nagging feeling that I should be doing it. Finally, when I can no longer make excuses and have to face reality, I sit down at my computer and start typing. I don't brainstorm on paper because when I do, the problem of picking out anything usable is too time consuming. I just write and keep erasing until I have some sentences that make sense. Usually, at some point in the writing, my thoughts begin to flow, and then the task is much easier than when the page is blank and I can't think of an intelligent sentence.

How I Wrote This Essay

Since I wrote this essay over the Christmas holiday, I had a chance to mull over some ideas with my parents and some friends. I realized that being nineteen, I was a few years short of being a true Generation Xer; therefore, I could be tough on this group who seem to feel that life owes them money without hard work and authority without responsibility. I got a kick out of poking fun at Generation X. In fact, I was beginning to be a little too sarcastic, so I toned down my attitude. I just kept writing down ideas and trying to find examples to support my assertions until, before I knew it, I had completed the assignment to my satisfaction.

My Writing Tip

Always make sure that your papers are backed up on a floppy disk in your computer. Begin a writing assignment soon after it is given to you; otherwise, you tend to forget the context in which it was assigned. If you can't begin right away, at least think about what you will write—while you are driving or just waiting somewhere. Often ideas need to "hatch" before they are placed on paper.

CHAPTER WRITING ASSIGNMENTS

1. Choose one of the following subjects and develop an essay by dividing the subject into categories:
   a. anxieties
   b. colleges
   c. humor
   d. values
   e. violence
   f. fashions
   g. children
   h. books
   i. movies
   j. painting styles
   k. political systems

2. Write an essay in which you contrast one of the following pairs of concepts:
   a. jealousy-envy
   b. liberty-license

    c. servant-slave
    d. democracy-demagoguery
    e. art-craft
    f. politician-statesman
    g. talent-ability

3. Write a causal analysis for one of the following conditions:
    a. The poor writing habits of today's students
    b. The lack of popular financial support for museums, concerts, and other art forms
    c. The fall of the U.S dollar overseas
    d. The need for prison reform
    e. The worldwide popularity of rock music
    f. The rise in child pornography
    g. The failure of the rapid transit system in most large cities
    h. The need to conserve our beaches
    i. Our tendency to buy throwaway items
    j. Homelessness

WRITING ASSIGNMENTS FOR A SPECIFIC AUDIENCE

1. Write a letter addressed to the president of your college, listing the major causes of your disgruntlement with the college. Consider such causes as high student parking fees, poor cafeteria food, ever-increasing cost of tuition, or lack of tutoring services for difficult courses. If you feel completely satisfied, then write a letter listing the causes for your high degree of satisfaction.

2. Write an imaginary letter to a younger sibling, contrasting college with high school. Be sure to choose appropriate bases for the contrast, such as academic rigor, social life, relationships with teachers, and independence.

COLLABORATIVE WRITING PROJECT

Join a group of four other students. After reading all the material on Generation X, brainstorm about how this generation can be defined and what, if any, are its characteristics. Then assign one member to write an essay based on the group discussion. When the rough draft is finished, the entire group should work on rewriting and editing it until the final draft accurately represents the positions and ideas of all four members.

Chapter Nine

ARGUMENTATION

INTRODUCTION TO ARGUMENTATION

Argumentation is a term of rhetorical intent, not of form. It refers to any essay or speech whose aim is to sway or persuade a reader. Because writers resort to many techniques and devices to achieve this aim, the argumentation essay tends to be a mixture of rhetorical forms; that is, you are likely to find the writer defining, describing, narrating, or even dividing during the course of the argument. The tone of the essay can vary from the savage sarcasm of Jonathan Swift's "A Modest Proposal" to the chilling, matter-of-fact tone of Andrew Vachss's "Sex Predators Can't Be Saved." And the subject matter can include any topic from the nearly infinite spectrum of issues about which people argue.

What elements are most likely to sway us in an argumentative essay, to make us change our minds and believe a writer's arguments? It is difficult to answer this question, but research suggests some clues. First, there is our perception of the writer's credentials to hold an opinion on the subject. If we think the writer competent and qualified on the subject—a medical doctor writing on a medical topic, for example—we are more likely to believe the advocated opinion. Should you hold a particular qualification to write on the subject, then mentioning it will probably help. You do not have to blare out your credentials, but can do it subtly. For example, in his essay on the sexual predators, Vachss tells us that he has interviewed many sex predators over the years, which revelation leaves us more likely to accept his contentions about them. If you are not an expert yourself, then quoting an expert can certainly lend weight to your view.

Another element that inclines us to believe an argumentative essay is the quality of its reasoning. If the writer's logic is sound, if the facts and supporting details strike us as reasonable and strong, then we are likely to be swayed by the conclusions. This is not as self-evident a proposition as it sounds. People who ardently believe one side of an issue frequently persuade themselves that the facts supporting the other are wrong. But presenting your facts in all their glory, while making the links between the propositions of your argument instantly clear, will make it harder for anyone to easily dismiss your conclusions. For example, in her essay "How the Superwoman Myth Puts Women Down," Sylvia Rabiner draws a valid logical connection between the media's glamorization of high-level professional women and the feeling of inferiority this "hype" instills in women destined to low-level careers. She bolsters her argument with appropriate examples and facts from the workplace.

Finally, arguments are persuasive if they appeal to our self-interests. We are more likely to believe an argument if we think there is something in it for us. This insight explains why arguers huff and puff to portray themselves and their views as if they agreed exactly with our self-interests, even if the correspondence is frequently far-fetched. The underlying appeal of Jonathan Swift's ironic proposal, for instance, is to the self-interests of Irish citizens who Swift thinks would be better off in a unified Ireland free from British exploitation.

The essays in this chapter both teach and exemplify argumentation. Richard Altick, in "Obstacles to Clear Thinking," acquaints us with argumentative trickery; John Sherwood, in "Introduction to Logic," shares with us the legitimate sources of belief. Swift savagely attacks the policy of the eighteenth-century English towards a destitute and starving Ireland, while Judy Syfers sarcastically catalogues the stereotypic traits we unreasonably expect from a wife. Andrew Vachss makes a chilling argument for permanently incarcerating sexual predators, and Sylvia Rabiner attacks the myth of the Superwoman who is touted by the media as "having it all." Finally, James Michie, in "Dooley Is a Traitor," creates a poetic persona who beguiles us with antiwar arguments. Homelessness and its painful effects are discussed in the Issues section. The efforts of all of these writers to persuade us teaches argumentation in the best possible way by good example.

A D V I C E

▼▼▼

Richard D. Altick

OBSTACLES TO CLEAR THINKING

RICHARD DANIEL ALTICK (b. 1915), American literary historian and biographer, is emeritus professor of English at Ohio State University since 1968. His works include *The Scholar Adventurers* (1959); *The English Common Reader: A Social History of the Mass Reading Public, 1800–1900* (1957); and *Preface to Critical Reading* (1969), from which this selection is excerpted.

This article identifies some of the common types of logical errors that you are likely to encounter in political debate, in the media, and even in everyday argument. Learning the formal names of these errors is unimportant; what is important is being able to recognize these common logical slips well enough to avoid them in your own reasoning.

1 In addition to the many pitfalls awaiting the unwary in formal inductive and deductive thinking, there are a number of common errors which perhaps can be called "abuses of logic" only by courtesy; some of them, at least, may best be described as sheer avoidances of logic.

2 1. Among them, an important class involves the *introduction of irrelevant and irrational evidence.* In the chapter on connotation, we have met a number of examples of such errors. There they were termed "name-calling" and "glittering generalities." Here we shall give them the labels they have in the books on clear thinking. But it is far less important to remember their names than it is to be able to recognize instances of them when we meet them—and to react to them as intelligent readers should react.

3 a. The *argumentum ad hominem.* Here the writer or speaker departs from his task of proving the point at issue to prejudice his audience against his opponent. In American politics, this argument (which is too dignified a word for it!) is called "mud slinging." If, for example, in attacking his opponent's position on the reduction of the national debt, a candidate refers to Mr. X's intimate connection with certain well-known gamblers, he ceases to argue his case on its objective merits and casts doubt upon his opponent's personal character. His object is not primarily to hurt Mr. X's feelings, but to arouse bias against Mr. X in his hearer's mind. Every critical reader or listener must train himself to detect and reject these irrelevant aspersions. It may be, indeed, that Mr. X *has* shady connections with the underworld. But that has nothing to do with the abstract rights or wrongs of his position on a national

issue. Although, as the history of American politics shows, it is a hard thing to do, issues should be discussed apart from character and motives. The latter are also important, since obviously they bear upon a candidate's fitness for public office, but they call for a separate discussion.

4   b. The *argumentum ad populum*. This too involves an appeal to the feelings, passions, and prejudices, rather than the reason, of the group addressed; but whereas the preceding argument is directed specifically against one's opponent, the *ad populum* argument has a wider range. The writer uses emotionally weighted words to bias his audience in favor of or against a person (not necessarily his opponent), an idea, a political party, a class, a nation. The monotonously repeated phrases of Communist propaganda against Americans—"Wall Street monopolists," "rich gangsters," "capitalistic warmongers"—are the most familiar recent examples of the negative, or name-calling, aspect of this argument. But just as common is the other aspect—that of the glittering generality, by which a writer attempts to sway his readers to enthusiasm for something or someone. The twin language-devices of the *argumentum ad populum*, then, are the stenchbomb and the perfume atomizer. The constant task of the critical reader is to ignore the odor with which an idea has been sprayed and to concentrate on the idea itself.

5   The "transfer" device is a particular favorite of those who find it to their advantage to use the *argumentum ad populum*. Like the use of name-calling and the glittering generality, it depends for its effectiveness upon the reader's or hearer's willingness to associate one idea with another, even though the two are not logically connected. Essentially, it represents an attempt to clothe one's pet policy or principle in borrowed raiment which will lend it a strength and dignity it does not possess by itself.

6   A common example of transfer is the habit which political orators have of working into their speeches quotations from Scripture or from the secular "sacred writings" (the Declaration of Independence, the Preamble to the Constitution, the Gettysburg Address). Such quotations are depended upon to arouse favorable emotions in the breasts of the auditors, emotions which are then transferred to the orator's pet policy. Much of William Jennings Bryan's success as a public figure was due to the way in which he transformed an ordinary political campaign into a quasi-religious crusade by his "Cross of Gold" speech: "You shall not press down upon the brow of labor this crown of thorns; you shall not crucify mankind upon a cross of gold!" Actually, although the underlying idea, that the national monetary policy at the end of the nineteenth century worked to the serious disadvantage of the "common man," was entirely valid, the metaphor in which it was expressed was not. There is no connection between economics and the passion and crucifixion of Jesus. But the metaphor succeeded admirably

in rallying to Bryan's ranks millions of Americans to whom Biblical quotation and allusion had the most powerful of connotations. It is noteworthy that as the influence of the Bible upon men's emotional habits declines, knowing politicians make less use of Biblical references; but such standard emotion-rousers as mention of Valley Forge, the Founding Fathers, and Abraham Lincoln are still found sprinkled through much propaganda. Whether they have any logical connection with the issues discussed is, to the speaker and (he hopes) to his audience, irrelevant; what they do is shed their own emotional effulgence upon ideas and pleas which might not otherwise be so acceptable.

7   The advertiser employs the transfer device just as commonly. Perhaps the most familiar instance of it is the use of the picture of a beautiful girl, not merely to attract attention to the advertisement but also to place the reader in a receptive frame of mind. Whether the girl has anything to do with the subject of the advertisement does not matter—so long as the reader is pleasantly affected. At certain periods when patriotic sentiment runs high, as during a war, commercial advertisers use the emotional symbols of patriotism for their own needs. Not only do they use the national colors and pictures of, or references to, the fighting men; their text often is designed to arouse fervent patriotic emotions which can then be transferred to a particular product. The following advertisement, dominated by a large drawing of the eagle on the United States seal, once appeared in eastern newspapers:

Pride in the American Way

The way of life that is American, that expounds democracy, is a proud way of life. It is a manner of living so fine, so high in ideals and purpose that it stands over and above all others. The Grabosky Family, makers of Royalist cigars, are proud to be members of The American Family, proud to present a cigar so fine in quality that it stands above all others. Over 50 years of superb cigar-making experience lies behind Royalist . . . a proud name in a proud America.[1]

8   c. The *argumentum ad verecundiam.* This is a special instance of the more general "transfer" device. Here it is not a matter of borrowing prestige from one institution, such as religion or a nation, to adorn something else; instead, the prestige is specifically that of a great name, an "authority," which is expected to have weight with the public. On the general matter of authority we shall have more to say in a little while. At this point, we need only stress the importance of critically analyzing any appeal which uses quotations from men and women who have achieved fame in one field or another. One crucial question

---

[1] Note that the brand name of the cigar is not conspicuously in harmony with the sentiments expressed in the advertisement itself; yet it probably sells cigars. Why?

is: Is the quotation appropriate here? Does it have real relevance to the point at issue? It is all very well to quote Jefferson or Lincoln or Franklin Roosevelt in support of one's political stand—but it must be remembered that circumstances have changed immensely since these quotations were first uttered, and their applicability to a new situation is open to question. The implication is, This man, who we all agree *was* great and wise, said certain things which prove the justice of my own stand; therefore it behooves you to believe I am right. But to have a valid argument, the writer must prove that the word of the authorities whom he cites has a logical bearing on the present issue. If that is true, then he is borrowing not so much their popular prestige as their wisdom—which is perfectly permissible.

9   In essence, what the writer who invokes august authority for his point of view does is to imply that if the great men of the past were living today, they would write testimonials in behalf of his position. The familiar testimonials of present-day advertising are another instance of the transfer device. In some cases, the authority who testifies has some connection with the type of product advertised. The problem to settle here is, when we decide which brand of cigarette is best, how much weight may we reasonably attach to the enthusiastic statements of tobacco buyers, warehousemen, and auctioneers? In other cases, the testifying authority may have no formal, professional connection with the product advertised. An actor, who may very well be a master of his particular art, praises a whiskey, an after-shaving lotion, or a new convertible. He likes it, he says: but, we may ask, does the fact that he is a successful actor make him any better qualified than anyone who is *not* an actor to judge a whiskey, a lotion, or a car? Competence in one field does not necessarily imply competence in another.

10   Furthermore, in recent times it has been increasingly the custom for advertisers to borrow the prestige of science and medicine to enhance the reputation of their products. The American people have come to feel for the laboratory scientist and the physician an awe once reserved for bishops and statesmen. The alleged approval of such men thus carries great weight when it is a question of selling something, or (which is the same thing) inducing someone to believe something. Phrases such as "leading medical authorities say . . . " or "independent laboratory tests show . . . " are designed simply to transfer the prestige of science, which presumably is incapable of either error or corruption, to a toothpaste or a cereal. Seldom if ever are the precise "medical authorities" or "independent laboratories" named. But the mere phrases have vast weight with the uncritical. Similarly too the honorific "Dr." or "professor" implies that the person quoted speaks with all the authority of which learned men are capable—when as a matter of fact "doctorates" can be bought from mail-order colleges. Whenever, therefore, an attempt is made to convince by appeal to the prestige that

surrounds the learned, the reader should demand full credentials. Just *what* medical authorities say this? Can they be trusted? *What* independent laboratories made the test—and what, actually, did the test reveal? Who is this man that speaks as a qualified educator or psychologist or economist? Regardless of the fact that he is called "doctor," does he know what he is talking about?

11   In all cases where the persuasive power of reputation and authority is invoked in behalf of a policy or a product, it is profitable to remember that before he can testify in a court of law, a man about to provide specialized evidence, which may have an important bearing on the jury's decision, must establish his competence in his field. A pathologist, a psychiatrist, an engineer, is asked briefly to outline the nature of his special training and experience. It would not hurt if, when we encounter the appeal to authority in any type of persuasive writing, we adopted the strategy of the opposing lawyer and probed more deeply into the witness' genuine competence to speak on the particular issue that is before us. A few pages later on, we shall suggest some pertinent questions in this respect.

12   2. *Begging the question.* Here the statement which is ostensibly offered as a proposition to be proved actually assumes the proposition as already proven. "This ordinance will certainly reduce juvenile delinquency, because it provides for steps which will prevent crimes on the part of teenagers." In other words, A is good because A is good. "The reason why Sally is so mischievous is that she has just a little of the devil in her." "I would trust him with any of my personal affairs because he is certainly a reliable lawyer."

13   Every instance of name-calling or of the glittering generality involves question-begging. When a writer or speaker brands someone a "dangerous radical" or acclaims a policy as "the only way to escape national disaster" he is using words the truth of which he never questions—nor expects his audience to question. Yet all such words and phrases, weighted as they are with emotion and charged with controversy, stand very much in need of proof. And even if, when stripped of their irrelevant emotional wording, the ideas can be established as true, the argument remains sterile. Since its premise is identical with its conclusion, nobody who does not already accept the conclusion will accept the premise, and hence it convinces nobody.

14   3. *False analogy.* This fallacy consists of presenting a situation which is acknowledged to be true, and then, on the basis of it, commenting on another situation which is said to be similar. It is usually employed in an attempt to simplify and make more vivid a complex issue. Newspaper political cartoons are often nothing more than pictorial analogies. Often, of course, such analogies serve admirably to point up, dramatically and colorfully, the crux of a problem. The analogy of a governmental agency in the role of the legendary Dutch boy,

trying desperately to stop a leak in the dike ("national economy") while the waves of the sea ("inflation") are already spilling over the top of the dike, is plainly very useful. But the ever-present danger is that the analogy will assume a vital resemblance between the two objects of comparison, where none really exists. "Don't change horses in the middle of a stream" is a familiar cry in political campaigns when, pleading a national emergency, the partisans of the incumbent in office declare he cannot be superseded without grave danger to the country. There is, of course, a superficial similarity between the two situations: changing horses in the middle of a swift stream is dangerous, and so too may be changing public officials at certain junctures in national affairs. But riding horseback is not much like being president of the United States, and while there may be only one or two reasons why one should or should not change horses, there may be very many reasons, none of them having anything to do with horseback riding, why one man should be elected president and not another. Equally dangerous is any attempt to prove a point which is based on the fancy that the nations of the world are like school children, and that when one nation does not have its way it goes into a corner and sulks; or that two opponents, labor and capital, for example, may be likened to two prizefighters squaring off in the ring, with some government official or agency as referee. Such analogies are, we repeat, useful in dramatizing a situation; but it is always perilous to maintain that because two situations are "alike" in one or two respects, what is true of one is necessarily true of the other.

15   4. *Oversimplification.* False analogy may well be considered a particular type of oversimplification—than which there is no more common error. When we discussed in the beginning of this chapter the method of reasoning by hypothesis, we stressed the fact that no hypothesis can be considered sound unless we have taken into account all the factors that are related to it. Unfortunately, with our natural human indolence, to say nothing of our intellectual limitations, we are always eager to view questions in their simplest terms and to make our decisions on the basis of only a few of the many aspects which the problem involves. If that is true of problems of a practical nature, such as those we used to illustrate the use of the hypothesis, how much more true it is of those involving a problem of human conduct, or a grave decision facing the voters or the statesmen of a nation! Few of the decisions which we are called upon to make are so simple that we can say with confidence that one choice is completely right and the other is completely wrong. The problem of the so-called minority groups in America, for instance, is not simply one of abstract justice, as many would like to think it; it involves deeply complex questions of economics, sociology, and politics. Nor can we say with easy assurance: "The federal government should guarantee every farmer a decent income, even if the money comes from the pocketbooks of the

citizens who are the farmer's own customers"—or "It is the obligation of every educational institution to purge its faculty of everyone who holds leftist sympathies." Perhaps each of these propositions is sound, perhaps neither is; but before he adopts it as a settled conviction, the intelligent man or woman must canvass its full implications, just as he should do with any hypothesis. After the implications have been explored, it may be found that there is more evidence telling against the proposition than there is supporting it; in which case it should be abandoned. In any event, no one can call himself a conscientious citizen who fails to explore, so far as he is humanly able, the honest pros and cons of any issue he is called upon to help decide—and then to adopt the position he feels is best justified by the evidence he has surveyed.

16   Countless false generalizations concerning parties, races, religions, and nations—to say nothing of individuals—are the result of the deep-seated human desire to reduce a complex idea to its simplest terms. Democrats tend naturally to think all Republicans as progress-obstructing conservatives, when in fact many Republicans are more "liberal" than many Democrats. Many Protestants regard Catholics as bigoted and superstitious, even though the views they regard as "bigoted" and the practices they regard as "superstitious" may have their roots deep in the philosophical grounds of the Catholic religion. Similarly many Catholics regard Protestants as infidels or atheists, although there may be as much philosophical justification for Protestant doctrine as there is for Catholic. It is easier to condemn than to understand. But every man and woman has a pressing moral, as well as intellectual obligation to examine the basis of every judgment he or she makes: "Am I examining every aspect of the issue that needs to be examined—do I understand the pros and cons of the problem sufficiently to be able to make a fair decision—or am I taking the easiest way out?"

17   5. The innate intellectual laziness of human beings invites one further, crowning device of deception: the *distortion or the actual suppression of the truth.* If men will not actively demand the truth, why should persuaders provide them with it, when doing so would hurt their chances of success? And so it is usual in all forms of persuasion to prevent considerations which would damage the cause from reaching the minds of those who are to be persuaded.

18   a. One such device—there are many—is *card stacking* (also called "smoke screen"[2]), which is used by a group, a political party for instance, to divert attention from certain issues which it does not care to have discussed. Card stacking consists of laying heavy and insistent

---

[2] Although their purposes are the same, card stacking and the smoke screen have slightly different techniques. The first is usually prepared in advance; the second is impromptu, being devised to meet exigencies as they occur in the course of an argument.

emphasis upon certain selected topics, discussion of which can probably do the party no harm. The party then hopes that the public, its attention centered on these topics, will not bother about the less attractive side of the party's record or program. A state administration, running for re-election, may devote all its propaganda to boasting about the reduction in taxes which it has effected in an "economy program"—and it will assiduously fail to mention the way in which state services have deteriorated as a result of the "slashed budget." This same practice is evident in virtually every advertisement one reads. The attractive points of a product are dwelt upon unceasingly; the less attractive ones, never. An automobile may be streamlined and easy-riding, it may have fast pickup in traffic, it may have a wealth of gadgets—these facts will be proclaimed from every newspaper, magazine, and billboard; but that the car eats up gasoline and oil, has a poorly made engine block, and costs $200 more than other cars in the same price-class—these facts are religiously suppressed. But, as you will no doubt agree, they are worth knowing about.

19   b. Another closely related means by which attention is drawn from the whole truth is one dear to every practical politician: the *red herring*. The red herring is an irrelevant issue which is drawn across the path of an argument when one side or the other is becoming embarrassed and wishes to change the subject. In a campaign for the mayoralty of a large city, for example, Party A (which is in office) may find itself in serious trouble because Party B has successfully given evidence of its waste of public funds. Four days before the election, therefore, Party A suddenly "discovers" that Party B's candidate has been seen in night clubs with a lady who is not his wife. Party A hopes that the injection into the contest of another, more appealing, topic of discussion will allow the public to forget the serious accusations that have been leveled against it. Whether or not Party A is able to prove that the B candidate's private frailties (if they do exist) disqualify him from holding public office, the red herring will have served its purpose if it ends the embarrassing talk about Party A's own shortcomings.

20   c. A third such device is that of *wrenching from context*. A sentence or a phrase can easily mean one thing when it is quoted alone, and a quite different thing if it is read against the background of the whole discussion to which it belongs. An extreme example is a sentence from a newspaper review of a new movie: "For about five minutes 'Fruits of Desire' is a topnotch show, brilliantly acted and magnificently photographed. After that it degenerates into a dismal spectacle of Hollywood hokum." It would not be surprising to see the subsequent advertisements of the movie flaunting this headline: "'A top-notch show, brilliantly acted and magnificently photographed . . . a spectacle'—Smith, *Daily News*." The familiar "avoid foreign entanglements" advice in Washington's farewell address, when read in full context,

means something very different from what it means when quoted separately. And probably no public figure whose statements are quoted in the newspapers or on the radio has ever escaped the chagrin that comes from seeing prominence given to one or two paragraphs of his latest speech which, thus isolated, completely distort his total argument. Such quotations must always be read with the greatest caution. The only way to be sure that they fairly represent the author's viewpoint is to read the complete text of his speech as printed in, for instance, *The New York Times*.

(3,883 words)

VOCABULARY

aspersions (3)	ostensibly (12)	indolence (15)
raiment (5)	acclaims (13)	impromptu
effulgence (6)	fallacy (14)	(footnote 2)
behooves (8)	partisans (14)	assiduously (18)
august (9)	superseded (14)	chagrin (20)
invoked (11)	junctures (14)	

DISCUSSION

▼▼▼

John C. Sherwood

INTRODUCTION TO LOGIC

JOHN C. SHERWOOD (b. 1918) was born in Hempstead, New York, and educated at Yale University. Since 1961, he has taught at the University of Oregon. The following selection comes from his *Discourse of Reason* (1964).

Sherwood discusses the relationship between belief, values, and logic. He defines the difference between induction and deduction, between generalizations and judgments, and discusses the use of each in everyday reasoning.

1   Even for the most skeptical, belief is an absolute necessity for practical experience. At the very least, we have to have faith that the material

world will continue in its accustomed ways, that tomorrow as today iron will be hard and clay soft, that objects will continue to fall toward the earth instead of flying off into the sky. Even in the less certain and less easily analyzed realm of human character, we constantly act on beliefs—that a soft answer turneth away wrath, that a veteran soldier will fight bravely, that a mother will love and protect her children, that the mailman will deliver the mail instead of stealing it. Without belief, action would be paralyzed; we should never know what to do in a given situation. What really distinguishes the rational from the irrational thinker is not the presence or absence of belief, but the grounds on which belief is accepted.

2   There are some sources of belief which are either absolutely unsound or to be resorted to only when all other methods fail. A "hunch" is not an absolutely useless guide, because it may be based on knowledge which has temporarily slipped our minds, but we would be foolish to trust a hunch when objective evidence was available. Our casual impression of a prospective employee may be useful, but full knowledge of his previous record is more valuable. Tradition may be a proper guide in some areas of life, but we cannot accept witchcraft or even the Newtonian physics because our forefathers did. All too often we believe simply because we want to believe. It is comforting to think that "there is always room at the top" or that "there are no atheists in foxholes" or that "football makes good citizens." But such beliefs are the most treacherous of all beliefs, because we tend to protect them by ignoring contrary evidence until at some crisis the brute facts force themselves on our attention. An unfounded belief is not merely wrong morally; it is an unsafe guide to conduct.

3   What then are the legitimate sources of belief? In a scientific age we instinctively answer, evidence or investigation. We believe that a worker is reliable because we have seen him at work frequently over a considerable period of time; we believe that a certain remedy will cure a certain disease because trained observers have watched its operation in a large number of cases (here, as often, we have to trust the reports of others' investigations); we believe that haste makes waste because we have seen it happen so many times. In effect, we infer from a certain number of instances of a thing that a characteristic of the thing we have observed in those instances will also appear in other instances. This is the process of *induction*. Somewhat less often (unless we are very much given to theoretical reasoning) we use *deduction*. Where induction puts facts together to get ideas or *generalizations*, deduction puts ideas together to discover what other ideas can be inferred from them. If John is the son of David who is the son of William, then John must be the grandson of William—we know this without asking. If a student must pass composition to graduate, and Mr. X has not yet passed it, then Mr. X cannot yet graduate. In each case, given

the first two ideas or *premises*, we know that the third—the *conclusion*—must be true: no further investigation is needed. (If the conclusion proved not to be true, then we would assume that one of the premises was wrong; perhaps a student must take composition unless excused.)

4   In every mind there will be a few beliefs which cannot be proved either by induction or deduction: basic standards of value, ultimate articles of faith, matters of inner conviction which we would be hard put to prove but without which we could scarcely think or act. Religious principles might be thought of as the most obvious example, but philosophy and even science illustrate the same necessity. In plane geometry we must begin with axioms and postulates from which the rest of the system is deduced. It is an article of faith that "things equal to the same thing are equal to each other"; we must believe it or give up plane geometry. Virtually all induction, and hence all scientific conclusions and practically all action depend on a faith in the uniformity of nature—that the laws of matter will be the same tomorrow as today. It seems only common sense to assume that water will continue to freeze at 32° Fahrenheit hereafter, but there is no way of proving the assumption theoretically.

5   Induction and deduction are not merely the tools of the philosopher and the scientist, but in rough-and-ready half-conscious forms are part of the everyday thought processes of all sane human beings, however limited their education. It is not infrequently argued that logic in the more formal sense is neither necessary nor useful for human life, since "common" or "horse" sense can serve us far better in practical affairs. All this involves a half-truth. In the first place, we might question whether logic and common sense are really so opposed. If common sense has any value, it is because it is based on "experience"; in other words, having generalized from a series of seemingly like instances observed in the past, we apply the generalization to a further instance that has just come to our attention. What really distinguishes common sense from logic is that it tends to take shortcuts: it seldom bothers to work out all the steps in the argument. Certain processes work in our brains, and we acquire a sudden conviction that something is true. It is fortunate that we have common sense and "intuition" to depend on, for time does not always allow us to work things out logically or go hunting for evidence. It is certainly better to investigate a prospective employee thoroughly, but if we have to fill the job on the spot, we shall have to trust our impressions of his character. Very rarely (if we are wise) we may even trust our common sense in preference to what seems to be scientific evidence. Many a parent or teacher has finally nerved himself to go against the "scientific findings" of a child psychologist or educator. (But perhaps here what is wrong is not really science but its interpretation by self-appointed prophets.) Whole

areas of human decision lie outside of the range of logic and some-times even of common sense. One may be able to prove by critical prin-ciple that a book has every virtue that belongs to a masterpiece, and the book may in fact be quite unreadable. Science has not conquered all areas of human life. It is useless to tell a young man that a certain girl has all the qualifications of an ideal wife if he happens to hate her. Nevertheless, to scorn logic and hold to "horse sense" is a dangerous business. An appeal to common sense—or worst yet, intuition—all too often represents an attempt to evade the responsibility of looking at evidence or working out the problem rationally. Common sense some-times tells people peculiar things about such matters as family life and racial and economic problems. If by common sense we mean a kind of informal, everyday logic, then it is an absolute necessity of rational ex-istence; but if by it we mean a defiance of logic, it ought not to exist at all, and it is unhappily true that most of us use logic too little rather than too much.* To come down to the practical problem of communi-cation—which after all is our basic concern here—our personal intu-itions are probably of very little interest to our readers or listeners, who may even not be much impressed by our common sense, however much they may value their own. What they expect from us is logic and evidence.

6   By its very nature, logic deals in statements or *propositions;* they are the materials of deductive reasoning and the products of inductive reasoning. By a proposition we mean a group of words which can be affirmed or denied—of which it can be said it is either true or false. (Even if it is false, it is still a proposition.) Not all sentences are propo-sitions. A question or command is not a proposition; we cannot say that "Who is there?" is true or that "Do your homework!" is false. A proposition is roughly equivalent to the grammarian's *declarative sen-tence,* though not exactly equivalent, since a declarative sentence might contain several different propositions ("The sky is blue, and the grass is green") or express what is really a question or command ("The audi-ence will leave quietly").

7   Another important distinction is that between a proposition which is merely factual and one which implies a *judgment.* "He served at Valley Forge" and "He was a loyal soldier" are both statements, but not of the same kind. The first is a matter of fact: either he served or he did not, and there is the possibility at least of proving the matter one way

---

* Perhaps we should distinguish common sense, which does involve some conscious reasoning on evidence, from intuition, which involves no reasoning at all, but only a "feeling" that something is so. Intuition certainly ought to be a last resort, but some-times there is nothing else to follow. Often, if the intuition is sound, one can find ev-idence or construct an argument to confirm it. One ought to be able to defend it rationally, however irrational its origins.

or another to the satisfaction of all. The second is a little different; it passes a judgment since the word "loyal" implies praise for something the speaker approves of or judges good. Another speaker, fully apprised of the same facts, might differ because of a differing conception of what constitutes loyalty, and absolute proof one way or another is impossible, since an element of personal feeling will always enter in. We should not confuse this distinction between *fact* and *judgment* with the distinction between *established truth* and *mere opinion*. Fact here means "piece of verifiable information"; what makes it a fact is the concrete quality which makes conclusive proof at least theoretically possible. "Columbus died in 1491" and "Martians have six legs" are in this sense factual, though the one statement is known to be false and the other is at present impossible of verification. "George Washington was loyal" still involves a judgment, however much the statement is confirmed by evidence and however universally it is believed. A British writer in 1776 might plausibly have called Washington disloyal, and while we could find plenty of arguments to challenge the writer with, it is very possible that we should never come to an agreement with him. Unhappily for logic, the distinction between fact and judgment is far from clear-cut. The statement "He is intelligent" certainly contains an element of judgment; yet it is susceptible of confirmation by means of standard tests and might approach the status of a fact. It may be especially hard to distinguish between judgments and generalizations derived from a number of facts. Generalizations, like statements of single facts, differ from judgments in not necessarily implying any approval or disapproval. "A 1.5 concentration of alcohol in the blood usually impairs reactions" is a generalization; "It is wrong to drive in such a state" is a judgment.

8   Needless to say, judgments are not to be condemned; they are merely to be recognized for what they are. It may not always be easy to do this. When the educator says "The learner cannot be considered aside from his environment," he seems to be stating a generalization. But a little reflection reminds us that, rightly or wrongly, pupils are often judged without reference to their environment, and that to make sense the sentence must read "The learner *ought not* to be considered aside from his environment"—a form which clearly identifies it as a judgment. "Good children brush their teeth" has the form of a generalization and might actually represent the result of investigation on the dental habits of children known to be "good." Probably, however, it is a judgment, telling how the speaker thinks children ought to behave, and in a certain context the sentence might amount to a command. What is important is to make our meaning clear in the first place, and to show our readers that our evaluations have been rational. Judgments may be supported by evidence and argument; they need not be mere emotional reactions. The statement "He was

loyal" can be supported by a definition of loyalty and instances of loyal conduct.

9   It goes without saying that one cannot work logically with a statement which does not have a clear-cut, ascertainable meaning. Puritanical logicians sometimes deny cognitive meaning to any statement which cannot be proved true or false (or at least shown to be probable or improbable) by reference to material facts. Since such an assumption would throw out much philosophy and theology, we should hardly wish to go so far, but we should at least try to avoid those statements, all too common in controversy, which do nothing more than express feeling or prejudice. The following is technically a valid argument: X is a no-good rat; No-good rats should be hung; X should be hung. But we should hope that no jury would follow such reasoning. . . . One cannot deduce anything from a feeling.

(2,190 words)

VOCABULARY

prospective (2)   postulates (4)   impairs (7)
infer (3)   intuition (5)   ascertainable (9)
induction (3)   propositions (6)   puritanical (9)
deduction (3)   apprised (7)   cognitive (9)
premises (3)   plausibly (7)
axioms (4)   susceptible (7)

THE FACTS

1. What is the difference between a rational and an irrational thinker?

2. What are legitimate sources of belief?

3. What is induction? What is deduction? How do they differ?

4. The author says scientific induction depends on an act of faith. Faith in what?

5. What is the difference between "common sense" and "logic"?

6. What is a proposition? Where do propositions come from? What is the difference between a proposition and an axiom?

7. What is the difference between a fact and a judgment? Between a generalization and a judgment?

THE STRATEGIES

1. Examine the opening sentences of the first four paragraphs. What key word is repeated in each sentence? What effect does this repetition have on these paragraphs?

2. The author readily supports his generalizations with examples. What does this contribute to the selection?

3. What method of logic does this article most heavily rely on—induction or deduction?

4. In paragraph 3, the author uses the pronoun *we*. Whom does this *we* refer to? What effect does its use have on the examples?

5. In paragraph 2, the author gives three examples of unfounded beliefs: (a) "there is always room at the top"; (b) "there are no atheists in foxholes"; (c) "football makes good citizens." By what other name are these and similar beliefs known?

THE ISSUES

1. List five statements of fact that apply to your own life; then rephrase them as statements of judgment. How do they differ?

2. Discuss at least one instance in history when it was appropriate to abandon a belief because of contrary logic or when it was appropriate to abandon logic because of a contrary belief.

3. How important do you consider common sense in the daily affairs of society?

4. It has been said that pollsters have replaced the ancient prophets and oracles. How effective do you consider opinion polls in predicting the future?

5. When is it necessary to be skeptical about an assertion presented to you?

SUGGESTIONS FOR WRITING

1. Write an essay in which you clarify the difference between a *fact* and a *judgment*. Use examples to make the distinction precise.

2. Discuss at least one instance in your life where you either abandoned a belief because of contrary logic or abandoned logic because of a contrary belief.

E X A M P L E S

▼▼

Jonathan Swift

A MODEST PROPOSAL

For Preventing the Children of Poor People from Being a Burthen to Their Parents or the Country and for Making Them Beneficial to the Public

Considered one of the greatest satirists in the English language, JONATHAN SWIFT (1667–1745) was born in Dublin and educated at Trinity College. His satirical masterpiece, *Gulliver's Travels*, was published in 1726, by which time Swift was already regarded by the Irish as a national hero for his *Drapier's Letters* (1724). Originally published as a pamphlet, "A Modest Proposal" first appeared in 1729.

In this famous satire, Swift, assuming the role of a concerned and logical citizen, turns society's indifference to the value of human life into an outraged attack against poverty in Ireland.

1   It is a melancholy object to those who walk through this great town, or travel in the country, when they see the streets, the roads, and cabin doors crowded with beggars of the female sex followed by three, four, or six children, all in rags and importuning every passenger for an alms. These mothers, instead of being able to work for their honest livelihood, are forced to employ all their time in strolling, to beg sustenance for their helpless infants, who, as they grow up, either turn thieves for want of work or leave their dear native country to fight for the Pretender in Spain or sell themselves to the Barbadoes.[1]

2   I think it is agreed by all parties that this prodigious number of children, in the arms or on the backs or at the heels of their mothers and frequently of their fathers, is in the present deplorable state of the kingdom a very great additional grievance, and therefore whoever could find out a fair, cheap, and easy method of making these children sound and useful members of the commonwealth would deserve so well of the public as to have his statue set up for a preserver of the nation.

3   But my intention is very far from being confined to provide only for the children of professed beggars; it is of a much greater extent,

---

[1] Swift refers to the exiled Stuart claimant of the English throne, and to the custom of poor emigrants to commit themselves to work for a number of years to pay off their transportation to a colony.—Ed.

and shall take in the whole number of infants at a certain age who are born of parents in effect as little able to support them as those who demand our charity in the streets.

4   As to my own part, having turned my thoughts for many years upon this important subject and maturely weighed the several schemes of other projectors, I have always found them grossly mistaken in their computation. It is true, a child just dropped from its dam may be supported by her milk for a solar year, with little other nourishment, at the most not above the value of two shillings, which the mother may certainly get, or the value in scraps, by her lawful occupation of begging; and it is exactly at one year old that I propose to provide for them in such a manner as, instead of being a charge upon their parents or the parish or wanting food and raiment for the rest of their lives, they shall on the contrary contribute to the feeding, and partly to the clothing, of many thousands.

5   There is likewise another great advantage in my scheme, that it will prevent those voluntary abortions and that horrid practice of women murdering their bastard children, alas! too frequent among us, sacrificing the poor innocent babes, I doubt more to avoid the expense than the shame, which would move tears and pity in the most savage and inhuman breast.

6   The number of souls in this kingdom being usually reckoned one million and a half, of these I calculate there may be about two hundred thousand couple whose wives are breeders, from which number I subtract thirty thousand couple who are able to maintain their own children (although I apprehend there cannot be so many, under the present distresses of the kingdom); but this being granted, there will remain a hundred and seventy thousand breeders. I again subtract fifty thousand for those women who miscarry or whose children die by accident or disease within the year. There only remain a hundred and twenty thousand children of poor parents annually born. The question therefore is how this number shall be reared and provided for, which, as I have already said, under the present situation of affairs is utterly impossible by all the methods hitherto proposed. For we can neither employ them in handicraft or agriculture; we neither build houses (I mean in the country) nor cultivate land; they can very seldom pick up a livelihood by stealing, till they arrive at six years old, except where they are of towardly parts, although I confess they learn the rudiments much earlier, during which time they can, however, be properly looked upon only as *probationers;* as I have been informed by a principal gentleman in the County of Cavan who protested to me that he never knew above one or two instances under the age of six, even in a part of the kingdom so renowned for the quickest proficiency in that art.

7   I am assured by our merchants that a boy or a girl before twelve years old is no saleable commodity, and even when they come to this

age they will not yield above three pounds or three pounds and a half a crown at most on the exchange, which cannot turn to account either to the parents or the kingdom, the charge of nutriment and rags having been at least four times that value.

8   I shall now, therefore, humbly propose my own thoughts, which I hope will not be liable to the least objection.

9   I have been assured by a very knowing American of my acquaintance in London that a young, healthy child well nursed is, at a year old, a most delicious, nourishing, and wholesome food, whether stewed, roasted, baked, or boiled; and I make no doubt that it will equally serve in a fricassee or a ragout.

10   I do therefore humbly offer it to public consideration that of the hundred and twenty thousand children already computed, twenty thousand may be reserved for breed, whereof only one fourth part to be males, which is more than we allow to sheep, black cattle, or swine; and my reason is that these children are seldom the fruits of marriage, a circumstance not much regarded by our savages; therefore one male will be sufficient to serve four females. That the remaining hundred thousand may, at a year old, be offered in sale to the persons of quality and fortune through the kingdom, always advising the mother to let them suck plentifully in the last month, so as to render them plump and fat for a good table. A child will make two dishes at an entertainment for friends; and when the family dines alone, the fore- or hindquarter will make a reasonable dish, and seasoned with a little pepper or salt, will be very good boiled on the fourth day, especially in winter. I have reckoned, upon a medium, that a child just born will weigh twelve pounds, and in a solar year, if tolerably nursed, will increase to twenty-eight pounds.

11   I grant this food will be somewhat dear, and therefore very proper for the landlords, who, as they have already devoured most of the parents, seem to have the best title to the children.

12   Infant's flesh will be in season throughout the year, but more plentifully in March and a little before and after; for we are told by a grave author, an eminent French physician, that fish being a prolific diet, there are more children born in Roman Catholic countries about nine months after Lent than at any other season; therefore, reckoning a year after Lent, the markets will be more glutted than usual, because the number of Popish infants is at least three to one in this kingdom; and therefore it will have one other collateral advantage, by lessening the number of Papists among us. I have already computed the charge of nursing a beggar's child (in which list I reckon all cottagers, laborers, and four fifths of the farmers) to be about two shillings per annum, rags included; and I believe no gentleman would repine to give ten shillings for the carcass of a good fat child, which, as I have said, will make four dishes for excellent nutritive meat, when he has only

some particular friend or his own family to dine with him. Thus the squire will learn to be a good landlord and grow popular among his tenants; the mother will have eight shillings net profit and be fit for work till she produces another child.

13   Those who are more thrifty (as I must confess the times require) may flay the carcass, the skin of which, artificially dressed, will make admirable gloves for ladies and summer boots for fine gentlemen.

14   As to our city of Dublin, shambles[2] may be appointed for this purpose in the most convenient parts of it; and butchers, we may be assured, will not be wanting, although I rather recommend buying the children alive than dressing them hot from the knife as we do roasting pigs.

15   A very worthy person, a true lover of his country, and whose virtues I highly esteem, was lately pleased in discoursing on this matter to offer a refinement upon my scheme. He said that many gentlemen of his kingdom having of late destroyed their deer, he conceived that the want of venison might be well supplied by the bodies of young lads and maidens, not exceeding fourteen years of age nor under twelve, so great a number of both sexes in every country being now ready to starve for want of work and service; and these to be disposed of by their parents if alive, or otherwise by their nearest relations. But with due deference to so excellent a friend and so deserving a patriot, I cannot be altogether in his sentiments; for as to the males, my American acquaintance assured me, from frequent experience, that their flesh was generally tough and lean, like that of our schoolboys, by continual exercise, and their taste disagreeable; and to fatten them would not answer the charge. Then as to the females, it would, I think, with humble submission, be a loss to the public, because they would soon become breeders themselves, and besides, it is not improbable that some scrupulous people might be apt to censure such a practice (although indeed very unjustly) as a little bordering upon cruelty, which, I confess, has always been with me the strongest objection against any project, however so well intended.

16   But in order to justify my friend, he confessed that this expedient was put into his head by the famous Psalmanazar, a native of the island Formosa, who came from thence to London above twenty years ago and in conversation told my friend that in his country, when any young person happened to be put to death, the executioner sold the carcass to persons of quality as a prime dainty and that in his time the body of a plump girl of fifteen, who was crucified for an attempt to poison the emperor, was sold to his imperial Majesty's prime minister of state and other great mandarins of the court in joints from the

---

[2] Slaughterhouses.—Ed.

gibbet at four hundred crowns. Neither, indeed, can I deny that if the same use were made of several plump young girls in this town who, without one single groat to their fortunes, cannot stir abroad without a chair, and appear at playhouse and assemblies in foreign fineries which they never will pay for, the kingdom would not be the worse.

17   Some persons of a desponding spirit are in great concern about that vast number of poor people who are aged, diseased, or maimed, and I have been desired to employ my thoughts what course may be taken to ease the nation of so grievous an encumbrance. But I am not in the least pain upon the matter, because it is very well known that they are every day dying and rotting by cold, and famine, and filth, and vermin, as fast as can be reasonably expected. And as to the young laborers, they are now in almost as hopeful a condition; they cannot get work and consequently pine away for want of nourishment to a degree that if at any time they are accidentally hired to common labor, they have not strength to perform it; and thus the country and themselves are happily delivered from the evils to come.

18   I have too long digressed and therefore shall return to my subject. I think the advantages by the proposal which I have made are obvious and many, as well as of the highest importance.

19   For first, as I have already observed, it would greatly lessen the number of Papists, with whom we are yearly overrun, being the principal breeders of the nation as well as our most dangerous enemies, and who stay at home on purpose to deliver the kingdom to the Pretender, hoping to take their advantage by the absence of so many good Protestants, who have chosen rather to leave their country than stay at home and pay tithes, against their conscience, to an Episcopal curate.

20   Secondly, the poorer tenants will have something valuable of their own which by law may be made liable to distress and help to pay their landlord's rent, their corn and cattle being already seized and money a thing unknown.

21   Thirdly, whereas the maintenance of a hundred thousand children from two years old and upward cannot be computed at less than ten shillings apiece per annum, the nation's stock will thereby be increased fifty thousand pounds per annum, beside the profit of a new dish introduced to the tables of all gentlemen of fortune in the kingdom who have any refinement in taste. And the money will circulate among ourselves, the goods being entirely of our own growth and manufacture.

22   Fourthly, the constant breeders, beside the gain of eight shillings sterling per annum by the sale of their children, will be rid of the charge of maintaining them after the first year.

23   Fifthly, this food would likewise bring great custom to taverns, where the vintners will certainly be so prudent as to procure the best receipts for dressing it to perfection and consequently have their houses frequented by all the fine gentlemen who justly value themselves upon

their knowledge in good eating; and a skillful cook who understands how to oblige his guests will contrive to make it as expensive as they please.

24   Sixthly, this would be a great inducement to marriage, which all wise nations have either encouraged by rewards or enforced by laws and penalties. It would increase the care and tenderness of mothers toward their children when they were sure of a settlement for life to the poor babes, provided in some sort by the public, to their annual profit or expense. We could see an honest emulation among the married women, which of them could bring the fattest child to the market. Men would become as fond of their wives during the time of their pregnancy as they are now of their mares in foal, their cows in calf, or sows when they are ready to farrow, nor offer to beat or kick them (as is too frequent a practice) for fear of a miscarriage.

25   Many other advantages might be enumerated. For instance, the addition of some thousand carcasses in our exportation of barreled beef; the propagation of swine's flesh and improvement in the art of making good bacon, so much wanted among us by the great destruction of pigs, too frequent at our table, which are no way comparable in taste or magnificence to a well-grown fat yearling child, which, roasted whole, will make a considerable figure at a lord mayor's feast or any other public entertainment. But this and many others I omit, being studious of brevity.

26   Supposing that one thousand families in this city would be constant customers for infant's flesh, beside others who might have it at merry-meetings, particularly at weddings and christenings, I compute that Dublin would take off annually about twenty thousand carcasses and the rest of the kingdom (where probably they will be sold somewhat cheaper) the remaining eighty thousand.

27   I can think of no one objection that will possibly be raised against this proposal unless it should be urged that the number of people will be thereby much lessened in the kingdom. This I freely own, and it was indeed one principal design in offering it to the world. I desire the reader will observe that I calculate my remedy for this one individual kingdom of Ireland and for no other that ever was, is, or I think ever can be, upon earth. Therefore let no man talk to me of other expedients; of taxing our absentees at five shillings a pound; of using neither clothes nor household furniture except what is of our own growth and manufacture; of utterly rejecting the materials and instruments that promote foreign luxury; of curing the expensiveness of pride, vanity, idleness, and gaming in our women; of introducing a vein of parsimony, prudence, and temperance; of learning to love our country, in the want of which we differ even from Laplanders and the inhabitants of Tupinamba; of quitting our animosities and factions, nor acting any longer like the Jews, who were murdering one another at the very

moment their city was taken; of being a little cautious not to sell our country and conscience for nothing; of teaching landlords to have at least one degree of mercy toward their tenants; lastly, of putting a spirit of honesty, industry, and skill into our shop-keepers, who, if a resolution could now be taken to buy only our native goods, would immediately unite to cheat and exact upon us in the price, the measure, and the goodness, nor could ever yet be brought to make one fair proposal of just dealing, though often and earnestly invited to it.

28   Therefore, I repeat, let no man talk to me of these and the like expedients till he has at least some glimpse of hope that there will be ever some hearty and sincere attempt to put them in practice.

29   But as to myself, having been wearied out for many years with offering vain, idle, visionary thoughts and at length utterly despairing of success, I fortunately fell upon this proposal, which, as it is wholly new, so it has something solid and real, of no expense and little trouble, full in our own power, and whereby we can incur no danger in disobliging England. For this kind of commodity will not bear exportation, the flesh being of too tender a consistence to admit a long continuance in salt, although perhaps I could name a country which would be glad to eat up our whole nation without it.

30   After all, I am not so violently bent upon my own opinion as to reject any offer proposed by wise men which shall be found equally innocent, cheap, easy, and effectual. But before some thing of that kind shall be advanced in contradiction to my scheme and offering a better, I desire the author or authors will be pleased maturely to consider two points: first, as things now stand, how they will be able to find food and raiment for a hundred thousand useless mouths and backs; and secondly, there being a round million of creatures in human figure throughout this kingdom whose whole subsistence, put into a common stock, would leave them in debt two millions of pounds sterling, adding those who are beggars by profession to the bulk of farmers, cottagers, and laborers, with the wives and children who are beggars in effect, I desire those politicians who dislike my overture, and may perhaps be so bold as to attempt an answer, that they will first ask the parents of these mortals whether they would not at this day think it a great happiness to have been sold for food at a year old in the manner I prescribe, and thereby have avoided such a perpetual scene of misfortunes as they have since gone through by the oppression of landlords, the impossibility of paying rent without money or trade, the want of common sustenance, with neither house nor clothes to cover them from the inclemencies of the weather, and the most inevitable prospect of entailing the like of greater miseries upon their breed forever.

31   I profess in the sincerity of my heart that I have not the least personal interest in endeavoring to promote this necessary work, having no other motive than the public good of my country, by advancing

our trade, providing for infants, relieving the poor, and giving some pleasure to the rich. I have no children by which I can propose to get a single penny, the youngest being nine years old and my wife past childbearing.

(3,393 words)

VOCABULARY

importuning (1)	censure (15)	parsimony (27)
sustenance (1)	gibbet (16)	overture (30)
prodigious (2)	encumbrance (17)	inclemencies (30)
proficiency (6)	digressed (18)	
collateral (12)	propagation (25)	

THE FACTS

1. What premise is "A Modest Proposal" based on? What is the chief assumption of its argument?

2. Reread paragraph 11. Why do the landlords have "the best title to the children"?

3. Swift's satire redefines children in economic terms. What does this say about his view of the society he lived in?

4. What does the satire imply about religious feelings in Ireland during Swift's time?

5. Given the state of affairs as the author describes them, is his argument logical? Explain.

THE STRATEGIES

1. What is the effect of the word *modest* in the title?

2. Swift describes people with words like *breeder, dam, carcass, yearling child*. What effect do these words have?

3. Satire usually hints at the true state of things as it proposes its own alternatives. How does Swift hint at the true state of things? Give examples.

4. How would you characterize the tone of this piece?

5. Reread the final paragraph. What is its purpose?

THE ISSUES

1. Do you consider satire an effective way to call attention to social ills? Why or why not?

2. Which paragraphs reveal Swift's real suggestions for improving the economic condition of the Irish? How do these paragraphs fit into the general scheme of Swift's essay?

3. What condition existing in our country today would make an excellent subject for the kind of satire used by Swift? What satirical proposal can you suggest?

4. How persuasive do you consider this essay? Would a more straightforward essay be more effective? Why or why not?

5. Is Swift's essay simply a literary masterpiece, to be studied within its context, or does it have a message for us today?

SUGGESTIONS FOR WRITING

1. Infer from "A Modest Proposal" the state of life in Ireland during Swift's time. Make specific references to the article to justify your inferences.

2. Discuss the relationship implied in "A Modest Proposal" between society and the individual.

▼▼▼

Judy Syfers

I WANT A WIFE

JUDY SYFERS (b. 1937) is a freelance writer who espouses the feminist cause. Born in San Francisco, she studied at the University of Iowa, where she earned a B.F.A. in painting (1962). In 1973, her feminist convictions led her to Cuba to study class relationships as a means of understanding how social change can occur. She is best known for the essay reprinted here, which became a classic and has been hailed as the feminist manifesto of the modern woman's emancipation from male domination.

> *Syfers' argument is based on the premise that all wives are completely devoted to their husbands and ardently diligent about promoting their husbands' causes and tending to their needs while all the time remaining glamorous and sexual. Once you accept that premise, then*

Syfers' argument makes perfect sense and seems incontrovertible. But more critical reading reveals some flaws in the argument. Pay particular attention to tone.

1   I belong to that classification of people known as wives. I am a Wife. And, not altogether incidentally, I am a mother.

2   Not too long ago a male friend of mine appeared on the scene fresh from a recent divorce. He had one child, who is, of course, with his ex-wife. He is obviously looking for another wife. As I thought about him while I was ironing one evening, it suddenly occurred to me that I, too, would like to have a wife. Why do I want a wife?

3   I would like to go back to school so that I can become economically independent, support myself, and, if need be, support those dependent on me. I want a wife who will work and send me to school. And while I am going to school I want a wife to take care of my children. I want a wife to keep track of the children's doctor and dentist appointments. And to keep track of mine, too. I want a wife to make sure that my children eat properly and are kept clean. I want a wife who will wash the children's clothes and keep them mended. I want a wife who is a good nurturant attendant to my children, who arranges for their schooling, makes sure they have an adequate social life with their peers, takes them to the park, the zoo, etc. I want a wife who takes care of the children when they are sick, a wife who arranges to be around when the children need special care, because, of course, I cannot miss classes at school. My wife must arrange to lose time at work and not lose the job. It may mean a small cut in my wife's income from time to time, but I guess I can tolerate that. Needless to say, my wife will arrange and pay for the care of the children while my wife is working.

4   I want a wife who will take care of *my* physical needs. I want a wife who will keep the house clean. A wife who will pick up after me. I want a wife who will keep my clothes clean, ironed, mended, replaced when need be, and who will see to it that my personal things are kept in their proper place so that I can find what I need the minute I need it. I want a wife who cooks the meals, a wife who is a *good* cook. I want a wife who will plan the menus, do the necessary shopping, prepare the meals, serve them pleasantly, and then do the cleaning up while I do my studying. I want a wife who will care for me when I am sick and sympathize with my pain and loss of time from school. I want a wife to go along when our family takes a vacation so that someone can continue to care for me and my children when I need a rest and change of scene.

5   I want a wife who will not bother me with rambling complaints about a wife's duties. But I want a wife who will listen to me when I feel the need to explain a rather difficult point I have come across in

my course of studies. And I want a wife who will type my papers for me when I have written them.

6   I want a wife who will take care of the details of my social life. When my wife and I are invited out by my friends, I want a wife who will take care of the babysitting arrangements. When I meet people at school that I like and want to entertain, I want a wife who will have the house clean, prepare a special meal, serve it to me and my friends, and not interrupt when I talk about the things that interest me and my friends. I want a wife who will have arranged that the children are fed and ready for bed before my guests arrive so that the children do not bother us. I want a wife who takes care of the needs of my guests so that they feel comfortable, who makes sure that they have an ashtray, that they are passed the hors d'oeuvres, that they are offered a second helping of the food, that their wine glasses are re-plenished when necessary, that their coffee is served to them as they like it.

7   And I want a wife who knows that sometimes I need a night out by myself.

8   I want a wife who is sensitive to my sexual needs, a wife who makes love passionately and eagerly when I feel like it, a wife who makes sure that I am satisfied. And, of course, I want a wife who will not demand sexual attention when I am not in the mood for it. I want a wife who assumes the complete responsibility for birth control, be-cause I do not want more children. I want a wife who will remain sex-ually faithful to me so that I do not have to clutter up my intellectual life with jealousies. And I want a wife who understands that *my* sexual needs may entail more than strict adherence to monogamy. I must, after all, be able to relate to people as fully as possible.

9   If, by chance, I find another person more suitable as a wife than the wife I already have, I want the liberty to replace my present wife with another one. Naturally, I will expect a fresh, new life; my wife will take the children and be solely responsible for them so that I am left free.

10   When I am through with school and have a job, I want my wife to quit working and remain at home so that my wife can more fully and completely take care of a wife's duties.

11   **My God, who *wouldn't* want a wife?**

(990 words)

VOCABULARY

nurturant (3)   entail (8)   adherence (8)
replenished (6)

THE FACTS

1. According to Syfers, what dual role does a wife play in the family?

2. What physical needs of the husband does the wife take care of?

3. What does Syfers say about the sexual expectations and behavior of husbands?

4. According to the author, for what details of a husband's social life are wives responsible?

5. According to the essay, what should happen if a more suitable wife comes along?

THE STRATEGIES

1. What part does hyperbole or exaggeration play in this essay?

2. How would you characterize the tone of this essay?

3. What pronoun does the author use to refer to a "wife"? Why?

4. How and where does the author use italics in this essay? To what effect?

5. What kinds of evidence does the author use to support her argument?

THE ISSUES

1. Do you think Syfers has fairly characterized the expectations men have of their wives, or has she grossly exaggerated?

2. Syfers' article was first published in 1970. Do you think her criticisms still apply today, or have things between men and women changed so much that they are now dated?

3. Would you want a spouse, male or female, as obliging and eager to please as the one Syfers parodies in her essay? Why or why not?

4. What qualities and characteristics would you expect to find in the perfect spouse?

SUGGESTIONS FOR WRITING

1. Write a similar essay, from a man's point of view, about wanting a husband.

2. Write a serious essay describing your ideal mate.

3. Write an essay telling why you would not want a wife like the one Syfers has described.

▼▼▼

Andrew Vachss

SEX PREDATORS CAN'T BE SAVED

ANDREW VACHSS (b. 1942) is a New York-based lawyer whose professional focus has been representing children. From 1965 to 1966, he served as a field interviewer and investigator for the Task Force on the Eradication of Syphilis for the U.S. Public Health Service in Ohio. He also worked for numerous community organizations concerned with youth problems. Since 1976, he has been in private law practice and has been a lecturer at numerous law schools in New York. His writing includes a book, *Life-Style Violent Juvenile: The Secure Treatment Approach* (1979) and two novels—*Flood* (1985) and *Strega* (in progress). He has written numerous magazine articles.

> *All of us have been horrified now and then by media accounts of violent sexual crimes, and our anger has turned into a wish for instant punishment to destroy these monsters of society. In Vachss' essay, a criminal lawyer provides what he considers the only possible solution to violent sex offenses.*

1   Westley Allan Dodd was scheduled to be hanged at 12:01 A.M. this morning at the Washington State Penitentiary in Walla Walla. Sentenced to execution for the torture-murder of three boys, Mr. Dodd has refused all efforts to appeal his case. He may not have exhausted his legal remedies, but he has certainly exhausted society's efforts at "rehabilitation."

2   A chronic, calcified sexual sadist, Mr. Dodd stated in a recent court brief, "If I do escape, I promise you I will kill and rape again, and I will enjoy every minute of it."

3   Mr. Dodd's threat demands a response because we know he is not unique. There can be no dispute that monsters live among us. The only question is what to do with them once they become known to us.

4   The death penalty is not a response. Racially and economically biased and endlessly protracted, it returns little for its enormous economic and social costs. Though it is effective—the killer will not strike again—the death penalty is limited to murderers; it will not protect us from rapists and child molesters who are virtually assured of release and who are almost certain to commit their crimes again.

5   If we do not intend to execute sex criminals, does our hope lie in killing their destructive impulses? Mr. Dodd and his ilk are sociopaths. They are characterized by a fundamental lack of empathy.

All children are born pure egoists. They perceive their needs to the exclusion of all others. Only through socialization do they learn that some forms of gratification must be deferred and others denied. When a child's development is incomplete or perverted—and child abuse is the most dominant cause in that equation—he or she tends not to develop empathy. There's a missing card, one that cannot be put back in the deck once the personality is fully formed.

6   While early childhood experiences may impel, they do not compel. In the end, evil is a matter of choice. Sociopaths can learn to project a veneer of civilization—for predators, it is part of their camouflage—but they will always lack the ability to feel any pain but their own, pursuing only *self*-gratification. Not all sociopaths choose sexual violence. For some, the outlet can be political or economic skullduggery. But those for whom blood or pain is the stimulus act no less efficiently and at a terrible and unacceptable cost.

7   Some predatory sociopaths can be deterred. None can be rehabilitated, since they cannot return to a state that never existed. The concept of coercive therapy is a contradiction; successful psychiatric treatment requires participants, not mere recipients. What makes sexual predators so intractable and dangerous is that, as Mr. Dodd candidly acknowledged, they like what they do and intend to keep doing it.

8   The obsession of sexual predators is typified in the case of Donald Chapman, a New Jersey rapist who was released in November after serving 12 years, the maximum for his crime. He underwent continual therapy in prison, and was utterly unaffected by it. He vows to continue to attack women—a threat that reflects his total absorption with sexual torture. As a result of his threat, he sits in his house in Wyckoff, N.J., surrounded by a 24-hour police guard.

9   A 1992 study of 767 rapists and child molesters in Minnesota found those who completed psychiatric treatment were arrested more often for new sex crimes than those who had not been treated at all. A Canadian survey that tracked released child molesters for 20 years revealed a 43 percent recidivism rate regardless of the therapy. The difference between those simply incarcerated and those subjected to a full range of treatment appears statistically negligible. And the more violent and sadistic the offense, the more likely it is to be repeated.

10   Another factor that thwarts rehabilitation is the need for offenders to seek higher and higher levels of stimulation. There is no observable waning of their desires over time: sexual predators do not outgrow their behavior. Thus, while most sadistic sex offenders are not first arrested for homicide, they may well try to murder someone in the future.

11   What about a traditional self-help program? Should we concentrate on raising their self-esteem? Imprisoned predators receive as much fan mail as rock stars. They are courted by the news media,

studied by devoted sociologists, their every word treasured as though profound. Their paintings are collected, their poetry published. Trading cards celebrate their bloody passage among us.

12   I recently received a letter from a young woman who gushed that, after a long exchange of letters, she was "granted visiting privileges" with Mr. Dodd and subsequently appeared on "Sally Jessy Raphael" "due to my relationship" with "Wes," who she believes is "sincere." So do I. We simply disagree about the object of his sincerity.

13   Sexual predators are already narcissistic; they laugh behind their masks at our attempts to understand and rehabilitate them. We have earned their contempt by our belief that they can change—by our confusion of "crazy" with "dangerous," and "sick" with "sickening."

14   If we don't intend to execute sexual predators, and we have no treatment, what is our final line of defense? Washington State has a so-called sexual predator law permitting indefinite confinement of sex offenders deemed to be dangerous if released. The law's critics argue that psychiatry has been a woefully inadequate forecaster. Others cite the constitutional problems of imprisonment based on prospective conduct.

15   Recently there has been much discussion of voluntary castration. Such a "remedy" ignores reality. Sexual violence is not sex gone too far, it is violence with sex as its instrument. Rage, sadism and a desire to control or debase others are the driving forces. Castration can be reversed chemically with black-market hormones, and sex murders have been committed by physically castrated rapists. People have been raped by blunt objects. And how do you castrate female offenders?

16   Our response to sexual predators must balance the extent and intensity of the possible behavior with the probability of its occurrence. An ex-prisoner likely to expose himself on a crowded subway may be a risk we are willing to assume. A prisoner with even a moderate probability of sexual torture and murder is not. Such violence is like a rock dropped into a calm pool—the concentric circles spread even after the rock has sunk. More and more victims will be affected.

17   When it comes to sexual violence, the sum of our social and psychiatric knowledge adds up to this: Behavior is the truth.

18   Chronic sexual predators have crossed an osmotic membrane. They can't step back to the other side—our side. And they don't want to. If we don't kill or release them, we have but one choice: Call them monsters and isolate them.

19   When it comes to the sexual sadist, psychiatric diagnoses won't protect us. Appeasement endangers us. Rehabilitation is a joke.

20   I've spoken to many predators over the years. They always exhibit amazement that we do not hunt them. And that when we capture them, we eventually let them go. Our attitude is a deliberate interference with Darwinism—an endangerment of our species.

21   A proper experiment produces answers. Experiments with sexual sadists have produced only victims. Washington State's sexual predator law will surely be challenged in the courts and it may take years before constitutional and criminological criteria are established to incarcerate a criminal beyond his or her sentence.

22   Perhaps no-parole life sentences for certain sex crimes would be a more straightforward answer. In any event, such laws offer our only hope against an epidemic of sexual violence that threatens to pollute our society beyond the possibility of its own rehabilitation.

(1,284 words)

VOCABULARY

rehabilitation (1)	impel/compel (7)	narcissistic (15)
calcified (2)	predators (7)	castration (16)
protracted (4)	camouflage (7)	osmotic (19)
ilk (5)	skullduggery (7)	appeasement (20)
sociopaths (5)	intractable (8)	
empathy (5)	recidivism (10)	

THE FACTS

1. What particular crime does the essay analyze? How does this crime differ from other crimes?

2. What are the main causes that lead human beings to become sex offenders? When are these causes developed?

3. According to the author, do sex offenders have a choice in the way they act?

4. According to Allan Dodd's testimony, why will he continue to kill and rape?

5. According to the author, what has research found out about the efficacy of psychiatric treatment for violent sex criminals?

THE STRATEGIES

1. Where does the author place the proposition (main point) of his argument? How does this placement affect his argument?

2. What kinds of argumentative strategies does the author use to support his proposition? Cite specific strategies.

3. What is the point of view from which the essay is written? How effective is this point of view? Give reasons for your answer.

4. How soon in the essay is the audience conditioned to the idea that sex offenders cannot be rehabilitated?

5. Where does the author use figurative language? Is this helpful or does it detract from the seriousness of the topic?

THE ISSUES

1. Do you agree completely with the author's view that there is no hope for the rehabilitation of sex offenders? Or do you believe the author has neglected some aspect of effective healing? Explain your answer.

2. How important is self-esteem in the socialization of human beings? Provide examples from your own experience to show what happens when self-esteem is not present and also examples to show the effect of having self-esteem.

3. What do you think of the idea of castrating violent sex offenders? Does such a policy seem logical, humane, and appropriate for our times? Explain your answers.

4. Why do you think the woman who became friends with Allan Dodd while he was in prison could possibly have been attracted to such a man?

5. What is your own solution to the problem of sex predators? How do you propose to protect society from their heinous crimes?

SUGGESTIONS FOR WRITING

1. Write an essay in which you argue for your own solution to the social menace posed by sex predators. Use facts, statistics, experience, and expert testimony to bolster your proposition. Also, be sure to take into account any opposition to your argument.

2. Write a letter to a person—real or imaginary—who is in prison because of a violent sex crime. While the letter will not be mailed, it should reveal your honest thoughts.

▼▼▼

Sylvia Rabiner

HOW THE SUPERWOMAN MYTH
PUTS WOMEN DOWN

SYLVIA RABINER (b. 1939), freelance writer and teacher, was born in New York and educated at Hunter College and New York University. Her articles have appeared in *Mademoiselle*, *Working Mother*, and *The New Republic*.

Any reader of popular magazines is familiar with the superwoman of whom the author writes. She is extolled as having everything: brains, brawn, children, career, husband, respect, fame, and money. She moves from boardroom to kitchen to nursery with equal ease. But is she real? Or is she merely a fantasy created by advertisers trying to profit from the feminist movement? This essay takes a long, hard, and discontented look at her.

1   Sunday afternoon. I'm making my usual desultory way through the Sunday *Times* when I come upon Linda Kanner. Ms. Kanner is prominently on display in The National Economic Survey, where she is referred to as a woman "in the vanguard of women taking routes to the executive suite that were formerly traveled by men." A quick run-through of the article reveals that she is a marketing consultant with an M.B.A. degree from Harvard and a degree from The Simmons School of Social Work. She is married to a physician who has an M.B.A., too. Somewhere along the way she has managed to find time to produce two sons, and all this glory is hers at age 31.

2   Well, there goes my Sunday afternoon. After reading about Ms. Kanner, I will be in a muddy slump until nightfall at least. Every time I come across one of these proliferating articles about the successful woman of today, I am beset by feelings of self-contempt, loathing, and failure. Moreover, I hate Ms. Kanner, too, and if she were in my living room at the moment, I would set fire to her M.B.A. I am a six-year-old child once again, listening while my mother compares me to one of my flawless cousins.

3   Let me tell you, it's getting harder all the time to be a successful woman. In the old days, a woman was usually judged by the man she had ensnared. If he was a good provider and she kept the house clean, was a good cook, and raised a few decent children, she was well regarded by her peers and most likely by herself as well. Now the mainstream Women's Movement has thrust forth a new role model: the

capitalist feminist. The career woman with a twist, she's not your old-time spinster who sacrificed marriage and motherhood for professional advancement, but a new, trickier model who has it all—a terrific career, a husband with a terrific career, and a couple of children as well.

4   We have Isabel Van Devanter Sawhill, successful economist, wife of New York University president John, and mother; or Letty Cottin Pogrebin, successful author, editor, activist, wife of lawyer Bert, and mother. A recent article in *Newsweek* investigated the life-styles of working couples with children. Their random democratic sampling included Kathy Cosgrove, vice-president of a public relations firm, wife of Mark, an advertising executive; Consuelo Marshall, Superior Court commissioner, wife of George, Columbia Pictures executive; Charlotte Curtis, associate editor of the *New York Times,* wife of William Hunt, neurosurgeon; and Patricia Schroeder, congresswoman, wife of lawyer Jim. Patricia, the article gushed, managed at 35 to "gracefully combine career, marriage, and family." The article was capped by a description of Carla Hills, Secretary of Housing and Urban Development, presidential possibility for the supreme court, wife of Roderick, chairman of the Securities and Exchange Commission, and mother of four. There was a photograph of Mrs. Hills presiding over her impeccable family at the dinner table. The article was swingy and upbeat. If they can do it, how about you? . . . Another afternoon ruined.

5   I turned for instruction to Letty Cottin Pogrebin, embodiment of the success game. Letty is now an editor at *Ms.* and author of two books—"How to Make It in a Man's World" and "Getting Yours." Those titles reveal Letty's commitment to self-advancement. She doesn't hesitate to tell her readers that she is a woman to emulate. Letty was an executive at 21. She married a man whom she adores and has three "happy, well-behaved, bright, and spirited kids." I gleaned all this from Letty's first book. Since Letty was also gracefully combining career, marriage, and family, I thought I might get some pointers from her.

6   Letty Cottin arrived at Bernard Geis in 1960. After six months she was promoted to the position of director of publicity, advertising, and subsidiary rights. She met her husband at a party and married him a couple of months later. She proceeded to have her first children (twins) as planned "early in marriage but after one full year as unencumbered newlyweds." Their next baby fit in perfectly after the three-year space between children which they deemed most desirable. She sums up: "It's better to be working than not working; it's better to be married than single; it's better to be a mommy as well as a Mrs. But it's best to be all four at once!"

7   Now, where does that leave me? My thumbnail autobiography follows: I am a child of my times, definitely more the rule than the exception to it. Raised in the '40s and '50s, the words *career* and *goal* were

not spoken when I was in the room. I got the standard New York City College Jewish Parental Advice to Daughters. "Take a few education courses. Then if . . . God forbid . . . anything should happen, you can always take care of yourself." Nora Ephron said that she always knew she wanted to write (Dorothy Parker was her idol). When her less motivated college friends went off after graduation and got married, Nora went off and wrote. A few remarkable women like Nora and Letty undoubtedly knew at the age of 18 or younger what profession they wanted to pursue, but most of us at Hunter College, as I recall, were thundering off in a herd to stand under the marriage canopy. A bunch of simpletons, you say? Not so. We had produced the school plays, edited the school newspapers, put together the creative publications, belonged to Arista, and frequently had our names on the honor roll. What was happening, then? Well, let's call it economics. We were the children of immigrant or near immigrant parents. Hard-working, uneducated or self-educated, they didn't know how to guide their bright daughters. The depression had been deeply felt and was well remembered. Their watchword was security. Dorothy Parker was my idol, too, but to my parents, writing was not a job. With encouragement from neither parents nor teachers, most of us sought security in marriage or teaching.

8   Now, I married neither wisely nor well, which to judge by current divorce statistics, proves me to be obstinately average. I worked to put my husband through graduate school, traveled where his career dictated, had two children as a matter of course and in the fall of 1969, although I had felt suffocated by my marriage, I protestingly and hysterically suffered its demise. My child support settlement would have done nicely to keep me in a cozy little tenement on Avenue C and 5th Street. I wanted to remain part of the middle class so I had to work: I had two children under the age of five and couldn't possibly pay a housekeeper. And I didn't really want a day-care center or babysitter with my boys eight or nine hours a day while I was at work. I wanted to be with them, so I found a job teaching night classes, and I tended home and sons during the day. A divorced woman with kids has a lot of things to think about. She is usually racing around trying to pay bills, do her job reasonably well, have some kind of social life, and be a loving mother too.

9   After 1969 I noticed that I never walked down a street, I ran. I ate standing up. I screamed at my sons a lot. The astute reader will detect here the subtle differences between Letty's life and mine. I admit I was failing in being a successful woman, I didn't have a terrific career, and I didn't have a husband with a terrific career. Where were all those dynamic, achieving wonderful men that the women in the news stories found and married? Not in the playgrounds and supermarkets where I spent my days, not in the classrooms where I spent my evenings, and

not in any of the other places I checked out with varying degrees of enthusiasm on the weekends when I had a babysitter. As for my long-range career goals—well, to tell the truth, I was grateful to have my teaching contract renewed each semester. My concession to getting ahead was to return to graduate school to earn my M.A. degree. I was able to indulge in this luxury only because the university at which I taught offered me free tuition. At $91 a credit, graduate school is hardly a priority of the divorced working mother. It appears that in addition to all my other errors in judgment, I've made the mistake of living in New York City during a recession. Last June I lost the teaching job that was supposed to be my security in case . . . God forbid . . . anything happened. After collecting unemployment insurance for five months, I am now typing, filing, and serving my boss his coffee four times a day.

10   Now, I ask you—do I need to read about the triumphant lives of Helen Gurley Brown or Mary Wells Lawrence? Statistics currently indicate that there are 7.2 million families headed by women. Most of us are clerks, secretaries, waitresses, salesgirls, social workers, nurses, and—if lucky enough to still be working—teachers. For us, the superwoman who knits marriage, career, and motherhood into a satisfying life without dropping a stitch is as oppressive a role model as the airbrushed Bunny in the *Playboy* centerfold, or That *Cosmopolitan* Girl. While I struggle to keep my boat afloat in rough waters with prevailing high winds, I am not encouraged to row on by media hypes of ladies who run companies, serve elegant dinners for 30, play tennis with their husbands, earn advanced degrees, and wear a perfect size eight. They exist, I know, a privileged, talented minority, but to encourage me by lauding their achievements is like holding Sammy Davis, Jr., up as a model to a junior high school class in Bed.-Stuy. What does it really have to do with them?

11   Women are self-critical creatures. We can always find reasons to hate ourselves. Single women believe they are failing if they don't have a loving, permanent relationship; working mothers are conflicted about leaving their children; divorced women experience guilt over the break-up of their marriages; housewives feel inadequate because they don't have careers; career women are wretched if they aren't advancing, and everyone is convinced she is too fat!

12   It is ironic that feminism, finally respectable, has been made to backfire in this way. The superwoman image is a symbol of the corruption of feminist politics. It places emphasis on a false ideal of individual success. We are led to believe that if we play our cards right, we'll get to the top, but in the present system it won't work; there just isn't that much room up there. And in our class society, those at the top probably were more than halfway up to start with. The superwoman image ignores the reality of the average working woman or

housewife. It elevates an elite of upper-class women executives. The media loves it because it is glamorous and false. In the end it threatens nothing in the system. In fact, all it does is give women like me a sense of inferiority.

(1,886 words)

VOCABULARY

desultory (1)	embodiment (5)	astute (9)
vanguard (1)	emulate (5)	concession (9)
proliferating (2)	unencumbered (6)	indulge (9)
impeccable (4)	demise (8)	

THE FACTS

1. By what measure does Rabiner feel a woman was judged a success or failure in the old days? How is she judged today?

2. What new role model has the feminist movement thrust on women?

3. According to Rabiner, why did most of the women of her generation pursue goals of marriage and motherhood rather than try to develop careers?

4. Why does Rabiner think the superwoman myth is so unfair to the vast majority of working women?

5. What does Rabiner find is so ironic about the image of the super-woman?

THE STRATEGIES

1. The article is tightly organized around a clear central idea. Where is this central idea stated?

2. What do paragraphs 4, 5, and 6 contribute to Rabiner's argument?

3. In paragraphs 7, 8, and 9 Rabiner gives a thumbnail sketch of her own life as a working mother. What implied relationship exists between these paragraphs and the three that preceded them?

4. This article is organized into four parts. What are they and what does each part do?

5. What specific details does Rabiner use in paragraph 11 to support her assertion that women are self-critical creatures?

THE ISSUES

1. Do you believe the picture is as bad as Rabiner portrays it? Explain your answer.

2. Do you agree with Rabiner's statement that feminism is finally respectable? When, if ever, was it *not* respectable?

3. What advantages can you cite for combining a career with marriage and family? What disadvantages?

4. What advice would you give your daughter about seeking a profession such as medicine or law?

5. How would you feel about going back to the standards of success described in paragraph 6? Explain your answer.

SUGGESTIONS FOR WRITING

1. Write an essay examining the pros and cons of the feminist movement, saying whether you think it has improved the lot of women, not affected it, or made it worse.

2. What is your idea of success in life? Write an essay specifying what you would have to do or become in order to consider yourself a success.

▼▼▼

James Michie

DOOLEY IS A TRAITOR

JAMES MICHIE (b. 1927), British poet and translator, is director of The Bodley Head Ltd. publishers, London, and a former lecturer at London University. His works include *Possible Laughter* (1959), *The Odes of Horace* (trans. 1964), and *The Epigrams of Martial* (trans. 1973).

> *In this humorous poem, a murderer makes a spirited defense against being compelled to fight a war not of his own making.*

"So then you won't fight?"
"Yes, your Honour," I said, "that's right."
"Now is it that you simply aren't willing,
Or have you a fundamental moral objection to killing?"
5 Says the judge, blowing his nose
And making his words stand to attention in long rows.

I stand to attention too, but with half a grin
(In my time I've done a good many in).
"No objection at all, sir," I said
10   "There's a deal of the world I'd rather see dead—
Such as Johnny Stubbs or Fred Settle or my last landlord, Mr. Syme.
Give me a gun and your blessing, your Honour, and I'll be killing
        them all the time.
But my conscience says a clear no
15   To killing a crowd of gentlemen I don't know.
Why, I'd as soon think of killing a worshipful judge,
High-court, like yourself (against whom, God knows, I've got no
        grudge—
So far), as murder a heap of foreign folk.
20   If you've got no grudge, you've got no joke
To laugh at after."
                                Now the words never come flowing
Proper for me till I get the old pipe going.
And just as I was poking
Down baccy, the judge looks up sharp with "No smoking,
25   Mr. Dooley. We're not fighting this war for fun.
And we want a clearer reason why you refuse to carry a gun.
This war is not a personal feud, it's a fight
Against wrong ideas on behalf of the Right.
Mr. Dooley, won't you help to destroy evil ideas?"
30   "Ah, your Honour, here's
The tragedy," I said. "I'm not a man of the mind.
I couldn't find it in my heart to be unkind
To an idea. I wouldn't know one if I saw one. I haven't one of my
        own.
35   So I'd best be leaving other people's alone."
"Indeed," he sneers at me, "this defence is
Curious for someone with convictions in two senses.
A criminal invokes conscience to his aid
To support an individual withdrawal from a communal crusade
40   Sanctioned by God, led by the Church, against a godless, churchless
        nation!"
I asked his Honour for a translation.
"You talk of conscience," he said. "What do you know of the
        Christian creed?"
45   "Nothing, sir, except what I can read,
That's the most you can hope for from us jail-birds.
I just open the Book here and there and look at the words.
And I find when the Lord himself misliked an evil notion
He turned it into a pig and drove it squealing over a cliff into the
50   ocean,

And the loony ran away
And lived to think another day.
There was a clean job done and no blood shed!
Everybody happy and forty wicked thoughts drowned dead.
55   A neat and Christian murder. None of your mad slaughter
Throwing away the brains with the blood and the baby with the
      bathwater.
Now I look at the war as a sportsman. It's a matter of choosing
The decentest way of losing.
60   Heads or tails, losers or winners,
We all lose, we're all damned sinners.
And I'd rather be with the poor cold people at the wall that's shot
Than the bloody guilty devils in the firing-line, in Hell and keeping
      hot."
65   "But what right, Dooley, what right," he cried,
"Have you to say the Lord is on your side?"
"That's a dirty crooked question," back I roared.
"I said not the Lord was on my side, but I was on the side of the
      Lord."
70   Then he was up at me and shouting,
But by and by he calms: "Now we're not doubting
Your sincerity, Dooley, only your arguments,
Which don't make sense."
('Hullo,' I thought, 'that's the wrong way round.
75   I may be skylarking a bit, but my brainpan's sound.')
Then biting his nail and sugaring his words sweet:
"Keep your head, Mr. Dooley. Religion is clearly not up
      your street.
But let me ask you as a plain patriotic fellow
80   Whether you'd stand there so smug and yellow
If the foe were attacking your own dear sister."
"I'd knock their brains out, mister,
On the floor," I said. "There," he says kindly, "I knew you were no
      pacifist.
85   It's your straight duty as a man to enlist.
The enemy is at the door." You could have downed
Me with a feather. "Where?" I gasp, looking round.
"Not this door," he says angered. "Don't play the clown.
But they're two thousand miles away planning to do us down,
90   Why, the news is full of the deeds of those murderers and rapers.
"Your Eminence," I said, "my father told me never to believe the
      papers
But to go by my eyes,
And at two thousand miles the poor things can't tell truth from lies."
95   His fearful spectacles glittered like the moon: "For the last time what
      right

Has a man like you to refuse to fight?"
"More right," I said, "than you.
You've never murdered a man, so you don't know what it is I won't
100   do.
I've done it in good hot blood, so haven't I the right to make bold
To declare that I shan't do it in cold?"
Then the judge rises in a great rage
And writes DOOLEY IS A TRAITOR in black upon a page
105   And tells me I must die.
"What, me?" says I.
"If you still won't fight."
"Well, yes, your Honour," I said, "that's right."

(896 words)

THE FACTS

1. Dooley is an admitted murderer, yet he still refuses to fight. Why? What is his primary objection to war?

2. How many arguments does the judge use in trying to persuade Dooley? What are they and in what order are they used?

3. Are the judge's arguments logical? Do they appeal to reason and evidence, or to emotion?

THE STRATEGIES

1. The poem is written in rhyming couplets. What does the rhyme contribute to the poem's tone?

2. How is Dooley characterized? What techniques are used?

3. How is the judge characterized? What techniques are used?

THE ISSUES

1. Evaluate critically the saying "All's fair in love and war." Has this attitude prevailed throughout history? Is it morally valid?

2. What is the poet's point in reflecting a pacifist view through a criminal rather than, say, a minister or a respected private citizen?

3. Do you perceive a difference between killing a rapist attacking your sister and killing an unknown enemy during war? Explain your answer.

SUGGESTIONS FOR WRITING

1. Analyze the logic in the exchanges between Dooley and the judge. Pinpoint the difference between their respective ways of thinking.

2. Assume that you are in Dooley's position and must argue against your participation in a war. Formulate an argument in your defense.

ISSUE FOR CRITICAL THINKING AND DEBATE

▼▼▼

HOMELESSNESS

Homelessness would seem to be a nondebatable issue. No one is seriously for it. Everyone is, in principle at least, against it. Where the debate begins is not on whether or not homelessness is terrible—everyone agrees that it is—but on its causes. And the division of opinion is predictably political. Conservatives, as a whole, blame homelessness on lapses and addictions in the individual; liberals tend to blame economic causes.

Adding to the muddle is the blurry definition of homelessness. Is a person homeless who lives in a government-funded shelter, say a hotel that houses the poor through a system of voucher payments from the state? Or is the homeless person one with no permanent residence who sleeps on the street, in a car, or a bus station? Most government statistics count both groups among the homeless. Yet government-funded housing, as some critics point out, may be drawing people into the ranks of the counted homeless who had been doubling-up with family members. The result is the more the government funds shelters for the homeless, the greater the homeless population seems to grow. (Ellickson, Robert, The homelessness muddle, *Public Interest*, April 1990).

How many people are homeless in America? No one knows for sure. Homelessness advocates say there are 3 million. Other studies have put the figure at around 400,000. The Department of Housing and Urban Development estimated in 1994 that there were about "600,000 people on the streets on any given night and that 7 million Americans experienced homelessness at some point in the latter half of the 1980s" (Who's homeless and why, *Christian Century*, September 7, 1994). These figures—whether high or low—are difficult to trust because they are always based on different methods of counting. Added to the

Dorothea Lange, Migrant Mother, Nipomo Valley, *1936. Gelatin silver print.*
© the Dorothea Lange Collection, The Oakland Museum of California, The City of
Oakland. Gift of Paul S. Taylor.

roster of the uncountable are those called "the invisible homeless," who
have no residence of their own but live in makeshift arrangements
with relatives.

The two essays in this section typify the usual debate about homelessness. The first essay, "Homeless: Expose the Myths," by a conservative writer, argues that the individual, not the system or the economy, is
to blame for homelessness. Having spent a night in New York's Grand

Central Station, the author reports that he saw no dispossessed yuppies, only dysfunctional people. The other point of view is represented by a newspaper columnist who chronicles how a middle-class, articulate young woman became homeless. Here the blame is laid at the doorstep of a badly run government bureaucracy and an out-of-kilter economy.

Which view is right? It is impossible to say. Certainly, one can imagine a scenario where an individual, even a family, can fall on hard times that result in homelessness. Yet anyone who lives in a city also knows from plain observation that many dysfunctional, tormented souls haunt the streets. Why homelessness exists in such an affluent country as ours may be impossible to explain. But one thing is certain: It should not exist.

▾▾

Joseph Perkins

HOMELESS: EXPOSE THE MYTHS

JOSEPH PERKINS (b. 1960) is a regular columnist for *The San Diego Union-Tribune*. According to the author, all of the homeless people out on our streets do not suffer from poverty as much as they suffer from mental illness or substance abuse.

1   Back in the days when the homeless problem was in vogue, I decided to investigate for myself whether the economic policies of Ronald Reagan were to blame for the growing legions of street people who seemed to have invaded America's cities.

2   So I spent a night at New York's Grand Central Station, which was a favorite gathering place for many of the city's homeless.

3   I quickly discovered that contrary to the news reportage at that time, the homeless were not "people like you and me" who simply had fallen upon hard times. I saw no yuppies in threadbare suits sifting through the trash bins. I saw no middle-class families huddled on benches.

4   What I did see were dozens upon dozens of pitiable men and women who were suffering from some dysfunction or another. Some were afflicted with mental problems. Others were drug or alcohol abusers. Clearly their homelessness owed not to economic dislocation, but simply to self-destruction.

5   It is now eight years later, yet homeless advocates continue to promulgate the myth that homelessness is primarily an economic problem rather than a mental health and substance-abuse problem.

6   Among the more prominent purveyors of this misinformation is the National Law Center on Homelessness and Poverty. It notes that 40

percent of poor people spend two-thirds of their income on housing. "This means that for growing millions of Americans, a missed paycheck, a health crisis or a high utility bill brings the threat of homelessness," the lawyers assert.

7   The law center advocates were less than happy with President Clinton's recent executive order calling for a homeless plan to be developed within nine months. They saw no reason why he shouldn't have given his imprimatur to a plan that they already have drawn up.

8   So what is the lawyers' solution? Have the federal government turn over former military bases and other vacant property to the homeless. Create a jobs program for them. Give them income assistance. Offer them day care and health care.

9   It's the typical liberal response to a problem—spend more money, create programs. They miss the boat. In 1963, there were as many poor people as there are today. Yet, in 1963, the only homeless people were the occasional bums and hobos.

10   Two things happened between 1963 and 1993 to give us today's homeless population: All but the most dangerous patients were disgorged from state mental hospitals, and illegal drug use exploded.

11   This is born out by a 1992 survey conducted by the U.S. Conference of Mayors. The mayors found that 28 percent of the homeless population in the cities were mentally ill and 41 percent substance abusers.

12   This means that at least seven of 10 street people have either a mental or chemical problem. Even if the economy were booming, jobs were plentiful and affordable housing abundant, these unfortunates probably would still be out on the streets.

13   By linking homelessness to poverty, advocates obscure the real root of the problem. If we really wanted to help the homeless, we would pay far more attention to their mental health and substance abuse problems.

(518 words)

VOCABULARY

vogue (1)	promulgate (5)	disgorged (10)
legions (1)	purveyors (6)	
dysfunction (4)	imprimatur (7)	

THE FACTS

1. How did the author find out whether government policies were really to blame for the growing street people population—as often claimed by liberals?

2. What was the author's first discovery? How long did this discovery take?

3. What about the National Law Center on Homelessness and Poverty annoys the author?

4. According to the author, what happened between 1963 and the present to change the statistics concerning the homeless population?

5. What is the author's answer to our desire to help the homeless?

THE STRATEGIES

1. This is an exceptionally brief essay. In your view, does the brevity of the essay ruin its ability to convince? Why or why not?

2. Why does the author word his proposition as a conditional clause ("If we really wanted to help the homeless . . .")? What might an alternate wording be?

3. How does the author maintain coherence between paragraphs 10 and 11?

4. What does the word "myths" refer to in the title of the essay?

5. How would you describe the author's style of writing?

THE ISSUES

1. The author says that in 1963 the only homeless people were occasional bums and hobos. How are bums and hobos different from today's homeless?

2. How much influence do economic policies have on people's standard of living?

3. What is the author's most compelling support for his proposition?

4. In your opinion, which is more effective—the liberal's response of spending more money on programs for the homeless or the conservative's response of tending to their mental illnesses? Give reasons for your stand.

5. What is your opinion of the suggestion that military bases be turned into housing for the poor? What other solution would you propose?

SUGGESTIONS FOR WRITING

1. Write an essay in which you propose a solution to the problem of begging so prevalent in our cities today. Support your argument with facts, experience, expert testimony, and logic.

2. Write an essay in which you describe a plan of action in case you should suddenly find yourself homeless and foodless. The plan should be based on reality, not fantasy.

▼▼

Linda Weltner

HOW SHE BECAME HOMELESS

LINDA WELTNER (1938–   ) was born in Worcester, Massachusetts, and educated at Wellesley, University of Michigan, and Harvard Divinity School. She is a freelance writer and author of a weekly column, "Ever So Humble," for the *Boston Globe*. A playwright, her plays include *As Lonely as American Pie* (1977), and *A Pox on Your Lips Now* (1980). She has also written books for young adults, including *The New Voice* (1981).

1   My friend Lanie was riding the bus one day when she noticed a young woman a few seats ahead. The woman's words drifted toward the back of the bus: "Getting evicted . . . can't afford day care . . . a shelter." When the woman began to gather up her belongings, Lanie moved impulsively.

2   "Look," she said, stepping into the aisle toward the woman, "I couldn't help overhearing. I want to help you in any way I can. Let me give you my name and phone number." The woman looked up, startled, then said, "I'll be at this number for a few weeks." Lanie wrote down the information.

3   "I don't know why. I felt instinctively I could trust her," Lanie explained to me later. "Would you be willing to be on my backup team?"

4   I hadn't known Lanie well, but because she'd come across many needy women in her job as a career counselor I trusted her judgment. So one day in August 1989 I found myself in the car beside her as we made our way to pick up 24-year-old Adrienne and her 6-month-old daughter, Janelle, at the apartment from which they were about to be evicted.

5   We went on a picnic in the park, sharing our life stories as if we'd known one another forever. That afternoon I learned how someone both bright and ambitious could find herself facing homelessness for the second time in her young life.

6   Adrienne's first experience with homelessness took her by surprise. At 21, she'd moved from a rented room into her first apartment. When she got a job as a receptionist at a prestigious Boston law firm, she found

a nicer apartment and gave notice on the old one without realizing that the verbal agreement she'd made with the new landlord was not binding. She was ready to move when she discovered that the new apartment had been given to someone else, and that her landlord had already rented her old place to another tenant.

7   Adrienne had already severed ties with her abusive mother and though she called several friends, none had room for another person. She couldn't afford a hotel; she needed to save her money for another apartment. The first night that she had no place to go, her friend John kept her company, sitting by her side on Boston Common and then keeping guard when she finally fell asleep. At work the next morning Adrienne called a church and was given the name of a temporary shelter, where she went that night. (The latest study by the U.S. Conference of Mayors estimates 18 percent of homeless people are employed.)

8   Every morning she picked a dress from the hand-me-down stack at the shelter, put a smile on her face, and didn't let on to a soul at work that she no longer had a home.

9   Adrienne called every church and charity she thought might be willing to help her, and by the end of 21 days—the limit she was allowed to stay at the shelter—she had enough money to pay the upfront expenses for an apartment.

10   Adrienne had learned during her stay at the homeless shelter that she was pregnant, but when the baby's father took little interest and no responsibility, she wasn't surprised. She'd never known her own father.

11   "I was determined to have the baby," she told us. She took a second job, nights, and began saving money. Fortunately, her law firm's health insurance covered the baby's birth, but she was so exhausted from working 14 hours a day that she became anemic and ran a fever the day she delivered. An organization called Birthright gave her clothing for the baby.

12   When Janelle was 2 months old, Adrienne tried leaving her with her sister so she could return to work, but the baby suffered visible neglect. Adrienne arranged for the sister of a friend at work to take over. Then one day the baby came home with a burn on her arm.

13   "I loved my work," Adrienne said, "and I really liked my boss, but I had a responsibility to my child that was more important. So I quit."

14   Listening to Adrienne's story, it was easy for me to see why 30 to 40 percent of the homeless are families or single parents with children. Adrienne was paying more than half of her $13,000 salary in rent. Day care for an infant, which costs at least $500 a month, would have taken all the rest.

15   Adrienne was unable to afford her new apartment once she left her job. She and Janelle were evicted, forced to move into a welfare hotel in downtown Boston. The state paid $70 a night for a dingy room with

barely enough space for a bed and chest. In order to use her days con-
structively Adrienne found a private organization that offered free
high-school-equivalency exam classes and child care.

16   It's hard to understand how someone so intelligent and well-
spoken could have slipped through the cracks at school, but Adrienne
traced her academic troubles to ninth grade, when a male friend of her
mother's commented on her "beautiful daughter."

17   "My mother said, 'There's no room for two women in this house,'"
Adrienne explained, "and after that I couldn't do my homework until
I'd done everything else around the house. When I tried to study, she'd
say things like, 'You think you're better than everyone else, don't you?'
I didn't go to school much after that."

18   Adrienne and Janelle had been at the welfare hotel for more than
two months and, since tenants weren't allowed to remain more than 90
days, Lanie and I began to feel anxious. We made phone calls and
followed leads to their inevitable dead ends. The funding for the housing vouchers that once had subsidized rent for the poor had virtually
disappeared.

19   We looked at apartments for weeks without finding anything in
our price range in places accessible by public transportation. Finally,
we found two apartments that seemed ideal. But when the landlord at
the first place heard the word *welfare,* he shook his head. He'd
promised the apartment to someone else, he said, feigning regret.

20   Twenty other families were competing for the second apartment.
Despite glowing references from Lanie and me, she never heard back
from the landlord.

21   In the meantime, a welfare check sent to Adrienne's old address
had never been forwarded. Lanie discovered that, with ten days to go
before her next check arrived, Adrienne had only four dollars to her
name. We had agreed not to get into the habit of handing Adrienne
money; we didn't see our role as dispensers of largess, or hers as a supplicant waiting for handouts. Still, this was clearly a special case, so
Lanie bought Adrienne a one-month mass-transit pass and I stocked
her room with disposable diapers and canned food. Luckily, Janelle
was still nursing.

22   Lanie and I talked often, trying to make sense of things that didn't
make sense: Adrienne had to make three long trips by public transportation to the welfare office to get a replacement check, even though
she didn't have the money to make the trips. The state, desperately
short of funds, was spending an exorbitant sum on a barely habitable
room for her. The money spent on the three months' emergency housing for Adrienne could have provided a $500 monthly housing voucher
to a family for a year. It was eye-opening, to say the least, to realize
that our concerted efforts still weren't making a dent, yet every day

people who are hungry, uneducated, and disorganized are expected to work the system, somehow, to meet their needs.

23   Eventually, my faith in people was renewed. When I wrote about Adrienne in my weekly *Boston Globe* column readers responded with great generosity. Without having asked for a penny, I received $1,100 to help Adrienne get resettled.

24   In the end, Adrienne found a place to live without our help. Conscientious and persistent, she visited the housing office in another town, made her case in person, and must have touched someone's heart, for the woman there not only gave her a voucher but also located one of the last subsidized apartments left before a freeze on vouchers was to go into effect.

25   At last Lanie and I found something we were good at: persuading our friends to give us their outgrown baby clothes, old toys, and discarded furniture. Some of my *Globe* readers delivered a bedroom set and a dining room table and chairs to Adrienne's door.

26   "I'm learning so much from you," Adrienne said the afternoon I showed her how to staple new fabric over the worn seats of her chairs.

27   "Are you kidding?" I replied. "Lanie and I are the ones getting an education."

28   So much that I take for granted is missing from Adrienne's world. She has had to deal with poor schools, inadequate housing, a devastating family life, and too little money. But that's only the broad outline of what sets her apart. The pain is in the small details—like not knowing a soul with a car when you have to move your furniture, or being on welfare and having your mother come to you for money. It's so hard to make a decent life for yourself when no one you know can be trusted to care for your child or to stay off drugs or to keep his or her word.

29   No one can make up for the deprivations of her childhood, but at least when Adrienne has good news she now has someone to tell. I think the most valuable thing Lanie and I have to offer her is the quality of our concern.

30   What we've gotten back is just as important. Many of my attitudes about my own life have changed fundamentally. For example, I used to shop as a form of entertainment. It took my friendship with Adrienne to make me aware that I already had more than I could ever use.

31   "Being a single mother is very demanding," Adrienne wrote in an essay with which she hoped to gain admission to Brandeis University's Transitional Year Program, a remedial program for promising students who otherwise wouldn't qualify for college. "Poverty and homelessness try to strip you of your dignity. However, during my ordeal an inner strength emerged and, looking at my daughter, my soul decided I could

not give up. From the day I knew I would be evicted I was on a mission to better our lives for the future."

32   Adrienne was accepted on full scholarship. Now there was only one obstacle still to be overcome: child care.

33   "This is too good to pass up," Lanie said. "You accept. Let Linda and me worry about raising the money for day care." But Adrienne's life continues to be mired in the complexities of being a single mother with little money.

34   Because there was no room in the campus day-care center when she started school, Adrienne had to get up at 5:00 every morning to take Janelle by public transportation to day care two towns away.

35   Yet she has plunged headfirst into her studies. I never know what new idea will have caught her fancy. "Have you ever heard of Marx's dialectic?" she asked me over the phone one day. "What about Freud's theory of the unconscious?" All these bits of knowledge are like brand new pennies to her.

36   "Jack," I said, lying beside my husband in bed late one night. "Is Adrienne going to have enough money for day care until she finishes school? What if they cut off her housing money?"

37   "Shhh," he replied. "We'll worry about that when the time comes."

38   But I couldn't sleep. What kind of society are we when a whole segment of the population is deprived of the opportunities other people take for granted?

39   According to the U.S. Conference of Mayors annual studies of 25 to 30 U.S. cities, the number of people requesting emergency shelter has increased 10 to 25 percent each year for the last nine years. And experts are telling us that Americans are suffering from "compassion fatigue." The American Civil Liberties Union has warned against a "national wave of intolerance against the homeless." How many have to be on our streets before we stop telling ourselves that only the undeserving go hungry, before we give up the belief that all homeless mothers and children have brought their suffering upon themselves? Does anyone still believe that our lives can continue undisturbed by the social mayhem around us? As I lay awake, feeling terribly alone with my thoughts, I prayed that the Clinton administration's promises would break through the silence of the night.

40   *Adrienne has successfully completed two years at Brandeis University. Janelle, now 5, was finally accepted into the day-care center on campus. She will attend kindergarten in September.*

41   *Last fall Adrienne found herself feeling exhausted by the demands of academic life and single motherhood. She is taking a year's leave of absence from Brandeis. In the meantime, she is looking for work and plans to take classes at a local college. Adrienne is hopeful she will*

return to Brandeis next year and plans to eventually receive a sociology degree.

42   *Lanie and I continue to be inspired by the courage and determination of our new friend.*

(2,220 words)

VOCABULARY

largess (21)   habitable (22)   dialectic (35)
supplicant (21)   deprivations (29)   mayhem (39)
exorbitant (22)   mired (33)

THE FACTS

1. How did the author come to learn of the plight of Adrienne?

2. How did Adrienne become homeless the first time?

3. Why did Adrienne decide to quit her job and take care of her baby?

4. To what incident does Adrienne trace her academic troubles in ninth grade?

5. Into which college was Adrienne finally admitted?

THE STRATEGIES

1. This article is not exactly an argument, but it nevertheless provides a rebuttal to the Perkins' essay with which it is paired. How does it do that?

2. What rhetorical pattern does this article logically follow?

3. Every now and again, the author mentions some fact about the homeless in America (see paragraph 7, for example.) Why does she do that? What does that tactic add to her essay?

4. In paragraph 10, the author casually mentions that Adrienne had become pregnant for an uncaring man. Why do you think this information is given so briefly, almost in passing?

5. What main underlying point is this article making? Where is it finally stated?

THE ISSUES

1. What does Adrienne seem to lack that most other people take for granted?

2. What do the government and the public owe someone like Adrienne?

3. The writer says she learned a lot from Adrienne. What are some of the lessons she seems to have learned?

4. How would you characterize Adrienne's mother?

5. The author implies that anyone, given a run of hard luck, could become homeless, a charge that Perkins staunchly denies. Could you become homeless? Why or why not?

SUGGESTIONS FOR WRITING

1. Write an essay about what society and the government owes someone like Adrienne, if anything. Explain your reasons.

2. Using the essay as your source of data, write an essay constructing the character of Adrienne.

First Draft

Antoinette Poodt, Furman University

People ^ Out on a Limb   *more specific title*

A disease ~~that~~ plagues our ~~nation~~. *people.* This disease can be seen in *not a complete sentence* every great city and far beyond that. As one walks the streets, it is all over the place. What is it ^ The Homeless! The main cause *?* of The Homeless is poverty. In 1993, according to the U.S. *Incorrect punctuation* Bureau of the Census, more than one million Americans fell into poverty. Despite the increasing economic growth and the decrease in unemployment, economic gaps are increasing. In 1993, the top fifth of all households held approximately 48% of the national income, whereas the share of national income going to the bottom fifth of ^ households (3.6%) was the lowest ever *the* *grammar* recorded. So it is evident for ~~one~~ to see that, *all* although there has been increasing economic growth, ~~none~~ of it has gone to the *little* *better word* poor. *Insert A*

bear   *? need more information*

Who is responsible for this and who should ~~bare~~ the burden is an issue that is unclear to many. ~~Even though~~ *Although* the responsibility is *evidently* unclear, ~~it is evident that~~ the gap in economic status between *Some of the following factors :* *Simplify/p* households can be blamed on ^ insufficient minimum wage, *clarification* insufficient affordable housing, and inadequate government

Poodt 2

benefits. In today's economy, ~~,due to the astronomically high~~ ~~the~~ cost of a college education, ~~has~~
,due to the astronomically high   P

~~become so astronomically high that~~ many people that come from
college. Insert B   *sounds better more info one word, P*

homeless families can not afford to attend, As a result, the jobs

chiefly available to them are minimum wage jobs. From January

1981 through March 1990, the minimum wage was frozen at

$3.35 an hour, while the cost of living increased by 48%. Then in

1990 the government decided to raise the minimum wage to

$4.25 an hour, which *hardly* ~~by no means~~ made up for ~~half of~~ the ground
Simplify updated information

lost during the inflation of the '80s. Even now the cost of living

has risen since 1991, ~~but minimum wage has stayed the same.~~ the
and it has taken six years for minimum wage to be raised to $5.25 an hour.

Government benefits, ~~is~~ another side of the issue, ~~and in the~~
unclear

~~past three years~~ have ~~shown~~ *taken* more cuts, *in the past three years* than in the past 25 years.
modify correctly

Rent increases have also risen immensely in the past few years,

making the issue hit closer to home than many ever imagined.
As a college student myself, who is earning below the poverty line,
~~The scarcest thing to me as a college student is that most college~~

~~cannot afford housing on my own, and~~ *her*
~~students fall far below the poverty line, can not find affordable~~
Clarification for reader

~~housing, and~~ receive *s* little or no government benefits, *I can empathize with the homeless in some way* When it

comes right down to it, the only difference between me and a

homeless person is, that I have a *family who cares.* ~~home and hope.~~
more personal

It is easy for me to sit in judgement when I see a "bum" on

the side of the street, *or for me* ~~I am not in his position and can~~ think to *to*
Too choppy correct to make more sense for reader

my self, *that* he should get a job, *because I am not in his position* ~~but when the reality is that could be~~

~~me I am not so quick to judge. I am not sure whose cross it is to~~
Insert C / The burden of the
cross is unclear to me,

~~bare~~ but I do believe that if one is *blessed* ~~fortunate~~ enough to have a
shift in point of view   *sounds better*

roof over *one's* ~~their~~ head, *one* ~~they~~ should want to help people who *are* ~~do~~
replace w/out repetition

less fortunate. ~~not.~~

As I see it,

~~Lacking hope and all chances of achieving ones dreams, that is~~ is they lack hope and the chance of achieving

the plight of the homeless, Should society have sympathy for their dreams.

them and would people feel different~~ly~~ if they walked in the shoes **Revise for a**

the **I think so!** **clear closing by**

of a homeless ~~person?~~ ~~Homeless people walk the streets daily~~ **combining ideas and getting rid of info.**

~~with people staring at them and experience people who turn~~ **This information is not necessary.**

~~their heads and never look them in the eye, those who look at~~

~~them in disgust and roll their eyes, and then the sympathizers~~

~~who smile an awkward "poor you" smile and quickly rush by. Not~~

~~a life anyone would freely choose. There are individual cases that~~

~~make the fight to help the homeless so controversial.~~ I have

always thought that America was the land of equal opportunity

where any one could do anything. This **was** ~~is~~ why the issue of the

was

Homeless ~~is~~ so difficult for me to understand. ~~Thinking about~~ **This is not necessary**

Now I know that the issue is more complicated than I ever realized.

~~this logically one thinks whose place is it to judge, not mine.~~

Insert A   We are becoming a polarized nation, with a great
divide developing between the "haves" and
"have nots."

Insert B   Moreover, children growing up in such an
environment are not stimulated enough to
attain the higher standards needed for scholarships
or grant money.

Insert C   When I think that I, or someone close to
me, could easily be in that position, then I
am not so quick to judge.

I

Final Draft

Antoinette Poodt, Furman University

People Out on a Limb

A disease plagues our people. This disease can be seen in every great city and far beyond that. As one walks the streets, it is all over the place. What is it? The Homeless! The main cause of the homeless is poverty. In 1993, according to the U.S. Bureau of the Census, more than one million Americans fell into poverty. Despite the increasing economic growth and the decrease in unemployment, economic gaps are increasing. In 1993, the top fifth of all households held approximately 48% of the national income, whereas the share of national income going to the bottom fifth of the households (3.6%) was the lowest ever recorded. So it is evident for all to see that, although there has been increasing economic growth, little of it has gone to the poor. We are becoming a polarized nation, with a great divide developing between the "haves" and the "have nots."

Who is responsible for this, and who should bear the burden is an issue that is unclear to many. Although the responsibility is unclear, evidently the gap in economic status between households can be blamed on some of the following factors: insufficient minimum wage, insufficient affordable housing, and inadequate government benefits. In today's economy, due to the astronomically high cost of a college education, many people that come from homeless families cannot afford to attend college. Moreover, children growing up in such an environment are not stimulated enough to attain the higher standards needed for scholarships or grant money. As a result, the jobs chiefly available to them are minimum wage jobs. From January 1981 through March 1990, the minimum wage was frozen at $3.35 an hour, while the cost of living increased by 48%. Then in 1990 the government decided to raise the minimum wage to $4.25 an hour, which hardly made up for the ground lost during the inflation of the '80s. Even now the cost of living has risen since 1991, and it has taken six years for the minimum wage to be raised to $5.25 an hour.

Government benefits, another side of the issue, have taken more cuts in the past three years than in the past 25 years. Rent increases have also risen immensely in the past few years, making the issue hit closer to home than many ever imagined. As a college student myself, who is earning below the poverty line, cannot afford housing on her own, and receives little or no government benefits, I can empathize with the homeless in some way. When it comes right down to it, the only difference between me and a homeless person is that I have a family who cares.

It is easy for me to sit in judgment when I see a "bum" on the side of the street, or for me to think to myself that he should get a job, because I am not in his position. When I think that I, or someone close to me, could easily be in that position, then I am not so quick to judge. The burden of the cross is unclear to me, but I do believe that if one is blessed enough to have a roof over one's head, one should want to help people who are less fortunate. I have always thought that America was the land of equal opportunity where anyone could do anything. This was why the issue of the homeless was so difficult for me to understand. Now I know that the issue is more complicated than I ever realized. As I see it, the plight of the homeless is they lack hope and the chance of achieving their dreams. Should society have sympathy for them and would people feel differently if they walked in the shoes of the homeless? I think so!

How I Write

Writing has always been a challenge for me, and it is usually very difficult for me to get started. Once I get the introduction down, however, the rest of the paper usually flows. Before I begin writing, I gather information about my topic, which I get from the Internet or the library. Then I go to my computer and begin typing. I cannot write in pen or pencil, and then type a paper. Instead I type as I write. This is easier for me because it is simple to make corrections as I go along. When writing a paper or essay, I usually begin with a story, quote, or statement that will grab the reader's attention. Then, taking into account the audience and depending on the type of writing I am to do, I follow with an outline covering specific points. If the paper is a story about me, or something I am very familiar with, I do not follow an outline.

After I write the first draft, I begin with a spell check followed by a computer grammar check. Then I print out the paper and do at least three to five revisions. Once I think the paper is good, I give it to someone else to read. I feel that I do much better on a paper when I spend a few days revising it instead of writing, revising, and turning it in all in one day. When I leave a paper for a while, and then go back to look at it, I see new things that I can do to improve it. Once I have made all the revisions, I read it over one more time and then turn it in.

How I Wrote This Essay

I began this paper by doing research to get some facts on the homeless. It took me a while to figure out what spin I was going to take. I actually started this essay three or four times before I found the spin I wanted to use. Once I got started on the one I wanted, the essay flowed for me. After a very rough first draft, I revised the paper six times. Then I had my mom read over it to make any last minute changes. While doing my corrections, my improvements were more instinctive than for any specific reason. When I thought I could not change it any more, I printed out the last copy.

My Writing Tip

One word of wisdom I can give to fellow writers is to learn to type on a computer as they write. Being a college student, I do not know where I would find the time if I had to write, say in pen or pencil, and then type. Corrections are so much quicker and easier to make when you can see them on the computer screen. It saves so much time, leading to less stress and hence better writing.

Another tip I would give is not to follow a cookie-cutter style of writing. Find your style, become comfortable with it, and use it whenever you write. Do not let one teacher discourage your writing ability because he or she doesn't like your style. We all have our own style. Write in your own style and your paper will turn out better than if you try to write like everyone else. In other words, trust your own personality.

CHAPTER WRITING ASSIGNMENTS

1. Write an essay discussing the idea that religion is a conditioned reflex.

2. Analyze the logic in "Dooley Is a Traitor."

3. Construct an argument for or against competitiveness in business.

4. Should a belief in creation be taught along with Darwin's theory of evolution? Write an essay arguing for or against this question.

5. Write an essay suggesting ways of achieving sexual equality.

TERM PAPER SUGGESTIONS

Investigate the major arguments related to any one of the following subjects:
a. The influence of the church in our country today
b. Animal experimentation
c. Better care for the poor
d. Increased emphasis on physical fitness
e. Careful monitoring of the ecosystems on our plane

    f. Equal rights for women (or another minority) in our country

    g. Maintaining ethnic identities in a pluralistic environment

    h. Smoke-free overseas flights

    i. The need for a national health program that allows for long-term health care.

WRITING ASSIGNMENTS FOR A SPECIFIC AUDIENCE

1. Write an essay arguing for a campus completely free from smoking. Your audience consists of the readers of your college paper. State your proposition clearly and support it with convincing evidence about the hazards of second-hand smoke.

2. You are a Native American. Write a letter to your local newspaper arguing that films about the early West depict Indians in an offensive way. Be specific with your facts and examples.

COLLABORATIVE WRITING PROJECT

This assignment requires a minimum of three students, each researching one aspect of homelessness in our cities: (1) homelessness due to job loss, (2) homelessness due to illness or some other catastrophe, or (3) homelessness due to laziness or irresponsibility or drug and alcohol abuse. The bulk of the research should represent specific statistics and examples. Have the three students make copies of their research for distribution to each other. After reading each other's work, have them come up with a team paper offering solutions to the problem, arguing that as citizens of a civilized and compassionate democracy, we have a sacred duty to end homelessness.

Chapter Ten

THE MEANING
OF WORDS

INTRODUCTION TO THE MEANING OF WORDS

In his autobiography, *Good-bye to All That,* the poet and translator Robert Graves tells of a professor who shunned conversational English in favor of words and phrases usually found only in books. Graves reports the following exchange between this pedantic soul and T. E. Lawrence, the well-known "Lawrence of Arabia," who was then in residence at Oxford. "Was it very caliginous in the metropolis?" asked the professor. "Somewhat caliginous, but not altogether inspissated," replied Lawrence tongue-in-cheek.

Its inanity aside, this exchange demonstrates not only the wonderful versatility of language that makes it possible for us to say simple things in complex ways, but also the awful ways in which some of us use words. Ideally, we should use words to make ourselves clear, to express ourselves honestly, to say truly what we feel and think. Unhappily, many of us use words to puff ourselves up, to hide our thoughts or feelings, and to impress our fellows. Language is essentially a plastic medium capable of being bent and twisted in the minds of speakers and writers. People will use words in their own peculiar ways, and not even the combined outrage of dictionaries and public opinion is likely to stop them.

Although we do not side with those purists who use no word until it has been branded with the imprimatur of a standard dictionary, we still think the abuse of words a pity. Language should be a living bridge between minds otherwise cut off from one another. It should not be a blur, a deliberate screen thrown up for reasons of vanity or deceit. You should write what you think and as well as you can think it. You should not write what you do not think, even if you write it well.

The writers in this section tackle language as a medium of expression that is also governed by various usages and practices, some sensible, some not. Richard Redfern, in "A Brief Lexicon of Jargon," humors us with a lesson on how to write wordily. Bill Bryson, in "Change in the English Language," shares with us the mythology behind some silly rules of usage. Debbie Price talks about how language and its misuse can demean and mislead. *Time* magazine's "Baffle-Gab Thesaurus" provides us with a chart that allows the creation of meaningless jaw-busting phrases. Later we get an amusing lesson from anthropologist Laura Bohannon in how culture affects words and beliefs. Then Jimmy Santiago Baca gives us an intimate account of how language changed his life. The chapter ends with a discussion of a controversial issue, affirmative action.

A D V I C E

▼▼▼

Richard K. Redfern

A BRIEF LEXICON OF JARGON
For Those Who Want to Speak and
Write Verbosely and Vaguely

RICHARD K. REDFERN (b. 1916) was born in Dixon, Illinois. He received his PhD in English from Cornell University in 1950. Between 1968 and 1981, he was professor of English at Clarion State College, Pennsylvania.

Through verbal irony this "Lexicon" tells how to avoid the vagueness and verbosity in much of today's bureaucratic language.

Area

1   The first rule about using *area* is simple. Put *area* at the start or end of hundreds of words and phrases. *The area of* is often useful when you want to add three words to a sentence without changing its meaning.

2

Instead Of	**Say or Write**
civil rights	the area of civil rights
in spelling and pronunciation	in the area of spelling and pronunciation
problems, topics	problem areas, topic areas
major subjects	major subject (*or* subject-matter) areas

3   Second, particularly in speech, use *area* as an all-purpose synonym. After mentioning scheduled improvements in classrooms and offices, use *area* for later references to this idea. A few minutes later, in talking about the courses to be offered next term, use *area* to refer to required courses, to electives, and to both required and elective courses. Soon you can keep three or four *area's* going and thus keep your audience alert by making them guess which idea you have in mind, especially if you insert, once or twice, a neatly disguised geographical use of *area:* "Graduate student response in this area is gratifying."

Field

4   If the temptation arises to say "clothing executive," "publishing executive," and the like, resist it firmly. Say and write "executive in the clothing field" and "executive in the field of publishing." Note that *the field of* (like *the area of*) qualifies as jargon because it adds length, usually without changing the meaning, as in "from the field of literature as a whole" and "prowess in the field of academic achievement" (which is five words longer than the "academic prowess" of plain English). With practice you can combine *field* with *area, level,* and other standbys:

> In the sportswear field, this is one area which is growing. (Translation from context: Ski sweaters are selling well.)
> [The magazine is] a valuable source of continuing information for educators at all levels and for everyone concerned with this field. (Plain English: The magazine is a valuable source of information for anyone interested in education.)

5   A master of jargon can produce a sentence so vague that it can be dropped into dozens of other articles and books: "At what levels is coverage of the field important?" Even in context (a scholarly book about the teaching of English), it is hard to attach meaning to *that* sentence!

In Terms Of

6   A sure sign of the ability to speak and write jargon is the redundant use of *in terms of*. If you are a beginner, use the phrase instead of prepositions such as *in* ("The faculty has been divided in terms of opinions and attitudes") and *of* ("We think in terms of elementary, secondary, and higher education"). Then move on to sentences in which you waste more than two words:

7

Instead Of	**Say or Write**
The Campus School expects to have three fourth grades.	In terms of the future, the Campus School expects to have three fourth grades. (5 extra words)
I'm glad that we got the response we wanted.	I'm glad that there was a response to that in terms of what we wanted. (6 extra words)

8   Emulate the masters of jargon. They have the courage to abandon the effort to shape a thought clearly:
     A field trip should be defined in terms of where you are.
     They are trying to get underway some small and large construction in terms of unemployment.
     When we think in terms of muscles, we don't always think in terms of eyes.

Level

9   Although *level* should be well known through overuse, the unobservant young instructors may need a review of some of its uses, especially if they are anxious to speak and write *on the level of* jargon. (Note the redundancy of the italicized words.)

10

Instead Of	**Say or Write**
She teaches fifth grade.	She teaches on the fifth grade level. (3 extra words)
Readers will find more than one meaning.	It can be read on more than one level of meaning. (4 extra words)
My students	The writers on my level of concern (5 extra words)

Long Forms

11   When the shorter of two similar forms is adequate, choose the longer; e.g., say *analyzation* (for *analysis*), *orientate* (for *orient*), *origination* (for *origin*), *summarization* (for *summary*). Besides using an unnecessary syllable or two, the long form can make your audience peevish when they know the word has not won acceptance or, at least, uneasy ("Is that a new word that I ought to know?"). If someone asks why you use *notate* instead of *note* (as in "Please notate in the space below your preference . . . "), fabricate an elaborate distinction. Not having a dictionary in his pocket, your questioner will be too polite to argue.

12   With practice, you will have the confidence to enter unfamiliar territory. Instead of the standard forms *(confirm, interpret, penalty, register,* and *scrutiny)*, try *confirmate, interpretate, penalization, registrate,* and *scrutinization.*

13   You have little chance of making a name for yourself as a user of jargon unless you sprinkle your speech and writing with vogue words and phrases, both the older fashions (e.g., *aspect, background, field, level, situation)* and the new (e.g., *escalate, relate to, share with; facility, involvement; limited, minimal)*. An old favorite adds the aroma of the cliché, while a newly fashionable term proves that you are up-to-date. Another advantage of vogue words is that some of them are euphemisms. By using *limited,* for example, you show your disdain for the directness and clarity of *small,* as in "a man with a limited education" and "a limited enrollment in a very large room."

14   Unfortunately, some vogue expressions are shorter than standard English, but their obscurity does much to offset the defect of brevity.

15

Instead Of	**Say or Write**
The children live in a camp and have both classes and recreation outdoors.	The children live in a camp-type situation.
She reads, writes, and speaks German and has had four years of Latin.	She has a good foreign-language background.
Many hospitals now let a man stay with his wife during labor.	The trend is to let the father have more involvement.

16   A final word to novices: dozens of words and phrases have been omitted from this brief lexicon, but try to spot them yourself. Practice steadily, always keeping in mind that the fundamentals of jargon—verbosity and needless vagueness—are best adorned by pretentiousness. Soon, if you feel the impulse to say, for example, that an office has one

secretary and some part-time help, you will write "Administrative cleri-
cal aids implement the organizational function." Eventually you can
produce sentences which mean anything or possibly nothing: "We
should leave this aspect of the definition relatively operational" or "This
condition is similar in regard to other instances also."

(1,117 words)

VOCABULARY

lexicon (title)	peevish (11)	novices (16)
jargon (title)	escalate (13)	verbosity (16)
redundant (6)	cliché (13)	
emulate (8)	euphemism (13)	

D I S C U S S I O N

▼▼

Bill Bryson

CHANGE IN THE ENGLISH LANGUAGE

BILL BRYSON (1951–   ), freelance writer, was born in Des Moines, Iowa, and
educated at Drake University. In 1977, he immigrated to England. His books include *The Penguin Dictionary of Troublesome Words* (1984), and *The Mother Tongue:
English and How It Got That Way* (1990), from which this excerpt is taken.

> *A sentence may not end with a proposition; it may not begin with a
> conjunction; it is wrong to split an infinitive; "hopefully" used at the
> beginning of a sentence is wrong: These and other picky questions of
> usage are tackled in this excerpt from a book on the English Lan-
> guage. In the minds of some people, many of these rules have become
> sacred cows. Yet as we learn, no grammatical justification, other
> than personal preference, exists for any of them.*

1   In the late 1970s, President Jimmy Carter betrayed a flaw in his linguistic armory when he said: "The government of Iran must realize that it
cannot flaunt, with impunity, the expressed will and law of the world
community." *Flaunt* means to show off; he meant *flout*. The day after he
was elected president in 1988, George Bush told a television reporter he

couldn't believe the enormity of what had happened. Had President-elect Bush known that the primary meaning of *enormity* is wickedness or evilness, he would doubtless have selected a more apt term.

2   When this process of change can be seen happening in our lifetimes, it is almost always greeted with cries of despair and alarm. Yet such change is both continuous and inevitable. Few acts are more salutary than looking at the writings of language authorities from recent decades and seeing the usages that heightened their hackles. In 1931, H. W. Fowler was tutting over *racial*, which he called "an ugly word, the strangeness of which is due to our instinctive feeling that the termination -al has no business at the end of a word that is not obviously Latin." (For similar reasons he disliked *television* and *speedometer.*) Other authorities have variously—and sometimes hotly—attacked *enthuse, commentate, emote, prestigious, contact* as a verb, *chair* as a verb, and scores of others. But of course these are nothing more than opinions, and, as is the way with other people's opinions, they are generally ignored.

3   So if there are no officially appointed guardians for the English language, who sets down all those rules that we all know about from childhood—the idea that we must never end a sentence with a preposition or begin one with a conjunction, that we must use *each other* for two things and *one another* for more than two, and that we must never use *hopefully* in an absolute sense, such as "Hopefully it will not rain tomorrow"? The answer, surprisingly often, is that no one does, that when you look into the background of these "rules" there is often little basis for them.

4   Consider the curiously persistent notion that sentences should not end with a preposition. The source of this stricture, and several other equally dubious ones, was one Robert Lowth, an eighteenth-century clergyman and amateur grammarian whose *A Short Introduction to English Grammar,* published in 1762, enjoyed a long and distressingly influential life both in his native England and abroad. It is to Lowth we can trace many a pedant's most treasured notions: the belief that you must say *different from* rather than *different to* or *different than,* the idea that two negatives make a positive, the rule that you must not say "the heaviest of the two objects," but rather "the heavier," the distinction between *shall* and *will,* and the clearly nonsensical belief that *between* can apply only to two things and *among* to more than two. (By this reasoning, it would not be possible to say that St. Louis is between New York, Los Angeles, and Chicago, but rather that it is among them, which would impart a quite different sense.) Perhaps the most remarkable and curiously enduring of Lowth's many beliefs was the conviction that sentences ought not to end with a preposition. But even he was not didactic about it. He recognized that ending a sentence with a preposition was idiomatic and common in both speech and informal writing. He suggested only that he thought it generally better and more

graceful, not crucial, to place the preposition before its relative "in solemn and elevated" writing. Within a hundred years this had been converted from a piece of questionable advice into an immutable rule. In a remarkable outburst of literal-mindedness, nineteenth-century academics took it as read that the very name *pre-position* meant it must come before something—anything.

5   But then this was a period of the most resplendent silliness, when grammarians and scholars seemed to be climbing over one another (or each other; it doesn't really matter) in a mad scramble to come up with fresh absurdities. This was the age when, it was gravely insisted, Shakespeare's *laughable* ought to be changed to *laugh-at-able* and *reliable* should be made into *relionable*. Dozens of seemingly unexceptionable words—*lengthy, standpoint, international, colonial, brash*—were attacked with venom because of some supposed etymological deficiency or other. Thomas de Quincey, in between bouts of opium taking, found time to attack the expression *what on earth*. Some people wrote *mooned* for *lunatic* and *foresayer* for *prophet* on the grounds that the new words were Anglo-Saxon and thus somehow more pure. They roundly castigated those ignoramuses who impurely combined Greek and Latin roots into new words like *petroleum* (Latin *petro* + Greek *oleum*). In doing so, they failed to note that the very word with which they described themselves, *grammarians*, is itself a hybrid made of Greek and Latin roots, as are many other words that have lived unexceptionably in English for centuries. They even attacked *handbook* as an ugly Germanic compound when it dared to show its face in the nineteenth century, failing to notice that it was a good Old English word that had simply fallen out of use. It is one of the felicities of English that we can take pieces of words from all over and fuse them into new constructions—like *trusteeship*, which consists of a Nordic stem *(trust)*, combined with a French affix *(ee)*, married to an Old English root *(ship)*. Other languages cannot do this. We should be proud of ourselves for our ingenuity and yet even now authorities commonly attack almost any new construction as ugly or barbaric.

6   Today in England you can still find authorities attacking the construction *different than* as a regrettable Americanism, insisting that a sentence such as "How different things appear in Washington than in London" is ungrammatical and should be changed to "How different things appear in Washington from how they appear in London." Yet *different than* has been common in England for centuries and used by such exalted writers as Defoe, Addison, Steele, Dickens, Coleridge, and Thackeray, among others. Other authorities, in both Britain and America, continue to deride the absolute use of *hopefully. The New York Times Manual of Style and Usage* flatly forbids it. Its writers must not say, "Hopefully the sun will come out soon," but rather are instructed to resort to a clumsily passive and periphrastic construction such as "It is to be hoped that the sun will come out soon." The reason? The

authorities maintain that *hopefully* in the first sentence is a misplaced modal auxiliary—that it doesn't belong to any other part of the sentence. Yet they raise no objection to dozens of other words being used in precisely the same unattached way—*admittedly, mercifully, happily, curiously,* and so on. The reason *hopefully* is not allowed is because, well, because somebody at *The New York Times* once had a boss who wouldn't allow it because his professor had forbidden it, because *his* father thought it was ugly and inelegant, because *he* had been told so by his uncle who was a man of great learning . . . and so on.

7   Considerations of what makes for good English or bad English are to an uncomfortably large extent matters of prejudice and conditioning. Until the eighteenth century it was correct to say "you was" if you were referring to one person. It sounds odd today, but the logic is impeccable. *Was* is a singular verb and *were* a plural one. Why should *you* take a plural verb when the sense is clearly singular? The answer—surprise, surprise—is that Robert Lowth didn't like it. "I'm hurrying, are I not?" is hopelessly ungrammatical, but "I'm hurrying, aren't I?"— merely a contraction of the same words—is perfect English. *Many* is almost always a plural (as in "Many people were there"), but not when it is followed by *a,* as in "Many a man was there." There's no inherent reason why these things should be so. They are not defensible in terms of grammar. They are because they are.

8   Nothing illustrates the scope for prejudice in English better than the issue of the split infinitive. Some people feel ridiculously strongly about it. When the British Conservative politician Jock Bruce-Gardyne was economic secretary to the Treasury in the early 1980s, he returned unread any departmental correspondence containing a split infinitive. (It should perhaps be pointed out that a split infinitive is one in which an adverb comes between *to* and a verb, as in *to quickly look.*) I can think of two very good reasons for not splitting an infinitive.

1. Because you feel that the rules of English ought to conform to the grammatical precepts of a language that died a thousand years ago.
2. Because you wish to cling to a pointless affectation of usage that is without the support of any recognized authority of the last 200 years, even at the cost of composing sentences that are ambiguous, inelegant, and patently contorted.

9   It is exceedingly difficult to find any authority who condemns the split infinitive—Theodore Bernstein, H. W. Fowler, Ernest Gowers, Eric Partridge, Rudolph Flesch, Wilson Follett, Roy H. Copperud, and others too tedious to enumerate here all agree that there is no logical reason not to split an infinitive. Otto Jespersen even suggests that, strictly speaking, it isn't actually possible to split an infinitive. As he puts it: "'To' . . . is no more an essential part of an infinitive than the

definite article is an essential part of a nominative, and no one would think of calling 'the good man' a split nominative." [*Growth and Structure of the English Language,* page 222]

10   Lacking an academy as we do, we might expect dictionaries to take up the banner of defenders of the language, but in recent years they have increasingly shied away from the role. A perennial argument with dictionary makers is whether they should be *prescriptive* (that is, whether they should prescribe how language should be used) or *descriptive* (that is, merely describe how it is used without taking a position). The most notorious example of the descriptive school was the 1961 *Webster's Third New International Dictionary* (popularly called *Webster's Unabridged*), whose editor, Philip Gove, believed that distinctions of usage were elitist and artificial. As a result, usages such as *imply* as a synonym for *infer* and *flout* being used in the sense of *flaunt* were included without comment. The dictionary provoked further antagonism, particularly among members of the U.S. Trademark Association, by refusing to capitalize trademarked words. But what really excited outrage was its remarkable contention that *ain't* was "used orally in most parts of the U.S. by many cultivated speakers."

11   So disgusted was *The New York Times* with the new dictionary that it announced it would not use is but would continue with the 1934 edition, prompting the language authority Bergen Evans to write: "Anyone who solemnly announces in the year 1962 that he will be guided in matters of English usage by a dictionary published in 1934 is talking ignorant and pretentious nonsense," and he pointed out that the issue of the *Times* announcing the decision contained nineteen words condemned by the *Second International.*

12   Since then, other dictionaries have been divided on the matter. *The American Heritage Dictionary,* first published in 1969, instituted a usage panel of distinguished commentators to rule on contentious points of usage, which are discussed, often at some length, in the text. But others have been more equivocal (or prudent or spineless depending on how you view it). The revised *Random House Dictionary of the English Language,* published in 1987, accepts the looser meaning for most words, though often noting that the newer usage is frowned on "by many"—a curiously timid approach that at once acknowledges the existence of expert opinion and yet constantly places it at a distance. Among the looser meanings it accepts are *disinterested* to mean uninterested and *infer* to mean imply. It even accepts the existence of *kudo* as a singular—prompting a reviewer from *Time* magazine to ask if one instance of pathos should now be a patho.

13   It's a fine issue. One of the undoubted virtues of English is that it is a fluid and democratic language in which meanings shift and change in response to the pressures of common usage rather than the dictates of committees. It is a natural process that has been going on

for centuries. To interfere with that process is arguably both arrogant and futile, since clearly the weight of usage will push new meanings into currency no matter how many authorities hurl themselves into the path of change.

(2,121 words)

VOCABULARY

impunity (1)	etymological (5)	inherent (7)
salutary (2)	castigated (5)	precepts (8)
hackles (2)	ignoramuses (5)	ambiguous (8)
stricture (4)	felicities (5)	patently (8)
pedant's (4)	exalted (6)	nominative (9)
didactic (4)	deride (6)	contentious (12)
immutable (4)	periphrastic (7)	equivocal (12)
resplendent (5)	impeccable (7)	

THE FACTS

1. What two presidents are mentioned as committing linguistic errors?

2. What word did noted language authority H. W. Fowler tut-tut about in 1931?

3. Who establishes the rules of usage such as, for example, that an infinitive must not be split?

4. To what writer can the pedant's most cherished beliefs about usage such as preferring "different from" rather than "different to" or "different than" be traced?

5. Which American newspaper flatly forbids the absolute use of "hopefully" in a sentence?

THE STRATEGIES

1. In making his points about language use, what is the writer's principal method of backing up his assertions?

2. How would you characterize the structure of the author's paragraphs?

3. In paragraph 2, referring to authorities on language, the writer remarks that certain changes "heightened their hackles." What does

this phrase mean? What is the usual expression, and why doesn't he use it here?

4. In paragraph 8, the writer gives two very good reasons for not splitting an infinitive. How would you characterize his tone here?

5. What kind of evidence is cited by the writer in paragraph 9 to show that the split infinitive rule is silly?

THE ISSUES

1. In what way can language be said to reflect class?

2. Which of these rules do you practice in your own writing? Why?

3. What legitimate reason can you think of to oppose change in the language?

4. How has your own language changed since you've been in college? How do you expect college to change it?

5. The author points out that English lacks an academy, meaning a panel of experts to oversee the language and rule on disputed usage points such as the French have. Do you think an academy would help or hinder the cause of English? Why or why not?

SUGGESTIONS FOR WRITING

1. Write an essay giving examples of words and phrases you might use in your speech but not in your writing. Explain why.

2. Write an essay about any usage points you practice in your own writing because of the influence of a former teacher.

▼▼

Deb Price

CLEANING A CATALOG OF ILLS

DEB PRICE (1958–   ), nationally syndicated columnist who writes a weekly column for the *Detroit News,* was born in Lubbock, Texas, and educated at Stanford University. She is the co-author of *And Say Hi to Joyce* (1995).

This essay, from a weekly newspaper column, points out the discovery of some odd associations made by the Library of Congress in its cataloging of subject headings. As the writer tells it, the discovery was made by a professional cataloger who has campaigned long and hard to have the offensive headings changed. The essay illustrates, once again, the tremendous power of words and how misuse of them can drastically affect perception.

1   With his nose buried in a card catalog, librarian Sandy Berman caught a whiff of something rotten while working at the University of Zambia 25 years ago. He smelled raw prejudice and realized to his horror that it was being imported from a hallowed American institution, the Library of Congress.

2   Since the turn of the century, English-language libraries around the world have cataloged their book collections by adopting the same subject headings as the Library of Congress. While this uniformity simplifies the work of librarians and researchers, it also means that even a putrid blunder at the Library of Congress gets duplicated at countless smaller libraries.

3   Berman's upsetting discovery back in 1969 was that, because the Zambian library followed the Library of Congress' catalog, he was obligated to categorize books about black South Africans under a racist term, "kafirs."

4   "I felt I was being compelled to do something essentially inaccurate and dishonest and, in a way, immoral," he recalls. He immediately sensed that by nosing around a bit more he'd uncover "a whole lot more muck."

5   Berman laid bare his discoveries about the Library of Congress' offensive terminology in his 1971 book, "Prejudices and Antipathies." He pointed to dozens of card catalog subject headings written in the language of the oppressor.

6   For example, "Jewish Question," a chilling phrase straight out of the mouth of Nazi propagandist Joseph Goebbels, and "Race Question," which Berman notes "smacks of white supremacy." Under "Sexual Perversion" he found the heterosexist notation, "See also Homosexuality."

7   Book-loving Berman is a matchmaker at heart. As a professional cataloger, he wants to make it easy for library patrons to connect with whatever they want to read and believes that anyone searching for works on a subject has a right "not to be offended, prejudiced, confused, misled or repelled by the very terminology used to denote specific categories."

8   If the giant Library of Congress hadn't stubbornly resisted Berman's good ideas, this David-and-Goliath saga would have ended with the little guy's total triumph decades ago. Instead, Berman has had to keep slinging suggestions, firing off petitions.

9   His successes are a testament to persistence and the power of one person to trigger much-needed change: "Race Relations" replaced "Race Question" about a decade after his first volley. "Jewish Question" left

the catalog in 1983. And after an 18-year siege, Berman defeated "Yellow Peril" in 1989.

10   Deleting the "perversion-homosexuality" link was an early victory for Berman, but he's still bothered by obstacles put in the way of gay readers. He first took an interest in helping gay people locate gay books in the mid 1960s, when he saw soldiers in U.S. Army libraries in Germany struggle to find gay novels without coming out of the closet.

11   The chief cataloger in Minnesota's Hennepin County Library for the past 21 years, Berman keeps prodding the "big, old, bureaucratic" Library of Congress to weed out headings that reek. "Criminal Justice Administration," for instance, still advises, "See also Lynching."

12   Berman's tireless campaign is a monument to true justice and simple fairness. Its successes smell mighty sweet.

(518 words)

VOCABULARY

hallowed (1)   Kafirs (3)   antipathies (5)

putrid (2)

THE FACTS

1. Where was the librarian working when he first noticed the odd classifications in the catalog of the Library of Congress?

2. Why does a blunder by the Library of Congress have such far-reaching effects?

3. What controversial and racist classification did Berman find under the heading of "Race Question"?

4. How did the Library of Congress react to Berman's findings?

5. What link did the catalog of the Library of Congress establish with homosexuality?

THE STRATEGIES

1. What technique does the writer use in her opening paragraph to draw us into the column?

2. How does the writer tie the beginning to the end of her essay?

3. This essay was originally published as a newspaper column. What are some of its characteristics that are associated with column writing?

4. Under what rhetorical type would you classify this essay? Why?

5. The writer uses no transitions between her paragraphs. How do you think she's able to get away with that?

THE ISSUES

1. What is your opinion of Berman's discovery? Do you think it important or trivial?

2. Which of the cataloging errors mentioned do you think the gravest? Why?

3. How do you think these inaccurate catalog entries evolved?

4. Why are we more likely today to see the catalog entries the author cites as injustices?

5. Why do you think the Library of Congress has been resistant to making the changes that Berman suggested?

SUGGESTIONS FOR WRITING

1. Write an essay on libraries.

2. In an essay, argue that Berman's findings are trivial or important.

▼▼

BAFFLE-GAB THESAURUS

We present the "Baffle-Gab Thesaurus" as an amusing exercise. Try writing a letter of complaint to an imaginary firm, flooding your content with combinations from this obfuscating word guide. (And if you do not already know the word obfuscating, *look it up.) (From* Time, *September 13, 1968.)*

1   As any self-respecting bureaucrat knows, it is bad form indeed to use a single, simple word when six or seven obfuscating ones will do.

2   But where is the Washington phrasemaker to turn if he is hung up for what Horace called "words a foot and a half long"? Simple. Just glance at the Systematic Buzz Phrase Projector, or S.B.P.P.

3   The S.B.P.P. has aptly obscure origins but appears to come from a Royal Canadian Air Force listing of fuzzy phrases. It was popularized in Washington by Philip Broughton, a U.S. Public Health Service official, who circulated it among civil servants and businessmen. A sort of

mini-thesaurus of baffle-gab, it consists of a three-column list of 30 overused but appropriately portentous words. Whenever a GS-14 or deputy assistant secretary needs an opaque phrase, he need only think of a three digit number—any one will do as well as the next—and select the corresponding "buzz words" from the three columns. For example, 257 produces "systematized logistical projection," which has the ring of absolute authority and means absolutely nothing.

4   Broughton's baffle-gab guide:

A	B	C
0) Integrated	Management	Options
1) Total	Organizational	Flexibility
2) Systematized	Monitored	Capability
3) Parallel	Reciprocal	Mobility
4) Functional	Digital	Programming
5) Responsive	Logistical	Concept
6) Optional	Transitional	Time-Phase
7) Synchronized	Incremental	Projection
8) Compatible	Third-Generation	Hardware
9) Balanced	Policy	Contingency

(238 words)

E X A M P L E S

▼▼

Laura Bohannan

SHAKESPEARE IN THE BUSH

LAURA BOHANNAN (b. 1922) is a cultural anthropologist who was born in New York and educated at the University of Arizona and at Oxford. Since 1969, she has been teaching at the University of Illinois.

Cultural anthropologists are all concerned with meaning, with the difficult task of translation from one language to another. In this classic of anthropology, Laura Bohannan shows the difficulty of translating the meaning of Hamlet *to the Tiv in West Africa. The article forcefully demonstrates that different cultures live in separate worlds of meaning.*

1   Just before I left Oxford for the Tiv in West Africa, conversation turned to the season at Stratford. "You Americans," said a friend, "often have difficulty with Shakespeare. He was, after all, a very English poet, and one can easily misinterpret the universal by misunderstanding the particular."

2   I protested that human nature is pretty much the same the whole world over; at least the general plot and motivation of the greater tragedies would always be clear—everywhere—although some details of custom might have to be explained and difficulties of translation might produce other slight changes. To end an argument we could not conclude, my friend gave me a copy of *Hamlet* to study in the African bush: it would, he hoped, lift my mind above its primitive surroundings, and possibly I might, by prolonged meditation, achieve the grace of correct interpretation.

3   It was my second field trip to that African tribe, and I thought myself ready to live in one of its remote sections—an area difficult to cross even on foot. I eventually settled on the hillock of a very knowledgeable old man, the head of a homestead of some hundred and forty people, all of whom were either his close relatives or his wives and children. Like the other elders of the vicinity, the old man spent most of his time performing ceremonies seldom seen these days in the more accessible parts of the tribe. I was delighted. Soon there would be three months of enforced isolation and leisure, between the harvest that takes place just before the rising of the swamps and the clearing of new farms when the water goes down. Then, I thought, they would have even more time to perform ceremonies and explain them to me.

4   I was quite mistaken. Most of the ceremonies demanded the presence of elders from several homesteads. As the swamps rose, the old men found it too difficult to walk from one homestead to the next, and the ceremonies gradually ceased. As the swamps rose even higher, all activities but one came to an end. The women brewed beer from maize and millet. Men, women, and children sat on their hillocks and drank it.

5   People began to drink by dawn. By midmorning the whole homestead was singing, dancing, and drumming. When it rained, people had to sit inside their huts: there they drank and sang or they drank and told stories. In any case, by noon or before, I either had to join the party or retire to my own hut and my books. "One does not discuss serious matters when there is beer. Come drink with us." Since I lacked their capacity for the thick native beer, I spent more and more time with *Hamlet*. Before the end of the second month, grace descended on

me. I was quite sure that *Hamlet* had only one possible interpretation, and that one universally obvious.

6   Early every morning, in the hope of having some serious talk before the beer party, I used to call on the old man at his reception hut— a circle of posts supporting a thatched roof above a low mud wall to keep out wind and rain. One day I crawled through the low doorway and found most of the men of the homestead sitting huddled in their ragged cloths on stools, low plank beds, and reclining chairs, warming themselves against the chill of the rain around a smoky fire. In the center were three pots of beer. The party had started.

7   The old man greeted me cordially. "Sit down and drink." I accepted a large calabash full of beer, poured some into a small drinking gourd, and tossed it down. Then I poured some more into the same gourd for the man second in seniority to my host before I handed my calabash over to a young man for further distribution. Important people shouldn't ladle beer themselves.

8   "It is better like this," the old man said, looking at me approvingly and plucking at the thatch that had caught in my hair. "You should sit and drink with us more often. Your servants tell me that when you are not with us, you sit inside your hut looking at a paper."

9   The old man was acquainted with four kinds of "papers": tax receipts, bride price receipts, court fee receipts, and letters. The messenger who brought him letters from the chief used them mainly as a badge of office, for he always knew what was in them and told the old man. Personal letters from the few who had relatives in the government or mission stations were kept until someone went to a large market where there was a letter writer and reader. Since my arrival, letters were brought to me to be read. A few men also brought me bride price receipts, privately, with requests to change the figures to a higher sum. I found moral arguments were of no avail, since in-laws are fair game, and the technical hazards of forgery difficult to explain to an illiterate people. I did not wish them to think me silly enough to look at any such papers for days on end, and I hastily explained that my "paper" was one of the "things of long ago" of my country.

10   "Ah," said the old man. "Tell us."

11   I protested that I was not a storyteller. Storytelling is a skilled art among them; their standards are high, and the audiences critical—and vocal in their criticism. I protested in vain. This morning they wanted to hear a story while they drank. They threatened to tell me no more stories until I told them one of mine. Finally, the old man promised that no one would criticize my style "for we know you are struggling with our language." "But," put in one of the elders, "you must explain what we do not understand, as we do when we tell you our stories." Realizing that here was my chance to prove *Hamlet* universally intelligible, I agreed.

12   The old man handed me some more beer to help me on with my storytelling. Men filled their long wooden pipes and knocked coals from the fire to place in the pipe bowls; then, puffing contentedly, they sat back to listen. I began in the proper style, "Not yesterday, not yesterday, but long ago, a thing occurred. One night three men were keeping watch outside the homestead of the great chief, when suddenly they saw the former chief approach them."

13   "Why was he no longer their chief?"

14   "He was dead," I explained. "That is why they were troubled and afraid when they saw him."

15   "Impossible," began one of the elders, handing his pipe on to his neighbor, who interrupted, "Of course it wasn't the dead chief. It was an omen sent by a witch. Go on."

16   Slightly shaken, I continued. "One of these three was a man who knew things"—the closest translation of scholar, but unfortunately it also meant witch. The second elder looked triumphantly at the first. "So he spoke to the dead chief saying, 'Tell us what we must do so you may rest in your grave,' but the dead chief did not answer. He vanished, and they could see him no more. Then the man who knew things—his name was Horatio—said this event was the affair of the dead chief's son, Hamlet."

17   There was a general shaking of heads round the circle. "Had the dead chief no living brothers? Or was this son the chief?"

18   "No," I replied, "That is, he had one living brother who became the chief when the elder brother died."

19   The old men muttered: such omens were matters for chiefs and elders, not for youngsters; no good could come of going behind a chief's back; clearly Horatio was not a man who knew things.

20   "Yes, he was," I insisted, shooing a chicken away from my beer. "In our country the son is next to the father. The dead chief's younger brother had become the great chief. He had also married his elder brother's widow only about a month after the funeral."

21   "He did well," the old man beamed and announced to the others, "I told you that if we knew more about Europeans, we would find they really were very like us. In our country also," he added to me, "the younger brother marries the elder brother's widow and becomes the father of his children. Now, if your uncle, who married your widowed mother, is your father's full brother, then he will be a real father to you. Did Hamlet's father and uncle have one mother?"

22   His question barely penetrated my mind; I was too upset and thrown too far off balance by having one of the most important elements of *Hamlet* knocked straight out of the picture. Rather uncertainly I said that I thought they had the same mother, but I wasn't sure—the story didn't say. The old man told me severely that these genealogical details made all the difference and that when I got home

I must ask the elders about it. He shouted out the door to one of his younger wives to bring his goatskin bag.

23   Determined to save what I could of the mother motif, I took a deep breath and began again. "The son Hamlet was very sad because his mother had married again so quickly. There was no need for her to do so, and it is our custom for a widow not to go to her next husband until she has mourned for two years."

24   "Two years is too long," objected the wife, who had appeared with the old man's battered goatskin bag. "Who will hoe your farms for you while you have no husband?"

25   "Hamlet," I retorted without thinking, "was old enough to hoe his mother's farms himself. There was no need for her to remarry." No one looked convinced. I gave up. "His mother and the great chief told Hamlet not to be sad, for the great chief himself would be a father to Hamlet. Furthermore, Hamlet would be the next chief: therefore he must stay to learn the things of a chief. Hamlet agreed to remain, and all the rest went off to drink beer."

26   While I paused, perplexed at how to render Hamlet's disgusted soliloquy to an audience convinced that Claudius and Gertrude had behaved in the best possible manner, one of the younger men asked me who had married the other wives of the dead chief.

27   "He had no other wives," I told him.

28   "But a chief must have many wives! How else can he brew beer and prepare food for all his guests?"

29   I said firmly that in our country even chiefs had only one wife, that they had servants to do their work, and that they paid them from tax money.

30   It was better, they returned, for a chief to have many wives and sons who would help him hoe his farms and feed his people; then everyone loved the chief who gave much and took nothing—taxes were a bad thing.

31   I agreed with the last comment, but for the rest fell back on their favorite way of fobbing off my questions: "That is the way it is done, so that is how we do it."

32   I decided to skip the soliloquy. Even if Claudius was here thought quite right to marry his brother's widow, there remained the poison motif, and I knew they would disapprove of fratricide. More hopefully I resumed, "That night Hamlet kept watch with the three who had seen his dead father. The dead chief again appeared, and although the others were afraid, Hamlet followed his dead father off to one side. When they were alone, Hamlet's dead father spoke."

33   "Omens can't talk!" The old man was emphatic.

34   "Hamlet's dead father wasn't an omen. Seeing him might have been an omen, but he was not." My audience looked as confused as I sounded. "It *was* Hamlet's dead father. It was a thing we call a 'ghost.'"

I had to use the English word, for unlike many of the neighboring tribes, these people didn't believe in the survival after death of any individuating part of the personality.

35   "What is a 'ghost'? An omen?"

36   "No, a 'ghost' is someone who is dead but who walks around and can talk, and people can hear him and see him but not touch him."

37   They objected. "One can touch zombis."

38   "No, no! It was not a dead body the witches had animated to sacrifice and eat. No one else made Hamlet's dead father walk. He did it himself."

39   "Dead men can't walk," protested my audience as one man.

40   I was quite willing to compromise. "A 'ghost' is the dead man's shadow."

41   But again they objected. "Dead men cast no shadows."

42   "They do in my country," I snapped.

43   The old man quelled the babble of disbelief that arose immediately and told me with that insincere, but courteous, agreement one extends to the fancies of the young, ignorant, and superstitious, "No doubt in your country the dead can also walk without being zombis." From the depths of his bag he produced a withered fragment of kola nut, bit off one end to show it wasn't poisoned, and handed me the rest as a peace offering.

44   "Anyhow," I resumed, "Hamlet's dead father said that his own brother, the one who became chief, had poisoned him. He wanted Hamlet to avenge him. Hamlet believed this in his heart, for he did not like his father's brother." I took another swallow of beer. "In the country of the great chief, living in the same homestead, for it was a very large one, was an important elder who was often with the chief to advise and help him. His name was Polonius. Hamlet was courting his daughter, but her father and her brother . . . [I cast hastily about for some tribal analogy] warned her not to let Hamlet visit her when she was alone on her farm, for he would be a great chief and so could not marry her."

45   "Why not?" asked the wife, who had settled down on the edge of the old man's chair. He frowned at her for asking stupid questions and growled, "They lived in the same homestead."

46   "That was not the reason," I informed him. "Polonius was a stranger who lived in the homestead because he helped the chief, not because he was a relative."

47   "Then why couldn't Hamlet marry her?"

48   "He could have," I explained, "but Polonius didn't think he would. After all, Hamlet was a man of great importance who ought to marry a chief's daughter, for in his country a man could have only one wife. Polonius was afraid that if Hamlet made love to his daughter, then no one else would give a high price for her."

49   "That might be true," remarked one of the shrewder elders, "but a chief's son would give his mistress's father enough presents and patronage to more than make up the difference. Polonius sounds like a fool to me."

50   "Many people think he was," I agreed. "Meanwhile Polonius sent his son Laertes off to Paris to learn the things of that country, for it was the homestead of a very great chief indeed. Because he was afraid that Laertes might waste a lot of money on beer and women and gambling, or get into trouble by fighting, he sent one of his servants to Paris secretly, to spy out what Laertes was doing. One day Hamlet came upon Polonius's daughter Ophelia. He behaved so oddly he frightened her. Indeed"—I was fumbling for words to express the dubious quality of Hamlet's madness—"the chief and many others had also noticed that when Hamlet talked one could understand the words but not what they meant. Many people thought that he had become mad." My audience suddenly became much more attentive. "The great chief wanted to know what was wrong with Hamlet, so he sent for two of Hamlet's age mates [school friends would have taken long explanation] to talk to Hamlet and find out what troubled his heart. Hamlet, seeing that they had been bribed by the chief to betray him, told them nothing. Polonius, however, insisted that Hamlet was mad because he had been forbidden to see Ophelia, whom he loved."

51   "Why," inquired a bewildered voice, "should anyone bewitch Hamlet on that account?"

52   "Bewitch him?"

53   "Yes, only witchcraft can make anyone mad, unless, of course, one sees the beings that lurk in the forest."

54   I stopped being a storyteller, took out my notebook and demanded to be told more about these two causes of madness. Even while they spoke and I jotted notes, I tried to calculate the effect of this new factor on the plot. Hamlet had not been exposed to the beings that lurk in the forest. Only his relatives in the male line could bewitch him. Barring relatives not mentioned by Shakespeare, it had to be Claudius who was attempting to harm him. And, of course, it was.

55   For the moment I staved off questions by saying that the great chief also refused to believe that Hamlet was mad for the love of Ophelia and nothing else. "He was sure that something much more important was troubling Hamlet's heart."

56   "Now Hamlet's age mates," I continued, "had brought with them a famous storyteller. Hamlet decided to have this man tell the chief and all his homestead a story about a man who had poisoned his brother because he desired his brother's wife and wished to be chief himself. Hamlet was sure the great chief could not hear the story without making a sign if he was indeed guilty, and then he would discover whether his dead father had told him the truth."

57   The old man interrupted, with deep cunning, "Why should a father lie to his son?" he asked.

58   I hedged: "Hamlet wasn't sure that it really was his dead father." It was impossible to say anything, in that language, about devil-inspired visions.

59   "You mean," he said, "it actually was an omen, and he knew witches sometimes send false ones. Hamlet was a fool not to go to one skilled in reading omens and divining the truth in the first place. A man-who-sees-the-truth could have told him how his father died, if he really had been poisoned, and if there was witchcraft in it; then Hamlet could have called the elders to settle the matter."

60   The shrewd elder ventured to disagree. "Because his father's brother was a great chief, one-who-sees-the-truth might therefore have been afraid to tell it. I think it was for that reason that a friend of Hamlet's father—a witch and an elder—sent an omen so his friend's son would know. Was the omen true?"

61   "Yes," I said, abandoning ghosts and the devil; a witch-sent omen it would have to be. "It was true, for when the storyteller was telling his tale before all the homestead, the great chief rose in fear. Afraid that Hamlet knew his secret, he planned to have him killed."

62   The stage set of the next bit presented some difficulties of translation. I began cautiously. "The great chief told Hamlet's mother to find out from her son what he knew. But because a woman's children are always first in her heart, he had important elder Polonius hide behind a cloth that hung against the wall of Hamlet's mother's sleeping hut. Hamlet started to scold his mother for what she had done."

63   There was a shocked murmur from everyone. A man should never scold his mother.

64   "She called out in fear, and Polonius moved behind the cloth. Shouting, 'A rat!' Hamlet took his machete and slashed through the cloth." I paused for dramatic effect. "He had killed Polonius!"

65   The old men looked at each other in supreme disgust. "That Polonius truly was a fool and a man who knew nothing! What child would not know enough to shout, 'It's me!'" With a pang, I remembered that these people are ardent hunters, always armed with bow, arrow, and machete; at the first rustle in the grass an arrow is aimed and ready, and the hunter shouts "Game!" If no human voice answers immediately, the arrow speeds on its way. Like a good hunter Hamlet had shouted, "A rat!"

66   I rushed in to save Polonius's reputation. "Polonius did speak. Hamlet heard him. But he thought it was the chief and wished to kill him to avenge his father. He had meant to kill him earlier that evening . . . " I broke down, unable to describe to these pagans, who had no belief in individual afterlife, the difference between dying at one's prayers and dying "unhousell'd, disappointed, unaneled."

67   This time I had shocked my audience seriously. "For a man to raise his hand against his father's brother and the one who has become his father—that is a terrible thing. The elders ought to let such a man be bewitched."

68   I nibbled at my kola nut in some perplexity, then pointed out that after all the man had killed Hamlet's father.

69   "No," pronounced the old man, speaking less to me than to the young men sitting behind the elders. "If your father's brother has killed your father, you must appeal to your father's age mates; *they* may avenge him. No man may use violence against his senior relatives." Another thought struck him. "But if his father's brother had indeed been wicked enough to bewitch Hamlet and make him mad that would be a good story indeed, for it would be his fault that Hamlet, being mad, no longer had any sense and thus was ready to kill his father's brother."

70   There was a murmur of applause. *Hamlet* was again a good story to them, but it no longer seemed quite the same story to me. As I thought over the coming complications of plot and motive, I lost courage and decided to skim over dangerous ground quickly.

71   "The great chief," I went on, "was not sorry that Hamlet had killed Polonius. It gave him a reason to send Hamlet away, with his two treacherous age mates, with letters to a chief of a far country, saying that Hamlet should be killed. But Hamlet changed the writing on their papers, so that the chief killed his age mates instead." I encountered a reproachful glare from one of the men whom I had told undetectable forgery was not merely immoral but beyond human skill. I looked the other way.

72   "Before Hamlet could return, Laertes came back for his father's funeral. The great chief told him Hamlet had killed Polonius. Laertes swore to kill Hamlet because of this, and because his sister, Ophelia, hearing her father had been killed by the man she loved, went mad and drowned in the river."

73   "Have you already forgotten what we told you?" The old man was reproachful. "One cannot take vengeance on a madman; Hamlet killed Polonius in his madness. As for the girl, she not only went mad, she was drowned. Only witches can make people drown. Water itself can't hurt anything. It is merely something one drinks and bathes in."

74   I began to get cross. "If you don't like the story, I'll stop."

75   The old man made soothing noises and himself poured me some more beer. "You tell the story well, and we are listening. But it is clear that the elders of your country have never told you what the story really means. No, don't interrupt! We believe you when you say your marriage customs are different, or your clothes and weapons. But people are the same everywhere; therefore, there are always witches and it is we, the elders, who know how witches work. We told you it was the

great chief who wished to kill Hamlet, and now your own words have proved us right. Who were Ophelia's male relatives?"

76   "There were only her father and her brother." Hamlet was clearly out of my hands.

77   "There must have been many more; this also you must ask of your elders when you get back to your country. From what you tell us, since Polonius was dead, it must have been Laertes who killed Ophelia, although I do not see the reason for it."

78   We had emptied one pot of beer, and the old men argued the point with slightly tipsy interest. Finally one of them demanded of me, "What did the servant of Polonius say on his return?"

79   With difficulty I recollected Reynaldo and his mission. "I don't think he did return before Polonius was killed."

80   "Listen," said the elder, "and I will tell you how it was and how your story will go, then you may tell me if I am right. Polonius knew his son would get into trouble, and so he did. He had many fines to pay for fighting, and debts from gambling. But he had only two ways of getting money quickly. One was to marry off his sister at once, but it is difficult to find a man who will marry a woman desired by the son of a chief. For if the chief's heir commits adultery with your wife, what can you do? Only a fool calls a case against a man who will someday be his judge. Therefore Laertes had to take the second way: he killed his sister by witchcraft, drowning her so he could secretly sell her body to the witches."

81   I raised an objection. "They found her body and buried it. Indeed Laertes jumped into the grave to see his sister once more—so, you see, the body was truly there. Hamlet, who had just come back, jumped in after him."

82   "What did I tell you?" The elder appealed to the others. "Laertes was up to no good with his sister's body. Hamlet prevented him, because the chief's heir, like a chief, does not wish any other man to grow rich and powerful. Laertes would be angry, because he would have killed his sister without benefit to himself. In our country he would try to kill Hamlet for that reason. Is this not what happened?"

83   "More or less," I admitted. "When the great chief found Hamlet was still alive, he encouraged Laertes to try to kill Hamlet and arranged a fight with machetes between them. In the fight both the young men were wounded to death. Hamlet's mother drank the poisoned beer that the chief meant for Hamlet in case he won the fight. When he saw his mother die of poison, Hamlet, dying, managed to kill his father's brother with his machete."

84   "You see, I was right!" exclaimed the elder.

85   "That was a very good story," added the old man, "and you told it with very few mistakes. There was just one more error, at the very end. The poison Hamlet's mother drank was obviously meant for the survivor

of the fight, whichever it was. If Laertes had won, the great chief would have poisoned him, for no one would know that he arranged Hamlet's death. Then, too, he need not fear Laertes' witchcraft; it takes a strong heart to kill one's only sister by witchcraft.

86   "Sometime," concluded the old man, gathering his ragged toga about him, "you must tell us some more stories of your country. We, who are elders, will instruct you in their true meaning, so that when you return to your own land your elders will see that you have not been sitting in the bush, but among those who know things and who have taught you wisdom."

(4,614 words)

VOCABULARY

hillock (3)	motif (23)	patronage (49)
accessible (3)	retorted (25)	unhousell'd (66)
calabash (7)	soliloquy (26)	unaneled (66)
hazards (9)	fratricide (32)	toga (86)
genealogical (22)	zombis (37)	

THE FACTS

1. In relating her experience with a primitive tribe in West Africa, what point does Bohannan make about language and culture?

2. While the author tells her story, we learn a great deal about the customs and beliefs of the Tiv. What are some of these customs and beliefs?

3. What is the proper style of beginning a story among the Tiv? What is our equivalent?

4. What causes the repeated breakdown in communicating the Hamlet story?

5. What desire on the part of the elders is revealed in the final paragraph?

THE STRATEGIES

1. What is the purpose for such a long introductory description of the homestead where the Hamlet story is told?

2. The story consists largely of narrative development. What other technique is used? What is its purpose?

3. Why is there no accurate Tiv translation for *school friends?*

4. If you had to translate the word *restaurant* for primitive people, what might you say?

5. What is the implied meaning of the final sentence in the selection?

6. Laura Bohannan is an anthropologist. Toward what level of education in her audience does she aim?

THE ISSUES

1. How could the Hamlet story be made comprehensible to a tribe like the Tiv?

2. Do you agree with the Englishman of the first paragraph or with Bohannan about whether or not the general plot of great stories can be understood by all people, human nature being what it is? Give reasons for your answer.

3. What advantages accrue from a culture with an oral tradition of story telling? Explain your answer.

4. How would you explain a ghost to a child? Be specific.

5. Which of the following stories would you choose to tell a group of primitive people so that they could understand it? Give reasons for your choice:
   a. Little Red Riding Hood
   b. The Scarlet Letter
   c. David and Goliath
   d. Romeo and Juliet

SUGGESTIONS FOR WRITING

1. Summarize the plot of *Othello* or some other famous play or story so that someone who does not understand English well can understand it.

2. Using all the details gathered from your reading of this essay, write a vivid description of the Tiv tribe.

▼▼

Jimmy Santiago Baca

COMING INTO LANGUAGE

JIMMY SANTIAGO BACA (b. 1952) is one among several admired Barrio writers, so-called because they emerged from the poverty and squalor of barrio life to portray their background with power and vividness. An ex-convict, he taught himself to read and write while in prison, eventually winning the American Book Award of 1988. Part Chicano and part Indian, Baca was abandoned by his parents when he was two and lived with his grandparents. By the time he was five, his mother had been murdered by her second husband, his father was dead of alcoholism, and Baca lived in an orphanage, which he escaped to survive on the streets. In time, he landed in prison on a drug charge (which he claimed was false) and was sent to maximum security and later placed in isolation because of his combative nature. Through an outside mentor, his writings gradually received international attention, and he was released from prison. Despite his tragic life, his writing—mostly poetry—dwells on rebirth rather than bitterness. Among his works are: *Immigrants in Our Own Land* (1979), *Swords of Darkness* (1981), *What's Happening?* (1982), *Martin and Meditations on the South Valley* (1987), *Black Mesa Poems* (1989), and *Working in the Dark: Reflections of a Poet of the Barrio* (1990), from which the following essay is taken.

> *What follows is a horrifying yet heart-warming autobiographical account of the author's personal journey toward poetic birth. We are allowed an intimate glance into a man's scarred and demon-filled soul and we witness how he faces the horrors of prison life, including solitary confinement and the mental ward. We see and feel his torment and hellish despair, but we also watch his slow development as a writer as he is purged of crime and violence through an appreciation of the beauty of language.*

1   On weekend graveyard shifts at St. Joseph's Hospital I worked the emergency room, mopping up pools of blood and carting plastic bags stuffed with arms, legs, and hands to the outdoor incinerator. I enjoyed the quiet, away from the screams of shotgunned, knifed, and mangled kids writhing on gurneys outside the operating rooms. Ambulance sirens shrieked and squad car lights reddened the cool nights, flashing against the hospital walls: gray—red, gray—red. On slow nights I would lock the door of the administration office, search the reference library for a book on female anatomy and, with my feet propped on the desk, leaf through the illustrations, smoking my cigarette. I was seventeen.

2   One night my eye was caught by a familiar-looking word on the spine of a book. The title was *450 Years of Chicano History in Pictures.* On the cover were black-and-white photos: Padre Hidalgo exhorting Mexican peasants to revolt against the Spanish dictators; Anglo vigilantes hanging two Mexicans from a tree; a young Mexican woman with rifle and ammunition belts crisscrossing her breast; César Chávez and field workers marching for fair wages; Chicano railroad workers laying creosote ties; Chicanas laboring at machines in textile factories; Chicanas picketing and hoisting boycott signs.

3   From the time I was seven, teachers had been punishing me for not knowing my lessons by making me stick my nose in a circle chalked on the blackboard. Ashamed of not understanding and fearful of asking questions, I dropped out of school in the ninth grade. At seventeen I still didn't know how to read, but those pictures confirmed my identity. I stole the book that night, stashing it for safety under the slop-sink until I got off work. Back at my boardinghouse, I showed the book to friends. All of us were amazed; this book told us we were alive. We, too, had defended ourselves with our fists against hostile Anglos, gasping for breath in fights with the policemen who outnumbered us. The book reflected back to us our struggle in a way that made us proud.

4   Most of my life I felt like a target in the cross hairs of a hunter's rifle. When strangers and outsiders questioned me I felt the hang-rope tighten around my neck and the trapdoor creak beneath my feet. There was nothing so humiliating as being unable to express myself, and my inarticulateness increased my sense of jeopardy, of being endangered. I felt intimidated and vulnerable, ridiculed and scorned. Behind a mask of humility, I seethed with mute rebellion.

5   Before I was eighteen, I was arrested on suspicion of murder after refusing to explain a deep cut on my forearm. With shocking speed I found myself handcuffed to a chain gang of inmates and bused to a holding facility to await trial. There I met men, prisoners, who read aloud to each other the works of Neruda, Paz, Sabines, Nemerov, and Hemingway. Never had I felt such freedom as in that dormitory. Listening to the words of these writers, I felt that invisible threat from without lessen—my sense of teetering on a rotting plank over swamp water where famished alligators clapped their horny snouts for my blood. While I listened to the words of the poets, the alligators slumbered powerless in their lairs. Their language was the magic that could liberate me from myself, transform me into another person, transport me to other places far away.

6   And when they closed the books, these Chicanos, and went into their own Chicano language, they made barrio life come alive for me in the fullness of its vitality. I began to learn my own language, the bilingual words and phrases explaining to me my place in the universe.

Every day I felt like the paper boy taking delivery of the latest news of the day.

7   Months later I was released, as I had suspected I would be. I had been guilty of nothing but shattering the windshield of my girlfriend's car in a fit of rage.

8   Two years passed. I was twenty now, and behind bars again. The federal marshals had failed to provide convincing evidence to extradite me to Arizona on a drug charge, but still I was being held. They had ninety days to prove I was guilty. The only evidence against me was that my girlfriend had been at the scene of the crime with my driver's license in her purse. They had to come up with something else. But there was nothing else. Eventually they negotiated a deal with the actual drug dealer, who took the stand against me. When the judge hit me with a million-dollar bail, I emptied my pockets on his booking desk: twenty-six cents.

9   One night in my third month in the county jail, I was mopping the floor in front of the booking desk. Some detectives had kneed an old drunk and handcuffed him to the booking bars. His shrill screams raked my nerves like a hacksaw on bone, the desperate protest of his dignity against their inhumanity. But the detectives just laughed as he tried to rise and kicked him to his knees. When they went to the bathroom to pee and the desk attendant walked to the file cabinet to pull the arrest record, I shot my arm through the bars, grabbed one of the attendant's university textbooks, and tucked it in my overalls. It was the only way I had of protesting.

10   It was late when I returned to my cell. Under my blanket I switched on a pen flashlight and opened the thick book at random, scanning the pages. I could hear the jailer making his rounds on the other tiers. The jangle of his keys and the sharp click of his boot heels intensified my solitude. Slowly I enunciated the words . . . p-o-n-d, ri-pple. It scared me that I had been reduced to this to find comfort. I always had thought reading a waste of time, that nothing could be gained by it. Only by action, by moving out into the world and confronting and challenging the obstacles, could one learn anything worth knowing.

11   Even as I tried to convince myself that I was merely curious, I became so absorbed in how the sounds created music in me and happiness, I forgot where I was. Memories began to quiver in me, glowing with a strange but familiar intimacy in which I found refuge. For a while, a deep sadness overcame me, as if I had chanced on a long-lost friend and mourned the years of separation. But soon the heartache of having missed so much of life, that had numbed me since I was a child, gave way, as if a grave illness lifted itself from me and I was cured innocently believing in the beauty of life again. I stumblingly repeated the author's name as I fell asleep, saying it over and over in the dark: Words-worth, Words-worth.

12   Before long my sister came to visit me, and I joked about taking her to a place called Kubla Khan and getting her a blind date with this *vato* named Coleridge who lived on the seacoast and was *malias* on morphine. When I asked her to make a trip into enemy territory to buy me a grammar book, she said she couldn't. Bookstores intimidated her, because she, too, could neither read nor write.

13   Days later, with a stub pencil I whittled sharp with my teeth, I propped a Red Chief notebook on my knees and wrote my first words. From that moment, a hunger for poetry possessed me.

14   Until then, I had felt as if I had been born into a raging ocean where I swam relentlessly, flailing my arms in hope of rescue, of reaching a shoreline I never sighted. Never solid ground beneath me, never a resting place. I had lived with only the desperate hope to stay afloat; that and nothing more.

15   But when at last I wrote my first words on the page, I felt an island rising beneath my feet like the back of a whale. As more and more words emerged, I could finally rest: I had a place to stand for the first time in my life. The island grew, with each page, into a continent inhabited by people I knew and mapped with the life I lived.

16   I wrote about it all—about people I had loved or hated, about the brutalities and ecstasies of my life. And, for the first time, the child in me who had witnessed and endured unspeakable terrors cried out not just in impotent despair, but with the power of language. Suddenly, through language, through writing, my grief and my joy could be shared with anyone who would listen. And I could do this all alone; I could do it anywhere. I was no longer a captive of demons eating away at me, no longer a victim of other people's mockery and loathing, that had made me clench my fist white with rage and grit my teeth to silence. Words now pleaded back with the bleak lucidity of hurt. They were wrong, those others, and now I could say it.

17   Through language I was free. I could respond, escape, indulge; embrace or reject earth or the cosmos. I was launched on an endless journey without boundaries or rules, in which I could salvage the floating fragments of my past, or be born anew in the spontaneous ignition of understanding some heretofore concealed aspect of myself. Each word steamed with the hot lava juices of my primordial making, and I crawled out of stanzas dripping with birth-blood, reborn and freed from the chaos of my life. The child in the dark room of my heart, that had never been able to find or reach the light switch, flicked it on now; and I found in the room a stranger, myself, who had waited so many years to speak again. My words struck in me lightning crackles of elation and thunderhead storms of grief.

18   When I had been in the county jail longer than anyone else, I was made a trustee. One morning, after a fist fight, I went to the unlocked and unoccupied office used for lawyer-client meetings, to think. The

bare white room with its fluorescent tube lighting seemed to expose and illuminate my dark and worthless life. And yet, for the first time, I had something to lose—my chance to read, to write; a way to live with dignity and meaning, that had opened for me when I stole that scuffed, second-hand book about the Romantic poets. In prison, the abscess had been lanced.

19   "I will never do any work in this prison system as long as I am not allowed to get my G.E.D." That's what I told the reclassification panel. The captain flicked off the tape recorder. He looked at me hard and said, "You'll never walk outta here alive. Oh, you'll work, put a copper penny on that, you'll work."

20   After that interview I was confined to deadlock maximum security in a subterranean dungeon, with ground-level chicken-wired windows painted gray. Twenty-three hours a day I was in that cell. I kept sane by borrowing books from the other cons on the tier. Then, just before Christmas, I received a letter from Harry, a charity house samaritan who doled out hot soup to the homeless in Phoenix. He had picked my name from a list of cons who had no one to write to them. I wrote back asking for a grammar book, and a week later received one of Mary Baker Eddy's treatises on salvation and redemption, with Spanish and English on opposing pages. Pacing my cell all day and most of each night, I grappled with grammar until I was able to write a long true-romance confession for a con to send to his pen pal. He paid me with a pack of smokes. Soon I had a thriving barter business, exchanging my poems and letters for novels, commissary pencils, and writing tablets.

21   One day I tore two flaps from the cardboard box that held all my belongings and punctured holes along the edge of each flap and along the border of a ream of state-issue paper. After I had aligned them to form a spine, I threaded the holes with a shoestring, and sketched on the cover a hummingbird fluttering above a rose. This was my first journal.

22   Whole afternoons I wrote, unconscious of passing time or whether it was day or night. Sunbursts exploded from the lead tip of my pencil, words that grafted me into awareness of who I was; peeled back to a burning core of bleak terror, an embryo floating in the image of water, I cracked out of the shell wide-eyed and insane. Trees grew out of the palms of my hands, the threatening otherness of life dissolved, and I became one with the air and sky, the dirt and the iron and concrete. There was no longer any distinction between the other and I. Language made bridges of fire between me and everything I saw. I entered into the blade of grass, the basketball, the con's eye and child's soul.

23   At night I flew. I conversed with floating heads in my cell, and visited strange houses where lonely women brewed tea and rocked in wicker rocking chairs listening to sad Joni Mitchell songs.

24   Before long I was frayed like a rope carrying too much weight, that suddenly snaps. I quit talking. Bars, walls, steel bunk and floor

bristled with millions of poem-making sparks. My face was no longer familiar to me. The only reality was the swirling cornucopia of images in my mind, the voices in the air. Mid-air a cactus blossom would appear, a snake-flame in blinding dance around it, stunning me like a guard's fist striking my neck from behind.

25   The prison administrators tried several tactics to get me to work. For six months, after the next monthly prison board review, they sent cons to my cell to hassle me. When the guard would open my cell door to let one of them in, I'd leap out and fight him—and get sent to thirty-day isolation. I did a lot of isolation time. But I honed my image-making talents in that sensory-deprived solitude. Finally they moved me to death row, and after that to "nut-run," the tier that housed the mentally disturbed.

26   As the months passed, I became more and more sluggish. My eyelids were heavy, I could no longer write or read. I slept all the time.

27   One day a guard took me out to the exercise field. For the first time in years I felt grass and earth under my feet. It was spring. The sun warmed my face as I sat on the bleachers watching the cons box and run, hit the handball, lift weights. Some of them stopped to ask how I was, but I found it impossible to utter a syllable. My tongue would not move, saliva drooled from the corners of my mouth. I had been so heavily medicated I could not summon the slightest gesture. Yet inside me a small voice cried out, I am fine! I am hurt now but I will come back! I am fine!

28   Back in my cell, for weeks I refused to eat. Styrofoam cups of urine and hot water were hurled at me. Other things happened. There were beatings, shock therapy, intimidation.

29   Later, I regained some clarity of mind. But there was a place in my heart where I had died. My life had compressed itself into an unbearable dread of being. The strain had been too much. I had stepped over that line where a human being has lost more than he can bear, where the pain is too intense, and he knows he is changed forever. I was now capable of killing, coldly and without feeling. I was empty, as I have never, before or since, known emptiness. I had no connection to this life.

30   But then, the encroaching darkness that began to envelop me forced me to re-form and give birth to myself again in the chaos. I withdrew even deeper into the world of language, cleaving the diamonds of verbs and nouns, plunging into the brilliant light of poetry's regenerative mystery. Words gave off rings of white energy, radar signals from powers beyond me that infused me with truth. I believed what I wrote, because I wrote what was true. My words did not come from books or textual formulas, but from a deep faith in the voice of my heart.

31   I had been steeped in self-loathing and rejected by everyone and everything—society, family, cons, God and demons. But now I had

become as the burning ember floating in darkness that descends on a dry leaf and sets flame to forests. The word was the ember and the forest was my life.

32   I was born a poet one noon, gazing at weeds and creosoted grass at the base of a telephone pole outside my grilled cell window. The words I wrote then sailed me out of myself, and I was transported and metamorphosed into the images they made. From the dirty brown blades of grass came bolts of electrical light that jolted loose my old self; through the top of my head that self was released and reshaped in the clump of scrawny grass. Through language I became the grass, speaking its language and feeling its green feelings and black root sensations. Earth was my mother and I bathed in sunshine. Minuscule speckles of sunlight passed through my green skin and metabolized in my blood.

33   Writing bridged my divided life of prisoner and free man. I wrote of the emotional butchery of prisons, and of my acute gratitude for poetry. Where my blind doubt and spontaneous trust in life met, I discovered empathy and compassion. The power to express myself was a welcome storm rasping at tendril roots, flooding my soul's cracked dirt. Writing was water that cleansed the wound and fed the parched root of my heart.

34   I wrote to sublimate my rage, from a place where all hope is gone, from a madness of having been damaged too much, from a silence of killing rage. I wrote to avenge the betrayals of a lifetime, to purge the bitterness of injustice. I wrote with a deep groan of doom in my blood, bewildered and dumbstruck; from an indestructible love of life, to affirm breath and laughter and the abiding innocence of things. I wrote the way I wept, and danced, and made love.

(3,131 words)

VOCABULARY

incinerator (1)	enunciated (10)	treatises (20)
inarticulateness (4)	primordial (17)	regenerative (30)
lairs (5)	subterranean (20)	creosoted (32)
extradite (8)	samaritan (20)	metamorphosed (32)

THE FACTS

1. Why did the author drop out of school in ninth grade?

2. What reason does the author offer for his having been sent to prison on a murder charge?

3. Who are Wordsworth and Coleridge? How do they relate to the author?

4. What was the "island" on which the author finally could rest while he was in jail? (See paragraph 15.)

5. When a prison guard finally took the author out to the exercise field, why couldn't he talk or even make the slightest gesture?

THE STRATEGIES

1. Who is the voice in this essay? What kind of person is revealed? How do you feel about him? Why does he seem to be writing the essay?

2. The author's experience is rendered in separate steps that could be called "the process of regeneration." What are the steps? List them individually as you discern them.

3. Where in this essay does the author reveal his poetic talent? Find specific examples of poetic utterances.

4. How does the author indicate the passage of time?

5. What do you think the author meant when he made the following statement: "Most of my life I felt like a target in the cross hairs of a hunter's rifle"? Explain this statement in your own words.

THE ISSUES

1. Which aspect of the author's artistic journey do you consider the climax of his experience as related in this essay? In other words, at which point does he recognize the possibilities inherent in language? Give reasons for your choice.

2. How can you explain the author's grasp of English grammar despite the fact that he was a school dropout?

3. How would you characterize the essence of Baca's life before he became a writer? How was it possible for him to become a writer?

4. What is your opinion of the punishment meted out by the author's teachers from the time he was seven years old? What typical results does this kind of pedagogy win?

5. Do you consider it a good idea to encourage prison inmates to develop their talents while in prison? Why or why not? If you believe the idea to have merit, what process would you suggest for assessing and promoting the prisoners' talents? If you believe the idea has no merit, indicate why.

SUGGESTIONS FOR WRITING

1. Write an essay in which you praise Baca for the vivid, poetic, and powerful language he uses. Illustrate your thesis with examples from the essay.

2. Write an essay either attacking or defending our prison system in the way it helps inmates to improve themselves intellectually.

▼▼

Carl Sandburg

THREES

CARL SANDBURG (1878–1967), American poet and biographer, was born in Galesburg, Illinois, to poor Swedish immigrants. He won a Pulitzer Prize for his *Complete Poems* (1950) and also for his ambitious multivolume biography of Abraham Lincoln (1926–1939).

This poem touches on the ideals that humans live by and are prepared to die for.

I was a boy when I heard three red words
a thousand Frenchmen died in the streets
for: Liberty, Equality, Fraternity—I asked
why men die for words.

5 I was older; men with mustaches, sideburns,
lilacs, told me the high golden words are:
Mother, Home, and Heaven—other older men with
face decorations said: God, Duty, Immortality
—they sang these threes slow from deep lungs.

10 Years ticked off their say-so on the great clocks
of doom and damnation, soup and nuts: meteors flashed
their say-so: and out of great Russia came three
dusky syllables workmen took guns and went out to die
for: Bread, Peace, Land.

15 And I met a marine of the U.S.A., a leatherneck with
a girl on his knee for a memory in ports circling the
earth and he said: Tell me how to say three things
and I always get by—gimme a plate of ham and eggs—
how much?—and, do you love me, kid?

(164 words)

THE FACTS

1. What is the theme of this poem?

2. At this stage in your life, on which of the word-clusters mentioned do you place *highest* value? Why?

3. What values are implied by each word-cluster?

4. What kind of person does the marine of the last stanza appear to be?

THE STRATEGIES

1. Who is the speaker in the poem? What does he represent?

2. What is the connotation of "mustaches, sideburns, / lilacs" in the second stanza?

3. What is the effect of juxtaposing such words as "doom and damnation" with "soup and nuts"?

4. Why does the poet allude to Russia in the third stanza?

5. How does the poet indicate the passing of time?

THE ISSUES

1. What is the association of Frenchmen with the words Liberty, Equality, Fraternity?

2. As people age, do they tend to become more idealistic or more cynical? Give reasons for your answer.

3. Are the syllables alluded to in the third stanza still "dusky" today?

4. How does this poem relate to the chapter we are studying?

SUGGESTIONS FOR WRITING

1. Write an analysis of the meaning of this poem.

2. Write an essay on the three most important words in your life and explain why they are so important to you.

ISSUE FOR CRITICAL
THINKING AND DEBATE

▼▼

AFFIRMATIVE ACTION

Affirmative action is a spin-off from the Fourteenth Constitutional Amendment, which guarantees the civil rights of blacks. No longer are employers or schools able to say, "Well, we tried to hire or admit minority candidates, but they just didn't apply or they weren't well enough qualified." As the word "action" in the term suggests, the system requires employers or admissions officers to actively compensate for past discriminations by advertising formally instead of through mere word of mouth, by recruiting at institutions where minorities reside, and by abolishing discriminatory tests. In the past thirty years, affirmative action has gradually led to the quota system—that is, proposing numerical goals for hiring minorities or women. This new approach has resulted in angry outbursts by people who feel that affirmative action is leading to reverse discrimination. In fact, a 1978 Supreme Court Decision ruled in favor of a white medical student who sued the University of California because he felt that he had been grievously hurt by a quota system which allowed a minority student less qualified than he to enroll.

Today the question of whether affirmative action truly provides equal opportunity to under-represented minorities is still anxiously being debated, especially when the system requires employers to hire a specific number of minority applicants.

The Problem We All Live With (1964), Norman Rockwell's famous painting of the little black girl being escorted to school by four burly U.S. Marshals, represents the early roots of affirmative action—making sure that black students were admitted to the same schools as whites. It is difficult for us today to remember that not so long ago in our history, black children were excluded from schools belonging to white neighborhoods, just as they were excluded from the front of the bus and from drinking at white water fountains. Probing the painting, one is struck by the little girl's innate dignity as she strides along, hair neatly tied into pigtails and wearing a primly starched dress, ready to do her part in the classroom. Her pose expresses determination and a sense of self-worth.

The three essays that follow the Rockwell painting reflect three different points of view on affirmative action. Anna Quindlen's "Great White Myth" argues forthrightly that the idea, widely espoused, that blacks are not as talented as whites is a myth in need of immediate

Norman Rockwell, The Problem We All Live With. *Original oil painting for* Look, *1964. Printed by permission of the Norman Rockwell Family Trust. Copyright © 1997 the Norman Rockwell Family Trust. Photo courtesy of The Norman Rockwell Museum at Stockbridge.*

remedy, even if doing so annoys some whites. In another approach, Wilma J. Moore, a grandmother concerned about her grandchildren's education, worries that affirmative action, when pushed to its logical conclusion, may well lead to ethnic persecution rather than racial balance. Finally, the student essay argues that affirmative action is not only appropriate but also desirable because discrimination is still prevalent in our society.

▼▼

Anna Quindlen

THE GREAT WHITE MYTH

ANNA QUINDLEN (b. 1953) is an American journalist based at the *New York Times.* She writes a syndicated column titled "Public and Private," noted for its unaffected style and for addressing universal problems through every-day incidents. Quindlen has written a best-selling novel, *Object Lessons* (1991), and her columns have been collected in a book, *Living Out Loud* (1988).

1   In a college classroom, a young white man rises and asks about the future. What, he wants to know, can it possibly hold for him when most

of the jobs, most of the good positions, most of the spots in professional schools are being given to women and, most especially, to blacks?

2   The temptation to be short, sarcastic, incredulous in reply is powerful. But you have to remember that kids learn their lessons from adults. That's what the mother of two black children who were sprayed with white paint in the Bronx said last week about the assailants, teenagers who called her son and daughter "nigger" and vowed they would turn them white. "Can you imagine what they are being taught at home?" she asked.

3   A nation of laws, we like to believe that when they are changed, attitudes will change along with them. This is naïve. America continues to be a country whose people are obsessed with some spurious pecking order. Leaving, at the bottom: blacks to be taught at age 12 and 14 through the utter humiliation of having their faces cleaned with paint thinner that there are those who think that even white in a bottle is better than not white at all.

4   Each generation finds its own reasons to hate. The worried young white men I've met on college campuses in the last year have internalized the newest myth of American race relations, and it has made them bitter. It is called affirmative action, a.k.a. the systematic oppression of white men. All good things in life, they've learned, from college admission to executive position, are being given to black citizens. The verb is ubiquitous: given.

5   Never mind that you can walk through the offices of almost any big company and see a sea of white faces. Never mind that with all that has been written about preferential treatment for minority law students, only about 7,500 of the 127,000 students enrolled in law school last year were African-American. Never mind that only 3 percent of the doctors in this country are black.

6   Never mind that in the good old days preferential treatment was routinely given to brothers and sons of workers in certain lines of work. Perceptions of programs to educate and hire more black citizens as, in part, an antidote to decades of systematic exclusion have been inflated to enormous proportions in the public mind. Like hot air balloons they fill up the blue sky of the American landscape with the gaudy stripes of hyperbole. Listen and you will believe that the construction sites, the precinct houses, the investment banks are filled with African-Americans.

7   Unless you actually visit them.

8   The opponents of affirmative action programs say they are opposing the rank unfairness of preferential treatment. But there was no great hue and cry when colleges were candid about wanting to have geographic diversity, perhaps giving the kid from Montana an edge. There has been no national outcry when legacy applicants whose transcripts were supplemented by Dad's alumni status—and cash contributions to the college—were admitted over more qualified comers. We

somehow only discovered that life was not fair when the beneficiaries happened to be black.

9   And so the chasm widens. The old myth was the black American incapable of prosperity. It was common knowledge that welfare was purely a benefits program for blacks; it was common knowledge although it was false. The percentage of whites on public assistance is almost identical to the percentage of blacks.

10   The new myth is that the world is full of black Americans prospering unfairly at white expense, and anecdotal evidence abounds. The stories about the incompetent black co-worker always leave out two things: the incompetent white co-workers and the talented black ones. They also leave out the tendency of so many managers to hire those who seem most like themselves when young.

11   "It seems like if you're a white male you don't have a chance," said another young man on a campus where a scant 5 percent of his classmates were black. What the kid really means is that he no longer has the edge, that the rules of a system that may have served his father well have changed. It is one of those good-old-days constructs to believe it was a system based purely on merit, but we know that's not true. It is a system that once favored him, and others like him. Now sometimes—just sometimes—it favors someone different.

(755 words)

VOCABULARY

incredulous (2)	preferential (5)	beneficiaries (8)
spurious (3)	hyperbole (6)	anecdotal (10)
ubiquitous (4)	precinct (6)	

THE FACTS

1. What is the question asked by the young white man in a college classroom (paragraph 1)?

2. The author states that "each generation finds its own reasons to hate." What is the reason for the bitterness revealed by worried white males on college campuses?

3. What percentage of doctors in this country are black?

4. According to the author, is it true that the construction sites, the precinct houses, and the investment banks of the United States are presently filled with African Americans?

5. What is the new myth of today? What is the reality?

THE STRATEGIES

1. What about the author's style is indicative of her profession?

2. What is the purpose of repeating "Never mind" three times in paragraph 5 and again once at the start of paragraph 6?

3. What is the effect of paragraph 7?

4. Where in the essay does the author use figurative language? What is the effect?

5. What is Quindlen's proposition? Where is it stated?

THE ISSUES

1. The author states that America is a nation obsessed with some spurious pecking order (see paragraph 3). What aspects of our country indicate that we are also a nation committed to human rights and to the value of individuals?

2. If the author is right in asserting that "each generation finds its own reason to hate," then what reason to hate do you find in your generation? Be specific in citing these reasons. If you believe her assertion is wrong, state why.

3. In your view, can one be opposed to affirmative action and still be a supporter of civil rights? Explain your answer.

4. What is your reaction to the author's implication, in the final paragraph of her essay, that it is quite all right for whites no longer to have an edge over blacks?

5. In an ideal world, how do you believe equality of school and job opportunity should be handled? What laws would you support?

SUGGESTIONS FOR WRITING

1. Write an essay in which you answer the question, "Do people in the United States have equal opportunities to achieve success?" Bolster your argument with facts, expert testimony, and experience.

2. Write an essay either for or against quota systems in hiring underrepresented minorities.

▼▼

Wilma J. Moore

THE ROUTE TO 9066

WILMA J. MOORE (b. 1936) is a free-lance writer residing in Santa Rosa, California. She received a B.A. in Humanities and Spanish from the University of San Francisco, but chose to make a career of being a housewife, mother, and grandmother. She is presently fulfilling one of her intellectual interests, archaeology, by serving as president of the Archaeological Association of America, North Coast Chapter. She loves to read, think about what she has read, and then write about it. Several of her essays have been published in *The Freeman*, a periodical voicing conservative thought.

1   Recently I had occasion to fill out an application form on behalf of my grandson for admission to a private elementary school. At the bottom of the application was a statement that the school ". . . is committed to achieving a well-balanced student population which reflects the ethnic and cultural diversity of San Francisco." At first glance this statement appears to be simply a rephrasing of the traditional policy of granting equal opportunity regardless of race, color, or creed. However, a second reading of those words reveals a very subtle shift from a policy of colorblindness to a policy of intense color awareness.

2   In spite of the dubious rationality of attempting to duplicate a city's racial percentages in the classroom, there are probably a number of good reasons that "ethnic diversity" could be considered a reasonable goal. One might be that a knowledge and understanding of cultures created by people of different races and different geographic locations is part of the definition of a liberal education. Another might be the wish to right past wrongs against many racial groups whose children were denied the advantages of a private education for no other reason than that they were born to non-Anglo-Saxon Protestant parents. A third reason might be to contribute to the elimination of racial prejudice and thus to the enhancement of world peace. There may even be other noble objectives that at the moment do not occur to me.

3   It would seem that, if one wished to offset a predominantly WASP student body, ensure cultural enrichment, and create an environment where racial tolerance could flower, one would actively seek those families in the community who had just immigrated to this country and who carried with them the language and customs of a different culture. One might also expect these schools to try to enroll children from households in which the members spoke a foreign language or in which the members still adhered to foreign religious or social customs

though they had been in this country for some time. However, it seems that satisfying their positive goals does not require "progressive" schools to follow either of these positive criteria. Instead it means satisfying a negative one, i.e., that a prospective student *not* have an English-speaking white Anglo-Saxon Protestant lineage.

4   If their family names are Stroganov, Patel, or Yamamoto the children must have an enriching cultural heritage to bring to the school to balance the culture shared by the Smiths, Browns, and Joneses who are already on the student roster. Never mind that the Stroganovs have never spoken a word of Russian and never eat borscht, that the Patel child's mother is a corporate lawyer who wouldn't be caught dead in a sari and that no one in the family likes curry, and that the parents and children in the Yamamoto clan have never been to Japan, attend a Methodist church every Sunday, listen mostly to rock and roll music, and number hamburgers and French fries among their favorite foods. Never mind these or any of the other features that characterize their lives as American and not as some other culture. They fulfill the criterion as representatives of Eastern European, Indian, and Japanese culture, so they'll balance the student population nicely.

5   The disturbing premise that underlies this policy is that ethnic origin carries with it certain irrevocable cultural characteristics. If one is born of Russian parents one must somehow carry with him the genes of a Russian persona which inevitably produces Russian "culture." Because a child has Indian parents or an Indian ancestor, he or she will therefore be the carrier of a distinctive Indian essence. If one has an Oriental name and facial features, then this person also has an "Oriental perspective" on life.

6   When I hear arguments in favor of an admissions policy like that of the school my grandson might attend, I hear the voices of reasonable people in a different historical context whose noble objectives justified something that turned out to be just the opposite. As uncomfortable as it may be for the morally righteous of today to contemplate, an admissions policy that uses race or ethnic origin as a criterion has as its foundation the premise that justified Executive Order 9066, which set in motion the relocation of anyone of Japanese descent from the West Coast in 1942.

7   In California just after Pearl Harbor, one argument repeated *ad nauseam* by radio commentators, in letters to the editor, in newspaper editorials, and in magazine articles was that blood ties were stronger than political or social ones, and that no matter how long people of Japanese descent had lived in this country, no matter how many generations their families might count on this soil, they were still Japanese, and a part of them would forever owe allegiance to the Emperor of Japan. Since they were not "one of us," their loyalty was to be questioned, their civil liberties revoked, their property confiscated, their movements restricted, and ultimately their lives uprooted and their

persons segregated—all because, by an accident of fate, they had the racial lineage of a political enemy.

8   The premise that children born of a certain racial caste are destined to share exclusive cultural preferences, personality characteristics, or a certain perspective on life is patently false. Yet thoughtful people everywhere seem unwittingly to be advocating an academic admissions criterion based squarely on that premise. The heterogeneity which characterized the life of persons of Japanese descent in the United States at the beginning of 1942 was ignored, submerged beneath a mountain of misconceptions regarding some ineluctable relationship between race and culture, between ethnic origin and values, between family origin and behavior.

9   Ethnic diversity on this level is a superficial goal resting on a fallacious premise which is ominous in its implications. Today the premise of inborn cultural characteristics may net a relatively benign result. Tomorrow it may reap a harvest of misery and shame. Today it may produce an ethnically balanced and peacefully interacting student body. Tomorrow it may erupt in a movement toward racial exclusion. Today this policy intends to educate children in the ways of enlightened civilization which liberates the individual from any stigma attached to a racial or cultural stereotype. Tomorrow, this same policy might educate children in the ways of collectivist tribal barbarity by identifying each other by that very stereotype.

10   The advocates of Executive Order 9066 justified their actions just as the advocates of "ethnic and cultural diversity" do today. In the process they became blind to their own racism and hardened to the results of the despotism generated by their erroneous assumptions. Let's hope modern school administrators and parents will recognize their own faulty logic in time before the color-blind society they so fervently hope to engineer becomes one that makes the blood lines of one's ancestors more important than the working of one's mind.

(1,147 words)

VOCABULARY

dubious (2)	confiscated (7)	fallacious (9)
rationality (3)	lineage (7)	benign (9)
borscht (4)	caste (8)	stigma (9)
criterion (4)	patently (8)	collectivist (9)
premise (5)	unwittingly (8)	barbarity (9)
irrevocable (5)	heterogeneity (8)	despotism (10)
essence (5)	ineluctable (8)	

THE FACTS

1. What experience triggered off the author's argument concerning affirmative action?

2. What hypothetically good reasons might exist for attempting to achieve a student population that reflects the racial balance of the community? Name at least one.

3. Why doesn't the author believe that coming from a certain ethnic background guarantees an expression of that background?

4. To what other historical action does the author compare the policy of creating a racial or ethnic balance in our schools?

5. What did the advocates of Executive Order 9066 have in common with today's advocates of "ethnic and cultural diversity"?

THE STRATEGIES

1. What does the title of the essay presume on the part of the reader? Is the presumption warranted?

2. Since the author's stance is against affirmative action, why does she list some good reasons for wanting to achieve racial percentages in the classroom? Doesn't presenting these reasons defeat her purpose?

3. What rhetorical techniques does the author use in paragraph 9 to achieve emphasis and clarity?

4. The author is primarily a housewife and mother. Does her style reflect the stereotypical ideas about housewives? Explain your answer.

5. How would you re-phrase the author's argument into your own words? Use only one full sentence.

THE ISSUES

1. In what way does Moore disagree with Quindlen? Demonstrate the major difference in their assumptions.

2. If you were African American, Native American, Hispanic, or female, whom would you rather have as your advocate—Quindlen or Moore? Give reasons for your choice.

3. How can we rationalize the actions of our government in 1942, when Executive Order 9066 was given?

4. What is your view on racial destiny? Do you believe that if a person bears certain racial bodily features, then that same person inevitably reflects the cultural tendencies of that race? Or, do you believe that members of races create a heterogeneous group?

5. How do you think recipients of affirmative action feel about the benefits they have received? How would you feel?

SUGGESTIONS FOR WRITING

1. Write an essay in which you take the position that affirmative action, especially the quota system, is demoralizing to the recipient.

2. Write an essay in which you argue that affirmative action is worth the trouble it causes because it symbolizes our nation's commitment to civil rights.

|

First Draft

Becky Winkler, University of Georgia

Affirmative Action and Women

Not as
redundant Taking a stand for or against affirmative action is not an easy

thing to do. Many different people publish ~~many~~ differ*ing*
sounds
better perspectives and it is not hard to get confused amongst
takes a *all the voices*
stand ~~everybody else's consequences and realities.~~ I myself have

wavered over time and only recently have come to a firm *was*
that Affirmative Action *ambiguous*
decision ~~as to what I feel~~ is ~~just~~ for the majority (you can never
right
Correct make everyone happy).
capitalization
First, let us define what affirmative action is. According to

Teresa Amott and Julie Matthaei in their book <u>Race Gender and</u>
smoother *are programs intended to better the positions of women*
<u>Work</u> (1996), affirmative action programs, encompass a broad
and minorities in the workforce. They

spectrum, ~~This~~ includ*ing* public policies such as set asides and

contract compliance. Set asides force government organizations

to purchase a certain percentage of their goods and services

from minority or women owned companies. Contract
needs
to be Compliance obligates companies that do business with the
lowercase *employee base*
government to diversify their ~~workers~~. Affirmative Action
sounds *an array of*
better, programs also include voluntary efforts made by privately owned
Wordy *influence*
businesses and educational institutions. These actions ~~can be~~

Winkler 2

~~seen in~~ hiring or promotion efforts and ~~in~~ admissions policies. *corrects*

Steps taken toward affirmative action can be as simple as more *capitalization*

widely publicizing job openings or using a greater variety of

qualifications for admission ~~in order~~ to broaden and diversify *sounds better*

~~their~~ workforce or student body. Lastly, affirmative action also *corrects it*

includes legislation to prevent discrimination or attack it where it

has been found. *corrects*

    For those ~~against~~ affirmative action (who think) ~~it~~ is *capitalization*

unnecessary, I ask ~~you~~ this: If equality is so prevalent already,

then why do white women still earn only $.75 ~~on the~~ *for every* dollar ~~that~~

~~every~~ white man earns? (RGW, 1996) ~~The reality of what~~ *Insert A for clarification*

~~minority women earn compared to whit men is even more~~ *correct spelling*

~~heartbreaking.~~

   Insert B for detail, enhancing paper

    Affirmative action is necessary and, slowly but surely, it is *corrects*

With AA, many more primary *capitalization*

gaining effectiveness. ~~Although the proportions are still not~~ *clarifies*

sector jobs are now held by women *than* ever *before.*

~~equal to the representation of white males, primary sector jobs~~

~~are now open to and held by white women and women of color.~~

Before affirmative action, this would never have been possible *corrects capitalization*

(RGW, 1996). Primary sector jobs are those that offer high

salaries, security, upward mobility, high status, and autonomy.

These gains are especially evident in the public government *sounds better*

where

sector of the economy, ~~since their~~ affirmative action programs *corrects capitalization*

For example,

are stringent and mandatory. In 1990, government and private *clarifies*

nonprofit agencies employed 90% of Black professional women,

74% of Black female technical workers, and 50% of Black female

statistic *it is*

managers (RGW, 1996). This is ~~both~~ good news; yet sad that *clarifies*

Winkler 3

tr   these ‸women can /only \ find jobs/ where people are required to   **adds detail**
~~equally qualified~~ [equally qualified inserted above]

hire them.

unecessary ~~As has been shown,~~ it would be a shame if affirmative action   **corrects capitalization**

programs were thrown away now that they are finally beginning

to show results of equality, however concentrated ~~it~~ *they* may be in   **corrects pronoun**

certain areas of our economy. I wish affirmative action programs   **corrects capitalization**

were not necessary, but the reality is that discrimination is still

highly prevalent in our society, ~~and~~ until the day comes when   **makes more sense**

employers are blind to race and gender, we will continue to be in

dire need of affirmative action programs in <u>every</u> sector of the   **corrects capitalization**
economy.

__Insert A__ For the same work, Native American women earn 62%, Black women earn 64%, and Chicanas earn 50% of what white men earn.

__Insert B__ ¶ (new paragraph) Opponents of Affirmative Action often use the myth of the model minority to prove AA programs are not really needed. This theory began by asserting that Japanese people, and later the entire Asian population, achieve on par with majority groups without the help of Affirmative Action. Asians as a group are praised for their high standards of academic achievement so often that this expectation has become a stereotype that applies to every individual of the race. This stereotype has both positive and negative effects. It masks the poverty Asians in this country often suffer and hides the prevalence of self-exploitation. It also has a negative effect on minorities as a whole, because they are all expected to be able to reach the same level of achievement that some Asian students have and are termed lazy and unintelligent if they don't (<u>RGW</u>, 1996).

I

Final Draft

Becky Winkler, University of Georgia

Affirmative Action and Women

Taking a stand for or against Affirmative Action is not an easy
thing to do. Many different people publish differing perspectives
and it is not hard to get confused amongst all the voices. I myself
have wavered over time and only recently have come to a firm
decision that Affirmative Action is right for the majority (you can
never make everyone happy).

First, let us define what Affirmative Action is. According to
Teresa Amott and Julie Matthaei in their book <u>Race Gender and
Work</u> (1996), Affirmative Action programs are programs
intended to better the positions of women and minorities in the
work force. They encompass a broad spectrum, including public
policies such as set asides and contract compliance. Set asides
force government organizations to purchase a certain percentage
of their goods and services from minority or women owned
companies. Contract compliance obligates companies that do
business with the government to diversify their employee base.
Affirmative Action programs also include an array of <u>voluntary</u>
efforts made by privately owned businesses and educational
institutions. These actions influence hiring or promotion efforts
and admissions policies. Steps taken toward Affirmative Action
can be as simple as more widely publicizing job openings or using

a greater variety of qualifications for admission to broaden and diversify the workforce or student body. Lastly, Affirmative Action also includes legislation to prevent discrimination or attack it where it has been found.

For those who think Affirmative Action is unnecessary, I ask this: If equality is so prevalent already, then why do white women still earn only $.75 for every dollar white men earn? For the same work, Native American women earn 62%, Black women earn 64%, and Chicanas earn 50% of what white men earn (RGW, 1996).

Opponents of Affirmative Action often use the myth of the model minority to prove AA programs are not really needed. This theory began by asserting that Japanese people, and later the entire Asian population, achieve on par with majority groups without the help of Affirmative Action. Asians as a group are praised for their high standards of academic achievement so often that this expectation has become a stereotype that applies to every individual of the race. This stereotype has both positive and negative effects. It masks the poverty Asians in this country often suffer and hides the prevalence of self-exploitation. It also has a negative effect on minorities as a whole, because they are all expected to be able to reach the same level of achievement that some Asian students have and are termed lazy and unintelligent if they don't (RGW, 1996).

Affirmative Action is necessary and, slowly but surely, it is gaining effectiveness. With AA, many more primary sector jobs are now held by women than ever before. Before Affirmative Action, this would never have been possible (<u>RGW</u>, 1996). Primary sector jobs are those that offer high salaries, security, upward mobility, high status, and autonomy. These gains are especially evident in the public government sector of the economy, where Affirmative Action programs are stringent and mandatory. For example, in 1990, government and private nonprofit agencies employed 90% of Black professional women, 74% of Black female technical workers, and 50% of Black female managers (<u>RGW</u>, 1996). This statistic is good news; yet it is sad that these equally qualified women can find jobs only where people are required to hire them.

It would be a shame if Affirmative Action programs were thrown away now that they are finally beginning to show results of equality, however concentrated they may be in certain areas of our economy. I wish Affirmative Action programs were not necessary, but the reality is that discrimination is still highly prevalent in our society. Until the day comes when employers are blind to race and gender, we will continue to be in dire need of Affirmative Action programs in <u>every</u> sector of the economy.

How I Write

Unless I have a long paper to write (over 4 pages), I prefer to write my rough draft by hand. For some strange reason, I am more comfortable with a pad of regular lined paper and a black pen than I am with any modern day technology. I prefer to save the assistance of the computer until I know exactly what I want to say and how I want to say it.

When I have my materials at hand, I sit in a well-lit area and begin to write whatever is in my head. I like to work wherever I feel like on that particular day. I can work equally well at home, in the library, at the local café, or outdoors. I don't like to pay too much attention to how correct my writing is until I get all my initial outbursts on paper. If I concentrate too hard on how my ideas conform to standards, I lose the spirit of my statement. This, of course, explains the extraordinary amount of corrections my work always needs.

I also like to get others to proofread my paper after I'm through with it. I believe an outside perspective is good for the writing because others will often see changes you might have initially overlooked. You can always make an executive decision regarding others' suggestions; you don't have to listen to everything everyone says. After all, your writing is your own creation.

How I Wrote This Essay

After I learned what my topic was, I started to look around and see if I already had any related resources. I remembered a textbook I am currently using for a course had something about Affirmative Action in it, so I started looking there. Luckily, it had enough information in it that I didn't have to search anywhere else.

I began to jot down specific examples to back up my beliefs, using the index of the book to locate what I needed. Gradually, a certain framework appeared in my head, so using that, I began my rough draft. Part of my revising I do while I write the rough draft by going back from time to time and rereading what I've written. I wrote only one draft, but the revisions you see are the results of about six attempts of proofreading. The easiest part was knowing what direction I wanted the paper to take—that which supports Affirmative Action. The hardest part was picking and choosing among the details to find those that served my purpose best.

My Writing Tip

The main suggestion I have is to make yourself fully comfortable before you begin to write. Your writing will sound much more natural if you feel natural writing it. Make yourself some tea or hang out on your favorite couch while you work; put some relaxing music on in the background or go to a favorite spot. Whatever it takes to make you relax, do it.

CHAPTER WRITING ASSIGNMENTS

▼▼▼

1. Write an essay indicating how a study of semantics can prevent quarrels between persons as well as governments. Use specific examples to strengthen your points.

2. Using all of the information gleaned from this chapter, write an essay in which you demonstrate how a knowledge of semantics can help improve writing.

WRITING ASSIGNMENTS FOR A SPECIFIC AUDIENCE

▼▼▼

1. Write a letter addressed to the Admissions Officer of an imaginary professional school to which you were not admitted because your slot was filled by an under represented minority student. You are disappointed because your grades and examination scores were higher than those of the admitted student. Begin your letter with "Dear Admissions Officer."

2. Prepare a written address to a group of junior high school students explaining the concept of affirmative action to them. Make sure that your examples are appropriate and that your vocabulary is at the right level.

COLLABORATIVE WRITING PROJECT

▼▼▼

1. Divide the class into groups of all males or all females. Have each group reread Judy Syfers' essay "I Want a Wife" (pp. 646–48). Then have the male groups come up with examples for writing an essay titled, "I Want a Husband" while the female groups find examples for writing an essay titled, "I Want to Be a Wife." Once the examples have been noted, have each student develop his or her essay.

2. Having read Jimmy Santiago Baca's "Coming Into Language," (pp. 712–18) join a group of five or six other students with whom you discuss the author's use of language. Make a list of the passages everyone in your group considers particularly vivid, powerful, or memorable. Then write an essay analyzing the language and indicating how it affected you, using the passages pointed out by the group as evidence.

▼▼▼

OPTIONAL ASSIGNMENTS

ASSIGNMENT I

▼▼

THE RESEARCH PAPER

WHY ENGLISH INSTRUCTORS ASSIGN RESEARCH PAPERS

Students rarely greet the research paper with joy, but it still remains one of the most important of all college assignments. Writing one entails thinking critically about a subject, tracking down and evaluating facts for relevance and truth, organizing materials in support of a thesis, and cultivating a readable style. Success in college depends largely on the acquisition of these skills, which are also essential for accomplishment in business, the major professions, and even in private life. Salespeople often research a market and analyze it for trends; lawyers track down facts and organize them in preparing briefs and contracts; journalists depend on investigative research to gather material for stories. Engineers, nurses, secretaries, actors, architects, insurance agents—virtually all the professions rely on and use the research techniques exemplified in this chapter.

HOW TO CHOOSE YOUR TOPIC

Typically, English instructors grant students the freedom to choose their own research topics, thus promoting exploration and self-discovery. If such a choice is indeed available to you, we recommend some preliminary browsing through the library until you come across a subject that arouses your curiosity—be it primitive Indians, the reign of the last empress of China, some influential sports figure, the complexities of the New York stock exchange, children's psychological problems, or the fiction or poetry of a modern writer. Here are some tips on finding a suitable topic:

1. Try working with a familiar subject. For instance, you may have been fascinated by historical attempts of the super-rich to manipulate the U.S. economy such as the Gould-Fisk scheme to corner gold in 1869, with the consequent Black Friday market panic. Now you must find out more about Jay Gould, who became symbolic of autocratic business practices and was hated by most American businesspeople. Research will supply the necessary information.

2. If familiarity fails, try an entirely new area. Perhaps you have always wanted to learn about Lenin's philosophy of government, genetic engineering, evolution in the Paleozoic era, the Roman empress Galla Placidia, the causes of earthquakes, pre-Columbian art, or the historical causes for the political unrest in Ireland. A research paper finally gives you the opportunity.

3. Use books and magazines to suggest possible topics. The library is a gold mine of hidden information. Browse through book stacks and magazine racks. Some topic of interest is bound to leap out at you.

Avoid topics for which a single source can provide all the needed information; those that require no development but end as soon as started; those so popular that everything about them has already been written and said; those so controversial that you have only fresh fuel to add to the already raging fire; or those decidedly unsuited to your audience, as for example, a paper advocating radical revision of the U.S. Constitution and written for a teacher who is a conservative Republican.

HOW TO NARROW YOUR SUBJECT

Good research papers deal with topics of modest and workable proportions. To attempt a paper on the galaxies of the universe or on World War II is to attempt the impossible. A simple but practical way to narrow your subject is to subdivide it into progressively smaller units until you reach a topic specific enough for a paper. The following diagram on the sport of fencing illustrates what we mean:

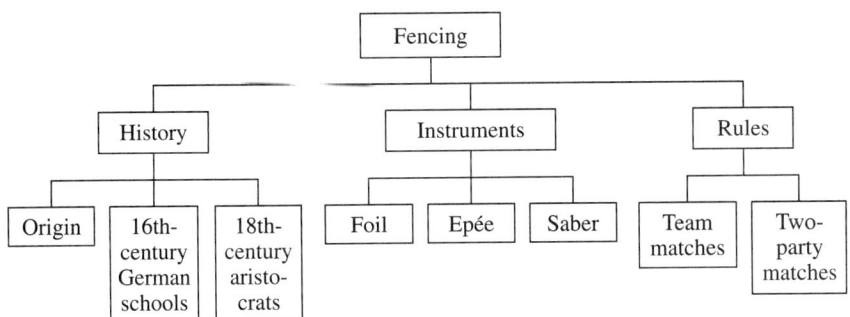

Any of the entries found on the lowest subdivision is a properly narrowed subject. For instance, you could write a useful paper on the sixteenth-century German schools that taught fencing to European gentlemen, or on the use of the saber in fencing, or on the rules of modern team fencing. But a paper just on fencing would be overly ambitious and tricky to write.

Another point to bear in mind is that unlike the typical class-written paper, in which you must first formulate a thesis and then write the text, the research paper completely reverses this process: you first gather evidence, study it, and only then deduce a thesis. The assembled facts, statistics, graphs, schematics, arguments, expert testimony, and so on will suggest a conclusion that will be your thesis. What you learn in this process of writing the research paper is not only how to write, but also how to infer a reasonable conclusion from a body of evidence.

THE PROCESS OF WRITING THE PAPER

You have narrowed your subject. You do not yet have a thesis or a definite topic, but you have a likely subject area to explore. You can do it in these simple steps:

Find and Evaluate Sources

To do this you must spend time in a library, which is your systematized retrieval network. Materials for your subject will be listed in the card catalog, in appropriate indexes, in reference works, on shelves, in files, and—in many libraries—on a computer screen. Evaluate each source by scanning titles, tables of contents, chapter headings, or article summaries. Check the date of publication to make sure that the information in the source is still valid. Ask the reference librarian for help. As you work, list each possible source on its own bibliography card, providing the information necessary for easy retrieval. Here is an example:

813.409
Sch.   *College Library*

Schneider, Robert W. Five Novelists of the
*   Progressive Era.*
*   New York: Columbia University Press, 1965*
Chapter 5 evaluates the novels of Winston
Churchill, stating why they were loved by
contemporaries but scorned by succeeding
generations.

Take Notes

Using your pile of bibliography cards, retrieve the books, magazines, pamphlets, and other identified sources and place them in front of you. Skim the source to get the drift of its content. Decide if it contains material relevant enough to warrant a more detailed reading. Once you have skimmed your sources, you can start taking four basic kinds of notes: (1) summary, in which you record the gist of a passage; (2) paraphrase, in which you restate in your own words what the source says; (3) direct quotation, in which you copy the exact words of a source; and (4) personal comments, in which you express your own views on the subject or source.

Write down your notes on cards, which can be easily shuffled or discarded when you get down to the business of writing the paper. For easier reorganization of your notes, restrict each card to a single idea. To guard against unintentional plagiarism, copy down only exact quotations from your sources while digesting and expressing all other ideas in your own words. At some point at this stage (it varies from paper to paper), a thesis will occur to you. When it does, jot it down on a card for permanent reference. This will be the starting point of your paper.

Write the First Draft

With a jumble of notes strewn on your desk, you may feel bewildered about what to include or exclude as you tackle your first draft. This may well be the time for an outline, which can either be adjusted later to fit your paper or your paper subsequently adjusted to fit your outline. In any case, by now you should have become something of an expert on your subject. Start composing your first draft, following your outline. If you are using computerized word-processing, you can easily correct or rewrite; if you are using a typewriter, you will more likely progress by writing, striking out, and rewriting. As you write, you will be backing up your own opinions and views with source material uncovered by your research and recorded in your notes.

Use Proper Documentation

Except for statements that are common knowledge ("Abraham Lincoln was shot by Wilkes Booth"), all information taken from your sources—whether quoted, paraphrased, or summarized—must be accompanied by a source citation given in parentheses and conforming to the proper format. We provide two sample papers in this chapter—one in the Modern Language Association (MLA) format, the other in the American Psychological Association (APA) format. Use the MLA author-work format if your instructor tells you to, or if your paper is on a subject in the liberal arts, such as literature, philosophy, history, religion, or fine arts. For a paper in a more scientific field, such as psychology, sociology, or anthropology, the APA author-date format should be used. In any event, check with your instructor about the documentation format that is expected and appropriate. One caution: Do *not* mix styles.

Both the MLA and APA documentary styles are represented in this appendix by two carefully annotated student papers serving as general models and illustrating most of the documenting problems you are likely to encounter. For more complex citations, we recommend that you consult a style sheet or a research paper handbook. Both MLA and APA have gone to a system of parenthetical documentation, which gives brief but specific information about the sources within the text itself. The MLA style cites the author's surname or the title of a work, followed by a page number; the APA style cites the author's surname, followed by a date and a page number. In both styles, the author's name, work, and date can be omitted from the parentheses if they have already been supplied within the text. The rule of thumb is this: If the citation cannot be smoothly worked into the text, it should be supplied within parentheses. This kind of parenthetical documentation is obviously easier and simpler than either footnotes or endnotes because the citation can be given as the paper is being written and is not tediously repeated in three places: the text, the note, and the bibliography. Moreover, the writer does not have to contend with typing in superscript notes (always a chore) or keeping track of a note sequence.

Flexibility in citations is a characteristic shared by both the MLA and APA styles. For example, you might choose to cite the author's name in the text while putting the page (MLA) or year and page (APA) in parentheses:

MLA example:
In her *Autobiography*, Agatha Christie admits that often she felt the physical presence of Hercule Poirot (263).

APA example:
According to *800-Cocaine* by Mark S. Gold (1985, p. 21), cocaine has exploded into a full-blown business with brand names.

Or you might choose to include the title of the citation in the parentheses:

MLA example:
The author began to realize how much she liked Poirot and how much a part of her life he had become (Christie, *Autobiography* 421).

APA example:
During the airing of ABC's *Good Morning, America* (Ross & Bronkowski, 1986), case histories were analyzed in an extremely serious tone.

In any case, the overriding aim should be to cite the necessary information without interrupting the flow of the text. What cannot elegantly be worked into the text is cited within parentheses.

Prepare "Works Cited" or "References"

The sources cited in your text must be alphabetically listed in full at the end of your paper. Under the MLA style of documentation, the list is entitled "Works Cited"; under the APA style, it is entitled "References." Both styles require the same general information but differ slightly in details of capitalization and order. MLA entries, for example, begin with a surname, followed by a full Christian name; on the other hand, APA requires a surname, followed only by initials. In MLA entries the author's name is followed by the title of the work, whereas in APA entries the author's name is followed by the date. Other differences are also minor: MLA requires titles of books or periodicals to be underlined, articles or chapters to be placed within quotation marks, and all words of a title to be capitalized. On the other hand, APA underlines the titles of books and magazines but uses no quotation marks around the titles of chapters or articles within these longer works. APA capitalizes only the first word of a book or article title and the first word of a subtitle (if there is one) while typing all other words in lowercase. See the sample student papers for specific examples of how to handle various bibliographical matters.

Write the Final Copy

Revising and editing your paper is the final step. Do not be easy on yourself; pretend, instead, that the paper is someone else's and badly in need of work. Check for logical progression, completeness of development, and mechanical correctness. The task of rewriting and revising can be simplified if you know how to use a word processor, which will spare you the tedious chore of retyping every page that needs changing. Still, the only way to produce an excellent paper is to pore over it paragraph by paragraph for weaknesses or faults. After careful review and editing, type the final copy using one of the formats exemplified by the two student papers. If you are following the APA format, you will need to write an abstract summarizing your findings (see student sample, pages 775–801). Remember that the appearance of a paper can add to or detract from its quality. Here are some important tips on manuscript appearance:

1. Use 8½ by 11 (20 pound), white nonerasable bond. Double space throughout the paper, except where indicated otherwise on the student sample.

2. Except for page numbers, use one-inch margins at the top, bottom, and sides of the paper. (For page numbers, see item 6.)

3. Use a clean typewriter ribbon (fresh computer ribbon) and type only on one side of the paper. Avoid fancy typefaces such as script.

4. Place a balanced and uncluttered outline before the text of the paper. Double-space throughout the outline. (See item 6 for paginating the outline.)

5. Do not use a title page unless your instructor specifies otherwise. Instead, type your name, the instructor's name, course number,

and date on the first page of the outline, repeating this information in the upper left-hand corner on the first page of the text. The title should be centered and double-spaced below the date. (See sample papers.)

6. Number pages consecutively throughout the paper in the upper right-hand corner. Do not follow page numbers by hyphens, parentheses, periods, or other characters. Number the outline with lower-case Roman numerals *(i, ii, iii,* and so on). Number the first page of the paper itself, beginning with an Arabic *1* and on throughout the entire paper, including "Works Cited" or "References."

7. Double-check the appropriate format (MLA or APA) for citing and documentation.

SAMPLE STUDENT PAPERS

Following are facsimiles of two student papers, the first in the Modern Language Association (MLA) style, the second in the American Psychological Association (APA) style. Both papers are complete with sentence outline, text, and final bibliographic listings. Both papers have been annotated to draw your attention to variations in style, content, and format.

Modern Language Association (MLA) Style

1

▼▼▼

* The first page seen by your teacher is the outline of your paper. Paginate the outline with small roman numerals. Write your name in the top left-hand margin, followed by the course title and number, your teacher's name, and the date when the paper is due.

2

▼▼▼

Center the title of your paper and quadruple space before the thesis. A good title should tell the reader what the paper is about. Double space throughout the outline.

3

▼▼▼

The thesis consists of a single declarative sentence preceded by the word *Thesis*. The rest of the outline follows the rules for correct sentence outlining. Some instructors allow topic outlines, which consist of phrases rather than full sentences. Do not make the outline too long. A rule of thumb is that for every five pages of writing you have one page of outline. The outline leaves out the details of the paper, mentioning only major points.

---

* The Arabic numerals in the margins of the research paper correspond to the comments that follow.

i

1 Elynor Baughman

   English 101

   Professor McCuen

   May 21, 1987

2   The Bilingually Handicapped Child

3 Thesis: Early compensatory educational programs give the

            bilingual child a head start that will better prepare the

            child for handling schoolwork.

   I. Empirical evidence indicates that bilingualism obstructs a

       child's speech development.

       A. There are varying degrees of bilinguals.

           1. Coordinate bilinguals speak two languages

               independently of one another.

           2. Compound bilinguals tend to mix the words of their

               two languages.

       B. Bilinguals have difficulty with tests involving vocabulary

           and concepts.

   II. Unlike children of many European countries, a child in a bilin-

        gual community in the United States is under a double strain.

        A. The language and values expected at school are different

            from those expected at home.

            1. A "heritage of conflict" separates the bilinguals from

                the rest of the community.

            2. The bilinguals have limited contact with English.

ii

      B. Every individual needs some degree of proficiency in the dominant language.

      C. The parents' role is important in helping children master a language.

III. There are several programs of early compensatory education for the bilingual child.

      A. English as a Second Language programs exist for the bilingual.

          1. Such programs do not address the problem of biculturalism, which makes translation difficult.

          2. Shifts from one language to another often confuse the child.

      B. The University of Michigan is experimenting with a bilingual program based on both cultures and languages.

      C. Preschool education programs provide formal training for bilingual children that enhance their chances of success.

      D. Bicultural, bilingual television programs for Hispanic-American children have been started.

      E. Early compensatory language education seems to be the best approach and should be given the highest priority.

4

▼▼▼

College papers require no title page. Simply write your name in the top left-hand margin of the first page, followed by the course title and number, your teacher's name, and the date the paper is due—all of this information double spaced, each entry on a separate line. Then double space again, center the title (capitalizing only the first, last, and principal words and without underlining), and quadruple space. Then begin the introduction of the paper. Double spacing is used throughout the body of the paper. A 1" margin is required on all sides. Start numbering the body of the paper with "1" typed in the upper right-hand corner of the first page. Beginning with page 2, type your last name before the page number (so that misplaced pages can be easily found). When you hand in the paper, do not staple it or place it in a folder; just use a large paper clip.

5

▼▼▼

The first paragraph captures the reader's interest by drawing attention to the difficult plight of children handicapped at school because they don't handle the English language adequately. The last sentence of this opening paragraph is the thesis. It is placed in the classical position at the end of the opening paragraph, where it can control the rest of the essay. Since the student author is taking a stand on the issue of training bilingual students, her paper results in an argumentative paper rather than a report. The parenthetical citations refer the reader to a bibliographical "Works Cited" list at the end of the paper. Integrating documentary sources into the flow of the paper takes considerable skill. Sometimes you may wish to mention the full name of an author in your text. If so, only the page numbers of the citation need be mentioned within parentheses. Usually it is best to introduce the full name of an author the first time a source is used; then subsequent citations will mention (within parentheses) only the page numbers, or the title followed by the page numbers. Notice that the final period follows the final parenthesis of the citation except in case of a long quotation set off from the main text (see annotation 7). Study the parenthetical documentation of this paper to see the various possibilities for handling source citations.

6

▼▼▼

The second paragraph introduces the author's first major subidea, that bilingualism obstructs a child's speech development. This subidea is preceded by a statement that serves as transition from the thesis to the first major subidea. Such transitions are important for smooth and coherent development. Without them, the paper would hop and skip abruptly.

I

4   Elynor Baughman

English 101

Professor McCuen

May 21, 1987

The Bilingually Handicapped Child

5   Children who cannot communicate in English are unlikely to
do well in school. According to sociologist Joyce Hertzler, if a
child has to use one language at home and another at school, he
must be able to express himself adequately in both or face
censure (432–33). A study entitled "Bilingual Education"
indicates that approximately five million children in the United
States attend public schools and speak a language other than
English in their homes and communities (School and Society
290). Many of these children are handicapped in communication
and thought processes and have to repeat the early grades in
school several times. Coming from a different cultural and
language background that renders them unable to conceptualize
in English, bilingual children consequently tend to lag behind
their monolingual peers. Early compensatory educational
programs give the bilingual child a head start that will better
prepare the child for handling schoolwork.

6   The acquisition of skill in two languages often imposes a
considerable burden upon a child. Having to keep up their

7

▼▼▼

The author observes research convention by introducing the source of a long
or important quotation, especially when referring to the source for the first
time. Such an introduction adds not only coherence but also a note of authority. Typical introductions are as follows:

> As Dr. Leonard Smith states . . .
> According to research analyst Rose Darkwood . . .
> Anthropologist Margaret Mead observes that . . .
> Gilbert Highet explains . . .

Any quotation longer than three lines should be indented ten spaces (left-
hand margin only) and should *not* be enclosed in quotation marks. Do *not*
single space long quotations. The parenthetical citation follows the final period of the quotation. When a work has been authored by two people, both
last names are cited.

8

▼▼▼

Notice that in this paragraph and in other paragraphs that follow the quoted
material is brief and so well integrated into the grammatical structure of the
writer's text that no formal introduction is necessary.

Baughman 2

7   mother tongue while also learning a new language obstructs the
speech development of many children. In 1969, behaviorist
Catherine Landreth made the following observation:

> If two languages are spoken in the home, or if the child is
> forced to learn a foreign language while he is still learning
> his mother tongue, he gets confused and his skill in both
> languages is retarded. (Morgan and King 66)

8   A study of bilingual Chinese children in Hawaii and
monolingual children on the mainland found that in either
language, "the bilingual group was below the average of
monolinguals of the same age" (Landreth 194). Only "the
superior bilingual child," who is more adept at concept
formation and has a greater mental flexibility, is capable of
performing as well as or better than the monolingual child
(Landreth 194).

A bilingual person is usually one who is able to understand
and speak two languages with native-like control. Donald Dugas
suggests that there are varying degrees of bilingualism. The
"coordinate bilingual" has two distinct and separate sets of
speech habits. He speaks the two languages independently of
one another. The "compound bilingual" tends to mix the words
or constructions of one language within another (294). Many
American immigrants are compound bilinguals. They gave up the
use of their native language and learned English imperfectly, and
therefore speak neither language well. A "bilingual experience,"
according to Leonard Kosinski, is a situation in which children

9

The second major subidea is introduced. First the writer indicates how children may handle a foreign language in Europe; then she shows how the situation in the United States differs from that of Europe. The contrast is accentuated by the word *but*. Other useful contrast words include *however, on the other hand, whereas,* and *unlike.*

who speak English at school hear a foreign language spoken in the home (14T).

Children who come from homes where little or no English is spoken have considerable difficulty with test items that involve vocabulary. When children have to function in two incompatible language systems, their bilingualism must be taken into account in the evaluation of their test results (Landreth 195).

9   In many European countries, children master several languages with ease, but there is no marked cultural discrimination involved and the several languages are used with seemingly equal facility in the community. Faye Bumpass, a teacher of English as a Second Language, believes that acquiring native-like control of several languages without great social or psychic strain is not difficult if the conditions for learning them are consistent (4). But, if the language and values expected at school are different from those expected at home, the child is under a double strain. These dual values seem to be detrimental to success. Thomas P. Carter, who studied the language problems of Mexican-American students, states that Americanization has been much easier for non-English-speaking people who have not resisted acculturation (1).

A division of communities into contrasting groups leads to a lack of understanding and to the development of prejudicial attitudes. In the Southwest, where these groups have had a "heritage of conflict," cultural differences tend to keep them apart, with the result that one group may have limited contact

10

Since part of her thesis focuses on the importance of "early" compensatory help for the bilingual child, the author now brings in the issue of how parents can help give the child a head start. The author's reference to a study of Los Angeles schools gives the paper strong support: these schools continue to train a huge number of immigrant students and are thus familiar with the problem of bilingualism.

11

The paragraph introduces the third and final major subidea, namely that there are several programs of early compensatory education for the bilingual child. This section of the paper is the longest because it is the bedrock support for the thesis.

Baughman 4

with the English language. If a child has inadequate stimulation in the language he is being taught at school, there will be definite deficiencies in his speech development (Manuel 12).

Proficiency in the dominant language is important for the welfare of both the individual and the community. Every individual must not only prepare to earn a living in the society in which he lives, but must be able to communicate in the dominant language if he is to obtain a job and function effectively.

Parents are a major influence in shaping the language facility of their children. They can strongly encourage their children to master the language taught in school and can address them in English some of the time. Limited early contact with English and inadequate stimulation results in deficiencies in the language. If there is insufficient verbal interaction in English between the parents and the child, the child will hesitate to use the language. If two languages are spoken in a home, it is better for the child to hear one language exclusively from one of the parents. The importance of children hearing English in the home was determined in a Los Angeles school study in 1968. The study revealed that "the exclusive use of English contributes consistently and positively for Mexican-American pupils at all grade levels" (Carter 19).

There are several early compensatory programs designed to help the bilingually handicapped child. Many of these programs are funded by the federal government. Most of the

12

▼▼

This page and the next consist mostly of paraphrasing, which means that the student has assimilated the information of some important source and has rewritten it in her own writing style, using her own words instead of the author's. Following each paraphrase, she provides proper documentation to credit the source for the information used. Using someone else's ideas without providing proper documentation is considered plagiarism, a serious wrong in scholarship.

Baughman 5

compensatory programs teach the bilingual child English as a second language. In English as a Second Language programs, the child's first language is used primarily until his ability in English permits the use of both languages. At this stage translation is important.

12   Although much of the new language may duplicate words and concepts the child already knows in his first language, there will be many words and concepts that do not carry the same cultural meaning (Carter 109). Some translations then will be like mutations that go off in different directions. For instance, some Spanish words, such as <u>simpatico</u>, have no literal translation in English. Bilingualism is consequently often accompanied by biculturalism, which makes translation from one language to another difficult, if not impossible (Hertzler 428). Shifting from one language to another in school may also confuse a child and make him slower in acquiring facility in the new language (Manuel 128). The child's tendency is to translate from one language to the other rather than to think in the new language. Encouraging the use of English as soon as possible benefits the bilingual child because constant practice in the new language makes fluency attainable sooner.

With federal funding, the University of Michigan has been experimenting with a bilingual education program that teaches the curriculum in two languages (Dugas 294). The theory is that drawing the curriculum from American and foreign cultures, and

13

▼▼

Although most of the material on this page reflects the ideas of outside sources, important commentary is nevertheless provided by the student author following the parenthetical citations. It is this commentary that gives the paper its point of view and argumentative edge. As is proper in a formal research paper, the author expresses her opinions without using the personal pronouns *I, me,* and *my.*

14

▼▼

Because of the importance of the study involved, the student quotes Carter rather than paraphrasing him.

Baughman 6

13   having both English- and non-English-speaking students attend, may result in a more complete liberal education. Perhaps bilingual programs such as this one will widen the bilingual's horizons culturally as well as linguistically and help to reduce the social hostility against the bilingual child.

     Preschool education programs for bilinguals provide formal school opportunities prior to entrance into the first grade. A close relationship exists between oral language ability and the successful development of reading skills. There is some evidence that preschool programs enhance the bilingual's potential for success in the first grade.

       A study in nine New Mexico towns found that first and second graders with a year of preschool language instruction achieved much better than the control group

14   that had no such experience. (Carter 152)

     Preschool programs develop the bilingual's speaking vocabulary, his interest in books, and his communication and listening skills.

     The first national bilingual, bicultural Spanish-English educational television program started in the fall of 1973. According to an editorial in the <u>Los Angeles Times</u> written by Bella Stumbo, the program was geared to children from preschool up to eight years of age. The theory was that television programming can provide a stimulating linguistic environment that offers good language models. Children have

15

▼▼

When referring to a newspaper article, cite the section (or edition) as well as the page number—for easier retrieval.

16

▼▼

The student uses ellipsis points, consisting of three spaced periods (people . . .) to indicate that she has left out a passage from the quotation. The material was eliminated because it was irrelevant to the point being made. If the student had left out an entire sentence, the ellipsis would follow a regular period (people. . . .).

17

▼▼

When a work has been authored by three people, list all three last names within parentheses following the citation. For works authored by more than three people, use "et al."(Smith et al.).

18

▼▼

The final paragraph neatly wraps up the paper's argument by reasserting its thesis in forceful and straightforward language.

Baughman 7

15 very flexible speech habits in their early years and can be
taught to produce sounds by imitation. With television,
moreover, the child has the advantage of seeing the instructor's
mouth and facial movements when words are being pronounced
(pt. 1:4). Television has an enormous potential for helping
children learn a foreign language without making it a chore. The
hope is that the television medium will eventually present good
educational programs that will help the bilingually handicapped
child.

16 According to Leonard Bloomfield, "the bilingual acquires his
second language in early childhood—after early childhood few
people . . . reach perfection in a foreign language" (56). Young
children have keen auditory perception, few inhibitions, and
eagerness, which enable them to learn a new language easily.
The first impact of any language on a child always comes by way
of a conversational approach. By the age of five most children
17 have mastered the fundamental rules of grammar without any
direct training (Mussen, Conger, and Kagan 202). A child's
progress in language during the preschool years is astounding,
and for this reason early compensatory education for the
bilingually handicapped should be given a very high priority.
Introducing a new language before speech habits are formed has
many psychological advantages and will enable the child to speak
without an accent (Manuel 123).

18 Although many studies have treated the linguistic
development of children from the point of view of bilingualism,

much of what has been written about any phase of bilingualism seems to be based on speculative thinking, and it is doubtful whether all of the assumptions are sound. Most of the programs offered to aid the bilingually handicapped are at first- and second-grade levels and may already be too late to help the child. Early compensatory education, offered at the preschool level, would bring bilingually handicapped children up to a level where they would be reached by existing educational practices. If the oral phase of learning a language can be mastered before a child starts school, the other related phases (reading and writing) should follow with relative ease.

19

▼▼

The heading "Works Cited" is centered on the page two inches from the top, followed by quadruple spacing. The entire page is double spaced, within as well as between bibliographic entries. Bibliographic entries differ from note entries not so much in content as in form. See explanation 21 for typical bibliographic form. The second and subsequent lines of each bibliography entry are indented five spaces. The entries appear in alphabetical order according to the first letter of the entry. Left and right margins are one inch.

20

▼▼

Typical entry for an unsigned magazine article. Notice that the year is followed by a colon and then the page number(s).

21

▼▼

Typical entry for a book with one author. Notice that the last name of the author appears first, followed by a comma and the author's first name. Periods followed by two spaces separate the major components of the entry (name. title. facts of publication.). No page reference is supplied. Names of well-known publishers are abbreviated ("Holt" for "Holt, Rinehart, and Winston").

22

▼▼

Typical entry for a signed article in a periodical issued quarterly. Notice that for all articles appearing in periodicals, magazines, or newspapers, the pages of the *entire* article must be given, not just the page(s) referred to in the research paper. Since the periodical is issued quarterly, the volume number precedes the publication date (within parentheses) and a colon separates the publication date from the page numbers.

23

▼▼

Typical entry for a book with two authors. Notice the name of the second author appears in its normal order with the Christian name first, preceded by a comma and the word *and*. If a book is by more than three authors, use the name of the first author (last name first), followed by "et al." (Witt, Charles B., et al.).

Baughman 9

19

Works Cited

20

"The Argument for Bilingual Education." <u>Saturday Review</u> 29 Apr.
1972: 54.

"Bilingual Education." <u>School and Society</u> 100 (Summer 1972):
290–95.

21   Bloomfield, Leonard. <u>Language</u>. New York: Holt, 1961.

Bumpass, Faye L. <u>Teaching Young Students English as a Foreign
Language</u>. New York: American Book, 1963.

Carter, Thomas P. <u>Mexican-Americans in School: A History of
Educational Neglect</u>. New York: College Entrance
Examination Board, 1970.

22   Dugas, Donald. "Bilingualism and Language Learning." <u>School and
Society</u> 95 (Summer 1967): 294–96.

Hertzler, Joyce O. <u>A Sociology of Language</u>. New York: Random,
1965.

Kosinski, Leonard V. "New Look at the Bilingual Student." <u>Senior
Scholastic</u> 4 Oct. 1963: 14T.

Landreth, Catherine. <u>Early Childhood Behavior and Learning</u>.
New York: Knopf, 1969.

Manuel, Herschel T. <u>Spanish-Speaking Children of the Southwest</u>.
Austin, Texas: University of Texas Press, 1965.

23   Morgan, Clifford T., Richard A. King, John Schopler, and John R.
Weisz. <u>Introduction to Psychology</u>. 7th ed. New York:
McGraw-Hill, 1986.

24

▼▼

Typical entry for a book in an edition other than the first. Notice that the edition is preceded as well as followed by a period (*Child Development and Personality.* 6th ed.).

25

▼▼

Typical entry for a newspaper article. Notice that the section of the paper is cited as well as the page.

24   Mussen, Paul Henry, John Janeway Conger, and Jerome Kagan.

Child Development and Personality. 6th ed. New York:

Harper & Row, 1984.

25   Stumbo, Bella. "Nueva Programa for Children of Two Cultures."

Los Angeles Times 24 Nov. 1972, pt. 4:1.

American Psychological Association (APA) Style

1

▼▼

* A running head—an abbreviated version of the title—is placed at the top right-hand side of each page. Do not use more than 50 characters (including spaces) for the running head.

2

▼▼

The page number is placed one double-space line below the running head.

3

▼▼

The first page of the paper is the title page. It includes the title of the paper, the name of the student, the name of the class, the name of the institution, and the date.

---

* The Arabic numerals in the margins of the research paper correspond to the comments that follow.

1   Dian Fossey

2   1

3   Dian Fossey: A Scientist

Who Stopped Caring About Science

Margie Vickers

English 101

Glendale Community College

December 14, 1987

4

▼▼

Following the title page is the abstract, a brief summary of the paper's major ideas. The heading *Abstract* is centered at the top of the page.

5

▼▼

The abstract itself is written in coherent paragraph form but leaves out the details of the research.

4

5

Abstract

Dian Fossey, an occupational therapist turned anthropologist, was dedicated to single-handedly preserving the mountain gorilla of Africa, an obsession that may have led to her brutal, unsolved murder.

With anthropologist Louis Leakey as her mentor, Fossey overcame linguistic as well as political barriers to follow her anthropological goals of preserving gorillas as a species and studying them in their natural habitat. Much of Fossey's success has been attributed to her ability to anthropomorphize the gorilla and, in some respects, to act like a gorilla herself, keeping low to the ground and imitating the gorillas' vocalizations. Her mysterious and brutal murder on December 17, 1985, led to international speculation about the motive for such an act. Some colleagues blamed her soured human relationships, accusing her of having a split personality. Others believed she was killed by angry poachers whose hunting of gorillas she had thwarted. But the Rwandan government's tribunal accused her student researcher, Wayne McGuire, who had escaped to the United States and thus avoided standing trial. To this day. Fossey's murder remains unsolved. In the end, this dedicated researcher sacrificed her life for the well-being of the African mountain gorilla.

6

The body of the paper begins on page 3. The full title of the page is centered at the top of the page.

7

The introductory paragraph contains no documentation, as it is the student's own conclusion. The final sentence is the thesis of the paper. Notice that it is worded slightly differently from the thesis in the outline, but the idea is the same.

8

The citation refers to specific pages in two separate authors' works. Since both sources agree on Fossey's yearly income and on her $8,000 loan, both are mentioned.

9

Since the author and year are given earlier, only the page is cited here.

10

This is a typical full parenthetical citation for a magazine article. The order is as follows: author, year, page. Notice that the sentence period follows the final parenthesis.

6

Dian Fossey: A Scientist Who
Stopped Caring About Science

7   Dian Fossey was a controversial, many-faceted loner. She
never endeared herself to human society, nor did she try to be
accepted by it. Her life had only two purposes: to map
scientifically the lives of gorillas, and to conserve their existence
and habitat. This woman's obsessive, single-handed dedication to
the mountain gorilla may have led to her brutal, unsolved murder.

At the age of 31, it occurred to Dian Fossey that half her life
had passed uneventfully. After reading George Shaller's book on
the mountain gorilla, she decided to fly to Africa. To finance the
trip, she took out an $8,000 loan against her $5,200 yearly
8   income as an occupational therapist (Hayes, 1986, p. 65, and
Smith, 1986, p. 35). Virginia Morell (1986), a journalist interested
in Fossey's work, called her "a lover of animals since childhood"
who had traveled to East Africa "simply to see vast herds of
wildlife and visit the Leakeys' well-known digs at Olduvai
9   Gorge" (p. 20). From this trip and conversations with Leakey, a
seed was planted in Fossey's mind to return someday to study
the gorillas (Morell, 1986, p. 20).

Louis Leakey, East Africa's resident expert on the origins of
early man and a key figure in launching long-term primate
10   studies, appreciated women who appreciated animals (Hayes,
1986, p. 65). Since his success with Jane Goodall and her

11

▼▼

The subject of the research paper is always referred to by her surname without title ("Fossey") or by her full name ("Dian Fossey"), but never merely by her first name ("Dian").

12

▼▼

Numbers that can be written out in two words or less may be spelled out; otherwise they must be expressed as numerals. Any passage with many numbers should have them expressed as numerals.

chimpanzees, he had been looking for a woman to observe gorillas. Leakey was of the belief that women were better suited than men to observing apes because he saw them as more perceptive about social bonds, more patient, and less threatening to male leaders of primate groups (Morell, 1986, p. 21). After a reacquaintance with Leakey at a lecture in 1966, Fossey was immediately hired, and eight months later sent on her way to Africa. Before her departure, Leakey tested the sincerity of her resolution by asking her to have her appendix removed as a precaution against developing appendicitis and needing surgery out in the jungle (McGuire, 1987, p. 36). Fossey, who was engaged to be married to the scion of a British family with extensive holdings in Rhodesia, immediately broke off her engagement to accept Leakey's challenge (Brower, 1986, p. 53).

11   From every standpoint, Fossey was ill-prepared for Africa. She had no training in the science of animal behavior, spoke no African languages, and knew nothing about camping. She was totally dependent on Leakey's guidance. Yet Leakey provided her only with a two-day course in field observation, given by Jane Goodall, and a Land Rover to take her from Nairobi six hundred miles into the Congo (Hayes, 1986, p. 65).

12   The trek to camp Karisoke, where her field work was to proceed, was extremely arduous. Just to reach the trailhead

13

▼▼

Words in a foreign language must be underlined.

Dian Fossey

5

to Karisoke required a four-hour bus ride. Then followed a 2,000-feet climb through sometimes impenetrable vegetation. At this altitude of 10,000 feet, the weather was often wet, misty, and bone chilling (McGuire, 1987, p. 30)—typical conditions Fossey would experience while observing gorillas. The camp, located in Rwanda's Parc National des Volcans, was narrowly limited to a stretch 25 miles in length and from 6 to 12 miles in width (Hayes, 1986, p. 65). It was here that Fossey set up housekeeping. But she had barely settled in when, six months after arriving, the Congo was in a state of revolution (Hayes, p. 65). On July 19, 1966, Fossey was escorted down to the military post of Rumangabo and placed under house arrest. She was held for two weeks, in which time she was beaten and raped. Acquaintances later claimed that this trauma had a profound affect on Fossey's future attitude toward all Africans (Hayes, p. 65). Other difficulties prevailed.

13

For instance, in Rwanda Fossey found signs of <u>sumu</u> or witchcraft. These signs included crossed sticks leading to poacher traps that signified death to any who tampered, buried animal ribs that reputedly could kill meddlers, and poisons that her African staff said could make them waste away (Morell, 1986, p. 20). Despite all of these obstacles, Fossey began her work.

While the mountain gorilla was officially protected, the Rwandan government felt that the people needed more

14
▼▼

Since the "1981" date was supplied earlier in the same paragraph, only the author and page are cited here.

and for agriculture and more meat for food to feed the overpopulated area (Fossey, 1981, p. 514). This emphasis resulted in less area for the gorilla to live and more encroachment of poachers hunting for antelope. Tradition and circumstances complicated the poachers' motivation in gorilla killing. Sometimes young gorillas were caught in traps meant for antelopes. Other times, hunters under the influence of hashish just killed for the thrill of killing (Fossey, p. 515). The promise of money in exchange for capturing young gorillas, to be sent to zoos or European pet shops, lured a number of natives. The black market offered $1,200 for a gorilla head and $600 for a hand (McBee, 1986, p. 74). Before long, the gorilla perched dangerously on the edge of extinction, a problem Fossey faced and tried to head off.

In her early research, Fossey discovered that the powerful but shy gorillas responded to her attentions when she herself acted like a gorilla. She learned to imitate gorilla vocalizations (hoots, grunts, belches), to munch the foliage they ate, and to keep low to the ground (Fossey, 1981, p. 515). Fossey's ability to act like a gorilla became a primary cause for her success as an anthropologist. It was also her downfall. A dominant factor in Fossey's becoming obsessed with gorillas was her succumbing to anthropomorphism—that is, humanizing the gorilla. This natural, irresistible urge is dangerous in science, particularly in the behavioral sciences; it is anti-science.

15

This is a quotation within a work. David Watts is mentioned to let the reader know that he is *not* the author of the work in which the quotation appears. Morell is the author. "Fossey" appears in brackets to clarify the "she" pronoun. Brackets indicate editorial addition.

16

Quotation by subject of paper within another author's work.

17

Quotation by subject within her own work.

18

Example of placing the date immediately following the author's name. This convention is popular with scientific papers.

19

Author and page have been cited earlier; thus, only the page is needed.

Dian Fossey

7

The researcher loses the ability to differentiate between the object observed and the person observing it. With women researchers who are childless, this is particularly true. David Watts, a research assistant at the University of Michigan, drew the following conclusion about Fossey: "Everyone who studies the gorillas falls in love with them. I think she [Fossey] took this to an extreme. She used gorillas as replacements for the human relationships she didn't have" (Morell, 1986, p. 21). Fossey's favorite gorilla, Digit, was killed by poachers on December 31, 1977. He was buried behind her cabin. Fossey was said to have lamented, "From that moment on, I came to live within an insulated part of myself" (Hayes, 1986, p. 68). On another occasion Fossey said, "Digit was a favorite among the habituated gorillas I was studying; in fact, I was unashamed to call him 'my beloved Digit'" (Fossey, 1981, p. 501).

Fossey shared her work with many students, but their relationships with her soured because she was perceived as a taskmaster with field research standards so high that they could not be kept. According to Goodall (1986), Fossey's definition of field work was: "You simply drive yourself to exhaustion and drive others in the same manner" (p. 132). Her courage to refuse to give way to threats from native poachers, who resented her protection of the gorillas, and her stamina in facing the charge of an angry silverback, were

20

▼▼▼

This section contains several quotations attempting to shed light on the subject's personality. Notice that all of the quotations are smoothly and grammatically integrated into text. They are properly documented.

21

▼▼▼

Since this information refers to the same author, work, and year as the citation immediately preceding, only the page is given.

Dian Fossey

8

were legendary (Goodall, p. 132). In brief, her co-workers simultaneously admired and resented her.

20   Wayne McGuire, a student researcher who for five months lived at the camp with Fossey, stated, "A lot of people get strange up here. It's the loneliness that is hardest to cope with. You forget how to speak English, forget how to interact with humans" (Brower, 1986, p. 53). Dian's hermitlike lifestyle was evident when she admitted, "I have no friends. The more you learn about the dignity of the gorilla, the more you want to avoid people" (Smith, 1986, p. 35). Research assistants Amy Vedder and Bill Weber believed there were two sides to Fossey's personality: "She could be charming and she could be hateful." They also felt that she was an alcoholic and suffered from insomnia (Hayes, 1986, p. 70). Fellow researcher Goodall (1986) described her as "a complex person with startling abruptness as she swung from one mood to another" (p. 132).

In her fierce determination to find and stop poachers, Fossey routinely combed the gorillas' favorite feeding grounds and cut animal traps almost as fast as they were set up (Fossey, 1981, p. 518). She found evidence in 64 gorilla skeletal specimens, collected throughout the Virunga mountains, that

21   poachers were responsible for at least two-thirds of the total gorilla deaths (p. 511). Fossey was so intent on saving the gorillas that she even exploited the natives' superstitions by terrorizing them with Halloween masks (Goodall, 1986, p. 134).

22

▼▼

Mention is made in the text that the citation comes from *Discover* magazine. Wayne McGuire is mentioned because he plays a leading role in the final days of Dian Fossey. Notice that all of the references are smoothly integrated into the text.

22

She bought beads to use as well as firecrackers (Morell, 1986, p. 21). In an article on Fossey, published in <u>Discover</u> magazine, Wayne McGuire is quoted as saying that he got "a feeling of eeriness here, a feeling of black magic. She [Fossey] believed in it, I think, and she had a local reputation for being a witch" (Brower, 1987, p. 48). Fossey used harsh methods of interrogation when dealing with poachers. She burned houses, commanded unauthorized patrols to cut traps, and bribed the government's own park guards to bring her captured poachers for interrogation (Brower, p. 53). It was said that she pistol-whipped poachers (McBee, 1986, p. 74). She was even accused of "nettle lashing." Her men would "whip the culprits with virulent nettles that sting on contact with the skin, like an electric shock" (Hayes, 1986, p. 68). On two occasions she held hostage the children of poachers. Certain graduate students who were not accepted by her spread stories that she administered mind-altering drugs (Hayes, p. 68).

Using vigilante tactics against poachers eventually put Fossey at odds with the Rwanda government. She came to believe that park officials were in collusion with poachers. A consortium, called the Mountain Gorilla Project, was formed with the help of the President of Rwanda. Fossey did not feel that this group was necessary. Moreover, she opposed its setting up of tourist groups who would come into "her domain" (Hayes, 1986, p. 68). The hostility on the government side was evident when the

23

The opening sentence of the paragraph is short and shockingly emphatic. Quotations are used when providing important aspects of the murder.

director of tourism, Laurent Habiyaremye, forced Fossey, who

suffered from emphysema, to trek down the mountain every

other month to renew her visa (McGuire, 1987, p. 30). Her

most acrimonious encounter with Habiyaremye took place at a

60th anniversary celebration for the park in which her camp was

located. She was not invited. Habiyaremye acknowledged

everyone and everything, but never mentioned Fossey. After the

ceremony, some government officials indicated some regret

about this obvious snub, and the President of Rwanda expressed

his annoyance with Habiyaremye. And a few weeks later, some

articles came out in the newspaper openly criticizing

Habiyaremye's behavior (McGuire, p. 40).

23   Shortly after 6:00 A.M. on December 17, 1985, Dian Fossey

was found brutally murdered in her cabin at the Karisoke

Research Center. A sheet of corrugated metal had been torn off

her bedroom wall in order to get to her (McGuire, 1987, p. 28).

"A brutal gash ran diagonally across her forehead" (McGuire,

p. 29). Virginia Morell, a fellow researcher, said, "No one who

knew Fossey well . . . was surprised by her violent end" (Hayes,

1986, p. 70). The fact that Fossey had so many enemies was

clearly the reason why those who knew her in Nairobi

considered her murder predictable, if not inevitable (Hayes,

p. 70). Her fellow worker, Wayne McGuire (1987), whose

relationship with Fossey is darkened by mysterious shadows,

claimed that Fossey was ill. He stated that before her murder,

24

Since McGuire was accused by the Rwandan government of murdering Fossey, his comments here are significant.

her weakened physical condition due to emphysema (she was a heavy smoker), along with her inability to sleep, left her gaunt and frail. She was unable to physically search out gorillas, and she became a virtual prisoner in the camp (McGuire, 1987, p. 31).

Colleagues and acquaintances suspected that poachers had murdered Fossey, but the Rwandan government had different ideas. In August of 1986 an arrest warrant was issued for Wayne McGuire. He was regarded as the principal author of the murder, and five accomplices (workers at the camp) were also charged. McGuire was accused of murdering Fossey in order to acquire her notes. Of the five Rwandans arrested, four were let go, and one committed suicide. The Rwandans, in looking for evidence associated with the murder, were very sloppy. They picked up everything in Fossey's room so no fingerprints could be found; they failed to follow or look into barefoot tracks leading from the scene; and they did not dust the murder weapon for fingerprints (McGuire, 1987, p. 44).

On December 18, 1986, a Rwandan tribunal convicted Wayne McGuire in absentia of Dian Fossey's murder and sentenced him to death by a firing squad. However, he had escaped to the United States (McGuire, p. 28). Ian Redmond, a biologist who spent two years at Karisoke, insisted, "The charge is nonsense. They've concentrated on trying to find someone who is not a Rwandan" (Smith, 1986, p. 35). Others questioned why, if he

25

▼▼

Notice how an accumulation of quotations are worked into the text.

26

▼▼

The student does not offer an opinion as to who murdered Fossey but prefers to leave the issue open-ended. The unsolved mystery adds an element of suspense to the paper.

were guilty, McGuire remained at the camp for some time after Fossey's murder and wondered what he could have gained from stealing her notes since he had constant access to them during his stay there (Smith, p. 35).

25   The Reverend Elton Wallace, a Seventh-day Adventist minister, spoke these words at Fossey's funeral: "Dian Fossey was born to a home of comfort and privilege, which she left by choice to live among a race facing extinction" (Hayes, 1986, p. 70). Goodall (1986) wrote, "She spent her last months where she wanted to be, near the magnificent animals to whom she had devoted her life" (p. 134). Harold Hayes (1986), editor of California magazine, wrote this about her death: "In defense of these animals, Fossey was herself beaten, robbed, raped, and ultimately murdered" (p. 70). Susanna McBee (1986) proclaimed that Fossey's death "has reunited conservation groups and galvanized Rwanda's government to take protective action" in behalf of Africa's wildlife (p. 74).

26   It must be stated that Dian Fossey was a dedicated researcher, who overcame enormous obstacles in order to pursue what she deemed important for the preservation of the mountain gorillas. In the end, she sacrificed her life for their well being. Her tragic murder remains unsolved, with accusing fingers pointing in different directions.

27

▼▼

The reference list follows the APA rules for listing sources:

- The title "References" appears centered on the page.
- The reference list is double-spaced throughout.
- Each unit of the citation ends with a period.
- Only those works actually cited in the paper appear in the reference list.
- The sources are listed in alphabetical order by the surname of the author. The surname is followed by initial(s) only, not full Christian names.
- The date of publication is enclosed in parentheses. For magazines, a comma follows the year, followed by the month—written out in full—and the date.
- Only the first word of a book or article title (and the first word of a subtitle, if there is one) is capitalized; the remaining words are typed entirely in lowercase letters. However, each word in the title of a periodical is capitalized.
- The titles of books and periodicals are underlined. No quotation marks are placed around the title of articles within these longer works.

The following items do not appear in the student research paper sample, but since they are common, we provide the appropriate format:

Book with a single author

Jones, E. (1931). <u>On the nightmare.</u> London: Hogarth.

Book with two or more authors

Terman, L. M. , & Merrill, M. A. (1937). <u>Measuring intelligence.</u> Cambridge, Mass.: The Riverside Press.

Edited book

Friedman, R. J., & Katz, M. M. (Eds.). (1974). <u>The psychology of depression: Contemporary theory and research.</u> New York: Wiley.

Article or chapter in an edited book

Waxer, P. (1979). Therapist training in nonverbal behavior. In A. Wolfgang (Ed.), <u>Nonverbal behavior: Applications and cultural implications</u> (pp. 221–240). New York: Academic Press.

Journal article, paginated anew in each issue

Rosenthal, G. A. (1983). A seed-eating beetle's adaptation to poisonous seed. <u>Scientific American, 249</u>(6), 56–67.

Journal article, paginated throughout the annual volume

Rodney, J., Hollender. B., & Campbell, P. (1983). Hypnotizability and phobic behavior. <u>Journal of Abnormal Psychology, 92</u>, 386–389.

Newspaper article

Goodman, E. (1983, December 123). Bouvia case crosses the "rights" line. <u>Los Angeles Times</u>, Part 2, p. 5.

Dian Fossey

13

27   References

Brower, M. (1986, February 17). The strange death of Dian
    Fossey: <u>A People Weekly</u>, pp. 46–54.

Fossey, D. (1981, April). The imperiled mountain gorilla. <u>National
    Geographic</u>, pp. 511–16, 518–22.

Goodall, J. (1986, May). Mountain warrior. <u>Omni</u>, pp. 132, 134.

Hayes, H. (1986, November). The dark romance of Dian Fossey.
    <u>Life</u>, pp. 64–66, 68, 70.

McBee, S. (1986, June 9). Great apes get new lease on life. <u>U.S.
    News and World Report</u>, p. 74.

McGuire, W. (1986, April). I didn't kill Dian. She was my friend.
    <u>Discover</u>, pp. 28–32, 34, 36–37, 40, 44–48.

Morell, V. (1986, April). Dian Fossey. Field science and death in
    Africa. <u>Science</u>, pp. 17, 20–21.

Smith, W. E. (1986, September 1). Case of the gorilla lady
    murder. <u>Time</u>, p. 35.

SUGGESTIONS FOR WRITING

1. Following the style advocated by your instructor, write a five- to eight-page research paper on one of the following psychological problems:
   a. Anorexia nervosa among teenage girls
   b. Loneliness and alienation among the elderly
   c. The effects of divorce on children under the age of ten
   d. Alcoholism among high school students
   Be sure to document any significant statement not your own.

2. Write a paper on the relationship between art and social class. Focus your research on the following queries:
   a. Does art reflect a class bias?
   b. Do different classes hold to different standards for judging art?
   c. Are these standards related to the ways different classes perceive the world?
   d. Is there a sociology of art?

3. Choosing any poem or short story in this book, write a literary analysis focusing on theme, character, action, or form.

APPENDIX WRITING ASSIGNMENTS

▾▾

Write a research paper, following the format suggested by your instructor. Above all, choose a topic in which you have a genuine interest. The following titles and restricted theses are presented to stimulate your own investigation:

Title	Thesis
"A Look at Thomas Wolfe"	The inconsistencies in Thomas Wolfe's writing can be directly attributed to constant family conflicts, to his doubts concerning his country's economic stability, and to his fear of not being accepted by his reading public.
"American Architectural Development"	The development of American architecture was greatly attenuated until the eighteenth century because of the lack of adequate transportation and manufacturing facilities, and the fact that city life had not formed prior to that century.

Title	Thesis
"Wordsworth and Coleridge: Their Diverse Philosophies"	Although Wordsworth and Coleridge were both Romantic poets, they believed in two completely different philosophies of nature.
"Why Jazz Was What We Wanted"	This paper deals with the various trends that led to the rise, development, and recognition of jazz as an important part of American musical culture during the nineteenth and twentieth centuries.
"The Influence of Imagism on Twentieth-Century Poetry"	Imagism, a self-restricted movement, has greatly influenced twentieth-century poetry.
"Automation and Employment"	The current fear of humans being displaced by machines, or what alarmists term the "automation hysteria," seems to be based on insubstantial reports.
"Needed: A New Definition of Insanity"	Our courts need a better definition of insanity because neither the M'Naghten Rule nor the psychological definition is adequate.
"The Proud Sioux"	In this paper I shall prove that the Sioux Indians, although confined to a shabby reservation, still fought on peacefully against their captors—the white man and his hard-to-accept peace terms.
"Women's Fashions After the World Wars"	The First World War and the Second World War had significant effects on women's fashions in America.
"Charlie Chaplin"	This paper deals with the various factors that made Charlie Chaplin the master of silent movies.
"The Funnies"	Today's funnies reflect a change in America's attitude toward violence, ethnic minorities, and ecology.
"The Decline of the Mayans"	The four most popular theories that have been advanced to explain the abrupt end of the Mayan civilization

Title	Thesis
	are: the effects of natural disaster, physical weaknesses, detrimental social changes, and foreign influence.
"Relief Paintings in Egyptian Mastabas"	The relief paintings found in the mastabas depict the everyday life of the Egyptian people.
"Athena"	The goddess Athena bestowed her favors not on those who worshipped her, but on those who fought for their beliefs.
"Goldfish"	Originally from China, goldfish have been bred into one of the most beautiful and marketable species of fish.

A S S I G N M E N T 2

▼▼

THE LITERARY PAPER

HOW TO WRITE A PAPER ABOUT LITERATURE

Literature is a difficult subject to write about. First, it is a subject about which there is no shortage of opinions. A famous play such as *Hamlet* has been so thoroughly studied and interpreted that it would take a tome or two to collect everything that has been written about it. Beginning writers must therefore always live in dread that what they have to say about a work may be blasphemously contrary to established opinion.

Second, the beginning writer is often unaware of the tradition or era into which a piece of literature falls. Yet to write intelligently about a piece of literature, a student must be able to distinguish the qualities of its literary tradition from the properties singular to the particular work. It is nearly impossible, for instance, to write comprehensibly about the work of a Romantic poet unless one knows something about the disposition of Romanticism.

But the beginning student is rarely called upon to perform any such feat of interpretation. Instead, what an instructor generally wishes to evoke from a student-writer is simply an intelligent exploration of a work's meaning, along with a straightforward discussion of one or two of its techniques. The student might therefore be asked to analyze the meaning of a sonnet and to comment briefly on its prosody; or to discuss the theme of a short story and to examine the actions and attitudes of a principal character; or to explain the social customs upon which a certain play is based.

Even so, there are numerous pitfalls awaiting the beginning commentator on literature. The first of these is a tendency to emote over a literary favorite. Students who have fallen victim to this trait will mistake sentimentality for judgment, and write enthusiastically about how much they like a particular work. But this is not what the teacher is generally looking for in a student's essay. What is desired is not an outpouring of affection, but the careful expression of critical judgment.

A second mistake beginning students of literature often make is assuming that one opinion about a literary piece is as valid and as good as another. It is only in literature classes that one finds such extreme democracy. Geologists do not assume that one opinion about a rock is the same as another; neither do chemists nor astronomers blithely accept every theory about chemicals and planets. This fallacious view of criticism has its origin in the mistaken belief that one's primary reaction toward literature is emotional. But the emotional response evoked by the literary work is not what a writing assignment is designed to draw out of a student. Instead, what the instructor is looking for is reasoned opinion based on a close reading of the text. Disagreements in interpretation can then be referred back to the text, and evidence can be gathered to support one view over another. It is very much like two lawyers getting together to interpret the fine print on a contract. It is not at all like two people trying to reconcile their differing reactions to anchovy pizza. Interpretations that cannot be supported by the text may be judged farfetched or simply wrong; those that can be supported may be judged *more* right.

But perhaps the most common mistake of the student-critic is a tendency to serve up inconsistent, unproven, and fanciful interpretations of the literary work. Often, these take the guise of rather exotic meanings that the student has inferred, for which scanty (if any) evidence exists. In its most extreme form, this tendency leads to rampant symbol-hunting, where the writer finds complex and knotty meanings bristling behind the most innocent statements. The only known cure for this is the insistence that all interpretations be grounded in material taken from the text itself. If you have devised an ingenious explanation or reading of a work, be certain that you can point to specific passages from it that support your interpretations, and always make sure that other passages do not contradict your thesis.

The In-Class Essay on Literature

Often students are asked to analyze and interpret literature in class-written essays. The literary work may consist of a poem, of a passage from a novel being read by the class, of a short story, or of a play. Depending on how the assignment is worded, the student may be required to find and express the theme, analyze an action, interpret a symbol, or comment on form.

Finding and Expressing a Theme

The theme of a literary work is its central or dominant idea, its comment on life. Finding and expressing this idea involves a form of literary algebra that requires students to think logically from cause to effect. Of course, writers say more than any summary theme can possibly express; nor should finding a theme involve smothering a writer's work under a crude and simplistic summary. Instead, in the summary you should compress what you interpret as the emphasis of the work into a few brief sentences.

Consider the poem "Design" (p. 600). A moth has been found dead in a spider's web spun on a heal-all flower. The poet wonders what could have brought the moth to this particular flower, where a web was spun and a spider was waiting. Why didn't the moth go to another, safer flower? This apparently trivial discovery leads the poem to speculate that destiny operates in random and mysterious ways, which is more or less the central emphasis or theme of the poem.

This theme can, of course, be stated in several different ways. So, for that matter, can the theme of any poem or other literary work. What you must do, after you have deciphered the theme of the work, is to make a statement and prove it. Proof can be supplied by quoting lines and passages from the work. The instructor can then reconstruct the process of thinking behind your conclusion. If you have misinterpreted the work, the proof allows the instructor to see how your misreading occurred.

Analyzing Character and Action

Fictional characters behave according to the same hopes, fears, hates, and loves that motivate real people. But the characters of fiction are found in exotic dilemmas real people hardly ever encounter. Consequently, fiction provides us with an opportunity to ponder how common people might react in uncommon situations; we can then draw moral lessons, psychological principles, and philosophical insights from their behavior. Without fiction, we would remain hemmed in by the narrow horizons of reality and experience.

By asking you to write an essay explaining why a certain character performed a certain action, your instructor is fostering valuable skills of social analysis. If you can understand the rage and jealousy of Othello or the isolated pride of Hester Prynne, you are better equipped to understand these emotions in yourself or in your acquaintances.

When you state that a certain character behaves a certain way, the burden of proof is on you. It is not enough to say that Hamlet was indecisive or weak, or that Lear was overweening and arrogant, or that the unidentified male character in "Hills Like White Elephants" is petty and selfish. In every instance, you must quote passages that prove your interpretation.

Interpreting Symbols

In its most literal sense, a symbol is a thing that stands for something beyond itself. The dove is a symbol of peace; the flag is the symbol of a country. In literature, a symbol is created when an author invests an object, an idea, or an action with a significance far beyond itself. A person may also be treated in such a way as to symbolize a class or a group of people.

Most of the time, symbolism is implicit in literature. The reader is left to unravel the meaning of the symbol. Indeed, the effect of a symbol would otherwise be ruined by preachiness. But occasionally an author will come out and say what a certain symbol means. For instance, in "Ars Poetica" (pp. 486–87), the poet tells us explicitly that "An empty doorway and a maple leaf" are symbols that stand for "all the history of grief."

In the interpretation of symbols, it is less a matter of who is right or wrong than of who has proven a point and who has not. Symbols rarely have cut-and-dried, unarguable meanings. Considerable variation in the interpretation of symbols is not only possible, but extremely likely. Whatever your interpretation, however, it must be supported by material quoted from the text.

Commenting on Form

For the most part, this type of assignment applies to poetry, where the student has numerous opportunities to express a knowledge of the terms and concepts of prosody. (Fiction and drama contain fewer nameable techniques.) In writing about a poem, you may be asked to describe its verse form or its meter, or to label and identify various tropes and figures of speech.

Wherever possible, use the formal names of any techniques present in a work. If you know that the poem you are analyzing is an Italian sonnet, it does no harm to say so. If you know that a certain action in a play occurs in its *denouement,* you should not be bashful about using that term. If a story begins *in media res* and then proceeds in *flash-backs,* you should say so. Your use of such labels will show an instructor that you have not only mastered the meaning of the work, but have also grasped its form.

In summary, when writing about literature, you should do more than simply ascribe a certain interpretation to the literary work. Your prime purpose should be to prove that your reading of the work is reasonable and logical. Passages from the work should be liberally quoted to support your paper's interpretation of it. Above all, never assume that any reading of a work, no matter how unsupported or farfetched, will do.

Bear one thing in mind before you begin to write your paper: Famous literary works, especially works regarded as classics, have been thoroughly studied to the point where prevailing opinion on them has assumed the character of orthodoxy. What may seem to you a brilliant insight may, in fact, be nothing more than what critics have been saying about the writer and his or her works for years. Saying that Hemingway's male characters suffer from *machismo* is a little like the anthropology student opining that humans are bipedal. Both remarks are undoubtedly true, but they are neither original nor insightful. You should, therefore, check out the prevailing critical opinions on a writer before attempting to dogmatize on your own.

THE LITERARY PAPER

The following literary paper is one student's response to the following assignment: "Write a 500-word critical analysis of Eudora Welty's 'A Worn Path,' (see pp. 369–76) focusing on character, action, mood, setting, and literary techniques such as diction, figurative language, and symbolism. Choose those strategies that best illumine the theme of the narrative."

1

▼▼▼

* The introductory paragraph captures the reader's attention by creating a "jewel" metaphor. It also presents the reviewer's unqualified literary judgment—that "A Worn Path" is an excellent, moving story.

2

▼▼▼

Paragraph two provides a summary of the story's literal level, allowing even the uninitiated reader to comprehend the reviewer's coming comments and interpretations.

---

* The Arabic numerals in the margins of the research paper correspond to the comments that follow.

1

Douglas B. Inman

English 102

Professor McCuen

March 15, 1988

A Worn, but Lightly Traveled Path

1   In this day when mediocrity is praised as inspiration and chaos as art, it is refreshing to find among the literary dung heaps a jewel, shining and glittering and making one forget, for the moment, the overwhelming stench and filth that threatens to suffocate, and squeeze the very life from one's literary soul. Eudora Welty's "A Worn Path" is such a rare jewel. Here is a story that exudes craftsmanship from every pore. It is filled with finely turned phrases, distinctly vivid imagery, and carefully constructed moods; but, more importantly, it tells its story well, communicating on many different levels. Ms. Welty demonstrates a firm command of the art of storytelling, and the way she weaves this particular tapestry of words will convince the reader that here is a lady who could turn a sow's ear into silk.

2   "A Worn Path" is the portrait of Phoenix Jackson, an old Negro woman, seen making a trip to town to retrieve badly needed medicine for her ailing grandchild. Burdened by age and faced with obstacles, she nevertheless presses on, stoically pursuing her goal. On the most obvious level, this is the story of an eccentric but delightful woman whose spirit

3

▼▼

Paragraph three begins the most important part of this critical review. The student has chosen to focus on the symbolic level of the story. For him, the importance of the narrative lies in its relationship to the history of black freedom in America.

4

▼▼

Here, as in several other passages, the reviewer carefully quotes from the story in order to bolster his argument—that the plight of Phoenix Jackson is also the history of blacks in America. Notice that each quotation is smoothly integrated into the main text of the essay. Note also that when Phoenix Jackson, the character, is speaking, the student writer uses single quotation marks within double quotation marks. But when the student is quoting the narrator, he uses double quotation marks only. In this way the reader can distinguish what the narrator says from what the character says in monologue or dialogue.

5

▼▼

The reviewer is straightforward in his explication of the thorn bush as a significant individual symbol within the total allegorical framework.

Inman 2

belies her advanced years. She makes the long and arduous trip to town despite the great distance, the many obstacles she encounters, and an encroaching senility that gently touches the soul of the reader. She climbs hills, crosses a creek by way of a suspended log, crawls under a barbed wire fence, marches through fields, confronts a stray dog, and comes to grips with exhaustion, hallucinations, and a failing memory. And throughout these ordeals, the author reveals a character filled with pride and dignity.

3   But there is another story here, one played out on a much deeper level. It is the story of black people in America, and their struggle for freedom and equality. The path Phoenix follows is the road of life for her people, and the obstacles she encounters on the way become the challenges of being black.

4   For instance, she comes to a hill. "'Seems like there is chains about my feet, time I get this far,'" she says, and we know that it is the hill out of slavery that she must climb. And she does it, although "'something,'" white people perhaps, "'pleads I should stay.'" And when she gets to the top, she turns and gives a "full, severe look behind her where she had come." Doubtless this action represents the black race scrutinizing in retrospect some especially difficult scene in the drama of their freedom. Phoenix encounters opposition to her

5   newfound freedom in the form of a thorny bush, and here her dress is a symbol of that freedom, as she struggles to free herself from the thorns without tearing her garment. But

6, 7

▼▼▼

Two more symbols—the marble cake and the scarecrow—are interpreted.

8

▼▼▼

The reviewer alludes to Egyptian mythology in order to draw attention to the special significance of the heroine's name.

9

▼▼▼

The reviewer points out other bird symbols and interprets them. Even the little grandson is seen as a bird symbol. Again, quotations from the story are used as primary sources to support the reviewer's claims.

she maintains her dignity, showing no spite for the thorns, saying "'you doing your appointed work. Never want to let folks past—.'" And finally, trembling from the experience, "she stood free."

6   But freedom for blacks is an illusive thing, as the reader understands when a small boy seems to bring Phoenix a slice of marble-cake, "but when she went to take it there was just her own hand in the air." Like the cake, freedom for the blacks has historically often been a seductive picture that seemed real; yet, when the blacks tried to claim it, it dissolved back into fantasy.

7   Phoenix passes through the childhood of her race when she traverses fields of "withered cotton" and "dead corn." She encounters "something tall, black, and skinny," and it is both a scarecrow and the image of slavery past. "'Who be you the ghost of?'" she asks, but there is only silence and the scarecrow dancing in the wind. And here Phoenix is the Negro of the past giving way to the future, as she intones, "'Dance, old scarecrow, while I dancing with you.'"

8   In this story, birds are used repeatedly to symbolize freedom. The character's very name, Phoenix, is an illustration of this strategy, for the phoenix was a bird in Egyptian mythology which, every five hundred years, would consume itself in fire and then rise renewed from the ashes, as blacks rose from

9   slavery after the Civil War. Other bird symbols occur. For instance, Phoenix comes to a place where quail are walking about, and she tells then, as she would young Negroes, "'Walk

10

▼▼▼

The reviewer begins to summarize by focusing on the mood of the story, calling it "optimistic." In other words, the summary appraisal is that this is a story of hope and triumph, not of bitterness and despair.

pretty. This is the easy place. This is the easy going,'" referring
to the new time of freedom after the Civil War. And when she
encounters a white hunter, she sees in his sack a bobwhite,
"with its beak hooked bitterly to show it was dead," indicating
that even though slavery has been abolished, whites still
managed to oppress blacks, and the struggle for black freedom is
not yet complete.

Phoenix's grandson represents the new generation of blacks
who never knew slavery, but still feel its impact, and he too is
portrayed as a bird of freedom. "'He suffer and it don't seem to
put him back at all. He got a sweet look. He going to last. He
wear a little patch quilt and peep out, holding his mouth open
like a little bird,'" she tells a nurse in town.

10   Overall, the story is an optimistic outlook on the black
experience. Though much of the action focuses on earlier
hardship. it ends with hope for the future, as can be seen when
Phoenix finally reaches town. There, it is Christmas time, while
during her journey it is simply a cold December day. In town,
dozens of black children whirl around her in the street, bells are
ringing, and colorful lights abound. "'Here I be,'" she says,
indicating the end of the journey, the attaining of freedom and
new life. And already the past is being forgotten; all the slavery,
the fight for freedom, the long and painful road to happiness is
but a dim memory. "'It was my memory had left me,'" she says
near the end, "'There I sat and forgot why I made my long trip.'"

"'Forgot?'" asks the nurse. "'After you came so far?'"

11

The final paragraph makes the point that it is Phoenix Jackson, the heroine and major character of the story, who gives the story its meaning and beauty. The concluding sentence brings the analysis full circle by using the same jewel/gem metaphor used in the introduction.

11   This is the story of a courageous and dignified old woman on
a long journey, but it is also the story of a courageous and
dignified race, and their long struggle for freedom and equality.
With wonderful artistry, Eudora Welty takes the reader along,
to travel this worn path of struggle that has been trudged by so
many peoples over the ages. She shows the dignity in the
struggle and the hope of a new generation. And she does so
with the craftsmanship of a fine watchmaker. One cannot help
but be changed in some way by this beautiful story. "A Worn
Path" is truly a gem.

Glossary

▼▼

abstract Words or phrases denoting ideas, qualities, and conditions that exist but cannot be seen. *Love,* for example, is an abstract term; so are *happiness, beauty,* and *patriotism.* The opposite of abstract terms are concrete ones—words that refer to things that are tangible, visible, or otherwise physically evident. *Hunger* is abstract, but *hamburger* is concrete. The best writing blends the abstract with the concrete, with concrete terms used in greater proportion to clarify abstract ones. Writing too steeped in abstract words or terms tends to be vague and unfocused.

ad hominem **argument** An argument that attacks the integrity or character of an opponent rather than the merits of an issue. (*Ad hominem* is Latin for "to the man.") It is also informally known as "mud-slinging." See "Obstacles to Clear Thinking," by Richard Altick in Chapter 9.

ad populem **argument** A fallacious argument that appeals to the passions and prejudices of a group rather than to its reason. An appeal, for instance, to support an issue because it's "the American Way" is an *ad populem* argument. For more, see Chapter 9, especially Richard Altick's "Obstacles to Clear Thinking."

allusion A reference to some famous literary work, historical figure, or event. For example, to say that a friend "has the patience of Job" means that he is as enduring as the biblical figure of that name. Allusions must be used with care lest the audience miss their meaning.

ambiguity A word or an expression having two or more possible meanings is said to be ambiguous. Ambiguity is a characteristic of some of the best poetry, but it is not a desired trait of expository writing, which should clearly state what the writer means.

analogy A comparison that attempts to explain one idea or thing by likening it to another. Analogy is useful if handled properly, but it can be a source of confusion if the compared items are basically unalike.

argumentation Argumentation is the writer's attempt to convince his reader to agree with him. It is based upon appeals to reason, evidence proving the argument, and sometimes emotion to persuade. Some arguments attempt merely to prove a point, but others go beyond proving to inciting the reader to action. At the heart of all argumentation lies a debatable issue.

audience   The group for whom a work is intended. For a writer, the audience is the reader whom the writer desires to persuade, inform, or entertain. Common sense tells us that a writer should always write to the level and needs of the particular audience for whom the writing is meant. For example, if you are writing for an unlettered audience, it is pointless to cram your writing with many literary allusions whose meanings will likely be misunderstood.

balance   In a sentence, a characteristic of symmetry between phrases, clauses, and other grammatical parts. For example, the sentence "I love Jamaica for its weather, its lovely scenery, and its people" is balanced. This sentence—"I love Jamaica for its weather, its lovely scenery, and because its people are friendly"—is not. See also **parallelism.**

causal analysis   A mode of developing an essay in which the writer's chief aim is to analyze cause or predict effect. For example, in "Why Tigers Become Man-Eaters," Jim Corbett's chief aim is to explain why some tigers start to prey on people.

cliché   A stale image or expression, and the bane of good expository writing. "White as a ghost" is a cliché; so is "busy as a bee." Some clever writers can produce an effect by occasionally inserting a cliché in their prose, but most simply invent a fresh image rather than cull one from the public stock.

coherence   The principle of clarity and logical adherence to a topic that binds together all parts of a composition. A coherent essay is one whose parts—sentences, paragraphs, pages—are logically fused into a single whole. Its opposite is an incoherent essay—one that is jumbled, illogical, and unclear.

colloquialism   A word or expression acceptable in informal usage but inappropriate in formal discourse. A given word may have a standard as well as a colloquial meaning. *Bug,* for example, is standard when used to refer to an insect; when used to designate a virus, for example "She's at home recovering from a *bug,*" the word is a colloquialism.

comparison/contrast   A rhetorical mode used to develop essays that systematically match two items for similarities and differences. See the comparison/contrast essay examples in Chapter 8.

conclusion   The final paragraph or paragraphs that sum up an essay and bring it to a close. Effective conclusions vary widely, but some common tacks used by writers to end their essays include summing up what has been said, suggesting what ought to be done, specifying consequences that are likely to occur, restating the beginning, or taking the reader by surprise with an unexpected ending. Most important of all, however, is to end the essay artfully and quietly without staging a grand show for the reader's benefit.

concrete   Said of words or terms denoting objects or conditions that are palpable, visible, or otherwise evident to the senses. *Concrete* is the opposite of *abstract*. The difference between the two is a matter of degrees. *Illness,* for example, is abstract; *ulcer* is concrete; "sick in the stomach" falls somewhere between the two. The best writing usually expresses abstract propositions in concrete terms.

connotation   The implication or emotional overtones of a word rather than its literal meaning. *Lion,* used in a literal sense, denotes a beast (see **denotation**). But to say that Winston Churchill had "the heart of a lion" is to use the connotative or implied meaning of *lion*. See Chapter 10, "The Meaning of Words."

deduction   Something inferred or concluded. Deductive reasoning moves from the general to the specific. For more, see "Introduction to Logic" by John C. Sherwood in Chapter 9.

denotation   The specific and literal meaning of a word, as found in the dictionary. The opposite of *connotation*.

description   A rhetorical mode used to develop an essay whose primary aim is to depict a scene, person, thing, or idea. Descriptive writing evokes the look, feel, sound, and sense of events, people, or things. See Chapter 6 for instructions on how to write a descriptive essay.

diction   Word choice. Diction refers to the choice of words a writer uses in an essay or other writing. Implicit in the idea of diction is a vast vocabulary of synonyms—different words that have more or less equivalent meanings. If only one word existed for every idea or condition, diction would not exist. But since we have a choice of words with various shades of meaning, a writer can and does choose among words to express ideas. The diction of skilled writers is determined by the audience and occasion of their writing.

division and classification   A rhetorical mode for developing an essay whose chief aim is to identify the parts of a whole. A division and classification essay is often an exercise in logical thinking. See, for example, "Thinking as a Hobby," by William Golding in Chapter 8.

documentation   In a research paper, the support provided for an assertion, theory, or idea, consisting of references to the works of other writers. Different styles of documentation exist. Most disciplines now use the parenthetical style of documentation—see the sample research paper, "The Bilingually Handicapped Child," in the Appendix—where citations are made within the text of the paper rather than in footnotes or endnotes.

dominant impression   The central theme around which a descriptive passage is organized. For example, a description of an airport lobby would most likely use the dominant impression of rush and bustle, which it would support with specific detail, even though the lobby may contain pockets of peace and tranquility. Likewise, a description of Cyrano de Bergerac—the famous dramatic lover whose nose was horrendously long—would focus on his nose rather than on an inconspicuous part of his face.

emotion, appeal to   An appeal to feelings rather than to strict reason; a legitimate ploy in an argument as long as it is not excessively and exclusively used.

emphasis   A rhetorical principle that requires stress to be given to important elements in an essay at the expense of less important elements. Emphasis may be given to an idea in various parts of a composition. In a sentence, words may be emphasized by placing them at the beginning or end or by judiciously italicizing them. In a paragraph, ideas may be emphasized by repetition or by the accumulation of specific detail.

essay   From the French word *essai,* or "attempt," the essay is a short prose discussion of a single topic. Essays are sometimes classified as formal or informal. A formal essay is aphoristic, structured, and serious. An informal essay is personal, revelatory, humorous, and somewhat loosely structured.

evidence   The logical bases or supports for an assertion or idea. Logical arguments consist of at least three elements: propositions, reasoning, and evidence. The first of these consists of the ideas that the writer advocates or defends. The logical links by which the argument is advanced make up the second. The statistics, facts, anecdotes, and testimonial support provided by the writer in defense of the idea constitute the evidence. In a research paper, evidence consisting of paraphrases or quotations from the works of other writers must be documented in a footnote, endnote, or parenthetical reference. See also **argumentation.**

example   An instance that is representative of an idea or claim or that otherwise illustrates it. The example mode of development is used in essays that make a claim and then prove it by citing similar and supporting cases. See, for example, the essays in Chapter 7.

exposition   Writing whose chief aim is to explain. Most college composition assignments are expository.

figurative   Said of a word or expression used in a nonliteral way. For example, the expression "to go the last mile" may have nothing at all to do with geographical distance, but may mean to complete an unfinished task or job.

focus   In an essay, the concentration or emphasis upon a certain subject or topic.

generalization   A statement that asserts some broad truth based upon a knowledge of specific cases. For instance, the statement "Big cars are gas guzzlers" is a generalization about individual cars. Generalizations are the end products of inductive reasoning, where a basic truth may be inferred about a class after experience with a representative number of its members. One should, however, beware of rash or faulty generalizations— those made on insufficient experience or evidence. It was once thought, for example, that scurvy sufferers were malingerers, which led the British navy to the policy of flogging the victims of scurvy aboard its ships. Later, medical research showed that the lethargy of scurvy victims was an effect rather than the cause of the disease. The real cause was found to be a lack of vitamin C in their diet.

image   A phrase or expression that evokes a picture or describes a scene. An image may be either literal, in which case it is a realistic attempt to depict with words what something looks like, or figurative, in which case an expression is used that likens the thing described to something else (e.g., "My love is like a red, red rose").

induction   A form of reasoning that proceeds from specific instances to a general inference or conclusion. Inductive reasoning is the cornerstone of the scientific method, which begins by examining representative cases and then infers some law or theory to explain them as a whole. See the article "Introduction to Logic" in Chapter 9.

interparagraph   Between paragraphs. A comparison/contrast, for example, may be drawn between several paragraphs rather than within a single paragraph. For an example of an interparagraph comparison/contrast, see "Grant and Lee: A Study in Contrasts" in Chapter 8.

intraparagraph   Within a single paragraph. For an example of an intraparagraph comparison/contrast, see Emerson's essay "Conservatism and Liberalism" in Chapter 8.

inversion   The reversal of the normal order of words in a sentence to achieve some desired effect, usually emphasis. Inversion is a technique long used in poetry, although most modern poets shun it as too artificial. For examples of inversion, see Shakespeare's "That Time of Year" (Sonnet 73) in Chapter 4.

irony   The use of language in such a way that apparent meaning contrasts sharply with real meaning. One famous example (in Shakespeare's *Julius Caesar*) is Antony's description of Brutus as "an honorable man." Since Brutus was one of Caesar's assassins, Antony meant just the opposite. Irony is a softer form of sarcasm and shares with it the same contrast between apparent and real meaning.

jargon   The specialized or technical language of a specific trade, profession, class, or other group of people. Jargon is sometimes useful, but when used thoughtlessly it can become meaningless expression bordering on gibberish, as in the following sentence from a psychology text: "His male sibling's excessive psychogenic outbursts were instrumental in causing him to decompensate emotionally." A clearer statement would be the following: "His brother's temper eventually caused him to have a nervous breakdown."

literal   *Literal* and *figurative* are two opposing characteristics of language. The literal meaning is a statement about something rendered in common, factual terms: "A good writer must be aggressive and daring." The figurative meaning is clouded in an image: "A good writer must stick out his neck." See **figurative.**

logical fallacies   Errors in reasoning used by speakers or writers, sometimes in order to dupe their audiences. Most logical fallacies are based on insufficient evidence ("All redheads are passionate lovers"); or irrelevant information ("Don't let him do the surgery; he cheats on his wife"); or on faulty logic ("If you don't quit smoking, you'll die of lung cancer"). See Richard Altick's "Obstacles to Clear Thinking," in Chapter 9.

metaphor A figurative image that implies the similarity between things otherwise dissimilar, as when the poet Robert Frost states, "I have been acquainted with the night," meaning that he has suffered despair.

mood of a story The pervading impression made on the feelings of the reader. For instance, Edgar Allan Poe often created a mood of horror in his short stories. A mood can be gloomy, sad, joyful, bitter, frightening, and so forth. A writer can create as many moods as his emotional range suggests.

mood of verbs A verb form expressing the manner or condition of the action. The "moods of verbs" are *indicative* (statements or questions); *imperative* (requests or commands); and *subjunctive* (expressions of doubt, wishes, probabilities and conditions contrary to fact).

narration An account of events as they happen. A narrative organizes material on the basis of chronological order or pattern, stressing the sequence of events and pacing these events according to the emphasis desired. Narration is often distinguished from three other modes of writing: argumentation, description, and exposition. See "How to Write a Narration," Chapter 6.

objective and subjective writing Two different attitudes toward description. In *objective* writing the author tries to present the material fairly and without bias; in *subjective* writing the author stresses personal responses and interpretations. For instance, news reporting should be objective whereas poetry can be subjective.

pacing The speed at which a piece of writing moves along. Pacing depends on the balance between summarizing action and representing the action in detail. See "How to Write a Narration," Chapter 6.

parallelism The principle of coherent writing requiring that coordinate elements be given the same grammatical form, as in Daniel Webster's dictum, "I was born an American; I will live an American; I will die an American."

paraphrase A restatement of a text or passage in another form or other words, often to clarify the meaning. Paraphrase is commonly used in research papers to assimilate the research into a single style of writing and thereby avoid a choppy effect. See also **plagiarism.**

personification Attributing human qualities to objects, abstractions, or animals: "'Tis beauty calls and glory leads the way."

plagiarism Copying words from a source and then passing them off as one's own. Plagiarism is considered dishonest scholarship. Every writer is obligated to acknowledge ideas or concepts that represent someone else's thinking.

point of view The perspective from which a piece of writing is developed. In nonfiction the point of view is usually the author's. In fiction the point of view can be first- or third-person point of view. In the first-person point of view, the author becomes part of the narration and refers to himself as "I." In the third-person point of view the narrator simply observes the action of the story. Third-person narrative is either *omniscient* (when the narrator knows everything about all of the characters) or *limited* (when the narrator knows only those things that might be apparent to a sensitive observer).

premise   An assertion or statement that is the basis for an argument. See **syllogism.**

process   A type of development in writing that stresses how a sequence of steps produces a certain effect. For instance, explaining to the reader all of the steps involved in balancing a checkbook would be a *process* essay. See Chapter 6 for examples of process writing.

purpose   The commitment on the part of authors to explain what they plan to write about. Purpose is an essential part of unity and coherence. Most teachers require student writers to state their purpose in a statement of purpose, also called a *thesis:* "I intend to argue that our Federal Post Office needs a complete overhaul."

red herring   A side issue introduced into an argument in order to distract from the main argument. It is a common device of politicians: "Abortion may be a woman's individual right, but have you considered the danger of the many germ-infested abortion clinics?" Here the side issue of dirty clinics clouds the ethical issue of the right or wrong of having an abortion. See Richard Altick's "Obstacles to Clear Thinking," pp. 623–31.

repetition   A final review of all of the main points in a piece of writing; also known as *recapitulation.* In skillful writing, repetition is a means of emphasizing important words and ideas, of binding together the sentences in a passage, and of creating an effective conclusion. Its purpose is to accumulate a climactic impact or to cast new light upon the material being presented.

rhetoric   The art of using persuasive language. This is accomplished through the author's diction and sentence structure.

rhetorical question   A question posed with no expectation of receiving an answer. This device is often used in public speaking in order to launch or further discussion: "Do you know what one of the greatest pains is? One of the greatest pains to human nature is the pain of a new idea."

satire   Often an attack on a person. Also the use of wit and humor in order to ridicule society's weaknesses so as to correct them. In literature, two types of satire have been recognized: *Horatian satire,* which is gentle and smiling; *Juvenalian satire,* which is sharp and biting.

simile   A figure of speech which, like the metaphor, implies a similarity between things otherwise dissimilar. The simile, however, always uses the words *like, as,* or *so* to introduce the comparison: "As a jewel of gold in a swine's snout, *so* is a fair woman which is without discretion."

slanting   The characteristic of selecting facts, words, or emphasis to achieve a preconceived intent:

favorable intent: "Although the Senator looks bored, when it comes time to vote, he is on the right side of the issue."

unfavorable intent: "The Senator may vote on the right side of issues, but he always looks bored."

specific   A way of referring to the level of abstraction in words; the opposite of *general*. A *general* word refers to a group or a class whereas a *specific* word refers to a member of a group or class. Thus, the word *nature* is general, the word *tree* more specific, and the word *oak* even more specific. The thesis of an essay is general, but the details supporting that thesis are specific. See also **abstract** and **concrete.**

standard English   The English of educated speakers and writers. Any attempt to define standard English is controversial because no two speakers of English speak exactly alike. What is usually meant by "standard English" is what one's grammar book dictates.

statement of purpose   What an author is trying to tell his audience; the main idea that he claims to support in his essay. Traditionally, what distinguishes a statement of purpose from a **thesis** is wording, not content. A statement of purpose includes such words as "My purpose is . . ." or "In this paper I intend to . . ." A statement of purpose is often the lead sentence of an essay. See Chapter 3, "Purpose and Thesis."

straw man   An opposing point of view, set up so that it can easily be refuted. This is a common strategy used in debate.

style   The expression of an author's individuality through the use of words, sentence patterns, and selection of details. Our advice to fledgling writers is to develop a style that combines sincerity with clarity. See F. L. Lucas's "What Is Style?" in Chapter 2.

subordination   Expressing in a dependent clause, phrase, or single word any idea that is not significant enough to be expressed in a main clause or an independent sentence:

lacking subordination: John wrote his research paper on Thomas Jefferson; he was interested in this great statesman.

with subordination: Because John was interested in Thomas Jefferson, he wrote his research paper on this great statesman.

syllogism   In formal logic, the pattern by which a deductive argument is expressed:

All men are mortal (major premise)

John Smith is a man (minor premise)

Therefore John Smith is mortal (conclusion)

symbol   An object or action that in its particular context represents something else. For instance, in Ernest Hemingway's novel *Farewell to Arms* the rain represents impending disaster because when it rains something terrible happens.

synonym   A word or phrase that has the same meaning as another. For instance, the words *imprisonment* and *incarceration* are synonyms. The phrases "fall short of" and "miss the mark" are synonymous.

syntax   The order of words in a sentence and their relationships to each other. Good syntax requires correct grammar as well as effective sentence patterns, including unity, coherence, and emphasis.

theme See **thesis.**

thesis The basic idea of an essay, usually stated in a single sentence. In expository and argumentative writing, the thesis (or *theme*) is the unifying force that every word, every sentence, and every paragraph of the essay must support.

tone In writing, *tone* is the reflection of the writer's attitude toward subject and audience. The tone can be personal or impersonal, formal or informal, objective or subjective. Tone may also be expressed by a tone of voice, such as irons', sarcasm, anger, humor, satire, hyperbole, or understatement.

topic sentence The *topic sentence* is to a paragraph what the *thesis* or *theme* is to the entire essay—that is, it expresses the paragraph's central idea.

transition Words, phrases, sentences, or even paragraphs that indicate connections between the writer's ideas. These transitions provide landmarks to guide the reader from one idea to the next so that the reader will not get lost. The following are some standard transitional devices:

time: soon, immediately, afterward, later, meanwhile, in the meantime

place: nearby, on the opposite side, further back, beyond

result: as a result, therefore, thus, as a consequence

comparison: similarly, likewise, also

contrast: on the other hand, in contrast, nevertheless, but, yet, otherwise

addition: furthermore, moreover, in addition, and, first, second, third, finally

example: for example, for instance, to illustrate, as a matter of fact, on the whole, in other words

understatement A way of deliberately representing something as less than it is in order to stress its magnitude. Also called *litotes*. A good writer will restrain the impulse to hammer home a point and will use understatement instead. An example is the following line from Oscar Wilde's play *The Importance of Being Earnest:*

"To lose one parent, Mr. Worthing, may be regarded as a misfortune; to lose both looks like carelessness."

unity The characteristic in writing of having all parts contribute to an overall effect. An essay or paragraph is described as having *unity* when all of its sentences develop one central idea. The worst enemy of unity is irrelevant material. A good rule is to delete all sentences that do not advance or prove the thesis or topic sentence of an essay.

voice The presence or the sound of self chosen by an author. Most good writing sounds like someone delivering a message. The aim in good student writing is to sound natural. Of course, the voice will be affected by the audience and occasion for writing. See Chapter 2, "The Writer's Voice."

Literary Credits

▼▼▼

Deb Price, "Cleaning a Catalog of Ills" from *The Atlanta Constitution* (October 20, 1994). Copyright © 1994. Reprinted with the permission of *The Detroit News*.

Anna Quindlen, "The Great White Myth" from *The New York Times* (January 15, 1992). Copyright © 1992 by The New York Times Company. Reprinted with the permission of *The New York Times*.

Sylvia Rabiner, "How the Superwoman Myth Puts Women Down" from *The Village Voice* (May 24, 1976). Reprinted with the permission of *The Village Voice*.

Richard K. Redfern, "A Brief Lexicon of Jargon" from *College English* (May 1967). Copyright © 1967 by the National Council of Teachers of English. Reprinted with the permission of NCTE.

Alastair Reid, "Curiosity" from *Weathering: Poems and Translations* (New York: Dutton, 1978). Originally in *The New Yorker* (November 14, 1959). Copyright © 1959, 1978 by Alastair Reid. Reprinted with the permission of *The New Yorker*. All rights reserved.

Adrienne Rich, "Living in Sin" from *Collected Earlier Poems: 1950–1970*. Copyright © 1993, 1955 by Adrienne Rich. Reprinted with the permission of W. W. Norton & Company, Inc.

Paul Roberts, "How to Say Nothing in Five Hundred Words" from *Understanding English*. Copyright © 1958 by Paul Robert. Reprinted with the permission of HarperCollins Publishers, Inc.

Roxanne Roberts, "The Grieving Never Ends" from *The Los Angeles Times* (June 12, 1996). Reprinted with the permission of the Los Angeles Times Syndicate.

Carl Sandburg, "Threes" from *Smoke and Steel*. Copyright © 1920 by Harcourt Brace and Howe, renewed 1948 by Carl Sandburg. Reprinted with the permission of Harcourt Brace & Company.

John C. Sherwood, "Introduction to Logic" from *Discourse of Reason*. Copyright © 1960 by John C. Sherwood. Reprinted with the permission of HarperCollins Publishers, Inc.

Albert Speer, "The Deception of Hitler," translated by Richard and Clara Winston, from *Spandau: The Secret Diaries*. Copyright © 1976 by Richard and Clara Winston. Reprinted with the permission of Simon & Schuster, Inc.

May Swenson, "Pigeon Woman" from *New and Selected Things Taking Place* (Boston: Little, Brown and Company). Originally published in *The New Yorker* (1962). Copyright © 1962 by May Swenson. Reprinted with the permission of The Literary Estate of May Swenson.

Wislawa Szymborska, "In Praise of Dreams," translated by Stanislaw Baranczak and Claire Cavanagh, from *View with a Grain of Sand*. Copyright © 1993 by Wislawa Szymborska. English translation copyright © 1996 by Stanislaw Baranczak and Claire Cavanagh. Reprinted with the permission of Harcourt Brace and Company.

Amy Tan, "The Red Candle" from *The Joy Luck Club*. Copyright © 1989 by Amy Tan. Reprinted with the permission of The Putnam Publishing Group.

John Taylor, "Are You Politically Correct?" from *New York* (January 21, 1991). Copyright © 1991 by K-III Magazine Corporation. Reprinted with the permission of *New York*.

Index